Creole Subjects in the Colonial Americas

Published for the Omohundro Institute
of Early American History
and Culture, Williamsburg, Virginia,
by the University of North Carolina Press,
Chapel Hill

Creole Subjects in the Colonial Americas

EMPIRES, TEXTS, IDENTITIES

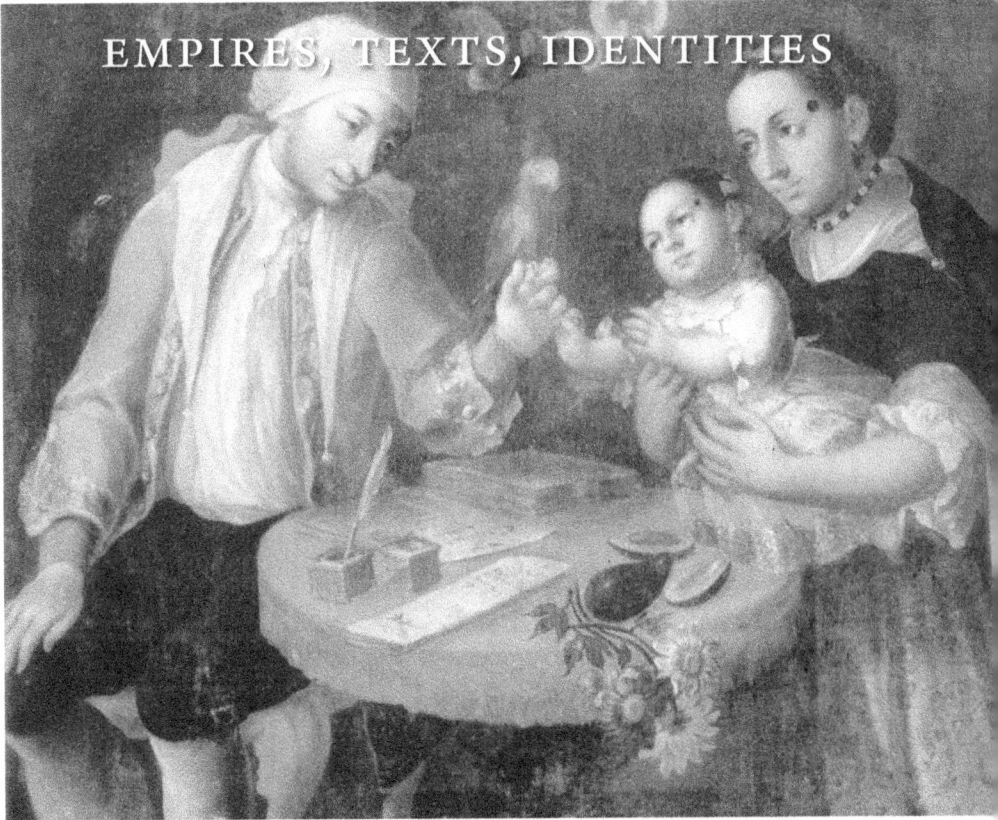

Edited by Ralph Bauer and José Antonio Mazzotti

The Omohundro Institute of Early American History and Culture is sponsored jointly by the College of William and Mary and the Colonial Williamsburg Foundation. On November 15, 1996, the Institute adopted the present name in honor of a bequest from Malvern H. Omohundro, Jr.

© 2009 The University of North Carolina Press
Set in Arno Pro
by Keystone Typesetting, Inc.
Manufactured in the United States of America

Complete cataloging information for this title is available from the Library of Congress.

ISBN 978-0-8078-3213-4 (cloth: alk. paper)
ISBN 978-0-8078-5968-1 (pbk.: alk. paper)

The paper in this book meets the guidelines for permanence and durability of the Committee on Production Guidelines for Book Longevity of the Council on Library Resouces.

The University of North Carolina Press has been a member of the Green Press Initiative since 2003.

cloth   13 12 11 10 09   5 4 3 2 1
paper   13 12 11 10 09   5 4 3 2 1

Publication of this book was aided by a grant from the Program for Cultural Cooperation between Spain's Ministry of Culture and United States Universities.

ACKNOWLEDGMENTS

We would like to thank the Society of Early Americanists for sponsoring the First Early Ibero / Anglo Americanist Summit in Tucson, Arizona (2002), the event out of which this collection of essays originally grew. Also, we would like to thank Fredrika J. Teute for her continual support of the project over the many years it has taken for it to take shape, as well as Karen Ordahl Kupperman, David Boruchoff, Jorge Cañizares-Esguerra, Thomas Scanlan, and Ivy Schweitzer for their helpful suggestions. Finally, we would like to thank Gil Kelly and the editorial staff of the Omohundro Institute of Early American History and Culture for all their excellent work on the project.

CONTENTS

LIST OF ILLUSTRATIONS

Creole Subjects in the Colonial Americas

RALPH BAUER AND JOSÉ ANTONIO MAZZOTTI

INTRODUCTION

Creole Subjects in the Colonial Americas

I do not marvel at the great defects and imbecility of those who are born in
these lands . . . because the Spaniards who inhabit them, and even more those
who are born here, assume these bad inclinations. Those who are born here become
like the Indians, and although they look like Spaniards, in their constitution they
are not; those who are born in Spain, if they do not take care, change within a few
years after they arrive in these parts; and this I think is due to the climate
or the constellations in these parts.—Bernardino de Sahagún (1590)

Why and how people who have descended from the Old World change
once they are transplanted to the New already occupied the Spanish natural
historians and ethnographers of the New World during the sixteenth century.
Early modern writers such as Bernadino de Sahagún, Gonzalo Fernández de
Oviedo y Valdes, and José de Acosta provided the earliest theories of "creolization"—the process of cultural change in different geographic locations that has
interested anthropologists, cultural geographers, and linguists up to the present
time. But, while modern scholars have often celebrated creolization in the New
World as "creative adaptations," evidencing human innovation and cultural
diversification, in early modern times the fact that transplanted Europeans
changed in the Americas was typically seen as profoundly disturbing, as evidence of a cultural "degeneration."[1]

The idea that human bodies and minds degenerated in the New World was
based on two suppositions, both ultimately rooted in classical antiquity. The
first one, humoral theory, was derived from the scientific thought of Aristotle,
Hippocrates, Galen, and others who held that a person's physiological and
psychological constitution was determined by the qualities of the natural environment or astrological constellation. The second supposition, rooted in
Greco-Roman notions of barbarity and corroborated by early modern travel

1. The literature on degeneration is vast. For some seminal titles, see the Terminological and
Bibliographical Notes at the end of this essay.

reports, alleged the savagery of the Americas' indigenous peoples. By way of logical deduction, early modern natural philosophers concluded that the natural environment and the skies of the New World were inhospitable to the development of human culture. Cultural changes observed in transplanted Europeans were, in this ethnocentric scheme, inevitably interpreted as a cultural decline. The polemic about creolization famously culminated during the eighteenth century, when it became a prominent topos in neoclassical natural philosophy. Thus, the debate over creole culture represents, as Karen Ordahl Kupperman has observed, a theme of "powerful continuity in European response" to America, as "European intellectuals, seeing difference as degeneracy, continued to treat America as a screen on which to project their own fears and fantasies."[2]

If the early modern debate over creolization was thus a wider Atlantic phenomenon that not only spanned the three centuries of European colonial rule in the Americas but also cut across the boundaries of the various European empires, how did those defined as creoles in the various European imperial realms in the Americas respond to this early modern ideology? What are the historical similarities, as well as the differences, between the notions about creolization as they arose in each of the European empires? How did early modern thinking about creolization in the New World evolve from the sixteenth to the nineteenth century? How did this debate inflect the development of a colonial sense of communal identity, local patriotism, New World nationalism, and literary expression in the various parts of the colonial Americas? Finally, how did it shape the creoles' relation with the European metropolis and place of origin as well as with peoples of non-European origin living in the Americas?

This collection of essays gathers responses to these questions by early Americanists working in Spanish, Portuguese, and Anglo-American colonial literature, in order to explore comparatively the ideological, literary, and scientific constitution of various early modern notions about creolization and forms of creole subjectivity in colonial Latin and British America.[3] Examining the literary rec-

2. William Robertson, *The History of the Discovery and Settlement of America* (1777; New York, 1829), 123; Karen Ordahl Kupperman, "Introduction: The Changing Definition of America," in Kupperman, ed., *America in European Consciousness, 1493–1750* (Chapel Hill, N.C., 1995), 1–27, esp. 23.

3. We use the expression "early modern period" to refer to the initial westernization of the Americas from the sixteenth to the eighteenth century in purposeful contrast to the general tendency within Latin American historiography and criticism to rely on such concepts as "ancien régime" or "sociedades de antiguo régimen." The idea of an "early modernity" could be quite misleading when applied to Latin America, for it would distort the peculiar and contradictory processes of the region's modernization as compared to the United States or the original Euro-

ord produced by and about creole subjects in the various European imperial realms of Spain, Portugal, and England in the New World, this collection hopes to make a contribution to several continuing discussions. First, it aims to broaden the critical debate about creole subjectivity, which has long held more currency in the literary study of colonial Latin America than in colonial British America. Second, it strives to extend the perspective of literary history to the advances made by modern historians who have called for a fresh look at Euro-American creoles in light of the intensified study of subaltern subjects in the colonial Americas. Third, it means to respond to historians' calls for comparative, hemispheric, and Atlantic perspectives on the study of the colonial Americas that would transcend both modern and early modern national and imperial boundaries. And, finally, it contributes an early American literary perspective to the comparative, hemispheric, or inter-American study of American literatures that has so far concentrated on the national periods of the nineteenth and twentieth centuries. In this volume, we are happy to bring Luso-, Spanish-, and British-American literature into a comparative focus and hope that it will serve as a model for similar scholarship on colonial French and Dutch literature.[4]

Together, these essays represent a composite overview of the pervasive themes of creolism and creolization in the ideological context of early modern settler colonialism. As such, we trust that this collection will stand as a platform for further research and study in comparative hemispheric as well as Atlantic scholarship, both historical and literary.

Creoles and Creolization: Definitions

Most likely derived from a Latin root (*creare,* to make, to create, that is, something new), the word *creole* made its first appearance in modern Western languages as a Portuguese neologism *(crioulo)* in a colonial New World context—to distinguish black slaves born in Brazil from those brought from Africa. Although crioulo slaves were sometimes favorably compared to African-born slaves for already being seasoned in the New World environment and therefore less susceptible to disease, they were more often seen as prone to rebelliousness and moral vice. In the course of its sixteenth-century translation from the Portuguese into the Spanish context, the word *criollo* soon came to designate not only slaves of African descent but also settlers of European

---

pean imperial model. In this collection, however, "early modern period" will be used only in its chronological sense.

4. On creole subjects in colonial Latin American studies, see the Terminological and Bibliographical Notes at the end of this Introduction.

ancestry born in the Americas. Its earliest documentations in this sense appear in letters written during the 1560s by Spanish officials from New Spain, who observed that the Spanish sector of the colonial population was now "different from that before" because the "creoles, who are those that are born there, . . . have never known the king nor ever hope to know him, and are quick to listen to and believe those who are malintentioned." Its earliest documentation in print has been traced to the *Geografía y descripción universal de las Indias* (1570), by the royal chronicler Juan López de Velasco, who claimed that the Spaniards born in the Indies, "who are called creoles, turn out like the natives even though they are not mixed with them [by] declining to the disposition of the land." By the end of the sixteenth century, the American-born creoles had come to be regarded as a distinct group in most regions of the Ibero-American empires who had assumed, as Anthony Pagden has written, a "single, if varied, character" that had acquired "all those supposed shortcomings of the Indians that were thought to derive from psychological weakness or deformation, above all their moral and social instability."[5]

The alleged change that Spaniards underwent in the Americas was not lost on Spain's European imperial rivals. The earliest documentation of the word *creole* in English occurs in E. Grimstone's 1604 translation of José de Acosta's *Historia natural y moral* (1590), which makes reference to "Crollos" as designating "Spaniards borne at the *Indies.*" By the end of the seventeenth century, English writers were using the word also in reference to British-American colonials—often to express a "deep skepticism" about the survival of British character among the English progeny born in the Caribbean, Virginia, and New England. But, despite the gradual domestication of the word in the English language, it generally retained a broadly foreign, and a distinctly Ibero-

5. Anthony Pagden, "Identity Formation in Spanish America," in Nicholas Canny and Pagden, eds., *Colonial Identity in the Atlantic World, 1500–1800* (Princeton, N.J., 1987), 57, 81. The Inca Garcilaso de la Vega writes during the early seventeenth century that the term "criollo" was first used "in order to . . . distinguish between those blacks born in the Indies and those born in Guinea because the latter are more honest and of better quality, having been born in their native country," in Garcilaso de la Vega, el Inca, *Obras completas del Inca Garcilaso de la Vega,* ed. P. Carmelo Saenz de Santa Maria (Madrid, 1960), I, 281; Lope García de Castro, quoted in Bernard Lavallé, *Las promesas ambiguas: ensayos sobre el criollismo colonial en los Andes* (Lima, 1993), 16–25 (our translation); Juan López de Velasco, *Geografía y descripción universal de las Indias recopiladas por el cosmógrafo-cronista Juan López de Velasco desde el año de 1571 al de 1574* (Madrid, 1894), 37–38. For discussions of the history of the concept of the creole in Spanish America, see José Juan Arrom, *Certidumbre de América: estudios de letras, folklore, y cultura,* 2d ed. (Madrid, 1971), 50–54. On colonial Brazil, see Stuart B. Schwartz, "Colonial Identities and *Sociedad de Castas,"* *Colonial Latin American Review,* IV (1995), 185–201; A. J. R. Russell-Wood, "Centers and Peripheries in the Luso-Brazilian World, 1500–1808," in Christine Daniels and Michael V. Kennedy, eds., *Negotiated Empires: Centers and Peripheries in the Americas, 1500–1800* (New York, 2002), 109–110.

American, connotation until the eighteenth century. This is evident in the spelling of the word in many seventeenth- and eighteenth-century English texts, such as Cotton Mather's famous early-eighteenth-century designation of certain behaviors among the colonials by which he found himself surrounded as "*Criolian* degeneracies" (from the Spanish *criollo,* rather than the French *créole*). However, whereas in the Ibero-American context the pejorative connotations of the word had consisted primarily in allegations of a lapse in piety or loyalty to king and country, the particular connotations that the word assumed in the predominantly Protestant context of early British America are still manifest today in one of the *Oxford English Dictionary*'s definitions of the verb *to creolize:* "to spend the day in a delectable state of apathy."[6]

Throughout the Americas, then, the word *creole* (and the various vernacular derivations from the Portuguese word *crioulo*) originated during the sixteenth century to designate a person of Old World descent who was born in the Americas, and the idea of creolization usually carried pejorative implications. During the sixteenth and seventeenth centuries, the causes for real or perceived changes in Old World bodies and minds in the New World were usually found in a combination of environmental and astrological explanations, which placed a premium not only on the time but also on the place of an individual's birth within the early modern matrix of terrestrial, sublunary, and supralunary constellations. Nevertheless, remarks about the negative influences of the New World environment were then usually qualified by reflections on the efficacy of human moral choice to overcome them.[7]

By contrast, during the eighteenth century, as natural history was increasingly being stripped of its astrological aspects, the significance of the time and place of an individual's birth gradually lost significance relative to the ever-present influences of the natural environment on individuals and entire cultures after birth. Human beings were now seen to be like plants, entirely dependent

6. José de Acosta, *The Natural History of the East and West Indies* (1590), trans. E. G[rimstone] (London, 1604), 278; Carole Shammas, "English-Born and Creole Elites in Turn-of-the-Century Virginia," in Thad W. Tate and David L. Ammerman, eds., *The Chesapeake in the Seventeenth Century: Essays on Anglo-American Society* (Chapel Hill, N.C., 1979), 274–296, esp. 284; Cotton Mather, *Magnalia Christi Americana; or, The Ecclesiastical History of New England* (Hartford, Conn., 1853–1855), I, 13, 25. On the concept of the "creole" in eighteenth-century and early-nineteenth-century Anglo America and the Caribbean, see Sean X. Goudie, *Creole America: The West Indies and the Formation of Literature and Culture in the New Republic* (Philadelphia, 2006), esp. 8–9.

7. Thus, Sahagún lamented that, while the "native Indians of old knew how to remedy the damage that this land imprints on those who live in it, obviating natural things with contrary exercises, we let ourselves be carried along by our bad inclinations." Bernardino de Sahagún, *Historia general de las cosas de Nueva España* (1590) (Mexico City, 1938), III, 82.

on their climate and soil. Thus, the term *creole* frequently came to refer not only to persons born in the New World but also to those who had been transplanted there and, thus, been subject to its peculiar natural influences for an extended period. The environmental determinism of Enlightenment philosophes such as Montesquieu, Raynal, Voltaire, and Buffon led to the inevitable conclusion that Americans of whatever ancestry were "destined" (in the words of William Robertson) "to remain uncivilized" because of New World climates and soils.[8]

Before the nineteenth century, the word *creole* was thus less a racial designation (in the sense of modern distinctions based on biological or genetic factors, such as white or black skin) than it was a geocultural designation denoting a place of birth or habitation. The particular racial connotations that the word often has today are largely due to semantic shifts of the nineteenth century, mainly in the context of the French Caribbean and Louisiana. Despite this terminological diffusion in the modern usage of the word, however, the *concept* of creolization has continued to be hotly debated in modern linguistic, historical, and anthropological scholarship since the early twentieth century.[9] In historical anthropology, for example, the concept has been used in order to emphasize New World cultural creations and thus cultural differences between the Old World and the New. It thereby has often found itself in opposition to and competition with various diasporic models of New World cultural formation. The controversy reaches back at least to the famous debate between the sociologist E. Franklin Frazier and the anthropologist Melville Herskovits during the 1930s. The former, in his study *The Free Negro Family* (1932), had argued that the "acculturation" forced upon African slaves in the New World formed the beginning of African-American culture in the New World, but the latter, in his celebrated critique of Frazier, *Acculturation: The Study of Culture Contact* (1938), emphasized the continuities connecting African-American cultures with the African roots, giving impetus to a so-called retentionist school in subsequent anthropological scholarship.[10]

8. On the role of astrology in the discourse of creolization, see Jorge Cañizares Esguerra, "New Worlds, New Stars: Patriotic Astrology and the Invention of Indian and Creole Bodies in Colonial Spanish America, 1600–1650," *American Historical Review*, CIV (1999), 33–68; on the increasing importance of environmental and physiological aspects during the nineteenth century, see Antonello Gerbi, *The Dispute of the New World: The History of a Polemic, 1750–1900* (1955), trans. Jeremy Moyle (Pittsburgh, 1973).

9. For a discussion of the scholarship on creolism, see the Terminological and Bibliographical Notes at the end of this essay.

10. E. Franklin Frazier, *The Free Negro Family: A Study of Family Origins before the Civil War* (Nashville, Tenn., 1932); Melville J. Herskovits, *Acculturation: The Study of Culture Contact* (1938; Gloucester, Mass., 1958).

However, between the 1940s and 1990s, anthropologists such as Fernando Ortiz, Edmund Brathwaite, and Sidney Mintz and Richard Price—though all acknowledging cultural continuities from the Old World to the New—reemphasized the importance of new cultural formations, proposing various models that they called "transculturation," "creolization," and "culturation," respectively. The debate continued, as some historians, such as David Hackett Fischer and Michael A. Gomez, suggested that Europeans and Africans, respectively, retained Old World identities and cultures, whereas others, such as T. H. Breen, David Buisseret, Daniel H. Usner, Jr., Mary L. Galvin, Richard Cullen Rath, and J. L. Dillard, emphasized "creative adaptation," cultural "syncreticism," and "bricolage" as the characteristic features of New World cultural beginnings.[11]

Postcolonial Theory, Creole Subjects, and Comparative Early American Literary Studies

This collection of essays, for the most part by literary historians, is concerned less with the actual cultural processes of creolization in the New World that have occupied historians and anthropologists than with the *idea* of the creole (and of creolization) in the early Americas as an imperialist discourse of colonial difference. As such, the concept has traditionally had more

11. Sidney Mintz and Richard Price, *The Birth of African-American Culture: An Anthropological Perspective* (Boston, 1992); and Fernando Ortiz, *Contrapunteo cubano del tabaco y el azúcar* (1940; Caracas, 1987). For a discussion of theories of cultural creolization in modern times, see David Buisseret and Steven G. Reinhardt, eds., *Creolization in the Americas* (College Station, Tex., 2000), 3–18; Michael A. Gomez, *Exchanging Our Country Marks: The Transformation of African Identities in the Colonial and Antebellum South* (Chapel Hill, N.C., 1998); David Hackett Fischer, *Albion's Seed: Four British Folkways in America* (New York, 1989); T. H. Breen, "Creative Adaptations," in Jack P. Greene and J. R. Pole, eds., *Colonial British America: Essays in the New History of the Early Modern Era* (Baltimore, 1984), 195–234; Breen and Timothy Hall, *Colonial America in an Atlantic World: A Story of Creative Interaction* (New York, 2004); Edward Brathwaite, *The Development of Creole Society in Jamaica, 1770–1820* (Oxford, 1971), esp. 295–305. Ira Berlin has coined the term "Atlantic creoles" in reference to people of African descent who act as go-betweens in the cultural interactions between Europeans and Africans in an early modern Atlantic commercial context; see *Many Thousands Gone: The First Two Centuries of Slavery in North America* (Cambridge, Mass., 1998). However, he does not produce any evidence that the people he refers to as "Atlantic creoles" were actually so called in their times. We therefore follow Buisseret, Usner, Galvin, Rath, and Dillard, who have proposed using "the concept of 'creolization'" and the term *Creole* in this historical sense—as referring to "people born in America of European or of African origins"—and who have investigated not only the cultural exchanges between different groups in the Americas but also the influence of the environment, such as the diversity of climates, topography, and availability of material resources (see their essays in Buisseret and Reinhardt, eds., *Creolization in the Americas*).

currency in early Ibero-American than in Anglo-American scholarship. Yet, we want to propose the early modern discourse of creolization and the creole subject as categories for the study of both realms as well as for comparative literary analysis of the literatures of the colonial Americas. Our focus here is primarily on the Euro-American creole elites and their ambiguous subject positions within the imperial geopolitical and the colonial social order.

Such a focus on the Euro-American creole elites may at first seem like an anachronistic choice. After all, scholars of colonial Latin American and of colonial Anglo-American literature, energized in part by the postcolonial debate taking place across the humanities and human sciences, have tended to focus their attention on the various subaltern groups in the colonial Americas. In early Anglo-American literary studies, for example, this turn has produced important and necessary new scholarship that has considerably advanced the historical understanding of the significant diversity of literacies and literary cultures. Some scholars have even rejected the notion of "literature" altogether for its Eurocentric connotations, instead embracing the notion of "writing" (in its broadest sense) in order adequately to appreciate the diversity of early American rhetorical practices. One effect of this has been an unprecedented expansion of the early American canon to include many African-American, native American, and women writers who had previously been excluded but whose perspectives competed with those of the elites. More important for our purposes, this scholarship on subaltern literatures and coloniality has raised new questions also about the elites, long familiar to literary historians since the seminal works of scholars such as Perry Miller and David Levin (on New England) as well as Leo Lemay (on the Middle Colonies and the Chesapeake). As the historian Trevor Burnard has argued, it is in "light of [this] new knowledge" about colonialism and early American culture that we "need to look afresh at elites" in British America.[12]

Similarly, colonial Latin American literary scholarship has since the late 1980s

---

12. Trevor Burnard, *Creole Gentlemen: The Maryland Elite, 1692–1776* (New York, 2002), 1. For only some modern examples of this paradigm shift in early Anglo-American literary studies, see Helen Jaskoski, ed., *Early Native American Writing: New Critical Essays* (Cambridge, 1996); Hilary E. Wyss, *Writing Indians: Literacy, Christianity, and Native Community in Early America* (Amherst, Mass., 2000); Philip Gould, *Barbaric Traffic: Commerce and Antislavery in the Eighteenth-Century Atlantic World* (Cambridge, Mass., 2003); Vincent Carretta and Philip Gould, eds., *Genius in Bondage: Literature of the Early Black Atlantic* (Lexington, Ky., 2001); Joanna Brooks, *American Lazarus: Religion and the Rise of African-American and Native American Literatures* (New York, 2003). For important revisions of the idea of "literature" itself in the early Americas, see also Sandra M. Gustafson, *Eloquence Is Power: Oratory and Performance in Early America* (Chapel Hill, N.C., 2000).

undergone a paradigm shift. Literary scholars have found new value in the enormous wealth of indigenous and mestizo authors who had traditionally been of interest primarily to anthropologists—authors such as Felipe Waman Puma de Ayala (circa 1550–circa 1616), Fernando Alvarado Tezozomoc (sixteenth century), Titu Cusi Yupanqui (circa 1530–1571), and Joan de Santacruz Pachacuti (late sixteenth–early seventeenth century). In addition, many colonial Latin Americanists began taking a more interdisciplinary approach in their work in order to shed light on the complex webs of meanings generated by texts both literary and nonliterary (in the traditional sense of the terms). The conventional paradigms of "author" and "text" were replaced by "subject" and "discourse," aiming at the importance of indigenous orality. Eventually, the widely accepted notion of discourse was further broadened by the idea of "semiosis" in an effort to recognize colonial Latin America's nonalphabetical archives (codexes, khipu, drawings, and so on) as part of the totality of cultural production that took place after 1492.[13]

At the same time, this postcolonial paradigm shift has resulted in the reevaluation of the creole elites also in colonial Latin American scholarship, as important new studies have revisited texts by canonical authors—such as Sor Juana Inés de la Cruz, Carlos de Sigüenza y Góngora, and Pedro de Peralta—though armed with a new set of questions. Such contributions have enriched and expanded the colonial field in important ways, renovating questions about the location of these creole authors within a totality of colonial writings and examining in greater detail the internal contradictions and ambiguities that such canonical texts present.[14]

13. See Walter D. Mignolo, "Afterword," *Dispositio,* nos. 36–38 (1989), 333–337; Mignolo, "La semiosis colonial: la dialéctica entre representaciones fracturadas y hermenéuticas pluritópicas," in Beatriz González Stephan and Lúcia Helena Costigan, eds., *Crítica y descolonización: el sujeto colonial en la cultura latinoamericana* (Caracas, 1992), 27–47; Mignolo, "Colonial and Postcolonial Discourse: Cultural Critique or Academic Colonialism?" *Latin American Research Review,* XXVIII (1993), 120–131; Mignolo, *The Darker Side of the Renaissance: Literacy, Territoriality, and Colonization* (Ann Arbor, Mich., 1995). For a basic understanding of this paradigm shift, see Rolena Adorno, "Nuevas perspectivas en los estudios coloniales literarios hispanoamericanos," *Revista de crítica literaria latinoamericana,* XVIII (1988), 11–28, and *Guaman Poma: Writing and Resistance in Colonial Peru* (Austin, Tex., 1986); Raquel Chang-Rodríguez, *La apropiación del signo: tres cronistas indígenas del Perú* (Tempe, Ariz., 1988), and *El discurso disidente: ensayos de literatura colonial peruana* (Lima, 1991); Mercedes López-Baralt, *Icono y conquista: Guamán Poma de Ayala* (Madrid, 1988).

14. Many of these studies suggest that creoles' postures toward the indigenous population varied in accordance with the need to ally, defy, or negotiate with Spanish metropolitan power. Spanish-American creoles often maintained a complicit silence with official colonial discourse, but at other times they produced their own characterizations—some paternalistically favorable, others scornful—of the poor and dominated colonial subjects. A brief survey of innovative

However, if the effects of the postcolonial and subaltern studies movements have thus energized colonial American literary studies within the various disciplines, the encounter between postcolonial theory and colonial American studies has also brought into focus the historical *specificity* of the "first," or "early modern," European empires in the early Americas within the history of European imperialism at large and, thus, the *limitations* of postcolonial theory as it had emerged from the specific historical and ideological context of the Second British Empire in Asia and Africa (1776–1914) as a comparative theoretical framework for understanding the colonial Americas. In particular, the conceptual binary "colonizer/colonized" that has frequently informed the postcolonial debate appears anachronistic for understanding the crucial though ambiguous position of colonial creoles within the geopolitical order of early modern imperialism.[15] At times, the uncritical transposition of the postcolonial theoretical apparatus onto the colonial Americas has had the effect of mystifying the thoroughly imperial ideology underwriting many ostensibly anticolonial discourses (such as the Lascasian historiographic tradition, for instance) and the oppositional or anti-imperial tendencies of many ostensibly colonial discourses (such as the criollo epic tradition in Spanish America that celebrated the fabulous exploits of the first conquerors). Even the more-nuanced theories of hybridity articulated by postcolonial theorists such as Homi Bhabha and Gayatri Chakravorty Spivak, who exposed the colonialist aspects of Enlightenment ideas of universal reason, have come to require a conceptual adjustment as a historical hermeneutic when attempting to understand the absolutist transcendental motives that drove European expansionism during the early modern period.[16]

---

readings on canonical authors would include Stephanie Merrim, *Early Modern Women's Writing and Sor Juana Inés de la Cruz* (Nashville, Tenn., 1999); Yolanda Martínez–San Miguel, *Saberes americanos: subalternidad y epistemología en los escritos de Sor Juana* (Pittsburgh, 1999); Kathleen Ross, *The Baroque Narrative of Carlos de Sigüenza y Góngora* (Cambridge, 1993); Jerry M. Williams, ed., *Peralta Barnuevo and the Art of Propaganda: Politics, Poetry, and Religion in Eighteenth-Century Lima: Five Texts* (Newark, Del., 2001); Mabel Moraña, "Barroco y conciencia criolla en Hispanoamérica," *Revista de crítica literaria latinoamericana*, XVIII (1988), 229–251, and *Viaje al silencio: exploraciones del discurso barroco* (Mexico City, 1998), esp. chap. 2.

15. Although the works of postcolonial critics of so-called Second World literature, such as Stephen Slemon and Nicholas Thomas, present an exception to this generalization, their archive, too, was drawn primarily from the British settler colonies in Australia and Africa during the nineteenth and twentieth centuries; see Slemon, "Unsettling the Empire: Resistance Theory for the Second World," *World Literature Written in English*, XXX, no. 2 (Autumn 1990), 30–41; Thomas, *Colonialism's Culture: Anthropology, Travel, and Government* (Oxford, 1994).

16. See Rolena Adorno, "Peaceful Conquest and Law in the Relación (Account) of Alvar Núñez Cabeza de Vaca," in Francisco Javier Cevallos-Canau et al., eds., *Coded Encounters: Writing, Gender, and Ethnicity in Colonial Latin America* (Amherst, Mass., 1994), 75–86, "Discourses

Finally, the very adjective "colonial" has become problematic as a common conceptual denominator for comparative historicist scholarship when applied to the heterogeneous societies that formed in the early Americas.[17] The concept of "colonial America," in both the Anglo- and the Ibero-American context, was first invented as a historical category from the vantage point of the nineteenth century, designating a period that preceded or led up to independence and the nation-state. But postcolonial criticism understood the adjective "colonial" not so much in absolute chronological terms (in opposition to "postcolonial") as in terms of a comparative cultural geography—the colonial-postcolonial peripheries in opposition to the centers of imperial power in Europe. Its comparative geopolitical framework was thereby enabled by limiting its understanding of "empire" to one specific manifestation of the phenomenon. Thus, in the most prominent examples of the postcolonial debate, "empire" denoted the coherent cultural and geopolitical system defined as British that connected various colonies (in India, in Africa, in the Caribbean, and so on) to one another in their common subordinate and dependent status to one center (London) during the nineteenth and twentieth centuries. Rarely did these theories take into consideration other forms of imperial domination. Although the postcolonial critiques emanating from the francophone colonial world in Africa and in the Caribbean, such as those of Albert Memmi, Frantz Fanon, and Aimé Césaire, were in this regard less parochial, they purchased their broader perspectives by basing their analyses less in a historicist than in a psychoanalytical-existentialist framework. Finally, the contributions from modern Latin America to the postcolonial debate by critics such as Enrique Dussel, Roberto Fernández Retamar, and perhaps even as far back as José Enrique Rodó have seemed primarily concerned with the common though difficult position of the Latin American nation-states in modern times, particularly in their relationship to the United States, and less with early modern forms of imperial domination.[18]

---

on Colonialism: Bernal Díaz, Las Casas, and the Twentieth-Century Reader," *MLN*, CIII (1988), 239–258, and "Reconsidering Colonial Discourse for Sixteenth- and Seventeenth-Century Spanish America," *Latin American Research Review*, XXVIII (1993), 135–145. See also Ralph Bauer, *The Cultural Geography of Colonial American Literatures: Empire, Travel, Modernity* (Cambridge, 2003), 30–76.

17. As initially formulated by Peruvian critic Antonio Cornejo Polar, "cultural and structural heterogeneity" works as a theoretical approach that posits that many historic times and discursive systems can coexist independently; their coexistence need not suggest a harmonious synthesis. See *Escribir en el aire: ensayo sobre la heterogeneidad socio-cultural de las literaturas andinas* (Lima, 1994).

18. Albert Memmi, *The Colonizer and the Colonized*, trans. Howard Greenfield (New York,

Unlike the colonies of the Second British Empire, from which postcolonial criticism has drawn most of its conceptual vocabulary, the various European domains in the New World were vastly different from one another culturally; politically, they connected, not to one and the same, but rather to different imperial centers in Europe (that is, Spain, England, France, the Netherlands). Thus, although historians today commonly speak of "colonial" Latin or British America, it is impossible to juxtapose these domains on the basis that they were all "colonial" without first inquiring what "colonial" meant in each imperial context. For the Spanish-American case, this debate dates back to the publication of Argentine historian Ricardo Levene's book *Las Indias no eran colonias* (1951) [The Indies Were Not Colonies]. Levene wrote in response to the widespread use of this term within the traditional, anti-imperialist rhetoric of Spanish-American nationalism. He was part of a growing movement among conservative sectors of the local intelligentsia to glorify Argentina's Spanish heritage. Later historians writing in the context of the wider postcolonial debate have not only reiterated this point with regard to "colonial" Spanish America but also problematized the term in reference to British America before the eighteenth century. Thus, Anthony Pagden and Jorge Klor de Alva have each pointed out that, although the Spanish and Portuguese conquests of the New World preceded and were more extensive than the early British settlements, all three branches of European expansion belonged to the first wave of imperialism that was in many ways antithetical to the Second British Empire from which postcolonial criticism and theory emerged. As inflected by the historical context of the Second British Empire, the term "colonial subject" pertained, of course, primarily to non-European peoples under European imperial domination, not to European colonists outside Europe, who shared with the metropolis their language, cultural origins, and race—the very terms on the basis of which colonial difference was constructed in nineteenth- and twentieth-century colonialist ideologies.[19]

It is telling that, although the word *colony* (and its derivatives) had had a long history in Western languages in reference to the Greek and Roman forms of

---

1972); Frantz Fanon, *Peau noire, masques blancs* (Paris, 1952); Aimé Césaire, *Discourse on Colonialism,* trans. Joan Pinkham (New York, 1972); Roberto Fernández Retamar, *Caliban and Other Essays,* trans. Edward Baker (Minneapolis, Minn., 1989); Enrique Dussel, *The Invention of the Americas: Eclipse of "the Other" and the Myth of Modernity,* trans. Michael D. Barber (New York, 1995); José Enrique Rodó, *Ariel* (1900; Barcelona, 1926).

19. Ricardo Levene, *Las Indias no eran colonias* (Buenos Aires, 1951); Anthony Pagden, *Lords of All the World: Ideologies of Empire in Spain, Britain, and France, c. 1500–c. 1800* (New Haven, Conn., 1995), 6, 128; Jorge Klor de Alva, "Colonialism and Postcolonialism as (Latin) American Mirages," *Colonial Latin American Review,* I (1992), 3–23.

expansionism in the Mediterranean, it was used with conspicuous infrequency in texts relating to the territories claimed by European powers in the New World or their communities before the eighteenth century. This is significant because it suggests that a *colony* (in the classical senses of the word) was not what naturally came to early modern writers' minds when they thought about the Americas. For the Spanish case, this classical understanding of the word in early modern Europe was still in evidence in Sebastián de Covarrubias's *Tesaurus de la lengua castellana*. On the one hand, it defined a colony as a "pueblo o término de tierra que se ha poblado de gente extranjera, sacada de la ciudad, que es señora de aquel territorio o llevada de otra parte" [a town or parcel of land that has been populated by a foreign people taken from the city that has dominion over that territory or from some other place]. In this sense, the meaning connotes the transplantation of soldiers and citizens into distant territories but not necessarily the transplantation of institutions or the transformation of the dominated people. On the other hand, there was an altogether equally important definition current in seventeenth-century Spanish: "También se llamaba colonias las que pobladas de sus antiguos moradores les avia el pueblo romano dado los privilegios de tales." [The name colonies also referred to those places populated by their ancient inhabitants, to whom the Romans had granted the privileges corresponding to such peoples.] In short, a "colony" was understood in seventeenth-century Spain either as an enclave with no necessary transformation of native religious and social practices or a subjugated province whose native population was granted the privilege of retaining some of its ancient customs (such as its institutions and methods of social organization). While both meanings seem to have circulated during the sixteenth and seventeenth centuries, and while the latter would certainly seem more fitting than the former in regard to early Spanish America, neither one appears to have accurately described Spain's ultimate goal in the Americas from the point of view of the sixteenth and seventeenth centuries.[20]

Perhaps due in part to the century-old Manichean struggle of the *reconquista* (Reconquest) between Christendom and Islam on the Peninsula, Spain's goal in the New World was both more socially ambitious and more religiously zealous than the classical model. When, in 1530, Peter Martyr of Anghiera first applied the word *colony* to refer to the Villa Rica de la Veracruz (the first European settlement that had been founded on the continental mainland by

20. The etymology of *colony*, from the Latin *colonus* (farmer), implies a specific interest in land, not in the native peoples who inhabit that land. Sebastián de Covarrubias, *Tesaurus de la lengua castellana* (Madrid, 1611).

Hernando Cortés), his use still denotes a "town" or "settlement" of Spaniards: "De Colonia deducenda, Progubernatore Cubae Dieco Velasquez incõsulto, consilium ineunt." [They discussed the founding of a colony, although they did not include the vice-governor of Cuba, Diego Velázquez.] And later, "Ad leucas inde duodecim in gleba fortunatissima fundãdae Coloniae locum designant." [Twelve leagues from there, in a very fertile section of land, they marked the spot to found a colony.] However, Peter Martyr's larger narrative also implied that this "colony" was only the necessary first step in a much grander project to eventually evangelize and assimilate the indigenous peoples. Thus, in addition to the coerced labor and tribute, Spanish domination ultimately sought the elimination of native "idolatrous" practices, forms of social organization, and patterns of settlement. To this end, groups of indigenous people were transplanted into *reducciones,* or urban Indian settlements, under the control of Spanish officials or mendicant monks. The overarching narrative that justified such a radical reorganization of native peoples was, of course, the triumphant implantation of Catholicism and the transformation of indigenous peoples from *rústicos* (uncivilized) or *menores* (minors) into mature political subjects, a transformation that required their proximity to, and surveillance by, "civilized" (that is, Christian) people. Whether it involved the mendicant orders, the secular clergy, or imperial officials, the common imperial design was the transformation of the American Indians (despite frequent disagreements about the best way to achieve it).[21]

Although in modern times this ambitious utopian project of social reorganization and economic exploitation of native peoples would come to be known as an integral part of "colonialism," at no time was it identified with the word *colony* during the Hapsburg era. Legally, the conquered territories of the New World were generally referred to as either the "reinos de la Corona de Castilla" [kingdoms of the crown of Castile] or simply as the "virreinatos" [viceroyalties]. In terms of their peculiar political and social organization, the first viceroyalty of New Spain (including Mexico and Mesoamerica) was created in 1534, and a second viceroyalty of Peru (including all of South America excluding Portuguese Brazil) was created in 1542. Until the early eighteenth century, these were the only two viceroyalties in Spanish America. They were conceptualized and designed, at least in legal theory, like other outlying Spanish provinces, with much of the same legislation as the central kingdom but with their own specific laws as well. When the word *colony* did come to be used more frequently during

---

21. Peter Martyr, *Opera: Legatio babylonica [1516], De orbe novo decades octo [1530], Opus epistolarum [1530],* facs. ed. (Graz, 1966), decade 4, chap. 7, fol. 6ov [154].

the eighteenth century in reference to Spanish America, it was in the context of what has been called the "second conquest" by the Bourbon dynasty, which attempted to secularize imperial administration and maximize metropolitan profit from colonial trade by reforming the mercantilist economy.[22]

The case of Brazil under the Portuguese crown presents similar features but has peculiarities all of its own. Since the fifteenth century, Portugal had been involved in the exploration and occupation of small portions of territory in Africa and Asia, erecting a series of *feitorias,* or coastal trading posts. When Alvarez de Cabral discovered new lands on the other side of the Atlantic in 1500, the Portuguese crown did not pay much attention. What it did do was assign donatary captaincies to *fidalgos,* or lesser nobles, who could then distribute these lands among their favored dependents in the form of grants, or *sesmerias,* often of huge extensions. In this way, the crown allowed for new feitorias to be established for the extraction of brazilwood (the tree that gave its name to the country) and the cultivation of sugarcane. The first five decades of Portuguese rule in Brazil were the setting for the decimation of indigenous groups through new diseases, forced labor, and war. Not until 1549 did the crown begin to take its possessions in the New World more seriously, sending a fleet under the command of Governor Tomé de Souza to centralize and oversee the administration of the new territories. Sugar was becoming a precious commodity in European markets, and continual and growing flows of African slaves were imported to increase production in the *engenhos,* or sugar mills, that flourished along the northeast coast of Brazil, especially in the Pernambuco region. The Jesuits arrived with Souza and took over the campaign for evangelization and protection of the Indians. Even before the Spanish annexation of Portugal between 1580 and 1640, Portuguese kings had shown concern for the

---

22. In 1719, the northern part of the viceroyalty of Peru was separated to create the new viceroyalty of Nueva Granada; in 1776, the southern section was separated to form the viceroyalty of Río de la Plata. Anthony Pagden defines the political status of the Spanish possessions in the New World: "The Spanish-American dominions were not colonies—that term is never used to describe any of the Habsburg possesions—but discrete parts of the crown of Castile. As early as the 1560s they had come to be seen by their inhabitants as quasi-autonomous kingdoms, part of what came to be called 'Greater Spain,' *Magnae Hispaniae,* no different, whatever the realities of their legal status, from Aragon, Naples, or the Netherlands"; see *Spanish Imperialism and the Political Imagination: Studies in European and Spanish-American Social and Political Theory, 1513–1830* (New Haven, Conn., 1990), 91. See also Pagden, "Identity Formation in Spanish America," in Canny and Pagden, eds., *Colonial Identity in the Atlantic World,* 63–64. On the Bourbons' "second conquest," see John Lynch, *Spanish Colonial Administration, 1782–1810: The Intendant System in the Viceroyalty of the Río de la Plata* (London, 1958), 4; John R. Fisher, *The Economic Aspects of Spanish Imperialism, 1492–1810* (Liverpool, 1997); Lester D. Langley, *The Americas in the Age of Revolution, 1750–1850* (New Haven, Conn., 1996).

physical and spiritual well-being of their new vassals. In 1511, Manuel I had discouraged the mistreatment of Indians, and, in 1570, King Sebastião prohibited the enslavement of any Indians except those taken prisoners in a just war.[23]

Not unlike the Spanish experience in the Reconquista, or the Portuguese experience in Africa and Asia, the English, too, had had, by 1600, some experience with the acquisition of new dominions by means other than inheritance. In some regards, the English conquest in Wales and Ireland during the sixteenth century raised questions about the nature of colonial territories and their settler communities that would later translate into a New World context. Thus, the sixteenth-century "New" English settlers, soldiers, and administrators recently arrived in Ireland frequently characterized the "Old" English feudal elite, who had established themselves there since the twelfth-century Anglo-Norman conquests, as tainted with the blood and culture of the Gaelic Irish, who were seen as barbaric by both the Old and the New English. Perhaps one of the most famous articulations of this idea of colonial difference in Ireland can be found in Edmund Spenser's *View of the Present State of Ireland,* in the dialogue between the two characters Eudoxus and Irenius:

> *Eudox:* What is this that ye say of so many as remain English of them?
>   Why are not they that were once English abiding English still?
> *Iren:* No, for the most part of them [the Old English] *are degenerated*
>   *and grown almost mere [Gaelic] Irish,* yea and more malicious to the
>   [New] English than the very Irish themselves.
> *Eudox:* What hear I? And is it possible that an Englishman brought up
>   naturally in such sweet civility as England affords could find such
>   liking in that barbarous rudeness that he should forget his own
>   nature and forgo his owne nation? How may this be, or what, I pray
>   you, may be the cause hereof?
> *Iren:* Surely nothing but that first evil ordinance and institution of that
>   commonwealth. But thereof now is here no fit place to speak, lest by
>   the occasion thereof offering matter of a long discourse, we might be
>   drawn from this that we have in hand, namely the handling of abuses
>   in the customs of Ireland.

As Nicolas Canny has explained, this discourse about the degeneracy of the Old English emerged in the context of an intense political conflict between the Old

23. E. Bradford Burns, *A History of Brazil,* 3d ed. (New York, 1993), 40, 54; see also James Lockhart and Stuart B. Schwartz, *Early Latin America: A History of Colonial Spanish America and Brazil* (Cambridge, 1983), 192, 232; Thomas E. Skidmore, *Brazil: Five Centuries of Change* (Oxford, 1999), 25, 31.

English feudal elite and the recently arrived English-borns who saw the Old English as an obstacle to their own social advancement in the colony. In this sense, there existed, as Canny notes, certain parallels between the Irish historical experience during the sixteenth century and the colonial American situation that would emerge during the seventeenth.[24]

But, despite some parallels between the Irish example and the American colonial enterprise, both were ultimately, as early modern English observers such as Francis Bacon quickly recognized, as different "as Amadis de Gaul differs from Caesar's Commentaries." While the Elizabethan colonies in Ireland were sometimes compared to the Roman prototype, America was not regarded as previously owned and lawfully inhabited, on the premise that the American Indians were heathens. Initially, the planting of the English settlements in the New World was therefore explicitly limited to territories not formerly claimed by a Christian prince—although the English also frequently challenged the legitimacy of Pope Alexander VI's Bull of Donation dividing the New World between Spain and Portugal, Alexander being, as Englishmen pointed out, "himselfe a spaniarde borne."[25]

Unlike the Roman colonies, which were provinces of native populations held in subjection by Rome but extended certain benefits of Roman citizenship, the American plantations were understood to be extracts of English people in a land perceived as "new" and "vacant." Insofar as Englishmen used the word *colony* in reference to their possessions in America, they did so interchangeably

24. Edmund Spenser, *A View of the Present State of Ireland* [1596], ed. W. L. Renwick (Oxford, 1970), 48, emphasis added; Nicholas Canny, "Identity Formation in Ireland: The Emergence of the Anglo-Irish," in Canny and Pagden, eds., *Colonial Identity in the Atlantic World*, 159–212, esp. 160, 169–170.

25. James Spedding, Robert Leslie Ellis, and Douglas Denon Heath, eds., *The Works of Francis Bacon* (London, 1858; rpt. Stuttgart-Bad Cannstatt, 1963), IV, 254; Richard Hakluyt, *A Particuler Discourse concerninge the Greate Necessitie and Manifolde Commodyties That Are Like to Growe to This Realme of Englande by the Westerne Discoveries Lately Attempted: Written in the Yere 1584: Known as Discourse of Western Planting*, ed. David B. Quinn and Alison M. Quinn (London, 1993), 97. See also Nicholas Canny, "Writing Atlantic History; or, Reconfiguring the History of Colonial British America," *Journal of American History*, LXXXVI (1999–2000), 1093–1114, esp. 1095. On the differences between the Roman model and the Anglo-American colonies, see also Jack P. Greene, *Peripheries and Center: Constitutional Development in the Extended Polities of the British Empire and the United States, 1607–1788* (Athens, Ga., 1986), 9; Stephen Saunders Webb, *The Governors-General: The English Army and the Definition of the Empire, 1569–1681* (Chapel Hill, N.C., 1979); David Armitage, *The Ideological Origins of the British Empire* (Cambridge, 2000). For some of the principal scholarship on the English conquest of Ireland, see also Nicholas P. Canny, *The Elizabethan Conquest of Ireland: A Pattern Established, 1565–76* (New York, 1976); Canny, *Kingdom and Colony: Ireland in the Atlantic World, 1560–1800* (Baltimore, 1988); K. R. Andrews, N. P. Canny, and P. E. H. Hair, eds., *The Westward Enterprise: English Activities in Ireland, the Atlantic, and America, 1480–1650* (Detroit, 1979).

with the more commonly used word *plantation*. Thus, Thomas Hobbes, in *Leviathan,* used the example of "Colonies sent from *England,* to plant *Virginia,* and *Sommer-Ilands"* in order to prove that assemblies were less "natural" a form of government than monarchy and went on to explain what he meant by the terms "colony" and "plantation":

> The Procreation, or Children of a Commonwealth, are those we call *Plantations,* or *Colonies;* which are numbers of men sent out from the Common-wealth, under a Conductor, or Governour, to inhabit a Forraign Country, either formerly voyd of Inhabitants, or made voyd then, by warre. And when a Colony is setled, they are either a Common-wealth of themselves, discharged of their subjection to their Soveraign that sent them, (as hath been done by many Common-wealths of antient time,) in which case the Common-wealth from which they went was called their Metropolis, or Mother, and requires no more of them, then Fathers require of the Children, whom they emancipate, and make free from their domestique government, which is Honour, and Friendship; or else they remain united to their Metropolis, as were the Colonies of the people of *Rome;* and then they are no Common-wealths themselves, but Provinces, and parts of the Common-wealth that sent them. So that the Right of Colonies (saving Honour, and League with their Metropolis,) dependeth wholly on their Licence, or Letters, by which their Soveraign authorised them to Plant.

For Hobbes, the definition of a plantation/colony had apparently less to do with the ethnic nature of the colonists in the "Foraign Country" (settler or aboriginal) than with the degree of the colony's political dependency on the metropolis. His definition *presumes* that a colony/plantation would have primarily referred to an exclusively English people who had left the metropolis to settle in a foreign land, not to people who were indigenous to that land—which is understood to be "formerly voyd of Inhabitants, or made voyd then, by warre."[26]

However, the overall preference for the word *plantation* over the word *colony* (usually italicized in early modern English print) until the middle of the seventeenth century suggests that the classical model appears to have conveyed only inadequately the initial ideological program of English expansionism in the New World. The sixteenth-century English promoters of empire were, for all of their anti-Spanish rhetoric, profoundly informed by the Spanish messianic

26. Thomas Hobbes, *Leviathan,* ed. C. B. Macpherson (London, 1985), 279–280, 301–302.

model, by the imperative of rivaling everything that Spain had done in the New World—except for doing it the *Reformed* way.[27]

Thus, the first reason for an English plantation in America listed in Richard Hakluyt's programmatic pamphlet *A Discourse of Western Planting* (1584) was the "inlargemente of the [Reformed] gospell of Christe" among the American Indians. Of the twenty-one reasons Hakluyt cites in favor of Western planting, more than half make explicit reference to Spain and its empire in the Americas: Spanish control over trade with the New World would be limited, the treasures that Charles V had extracted from the exploitation of mines would be equaled, the advances of the "popishe Clergye" among the American Indians would be checked, and the Spaniards' "moste outragious and more then Turkishe cruelties in all the west Indies" would be avenged. In his calls upon the English to take seriously their Protestant evangelical mission to the native Americans, Hakluyt advocated "to handle them gently, while gentle courses may be found to serve," though he was also aware from the Spanish example that, "if gentle polishing will not serve, then we shall not want hammerours and rough masons enow . . . to square and prepare them to our Preachers hands."[28]

Once the Virginia Company (an organization of private stockholders and investors) was founded in 1606, it employed a host of Anglican ministers, printed their sermons and pamphlets, and paid them with cash or stock to promote England's evangelical mission in the New World. This mission became subsequently anchored in Virginia's second charter, which stated, "The principal effect which we can desire or expect of this action is the conversion and reduction of the people in those parts unto the true worship of God and christian religion." Even when granting a group of Dissenting Puritans a charter in 1629, Charles I stipulated that the "principal end of the Plantation" in New England was to "win and incite the *Natives* of that Country to the knowledge and Obedience of the only true God." Finally, in 1650 Parliament passed an act appointing the "Corporation for Propagation of the Gospel amongst the Hea-

---

27. Significantly, all of Jack Greene's examples documenting the use of the word "colony" and "colonizing" originate from the eighteenth century; see Greene, *Peripheries*, 9, 221n. 5. Hakluyt, however, writes: "Nowe the meanes to sende suche as shall labour effectually in this busines ys by plantinge one or twoo Colonies of our nation uppon that fyrme, where they may remaine in safetie, and firste learne the language of the people nere adjoyninge . . . and by little and little acquainte themselves with their manner, and so with discrecion and myldenes distill into their purged myndes the swete and lively liquor [lignes?] of the gospell." *Discourse of Western Planting*, ed. Quinn and Quinn, 9.

28. Hakluyt, *Discourse of Western Planting*, ed. Quinn and Quinn, 57; *Virginia Richly Valued, by the Description of the Maine Land of Florida, Her Next Neighbour . . . Translated out of Portugese by Richard Hakluyt* (London, 1609), epistle dedicatory, n.p.

then Natives in New England," under which regular funds were provided for the New England missions to the Indians. Thus, the English idea of a "plantation" in America was initially invested with a utopianism and messianism that the classical idea of a "colony" would have conveyed only imperfectly—the Western planting of the Protestant seed in the heathen soils of America.[29]

During the second part of the century the word *colony* increasingly seems to replace *plantation* in reference to an exclusively English settlement in the Americas. While the word *plantation* itself now assumes the secular and economic connotation of what Philip D. Curtin has called a "plantation complex"—a privately owned estate whose purpose is the protoindustrial agricultural production of consumer goods based on slave labor (as in a sugar or tobacco plantation)—the civic connotation of the word *colony* now makes it interchangeable with *province,* as England's apostolic mission seems to take second or third place behind the goals of expanding the English dominion and trade in a "new kind of empire" built primarily for mercantile objectives. Charles II's 1681 "Charter for the Province of Pennsylvania," for example, specifies three reasons for the establishment of the "Colonie" but lists evangelization last: A "Desire to enlarge our *English* Empire, and promote such usefull comodities as may bee of Benefit to us and Our Dominions, as also to reduce the savage Natives by gentle and just manners to the Love of Civil Societie and Christian Religion."[30]

Throughout the early Americas, it was precisely the stark contrast between Europe's early utopian designs for a New World and the inevitable shortfalls of that utopian project that raised, for the first time, the perennial European question whether the discovery of America—still in 1552 famously hailed by Francisco López de Gómara as "the greatest event since the creation of the world" (excepting the birth of Christ)—was not, after all, anything but a colos-

29. Keith Kavenagh, ed., *Foundations of Colonial America: A Documentary History* (New York, 1973), 1715. See also Louis B. Wright, *Religion and Empire: The Alliance between Piety and Commerce in English Expansion 1558–1625* (Chapel Hill, N.C., 1943); John Parker, "Religion and the Virginia Colony, 1609–10," in Andrews, Canny, and Hair, eds., *The Westward Enterprise,* 245–270; New England charter quoted in Cotton Mather, *The Triumphs of Reformed Religion, in America: The Life of the Renowned John Eliot . . .* (Boston, 1691), 77.

30. Philip D. Curtin, *The Rise and Fall of the Plantation Complex: Essays in Atlantic History* (Cambridge, 1990), 14. The literature on this transformation is extensive. For only a few modern examples, see David Hancock, "A World of Business to Do": William Freeman and the Foundations of England's Commercial Empire, 1645–1707," *William and Mary Quarterly,* 3d Ser., LVII (2000), 3–34; Eric Hinderaker, "The 'Four Indian Kings' and the Imaginative Construction of the First British Empire," *WMQ,* 3d Ser., LIII (1996), 487–526; Armitage, *Ideological Origins.* Charter in Kavenagh, ed., *Foundations of Colonial America,* 849.

sal mistake. As Samuel Purchas argued during the early seventeenth century, the Spaniards had given to the New World "an Iron Age for a golden,"

> imposing a heavy yoke of servitude which hath consumed worlds of people in this New World, and made the Name of CHRIST and *Christian* to stinke amongst them: yea, they abhorre the Sea it selfe, for bringing forth such monsters, as they thinke the Spaniards: whom for their execrable wickednes, they esteemed, not to come of humane generation, but of the froth of the Sea, and therefore call them *Viracochie*, or Seafroth.

Purchas's lamentation of Spanish shortfalls was, of course, intended to provide an ideological pretext for Protestant encroachments on Spanish-American territories. Almost twenty years before Purchas, Walter Ralegh had even argued that the English reformers would restore the "legitimate" rule of the native Inca elite, who had wrongly been supplanted by Spanish usurpers.[31]

Ironically, however, the common charge that things had not gone according to God's design in the New World because of human depravities originated, not with Protestant English historians, but rather with a historiographic tradition that had emerged from within Spain herself. Even as early as the works of Peter Martyr, the Spanish imperial historians had criticized the conquerors (and later their descendants), such as Cortés, for their alleged "treachery and false dealings" in disobeying imperial authority, enriching themselves by exploiting the Indians without regard for their physical and spiritual well-being and even for mixing with them without inhibitions. Later court historians, such as Juan López de Velasco, Antonio de Herrera y Tordesillas, and Gil González Dávila, advanced an even more pessimistic judgment of the first conquerors, suggesting that they and their creole descendants had succumbed to the "American" disorder and immorality that the Spanish conquerors had been sent to redeem;

---

31. Gómara quoted in J. H. Elliott, *The Old World and the New, 1492–1650* (Cambridge, 1970), 10; Samuel Purchas, *Purchas His Pilgrimage; or, Relations of the World and the Religions Observed in All Ages and Places, Discovered, from the Creation unto this Present: This First Containing a Theologicall and Geographical Historie of Asia, Africa, and America, with the Islands Adjacent* (London, 1613), 606; Walter Ralegh, *The Discoverie of the Large, Rich, and Bewtiful Empyre of Guiana*, ed. Neil L. Whitehead (Norman, Okla., 1997), 134. On the role of Ralegh, Drake, and other British interlopers in the internal tensions of viceregal Peru and in the formation of a creole identity, see José Antonio Mazzotti, "The Dragon and the Seashell: British Corsairs, Epic Poetry, and Creole Nation in Viceregal Peru," in Álvaro Félix Bolaños and Gustavo Verdesio, eds., *Colonialism Past and Present: Reading and Writing about Colonial Latin America Today* (New York, 2002), 197–214.

they had, in effect, been "conquered" by the very America invented in the discourses of the conquest, by a place where the devil's unrestrained force had turned upside down God's natural order.[32]

Empires and Creole Subjects

Judgments such as these by the court-based imperial historians rested partially on the devastating testimonies by well-meaning monks such as Fray Antón de Montesinos and Bartolomé de las Casas, whose admirable and passionate defense of the Indians precipitated a remarkable "struggle for justice" within the Spanish Empire. This "struggle for justice" culminated in a series of high-profile debates taking place in Valladolid in 1550–1551, which were to decide whether the American Indians were, in the Aristotelian sense, "natural slaves" and, thus, whether their conquest by the Spanish conquerors had been a "just" war. However, as many modern historians have pointed out, there was more at stake in this struggle than merely the crown's humanitarian concern on behalf of the American Indians. What was equally at stake was the crown's interest in a geopolitical struggle as it had arisen from the internal constitutional tensions and contradictions of a transoceanic empire of unprecedented geographic and cultural dimensions. For, despite the *theoretical* equality of the Spanish-American viceroyalties vis-à-vis Spain's possessions in Europe, it was apparent that they were not carbon copies of fifteenth-century Mediterranean viceroyalties and Aragonese possessions (such as Naples, Milan, Sicily, Sardinia, Piombino, and Mallorca). The Spanish Americas had their idiosyncratic features, which became increasingly pronounced over time and, hence, subject to particularist legislation. For example, while Naples and Milan had retained their indigenous political institutions, those of the American Indians were systematically replaced by Spanish institutions in the course of the sixteenth century.[33]

The Americas were furthermore unique in the division of imperial subjects into the "república de españoles" and the "república de indios." The leading political offices were thereby invariably occupied by Spaniards sent from Spain,

32. On the idea of America as a mistake, see Henry Steele Commager and Elmo Giordanetti, eds., *Was America a Mistake? An Eighteenth-Century Controversy* (Columbia, S.C., 1967). Peter Martyr, *De Novo Orbe; or, The Historie of the West Indies*, trans. M. Lok and R. Eden, ed. Richard Hakluyt (London, 1612), 168.

33. See Lewis Hanke, *The Spanish Struggle for Justice in the Conquest of America* (Philadelphia, 1965); D. A. Brading, *The First America: The Spanish Monarchy, Creole Patriots, and the Liberal State, 1492–1867* (Cambridge, 1991), 68–72; Sigfrido Radaelli, *La institución virreinal en las Indias: antecedentes históricos* (Buenos Aires, 1957), 18.

not by the native-born elites. Finally, the mercantilist organization of trade that prohibited interregional commerce among the Spanish-American viceroyalties and that channeled all economic activity through the Casa de la Contratación in Seville accorded the American territories a peculiar status of economic dependency within the empire. As a consequence, the Spanish-American possessions were characterized by a similar kind of foreign domination and exploitation that we identify today with "colony," informed as it is by the model of the Second British Empire.[34]

This is most patent for the experiences of American Indians, whose internal differences between indigenous groups began to be blurred by the common denominator of being an "Indian" (born in the Indies) and being exploited by the same entity, that is, Spanish authorities—despite the eloquent efforts by the crown to implement protective laws and the brave testimonies of clergymen denouncing the abuse of the Indians. But in the experiences of the creoles, too, there was a growing ambiguity in their status as imperial citizens vis-à-vis the inhabitants of the Spanish territories in Europe. Thus, the debate over the justness of the Spanish conquest of the New World was intimately linked with the crown's attempt to roll back the former neofeudal privileges it had granted to the conquerors and their descendants, especially the grants of a perpetual *encomienda,* wherein a Spanish official (generally a conqueror) was given charge over a particular part of the indigenous population, collecting the royal tribute in return for protecting and evangelizing these new vassals of the king. This economic system, in conjunction with the system of *repartos,* or land grants handed out to the conquerors, had created a group of New World aristocrats with so much wealth and power that they even dared to challenge the crown itself (in the 1544–1548 rebellion of Gonzalo Pizarro in Peru) and to propose perpetual ownership of the lands for themselves (in a 1555 proposal by Peruvian encomienda holders, or *encomenderos,* to the crown).[35]

The aristocratic pretensions of this New World elite were from the beginning considered suspect not only by the crown, which had long been attempting to bring under tighter control the feudal houses of Spain, but also by the Old World nobility, who were well aware of the lowly social origins of most of

34. This domination is especially marked for the examples of South Africa and India. For a summary of the periods and modalities of British imperialism, see Simon C. Smith, *British Imperialism, 1750–1970* (Cambridge, 1998), esp. chaps. 1–3, The British Library of Information, and P. J. Marshall, ed., *The Cambridge Illustrated History of the British Empire* (Cambridge, 1996), 318–337.

35. Brading, *The First America,* 68–72.

the American conquerors. During the sixteenth century, Peninsular Spaniards scoffed at the fact that in the Americas any creole who held a few Indians in encomienda referred to himself as a "Don"—a title that was on the Peninsula still reserved for the nobility during the sixteenth century. The creoles' legitimacy as a neofeudal elite thus hinged rather precariously, not on a natural right of birth, but exclusively on a spotless record in imperial service. Indeed, the original encomiendas had been granted on the condition that the grantees had served the monarch in a "just war" (such as was the Reconquest of Spain from the Moors) and that they were upholding their duty of caring for the spiritual well-being of the natives. If, on the other hand, the conquest of America had been an unjust war and, particularly, if the conquerors had fallen short of their obligations vis-à-vis the American Indians, it was, as the court historian Antonio de Herrera y Tordesillas pointed out during the early seventeenth century, "legitimate reason to deprive them of their encomiendas; wherefore the king ordered that care be taken to find out whether the encomenderos complied with the obligation with which they were charged." Indeed, in 1542, the crown passed the so-called New Laws, which were aimed primarily at dismantling the neofeudal institution of encomienda. While the crown had to make several compromises with the conquerors and their descendants (due in part to its fear of more rebellions), the latter were convinced that these measures were a deliberate political attack on their neoaristocratic way of life.[36]

Whatever the ultimate intentions that inspired this metropolitan legislation might have been, the fact is that the New Laws did not result in population growth or better living conditions for indigenous communities. On the contrary, in the core regions of New Spain and Peru, the various new compromise solutions, such as the institution of the *repartimiento* (a rationed and rotational recruitment system that essentially divided the available native labor between the conquerors and the viceregal government), only increased the burden on the native communities and led to even more appalling social and demographic disintegrations. The decline of Indian populations, in turn, caused the social demise also of the neofeudal class of the conquerors, who had lived off the labor of the Indians they had held in encomienda. By the final decades of the sixteenth century, many creoles felt that their situation was dire. As Bernal Díaz del Castillo complained in his old age, they who had suffered the "great dangers and travails as well as hunger and thirst and endless toils" of the conquest were

---

36. J. H. Elliott, *Imperial Spain, 1469–1716* (London, 2002), 213; Pedro Henríquez-Ureña, *Literary Currents in Hispanic America* (Cambridge, Mass., 1946), 35; Antonio de Herrera y Tordesillas, *Historia general de los hechos de los castellanos en las islas y tierrafirme del mar oceano o "Decadas"* (1601–1615), ed. Mariano Cuesta Domingo (Madrid, 1991), IV, 215.

now "very poor, and burdened with sons and daughters to marry off, and grandchildren to maintain, and little rent to do it with, and so we pass our lives, in pain, in labor, and in sorrow."[37]

If these discontented conquerors were increasingly regarded with suspicion by the crown, their creole offspring's loyalty was equally cause for uneasiness. To be "creole," and in particular to be a direct descendant of a conqueror or one of the earliest *pobladores* (or settlers), was also to possess the feelings of belonging to the *patria*, or fatherland, and of being entitled to the privileges of *señorío* in the new kingdom. These were the feelings of many of the conquerors themselves. The claims made by American-born Spaniards for *prelación*, or preferential treatment, from the Spanish crown were a constant presence in almost every aspect of viceregal law and social organization.[38]

The late-sixteenth-century identity of the new creole subjects was thus founded upon the mythic memory of the "glorious" conquest. While this myth of the conquest remained strong in the creole historical imagination during the seventeenth century, the gradual abrogation of the old encomienda system forced the creole sector of the colonial population to adjust to the new order. The creoles' attempts at coping with the situation, however, were frequently met with additional imperial policies that ultimately frustrated their advancement. Some creoles found prominent positions as functionaries within

37. Bernal Díaz del Castillo, *Historia verdadera de la conquista de la Nueva España* (Buenos Aires, 1955), 672–673, our translation. As the overseer of the poor in the City of Kings (Lima) noted in a letter "written in his own hand" to Philip II, dated Dec. 12, 1588: "Justly, the needy ones from here ask that they be given a greater part of the resources, for many of them are the sons, brothers, and relatives of those who conquered and won over these lands and who have faithfully served your majesty with no gratification or reward. The number of these people is so great and their needs so extensive that, even if ten thousand silver pesos were distributed among them each year from the contributions collected, it would represent very little help in terms of the growing numbers of the Shameful Poor." Archive of Indies, Lima, 32.

On the encomienda in New Spain, see Charles Gibson, *The Aztecs under Spanish Rule: A History of the Indians of the Valley of Mexico, 1519–1810* (Stanford, Calif., 1964), 222–233, 323–326. On Peru, see Luis Millones, *Perú colonial: de Pizarro a Túpac Amaru II* (Lima, 1995), especially chap. 2; José de la Puente Brunke, *Encomiendas y encomenderos en el Perú: estudio social y político de una institución colonial* (Seville, 1992). A general view of the encomienda system can be found in the canonical work by Silvio A. Zavala, *La encomienda indiana* (1935), 2d ed. (Mexico City, 1973).

38. See Jacques Lafaye, *Quetzalcóatl and Guadalupe: The Formation of Mexican National Consciousness, 1531–1813*, trans. Benjamin Keen (Chicago, 1987), 7–8; Solange Alberro, *Del gachupín al criollo: o de cómo los españoles de México dejaron de serlo* (Mexico City, 1992); Bernard Lavallé, "Del 'espíritu colonial' a la reivindicación criolla a los álbores del criollismo peruano," *Histórica*, II (1978), 39–41. Viceroy Conde del Villar attested to this presence explicitly in a letter to Philip II dated May 12, 1588: "There are a great many claimants in this kingdom because the conquerors and first settlers have left children, each one of whom expects to be fully compensated for the service of his father." A.G.I., Lima, 32.

the vast imperial administrative apparatus of the Spanish Empire in the Americas, which has been compared to a Baroque "lettered city." However, the apex of this administrative pyramid always remained in Spain, and the leading offices were reserved for Peninsular Spaniards, who, all too often, represented particularly Peninsular interests. Other creoles came to hold prominent positions in the religious orders, especially the Jesuits—who would later be expelled from the Americas by the Bourbon dynasty in 1767 partially for that reason. Yet others figured prominently as merchants in viceregal commerce, even competing with the Peninsular merchants for economic domination in the New World. In New Spain, for example, the creoles' growing economic power was due in part to a lucrative Pacific trade in Chinese fabric and Peruvian minerals. This trade, however, was eventually stopped by royal decree in 1639, largely because it competed with the interests of Peninsular manufacturers and merchants.[39]

These socioeconomic factors combined to foment a distinct creole consciousness in the various parts of Spanish America that is reflected in various ways in the literary record. In Peru, many creoles began to declare their capital city of Lima to be the center of human civilization and the highest peak of New World religiosity. An extensive descriptive bibliography attests to the extent of creole exaltations of their cities and the physical richness of their lands. From Mexico, the examples extend from Bernardo de Balbuena's *Grandeza mexicana* to Sigüenza y Góngora's *Paraíso occidental* as well as to the works of Sor Juana Inés de la Cruz (discussed by Stephanie Merrim in her essay below); in Peru, from Rodrigo de Valdés's *Fundación y grandezas de Lima* to the poetic works of Pedro de Peralta y Barnuevo (discussed by Jerry Williams below). In all cases, the superlative descriptions of American cities and territories reveal not just the psychological profile of their authors but also the subjective locus of their articulations and, consequently, their constitution as discursive and social subjects. These particular features would clearly differentiate the creoles from the other social subjects within the viceroyalties (a point to which we will return below). The creoles argued that their innate talents and their familiarity with the land and indigenous populations made them more suitable to govern the Indians. Through such glorifications, lettered creoles sought the symbolic authority necessary to achieve more administrative access and a viceregal government more dedicated to the common good.[40]

39. Angel Rama, *The Lettered City*, ed. and trans. John Charles Chasteen (Durham, N.C., 1996); J. I. Israel, *Race, Class, and Politics in Colonial Mexico, 1610–1670* (New York, 1975), 99–101.

40. See Margarita Suárez, *Desafíos transatlánticos: mercaderes, banqueros, y el estado en el Perú virreinal, 1600–1700* (Lima, 2001); José Antonio Mazzotti, "La heterogeneidad colonial peruana y la construcción del discurso criollo en el siglo XVII," in Mazzotti and Juan Zevallos, eds., *Asedios a*

In short, Spanish-American creoles found diverse ways to negotiate with and confront Spanish power, whether as writers, merchants, officeholders, or landed elites. Lettered creoles, especially, responded time and again to the marginalization implied in the privileged, Eurocentric disdain, producing numerous pages of their own dedicated to exalting the character and appearance of the distinguished descendants of the conquerors. In doing so, these creole intellectuals carried out the immense task of creating a discursive corpus to articulate their own conception of Hispanic identity. Indeed, by the late seventeenth century, the Mexican creole patriot Carlos de Sigüenza y Góngora proudly referred to his New World community as "nuestra criolla nación" [our creole nation].[41]

In Brazil, a distinct creole identity also emerged largely in response to negative metropolitan biases toward colonial society. In addition to the presence of the indigenous and African populations, sixteenth-century incursions by French Huguenots and a seventeenth-century occupation of Recife and Rio de Janeiro by Dutch troops further served to consolidate a sense of collective identity among Brazilian elites. Theirs was an identity based upon a common religion (Catholicism), language (Portuguese), and ancestry (Lusitan nobility and regional origins). According to E. Bradford Burns, the expulsion of the Dutch from Recife in 1654 "awoke the first national sentiments among the varied and scattered inhabitants of the sprawling colony.... That achievement infused into the Brazilians a new pride that replaced their old feeling of inferiority before the Portuguese." The Brazilians that Burns refers to were not simply the remnants of an old aristocracy; they also included the enterprising sugar planters, who had become "an aristocracy with pretensions of noble status." The descendants of Brazil's landowning elite "went to Portugal to study." "Virtually all went to the University of Coimbra, the most famous and influential in Portugal, where 300 Brazilian-born students enrolled between 1772 and 1785."[42]

Unlike the Spanish who transplanted many of their cultural institutions in the New World, the Portuguese did not establish a single university or printing press

---

la heterogeneidad cultural: libro de homenaje a Antonio Cornejo Polar (Philadelphia, 1996), 173–175.

41. Carlos de Sigüenza y Góngora, *Seis obras,* ed. William G. Bryant (Caracas, 1984), 250. Although this American perspective surely differed in many respects from a Peninsular Spanish one, we should be careful not to assume that it necessarily prefigured the struggle for independence, nor that it in any sense suggested an essentialist kind of biological or spiritual kinship between creoles and the majority of underprivileged Amerindians, blacks, and *castas* ("castes," or racially mixed groups). By "nation" creole patriots such as Sigüenza y Góngora did not mean a nation-state separate from the empire but rather a nation equal in status and value to other nations (Castilians, Sicilians, and so forth) *within* the empire.

42. Burns, *A History of Brazil,* 40, 54; see also Lockhart and Schwartz, *Early Latin America,* 192, 232; Skidmore, *Brazil: Five Centuries of Change,* 25, 31.

in their American territories until the nineteenth century. Despite their local patriotism and their pride in being the greatest producers of the Portuguese Empire (providing sugar, cotton, coffee, and gold), the Brazilian white elite kept their close ties with the metropolis. It was not until the long administration of the marqués de Pombal (1750–1777) that the Portuguese crown allowed literature and the arts to flourish in Brazil. By that time, Indians were being pushed into learning Portuguese and persuaded to forget their own languages. The subsequent transfer, in 1808, of the Portuguese crown from Lisbon to Rio de Janeiro (due to Napoleon's invasion of the Iberian Peninsula) gave Brazil new status as the center of the Portuguese Empire and a kingdom parallel to the European metropolis. "For this elite [Brazilians of European descent] as for others, family links were crucial in gaining favors from state power. Family clans regularly infiltrated the state structure, turning it to their advantage. In Brazil, the colonists also had to nurture their links with the crown. By doing so successfully, they produced strong clans of long-standing influence. These clans were regional and contributed to the oligarchies that would dominate Brazil after independence." Although João VI returned to Portugal in 1821, his son Pedro remained in Brazil, declared Brazilian independence with the support of the local white elite, and became Pedro I, emperor of Brazil.[43]

Similarly, in British America, a creole consciousness developed largely as a phenomenon among the colonial elite in response to negative metropolitan attitudes about the creoles' social origins in Europe and to their cultural difference in the new environment in America. Also, as in Spanish America, these metropolitan attitudes were in part the result of the inevitable contrast between the utopian New Worlds that had been evoked by the early promoters of English expansionism and the actual shapes that colonial life assumed in historical reality. Finally, as in Spanish America, these stereotypes had geopolitical dimensions and consequences, as British-American creoles lost certain political privileges that they felt were due them. The troubling debate whether the English plantations had been failures began practically as soon as (or even before) the first permanent settlement at Jamestown had been founded and repeated disasters such as starvation, Indian massacres, and rebellions afflicted the colony. In the tracts published when the plantation was under the aristocratic regime of the Virginia Company (1606–1624), the "extreme choler and passion" that notoriously characterized colonial life were blamed on the lowly social origins of most of the colonists. The fact that many of the settlers had slipped old ties by migrating to America and the fact that many appeared to be

43. Skidmore, *Brazil: Five Centuries of Change*, 25.

the dregs of Old World societies prompted the aristocratic leadership to institute a stern regimen in the belief that they "would be useful only when subject to arbitrary rule." Such endeavors provoked obstinate opposition from the colonists, which, in turn, was decried as treasonable and was rigorously suppressed. Finally, in 1624, the crown stepped in, voiding the charter of the Virginia Company and declaring the colony royal property over opposition in Parliament and from the aristocratic investors.[44]

If the turbulence during Virginia's early years did much to crystallize common English notions that the colonies were the habitat of "convicts, whores, poorhouse veterans, and bankrupt citizens," the gradual economic stabilization with the rise of tobacco cultivation and trade modified these notions only insofar, as Carole Shammas has put it, that now the colonials were regarded as "worthless moneygrubbers who neglected social amenities and thought only of trade." By the time that the first native-born generation of English creoles came of age, Virginia had developed into a new though highly stratified plantation society. On the one hand, there was the newly rich planter class that fashioned itself in the style of the Old English gentry, sending its children to England for an aristocratic education and marriage match. On the other hand, the appropriation of enormous tracts of land by a few of the original settlers quickly led to social unrest among the newcomers to the colony, especially ex-servants who found themselves faced with dwindling opportunities to become independent freeholders. This tendency was further aggravated by the gradual replacement of English indentured servants by an increasing number of African slaves in the agricultural labor force, as the acquisition of slaves, though considered more economical in the long run, required a larger starting capital than many smaller plantation households could muster.[45]

44. Michael Zuckerman, "Identity in British America: Unease in Zion," in Canny and Pagden, eds., *Colonial Identity in the Atlantic World*, 115–157, esp. 141; Shammas, "English-Born and Creole Elites," in Tate and Ammerman, eds., *Chesapeake in the Seventeenth Century*, 277. See also David W. Galenson, *White Servitude in Colonial America: An Economic Analysis* (Cambridge, 1981); Nicholas Canny, "The Permissive Frontier: Social Control in English Settlements in Ireland and Virginia, 1550–1650," in Andrews, Canny, and Hair, eds., *The Westward Enterprise*, 17–44, esp. 18, 27; Michael Zuckerman, "The Fabrication of Identity in Early America," *WMQ*, 3d Ser., XXXIV (1977), 141; James Horn, *Adapting to a New World: English Society in the Seventeenth-Century Chesapeake* (Chapel Hill, N.C., 1994).

45. Shammas, "English-Born and Creole Elites," in Tate and Ammerman, eds., *Chesapeake in the Seventeenth Century*, 275; see also Burnard, *Creole Gentlemen*, 205–236; Jack P. Greene, *Pursuits of Happiness: The Social Development of Early Modern British Colonies and the Formation of American Culture* (Chapel Hill, N.C., 1988); T. H. Breen, *Tobacco Culture: The Mentality of the Great Tidewater Planters on the Eve of Revolution* (Princeton, N.J., 1985), 86; Lois Green Carr, Russell R. Menard, and Lorena S. Walsh, *Robert Cole's World: Agriculture and Society in Early Maryland* (Chapel Hill, N.C., 1991).

Similarly, in British Barbados the introduction of protoindustrial plantation-style sugar production had produced a planter class of approximately 175 individuals who together owned more than half of the insular territories and who each owned sixty slaves or more. While this class of planters aspired to social recognition as a new aristocracy, they visibly fell short in the traditional English social values attributed to that class. Instead, the planters there were known to live the extravagant boom-and-bust style of the noveau riche, which contrasted sharply with the abject conditions of servants, slaves, and even the struggling smaller planters with whom they shared the islands. The society that originated on the sugar islands was seen by English observers as a "fast-living, fast-dying tropical community" of profiteers, rogues, and prostitutes. It was, in the judgment of a contemporary, a "dunghill whereon England doth cast forth its rubbish" and even in the judgment of modern historians a "disastrous social failure" that had no counterpart in English experience.[46]

As in early Spanish America, then, in much of early British America the aristocratic pretensions of the creole elites and the legitimacy of their incipient political power in colonial society were regarded with extreme suspicion and even outright contempt by imperial administrators, most of whom were members of the Old World aristocracy. As second-generation colonials, most of them born in America, were replacing their immigrant parents in the colonial leadership, the perceived failures of colonial life by the standards of Old World (historical or utopian) models were now more often explained in terms of the colonials' American birth rather than their nonaristocratic lineage. Thus, while "English society had questioned the social origins of the immigrant elite," Shammas writes, "in the case of the native elite they questioned its Englishness." English contempt for the colonial planter aristocracy openly surfaced during Bacon's Rebellion, which erupted in Virginia in 1676, when bands of frontier settlers started a war against the neighboring Indians in open defiance of the authority of Governor Sir William Berkeley. This internal conflict strengthened metropolitan arguments that the Virginia pseudoaristocrats were incapable of handling their own affairs. The geopolitical ramification of the intense social and racial conflict in Virginia was a "full-scale reconsideration" of the relations between the American provinces and central administration. Although Virginia had lost its status as a charter colony and became royal property in 1624, local political institutions, such as the Virginia House of Burgesses, had provided conduits for representing the planters' interests. However, colo-

46. See Richard S. Dunn, *Sugar and Slaves: The Rise of the Planter Class in the English West Indies, 1624–1713* (Chapel Hill, N.C., 1972), 47–61, 77, 340.

nial offices of imperial administration became increasingly reserved to English-born aristocrats. Thus, from a whole generation of native-born Virginians, only the adventive Daniel Parke II (1669–1710) managed to enter the English political arena outside the colony.[47]

In New England, too, the perceived failures of the creole elite to bring about their apostolic Protestant errand had very concrete geopolitical ramifications. In the early decades of the seventeenth century, the New England colonies, while intimately connected in the transatlantic trading network, had remained relatively independent from metropolitan control, their political autonomy protected by their charters and their economies based on farming, fishing, and trade. However, the radical reformers' political autonomy came increasingly under attack after the Restoration of the Stuart monarchy in 1660, with the introduction of policies of religious toleration and economic mercantilism, such as the Navigation Acts. Not unlike the Spanish *Consejo de Indias* (Council of the Indies) in the 1540s, British authorities during the 1670s grew increasingly determined to bring colonial administration more closely into line with metropolitan interests. When, in 1675, King Philip's War broke out on the New England frontier and brought the colonies to the brink of annihilation, the New England elite was portrayed by imperial authorities and the popular press in London as an unqualified and even savage lot of bigots—as "Devouring Wolves"—who had mismanaged colonial Indian relations, causing harvests in dead Indian bodies rather than in living Indians' souls. In 1684, the charter of Massachusetts Bay was revoked, and the New England elite was left in perpetual struggle with the insular governors now sent to the colonies from London. It was in part the attempt to counterpoint these "late oppressors of New-England" that inspired Cotton Mather's patriotic biographies of New England's leading personages during the seventeenth century in his *Magnalia Christi Americana* (1702)—perhaps the most monumental expression of an emerging creole consciousness in colonial British America.[48]

Thus, in both Spanish and British America, a creole consciousness emerged largely in reaction to what colonials perceived to be unfair metropolitan biases

47. Shammas, "English-Born and Creole Elites," in Tate and Ammerman, eds., *Chesapeake in the Seventeenth Century*, 276, 287; Stephen Saunders Webb, *1676: The End of American Independence* (New York, 1984), 205.

48. Bernard Bailyn, *The New England Merchants in the Seventeenth Century* (New York, 1964); Hancock, "A World of Business," *WMQ*, 3d Ser., LVII (2000), 3–34; John J. McCusker and Russell R. Menard, *The Economy of British America, 1607–1789* (Chapel Hill, N.C., 1985), 111; Greene, *Peripheries and Center*, 13; Samuel Groom, *A Glass for the People of New England, in Which They May See Themselves* . . . (London, 1676), 16. See also Webb, *1676*; Mather, *Magnalia Christi Americana*, I, 573.

and policies: the result of a combination of factors, such as a European ethno-centrism that equated cultural difference with cultural degeneracy, the inevi-table Baroque disenchantment of the European utopianism that had under-written much of the cultural energy of Renaissance expansionism, and the deliberate exploitation of this disenchantment for the geopolitical purpose of imperial consolidation. Finally, the colonial ambiguity of creoles originated with the ill-defined nature of an unprecedented imperial project. Creoles were European by descent and citizens of empire; but, unlike the European imperial functionaries traveling in and writing about the New World, their cultural location within the empire was defined by what Benedict Anderson has called the "fatality of trans-Atlantic birth." Whereas the imperial functionary traveled for social advancement back in the metropolis, in a modern-day form of lateral and vertical "pilgrimage," Anderson suggests, the mobility of the creoles was blocked by the geographic, social, and even legal boundaries placed upon them by imperialist cultural ideologies and concrete colonial policies.[49]

The Colonial Sociology of Creole Subjectivity and the Question of Race

In order to bolster their claim to legitimacy as a ruling elite (and perhaps to compensate for the Peninsular disdain that often rested on them), creoles would insist that their loyalty and blood were purer even than the Spaniards'. In 1683, Juan Meléndez, a creole Dominican priest from Lima, declared,

> Hacemos pues mucho aprecio los Criollos de las Yndias de ser Españoles, y de que nos llamen assi, y nos tengan por tales, y en orden à conseruar esta sangre Española pura, y limpia se pone tanto cuydado, que no tiene ponderacion.

> We creoles of the Indies greatly appreciate being Spanish, and being called such and considered as such, and we go to any length to preserve the cleanliness and purity of this Spanish blood.

However, Meléndez also noted that creoles identified themselves as different from Peninsular Spaniards, who in their ignorance toward creoles were seen as "safios," or idiots, and less than human:

49. Benedict Anderson, *Imagined Communities: Reflections on the Origin and Spread of Nationalism* (London, 1983), 57.

Para distinguirnos de los mismos Españoles que nacieron en España, nos llamamos allà Criollos, voz que de cierto en España se ríen mucho: pero con la razón con que se ríen algunos de todo lo que no entienden: propiedad de gente safia indigna de tener figura de hombres.

In order to distinguish ourselves from the Spaniards born in Spain, we call ourselves creoles, a term that Spaniards undoubtedly laugh at very much; but they laugh using the same logic as those who laugh at everything they do not understand. This is typical of stupid people who do not deserve to figure as human beings.[50]

The varying interactions between creoles and peoples of non-European descent played an important role in the distinct evolution of creole subjectivities in various regions of the Americas. As several of the following essays show, a prominent response of both Spanish- and British-American creoles to their ambiguous coloniality is their assertion of an identity and cultural continuity with their Old World ancestors, particularly manifest in colonial Euro-American creoles' assertions of being white. It has been suggested elsewhere that the early modern invention of racial essence and purity as well as the identification of peoples in categories such as white and black were, paradoxically, the very products of a creolized subjectivity—a subjectivity shaped not so much by "general Old World notions about race and color," but rather by the experience of alterity in the New World "long after initial colonization." However, as some of the essays here suggest, the emergence of this discourse of race in the New World was not so much a product of natural creolization processes among peoples who became aware of their racial identity in the face of racial alterity—in the encounter of European, native American, and African peoples in the Americas—as it was a dialectical and often rhetorical response to environmental determinism in neoclassical natural history. The discourse of race throughout the Americas thus came to form the epistemological basis for colonial Euro-American political assertions of equality vis-à-vis Europeans within the geography and sociology of imperial power.[51]

---

50. Juan Meléndez, *Tesoros verdaderos de las Yndias: en la historia de la gran provinçia de San Iuan Bautista del Peru, de el orden de Predicadores* (Rome, 1681–1682), I, 353–354.

51. See T. H. Breen, "Creative Adaptations," in Greene and Pole, eds., *Colonial British America*, 221; see also Breen and Stephen Innes, *"Myne Owne Ground": Race and Freedom on Virginia's Eastern Shore, 1640–1676* (New York, 1980); Peter H. Wood, *Black Majority: Negroes in Colonial South Carolina from 1670 through the Stono Rebellion* (New York, 1974); for Spanish America, see Cañizares Esguerra "New World, New Stars," *AHR*, CIV (1999), 33–68. On the concept of race in

In colonial Spanish America, for example, where the particular colonial exchanges between Spanish, native American, and African cultures had produced a regionally highly variable mosaic of cultural and racial *mestizaje* (racial mixture), the category *criollo* was used to distinguish American-born peoples of European descent not only from Peninsular Spaniards, Africans, and Indians but also (and often primarily) from those of mixed ancestry (mainly mestizos) in an elaborate system of *castas* (castes) in which the criollos inhabited a privileged yet highly ambiguous position. Although creoles insisted on their pure Spanish ancestry, it was not unusual to hear about the dark origin of some creoles, as somewhere between 20 and 40 percent of all defined as criollo were in fact biologically mestizos whose assimilation as creoles was linked to their Spanish fathers' efforts to retain certain privileges in colonial society. This unofficial miscegenation was in part the result of an increasingly common practice on the part of imperial officials to sell "certificates of whiteness" *(cédulas de gracias al sacar)* to those who could not otherwise assume to be identified as such. Thus, in 1749 Jorge Juan and Antonio de Ulloa, two Peninsular Spaniards who participated in the Charles de La Condamine expedition to South America, reported:

> The largest proportion of the population consisted of mestizos and castes. In some cities they are mixtures of Indians and Spaniards; in others of Spaniards and Negroes; in still others of Spaniards, Indians, and Negroes; and finally of various mixtures of different castes. Over time Spaniards and Indians mix in a way that transforms the offspring completely into whites with coloring that, in the second generation, cannot be distinguished from that of Spaniards, yet they are not called Spaniards until the fourth generation.

Thus, the unofficial miscegenation had the effect that the category of "Spanish" (that is, creole) was gradually expanded in strictly biological terms in the Americas and had, by the eighteenth century, become semiofficial.[52]

Juan and Ulloa's observations are illustrated also in many of the contemporary casta paintings, which were intended to explain to Europeans the complexities of colonial Spanish American social hierarchies. In an anonymous eighteenth-century series about New Spain, for example, a "Spanish" man

---

colonial British America, see Dana D. Nelson, *The Word in Black and White: Reading "Race" in American Literature, 1638–1867* (New York, 1992).

52. Jorge Juan and Antonio de Ulloa, *Noticias secretas de América,* ed. Luis J. Ramos Gómez (Madrid, 1991), 65.

FIGURE 1. *De Español e Yndia nace Mestiza.* [Of a Spanish man and an Indian woman is born a Mestiza.] Casta Painting. Anonymous. Eighteenth Century. © Museo Nacional de Antropología, Madrid

mixing with an "Indian" woman is said to produce a "mestiza"; if that "mestiza" were to mix with a "Spanish" man, their offspring would be defined as a "castiza"; and if that "castiza" daughter were to mix with another "Spanish" man, their offspring would be considered a "Spaniard" (see Figures 1–3).

Overall, this particular series includes sixteen different varieties of castas. What is generally noteworthy about the casta paintings, which is a distinctly European genre, is that the word "white" is never used. As Ruth Hill has argued, the casta system was not a racial taxonomy in the modern sense of the word, but instead, a hierarchy of social status based on premodern concepts of ancestry or lineage that were defined, not by biological, but rather by cultural or social attributes ("Spanish," "Christian," "noble," and so forth). Nevertheless, the conferral of the official status of "Spaniard" upon children with a three-quarter Spanish and one-quarter Indian descent in Spanish America had the effect not only of biologically expanding the category of "Spanish" (that is, creole) but also of blurring the social distinctions between creoles and other

FIGURE 2. *Español y Mestiza producen Castiza.* [A Spanish man and a Mestiza produce a Castiza]. Casta Painting. Anonymous. Eighteenth Century. © Museo Nacional de Antropología, Madrid

castas, thereby lending a racial component to environmentalist theories about creole degeneracy and to further render the category of "criollo" as social status highly ambiguous and instable.[53]

One of the creoles' responses to this ambiguity of their social status is recorded by Juan and Ulloa in their tract *Noticias secretas,* which was suppressed from publication by the Bourbon monarchy in the eighteenth century. When attempting to emphasize the distinction of their families, they write, "The creoles have no better ground to rest upon than *merely to say that they are white,* and this sole prerogative entitles them to some distinction." Thus, in the

53. On casta paintings, see Ilona Katzew, *Casta Painting: Images of Race in Eighteenth-Century Mexico* (New Haven, Conn., 2004); María Concepción García Sáiz, *Las castas mexicanas: un género pictórico americano* (Milan, 1989); Manuel de Amat y Junient, Juan Carlos Estenssorro Fuchs, et al., *Los cuadros del mestizaje del Virrey Amat: la representación etnográfica en el Perú colonial* (Lima, 2000); Ruth Hill, *Hierarchy, Commerce, and Fraud in Bourbon Spanish America: A Postal Inspector's Exposé* (Nashville, Tenn., 2005). For discussions of the social significance of racial categories in colonial Latin America, see Langley, *The Americas,* 152–159; Magnus Mörner,

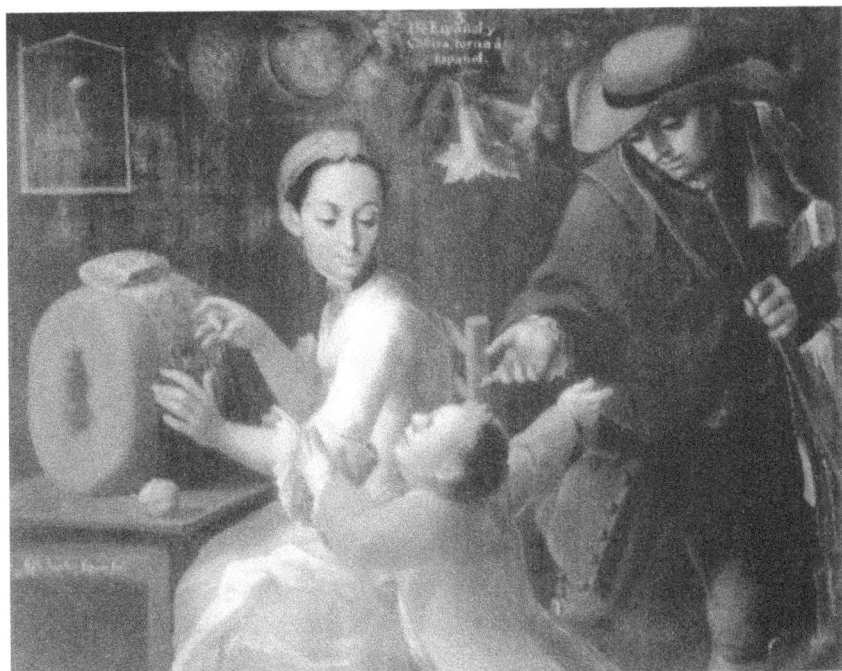

FIGURE 3. *De Español y Castiza torna a Español.* [Of a Spanish man and a Castiza is born a Spaniard.] Casta Painting. Anonymous. Eighteenth Century. © Museo Nacional de Antropología, Madrid

creoles' social imaginary, the metaphor of "blood" has assumed a meaning very different from what it meant in the European context. Whereas in the social imaginary of the Old World "blood" stood for family lineage ("noble" blood), religion ("Christian" blood), or nationality ("Spanish" blood), in the creoles' New World it has come to denote a new difference that we might recognize as an emergent, though not yet fully articulated and theorized, modern essentialist discourse of race—whiteness. Its ideological function in viceregal Spanish America was to realign geographic and social distinctions (Americans versus Europeans, nobility versus commoners) through a fiction of a transnational

---

Race Mixture in the History of Latin America (Boston, 1967); Amos Megged, "The Rise of Creole Identity in Early Colonial Guatemala: Differential Patterns in Town and Countryside," *Social History,* XVII (1992), 421–440. See also Anne Elizabeth Kuznesof, "Ethnic and Gender Influences on 'Spanish' Creole Society in Colonial Spanish America," *Colonial Latin American Review,* IV (1995), 153–176; Sarah Poot-Herrera, "Los criollos: nota sobre su identidad y su cultura," *Colonial Latin American Review,* IV (1995), 177–184; Schwartz, "Colonial Identities and *Sociedad de Castas,*" *Colonial Latin American Review,* IV (1995), 185–201.

kinship between Europeans and creoles across social and ancestral distinctions based on their common whiteness.[54]

The dialectical relationship between an imperialist discourse of creolization and an emerging creole discourse of race is also evident in eighteenth-century British-American letters and perhaps best illustrated by Thomas Jefferson's famous pronouncements in *Notes on the State of Virginia* (1785), in which he cites the writings of Juan and Ulloa about South America. Having defended native and (white) creole American culture from the Abbé Raynal's and the comte de Buffon's charge of degeneration by in effect denying the philosophes' logic of a detrimental influence of the New World environment, Jefferson turns to a consideration of African creoles in the New World. While expressing admiration for the moral integrity, religious piety, and loyalty of many of the Africans he personally knew, he belittles Africans' inherent capacity for genius in a series of disparagements, such as his infamous attack on the Boston poet Phillis Wheatley: "Religion indeed has produced a Phyllis Whately; but it could not produce a poet. The compositions published under her name are below the dignity of criticism. The heroes of the Dunciad are to her, as Hercules to the author of that poem." Considering the fact that under Roman slavery some slaves, such as Epictetus, Terence, and Phaedrus, were able to become accomplished writers, Jefferson dismisses the possibility that it might be the institution of slavery itself that inhibits the Africans' cultural development. The difference between Roman and African slaves, Jefferson argues, is that the former "were of the race of whites":

> It is not their [the Africans'] condition then, but nature, which has produced the distinction.—Whether further observation will or will not verify the conjecture, that nature has been less bountiful to them in the endowments of the head, I believe that in those of the heart she will be found to have done them justice.

Jefferson's patriotic defense of creole (Euro-American) character and culture is predicated on a particular rhetorical shift in which the eighteenth-century discourse about cultural creolization and degeneration is displaced by a modern discourse of race. If the American environment did not have a degenerative influence on human culture (as his discussions of native American and white creoles intend to demonstrate), but African-American creoles were obviously

54. The Spanish original reads here: "No tienen los criollos más fundamento para tal conducta que *el decir que son blancos,* y por esta sola prerrogativa son acreedores legítimos a tanto distintivo, sin pararse a considerar cuál es su estado." Juan and Ulloa, *Noticias secretas,* 432 (emphasis added).

(to Jefferson) inferior, it must be that Africans had arrived in the New World already as a distinct race, whose inferiority must be seen as essential and independent of environmental and geographical factors or social condition.[55]

Despite these analogies in the emergence of a discourse of race in Spanish and British-American creole social consciousness, however, there were, as the essays below illustrate, a number of important differences in the ways in which this consciousness manifested itself in each realm. First, because of the roughly one hundred years that separated the founding of the first Iberian and permanent English settlements in the New World, a distinct creole consciousness did not, as historians have noted, evolve in British America until the late seventeenth century. Also, unlike Spanish-American creoles, who gradually adopted the originally disparaging term "creole" as a badge of local patriotic pride to distinguish themselves from the Peninsulars, British-American colonials used the word itself only infrequently in reference to themselves. Insofar as they did use it, they usually did so in a pejorative or humorous way, often parodying common English stereotypes about colonials. Thus, William Byrd II of Westover in Virginia, the subject of Susan Scott Parrish's essay, slyly apologized in a letter to an English correspondent for "presuming to obtrude my Creolean Notions in Affairs so high above my humble sphere," and the long-term Maryland resident Ebenezer Cook, studied in Jeffrey Richards's essay, adopts the poetic persona of a haughty English tobacco merchant who presents an outrageously exaggerated account of colonial degeneracies in the Chesapeake.[56]

Generally speaking, the social distinctions between creoles and the European-born were less pronounced in British America than they were in Spanish America. Unlike in Spanish America, whose economy was based on mineral extraction, the English imperial dream of gold and silver in the New World had died with Sir Walter Ralegh's execution. The English promoters of empire therefore began to advocate fishing and the cultivation of agricultural consumer products, such as sugar, tobacco, and wheat, as the colonial British-American economic program. In an economy primarily based on agricultural production, British officials did not need to play as critical a role on the local level in the colonies as their counterparts did in Spanish America. Consequently, the British imperial administrative apparatus was far less elaborate than its Spanish

55. Thomas Jefferson, *Notes on the State of Virginia*, ed. William Peden (Chapel Hill, N.C., 1955), 140–143, 199–200.

56. Feb. 17, 1740/1, Byrd Letterbook, VI, Virginia Historical Society, Richmond. See also Shammas, "English-Born and Creole Elites," in Tate and Ammerman, eds., *Chesapeake in the Seventeenth Century*, 284; Zuckerman, "The Fabrication of Identity in Early America," *WMQ*, 3d Ser., XXXIV (1977), 183–214; Burnard, *Creole Gentlemen*; Mather, *Magnalia Christi Americana*, I, 13, 25.

counterpart, and the permanent presence of Europeans (other than immigrants) smaller than in Spanish America.[57]

Finally, distinct religious and cultural mentalities separating the Spanish from the British realm also led to distinct articulations of creole subjectivities in the Americas. Most important was the general difference between Catholic and Protestant predispositions toward paganism in general and native American cultures in particular. The Catholic empire of Spain had inherited from the Holy Roman Empire the long scholastic tradition of cultural syncretism, which was predicated on the Thomist theological notion of man's natural tendency toward God and the position that supernatural grace perfects, rather than destroys, nature. The Hapsburgs had tolerated—even embraced—local cultural diversity and syncretism on the condition of formal political submission and imperial integration. This syncretism became one of the foundations of a creole expression in New Spain—even when it involved, as Carlos Jáuregui shows in his essay, alleged Mexica practices of cannibalism. By contrast, as David Armitage has argued, an overall British ideology of empire was forged largely on the precepts of the Protestant Reformation, despite the later regional variations of the British colonies (Anglican Virginia, Puritan New England, Catholic Maryland)—and despite a few celebrated early English celebrants of native paganism, such as Thomas Morton. While in Catholic Spain the status of pagan culture was therefore the subject of much theological debate and the response to native American cultures various, the Protestant Reformation tended to reject Catholic compromises with any pagan practices as Satanist. Thus, in some areas of Spanish America, such as New Spain, the cultural aesthetics of the Counter-Reformation, the Baroque, licensed the creoles' appropriation of syncretist cultural symbols in their articulation of an identity distinct from Europeans—evident, for example, in the cult of the Virgin of Guadalupe. By contrast, in British America such an appropriation was rare until the dominance of the cultural aesthetics of the Reformation was mitigated by the rise of neoclassical universalism during the later eighteenth century—resulting, for example, in iconic appropriations of native American history and culture in the revolutionary epic.[58]

57. See James Lang, *Conquest and Commerce: Spain and England in the Americas* (New York, 1975).

58. See Fernando Cervantes, *The Devil in the New World: The Impact of Diabolism in New Spain* (New Haven, Conn., 1994); Armitage, *Ideological Origins*, 24–60. On the distinction between a Spanish-American "baroque" cultural aesthetic and a British American "gothic," see Claudio Véliz, *The New World of the Gothic Fox: Culture and Economy in English and Spanish America* (Berkeley, Calif., 1994).

In sum, the definition of the creole as a distinct social category remained in British America overall less intricately articulated than it was in Spanish America. While in British America, too, even elite creoles were frequently regarded as inferior to the English-born, the creoles' identity as being of (pure) European descent was in British America threatened less by biological mixture than it was by cultural creolization. Thus, observations about the Euro-American creoles' changes in complexion, dress, custom, or morality in comparison with the English-born were typically explained, not through racial mixture, but rather through the influence of climate, environment, and cultural contact with Africans and native Americans. This was due in part to the relatively greater racial exclusiveness that characterized British-American colonial societies from the very beginning. Although some of the early English attempts to secure colonial toeholds in the Americas were modeled on the Spanish example of conquering and subjugating native peoples in order to exploit their labor, the miserable failures of this model in the more sparsely populated regions of North America quickly led to a conceptual revision of the English colonial enterprise, in the course of which native American land, rather than labor, became the primary object of interest for English colonial adventurers.[59]

Also, as in Spanish America, in early British America, too, European women were a rare and prized commodity. (In Virginia, female indentured servants were frequently bought out of servitude before the end of their term by free suitors.) English colonists arrived in the New World more frequently as family units than did their Spanish counterparts, especially in some areas, such as New England. Finally, the institution of indentured servitude provided the single English woman with a social and economic opportunity (for lack of a better word) of coming to the New World that was not available to her Spanish counterpart. The result of these combined factors has been characterized by comparative historians of early American borderlands (perhaps too schematically) as a "frontier of exclusion" characterizing the British-American contact zones, as compared with a "frontier of inclusion" characterizing those of Spanish America. Finally, by the time the English entered the stage of imperial expansionism across the Atlantic, African slavery had been introduced into

59. See Shammas, "English-Born and Creole Elites," in Tate and Ammerman, eds., *Chesapeake in the Seventeenth Century,* 284; Zuckerman, "The Fabrication of Identity in Early America," *WMQ,* 3d Ser., XXXIV (1977), 183–214; Dunn, *Sugar and Slaves;* Burnard, *Creole Gentlemen.* Edmund S. Morgan has shown that the Chesapeake colonists during the first two decades of the seventeenth century envisioned a trading post colony—or a pseudofeudal "Promised Land" based on the labor of Indian "vassals" in the fashion of Spanish colonization—until tobacco found them; see *American Slavery, American Freedom: The Ordeal of Colonial Virginia* (New York, 1975), 1–107.

the New World for almost a century, even though African slaves would not surpass European indentured servants as the primary source of labor on British-American plantations until the end of the seventeenth century.[60]

As a result, racial difference implied in British America for the most part a legal status outside the imperial body politic. Unlike the mestizos, mulattoes, zambos, Negroes, and Indios of patrimonialist Spanish-American law, black slaves in liberal British-American law were, not imperial subjects of the crown, but rather the personal property of an individual colonist. While biological mixture between Europeans, Africans, and native Americans was frequent in British America, colonial laws such as the Virginia codes—stipulating that the offspring of a union between a (presumably black female) slave and a (presumably white male) free person followed the "condition of the mother"—had the effect that miscegenation in British-American plantation societies expanded biologically the social category of "black" rather than "white" as in Spanish America. Yet, in British America the gradually increasing presence of free blacks (especially in some urban areas of the Middle Colonies) also challenged the racialized rationalization of the creoles' privileged social status in the colonial order.[61]

The Essays

The essays in Part I of this volume, "New Worlds, New Empires, New Societies," investigate the continuities and connections between European ideologies of conquest in early Spanish and English discourses about the New World by presenting responses from various groups, both creole and non-creoles, to the debate about cultural difference in colonial societies. In the opening essay, "Cannibalism, the Eucharist, and Criollo Subjects," CARLOS JÁUREGUI investigates the transference of one of the most persistent tropes in the history of colonialism—cannibalism—from the European representations of native Americans in the sixteenth-century chronicles of the discovery and conquest to the representation of the European conquerors and creoles in Spanish historiography and, finally, in the seventeenth-century Eucharist plays

60. Alistair Hennessy, *The Frontier in Latin American History* (Albuquerque, N.Mex., 1978), 19; David J. Weber, *The Spanish Frontier in North America* (New Haven, Conn., 1992); Paula H. Covington, ed., *Latin American Frontiers, Borders, and Hinterlands* (Albuquerque, N.Mex., 1990); David J. Weber and Jane Rausch, eds., *Where Cultures Meet: Frontiers in Latin American History* (Wilmington, Del., 1994); Morgan, *American Slavery, American Freedom*; Galenson, *White Servitude in Colonial America*; McCusker and Menard, *The Economy of British America*.

61. Warren M. Billings, ed., *The Old Dominion in the Seventeenth Century: A Documentary History of Virginia, 1606–1700*, rev. ed. (Chapel Hill, N.C., 2007), 204.

of the famous Mexican poet and nun Sor Juana Inés de la Cruz. If there had all along been an uncanny resemblance between savage cannibalism and the Christian Eucharist in the European constructions of native American alterity, Jáuregui argues that Sor Juana's playful explorations of these resemblances manifest a "creole consciousness," "not because it recuperates any aspect of indigenous culture, but rather because it translates radical alterity (cannibalism) into the Catholic and imperial universalist continuity." Jáuregui's argument bears further testimony to the important role that the aesthetic of the Baroque played in the formation of Spanish-American creole expression by providing the colonial lettered elite a space for what he calls an "eccentric occidentalism," a "participatory yet differential practice" in which the "peripheral sender inscribes herself in the metropolis by way of cultural correspondence and participation in a conservative genre" such as Eucharist theater.

The interimperial ramifications of the emerging (Spanish) European discourse of creolization in the New World are the subject of the contribution of DAVID S. SHIELDS, "Sons of the Dragon; or, The English Hero Revived." Shields traces the unofficial myth of British imperialism—the heroic figure of the English privateer, especially Sir Francis Drake—in British and Anglo-American literary history from the sixteenth to the eighteenth century. The interplay between the two apparently contradictory narratives that initially dominated the English discourse of expansionism—the tale of the peaceful man of commerce and the tale of the daring, plundering sea dog—must be understood, Shields suggests, in the context of the "Black Legend" (leyenda negra) and its translation into the Protestant ideological context of empire. Thus, the White Myth of the English hero and the Black Legend of the degenerate Spaniard in the New World are two characters in the same story. English promoters and translators of empire in strategic positions, such as the defected Catholic monk Thomas Gage, spread the notion that the English conquest of Spanish America would equal a liberation of Spanish-American creoles as well as maroons, mestizos, and Indians, who were all eager to ally themselves with the English liberators from Spanish oppressions.

An unsuspected though interesting contribution to the debate surrounding Spanish-American creoles comes from an early-seventeenth-century native American perspective. The Andean writer Felipe Guaman Poma de Ayala opens, as RAQUEL CHANG-RODRÍGUEZ shows in her essay "Cruel Criollos in Guaman Poma de Ayala's First New Chronicle and Good Government," a unique window into the relationships developed between the ancient and new Americans in the viceroyalty of Peru. Contrasting Guaman Poma's representation of creoles with the representations of other Peruvian writers, most notably the mestizo Inca Garcilaso de la Vega and Juan de Espinosa Medrano (El Lunarejo), Chang-Rodríguez shows how Guaman Poma draws an intriguing distinction in word and images between the "criollos españoles" and the "Indios: criollos y criollas indios" that expands the familiar rhetoric and makes problematic the denomination by using it as a cultural category—transcending place of birth and parental origin. The equation of the creoles with the mestizo population, Chang-Rodríguez suggests, builds on Lascasian rhetoric to underscore one of Guaman Poma's main political arguments at issue in his text—that the native (Indian) lords, not the (creole) natives, are the only ones fit to govern Peru.

After the first three essays together offer three different perspectives (Spanish, English, and Andean) on Spanish-American creoles, the geographical focus switches to British-American creoles in the essay of JEFFREY H. RICHARDS, "Barefoot Folks with Tawny Cheeks: Creolism in the Literary Chesapeake, 1680–1750." Richards investigates a variety of responses to what he calls a "creole imaginary"—the formation of British ideas about cultural change and difference resulting from the particularities of the American landscape and climate, contact with native American and African inhabitants, the experience of plantation slavery, and life in the uncertainties of colonial class structure. Thus, Richards considers cardinal texts about creolization in the Chesapeake: a poem by the indentured servant James Revel about his experiences in Virginia, Aphra Behn's Restoration play about Bacon's Rebellion, *The Widdow Ranter,* Ebenezer Cooke's Hudibrastic poems about colonial Maryland, *The Sot-weed Factor* and *Sotweed Redivivus,* and the Anglican parson Thomas Cradock's "Maryland Eclogues in Imitation of Virgil's." Richards argues that, whereas Revel's suggestively titled *The Poor Unhappy Transported Felon's Sorrowful Account* manifests how the "migrant can successfully resist creolization," Behn's play chronicles a grudging recognition of processes of creolization. Cooke's poem, ostensibly an English satire about colonial life, evidences the parodic modes in which colonial creoles began to affirm their distinct identity in the face of European stereotypes; in contrast, Cradock's series of satiric poems manifests a straightforward first awareness of the social stratification of creole society in the Chesapeake.

While Richards demonstrates the wide generic as well as modal spectrum of British and British-American literary responses to creolization in America (poetic, dramatic, satiric, parodic), YOLANDA MARTÍNEZ–SAN MIGUEL, in "Colonial Writings as Minority Discourse?" provides a similarly broad overview of the literary consequences of creolization for Spanish-American letters. Martínez–San Miguel engages with the theoretical implications of the connections and continuities between European colonial discourse about the New World and colonial American writing. In particular, she considers the relevancy of the critical perspectives offered by recent comparativist, postcolonial, subaltern, and minority discourse theory to texts written in sixteenth- and seventeenth-century Latin America. Taking a neoformalist and linguistic approach to the identification of a distinctly creole colonial discourse, her essay analyzes the narrative and rhetorical structures of colonial texts for manifestations of colonial power relationships and of various colonial conditions distinctive of the Spanish Empire in the Americas. She first establishes that Christopher Columbus's aphasia in his *Diarios de viaje* on the one hand and Bartolomé de las Casas's excessive repetition and duplication of information in his *Brevísima relación de la destrucción de las Indias* on the other represent the two originary poles in a linguistic spectrum that defined the verbal strategies in European representations of the New World and that would become foundational also in the evolution of a creole, or Euro-American, discourse about the New World. From there, she surveys a number of canonical texts written by colonial creole (and mestizo) authors, including the Inca Garcilaso de la Vega (Peru) and Carlos de Sigüenza y Góngora (New Spain), demonstrating how these writers oscillate between a lack of words and excessive representation, between indigenous and metropolitan languages, between narrative and descriptive passages, and between silence, reticence, aphasia, and hyperbole on the one hand and repetition, amplification, intensification, and redundancy on the other. In the climax of her essay she explores the possibility of extending her linguistic theory of colonial subjectivity into the Anglo-American cultural context, by establishing points of contact with early accounts of colonization from both cultural traditions.

Martínez–San Miguel's shift to formal considerations in the literary response to creolization sets the stage for the essays in Part II, "The Cultural Geography of Creole Aesthetics." These essays investigate the regional diffusions of Old World literary aesthetics in the cultural environments of the New and show how colonial performances of metropolitan discursive and generic conventions are often rendered ambivalent in peripheral geocultural locations and, thus, are subtly distinct from the European aesthetic traditions they appear to be imitating. STEPHANIE MERRIM, in "Sor Juana Criolla and the Mexican Archive: Public Performances," aptly revisits in more detail the Baroque aesthetics of the works of Sor Juana Inés de la Cruz, such as *El Divino Narciso,* by placing them in their intertextual relations with a distinctly Mexican archive as diverse as Bernardo de Balbuena's epic celebrations of Mexico City, Baltasar Dorantes de Carranza's bitter historical narrative in defense of the conquerors' right to an encomienda, and landmark syncretist historiographers such as Juan de Torquemada. This Mexican archive, Merrim argues, is central for understanding Sor Juana's works as a mediation between New and Old Spain, as it affords her works a platform to represent Mexican culture to Spain. Thus, Sor Juana—often referred to by her contemporaries as the Tenth Muse—calls for a renewal of poetic space by making it patent and palpable to her European audience that New Spain had a distinct and legitimate cultural history to be reckoned with.

Colonial America's other Tenth Muse—the New England poet Anne Bradstreet—is the subject of the essay of JIM EGAN, "Creole Bradstreet: Philip Sidney, Alexander the Great, and English Identities." Unlike Merrim's Sor Juana, who turns to the cultural landscape of her New World homeland, Egan's Bradstreet turns to the Old World and to the classical past for a literary genealogy. By focusing on the two versions of Bradstreet's "Elegie upon That Honourable and Renowned Knight, Sir *Philip Sidney*" as they were published in Old and New England, respectively, as well as on the representation of Alexander the Great in "The Four Monarchies," Egan argues that Bradstreet's poetry engages with cultural anxieties about colonial degeneracy on the geographic periphery of empire by exploring, not so much the question of creolization per se, but what it meant to be English in the first place—a concept, Egan notes, that was still fluid during the seventeenth century. Bradstreet's turn "East," Egan concludes, challenges theories of creole identity formation that take a "Spanish model" as normative and that assume the active engagement with the cultural "contact zone" on the part of creole writers as an integral aspect of creole subjectivity.

Indeed, an active engagement with New World mestizaje and cultural syncretism as practiced by some creoles in Mexico has sometimes been misconceived as normative for creole literary expression in all of Ibero-America. This may be partly due to an overemphasis in colonial studies on the core regions such as New Spain, as LÚCIA HELENA COSTIGAN points out in her essay, "Self- and Collective Identity among New Christians in the Periphery of the Iberian Empires: Bento Teixeira, Ambrósio Fernandes Brandão, and Manuel Beckman." This overemphasis has resulted in a distorted picture of the diversity of formal manifestations of creole subjectivities and is partly owing to the relative neglect of peripheral regions, such as Brazil. Thus, as Costigan shows in her discussion of three writers from Brazil, Teixeira, Brandão, and Beckman, marginal groups such as "New Christians" (converted Jews and their descendants) did not seek to extend Old World social norms into the New but rather saw the Americas as a place where they could start a new life without the limitations that they faced in the Old World—resembling in this regard more the English Puritans than some of their Spanish-American counterparts in the urban core regions.

Similarly, LISA VOIGT critiques the scholarly overemphasis on the urban core regions of Spanish America in her "Spectacular Wealth: Baroque Festivals and Creole Consciousness in Colonial Mining Towns of Brazil and Peru," which scrutinizes the literature produced on the peripheries of viceregal power, such as the South American mining boomtowns of Potosí (in the viceroyalty of Peru) and Vila Rica and Mariana, in Minas Gerais (Brazil). Voigt corroborates the notion that a hybridization of European imperial discourses about the New World is at the root of creole cultural expression by demonstrating that the colonial festivals staged in these colonial towns replicated Peninsular Spanish religious and courtly spectacles of power on the part of the imperial crown and Catholic Church only ostensibly and ambivalently. As her closer look reveals, creole writers recording these festivals frequently used them as platforms for their own articulation of American difference—in affirming that the festivals actually surpassed their Peninsular counterparts, thus lending support to the claim of creole superiority in both piety and grandeur. In an analysis of the literary record of these celebrations—including Diego Mexía de Fernangil's *El Dios Pan*, Bartolomé Arzáns de Orsúa y Vela's *Historia de la Villa Imperial de Potosí* (1737), and two publications describing festivities in Minas Gerais, *Triunfo eucharístico* (1734) and *Áureo throno episcopal* (1749)—Voigt rejects reading these accounts as purely documentary and shows that the rhetorical goals of the texts do not necessarily correspond to those of the festivals, but rather reorient the meaning of "spectacular wealth" they describe.

The essays in Part III, "Creole Bodies: Race, Gender, Ethnicity," engage more specifically with the rhetorical strategies in which (male) colonial elites negotiate the duality of their social subject positions in both the local and the transatlantic context. Thus, KATHLEEN ROSS, in "Gender and Gossip in Criollo Historiography: Juan Suárez de Peralta's *Tratado del descubrimiento de las Indias y su conquista* (1589)," examines the stereotype of the effeminized criollo (or sissy) by taking examples from the *Tratado* dealing with Cortés's role in the conquest that have come to Suárez from oral sources and comparing them to the creole Carlos Sigüenza y Góngora's seventeenth-century commentary in *Piedad heroyca de don Fernando Cortés* (1693?) as well as to Cortés's own 1547 testament. She contrasts the weak position of the earlier criollo generation vis-à-vis imperial power with the more consolidated position of the Baroque criollo during the seventeenth century in order to illuminate the complex positioning of writers such as Peralta, who manifest a dual and ambivalent mentality that allowed them to identify what differentiated them as a group while continuing to fully support the imperial project of the crown.

These creole ambivalences with regard to Old World norms of cultural authority as well as later-generation creoles' uses of the mythic figures of Mosaic forefathers are also the subjects of the essay of TERESA A. TOULOUSE, "Female Captivity and 'Creole' Male Identity in the Narratives of Mary Rowlandson and Hannah Swarton." However, unlike their Catholic counterparts such as Sigüenza y Góngora, the Puritan sons of New England such as Cotton Mather had a vested interest in narratives, particularly of female captivity (such as Mary Rowlandson's), as they helped to produce, Toulouse argues, an exceptional form of creole male identity during an extraordinarily fraught period of political change and social competition. Appropriating the doubleness culturally ascribed to women and to captives alike, second- and third-generation New England men were enabled at once to express both their loyalty to their English-born, first-generation fathers and their desire to separate from and even to aggress against them. Thus, Toulouse concludes that the female captive's cultural ambivalence, which many critics have seen as transgressing colonial New England's patriarchal order, instead points to a transformation of this order by second- and third-generation male creoles, who seek to relocate the grounds of political authority from the invocation of the fathers to the competition among diverse sons in a new empire of commercial interest.

Thus, both Ross and Toulouse illustrate the duality of the subject position of the male creole elite within the imperial order. To shore up a legitimacy that was often considered suspect by the empire and under pressure from colonial social transformation on the local level, elite creoles frequently oscillated between Old World and New World forms of symbolic capital. In "The Ambivalent Nativism of Lucas Fernández de Piedrahita's *Historia general de las conquistas del Nuevo Reyno de Granada* (1688)," LUIS FERNANDO RESTREPO examines how creole writer Piedrahita inscribes Muisca culture (in present-day Colombia) in his *Historia general* (1688) in relation to his native informants and to previous chroniclers such as Fray Pedro de Aguado and Juan de Castellanos. Restrepo argues that Piedrahita's text reframes native knowledge and the story of conquest in new terms, seeking to produce a local history with universal value. However, this double aim, he shows, creates unresolved tensions within the narrative that shed light on the ambivalences of New Granada's creole society at large: on the one hand, it seeks recognition from the metropolis and, on the other, insists on equal but different cultural citizenship within the empire. The representation of Muisca culture in the creole text, Restrepo suggests, seeks in this context both to erase Muisca elements at the auto-biographical level and to set in writing the past Muisca "symbolic capital" of creole society.

An epistemological ambivalence of another kind in creole literary expression is discussed by SUSAN SCOTT PARRISH in her "William Byrd II and the Crossed Languages of Science, Satire, and Empire in British America." Parrish begins with a survey of contemporary English humoral theories in order to pursue the tensions in Byrd's *History of the Dividing Line* and *Secret History of the Line* between appropriations of metropolitan scientific language about the American landscape on the one hand and deconstructions of these languages on the other. Specifically, Parrish suggests that Byrd's histories appropriate the scientific language of natural history prescribed by the Royal Society of London when recording the 1728 journey undertaken by commissioners from both Virginia and North Carolina to settle a boundary line between the two colonies. On this level, his texts aim to "settle" metropolitan assumptions of how the American landscape can be known and appropriated linguistically—by affixing signs to places (in the form of blazes, cairns, names written upon maps, and so forth), by duly recording acts of surveying, chain laying, measuring, and map drafting, and by describing and cataloging animals, plants, and native American tribes. On the other hand, Byrd's texts also "unsettle" metropolitan assumptions about linguistic acts of possession, as he unsettles the new scientific assumptions about how knowledge is made and about the purity of language in its reference to nature.

Perhaps the most important difference between colonial creole and colonial native American subjectivities in the early Americas, as well as so-called post-colonial subjectivities emerging in the course of the Second British Empire and theorized in modern postcolonial theory, regards their respective poetics of nativism. Like these other (post)colonial subjectivities, colonial Euro-American creoles frequently appropriated the symbols of a precolonial and indigenous past as rhetorical sites of anti-imperial resistance. However, unlike these other subjectivities, their nativism was often beset by sociopolitical contradictions, and it frequently remained highly ambivalent.

This ambivalence is the focus of the last section, "Creole Politics of Memory and Knowledge." Thus, JOSÉ ANTONIO MAZZOTTI examines the origin and development of the El Dorado legend in colonial Spanish writings in "El Dorado, Paradise, and Supreme Sanctity in Seventeenth-Century Peru: A Creole Agenda." He demonstrates how the creoles of the Peruvian viceroyalty made use of the legend to help consolidate their own discursive identity and stake out their particular political claims. Although most studies have envisioned El Dorado as a phenomenon of the mid-sixteenth century, the emphasis in his essay is on the seventeenth century, by which time creoles had become major protagonists in the social and economic life of the viceroyalty. The myth of El Dorado (and others like the Paradise in the New World and Jauja, or land of abundance), he argues, provided creole intellectuals in Lima with a platform for their insistence upon certain "essential" differences between their land and the other kingdoms of the Spanish Empire. At the same time, the forms of racism that took root in the New World constituted the external face of creole self-definition, for the same discourse that exalted the white inhabitants of the New World achieved its effectiveness through the constant exclusion of other racial groups, Indians and blacks in particular.

By the eighteenth century, this Peruvian self-definition by way of rewriting history had also acquired distinctly cosmopolitan dimensions. As JERRY M. WILLIAMS shows in "Popularizing the Ethic of Conquest: Peralta Barnuevo's *Historia de España vindicada*," the eighteenth-century creole savant from Lima, Pedro de Peralta Barnuevo, fully inhabited the emerging intellectual culture of scientific modernity, especially French neoclassical science. On the one hand, Peralta's "historical-scientific method" was shaped by Bourbon norms that favored Cartesian thought, philosophy, and poetics. In this regard, Peralta's history of Spain and her glorious conquests, *Historia de España vindicada*, was undertaken as an act of imperial service and intended to be a gift to the monarchy, with the expectation that—through the intercession of influential friends—the crown would come to Peralta's aid in gratitude for his singing its praises. However, like a long line of American colonial creole writers before him, Peralta received no favorable response, compensation, or acknowledgment from the crown for his imperial services. This, Williams argues, forms the historical context for understanding how the confluence in Peralta's work of a philosophic, scientific, religious, and military notion of "conquest" in a history of Peninsular Spain comes to frame a distinct sense of a creole *nación*, or group identity, in early-eighteenth-century Peru.

Though colonial creoles such as Peralta were all too keenly aware of their unequal status as imperial citizens vis-à-vis their European counterparts, their critiques of imperial languages and affirmations of a creole nación are always bound up with the commitment to the imperial order and the mother country as well as with their debt to metropolitan culture. Nevertheless, their texts laid the epistemological, philosophical, and poetic groundwork for later writers during and after the national independence movements of the late eighteenth century in the United States and the early nineteenth century for most of Spanish America. The last two essays investigate the creole politics of memory in the postcolonial moment of the American independence movements. In "The 'Rebellious Muse': Time, Space, and Race in the Revolutionary Epic," RALPH BAUER compares the ideological appropriations of the native American past and of the New World landscape in the epic poetry of the Ecuadorian José Joaquín de Olmedo and the New Englander Joel Barlow. He suggests that the epic genre provided the revolutionary generations of creoles in the postcolonial Americas with a discursive vehicle that conveniently straddled the authority of historiographic discourse and poetic license in verisimilitude: they attempted to mystify the ideological ambiguities and contradictions inherent in the appropriation of a native American past in order to assert their cultural independence from the old centers of European imperial power. Both epic poets thereby reconceptualize the history of the New World from the spatial expansion of Europe to a progressive temporal plot of historical supersessions in the New World, albeit based on a Eurocentric model, and uphold race as the most important paradigm underlying historical evolution.

Finally, SANDRA M. GUSTAFSON, in "Natty in the 1820s: Creole Subjects and Democratic Aesthetics in the Early Leatherstocking Tales," revisits the fictional work of James Fenimore Cooper—particularly his novel *The Prairie*—against a school of critics who have seen his literary interest in native American culture exclusively in terms of a literary founding of a (white) United States American nation-state. By contrast, Gustafson's comparative perspective, which juxtaposes Cooper with a group of (Latin) American writers who articulated the political and cultural difference of the postcolonial Americas through references to indigenous traditions and the indigenous past, reveals a more sympathetic side of Cooper's fiction, one that does not merely anticipate the eradication of native peoples but is more ambivalent about the racial and gender taxonomies that his works nevertheless at times reinforce. Rather than turns to the alleged historical inevitabilities of a vanishing race in the past in order to validate (white-creole) United States civic life in the present, Cooper examines contemporary native political life for analogies to the emerging democracy of his own day. As Gustafson shows, it is significantly *The Prairie,* the one novel of Cooper's that most fully depicts native Americans as republicans in the aftermath of the Louisiana Purchase, that also engages with the question of integrating numerous Spanish-American characters into United States society, portraying a cautious mixing of creole societies.

Terminological and Bibliographical Notes

Creoles, Creolization, and Creolism

ETYMOLOGY

As we discuss above, the term *creole* originated in an Ibero-American context during the sixteenth century and came to refer, throughout the early modern Atlantic world, to European or African transplants in the New World. However, the usage of the term has become increasingly diffuse since the nineteenth century. In the United States, this diffusion has been caused in part by its specific regional usage in French Louisiana during the nineteenth century and its subsequent popularization throughout the United States by nineteenth-century novelists such as George Washington Cable (1844–1925), Grace King (1852–1932), and Lafcadio Hearn (1850–1904). In rural French Louisiana, *Créole* was first used to distinguish the original French settlers from the *Cajuns* (Acadians), who had immigrated later (and after some detours) from Canada during the later half of the eighteenth century. It thus referred to natives of rural French Louisiana in counterdistinction to newcomers. In the more stratified urban society of New Orleans, it was used specifically to designate the old francophone social elite. However, because of the gradual disappearance of this elite from New Orleans and French Caribbean influence and immigration during the nineteenth century, this latter sense of the term was gradually lost, and *créole* came to be used primarily in reference to people of African and mixed ancestry during the twentieth century.

The usages of the term in the francophone Caribbean context are themselves the result of a history, at times curious, of domestication of the term in French. As in English (see above), in French, too, the history of the term clearly points to an Ibero-American origin, the earliest documented source being again José de Acosta's *Historia natural y moral,* in Robert Regnault's 1598 translation *(Histoire naturelle et morale des Indes),* which retains Acosta's original "criollo" in reference to Spaniards born in the Americas. Also as in the English case, in the French context the word retained its distinctly foreign and Ibero-American connotation until the end of the seventeenth century, when it was gradually gallicized as *criole, criolle,* and finally *créole* in French Caribbean colonists' oral borrowing from the Spanish and Portuguese.

While the term *creole* was racially nonspecific also in the larger francophone context still during the eighteenth century—referring to anybody who is native to a colony and not a recent immigrant—in the course of the nineteenth century the term came to denote primarily people of African descent, especially in the wake of the Haitian Revolution (1804), when the white creoles all but disappeared from the island. Yet, on other French Caribbean islands, such as Martinique and Guadeloupe, the term continued to refer to whites. For some of the curious theories offered about the origins of the word by nineteenth- and twentieth-century French intellectuals, including those of the first president of the Réunion Academy, Jules Herman (1846–1924), who postulated that the word derived from a language spoken on a "southern continent where Réunion, South America, Africa, and the eastern parts of Madagascar and Hindoostan [India] formed one country," see Robert Chaudenson, *Creolization of Language and Culture,* trans. and rev. Salikoko S. Mufwene et al. (London, 2001), 1–13. Another useful discussion of this terminological history can be found in Raimond Arveiller, *Contribution à l'étude des termes de voyage en français, 1505–1722* (Paris, 1963).

USES IN MODERN SCHOLARSHIP

During the twentieth century, the term *creole* has been used most frequently by linguists in a very broad sense—to designate all languages that originated as the products of intercultural contact and trade. As such, from a linguistic point of view "creole" languages are similar to so-called pidgin languages, with the difference that the latter category designates makeshift languages that serve for interlinguistic communication but are not primary or native to any of the participating speakers, whereas the former designates languages that are actually native to a group of speakers. While modern linguists have invested a substantial amount of energy and enthusiasm in the study of creole and pidgin languages, both were initially considered marginal by early-twentieth-century linguists, whose attitudes resembled those of the early modern natural historians theorizing about creole cultures in the New World. See Leonard Bloomfield, *Language* (New York, 1933); Otto Jespersen, *Language: Its Nature, Development, and Origin* (London, 1922). For a discussion and critique of these early works, see Dell Hymes, "Preface," in Hymes, ed., *The Pidginization and Creolization of Languages: Proceedings of a Conference Held at the University of the West Indies, Mona, Jamaica, April 1968* (Cambridge, 1971), and David Decamp, "Introduction," 3–39, esp. 3–5.

As mentioned above, in the modern social sciences, the terms *creole, creolization,* and *creolism* have been used mainly to identify peoples and cultures transplanted from the Old World (mainly Africa and Europe), often thereby emphasizing cultural change in the New World over Old World cultural retention. Among historians of British America, a seminal work with regard to the Caribbean remains Edward Brathwaite, *The Development of Creole Society in Jamaica, 1770–1820* (Oxford, 1971). A more explicit model of New World "culturation" and "transculturation" was developed by Sidney Mintz and Richard Price, *The Birth of African American Culture: An Anthropological Perspective* (Boston, 1992); and earlier, for the case of Cuba, by Fernando Ortiz, *Contrapunteo cubano del tabaco y el azúcar* (1940; Caracas, 1987). Also of interest here are T. H. Breen, "Creative Adaptations: Peoples and Cultures," in Jack P. Greene and J. R. Pole, eds., *Colonial British America: Essays in the New History of the Early Modern Era* (Baltimore, 1984), 195–234; and David Buisseret and Steven G. Reinhardt, eds., *Creolization in the Americas* (College Station, Tex., 2000), 3–18. Some modern discussions of Euro-American creoles include Trevor Burnard, *Creole Gentlemen: The Maryland Elite, 1692–1776* (New York, 2002); Joyce E. Chaplin, *An Anxious Pursuit: Agricultural Innovation and Modernity in the Lower South, 1730–1815* (Chapel Hill, N.C., 1993); Bernard Bailyn and Philip D. Morgan, eds., *Strangers within the Realm: Cultural Margins of the First British Empire* (Chapel Hill, N.C., 1991).

In the humanities, the term has been used widely and with variable meanings. In the French Caribbean, the term has been frequently used to signify a postcolonial poetics of cultural identity that rejects essentialist or purist labels (such as "negritude"). The most prominent example here has probably been Édouard Glissant, *Poetics of Relation,* trans. Betsy Wing (Ann Arbor, Mich., 1997) as well as Jean Bernabé, Patrick Chamoiseau, and Raphaël Confiant, *Eloge de la créolité* (Paris, 1989).

In the Latin American context, the term *criollo* has been frequently used in historical and literary scholarship. Some of the seminal works by intellectual and cultural historians include D. A. Brading, *The First America: The Spanish Monarchy, Creole Patriots, and the Liberal State, 1492–1867* (Cambridge, 1991); Jacques Lafaye, *Quetzalcóatl and Guadalupe: The Formation of Mexican National Consciousness, 1531–1813,* trans. Benjamin Keen (Chicago, 1976); Solange Alberro, *Del gachupín al criollo: o de cómo los españoles de México dejaron de serlo* (Mexico City, 1992); and Jorge Cañizares-Esguerra, *How to Write the History of the New World: Histories, Epistemologies, and Identities in the Eighteenth-Century Atlantic World* (Stanford, Calif., 2001), and *Nature, Empire, and Nation: Explorations of the History of Science in the Iberian World* (Stanford, Calif., 2006).

Works by literary historians include José Juan Arrom, *Certidumbre de América: estudios de letras, folklore, y cultura,* 2d ed. (Madrid, 1971); Bernard Lavallé, *Las promesas ambiguas: ensayos sobre el criollismo colonial en los Andes* (Lima,

1993); José Antonio Mazzotti, ed., *Agencias criollas: la ambigüedad "colonial" en las letras hispanoamericanas* (Pittsburgh, 2000).

In literary scholarship on Anglo America, the creole has only recently gained wider currency. Examples of relevant scholarship include Ralph Bauer, *The Cultural Geography of Colonial American Literatures: Empire, Travel, Modernity* (Cambridge, 2003); Susan Scott Parrish, *American Curiosity: Cultures of Natural History in the Colonial British Atlantic World* (Chapel Hill, N.C., 2006); Sean X. Goudie, *Creole America: The West Indies and the Formation of Literature and Culture in the New Republic* (Philadelphia, 2006).

Comparative Hemispheric and Atlantic Scholarship

The debate about the possibility of a comparative hemispheric historiography about the Americas reaches back to the seminal works of Herbert E. Bolton, particularly his *Wider Horizons of American History* (New York, 1939) and "The Epic of Greater America," *American Historical Review*, XXXVIII (1932–1933), 448–474. The so-called Bolton thesis (positing a "basic unity" in the history of the Americas) has been hotly contested since, especially in Lewis Hanke, ed., *Do the Americas Have a Common History? A Critique of the Bolton Theory* (New York, 1964). Perhaps in part resulting from some of the sharp critiques offered in that collection, only relatively few historians followed Bolton's path until the recent rise of so-called Atlantic History. Two earlier examples include Richard M. Morse, *New World Soundings: Culture and Ideology in the Americas* (Baltimore, 1989); and Claudio Véliz, *The New World of the Gothic Fox: Culture and Economy in English and Spanish America* (Berkeley, Calif., 1994).

Still the most seminal and comprehensive historical treatment of the early modern idea of creolization from a comparative and Atlantic perspective, particularly in relation to the alleged "degenerative" influence of the New World's natural environment on the development of New World Cultures, is Antonello Gerbi, *The Dispute of the New World: The History of a Polemic, 1750–1900* (1955), trans. Jeremy Moyle (Pittsburgh, 1973). Although this work focuses on the debate during the eighteenth and nineteenth centuries, in *Nature in the New World: From Christopher Columbus to Gonzalo Fernández de Oviedo*, trans. Jeremy Moyle (Pittsburgh, 1985), Gerbi traces some of the roots of this Enlightenment controversy to the fifteenth and sixteenth centuries.

Some of the milestones in modern comparative Atlantic historical scholarship more generally include Nicholas Canny and Anthony Pagden, eds., *Colo-*

nial Identity in the Atlantic World, 1500–1800 (Princeton, N.J., 1987); Pagden, *Lords of All the World: Ideologies of Empire in Spain, Britain, and France, c. 1500– c. 1800* (New Haven, Conn., 1995); Patricia Seed, *Ceremonies of Possession in Europe's Conquest of the New World, 1492–1640* (Cambridge, 1995); Lester D. Langley, *The Americas in the Age of Revolution, 1750–1850* (New Haven, Conn., 1996); Jorge Cañizares-Esguerra, *Puritan Conquistadors: Iberianizing the Atlantic, 1550–1700* (Stanford, Calif., 2006); and J. H. Elliott's magisterial *Empires of the Atlantic World: Britain and Spain in America, 1492–1830* (New Haven, Conn., 2006).

Among literary historians, comparative scholarship on the early modern period includes Myra Jehlen, *American Incarnation: The Individual, the Nation, and the Continent* (Cambridge, Mass., 1986); Gordon Sayre, *Les Sauvages Américains: Representations of Native Americans in French and English Colonial Literature* (Chapel Hill, N.C., 1997), and *The Indian Chief as Tragic Hero: Native Resistance and the Literatures of America, from Moctezuma to Tecumseh* (Chapel Hill, N.C., 2005); Jonathan Hart, *Representing the New World: The English and French Uses of the Example of Spain* (New York, 2001); Ralph Bauer, *The Cultural Geography of Colonial American Literatures: Empire, Travel, Modernity* (Cambridge, 2003); Susan Castillo, *Colonial Encounters in New World Writing, 1500–1786: Performing America* (London, 2005).

Examples of hemispheric scholarship on later periods include José David Saldívar, *The Dialectics of Our America: Genealogy, Cultural Critique, and Literary History* (Durham, N.C., 1991); José C. Ballón, *Autonomía cultural americana: Emerson y Martí* (Madrid, 1986); Gustavo Pérez Firmat, ed., *Do the Americas Have a Common Literature?* (Durham, N.C., 1990); Vera Kutzinski, *Against the American Grain: Myth and History in William Carlos Williams, Jay Wright, and Nicolás Guillén* (Baltimore, 1987); Bell Gale Chevigny and Gari Laguardia, eds., *Reinventing the Americas: Comparative Studies of the Literature of the United States and Spanish America* (Cambridge, 1986); Renata R. Mautner Wasserman, *Exotic Nations: Literature and Cultural Identity in the United States and Brazil, 1830–1930* (Ithaca, N.Y., 1994); Hortense J. Spillers, ed., *Comparative American Identities: Race, Sex, and Nationality in the Modern Text* (New York, 1991); Lois Parkinson Zamora, *Writing the Apocalypse: Historical Vision in Contemporary U.S. and Latin American Fiction* (Cambridge, 1989); Earl E. Fitz, *Rediscovering the New World: Inter-American Literature in a Comparative Context* (Iowa City, Iowa, 1991); Eric Wertheimer, *Imagined Empires: Incas, Aztecs, and the New World of American Literature, 1771–1876* (Cambridge, 1999); Myra Jehlen, *American Incarnation: The Individual, the Nation, and the Continent* (Cambridge, Mass., 1986); Kirsten Silva Gruesz, *Ambassadors of Culture:*

The Transamerican Origins of Latino Writing (Princeton, N.J., 2002); Anna Brickhouse, *Transamerican Literary Relations and the Nineteenth-Century Public Sphere* (Cambridge, 2004); John Muthyala, *Reworlding America: Myth, History, and Narrative* (Athens, Ohio, 2006).

The French Colonial Experience

Although the current volume did not include scholarship on creolization in the French colonies, a basic bibliography on the French colonial experience in the Caribbean and Lousiana includes Oruno D. Lara, *La liberté assassinée: Guadaloupe, Guyanne, Martinique, et la réunion en 1848–1856* (Paris, 2005); Mary Rush Gwin Waggoner, ed., *Le Plus Beau Pais du Monde: Completing the Picture of Proprietary Lousiana, 1699–1722* (Lafayette, La., 2005); François Blancpain, *La colonie française de Saint-Domingue: de l'esclavage à l'indépendance* (Paris, 2004); Christine Daniels and Michael V. Kennedy, eds., *Negotiated Empires: Centers and Peripheries in the Americas, 1500–1800* (New York, 2002), which includes essays on English, French, Portuguese, and Dutch colonization. On the French in Brazil, see Frank Lestringant, *Jean de Léry; ou, l'invention du savage: essai sur l'histoire d'un voyage fait en la terre du Brésil,* 2d rev. and augm. ed. (Paris, 2005), which examines Jean de Léry's 1557 *Journal de bord en la terre de Brésil* and the projects of "la France Equinoccial" and "la France Antartique." On the Dutch colonial experience, see Gert Oostindie, *Paradise Overseas: The Dutch Caribbean, Colonialism, and Its Transatlantic Legacies* (Oxford, 2005); Oostindie and Inge Klinkers, *Decolonising the Caribbean: Dutch Policies in a Comparative Perspective* (Amsterdam, 2003), which includes an examination of the dismantling of the Dutch empire in the 1940s and 1950s.

PART I

New Worlds, New Empires, New Societies

CARLOS JÁUREGUI

Cannibalism, the Eucharist, and Criollo Subjects

¿y quién pensara,
que al Fruto de la Vida le quitara
lo hermoso la razón de apetecido?
—Sor Juana Inés de la Cruz

Cannibalia

Beyond the archaeological and anthropological disputes over evidence indicating that people might have been eating one another since prehistoric times, cannibalism has been one of those primary images, desires, and fears on which both subjectivity and culture are based. Powerful narrations and images of man-eating men have been present for centuries, across many cultures and cultural traditions, myths, tales, and artistic works. As a frequently used cultural metaphor, *cannibalism* constitutes a way to make sense of others and of ourselves as well; it is a trope that embodies the fear of the dissolution of identity, and, conversely, it is a model of incorporation of difference. Cannibalism is not a neutral term denoting man-eaters. It is a discursive construction that emerges as a colonial metaphor for the *Other* during the invasion and conquest of the New World. At first it appeared as a non-European term (*caniba*) used to identify an indigenous group (the Caribs), who by some accounts devoured their adversaries. The word later found its way into Spanish and other European vernaculars, replacing the Greek word *anthropophagos* and becoming a master trope for the New World. Indeed, in the sixteenth century, America was

I am indebted to the Robert Penn Warren Center for the Humanities, which funded my research for this essay, and to Mabel Moraña, Luis Fernando Restrepo, Andrés Zamora, Juliet Lynd, Joshua Lund, and Susana Hernández Araico for their valuable comments and suggestions. An initial version of this essay in Spanish titled "'El plato más sabroso': eucaristía, plagio diabólico, y la traducción criolla del caníbal" was published in *Colonial Latin American Review*, XII (2003), 199–231.

constructed culturally, religiously, and geographically as a kind of Cannibalia. Letters, chronicles, ethnographic accounts, laws, engravings, and maps all turn cannibalism into a central trope with which to represent the New World. For example, the first contact zone was named "Caribana" or "Caribe" (lands of cannibals), Brazil was cartographically marked "Canibalor terra," and "Aztec" society was for the most part portrayed through the imagery of sacrifice and ritual cannibalism.[1]

Certainly, canibalism has historically been a cornerstone of colonialism and of the very idea of savagery and civilization. Nevertheless, from the European visions of a monstrous and savage New World to the (post)colonial and post-modern narratives and contemporary cultural production, the metaphor of cannibalism has been not just a paradigm of otherness but also a trope of self-recognition and a central concept in the very definition of Latin American identities forged within the conflicts of coloniality. The cannibal, one might say, is at once a sign of America's anomaly (alterity) and a figurative device for the continent's westernization, or peripheral inscription in the West.[2]

---

1. The use of the word "Aztec" (from Aztlán) was generalized during the eighteenth and nineteenth centuries to refer to those who identified themselves as "Colhua Mexica"; for the purpose of this essay both words "Mexica" and "Aztec" will be used.

2. W[illiam] Arens's influential and controversial work *The Man-Eating Myth: Anthropology and Anthropophagy* (New York, 1979) represented the apex of "cannibal studies." With an incisive hermeneutic of suspicion, his book questioned the scientific consistency of the narratives on cannibalism and accused anthropological discourse of being a space for ethnocentric, Western, colonialist ideology. His book disrupted academic efforts of the 1970s to explain the nature and meanings of cannibalism in so-called primitive societies, such as Eli Sagan's *Cannibalism: Human Aggression and Cultural Form* (New York, 1974); as a system of demographic control arising from the need for protein, as in Marvin Harris, *Cannibals and Kings: The Origins of Cultures* (New York, 1977), or in Michael Harner, "The Enigma of Aztec Sacrifice," *Natural History*, LXXXVI, no. 4 (April 1977), 47–51; or as a symbolic ritual by which certain qualities of the person consumed might be obtained, as in Marshall Sahlins's "Culture as Protein and Profit," *New York Review of Books*, Nov. 23, 1978, 45–53. Since Arens's book, the veracity of the practice of cannibalism, the historical documents that report it, and the authority of these accounts have been strongly debated. The academic field could be described today as divided between those who are on what Maggie Kilgour calls the "did they or didn't they? debate" and those who set aside the question of historical veracity in favor of studying the different narratives about cannibalism. Within the first group some insist on assuming cannibalism as an ethnographically proven ritual system and try to explain it or pursue hard evidence to reveal different sorts of ritual cannibalism among remote indigenous peoples. Other scholars, however, examine the different roles that cannibalism plays in the construction of colonial authority. Among the latter, anthropologists such as Grannath Obeyesekere have studied the often-quoted testimonial evidence and classic colonial ethnonarra-tives about cannibals, suggesting their fictional and literary attributes; see Obeyesekere, "Can-nibal Feasts in Nineteenth-Century Fiji: Seamen's Yarns and the Ethnographic Imagination," in Francis Barker, Peter Hulme, and Margaret Iversen, eds., *Cannibalism and the Colonial World* (Cambridge, 1998), 63–86. Likewise, historians and literary critics have explored the use of the term "cannibal" as a justification for colonial aggression and have examined the recurrence and

This essay explores several variations on the theological conception of American anthropophagy as a marker of both similarity and difference between Europe and the New World, between Christianity and the aboriginal religions, and between the metropolis and its imperial periphery. The first three sections review the tensions between the Counter-Reformationist conceptions of the Eucharist and the syncretist readings of religious alterity and cannibalism, found in ethnographic and historiographic texts from sixteenth-century Mexico. The last part examines how in the New World Baroque—within the context of what has been called the emergence of criollo consciousness—the cannibal is recodified, or translated, symbolically as a conceptual character in two *loas* (dramatic prologues) by Sor Juana Inés de la Cruz.[3]

Anomalous Conversions, Mimetic Hybridity, and Sinister Commonality

In the rhetorical construction of alterity, relationships of continuity imply a process of relative identification with alterity: the *other* (with a lowercase *o*) constitutes one particularity within the continuous universal of humanity, Christianity, and empire; the Old World (European Christianity) could thereby be continued in the New World. Schemes of contiguity, by contrast, define the *Other* (with a capital *O*) as a limit; the Other cannot be subsumed by sameness. Alterity is, then, threatening and irreducible. As Hayden White affirms, these two types of schemes, continuity and contiguity, "engender dif-

---

representation of the cannibal in European imagery as well as in the colonial representations of the New World. See Peter Hulme, *Colonial Encounters: Europe and the Native Caribbean, 1492–1797* (London, 1986); Maggie Kilgour, *From Communion to Cannibalism: An Anatomy of Metaphors of Incorporation* (Princeton, N.J., 1990); Philip P. Boucher, *Cannibal Encounters: Europeans and Island Caribs, 1492–1763* (Baltimore, 1992); Frank Lestringant, *Cannibals: The Discovery and Representation of the Cannibal from Columbus to Jules Verne*, trans. Rosemary Morris (Berkeley, Calif., 1997); Barker, Hulme, and Iversen, eds., *Cannibalism and the Colonial World*; Zinka Ziebell, *Terra de canibais* (Porto Alegre, Brazil, 2002). I analyze the symbolic articulations of cannibalism in Latin-American cultural history and provide a critical account of the historical redefinition and ideological values of cannibalism not just as a master trope of colonialism and otherness but also as a shifting figurative device for the definition of Latin American identities: see Carlos Jáuregui, *Canibalia: canibalismo, calibanismo, antropofagia cultural, y consumo en América Latina* (Havana, Cordoba, 2005).

3. The loa was a short theatrical piece that at times was shown by itself but more typically preceded an *auto sacramental* (a sacramental play) or a comedy and often alluded in the text to its role as a prelude or introduction; see Alfonso Méndez Plancarte, introduction and notes, in Sor Juana Inés de la Cruz, *Obras completas*, ed. Méndez Plancarte (Mexico City, 1951–1957), III, 503 (hereafter cited as Sor Juana, *Obras*).

ferent possibilities for praxis: missionary activity and conversion on the one side, war and extermination on the other."[4]

The early years of the evangelization of America were replete with euphoria and optimism. The Franciscans envisioned the New World as a utopian opportunity for a new beginning of Christianity. Soon, however, a cloud of pessimism began to darken this Christian dawn in America. By the mid-1530s, clear indications began to emerge that idolatry was enduring, that it was even hidden within the Christian rites and celebrations of the Indians. The Franciscans, and later the Dominicans and the Jesuits, compiled studies, such as Bernardino de Sahagún's *Historia general de las cosas de la Nueva España* (circa 1575–1580, published 1829), with the explicit intention of eradicating "superstitions . . . and idolatrous ceremonies," consolidating the Church of Christ, "where the Synagogue of Satan has been so prosperous," and liberating the Mexicans from "the hands of the Devil." The evangelical effort thus came to be seen as a cosmic battle between God and Satan. This particular vision had its roots in certain variations on theological conceptions of the devil, idolatry, and sin during the late Middle Ages. The change in medieval tradition from the seven capital sins to the conception of sins against the Ten Commandments established idolatry as the first sin against God and facilitated its identification with diabolism by supposing that the devil was an entity opposite to God and that idolatrous practices were an anastrophe, or inversion, of the Christian rites. This vision was strengthened during the sixteenth century, especially as a result of the frustrations with the evangelization and the anxieties rising from within Counter-Reformation readings of religious difference.[5]

---

4. Hayden White, "The Noble Savage: Theme as a Fetish," in Fredi Chiapelli, ed., *First Images of America: The Impact of the New World on the Old* (Berkeley, Calif., 1976), 129. This brief explanation of relations of continuity and contiguity is merely descriptive and is not intended to be in any sense a taxonomy of models for conceiving alterity.

5. Bernardino de Sahagún, *Historia general de las cosas de la Nueva España,* ed. Alfredo López Austin and Josefina García Quintana (Madrid, 1988), 31, 34, 65. On the theological conceptions of idolatry as conceived in relation to the conquest and the evangelization in Mexico in the sixteenth century, see Fernando Cervantes, *The Idea of the Devil and the Problem of the Indian: The Case of Mexico in the Sixteenth Century* (London, 1991), 6, 13–19. The demonological vision of religious alterity can be found in most of the chronicles of the conquest as well as in the early historiography of the period. Francisco López de Gómara (1552), for example, maintains: "The Devil would frequently appear and speak to these Indians. . . . Deceived by his sweet words or the tasty foods of human flesh . . . , they desired to please him." [Aparecía y hablaba el diablo a estos indios muchas veces. . . . Ellos engañados con las dulces palabras o con las sabrosas comidas de carne humana . . . deseaban complacerle.] Francisco López de Gómara, *Historia general de las Indias y vida de Hernán Cortés* (Caracas, 1979), 328. Several religious treatises, such as Friar Andrés de Olmos (1491–1570), *Tratado de hechicerías y sortilegios* (1553), ed. George Baudot (Mexico City, 1990), also take up the demonological thesis.

As Francois Hartog states, the conversion, or *translatio*, of the Other fails, for alterity persists in various forms, both open and hidden, through mimesis and syncretism. The translated Other does not stop being alien, and his supplementarity thus becomes a threat. Within the colonial context this conundrum provided endless headaches for ethnographers such as Toribio de Motolinía (1495?–1569), Diego Durán (1537?–1588?), the aforementioned Sahagún (1499?–1590), and later for historians such as José de Acosta (1540–1600). Durán, like Motolinía before him, was justly worried about the impurity of faith on the part of the indigenous: "Many [Mexica rituals]," wrote Durán, "coincide so much with ours that they are hidden by them." [Muchos dellos [los ritos mexicas] frissan tanto con los nuestros, que estan encuviertos con ellos.] However, his anxiety was not inspired by hybridity as such, which is an effect of colonial discourses and practices, nor by mimicry, a strategy of colonial power/knowledge that is derived from the assimilation of the colonized in an imperfect way that thereby maintains his alterity—but rather by mimesis. The latter is seen as a strategy of resistance: mimesis perceived as imitation (in the Aristotelian sense) but also as dissimulation and camouflage. In the same sense that one of the meanings of *to mimic* is "to dissimulate" and that *mimetic* can be understood as "covered up," Catholicism would be a façade behind which religious alterity would hide. Conversion thus becomes a masking; that is to say, it is a perfidious imitation that has as its object the defiant perpetuation of difference.[6]

Durán spoke of a masked other, maintaining its alterity hidden behind fakery and appearances: "our main purpose: warning them about the mixtures that may be going on between our rituals and theirs, because pretending to celebrate the ceremonies of our Lord . . . they could in fact be inserting, mixing and

6. François Hartog, *The Mirror of Herodotus: The Representation of the Other in the Writing of History* (Berkeley, Calif., 1988), 237; Diego Durán, *Ritos y fiestas de los antiguos mexicanos* (1867–1880), ed. César Macazaga Ordoño (Mexico City, 1980), 71. Mimicry as it is conceived by Homi K. Bhabha—in the context of the British colonization of India—results in a threat to colonial power and its discourses because in mimicry lies the Lacanian paradox of the production of traces of sameness in otherness. Mimicry produces a differential supplementarity (the other is "almost the same, but not quite"), and it embodies a decentering mockery of colonial power; see Homi Bhabha, *The Location of Culture* (London, 1994), 86. Durán, like many of his contemporaries, is concerned about religious mimesis and false conversions: the camouflaged persistence of otherness. During the sixteenth and seventeenth centuries, several texts were published on the impurity of the conversions. Said impurity is the motive of colonial anxiety related to the supposed mimetic masking of the rites of American religions—identified with the devil—under different forms of Christian devotion. On mimesis as a rhetorical strategy of resistance, see Barbara Fuchs, *Mimesis and Empire: The New World, Islam, and European Identities* (Cambridge, 2001).

celebrating those of their idols" [nuestro principal yntento advertirles la mezcla que puede haver á casso de nuestras fiestas con las suyas que fingiendo estos celebrar las fiestas de nuestro Dios . . . entremetan y mezclen y celebren las de sus ydolos]. In other words, anxiety is not produced by the perception of sameness in alterity (the Other has my characteristics), but rather by the idea that Mexica traits are hidden below the false appearance of Christianity (the Other is hidden in the similarity, in the appearance of having been converted). There is no epistemological space more terrifying than resemblance. But when the otherness, thanks to which we recognize ourselves, masks itself by appropriating our image in order to resist, we at this point enter the realm of sheer horror. Not only was conversion failing, thanks to this resistance and mimesis, but also the conquistadors and evangelists were finding that Mexica religion itself approximated Catholicism in many respects. The most problematic of the mirroring effects of religious difference stemmed from human sacrifices, since it was assumed that they functioned "under the same principle" of Communion. Durán, like many other men of the cloth, was quick to clarify that these similarities existed only at the level of "form." The problem was that Catholicism defined itself against Protestantism precisely—among other things—in reference to the substantiality of forms.[7]

In accordance with the dogma of transubstantiation—adopted by the Roman Catholic Church in the Fourth Lateran Council (1215) and ratified in the First Council of Lyon (1274) as well as the Council of Trent (1545–1563)—at the Last Supper, Jesus Christ was said to have given his disciples his own flesh and blood through bread and wine: "Jesus took bread, and blessed it, and brake it, and gave it to the disciples, and said, Take, eat; this is my body. And he took the cup, and gave thanks, and gave it to them, saying, Drink ye all of it; For this is my blood of the new testament, which is shed for many for the remission of sins" (Matt. 26:26–28). The Council of Trent was categorical in its pronouncement: in this biblical passage there was no trope or figurative language. The church argued for a total and real *conversio substantialis* (substantial conversion) of the Eucharistic forms: "If any one denieth, that, in the sacrament of the most holy Eucharist, are contained truly, really, and substantially, the body and blood together with the soul and divinity of our Lord Jesus Christ, and consequently the whole Christ; but saith that He is only therein as in a sign, or in figure, or virtue; let him be anathema."[8]

7. Durán, *Ritos y fiestas*, 79.

8. In addition to Matt. 26:26–28, see also Mark 14:22, 24: "And as they did eat, Jesus took bread, and blessed, and broke it, and gave to them, and said, Take, eat: this is my body. . . . And he

The topic would become the object of inflamed controversies, among which can be mentioned those carried out between Roman Catholicism and Protestantism. Even among Reformed Christians there is not a single unified doctrine on this contentious matter. Christopher Rasperger's treatise on the two hundred different interpretations of the biblical passage narrating the Last Supper, titled *Ducentae verborum . . . hoc est corpus meum: interpretationes* (1577), gives an idea of the magnitude of the controversy during the sixteenth century.[9]

Even today, religious historiographers debate the biblical and patristic foundations and the tradition of the dogma in the primitive and early-medieval church. It is unclear whether, as some affirm, for centuries the doctrine of transubstantiation was more or less minor and believers in general would have stayed within the Hebrew tradition of symbolic interpretation, or, on the contrary (as some Catholic historians affirm) the predominant position was the acceptance of the real conversion of the bread and wine into the body and blood of Christ during the Consecration (Real Presence). The latter tradition

---

said unto them, This is my blood." This supper provides eternal life and communion with God: "For my flesh is meat indeed, and my blood is drink indeed. He that eateth my flesh, and drinketh my blood, dwelleth in me, and I in him" (John 6:54, 56). According to Luke 22:17–20 and 1 Cor. 11:23–25, Christ would have added on that occasion: "This do in remembrance of me," which is the biblical basis of the celebration of Mass. Historians and theologians have intensively studied the history of the Eucharist in the Catholic and Protestant churches. For a comprehensive overview of the celebration of Mass and its origins, see Josef A. Jungmann, *The Mass of the Roman Rite: Its Origins and Development (Missarum Sollemnia)* (Westminster, Md., 1986). Several specialized dictionaries are also particularly useful: *The Catholic Encyclopedia* (New York, 1907–1912); Gerald O'Collins and Edward G. Farrugia, *A Concise Dictionary of Theology* (New York, 1991); Donald Attwater, ed., *A Catholic Dictionary (The Catholic Encyclopaedic Dictionary)*, 3d ed. (New York, 1958); William J. Collinge, *Historical Dictionary of Catholicism* (Lanham, Md., 1997); Council of Trent, session 12, chap. 8, canon 1, in Raymond Phineas Stearns, ed., *Pageant of Europe* (New York, 1947), 152.

9. Christoph Rasperger, *Ducentae paucorum istorum et quidem clarissimorum Christi verborum . . . hoc est corpus meum: interpretationes . . .* (Ingolstadt, 1577). See also "The Real Presence of Christ in the Eucharist," *The Catholic Encyclopedia*, V (New York, 1909), 573–578. The Swiss Protestant reformer Huldreich Zwingli (1484–1531) conceived of the thesis of a commemorative supper and proposed that the bread and wine *meant*—but *were not*—the body and blood. He thereby seconded Johannes Oecolampadius (1482–1531), who elaborated the theory of the spiritual and not the physical presence of Christ. Martin Luther was the only one of the reformers to maintain the doctrine of the Real Presence of Christ in the Eucharist, albeit under the heterodox theory that the body and blood of Christ were offered to the communicant coexisting in, with, and under the forms of bread and wine, known as consubstantiation. Meanwhile, in Geneva, John Calvin was searching for a point of convergence between the literal interpretation of the substantial presence and the figurative or merely symbolic interpretation. He proposed that the Eucharist be celebrated as the mystery by which Christ is truly present in spirit; communion is a real and spiritual (but not physical) supper of Christ (*Institutio christianae religionis* [1536–1559], IV, chaps. 17, 18). For an account of Calvin's theories on this subject, see Kilian McDonnell, *John Calvin, the Church, and the Eucharist* (Princeton, N.J., 1967).

FIGURE 4. The Theft of the Eucharist. From *Host Desecration at Passau*. Woodcut. 1477. In *The Jewish Encyclopedia: A Descriptive Record of the History, Religion, Literature, and Customs of the Jewish People from the Earliest Times to the Present Day* (New York, 1901–1906), VI, foll. 482

would date back to the first century and apparently was subscribed to by fathers of the church like Ignatius of Antioch (second century) and Augustine, among others.[10]

It seems that, rather than a fundamental difference between two distinct traditions, the conflict emerged from a notable change in the idea of symbolic representation: for the primitive and early-medieval church, there was no Scholastic schism between the symbol and the represented. The *repraesentio*, argues Adolph Harnack, had the sense of "to make present": "At that time 'symbol' denoted a thing which is in some kind of way really what it signifies." If historians do not find great disputes or allegations that question the literalness of Communion during the first years of the church, it is because only at the beginning of the thirteenth century did the discussion become relevant and, above all, epistemologically and politically possible. To many, however, the reality of transubstantiation was not convincing; the idea that within the Eucharist there was a symbolic representation and not an actual materialization of the Last Supper continued to be discussed by theologians, priests, and the

10. Even though Augustine never mentions the term "transubstantiation" (which originated in the eleventh century) and although many allege that he favored a symbolic interpretation (making him a sort of precursor to the Reformation), it appears that he preferred the idea of the substantial conversion of the Eucharistic forms. In *Sermons*, no. 227, Augustine instructs: "That bread which you can see on the altar, sanctified by the word of God, is the body of Christ. That cup, or rather, what the cup contains, sanctified by the word of God, is the blood of Christ"; *Sermons* (Brooklyn, N.Y., 1990–1994), part 3, VI of The Works of Saint Augustine. See also *Sermons*, nos. 234, 272, Works, part 3, VII; *The City of God against the Pagans*, ed. and trans. R. W. Dyson (Cambridge, 1998), book 10, chap. 20. Gary Macy, *The Theologies of the Eucharist in the Early Scholastic Period: A Study of The Salvific Function of the Sacrament according to the Theologians, c. 1080–c. 1220* (Oxford, 1984), presents early scholastic literature on the Holy Sacrament; Miri Rubin, *Corpus Christi: The Eucharist in Late Medieval Culture* (Cambridge, 1992), studies the historical and theological aspects of the Communion during the late Middle Ages.

faithful during the following centuries. But the dogma was imposed to such an extent that many came to venerate the sacred forms and to believe that the sacrilegious could literally torture the host and make it bleed. Such a scenario appears in several engravings from 1477 that present, in sequence, the theft of the Eucharistic forms, their being handed over in a synagogue, and their bleeding in the presence of the Torah (the last engravings illustrate the merciless punishment of the thieves) (see Figure 4). Indeed, until the first decades of the sixteenth century, this was the reason for numerous massacres of Jews. Thanks to the insistence upon a thorough exegesis—which had gained force with the interpretive criticism and the study of the *Institutiones* of Roman law and the Bible—the ritual center of Catholicism was defined as a theophagic act, or better yet as an anthropotheophagic sacrifice in which God, incarnated in a man (Christ), is both host and guest (that is, victim of a sacrifice and also a sign of alliance or incorporation).[11]

With the discovery of America—and especially after the conquest of Mexico

11. Kilgour, *From Communion to Cannibalism,* 80 (Harnack's quote). By the beginning of the thirteenth century the church had already begun affirming its universalist pretensions, consolidated itself politically in Europe as an institution, and defined its Others (Christianity, especially for Spain, is the story of the European, of the non-Oriental—neither Muslim nor Jewish). The problem of the Eucharist—to explain how one participates and exactly what eating means in the Communion—allowed Innocent III (1160–1216) to test the authority of the papacy against "heterogeneities" internal to Christianity: that is, the Albigenses, the Catharists, the Waldenses, the Petrobrusians, and other groups on the margins of institutional discipline who refused to recognize either the priestly power to consecrate or the Real Presence, and who defied the hierarchical authority of the church. See Alberto Cardin, *Dialéctica y canibalismo* (Barcelona, 1994), 150. Cardin also recounts (149–157) how rumors of Jewish desecrations of the host, human sacrifices, and cannibalism were so prevalent that even the papacy intervened several times to discredit such stories. See also Reay Tannahill, *Flesh and Blood: A History of the Cannibal Complex* (Boston, 1996), 82–84.

and, later, in the context of the Catholic-Calvinist colonization of Brazil—this theological debate about the Eucharist was articulated with the problem of universalist imperialism and was thereby knotted up with the ethnic construction of American alterity. Paradoxically, while Catholic universalism defined itself in Europe by defending the realism of Eucharistic theophagy (eating of God), in America it nonetheless raged against what it perceived as a similar order of materiality in the Communion of Amerindian religions.[12]

The Envy of Satan: The Plagiarist *Simia Dei*

Since the first moment of the colonial encounter, blood sacrifices began to occupy a fundamental place in the imaginary of colonial Mexico. Conquistadors such as Hernando Cortés often alleged the practices of human sacrifices and anthropophagy in order to justify the war against the Mexicas and the civilizing mission of Spain; but, more important, the ritual aspects of Mexica cannibalism prompted extensive ethnographic and theological inquiries.[13]

The Aztec sacrifices took various forms, at times with rituals that provided the gods with a gift of the victim's blood. Sometimes the victim, seen as the living image of the god, was killed and skinned, and his or her hide was worn. In other instances, a figure or a prisoner of war was consecrated as a god and then eaten. The flesh of the god was provided by human victims, or else by mushrooms, tamales, or anthropomorphic figures made of corn or *bledos* (*Amaranthus deflexus*), sometimes drizzled with blood. Motolinía, along with Sahagún,

---

12. In 1555 the French navigator Nicholas Durand de Villegagnon attempted, under the protection of Henry II, to establish a French colony (France antarctique) in Rio de Janeiro Bay. Amid its internal divisions, the Portuguese finally eradicated the colony in 1561. Villegagnon had promised Calvin he would protect his ministers in their mission to found, on the *terre du brésil*, a society ruled in accordance with the Reformed religion. However, France antarctique turned out to be a renewal of the conflicts of the Counter-Reformation: Villegagnon defended the dogma of transubstantiation, which provoked the division of the colony; the Protestant ministers abandoned the fort and went inland to live with the Indians. This failed colonial experience gave way to various ethnographies of Tupinambá cannibalism (such as André Thevet, 1557, 1575; Jean de Léry, 1578) and to a religious and political debate between Protestants and Catholics. Furthermore, these ethnographies served as a motivation for diverse critiques of the religious wars in Europe and the European imperial enterprises in America. See Lestringant, *Cannibals*; my essay, "Brasil especular: alianzas estratégicas y viajes estacionarios por el tiempo salvaje de la Canibalia," in Carlos Jáuregui and Juan Dabove, eds., *Heterotropías: narrativas de identidad y alteridad latinoamericana* (Pittsburgh, 2003), 77–114.

13. Cortés is the first to refer to these sacrifices of a figure made of seed, mixed and kneaded with "blood from human hearts and bodies" [con sangre de corazones y de cuerpos humanos]. Hernán Cortés, *Cartas de relación* (Mexico City, 1993), 65.

observes that in Mexico they made corn tamales and "sang and said that those *bollos* became the flesh of Tezcatlipoca, who was their highest god or demon," and that "they ate those *bollos* in place of Communion" [cantaban y decían que aquellos bollos se tornaban carne de Tezcatlipoca, que era el dios o demonio que tenían por mayor / comían aquellos bollos, en lugar de comunión]. In the fifteenth month (Panquetzaliztli), dedicated to Huitzilopochtli, the body of the god, sculpted out of seeds, was eaten. The breaded idol was sprinkled with human blood, and later the priests broke it into "little pieces . . . [that] were administered as a communion to children and adults, men and women, the elderly and the young . . . with . . . such reverence, fear and joy . . . that it was remarkable to hear them saying that they were eating the flesh and bones of the god" [pedaçitos . . . [que] comulgauan . . . chicos y grandes, onbres y mugeres, biejos y niños . . . con tanta reuerencia, temor y alegria . . . que era cossa de admiracion diçiendo que comian la carne y los guessos del dios].[14]

Even more perturbing to the Spaniards was the ritual proximity between Mexica and Christian theophagy, "close to the Easter of Resurrection," during the fifth month, or Toxcatl, in honor of Tezcatlipoca (smoking mirror). Like the Roman soldiers in Durostorum (Low Moesia; modern Silistra, Bulgaria)—who, to celebrate the Saturnalia, chose among themselves a handsome man and dressed him in such a way that he looked like Saturn, gave him license to act out the god's character traits, and then sacrificed him (as James George Frazer recounts)—during the Mexica festivals the god was made to die in the person of its human representative. He was then resuscitated in the figure of another victim, who for one year would enjoy the fatal honor of divinity, with its various privileges and honors, only to die as did his predecessors. The altar of sacrifice (according to Durán) "was in the same form that our sacred Christian religion and Catholic Church uses" [era á la mesma forma que nuestra sagrada religion xiptiana y la yglesia católica usa]. The chosen one was transformed into a deity by virtue of physical similarity, careful education, and adoration: "they honored him like a god" [honrábanle como a dios] before the sacrifice.[15]

14. Toribio de Benavente Motolinía, *Historia de los indios de la Nueva España* (Madrid, 1988), 64, 82; Sahagún, *Historia general*, 82, 107–111. Durán also associates various scenes of cannibalism with the Mexica religion: the prisoners were "the tasty and warm food of the gods whose flesh was very sweet and delicate to them" [comida sabrosa y caliente de los dioses cuya carne les era dulçísima y delicada]; they were sacrificed and offered "as food for the idol and for those wicked butchers hungry to eat human flesh" [de comer al ydolo y a aquellos malditos carniceros hambrientos por comer carne humana]. Durán, *Ritos y fiestas*, 94.

15. Sahagún describes the Toxcatl in his *Historia general*, 85, 115–118. James George Frazer, *The Golden Bough: A Study in Magic and Religion* (New York, 1996), 677–679, 681; Durán, *Ritos y fiestas*, 99. See also the description of the said ceremony in José de Acosta, *Historia natural y moral*

Whereas the conversions were viewed suspiciously as a form of mimetic deception, Mexica religion itself was perceived as a mimicry of Catholicism. Peggy Sanday remarks that, like the Catholic Eucharist, the Aztec rite entails a bloody transubstantiation. While this of course is a generalization that misses the complexity and variety of the Mexica rites, it nonetheless accurately expresses the understanding of cannibalism exhibited by the evangelizing priests. The colonial reading of difference reduces all complexity to similarity; and, as we have stated, similarity is the antechamber to horror.[16]

In order to explain the supposed similarities between the religious practices of the Mexicas and the sacraments of the church, and to make this recognition intelligible, two hypotheses were proposed in the sixteenth century. According to the first, God had in some way revealed himself to the Indians, thus preparing them for the arrival of his word; the Eucharist thereby would replace ritual anthropophagy. The other possibility was that the similarities were the work of Satan (from the Hebrew שָׂטָן /Satan/; "adversary" or "contrary"). The first hermeneutic tradition was syncretist, and it lent itself to important developments, such as the conjectures about a pre-Columbian revelation of the word of God to the Indians and the presence of Thomas the apostle in America; the theses of Friar Bartolomé de las Casas, for whom the preevangelic anthropotheophagic sacrifice had a theological dimension; and the universalist interpretations of some Jesuit missionaries in the seventeenth century, who saw prefigurations of Christianity in the pagan rites. The second thesis converted religious difference into idolatry and a cult of evil, and it turned Mexica theophagic cannibalism into a satanic version of the Eucharistic sacrament (in the Hebrew sense of contrary to God, relative to the devil). Cannibalism, which has

---

de las Indias (Madrid, 1987), 378–383. The mask and the costume contained the power and the identity of the (re)presented. To (re)dress in this mask or appearance meant to embody this force *(ixtli)*, to become it; see Kay Almere Read, *Time and Sacrifice in the Aztec Cosmos* (Bloomington, Ind., 1998), 147.

16. Peggy Reeves Sanday, *Divine Hunger: Cannibalism as a Cultural System* (Cambridge, 1986), 18, 172. Several anthropological studies point out that the Mexica sacrifices—associated with hunting, war, and agricultural cycles—dramatized the flows of the cosmos with the continuous rhythms by which one consumes and is consumed, a movement that can be understood as the incessant flow, or continuum, of existence and the discontinuity of its forms. Food, ritual sacrifice, and periodic bloodletting were equivalent to the movement of the cosmos and prevented the *tlahtlacolli*, or the apocalypse of the Mexica-Tenocha universe. See Sagan, *Cannibalism*, 109; Sahlins, "Culture as Protein and Profit," *New York Review of Books*, Nov. 23, 1978, 45–53; Yolotl González Torres, *El sacrificio humano entre los mexicas* (Mexico City, 1985), 304; Sanday, *Divine Hunger*, 47–48; Read, *Time and Sacrifice*, 124, 127–136, 144.

never been defined by Catholicism as a sin in and of itself, was made one by constituting the "ultimate expression of idolatry."[17]

Although Durán recognized the possibility of a previous revelation or pre-figuration, the demonological discourse and the idea that the ritual was a perverse (American) copy of the Eucharist prevails:

> The reader should note how truly deformed is this demon-possessed ceremony, [which is a deformation of] the ceremony of our sacred church, that obliges us to receive the true body and blood of our Lord Jesus Christ true god and true man on Easter . . . from which we can conclude two things: either there was news (as I have stated) of our sacred Christian religion in this land, or our accursed adversary the devil made them do wrong in his service and cult, making himself adored and served, deforming the Catholic ceremonies of the Christian religion.

> Note el lector quan propiamente esta contrahecha esta cerimonia endemoniada la de nuestra yglesia sagrada que nos manda reciuir el berdadero cuerpo y sangre de nro. Señor Jsuxto verdadero dios y berdadero hombre por pascua florida . . . de lo qual se coligen dos cosas ó que huuo notiçia (como dexo dicho) de nuestra sagrada religion christiana en esta tierra o que el maldito de nro. aduersario el demonio las haçia contra haçer en su seruicio y culto haciendose adorar y seruir contra haciendo las católicas cerimonias de la christiana religion.[18]

Despite the range of intellectual attitudes, many colonial writers typically arrived at this conclusion. For them, the similarities could not have been of divine origin, first, because that commonality would undermine the conversions and, second, because it made no sense that God would copy himself, much less do so imperfectly. Mimicry is a thing of the devil, or *simia Dei,* as the fallen angel was called, alluding to his supposed apelike fondness for imitation. According to Sebastián de Covarrubias's *Tesoro de la lengua castellana o Española* (1611), "We call simian he who mimics another and wants to imitate him" [Llamamos simia al que remeda a otro y quiere imitarle]. Lucifer is defined precisely by his envy, by his desire to copy, to imitate and be like God: "How art thou fallen from heaven, O Lucifer, son of the morning! . . . For thou

17. Cervantes, *The Idea of the Devil,* 23. The often-repeated thesis of Thomas's apostolic work in America is presented, for example, in the writings of José de Acosta, Carlos de Sigüenza y Góngora, and Servando Teresa de Mier.

18. Durán, *Ritos y fiestas,* 96.

hast said in thine heart, I will ascend into heaven, I will exalt my throne above the stars of God: I will sit also upon the mount of the congregation, in the sides of the north: I will ascend above the heights of the clouds; I will be like the most High" (Isa. 14:12–14). However, as stated by Thomas Aquinas, this simian desire fails as the devil can muster up only a grotesque imitation of God.[19]

It was even understood that abstinence, confession, and chastity among the indigenous peoples were inspired by the jealousy that the devil had of the true virtues and penitence offered to God. In the specific case of the Eucharist, the devil carried out his copy of transubstantiation to an extreme by making it a bloody sacrifice, as if he wished to outdo the most sacred mystery. Thus the New World became host to the plagiarizing hand of Satan; the unspeakable rites of the Americans were actually perverse copies perpetrated by the simia Dei.[20]

Even the rational Jesuit José de Acosta, often inclined to syncretic explanations, would thus use the rhetoric of sacrilegious alterity to posit similarity as sinister, an aping "deformity" that can only simulate the truth: "The devil," he wrote in his *Historia natural y moral de las Indias* (1590), "has endeavored to resemble God in the forms of sacrifice, religion, and sacraments." [El demonio ha procurado asemejarse a Dios en el modo de sacrificios, y religión y sacramentos.] In Mexico as much as in Peru, Acosta suggested, the devil "has managed to mimic the sacraments of the Holy Church" [ha procurado remedar los sacramentos de la santa Iglesia] with ceremonies, offerings, services, "convents of virgins . . . invented for his service," imitations of penitence, an institution similar to the confession, lavatories, processions and flagellants, and so on. Of course, the most horrible of these simulations was the Mexican mockery of the Eucharist. Acosta gives a detailed account of the *guerras floridas* (Flower Wars), the capture of prisoners, the extraction of hearts to be offered up to the sun, and the practice of anthropophagy. The Jesuit angrily notes that the word *host* (*hostia*, "victim") is closely related to *huestes* ("enemies") and then goes on to dedicate several embittered anthological pages to a rant against the plagiarism of the Eucharist:

19. *Simia*, in Sebastian de Covarrubias Orzoco, *Tesoro de la lengua castellana o Española* (Barcelona, 1943), 939; Thomas Aquinas, *Summa Theologica* (Denver, Colo., 1995), part 1, quest. 63, art. 3.

20. As many historians point out, diabolism does not reach its peak during the Middle Ages, as it is often assumed, but rather between the fourteenth century and the end of the seventeenth, concomitant with the conquest and colonization of the New World. See Georges Minois, *Historia de los infiernos* (Barcelona, 1994); also Cervantes, *The Idea of the Devil*, on the relationship between the idea of the devil and indigenous culture and religion in Mexico during the sixteenth century.

What is most admirable about the envy and competency of Satan is that not only with idolatries and sacrifices, but also in some way with ceremonies, he has mimicked our sacraments that Our Lord Jesus Christ instituted and that his sacred church uses, especially the communion, the highest and most divine [which] he tried in a certain way to imitate.

Lo que más admira de la envidia y competencia de Satanás, es que no sólo en idolatrías y sacrificios, sino también en cierto modo de ceremonias, haya remedado nuestros sacramentos, que Jesucristo Nuestro Señor instituyó y usa su santa Iglesia, especialmente el sacramento de la comunión, que es el más alto y divino [y que] pretendió en cierta forma imitar.

Acosta describes the festivals in honor of Huitzilopochtli, which involved the creation of the corn idol, its consecration and supper. The "pieces of dough that they called the bones and flesh of Vitzilipuztli" [trozos de masa [que] llamaban los huesos y carne de Vitzilipuztli] were given

as a communion to all the people ... [and] they received it with such reverence, fear, and tears that it inspired admiration, as they said that they were eating the flesh and bones of god. ... Who could not but admire that the devil takes such care to make himself adored and received in the same way that Jesus Christ our God ordered and taught...?... Satan... always mixes his cruelties and filth because he is a homicidal spirit and the father of lies.

a modo de comunión a todo el pueblo ... [y] recibíanlo con tanta reverencia, temor y lágrimas, que ponía admiración, diciendo que comían la carne y los huesos de dios.... ¿A quién no pondrá admiración que tuviese el demonio tanto cuidado de hacerse adorar y recibir al modo que Jesucristo nuestro Dios ordenó y enseñó...?... Satanás... siempre mezcla sus crueldades y suciedades porque es espíritu homicida, y padre de la mentira.

The seriousness and vehemence of Acosta's writings against the devil and his mixtures permit one to suppose that he was, not simply placating the Inquisition, but rather responding to the threat of the specular traps of difference. "How one suffers," says Acosta, "when using this word (Communion) to describe such a diabolic act." Religious alterity appeared as a sinister mirror. Religious ethnographies such as Acosta's aimed to differentiate what the evil simia Dei had intermingled. Here, colonial discourse is not fraught with the fear of being devoured, but rather with horror at this promiscuous confusion, at the diminishing of difference. The thesis of diabolic plagiarism converted religious difference into a satanic cult, constructing the Mexica theophagic cannibalism as a sinister mimicry of the Eucharistic Sacrament. This demonological discourse recognizes similarity, but insists upon difference, and concludes with accusations of plagiarism.[21]

In his *Historia eclesiástica indiana* (1596–1604), the Franciscan friar Gerónimo de Mendieta—a friend of the Indians—also hotly denounced these "abominations that [the devil] ordained in his diabolical church, in competition with Christ's holy sacraments" [los execramentos que ordenó [el demonio] en su iglesia diabólica, en competencia con los santos Sacramentos [de] Cristo]. Similitude (of the sacraments) becomes sinister in the rhetoric of execrable alterity, a sinister deformity that simulates truth. Cannibalism, as a trope of identity/alterity, is a perturbing image and is essentially ambivalent: it is a mockery of the culture of the European conquistador and an American (that is to say, *different*) version of sameness; in other words, cannibalism is diabolic plagiarism. American difference is the discursive result of the theological dissimilation of similitude within the realm of evil and moral monstrosity.[22]

Divine Permission and the Prefiguration

Coincident with the emergent idea of an empire—above and beyond the rhetoric of conquest, the mission of which was to civilize, evangelize, and protect the Indians—another tradition of conceiving religious alterity recognized a commonality with the Mexica religion and saw its rites as prefigurations of Christianity. Las Casas's position (and later that of various Jesuits) was based on a scheme of continuity with the Other: Christ could be reached from the indigenous religion, for it already possessed the seeds of revelation. There was just a minor detail to be resolved: cannibalism. Las Casas accounted for this uneasy matter from four angles: cultural comparisons and relativism; the thesis that gave a biblical sense to the bellicosity of the Caribs; the recognition that some cannibal rites in Central America had a theological dimension; and the construction of a cannibal-conquistador.

---

21. Acosta, *Historia natural y moral*, 334–335, 360, 361, 363, 364. As mentioned, Acosta details several examples of indigenous mimicry of different sacraments (247, 364, 372, 381, among others); his account of the guerras floridas, treatment of prisoners, ritual killings, and cannibalism is accompanied by an ardent allegation against the diabolic mimicry of the Eucharist (352–359).

22. Gerónimo de Mendieta, *Historia eclesiástica Indiana* (1597) (Madrid, 1973), I, 66.

Las Casas's first strategy is to construct a textual journey to antiquity, a journey that seeks to dismiss the notion that cannibalism is original or unique to the New World, refuting "many [who] think that the practice of eating human flesh was originated in this land." According to the different types of barbarism defined in the epilogue to the *Apologética historia sumaria,* the Indians of the New World can be defined as barbarian only in relation to their paganism—which is not negative, because it indicates only a lack of revelation—and with respect to linguistic difference. Regarding the latter, Las Casas warns, "As barbarous as they are to us, we are to them" [tan bárbaros como ellos nos son, somos nosotros a ellos]. Las Casas's discussion of barbarity takes place in continuous and casuistic comparison to ancient civilizations. He establishes a long tradition of paganism and human sacrifice among the Greeks, Romans, Jews, Babylonians, and others, and he reminds the reader that cannibalism was not unknown to the Old World. For example, there was anthropophagy among the early settlers of France, Spain, and England as well as among Asian peoples such as the Scythians.[23]

Las Casas also claims that Caribs are not cannibals by "corrupt nature" or by "perverse constitution" [perversa complixión]. In other words, they are not monsters. His hypothesis is that there must have been a famine, or some calamity "like many times there has been in the world, and our Spaniards have done it [eaten human flesh] in these Indies and in Spain" [como muchas veces ha en el mundo acaecido, y nuestros españoles lo han hecho [comer carne humana] en estas Indias y en España]. To illustrate his point he mentions the "horrible and abominable" case of the Spaniards on Pánfilo de Narváez's expedition, told by Cabeza de Vaca in *Naufragios.* He also notes other reports of cannibalism, including incidents in France and Spain recorded by the ancient geographer Strabo, as well as Jerome's account of cannibalism in Scotland. Las Casas goes on to list events narrated by Herodotus, Pomponius Mela, and Sebastian Münster, all of which seem to him much more cruel than Carib cannibalism: "I do not know whether the Caribs of these lands who are tainted by it [eating human flesh] could go further, nor even as far." [No sé si los caribes destas tierras que della [la carne humana] están inficionados puedan llegar a más, ni a tanto.][24]

23. Bartolomé de las Casas, *Apologética historia sumaria* (Mexico City, 1967), II, 221, 654. Las Casas's typology of barbarism outlines the grounds for his sympathetic anthropology of otherness (II, 637–654); his "comparative approach" defines his vision of cannibalism, as he examines cases of anthropophagy among ancient classical civilizations, early inhabitants of Europe, and Asian civilizations (I, 467–470, 543–545, II, 140–172, 354–356).

24. Ibid., II, 352–356.

Additionally, in his *Historia de las indias* Las Casas maintains that the Caribs are God's instruments for punishing the sins of the Spaniards:

> Once the natural neighbors [of the Island of San Juan] were killed, God reserved for the exercise and punishment of the Spaniards those fierce peoples of the Caribbean islands of Guadalupe and Dominica and others around there, who infested many times that island, assaulting it. They killed some Spaniards and robbed and destroyed some of the estates and haciendas. . . . That is how God left some nations for the sins of the sons of Israel, so that they might bother, perturb, infest, rob, and punish them. . . . And God willing, with that damage and punishment we could pay for the havoc and calamity and destruction that we have caused on that island.

> Después de muertos los naturales vecinos della [la Isla de San Juan], dejó Dios para ejercicio y castigo de los españoles, reservadas las gentes de los caribes de las islas de Guadalupe y de la Dominica y otras de por allí, que infestaron muchas veces aquella isla, haciendo saltos; mataron algunos españoles y robaron y destruyeron algunas estancias y haciendas. . . . Así dejó Dios ciertas naciones por los pecados de los hijos de Israel, para que los inquietasen, turbasen, infestasen, robasen, castigasen. . . . Y pluguiese a Dios que con aquellos daños y castigos pagásemos solos los estragos y calamidades y destrucciones que habemos causado en aquella isla.

The recurring formula (from Columbus to Cieza de León) according to which the conquistador was a sort of instrument of God to punish the cannibals is here inverted. Las Casas locates the cannibals within an order of calamities. The fierceness of the cannibal is not his own; it is a divine instrument. The Caribs thus become the corrective punishment for the excesses of the colonizer.[25]

Regarding what was perceived as the more civilized Meso-American cannibalism, Las Casas—while not justifying it—points out that in Guatemala and New Spain cannibal feasts were religious rites and that more "horrible and abominable" was the cannibalism of the Old World. In Guatemala "they cooked, prepared, and ate the flesh . . . of the sacrificed as a holy thing, consecrated to their gods . . . they did it for religion and for no other reason" [la carne . . . de los sacrificados la cocían y aderezaban y la comían como cosa sanctísima y a los dioses consagrada, . . . que por religión y no por otra razón hacían]. If certainly he did not justify Mexica cannibalism, he offers a theological context to explain it: "[In] New Spain they did not eat [human flesh] just

25. Las Casas, *Historia de las Indias* (Caracas, 1986), II, 204.

for the sake of it, as I understand it, but rather they ate the flesh of those they sacrificed, as a sacred thing, more for religion than for any other reason." [[En] la Nueva España no la comían tan de propósito, según tengo entendido, sino la de los que sacrificaban, como cosa sagrada, más por religión que por otras causas.][26]

Las Casas's universalism regarding the perception of Amerindian religions can be juxtaposed to the thesis of diabolic intervention: idolatry is seen in the *Apologética* as "a natural and universal corruption present among all human beings . . . before the knowledge of God's revelation." Idolatry, therefore, is instigated, not by the devil, but rather by an innate religious sense. Moreover, Las Casas insinuates that religious cannibalism occurred "by divine permission, before the Gospel's word gave the world light." The idea of divine permission suggests that eating the flesh and blood of Christ substitutes anthropophagy as natural idolatry gives way to true knowledge of God. In his polemic with Juan Ginés de Sepúlveda, Las Casas dares, with intellectual audacity, to say that the sacrifices, although censurable, were proof of the high religiosity of the infidels because, by "giving their life to God, they make the greatest act of subjection and respect they can" [dando la vida a Dios, la hacen mayor subiectión y acatamiento que pueden].[27]

Again Las Casas draws on examples from antiquity to propose that, because of the lack of divine revelation that would otherwise prohibit it, it was understandable that idolaters would offer God the greatest and best offering, which is human life itself:

> The nations that offered men in sacrifice to their gods . . . had a noble
> and honorable estimation of the excellence and deity and deservedness
> (mistaken because they were idolaters) of their gods . . . because they
> offered, to those they understood to be gods, the most splendid and most
> precious and most valuable . . . of creatures . . . [and,] as has been said, by
> natural illumination [reason] judges that one should offer to God the
> best and the most worthy, being within the limits of natural law, in the
> absence of positive law, human or divine, which would prohibit or hinder
> the offering of men.

> Las naciones que a sus dioses ofrecían en sacrificio hombres . . . noble y
> digna estimación tuvieron de la excelencia y deidad y merecimiento

26. Las Casas, *Apologética*, II, 221, 354.

27. Ibid., I, 381, 466 (see also I, 375, 386); Las Casas, *Obra indigenista* (Madrid, 1985), 193. According to Las Casas, even though idolatry is a product of the natural religiosity of the human kind, the devil might take advantage of it (*Apologética*, I, 384–387), II, 263).

(puesto que idólatras engañados) de sus dioses . . . porque ofrecían, a los que estimaban ser dioses la más excelente y más preciosa y más costosa . . . de las criaturas . . . [y] como queda dicho, por la lumbre natural juzga [la razón] que a Dios se le debe ofrecer lo mas digno y lo mejor, estando dentro de los límites de la ley natural, faltando ley positiva, humana o divina, que ofrecer hombres prohíba o estorbe.[28]

Before the preaching of the Gospel, religious cannibalism appears as an anthropotheophagic sacrament and as a prefiguration of the Eucharistic supper, in the same way that indigenous penitence, mortifications, confessions, ablutions, and other religious rites are also referred to as forms of religiosity that anticipate Christianity. Las Casas—who takes care to not harm the Sacrament —barely insinuates that the body and blood of Christ replace anthropophagy in a relaylike exchange of natural idolatry for true spiritual and physical knowledge of God. A fragment of a fresco by Paolo Farinati (1595) in Villa Della Torre, Mezzane di Sotto (Verona) (see Figure 5) adeptly expresses this idea of correspondence and substitution between communion and cannibalism that Las Casas suggests: an indigenous man (functioning as an allegory of America) is shown leaving the cannibalistic banquet that appears on his left—where a human arm and torso are being roasted in a fire pit. As he turns his back on the feast, he grabs the crucifix to his right: America substitutes anthropophagy with the Eucharist.

Finally, in his evangelizing role, Las Casas finds himself face-to-face with the native, and he discovers, as Mario Cesareo has observed of other friars, that in the "step from the Satanic mask to the indigenous face, what is at stake is the inevitability of supposing the monstrous as a possibility of the self." Las Casas— addressing the moral monstrosity within what Enrique Dussel has called the "ego conquiro" ("I conquer")—produces one of the most radical refigurations of the cannibal trope. In Las Casas's writings the Indian is not a devouring Other, but a suffering and consumed victim. Anticipating Las Casas's idea that the colonizer could be more savage than the colonized, a letter the Dominicans wrote to Charles V on December 4, 1519, had called the encomenderos "butchers" and had identified colonial commodities with the exploited bodies who produced European wealth. "We think that if the silk were well wrung, Indian blood would flow from it." [[La] seda pensamos que si fuese bien esprymida, sangre de los yndios manaría.] American goods and wealth were soaked with blood and obtained at the expense of uncountable human lives,

28. Las Casas, *Apologética*, II, 244, 245.

FIGURE 5. *America*. Fragment. Paolo Farinati. Fresco. 1595. Villa Della Torre, Mezzane di Sotto, Verona. In Carlos Jáuregui, *Canibalia: canabalismo, calibanismo, antropofagía cultural y consumo en América Latina* (Havana, 2005)

consumed by the encomenderos. Las Casas gets the most out of this trope throughout his *Historia de las Indias:* "The peoples of San Juan, seeing that they were on their way to be consumed . . . decided to fight back." [Viendo las gentes de la isla de San Juan que llevaban el camino para ser consumidos . . . acordaron de se defender.] "By that time, the year of 1516, the Spaniards did not forget that they were guilty of the consumption of docile peoples." [Por ese tiempo y año de 1516, no olvidaban los españoles que tenían cargo de consumir la gente mansísima.] Elsewhere, in the famous *Brevísima relación de la destruición de las Indias,* he writes: "They [the Spaniards] were [involved] in these inhuman butcheries for about seven years. . . . Judge how many people they managed to *consume.*" [Estuvieron [los españoles] en estas *carnicerías* tan inhumanas cerca de siete años. . . . Júzguese cuánto sería el número de la gente que *consumirían.*]²⁹

Note here that for Las Casas the verb *to consume (consumir)* has the double meaning of annihilation and communion. In fact, *to consume* is defined by Covarrubias (1611) as the "act of taking the priest, the body of our Lord Christ, on the bread and the wine, during the holy sacrifice of Mass" [en el Sacrosanto Sacrificio de la missa el tomar el sacerdote el cuerpo de Christo nuestro Señor,

29. Mario Cesareo, *Cruzados, mártires y beatos: emplazamientos del cuerpo colonial* (West Lafayette, Ind., 1995), 18; Enrique Dussel, *1492: el encubrimiento del otro: hacia el origen del "mito de la modernidad"* (La Paz, 1994), 59; Joaquín Franciso Pacheco et al., eds., *Colección de documentos inéditos, relativos al descubrimiento, conquista, y organización de las antiguas posesiones españolas de América y Oceanía* (Madrid, 1864–1884), XXXV, 199–240. Karl Marx, using a similar metaphor to the Dominicans', but in relation to capital, will say that, if one thinks that money is stained with blood, capital "comes dripping from head to toe, from every pore, with blood and dirt"; Marx, *Capital,* trans. Ben Fowkes, I (New York, 1976), 926 (book 1, part 8, chap. 31). Bartolomé de las Casas, *Historia de las Indias,* II, 202, III, 333, and *Brevísima relación de la destruición de las Indias* (1552) (Madrid, 1992), 68.

debaxo de las especies del pan y el vino]. When Las Casas says that the encomenderos consume the Indians, his trope was depicting the colonial consumption of labor as a diabolic distortion of the Eucharist. In Lascasian discourse, the verb *to consume* is not metaphorically associated with a voracious savage, but rather with the conquistador. His selection of the verb *to consume* (*consumir*) in relation to the subject *conquistador* allows the latter to occupy the place previously assigned to the rapacious savage. The perverse copy of the Communion is thus that of the encomenderos and the conquistadors. According to Las Casas, they perverted Christ's mandate to his disciples to preach like sheep among wolves (Matt. 10:16). Instead, said the priest, they behave "like wolves and tigers and cruel lions famished during many days" [como lobos e tigres y leones crudelísimos de muchos días hambrientos]. The Spaniard represented in the *Brevísima* is a devourer of the innocent and a true cannibal. In this manner, Las Casas distances himself from the conquistador-cannibal and authorizes his church to speak for the Indian, to be the "prosthetic tongue" of the subjugated Other.[30]

Cannibalism and Criollo Consciousness

In the culture of the *Barroco de Indias* (New World Baroque) in the context of imperial decadence and what has been called "the emergence of a *criollo* consciousness," colonial tropes, especially cannibalism, are reexamined without the religious and militaristic paranoia of the sixteenth century. In the seventeenth century, an abstract and heroic version of the Indian emerged as the symbolic patrimony of the American elite, a concept unimaginable to earlier writers, judging from such examples as Bernardo de Balbuena's *Grandeza mexicana* (1604).[31]

An interesting example of a syncretic representation of alterity is found in Carlos de Sigüenza y Góngora's *Teatro de virtudes políticas, que constituyen a un príncipe* (1680), apparently produced with some collaboration from Sor Juana Inés de la Cruz. Sigüenza y Góngora (1645–1700) wrote the text to accompany a triumphal arch in honor of the arrival of Viceroy Tomás Antonio de la Cerda,

30. *Consumir* in Covarrubias, *Tesoro* (Barcelona, 1943), 351 (I owe this reference to Luis Fernando Restrepo); Las Casas, *Brevísima relación*, 16. Cesareo uses the expression "prosthetic body" to refer to the function of "tongue" and voice that some friars assigned to themselves in order to represent the indigenous, who were considered minors without legal standing of their own. Cesareo, *Cruzados, mártires y beatos*, 106.

31. See Guillermo Céspedes del Castillo, "La defensa de las Indias," in his *América hispánica (1492–1898)* (Barcelona, 1983); R. Trevor Davies, *La decadencia española, 1621–1700* (Barcelona, 1969); John Lynch, *The Hispanic World in Crisis and Change, 1598–1700* (Oxford, 1992).

marqués de la Laguna (1680). According to Sigüenza's description, represented on the arch was a succession (extending into the pre-Hispanic past) of rulers of New Spain, with Viceroy de la Cerda at the apex. Sigüenza positions the "Aztec State" in the Mexican viceregal genealogy. Even Huitzilopochtli, the blood-thirsty cannibal god—who for Durán and Mendieta had been the quintessential demonic image, the instigator of the abominable plagiarism of the Eucharist— here allegorizes the virtues of the prince. Sigüenza mentions José de Acosta and Bernal Díaz del Castillo as two of his sources. Both of these authors represent Huitzilopochtli as the devil of the Mexica religion, and yet this deity becomes a positive sign in criollo writing.[32]

In *Teatro de virtudes políticas* the evil and monstrous Huitzilopochtli becomes a political allegory of leadership. This is not to say, as Georgina Sabat de Rivers maintains, that Sigüenza was making an "apology for the Aztec world," nor that the cannibal is adopted as a sign of identity in the Baroque. What I am propos-ing here is that, for some *letrados,* there is an incipient symbolic appropriation of the indigenous (even of the cannibal) and, simultaneously, a partial over-coming of the colonial stereotype. This did not happen in works of classical Spanish theater, such as Lope de Vega's *El Nuevo Mundo descubierto por Cristó-bal Colón* (1614), Fernando de Zárate's *La conquista de México* (1668), or in the representations of America in the theater of Calderón. Rather, the phenomenon of appropriation corresponds to what has been called the emergence of criollo consciousness, which can be defined as a set of symbolic strategies and dis-courses for disputing and negotiating power; based on assertions of American particularism, criollos sought on the one hand cultural and political authority vis-à-vis the theocratic and cultural universal order of the empire and, on the other, inscription or participation within that same order.[33]

The emergence of this criollo consciousness can be described by its gestures better than by its goals; for instance, one of those gestures is the step from hor-ror at alterity to its symbolic appropriation and recodification by a sector of

32. Carlos de Sigüenza y Góngora, *Teatro de virtudes políticas, que constituyen á un príncipe advertidas en los monarcas antiguos del mexicano imperio* (Mexico City, 1986), 47–69. Note the contrast between Sigüenza's representation of Huitzilopochtli and that of his sources, Acosta and Díaz del Castillo; for example, Díaz del Castillo—who calls the Mexica god "Huichilobos," portrays the god as a demon and describes the abject spectacle of its cult, in *Historia verdadera de la conquista de la Nueva España* (Mexico City, 1995), 174–178. Although Sigüenza's sources cannot be considered the same as Sor Juana's, we should keep in mind that they shared references and ideas; on this matter, see Georgina Sabat de Rivers, *En busca de Sor Juana* (Mexico City, 1998), 289, 290.

33. Sabat de Rivers, *En busca de Sor Juana,* 267; Lope de Vega, *El Nuevo Mundo descubierto por Cristóbal Colón,* in Francisco Ruiz Ramón, ed., *América en el teatro clásico español: estudio y textos* (Pamplona, 1993), 269–330, and Fernando de Zárate, *La conquista de México,* 207–258.

what Angel Rama has famously called the "lettered city" of the Baroque. However, one does not find a criollo identity articulated by self-recognition in the Other. These approximations are symbolic, retrospective, and extremely ambivalent; they are always quivering on the edge of paranoia. While Sigüenza installed Huitzilopochtli in the genealogy of viceregal power, some flesh-and-blood New World Indians provided the viceroy with a different kind of welcome —in the form of an insurrection that he would never succeed in containing during his entire tenure. But, as we know, and Sigüenza makes this very clear in his own writings, the distance is vast between allegorical Indians and those armed and ready to revolt and burn Sigüenza's sacred Baroque library.[34]

In the work of Sor Juana Inés de la Cruz, symbolic appropriations, or, rather, recodifications, of the indigenous are similarly abundant. A notable sampling might be gathered from her *villancicos* (genre of devotional song), in which a criolla virgin is the leader of disparate voices (of blacks and Indians) from New Spain in a sort of poetic procession of integration. The Virgin is the point of confluence for New World heterogeneity. Similarly, the lettered criollo constructs his or her organic place as interpreter, translator, and privileged epistemological subject; he or she apprehends and then unites the ethnic, cultural, and linguistic hubbub of New Spain and renders the heterogeneous intelligible.[35]

34. Although the concept of the lettered city developed by Angel Rama in *La ciudad letrada* (Hanover, N.H., 1984) is useful, one ought to note that it does not correspond to a monolithic but corresponds to a heterogeneous sector of society and that, as Rolena Adorno points out, the concept "refers to a set of practices and mentalities that did not form one single ideological discourse, but rather were polyvocal"; it was "a labyrinth of ideological rivalries." See Rolena Adorno, "La *ciudad letrada* y los discursos coloniales," *Hispamérica: revista de literatura*, XVI, no. 48 (December 1987), 4, 5; see also Mabel Moraña, *Viaje al silencio: exploraciones del discurso barroco* (Mexico City, 1998), 58. Indeed, the repeated rebellions of the indigenous reminds us that the colonial letrado is located in a "besieged enclave" and that the integration of the Indian into the chorus of the Baroque fiesta, or into the allegorical monument, acts as a sort of symbolic compensation for this state of siege. For example, the religious pressures resulting from intolerant evangelization and the high tributary duties imposed on the Pueblo Indians gave rise to an extended indigenous insurrection that from 1680 to 1692 successfully challenged Spanish control of New Mexico: In 1680 there was a general revolt, led by an indigenous man from San Juan named Pope. For more than a decade, the viceregal establishment was incapable of controlling the insurrection and subjugating the Pueblo. Finally, in 1692, reconquest was made possible thanks to a combination of successful negotiations and a military campaign headed by Don Diego de Vargas. By that time, Carlos Sigüenza y Góngora had his own taste of Indian insurgency after witnessing a revolt (described in his tract *Alboroto y motín de los indios de México* [1692]) that led to the burning and destruction of papers and documents from the viceregal palace, some of which the author saved, burning his own fingers in the process. Thus, the "state of siege" describes a general condition of the Hispanic lettered city faced with insurgent heterogeneities. However, mutiny and insurrection are eruptions of violence within very dynamic and complex processes of negotiation and resistance.

35. Certainly—as Georgina Sabat de Rivers argues—in these villancicos there are carnival-

In what will be an inevitably partial analysis, I will refer to the intersection between the translation or allegorical construction of indigenous alterity and the manifestation of a criollo consciousness in Sor Juana's loas that precede the *autos* (plays) *El Cetro de José* (1692) and *El divino Narciso* (1690). Here Sor Juana takes on the problem of the similarity between the anthropotheophagic rites of the Aztecs and the Eucharist. Both loas are about the religious conversion of an American feminine character (América and Idolatría) through the benign means of persuasion by religious feminine dramatis personae (Fe and Religión); they are also about the substitution of Mexican cannibal rites with the Catholic Communion. Moreover, both exalt the mystery of transubstantiation.[36]

Méndez Plancarte affirms that Sor Juana had access to and indeed utilized *Monarquía indiana* (1615), by Friar Juan de Torquemada (1557–1664), a work that formed part of the library of the Golden Age in Spain and America and that reproduced the rhetoric of the sixteenth-century "war against the demon." With that text, Sor Juana would have had indirect access to Mendieta, Motolinía, and Durán (as suggested by Margo Glantz).[37] Indeed, Sor Juana was heiress to more than a century and a half of demonological rhetoric on religious alterity but also to a countertradition that in the sixteenth century had its most resolute defender in Las Casas and in the seventeenth century in the many missionaries and Jesuit educators who maintained a syncretist evangelical position toward the indigenous religions. It is therefore not an arduous hermeneutic task to see that Sor Juana takes up the latter tradition. But this syncretist humanism does not legitimate per se the thesis of a protonational Mexicanism in the work of Sor Juana that was put forth in the 1950s (by Agustín Cué Cánovas and Francisco López Cámara, among others). The loas, although they

esque and transgressive aspects. What is being emphasized here is that this transgression is articulated functionally in the culture of the Baroque; see *Estudios de literatura hispanoamericana: Sor Juana Inés de la Cruz y otros poetas barrocos de la colonia* (Barcelona, 1992), 193–198. Marie-Cécile Bénassy-Berling gives an overview of Sor Juana's representation of the indigenous in *Humanismo y religión en Sor Juana Inés de la Cruz* (Mexico City, 1983), 307–324.

36. *El divino Narciso* was first published in 1690 (Madrid); *El cetro de José* in the second volume of *Obras de soror Juana Ines de la Cruz* (Seville, 1692). Both loas maintain a structural and thematic relation to the autos sacramentales that they introduce. Other cases relevant to a comprehensive study of the perceptions of religious alterity would be texts by the evangelists of seventeenth-century Mexican missions and the work of intellectuals like Fernando de Alva Ixtlilxóchitl (1578–1650), who—with a tense and problematic sense of belonging to New Spain's elite—represents a criollo agency that negotiates and translates alternative imaginaries and a heterogeneous historical memory for New Spain.

37. Juan de Torquemada, *Monarquía indiana* (1615) (Mexico City, 1975); and see comment by Méndez Plancarte in Sor Juana, *Obras*, III, lxxiii. Margo Glantz, *Borrones y borradores: reflexiones sobre el ejercicio de la escritura (ensayos de literatura colonial, de Bernal Díaz del Castillo a Sor Juana)* (Mexico City, 1992), 178.

present American themes and express to different degrees an incipient Americanism, do not declare an "Americanist act of faith," nor do they manifest a "'nationalist' aspect" of Sor Juana, as Sabat de Rivers has somewhat hyperbolically alleged. This opinion reads the Baroque of New Spain teleologically as on a path toward the national. Moreover, it exaggerates the function of the characteristic Baroque trait of incorporating difference and the exotic; it confuses the translation of difference with the celebration or vindication of alterity.[38]

In Sor Juana's loa to *El cetro de José* (1692), the problem of sacramental similarity is debated in a dialogue between the conceptual characters Fe (Faith), Ley de gracia (Law of Grace, that is, Christian morality), Ley natural (Natural Law), Naturaleza (Nature), and Idolatría (Idolatry). Contrary to numerous readings, the loa allows for very little heterodoxy. Instead, it puts forth a dogmatic defense of the integrity of transubstantiation and exhibits a stereotypical critique of Mexica sacrifice, described by Fe as "blind idolatry" and as "barbarous" and "sacrilegious" rites:

> blind Idolatry: whose sacrilegious altars, despite your precepts, with human blood, showed that they are men of the most barbarous entrails more so than the most cruel beasts (for among these there is none who against its own kind turns its ferocious claws . . .).

>   ciega Idolatría:
> cuyas sacrílegas Aras,
> a pesar de tus preceptos
> manchadas de sangre humana,
> mostraban que son los hombres
> de más bárbaras entrañas
> que los brutos más crueles
> (pues entre éstos no se halla
> quien contra su especie propia
> vuelva las feroces garras . . .).[39]

The American character in indigenous costume, Idolatría, is declared "Plenipotentiary of all the Indians" [Plenipotenciaria / de todos los indios]. "Pleni-

38. Agustín Cué Canovas, "Juana de Asbaje y su tiempo," *El Nacional*, Nov. 29, 1951, 3, 6; Francisco López Cámara, "La conciencia criolla en Sor Juana y Sigüenza," *Historia mexicana*, VI (1957), 350–373; Sabat de Rivers, *En busca de Sor Juana*, 269–271, and also "Apología de América y del mundo azteca en tres loas de Sor Juana," *Revista de estudios hispánicos* (University of Puerto Rico), IX (1992), 267–291.

39. Loa to *El cetro de José*, in Sor Juana, *Obras*, III, 186. Translations are mine.

potentiary" (emissary or representative), yes, but in the allegorical sense of a character that exists only to be converted, reduced to sameness. For example, when the character Ley de gracia proposes to remove the Mexican sacrilegious idols and false gods and replace them with "the sacred image of Christ," Fe categorically responds to the advocates of simile and metaphor:

> More appropriate action—I think—is placing a Consecrated Form, which is not placing the image but the Real Substance.

> Más acertada
> acción tengo el colocar
> una Forma Consagrada,
> que no es colocar la Imagen
> sino la propia Substancia.[40]

The Consecrated Form is, not an image or symbol, but the sacred Substance, that is, the flesh of Christ, the "real thing." To the loa, inasmuch as it is a Counter-Reformationist work, the revelation of truth is insufficient. As José Antonio Maravall points out, referring to the culture of the Baroque in general, it was necessary to present such a truth performatively, "as an action."[41]

Let us take a look at another example of the Counter-Reformationist character of the loa to *El cetro de José.* At one point Idolatría proposes to continue with human sacrifices, since they are not in contradiction with the new religion (Catholicism):

> It does not contradict the precept that to this same deity [the Christian one] they offer the best sacrifices, which are those of human blood.

> No contradice al precepto,
> que a esa misma Deidad hagan
> los mejores Sacrificios,
> que son los de sangre humana.[42]

Idolatría, who appears to be an Indian woman educated in Scholasticism and the logical argumentation of Jesuit disputes (or at least a reader of Las Casas), adds that, because the human offerings are so high, the error of the ancient cult "was not in the sacrifice, but rather in the purpose, for it was offered to false deities" [no en el Sacrificio estaba, / sino en el objeto, pues / se ofreció

---

40. Ibid., III, 188, 189, 193.

41. José Antonio Maravall, *La cultura del barroco: análisis de una estructura histórica* (Barcelona, 1983), 153, 154.

42. Loa to *El cetro de José,* in Sor Juana, *Obras,* III, 193.

a Deidades falsas], and that now simply "exchanging the purpose is good enough" [mudar el objeto basta]. Naturaleza, seconded by Ley natural, responds by saying that the problem is not only the object but also the "inhuman offering" [la ofrenda inhumana]. According to Ley natural, life is a universal right: "All are men" [Todos / son Hombres], including the Tlaxcalans (enemies of Tenochtitlán), since, adds Naturaleza, "they all came from my entrails" [todos / salieron de mis entrañas].[43]

Idolatría, however, insists on the practice of cannibalism by employing a theological appeal that assimilates cannibalism with the Eucharist:

Among the foods, sacrificed meat is the tastiest dish . . . for making life long for all those who eat it.

> En las viandas,
> es el plato más sabroso
> la carne sacrificada,
>
> .   .   .   .
>
> para hacer la vida larga
> de todos los que la comen.[44]

Then Fe offers Idolatría a real sacrifice, more complete than anything that Idolatría has tasted before:

So I will place on the altars a holocaust so pure, a victim so exquisite, an offering so supreme, one that would be not just human but also divine; and one that would serve not only to calm, but also to satisfy the deity completely; and one that would provide not only the delights of a flavor, but infinite delights; and would give not only long life, but eternal life.

> Pues yo pondré en las Aras
> un Holocausto tan puro,
> una Víctima tan rara,
> una Ofrenda tan suprema,
> que no solamente Humana,
> mas también Divina sea;
> y no solamente valga
> para aplacar la Deidad,
> sino que La satisfaga
> enteramente; y no sólo

43. Ibid., 194, 195.
44. Ibid., 196.

delicias de un sabor traiga,
sino infinitas delicias;
y no solamente larga
vida dé, mas Vida Eterna.[45]

Fe is talking, obviously, about the Holy Eucharist. Idolatría doubts but finally concedes: if it is that good, and if the meal is real and anthropophagic, she will accept the Eucharist:

> Well, as long as I see that it is a human victim, that it pleases God, that I eat it, and it gives me eternal life (as you say), the dispute is over, and I will be satisfied!

> ¡Vamos, que como yo vea
> que es una Víctima Humana;
> que Dios se aplaca con Ella;
> que La como, y que me causa
> Vida Eterna (como dices),
> la cuestión está acabada
> y yo quedo satisfecha![46]

Fe has no problem keeping her promise, because, as we know, in the Eucharist "Christ is present," thanks to the mystery of transubstantiation.[47]

The work, then, does not—to repeat—"center on the theological recupera- tion of aspects of indigenous culture," as Carmela Zanelli argues, nor on the affirmation of difference. On the contrary, it constitutes a symbolic appropria-

45. Ibid., 197, 198.
46. Ibid., 199.
47. In the sonnet "A San Juan de Sahagún en consumir la Hostia Consagrada, por aparecérsele en ella Cristo visiblemente" [To St. John of Sahagún upon Consuming the Sacred Host, for Christ Visibly Appearing in It] Sor Juana states:

> O Juan! Eat, and do not look, for you make one sense jealous of the other; and who would think that the Fruit of Life could lose its beauty because it is craved? The sacrament is children's delight, and God provokes us to blindly deserve his nourishment, by eating.

> ¡Oh, Juan! Come, y no mires, que a un sentido
> le das celos con otro; y ¿quién pensara,
> que al Fruto de la Vida le quitara
> lo hermoso la razón de apetecido?
> Manjar de niños es el sacramento;
> y Dios, a ojos cerrados nos provoca
> a merecer, comiendo su alimento.

Fama, y obras póstumas del fénix de México, decima musa, poetisa Américana, sor Juana Inés de la Cruz (Madrid, 1700), 164.

tion of that difference for an orthodox defense of the dogma of transubstantiation, which, indeed, is the function of Eucharistic theater.[48]

In the culture of the Baroque, ethnic or religious alterity, like monstrosity, revolt, and transgression, often reinforces the absolutist pretension of incorporating and symbolically subduing all particularisms and subversions. The oft-mentioned Americanism of Sor Juana should be approached with the same caution, even with the evident poetic sympathy exhibited by Sor Juana toward the general rowdiness of Idolatría and her critique of the violence of the conquest:

> (Against my will) you took from me the crown that for so long I peacefully held [and] you the tyrant imposed your sovereignty in my domains preaching the Christian law, a law for which weapons opened for you a violent path.

> (A pesar de mis ansias)
> privándome la Corona,
> que por edades tan largas
> pacífica poseía,
> introdujiste tirana
> tu dominio en mis Imperios,
> predicando la Cristiana
> Ley, a cuyo fin te abrieron
> violenta senda las armas.[49]

Even though Idolatría recognizes that force opened the "path," she prefers a peaceful conquest: "Do not try with violence to alter the ancient customs." [No intentes con la violencia / inmutar la antigua usanza.] This humanist nuance does not in itself constitute rupture, but rather continuity with an intellectual tradition conscious of the questions of legitimacy that faced the conquest. A genealogy of this position would run through, for example, Francisco Vitoria, Las Casas, Bartolomé de Carranza, and Diego de Covarrubias, all, in one way

48. Carmela Zanelli, "La loa de 'El divino Narciso' de Sor Juana Inés de la Cruz y la doble recuperación de la cultura indígena mexicana," in José Pascual Buxó and Arnulfo Herrera, eds., *La literatura novohispana: revisión crítica y propuestas metodológicas* (Mexico City, 1994), 187. It is noteworthy to observe that neither loa fits easily within the parameters of the Eucharistic theater of New Spain, at the service of religious celebrations and the catechesis. The public for whom these works were written was, apparently, the Madrid court in the case of the auto to *El divino Narciso,* and the criollo lettered city and the viceregal court in the case of *El cetro de José.*

49. Loa to *El cetro de José,* 192.

or another, ideologues of the new imperial reason. Sor Juana quotes the imperial ideology in place since the middle of the sixteenth century.[50]

The other loa introduces the auto *El divino Narciso*, a play that underscores a cultural symmetry between the Greco-Roman antiquity absorbed by Christianity and the Mexican antiquity conquered by imperial Spain. *El divino Narciso*, as Yolanda Martínez–San Miguel states, "explains the institution of the Eucharist by establishing a parallel . . . between Narciso and Christ." The loa constitutes an American prelude that anticipates the religious dramatic allegory.[51]

There are two Indian characters in the loa to *El divino Narciso*: Occidente ("A handsome Indian, with a crown" [Indio galán, con corona]), according to Sabat de Rivers "a Mexica King"; and América, a defiant Indian woman (described in Spanish as "India bizarra: con mantas y cupiles"). Both characters are dancing and offering sacrifices to their gods when they are accosted by Religión and Celo. Here, the empire is represented militarily by Celo and spiritually by Religión. Celo, "Captain General" and conqueror, is pure force. Glantz notes that Celo evokes the image of Hernán Cortés. Religión (a "Spanish lady" [de dama española]), on the other hand, is the conceptualization of the Lascasian, evangelizing project, inclined to persuade the Indians, to, as she says, "invite them, in peace, to accept my faith" [convidarlos, de paz, / a que mi culto reciban].[52]

América resists conversion and invites Occidente to ignore Religión: "Obviously she [Religion] is crazy; forget about her, and let's continue with our rituals." [Sin duda es loca; ¡dejadla / y nuestros cultos prosigan!] Later she reproaches Celo: "You barbarous, crazy, blind man who with reasons not understood, wants to disturb the peace . . . we enjoy." [Bárbaro, loco, que ciego, / con razones no entendidas, / quieres turbar el sosiego / que . . . gozamos.][53]

Faced with the disastrous failure of his method of forced conversion, Celo prepares to execute América; but, before he can carry out the deed, and in historic correspondence with a second moment in the conquest, Religión intervenes:

50. Ibid., 193.

51. Sor Juana Inés de la Cruz, *El divino Narciso*, in *Obras*, III; Yolanda Martínez–San Miguel, "Articulando las múltiples subalternidades en el *Divino Narciso*," *Colonial Latin American Review*, IV (1995), 92.

52. Loa to *El divino Narciso*, in Sor Juana, *Obras*, III, 3–6; Sabat de Rivers, *En busca de Sor Juana*, 187; Glantz, *Borrones y borradores*, 180. Note the positive representation of Religión as a feminine and peaceful character, counter to the masculine, military subjectivity of *Celo* (see Martínez–San Miguel, "Articulando," *Colonial Latin American Review*, IV [1995], 91).

53. Loa to *El divino Narciso*, in Sor Juana, *Obras*, III, 8, 9.

Wait, don't kill her, for I need her alive! . . . because defeating her by force was your role, but subduing her through reason and persuasive kindness is mine.

¡Espera, no le des muerte,
que la necesito viva!

.　.　.　.　.　.　.

porque vencerla por fuerza
te tocó; mas el rendirla
con razón, me toca a mí,
con suavidad persuasiva.[54]

The pagan couple is then vanquished by Celo, but both make what we could call a conscientious objection: América declares:

Though captive I am crying for my freedom, my free will with rising liberty will adore my Gods!

　　Aunque lloro cautiva
mi libertad, ¡mi albedrío
con libertad más crecida
adorará mis Deidades![55]

Occidente, likewise, states:

I already said that your violence forces me to surrender, . . . but, although I grieve in captivity, you cannot prevent me from saying, here in my heart, that I worship the great God of seeds!

Yo ya dije que me obliga
a rendirme a ti la fuerza;

.　.　.　.　.　.　.　.

y así, aunque cautivo gima,
¡no me podrás impedir
que acá, en mi corazón, diga
que venero al gran Dios de las Semillas![56]

The proximity to Lascasian tradition is evident: Religión is the persuasive good colonizer, in contrast with Celo. Mabel Moraña has said of this loa that it

54. Ibid., 11.
55. Ibid., 12.
56. Ibid.

"relativizes the legitimacy of the implementation of the conquest" through a certain questioning of the violence of its campaigns. Glantz alleges that the loa is hence a universal defense of reasoned conversion and free will. The legal and theological defense of free will, however, is clearly not a thesis original to Sor Juana. Las Casas had sustained it more than 150 years before as the only mode for the religious conversion of alterity in his *De unico vocationis modo omnium gentium ad veram religionem* (circa 1537), and this was, indeed, an accepted theological thesis among many seventeenth-century Jesuits. Furthermore, the critique of the conquistadors (for their greed or their cruelty) is a common topic in Peninsular Baroque literature.[57]

The loa, although syncretist, to a certain extent takes up the tradition of the simia Dei. Religión, faced with the rites of America, manifests the thesis of diabolic plagiarism inherited from the archives of the sixteenth century: "Leave the profane cult that the Devil incites." [Dejad el culto profano / a que el Demonio os incita.][58] Further on:

My God! What kind of replicas, what kind of simulations or ciphers of our sacred Truths do those lies want to be? . . . Until what point does your malice want to imitate from God the sacred marvels?

¡Válgame Dios! ¿Qué dibujos,
qué remedos o qué cifras
de nuestras sacras Verdades
quieren ser estas mentiras?

. . . .

¿Hasta dónde tu malicia
quiere remedar de Dios
las sagradas Maravillas?[59]

Ambivalent toward the Mexica religious otherness, the loa also proposes the idea that cannibalism anticipates or is a prefiguration of the Eucharist, which corresponds to a conception of religious alterity in a relation of continuity with Catholicism. This circumstance has been the base for countless hyperboles. Sabat de Rivers proposes that both loas constitute an "apology for America" and "for the pre-Cortés world." Zanelli concurs, noting that in the loa to *El divino Narciso* Sor Juana "recuperates" both the "historical and the theological

---

57. Moraña, *Viaje al silencio*, 212, 213; Glantz, *Borrones y borradores*, 185, 186, 189; Bartolomé de las Casas, *Del único modo de atraer a todos los pueblos a la verdadera religión* (Mexico City, 1975).
58. Loa to *El divino Narciso*, in Sor Juana, *Obras*, III, 7.
59. Ibid., 13.

dimensions of the indigenous cultures." Susana Hernández Araico sees in both loas the "de/re/construction" of the festive European code of the allegorical representation of América as well as a critical consciousness of the Spanish conquest and an attempt to give historical and cultural specificity to the representation of America. Martínez–San Miguel insinuates that it might have been a "dramatization of the process of the conquest from the perspective of the colonized Indian."[60]

The implications here, which would frame Sor Juana as something of an indigenist, Latin Americanist antecedent to José Martí, or an intellectual from the tradition of the oppressed, find little textual support in the loa itself. As with the theological jurists of the sixteenth century, the discourse of the rights of the Other is, not a loose wheel of colonialism, but rather one of its best-oiled gears. The dramatic division between Religión and Celo corresponds to the old division of imperial labor. What has been seen as a political and religious heterodoxy is actually a quote from the Spanish Christian humanism of the sixteenth century that proposes a new imperial model (an evangelical one) in terms similar to those set out by Las Casas. Let us not forget that at the end of the loa América is converted and that the last scene concludes with América, Occidente, and Celo dancing in naked celebration of the integration of difference:

(América, Occidente, and Celo singing:) The Indies now know the one who is true God of Seeds!

(Cantan la América, y el Occidente y el Celo:)
        ya
conocen las Indias
al que es Verdadero
Dios de las Semillas![61]

If the loa to *El divino Narciso* displays a kind of Americanism or a sign of the "emergence of a *criollo* consciousness," it is not because it "recuperates" any

---

60. Sabat de Rivers, *En busca de Sor Juana,* 265, 282; Zanelli, "La loa de 'El divino Narciso' de Sor Juana," in Buxó and Herrera, eds., *La literatura novohispana,* 183; Susana Hernández-Araico, "El código festivo renacentista barroco y las loas sacramentales de Sor Juana: des/re/construcción del mundo europeo," in Ysla Campbell, ed., *El escritor y la escena II: actas del II Cong. de la Asociación Internacional de Teatro Español y Novohispano de los Siglos de Oro* (Ciudad Juárez, 1994), 79; Hernández-Araico, "La alegorización de América en Calderón y Sor Juana: Plus Ultra," *RILCE: Revista de Filología Hispánica,* XII (1996), 294, 295; Martínez–San Miguel, "Articulando," *Colonial Latin American Review,* IV (1995), 88. Martínez–San Miguel recognizes, however, that in the loa the "American Indian" is an "abstract category" (90).

61. Loa to *El divino Narciso,* in Sor Juana, *Obras,* III, 21.

aspect of indigenous culture, but rather because it translates radical alterity (cannibalism) into the Catholic and imperial universalist continuity.

Nonetheless, there is a notably indeterminate space in the Baroque games and parallelisms of the loa. Throughout the work, there is a repeated invitation to celebrate "the great god of seeds" [al gran Dios de las Semillas], whose name Sor Juana never clarifies. Among the logical referential candidates would be Huitzilopochtli, whose effigy was made of seeds ("semillas") and eaten in the *Teoqualo;* Tlaloc, the god of water and fertility; Quetzalcóatl, the benevolent god of agriculture; Saturn, god of agriculture in European antiquity; or Christ, the sower *(sembrador),* who plants his body in man through the Eucharistic feast. Only the loa's instructions, which indicate who is speaking, can differentiate between Christianity, European paganism, and Mexica religion. What is said about one god is not distinguished from what is said about another. Religión, like Diego Durán or José de Acosta, sees in all of this a demonic imitation of Catholic rites, but ends up defining the Eucharist as América and Occidente do—and using the same symbols and materials (bread, blood, seed, and redemption). What is more, Religión describes the Christian God as an agrarian deity:

> If the fields become fertile, if the fruit multiplies, if the crops grow, if the rain falls, it is all because of the work of his hand.

> Si los campos se fecundan,
> si el fruto se multiplica,
> si las sementeras crecen,
> si las lluvias se destilan,
> todo es obra de Su diestra.[62]

Through Sor Juana's baroque and intricate reasoning, we enter a hall of textual mirrors in which cannibalism and Communion dance arm-in-arm. Sor Juana approximates the Eucharist with anthropophagy. She is not the first to express this affinity, as Marie-Cécile Bénassy-Berling believes, for José de Acosta and Jean de Léry, among others, had already expressed it. But she is perhaps the first to do so from that early moment of an emergent American criollo consciousness.[63]

On the one hand, the American lettered city appeals to an epistemological privilege: the understanding of cultural codes that the Peninsular intellectuals cannot access. However, the point was not to separate from but rather to par-

---

62. Ibid., 14.

63. Bénassy-Berling, *Humanismo y religión,* 317. These ambiguities with respect to the Eucharist were tacitly recognized by the editor of the auto *El divino Narciso* put together for the 1924 Congreso Eucarístico Nacional in Mexico: the published text suppressed the introductory loa.

ticipate in the cultural, lettered imperial community in order to, as Martínez–San Miguel has pointed out, "negotiate with the metropolitan authorities a way to coordinate imperial interests with local interests." As indicated by John Beverley, the peripheral intellectual uses the metropolitan aesthetic codes to participate in a linguistic community (the imperial lettered city). The auto to *El divino Narciso*, written to be performed in the Spanish court (and with numerous citations from Calderón's *Eco y Narciso*), is a good example of this participatory yet differential practice of the letrado colonial elite. The criollo gesture is not countercolonial or against the empire, and it doesn't defy Catholic dogmas. Rather, it is a symbolic balancing act of cultural and political submission and a claim of perpipheral authority: "*I want to be part,* so I bring this translation of American difference to the table," it seems to be saying. The issue at play in the play is not Indian culture, but the desired criollo participation in the cultural imperial community.[64]

The loa could be described as a cultural missive with which the peripheral sender inscribes herself in the metropolis by way of cultural correspondence and participation in a conservative genre (Eucharistic theater)—at the same time that she produces the symbolic appropriation and construction of the "indigenous." Sender and receiver are thus in a participatory relationship of periphery and center. The loa makes this tension explicit: Celo questions Religión: "Don't you see any impropriety in the fact that the play is written in Mexico, but it would be performed in Madrid?" [¿Pues no ves la impropiedad / de que en Méjico se escriba / y en Madrid se represente?] Religión, with a Sor Juanesque innocence, responds with another question: "So it is such an odd event that something is produced in a certain place, but used in another?" [¿Pues es cosa nunca vista / que se haga una cosa en una / parte, porque en otra sirva?] Moreover, the character Religión insists that the play is not a "creation of audacity" [parto de la osadía], since it complies with an order from her excellency the countess de Paredes.[65]

64. Martínez–San Miguel, "Articulando," *Colonial Latin American Review,* IV (1995), 98; John Beverley, *Una modernidad obsoleta: estudios sobre el barroco* (Los Teques, Ven., 1997). On the Calderonian sources of Sor Juana's autos and her differences from Calderón with respect to the representation of América, consult Méndez Plancarte in Sor Juana, *Obras,* III, lxxiv; and A. A. Parker, "The Calderonian Sources of *El divino narciso* by Sor Juana Inés de la Cruz," *Romanistisches Jahrbuch,* XIX (1968), 257–274; Hernández-Araico, "La alegorización de América," *RILCE: Revista de Filología Hispánica,* XII (1996), 281–300.

65. Loa to *El divino Narciso,* in Sor Juana, *Obras,* III, 19. As is well known, a trick of the weak common in Sor Juana is her insistence that she is obeying an order; see Josefina Ludmer, "Tretas del débil," in Patricia Elena González and Eliana Ortega, eds., *La sartén por el mango: encuentro de escritoras latinoamericanas* (Río Piedras, P.R., 1984), 47–54.

Celo then replies: "How do you respond to the objection that you introduce the Indies and you want to take them to Madrid?" [¿Cómo salvas la objeción / de que introduces las Indias, / y a Madrid quieres llevarlas?], thereby alluding to the condition of the criollo intellectual, peripheral translator of a cultural difference that yet forms part of the empire.[66]

The publication of the loa to *El cetro* and the republication of the loa to *El divino Narciso* in 1692 (according to Hernández Araico, prepared for the second "centenary of Colón's navigation to the New World") signal the works' celebratory character or, at least, their commemoration of America's belonging to the empire. Religión defends the criollo boldness: "In matters of intelligence there are neither distances nor oceans that hinder." [Que a especies intelectivas / ni habrá distancias que estorben / ni mares que les impidan.] The insinuation is clear: just as the Christian faith has its use and place in the New World, discourse made in America can also serve Europe. At issue, then, is the intellectual authority of the criollo intellectual. Sor Juana reclaims her epistemological competence vis-à-vis the Peninsular ingenios, to whom América, with false modesty, begs pardon for "pretending with unrefined lines to describe such a Mystery" [querer con toscas líneas / describir tanto Misterio]. In the illustration that follows the cover of *Fama y obras póstumas* (1700), published after Sor Juana's death, she appears writing (with a plume and paper in hand), under an imperial arch whose pillars are adorned with a conquistador on her right (below the inscription "Europe") and an indigenous figure at her left (below the legend "America") (see Figure 6). The place of identity for the criollo intellectual (an imaginary construction, like the arch) appears in a location written between the commemoration of the conquest and the legacy of "the indigenous" (subordinated to the empire).[67]

The "parto de la osadía" [creation of audacity] (to use Sor Juana's expression) consists in writing from the margin, of bringing her American "conceptual character" to Europe, translating América from cannibal to Christian, and

66. Loa to *El divino Narciso,* in Sor Juana, *Obras,* III, 20. Octavio Paz signals early on: "It would be an error of historical perspective to confuse baroque aesthetics—which opened the door to the exoticism of the New World—with a nationalist preoccupation. . . . Rather the opposite can be said. But if [Sor Juana] has no consciousness of nationality, she is conscious, and very much so, of the universality of the Empire. Indians, criollos, mestizos, whites, and mulattos form a whole. Her preoccupation with pre-Cortés religions—visible in the loa that precedes *El divino Narciso*—has the same meaning. The function of the church is not diverse to that of the empire: to reconcile antagonisms, embrace differences in a superior truth." Octavio Paz, "Homenaje a Sor Juana Inés de la Cruz en su Tercer Centenario, 1651–1695," *Sur,* no. 206 (December 1951), 29–40.

67. Hernández-Araico "La alegorización de América," *RILCE: Revista de Filología Hispánica,* XII (1996), 290, 294. Loa to *El divino Narciso,* in Sor Juana, *Obras,* III, 20, 21.

FIGURE 6. Sor Juana Inés de la Cruz. Portrait. Designed by José Caldevilla, engraved by Clemens Puche. In *Fama, y obras pósthumas del fénix de México, decima musa, poetisa americana, Sor Juana Inés de la Cruz* (Madrid, 1700). Courtesy New York Public Library

symbolically placing alterity into the continuity of the universal, in other words, the continuity of Christianity and empire. The American anomaly is conjured up as an allegory (as a simulacrum of otherness) below the imperial arch. In what could be described as a kind of *eccentric* occidentalism, Sor Juana's cultural trope of cannibalism and heterogeneous Americanism reclaims a cultural space of commonality within the empire through the affirmation of an abstract difference, represented by allegorical Indians. Of course, the cannibal (or more generally the Indian) is "a metaphorical idea dressed up in rhetorical colors" [una idea / metaforica, vestida / de rétoricos colores], as Sor Juana said. What the letrado criollo reclaims, as part of its genealogy, is a translated difference, an archaeological and ahistorical version of colonized alterity. América and Idolotría are *conceptual characters*, fluffy versions of difference as abstract as the Americanism of the plays:[68]

And these persons introduced are not people but abstract figures, who illustrate what is sought to be said.

Y aquestas introducidas
personas no son más que
unos abstractos, que pintan
lo que se intenta decir.[69]

Any empathy with the indigenous therein is symbolic, and retrospective; an alliance, not with the historical subjects of the present, but with conceptual characters. Contemporary Indians revolt everywhere, and there are big insurrections even in the heart of Mexico City while Sor Juana and other criollos play with these colorful allegorical Indians: compensatory cultural artifacts for the exorcism of problematic Indians—laborers, insurrectionists, resilient and not-quite-converted Indians, and so forth. The Baroque constitutes its unconscious by way of a series of exclusions, one of which is the material conditions that make that self-celebratory imperial culture possible. Nonallegorical Indians do not offer themselves up like the rest of the Baroque cornucopia. They cannot enter into the sublime of the allegory, because they are the labor that makes the ciudad letrada possible, from its *arcos triunfales* to its poetic games; and hence they dwell in the Baroque's fields of horror, abjection, and unrepresentability. They inhabit the nightmares of the ciudad letrada as the rebellious Indians that spoiled Sigüenza y Góngora's appetite for the autochthonous.

68. Loa to *El divino Narciso*, in Sor Juana, *Obras*, III, 17.
69. Ibid., 20.

Confronted with the possible collapse of its material colonial conditions, the criollo lettered city acted as in a state of siege vis-à-vis insurrectional subjects.

The emergence of criollo consciousness can here be defined as the exorcism of the horror of the other by way of the compensatory appropriation-translation of colonial tropes. Sor Juana, anticipating one of the most recurrent discursive practices of nationalism, inserts into the family album—she renders familiar—distant and touched-up portraits of strange ancestors, dressed in "retóricos colores." But she does so in order to be part of the empire. Later, this stereotype would be converted into a cultural fetish, a fetish upon which would be displaced the obscure object of desire of Latin American nationalisms. Then, again, by the last decade of the seventeenth century this was only an ambivalent sign of the criollo desire to belong to the imperial cultural community.

DAVID S. SHIELDS

Sons of the Dragon; or,
The English Hero Revived

At first, two narratives dominated the welter of stories relating English imperial enterprise. One enjoyed semiofficial sanction—the tale of the English commercial empire of the seas, the peaceful "imperium pelagi," which was said to be so different and so much more ethical than Spain's conquered territories. The other began as an alternative official discourse but lost sanction during the Restoration, only to survive in the popular imagination. It was the adventure tale of the common English man who by daring, religious zeal, and martial mayhem won rank, riches, and renown wresting the world and its treasures for the nation. The former celebrated the moral work of a country civilizing the world through trade; the latter discovered national energy in the initiative of heroes. The two narratives contradicted each other. The former provided cover for England's exercise of maritime dominion; the latter promised glory and wealth to individual Englishmen who possessed audacity and valor. The former lauded the "arts of peace"; the latter, righteous violence.[1]

The interplay of the two narratives reveals the central tension in England's original imperial imagination. It also reveals a growing disparity between the metropolitan understanding of the imperial project and an Anglo-American creole sense of what the business of colonization and commerce was. For American agents of empire the alternative, or unofficial, myth warranted deviation from London policy. After the Restoration, it stood at the core of creolian self-understanding of enterprising Anglo-Americans.

The unofficial myth suffered eclipse early in the nineteenth century. Here I will offer an outline for its recovery, a skeleton narrative of occasions, texts, and hero figures that brings the adventure story back into awareness. The narrative will sound strange in parts, for it speaks of an English America in which Cuba

---

1. David S. Shields, *Oracles of Empire: Poetry, Politics, and Commerce in British America, 1690–1750* (Chicago, 1990), 21–35.

was to have been the first colony and Panama the key to the control of America's wealth and the world's trade. When it held greatest sway over the minds of Englishmen, it projected an Anglo-Protestant dominion extending from Chile to Nova Scotia. The development of the hero tale has remained obscure because it was too closely tied to a history of imperial misadventures, a history that has been repressed. One component of my task here is to recall the misadventures and judge their effect on the figure of the English adventurer.

All of the English adventurers were really one adventurer, Sir Francis Drake. Like the familiar "bound to rise" myth of American self-improvement generated out of Benjamin Franklin's *Autobiography*, the imperial adventurer tale was an avatar myth in which a sequence of latter-day English champions relived the life and dreams of the primordial national hero, Drake. All looked to the sea for destiny; all fought the Catholic enemy; all attempted to seize America from Spain; all strove to make grace and gold agree. We can see in a host of imperial adventure narratives the signal features of the hero myth: the concern with the mystery of divine favor, the accounting of the fateful life and death of heroes, the telling of the creation and destruction of peoples, the charting of a restless search for mastery over an elusive world.[2]

Drake was like a classical hero, a paradoxical combination of divinity and humanity. Son of a Puritan preacher, he seemed the darling of Providence, yet at the same time a man of worldly appetite and policy. His words and deeds confused the common distinctions between commonweal and private gain, religion and politics, worldly fame and heavenly glory. His deeds were recorded in a half-dozen chronicles by a host of witnesses: Walter Bigges, *A Summarie and True Discourse of Sir Frances Drakes West Indian Voyage*; Thomas Greepe, *The True and Perfecte Newes of the Woorthy and Valiaunt Exploytes, Performed . . . by . . . Syr Frauncis Drake*; *A Full Relation of Another Voyage into the Indies, Made by Sir Francis Drake*; Francis Fletcher, *The World Encompassed by Sir Francis Drake*.[3]

2. John G. Cummins, *Francis Drake: The Lives of a Hero* (New York, 1995), is the least politically tendentious and most sensitive modern biography to examine Drake as a cultural persona.

3. Walter A. Bigges, *A Summarie and True Discourse of Sir Francis Drakes West Indian Voyage* (London, 1589, 1652); Nicholas Breton, *A Discourse in Commendation of the Valiant as Vertuous Minded Gentleman, Maister Frauncis Drake, with a Rejoysing of His Happy Adventures* (London, 1581); Thomas Greepe, *The True and Perfecte Newes of the Woorthy and Valiaunt Exploytes, Performed . . . by . . . Syr Frauncis Drake: Not Onely at Sancto Domingo, and Carthagena, but also Nowe at Cales, and uppon the Coast of Spayne* (London, 1589); *A Full Relation of Another Voyage into the West Indies, Made by Sir Francis Drake . . .* (London, 1652); Francis Fletcher, *The World Encompassed by Sir Francis Drake, Being His Next Voyage to That to Nombre de Dios . . .* (London,

Drake's words pervade these works—speeches, conversations, letters, exhortations, expressions full of rhetorical elevation, guile, and brashness. His distinctive style and his aspiring values shine even in the briefest of his published works, a poem he wrote commending Sir George Peckham's *True Report* of Sir Humphrey Gilbert's expedition to Newfoundland (1583):

> Who seekes, by worthie deedes, to gaine renowne for hire:
> Whose hart, whose hand, whose purse is prest to purchase his desire
> If anie such there bee, that thristeth after *Fame*:
> Lo, heere a meane, to winne himselfe an everlasting name.
> Who seeks, by gaine and wealth, t'advaunce his house and blood:
> Whose care is great, whose toile no lesse, whose hope, is all for good
> If anie one there bee that covettes such a trade:
> Lo, heere the plot for common wealth, and private gaine is made.
> Hee, that for vertuees sake, will venture farre and neere:
> Whose Zeale is strong, whose practice trueth, whose faith is void of feere,
> If any such there bee, inflamed with holie care.
> Heere may hee finde, a readie meane, his purpose to declare.
> So that, for each degree this Treatise dooth unfolde:
> The path to *Fame*, the proofe of Zeale, and way to purchase golde.[4]

The myth erected from Drake's deeds and words projected several messages: (1) the power to found empires inheres in common men rather than kings, (2) the globe is the broadest register of that power, yet America is the particular arena in which heroism will come into its own, (3) martial valor and righteous violence serve as warrants to win, found, and rule nations, (4) this energy is understood to be a spiritual gift of zeal given by God to a Protestant champion against Spanish Catholic dominion in the West, (5) the hero must impose military dominion on the seas to secure the treasures of the land, (6) the distinction between material ambition and religious calling does not exist, (7) the hero discovers purpose in liberating persons from tyrannies of religious absolutism and governmental coercion, (8) the hero projects his potency by rising in the world, securing fame, then accomplishing great works, (9) his

---

1626). Drake's extensive paper trail induced twentieth-century scholars to supplement these early printed accounts with compilations of manuscript testimonies, such as John Hampden, ed., *Francis Drake, Privateer: Contemporary Narratives and Documents* (London, 1972); Kenneth R. Andrews, *The Last Voyage of Drake and Hawkins*, Hakluyt Society, 2d Ser., II, no. 142 (Cambridge, 1972).

4. Sir George Peckham, *A True Reporte of the Newfound Landes* (1583), The English Experience, no. 341, facs. rpt. (Amsterdam, 1971), iv.

power signifies divine favor and shows by contrast the impotency of kings and aristocracies, (10) while his power is expressed in the power to destroy, the hero also possesses a power to create, build, and reform. Destructions are tied to renovations and fired by a vision to create a Nova Albion, or a New World.

We should recognize the peculiar creolian features of this hero figure. He emerges precisely because of the jury-rigged character of early English empire —the lack of a formal navy, the absence (and later weakness) of a metropolitan colonial administration, the distance between the scene of heroic action and the locus of government, juridical review, and surveillance. The fact that he was not a member of court placed him somewhat outside the jealousies, rivalries, and constraints of obligation of the retinue around the monarch. As long as he kept the appearance of a loyal subject and made a show of supplying the state's percentage of the take and defying the Catholic enemy, he might use whatever means he chose, with few questions asked. In short, the Drakean hero was a creature of creolian duplicity as well as a man of martial energy.

The myth remained vital for two centuries, inciting several generations of mariners to aggression against the Spanish Empire in the Americas. Like Drake, who died in the unsuccessful attempt to seize and colonize Panama in 1592, the "sons of the dragon" never managed to accomplish the Protestant reconquest of the Catholic empire. Yet Drake's dream did not simply beach with the failure of William Grenville's thwarted design on Chile and Mexico in 1806–1807. The ambition fired an American progeny. The southern filibuster was the creole grandson of "el Draque," and he proved to be as pliable and improvisatory as his grandsire. Three generations of southern imperialists, from William Blount in the 1790s to William Walker in the 1850s, schemed the seizure of Spanish territories in the name of civilization and glory. If Britain failed to secure much Spanish territory in the Western Hemisphere, the United States did better. Florida, Texas, California, New Mexico, and Arizona came into the nation.

One reason the myth slipped into American hands was that Britain forgot the hero's promise to liberate natives and settlers from corrupt colonial rule, while American filibusters flooded the Caribbean and Central America intoxicated with the ideas of liberty loosed by the American Revolution. If they did not attach to some local liberator, they took the task upon themselves.

DRAKE WAS one of those persons so vital that he could not be kept dead. He had not long been deposited in his lead coffin off the shores of Panama in early 1596 when the press in Amsterdam announced *Franciscus Dracus Redivivus*. In 1626, when the English were erecting a colony on Providence Island (Isla de

Providencia) off the coast of central America and England was engaged in war with Spain, Philip Nichols resurrected him again in *Sir Francis Drake Revived.* But his most spectacular resuscitation took place during the Commonwealth. In 1653, at the moment Oliver Cromwell had himself named lord protector of England, the press once again conjured Drake from the waters off Panama "to stirre up" the English nation. He did not come as defender of the realm, the admiral who drove the Armada from the English Channel into the path of northern storms and destruction; rather, he came as the adventurer in America. *Sir Francis Drake Revived* summarized "foure severall Voyages . . . to the West-Indies"—the treasure raid at Nombre de Dios (in Panama), the voyage of circumnavigation that terrorized Peru, the 1585–1586 invasion of the West Indies, and the thwarted attempt to seize Panama for England in 1592—just as Cromwell was formulating the most ambitious undertaking of his rule, an invasion of the Indies and Central and South America. Cromwell determined to wrest America from Spain and create an Anglo-Protestant Western Hemisphere, calling the reconquest "The Western Design." An integral part of the design was inciting English men to arms against Spain. Cromwell called Drake from the dead to galvanize (as the title page says) "all Heroicke and active Spirits of these Times, to benefit their Country and eternize their Names by like Noble Attempts."[5]

Cromwell might have summoned Drake to excite English manhood, but the great mariner came to possess Cromwell himself. As early as 1648 the apostate English Dominican friar Thomas Gage had reanimated thoughts of seizing the Spanish-American treasure ports in *The English-American*. He promised that Hispanic creoles had become so disaffected with the rule of Spanish placemen and courtiers that they would welcome liberation by English. In 1652, *The World Encompassed,* Drake's account of the circumnavigation and seizure of the Peruvian silver shipment, reissued from the press, as did *A Full Relation of Another Voyage*. In 1653, with the last rebellions in the British Isles finally quashed, Cromwell needed an enterprise to occupy his potent and restive military; he needed a source of revenue that would preclude his calling another Parliament into being. Most of all, he needed a project worthy of his station, demonstrating that he was the divine vessel that would enact the Reformation

5. Sir Francis Drake, Philip Nichol, et al., *Sir Francis Drake Revived* . . . (London, 1653). This astonishing campaign has been understudied in English and American scholarship. It deserves a new examination. Consider that the one monographic treatment of the invasion is decades old: S. A. G. Taylor, *The Western Design: An Account of Cromwell's Expedition to the Caribbean* (Kingston, Jamaica, 1965).

throughout the world. Becoming Drake's avatar enabled Cromwell to see the way to all three ends. So in 1654 Thomas Gage was preparing a memorandum addressed to the lord protector outlining an invasion plan.[6]

In 1654 the lord protector appointed his brother-in-law John Desborough to head the conquest of Spanish America. Sixty ships were commandeered, eight thousand soldiers and sailors enlisted, and Admiral William Penn and General Robert Venables were given charge of the invasion. Three civilian commissioners, including the old Pilgrim governor, Edward Winslow, would supply civil oversight when the conquests succeeded. The flotilla embarked in 1654, arriving at the English colony of Barbados and impressing an additional four thousand troops from laborers on that island, Nevis, and Saint Lucia. The forces targeted the principal Spanish island fortress in the northern Caribbean, Hispaniola, assaulting out of the island's jungle, reenacting Drake's plan in his conquest of 1585. Where Drake had succeeded, Venables and Penn suffered disaster. The English fled from the island, Winslow died, and lightly defended Jamaica was seized to prevent the expedition from being a total debacle.[7]

Curiously, the failure of the Western Design amplified the mystique of Drake and the allure of his American exploits. Compulsively, ambitious Englishmen attempted to follow Drake's path to fame, often revisiting the targets of his invasion plan and Cromwell's design—Captain Edward Mansfield attacked Providence Island in 1666, Admiral Henry Morgan conquered Panama in 1671, buccaneer William Dampier attacked Panama in 1681, Admiral Edward Vernon seized Portobelo in 1739, Vernon and General Thomas Wentworth invaded (unsuccessfully) Cartagena in the War of Jenkins's Ear, and Prime Minister Grenville's army and navy attacked Argentina in 1806 (he had ordered a wholesale invasion of South America before the scheme fell apart).

What features of Drake's story proved so useful to subsequent adventurers? His resurrected person can tell us. Drake was the one English figure from history so vital that he broke through the Commonwealth's ban on theatrical representations. He addressed the English public in Sir William Davenant's opera, *The History of Sir Francis Drake: Exprest by Instrumental and Vocall Musick*. This piece must be understood in the context of the Anglo-Spanish War, the Western Design, and in conjunction with its theatrical companion

---

6. Thomas Gage, *The English-American* . . . (London, 1648); Thomas Gage, "Some Briefe and True Observations concerning the West-Indies, Humbly Presented to His Highnesse, Oliver, Lord Protector of the Commonwealth of England, Scotland, and Ireland," in Thomas Birch, ed., *A Collection of the State Papers of John Thurloe, Esq.* (London, 1742), III, 59–63.

7. Paul Sutton, *The Jamaica Campaign: The Cromwellian West Indies Attack, 1654–55* (Leigh-on-Sea, Essex, 1990).

piece of 1658, *The Cruelty of the Spaniards in Peru*. The latter was an operatic telling of the Black Legend—the indictment that the Spanish ventured into lands in the name of grace but destroyed their peace and order to get gold. Davenant showed that the supposed beneficiaries of Spain's Christian civilization knew only misery and stood in need of grace and liberty. The misery of the natives was an occasion for the Western Design.[8]

Cromwell's minions retranslated and published the master text of "la leyenda negra" (the Black Legend)—Bartolomé de las Casas's *Brevísima relación de la destrucción de las Indias* (1552) (English: *The Tears of the Indians*, 1656)—they bankrolled the London publication of John Eliot's mission writings about New England natives to supply a blueprint for the reconversion of Spanish America and cited John Milton's Latin tract declaring the reasons for an English war with Spain.[9]

The History of Sir Francis Drake portrays the one incident in Drake's career in which he appears most unequivocally as a liberator of oppressed natives—the famous seizure of the Spanish gold train in Nombre de Dios, Panama, in 1572. This incident won Drake his first renown. Allying with the local cimarrons, a mixed community of natives and African slave runaways, Drake's forces infiltrated the Panama jungle and ambushed the mule train carrying Peruvian silver and gold from the Pacific across the isthmus to the Atlantic dispatch port. Drake aided the victims of Spanish cruelty, countervailing the effects of the Black Legend on the victims. Immediately before engaging in battle, Drake declares:

> I despise
> That treasure which I now would make your Prize:
> Unworthy 'tis to be your chiefest aime,
> For this attempt is not for Gold, but Fame.

8. [William Davenant], *The History of Sir Francis Drake: Exprest by Instrumentall and Vocall Musick* . . . (London, 1659); Richard Frohock, "Sir William Davenant's American Operas," *Modern Language Review*, XCVI (2001), 323–333; [William Davenant], *The Cruelty of the Spaniards in Peru: Exprest by Instrumentall and Vocall Musick* . . . (London, 1658).

9. Bartolomé de las Casas had been previously translated and published in 1583 as *The Spanish Colonie*, during the strained period before Drake's invasion of the Indies and the invasion of the Armada. On the uses of John Eliot's mission writings in this context, see Kristina Bross, *Dry Bones and Indian Sermons: Praying Indians in Colonial America* (Ithaca, N.Y., 2004), chap. 1.

[John Milton], *A Declaration of His Highness, Setting Forth the Justice of the Commonwealth's Cause against Spain* (London, 1655). Milton produced a Latin translation, *Scriptum dom. protectoris reipublicae angliae, scotiae, hiberniae* . . . (London, 1655) but did not produce the codicils of the treaty. One or two vocal scholars have argued against Milton's authorship, but the consensus remains that it is his.

Fame, the service of justice, the imposition of self-control, and martial valor combine to form Drake's heroic identity for Davenant.[10]

One of Ralph Bauer's maxims about the comparative study of Anglo-American and Ibero-American literatures is germane here: the entire English literature of empire must be read as a gloss on the Spanish imperial literature. Drake's avowal of fame as his motive parodied the quest for "reputación" by the conquistadors. As the Black Legend instructs, the conquistadors sought notice for championing Christ and civility but won infamy, for the Indians were enslaved and degraded, not saved. Gold supplanted the Gospel in the adventurer's hearts. Drake disavowed gold and came as liberator, aiding natives and slaves against tyranny and greed.[11]

Drake said he despised gold, yet he seized vast treasures from the Spanish. What kept him from being considered just another corsair? He insisted that all seizures were recompense for the property (ships and slaves) taken from him by the Spanish in San Juan de Ulúa. He kept strict account of seized goods, prevented sailors from indulging in indiscriminate looting, and took care to turn booty over to the crown. The crown would gratefully permit him to take a portion of the gains. He did not execute prisoners, particularly gentlemen, and ensured that ladies were not molested. Then, too, he was the first commander to circle the earth. Finally, his militant Protestantism. The Spanish literature about Drake confronts, sometimes contests, each of these claims.[12]

The circumnavigation seized Spanish attention particularly. Magellan had not survived his attempt to circle to earth; Drake had. His undeniable energy, his audacity, his skill as a pilot, and his lack of sadism made him a memorable being. Martín del Barco Centenera admired the mariner's epic voyage in his *Argentina,* regretting that a lack of true faith permitted him to sink to piracy. Juan de Castellanos, in "Elegias de varones ilustres de Indias," was so admiring of Drake's circumnavigation that a large section was censored from his published *Discorso.* Lope de Vega's *La Dragontea* famously shows the strange mixture of wonder and animosity that Drake inspired. Like dragons of lore, Drake

---

10. [Davenant], *History of Drake,* 32.

11. Ralph Bauer, *The Cultural Geography of Colonial American Literatures: Empire, Travel, Modernity* (Cambridge, 2003). To make an obvious point: The Black Legend functioned differently in the hands of Anglo-Protestants than in the political and cultural contests between Hispanic creoles of America and the Spanish.

12. This care in maintaining legal and civil forms was in part because, as a commoner, Drake was perpetually suspect in the eyes of noble-born English courtiers whose reputation he eclipsed with his enterprise. His punctiliousness disarmed the more overt attacks of aristocrats and kept him from seeming a parvenu.

is fired by monstrous energy and love of gold. Indeed, the playwright is not so concerned with his heretical Protestantism as with his devotion to the goddess Greed (Codecia). A hunger for riches moves the beast in his furious itinerary of destructions. In Spanish eyes, Drake is guilty of precisely the crime that the Black Legend ascribes to the conquistadors, a love of gold that eclipses a zeal for grace.[13]

Lope de Vega debunks Drake's reputation as ally and liberator of the cimarrons, inventing an episode of Drake's fatal final assault on Panama in which the dragon revisits his old allies to enlist them in another alliance against the Spanish overlords. This time they rebuff Drake, praising the benefits of civilization that Spanish rule has brought. Domestic comfort—the "civil fuego"—has brought the blacks into willing subjecthood. The epic tells of a happenstance forgotten in English memory—the turning of the cimarrons away from alliance with English corsairs to faithful subjection to the Spanish crown in the 1580s.[14]

Davenant did not need to defend against the Spanish attack. The King of the Symerons attests that, just as Drake embodies freedom on the main, so the king seeks to maintain liberty on land. Drake's coming aids the king in this end. Taking gold is an instrument toward this end, "For nothing can afflict them more, / Then to deprive them of that store." Gold gives Spain the wherewithal to "afflict the peaceful world with war" and coerce peoples to its bidding. Yet liberty can pose a problem if there is no self-government. Drake's connection with the cimarrons conveys to them civility, not through subjection, but by the free emulation of virtue.[15]

Davenant's opera was penned after the failure of the Western Design, while the Anglo-Spanish war was being fought in and about Europe. Cromwell had entered into an alliance with France as unlikely as that between Drake and the cimarrons.

The failure of the Western Design left the Caribbean afloat with sailors and ships, and much pent-up ill will toward Spain that Cromwell's death and the restoration of Charles II in 1660 did little to dissipate. Indeed, the Drake-Cromwell Protestant animus translated to Anglo-America when the restored English monarchs began to manifest regard and appreciation for Europe's

---

13. Martin del Barco Centenera, *La Argentina y conquisto del Rio de la Plata* (Lisbon, 1602). The excised section from Castellanos was found in manuscript and published in the early twentieth century: Juan de Castellanos, *Discurso de el capitán Francisco Draque* (Madrid, 1921). Lope de Vega Carpio, *La Dragontea* (Madrid, 1935): this edition contains a helpful index containing contemporary correspondence by Spanish officials in America concerning Drake's activities.

14. Lope de Vega, *La Dragontea*, canto VII, stanzas 499–512.

15. [Davenant], *History of Drake*, 12.

Catholic powers. Two men associated with the Western Design would dominate the next phase of imperial adventure. They would form the creolian understanding of the imperial project. Captain Henry Morgan, a Welsh privateer, had served as a minor officer in the invasion fleet and settled in Jamaica after the debacle. Thomas Modyford, a Barbadian planter who had counseled Cromwell against concentrating his attack on Hispaniola, had his prescience rewarded by appointment to the governorship of the sole island captured in the great enterprise.

Modyford granted Morgan a charter to be a privateer, permitting him to prey upon Spanish shipping at a time when England was at peace with Spain and at war with the Dutch. The legacy of Drake and Cromwell was the belief (the creolian conviction) that in the Americas a state of perpetual animosity existed between the Catholic colonies and England. What Whitehall said at a given moment was a metropolitan fantasy that did not bear on the reality lived in the West Indies. A local legal procedure developed on a Drakean model. The privateer captains and American officials maintained a Drakean punctilio about making sure proper accounts were kept of seized treasures. Sir Thomas Modyford presided over the Admiralty court that divvied prize moneys: one-tenth for the lord high admiral, the duke of York; one-fifteenth for the king; and a substantial percentage as commissions to the members of the court, including a twenty-pound commission per adventure to the governor. If a privateer showed the initiative of a Drake, improvising an attack against a bastion of Spanish treasure or power, as Mansfield did in his recapture of Providence Island, the officialdom of Jamaica would legitimize the event, just as Elizabeth had legitimized Drake's assaults and seizures. If a corsair acted, however, without any commission, he was considered a pirate. Drake had shown that a warrant from the authority on land was carte blanche to act as he willed on the sea.[16]

The land-sea dichotomy that Drake's career described played out curiously in the careers of the privateers. Much of the regulation from Whitehall and Jamaica controlled the disposition of properties seized at sea. It did not speak of booty seized on land, because the doctrine of warfare conceived of land battles as affairs of state conducted under crown prerogatives. Drake's raid on Nombre de Dios was an unprecedented colonial adventure, an impromptu war without state sanction. Drake treated it like a seizure at sea, giving the crown its portion of the treasure, but the ramifications for policy were profound. American ad-

---

16. Peter Earle, *The Sack of Panamá: Sir Henry Morgan's Adventures on the Spanish Main* (New York, 1981), 40–54, 68–80; [A.] P. Thornton, "The Modyfords and Morgan," *Jamaican Historical Review*, II, no. 2 (1952), 36–60.

venturers improvised in Drake's shadow a new creolian understanding of warfare and spoils. Morgan realized that the legal vacuum surrounding raids and land-based seizures had provided him and his followers a loophole permitting their vast enrichment. He was not obliged to surrender his loot to an Admiralty court, and he could attract more men and more ambitious men with the prospect of plunder. So long as he reenacted the invasions of Drake and Cromwell, he could cover himself in the mantle of Protestant zealotry.

The ultimate warrant for violence remained religion. Spain prided itself on being the defender of the true faith in America. Drake, Cromwell, Morgan, and Vernon were champions of the Reformation. During episodes of violence—such as Morgan's sack of Portobelo—there would always be an iconoclastic moment when a church, chapel, cabin, or hacienda was stripped of its crucifix, or its statue of the Virgin, and wrecked as a sanctuary of superstition.

The court of Charles II was not so suffused with Protestant zeal. Prince Rupert, nephew of Charles I, alone of the royals had anything of the adventuring spirit; and powerful figures in the political establishment, the duke of Albemarle particularly, were friends of Spain, active in engineering a peace that Modyford and Morgan ignored, and in recalling and arresting Modyford when the English assaults in the Caribbean climaxed in Morgan's sack of Panama in 1671. Morgan and Modyford knew that they acted out a design imprinted in their desires but not necessarily in those of the metropolis.[17]

The Spanish, for their part, failed to realize that Drake's dream was not moving the highest levels of state policy. When Morgan succeeded in conquering Panama, winning the prize that had eluded Drake, the authorities in Peru fantasized a coordinated naval expedition up the west coast of South America. Morgan's army of buccaneers and an English navy would pincer Peru from land and sea, and the Spanish Empire in America would fall. But the flotilla off Chile was a single exploration vessel, and Morgan, disappointed at the lack of loot, appalled at the depredations of disease on his forces, and surprised by the destruction of the city by its residents and later his own forces, saw continued occupation as a fruitless exercise. He decamped. The idea of a colony, or even an English outpost in Panama, seemed hardly worth the continuing expense, if Spanish ships and cities could be so easily seized. One didn't need to secure the isthmus to have the treasure of Peru. One could sail to Panama at will, seize the treasure on the Atlantic side, or cross the isthmus and raid the East India fleets. This English corsairs did regularly in the 1680s.

While Morgan surrendered to Drake's ambition to make Panama an English

17. A. P. Thornton, *West-India Policy under the Restoration* (Oxford, 1956), 105–109.

settlement, he held fast to Drake's rationale for fighting Spain. In a series of official depositions transcribed for the Admiralty court in Jamaica and for Whitehall, he refreshed the rhetoric of adventure. He reveled in Protestant zeal and national purpose, and, like Drake, was forthright about taking an enemy's treasure. Panama shone with all its Drakean renown—"that famous and antient City . . . the greatest Mart for Silver and Gold in the whole World, for it receives all the goods into it that comes from Old *Spain* in the King's great Fleet, and likewise delivers to the Fleet all the Silver and Gold that comes from the Mines of *Peru* and *Potazi*."[18]

We should not underestimate the readership for official depositions. Morgan was a celebrity since taking Portobelo. The account of his conquest of Panama, a prize that neither Drake nor Cromwell managed to secure, must have riveted all who had access to it.

Whitehall was tolerant of American innovations so long as wealth and glory were the results. The most telling indicator of officialdom's knowledge of and sympathy for Morgan was its willingness to suppress other versions of events. It proceeded against Alexander Exquemelin, a surgeon on the Panama expedition. Disgruntled by the lack of financial reward from the adventure, Exquemelin remedied his low finances by publishing a sensationalist account of Morgan's deeds in *De Americaensche Zee-Roovers* (Amsterdam, 1678), translated as Jon Esquemeling, *Bucaniers of America* (London, 1684). Exquemelin made Morgan out to be a bloodthirsty pirate, the reputation that has gripped the popular imagination to this day. Yet the English publishers were forced to retract their characterizations when challenged in court for libel, and Morgan was appointed vice-governor of Jamaica.[19]

IF DRAKE operated as a model for privateer initiative and ideological warrant for enmity with the Spanish settlements in Anglo-America, he became an increasingly abstract figure in the metropolis. In London in the eighteenth century, Drake's person sometimes sublated from the myth, leaving his virtues and his imperial program. His character was figured in sublated form, as "antique valor," a quality that hovered around the two heroes that emerged from the War of Jenkins's ear—Admiral Edward Vernon and Admiral George Anson —but seems to have absented itself from the body of Britain's armed services,

18. Henry Morgan's Report on the Sack of Panama, Misc. Papers concerning the West Indies, MSS ADD 11268, British Library; *The Present State of Jamaica, to Which Is Added an Exact Account of Sir Henry Morgan's Voyage to Panama . . .* (London, 1683), 92–93.

19. Earle, *The Sack of Panamá,* 266.

occasioning fretting over the loss of the empire's martial "genius." The occasion of the War of Jenkins's ear was much the same as what had first sparked Drake's conflict with Spanish authorities in the 1570s, the monopoly on trade that Spain exerted in her colonies. For a nation that thrived on commerce such as England, the prohibition to engage in exchange with wealthy Spanish territories rankled. Smugglers attempted to circumvent it. Privateers overcame the monopoly by force. When Spain began cracking down on smuggling in the islands with a Garda Costa (privateer marine police fleet) after the 1729 Treaty of Seville, England began feeling bullied. After nearly a decade of aggravation, Edward Vernon (member for Portsmouth and rear admiral of the British navy, retired), rose in Parliament and declared that he could seize Portobelo, as Drake and Morgan had done, with six ships. In the pitch of war fever, Parliament took him at his word, reactivated his commission, and dispatched him to Panama.[20]

Vernon, despite a courtly background, was an old salt who had commanded vessels in the 1702 seizure of Gibraltar. He knew how to lead men, how to win battles, and how to hide his gentility behind his valor. In November 1739 he came upon Portobelo with his six ships and took the fort in a single day. Vernon then destroyed Fort Chagres on the Isthmus of Darien. Though Vernon's dispatches did not invoke Drake's memory, the periodical writers showed no such restraint. Samuel Johnson published his serial biography of Drake in the 1740–1741 issues of the most popular periodical in Britain, Gentleman's Magazine.[21]

In 1740, the war entered its most ambitious phase. Vernon regrouped at Jamaica to assemble an invasion fleet to reduce the great Colombian treasure port, Cartagena. But, just as the Western Design unraveled because the naval and land contingents could not coordinate, the invasion of Cartagena collapsed because of the incompetence of General Wentworth, who led the land assault. Drake had taken the city in the West Indian campaign of 1586. But Wentworth's scaling ladders were too short, and the spirit of the defenders was too stout. Plans to pincer South America between an attack on Panama by Vernon and on Peru by Admiral George Anson, coming up the west coast of South America, collapsed. The difficulty securing logistical support and troops had kept Vernon in Jamaica. Anson was late around Cape Horn and contented himself

---

20. Shields, *Oracles of Empire*, 185–194; Harold W. V. Temperley, "The Causes of the War of Jenkins' Ear, 1739," Royal Historical Society, *Transactions*, 3d Ser., III (1909), 197–236; Richard Pares, *War and Trade in the West Indies, 1739–1763* (London, 1963).

21. Samuel Johnson, "Life of Drake" (1740–1741), in J. R. Fleeman, ed., *The Early Biographical Writings of Dr. Johnson* (Farnborough, 1973).

with reenacting Drake's Pacific strategy, raiding Chile, Peru, and Mexico until he seized his own treasure ship, then performed his own circumnavigation of the globe.[22]

In a curious way, Vernon and Anson combined reconstitute Drake. Anson's lowly origins and his rise through the ranks by merit, his ability dealing with strange places, his curiosity about the world, and his good fortune at treasure hunting approximate the Drake of *The World Encompassed*. Vernon's audacity in battle, his zeal, and his oratory call to mind the Drake of the *Summarie and True Discourse*. Anson was the intermediate figure in the English trinity of global inquiry—Drake, Anson, Captain Cook. Vernon became the darling of the patriot writers, the man who inspired Thomas Arne's "Rule Britannia," who endeared himself to generations of English sailors by creating and dispensing grog (a measure of watered rum named after Vernon's grogram cloth coat). He seemed an old-style hero come back to find a world overrun by courtiers and genteel soldiers and ruled by a man who believed in bribing enemies rather than in bravery, Robert Walpole. Vernon was Britain's martial genius restored; Walpole, the man who made heroism unnecessary by paying off rivals.[23]

The patriots absolved Vernon of responsibility for the Cartagena debacle. Publication of *Authentic Papers Relating to the Expedition against Carthagena* (1744) made him seem the one active spirit in a campaign of ditherers and dolts. He was made a full admiral in 1745. But, when he attempted to mold public opinion toward pressuring reform of conditions in the navy with *Some Seasonable Advice from an Honest Sailor* (1746), his political enemies struck: he was stripped of admiral's rank. Being a fighter, he stood for Parliament and was repeatedly elected from Ipswich.[24]

Vernon was exquisitely conscious of his place in the history of English imperial enterprise. In his *New History of Jamaica, from the Earliest Account to the Taking of Porto Bello* (1740), he presented a continuum of purpose and conduct

22. Edward Vernon, *Authentic Papers Relating to the Expedition against Carthagena: Containing Original Letters between the Admiral and the General, Their Councils of War* . . . (London, 1744); see also Vernon, *A Letter to the Secretary of a Certain Board . . . Being a Proper Supplement to the Original Papers Relating to the Expedition to Carthagena, Cuba, and Panama* (London, 1744). In imperial strategy Drake came to represent the idea of a two-fronts conquest of Spanish America, with attacks on both Atlantic and Pacific ports.

23. Boyle Somerville, *Commodore Anson's Voyage into the South Seas and around the World* (London, 1934); Richard Walter, *A Voyage round the World in the Years MDCCXL, I, II, III, IV, by George Anson . . .* (London, 1748); *Some Excellent Verses on Admiral Vernon's Taking the Forts and Castles of Carthagena, in the Month of March, Last,* broadside (Boston, [1741]); [Edward] Vernon, *The Genuine Speech of the Truly Honourable Adm . . . l V . . . n, to the Sea-Officers . . .* (London, 1741).

24. [Edward Vernon], *A Specimen of Naked Truth, from a British Sailor, a Sincere Well-Wisher to the Honour and Prosperity of the Present Royal Family, and His Country* (London, 1746).

between Cromwell's Western Design and the campaign of conquest undertaken in the War of Jenkins's Ear. In court circles he seemed a troublesome relic crazed by an ancient violent dream. But, in America, others—George Washington's older half brother Lawrence, who also served in the Cartegena assault, for instance—thought him the savior of British manhood. Lawrence Washington named his plantation Mount Vernon in tribute and nurtured his younger brother in the ethic of valor according to the Vernon model. If valor was being supplanted among elite British males by Wentworthian gentility and Walpolesque policy, it would be nourished in American soil.[25]

Dreams of English dominion over Spanish territories dimmed because France at midcentury had eclipsed Spain as Britain's chief imperial rival. The old Anglo-Protestant animus against the evil empire, stoked by the Black Legend, had given way to an anti-Catholic rage about "Gallic Perfidy." In British America, geographical proximity split the mainland north and south in their feelings. New England became obsessed with Catholic menace to the north; the southern colonies and Indies remained fixed in their enmity to the Spanish south.

London lost its old ambition for the Spanish Caribbean in the wars with France. One incident reveals this more than any other. During the Seven Years' War, the British navy successfully conquered Cuba, where Drake had dreamed of establishing the first English colony in America, where Morgan had raided, and Vernon had suffered a setback. Once hostilities ceased, Britain returned it to Spain in exchange for Florida. Florida remained British until the American Revolution, when it was ceded back to Spain, an ally of the United States.

The Independence of the United States pared Britain's American empire to Canada and a handful of islands. Immediately, John Dalrymple of Cranstoun began to wonder how to recoup global glory and American wealth. In 1779 he proposed to Lord North a concerted attack on Central America. It was a scheme of Drakean portions, with coordinated expeditions crossing the Pacific and emanating from Jamaica to seize Peru and pincer Mexico. The plan captured the imagination of Lord Charles Townshend and nearly came to fruition before the peace of 1783 quelled the action. Dalrymple laid out the plan in an appendix to his 1788 *Memoirs of Great Britain and Ireland,* a text that lodged in the imperial imaginations of high officials in England and Spain.[26]

In 1806, the capture of the Rio de la Plata and Buenos Aires during the

25. David S. Shields, "George Washington: Publicity, Probity, and Power," in Tamara Harvey and Greg O'Brien, eds., *George Washington's South* (Gainesville, Fla., 2004), 143–154.

26. Andrew Jackson O'Shaughnessey, *An Empire Divided: The American Revolution and the British Caribbean* (Philadelphia, 2000), 237–247; John Dalrymple, *Memoirs of Great Britain and Ireland . . .* (London, 1771–1788).

Napoleonic Wars caused Prime Minister Sir William Grenville to activate Dalrymple's plan, with expeditions against Mexico and Valparaíso dispatched from Australia and India and an invasion of Argentina. Before the stupefying ambitious plan could be fully mobilized, the residents of Buenos Aires threw out the English expeditionary force and captured its leader. Grenville had made a fundamental miscalculation. His deputy William Windham had directed the English commander that he should "by no means . . . encourage any acts of insurrection or revolt, or any measures tending likely to any other change than that of placing the country under His Majesty's protection and government." The last great English effort to make South America English collapsed because Englishmen had forgotten Drake's modus—serving the cause of liberation enlists the aid of the local population against colonial authority.[27]

In the wake of the American Revolution, converting Spanish colonies into British dependencies was no longer an option. The British failure to aid the self-determination of the indigenous population was seen by South Americans as European lèse-majesté and by metropolitan champions of Britain's ancient liberties as a sign of political degeneracy. Anna Letitia Barbauld in *Eighteen Hundred and Eleven: A Poem* envisioned a transfer of liberty, in which the ancient political genius of the Old World crossed the Atlantic to enliven a liberated South America:

> Ardent, the Genius fans the noble strife,
> And pours through feeble souls a higher life,
> Shouts to the mingled tribes from sea to sea,
> And swears—Thy world, Columbus, shall be free.[28]

Ironically, one nation could engage in exercises of imperial absorption and simultaneously promote the cause of freedom. The "land of liberty," because it was free, might absorb subject territories into its body and vest the people with rights and privileges. At least certain agents of government believed this to be the case. Senator William Blount of Tennessee secured the honor in 1797 of being the first government representative in United States history to be impeached—for his private initiatives to liberate Florida from Spain. Like

---

27. Robert Craufurd, *An Authentic Narrative of the Proceedings of the Expedition under the Command of Brigadier-Gen. Craufurd; until Its Arrival at Monte-Video . . .* (London, 1808); Charles F. Mullett and John Dalrymple, "British Schemes against Spanish America in 1806," *Hispanic American Historical Review*, XXVII (1947), 269–278; Robert J. King, "An Australian Perspective on the English Invasions of the Rio de la Plata in 1806 and 1807." http://www.derro teros.perucultural.org.pe/textos/erroteros10/australian.doc +Sir+John+Dalrymple+australia

28. Anna Laetitia Barbauld, *Eighteen Hundred and Eleven: A Poem* (London, 1812), ll. 321–324.

Drake stirring up the cimarrons, Blount agitated among the Creeks and Cherokees, urging them to join English settlers in West Florida in a rebellion against their Spanish overlords. Blount's impeachment failed, because Americans knew that liberty meant taking action, even if that action were outside the bounds of treaty or law. The citizens of Tennessee elected him president of the state senate. In Blount's wake, freelance liberators began moving into Florida, the Louisiana Territory, Texas, the islands, trying to free land and treasure from decadent colonial powers and introducing Catholic subjects of the Spanish crown to Protestant grace, the Yankee dollar, and independence. American heroes took up the ethical component of imperialism, dressing it in the language of liberty.[29]

29. Buckner F. Melton, Jr., *The First Impeachment: The Constitution's Framers and the Case of Senator William Blount* (Macon, Ga., 1998).

RAQUEL CHANG-RODRÍGUEZ

Cruel Criollos in Guaman Poma de Ayala's *First New Chronicle and Good Government*

Felipe Guaman Poma de Ayala is one of the most polemic and admired native authors of the colonial period. *El primer nueva corónica y buen gobierno* [The First New Chronicle and Good Government] (1615–1616), his long illustrated history (1,190 pages, 398 pen-and-ink drawings by the author) of ancient Andean times and Inca and colonial rule, was discovered in 1908 in the Royal Library of Copenhagen by Richard A. Pietschmann and first published in facsimile in 1936 by the Institut d'Ethnologie of the Université de Paris under the supervision of Paul Rivet. Anthropologists consider it a primary source of information on the pre-Columbian and Andean world as well as on the first decades of colonization. Literary scholars regard it as a symbolic representation where the author criticizes colonial rule while submitting a plan for "good government" to the Spanish king Philip III, to whom the chronicle is addressed. Traditionally, historians have pointed out inaccuracies in Guaman Poma's work; however, modern research has explained how and why the author takes advantage of information available from native and European sources to present an Andean version of history. A key component of these inquiries, for me, is to understand the textual and iconic nuances through which an *indio ladino* (Hispanized Indian) represents the Andean past and reconfigures its colonial present. By combining the ancient ways of codifying knowledge with

An abbreviated version of this study was presented in Spanish at the symposium "Peru in Black and White and in Color: Unique Texts and Images in the Colonial Andean Manuscripts of Martín de Murúa and Guaman Poma," held at the Newberry Library, April 19–20, 2002, and sponsored by the University of Chicago, the Newberry Library, and the D'Arcy McNickle Center for American Indian History. I am grateful to its organizers, Tom Cummins and Juan Ossio, for their invitation to present my ideas in this forum. My thanks to Rolena Adorno for her assistance in securing the illustrations from *First New Chronicle and Good Government* for this essay and to Ivan Boserup for granting permission to reproduce them.

newly acquired European techniques, Guaman Poma places his readers at a unique cultural crossroads. This vantage point makes it possible for them to glimpse the mental categories used by the author and to understand his singular situation in colonial society—an educated Indian, who presents himself as an intermediary between the Andes and Spain. How this chronicler depicts and understands European otherness, gender differences, the new social subjects who are products of miscegenation, and the impact of foreign mores on the native population raises questions that have constantly remained with me when examining the ever-challenging writings and drawings by Guaman Poma. His views are particularly interesting because they offer a unique presentation of colonized subjects and their assigned role within a society in which the majority is often marginalized for several reasons—gender, ethnicity, genealogy, religion, place of birth.[1]

From the lexicon that evolved in the colonial period to name the new ethnic and cultural categories of the Spanish Indies, the word *criollo* attracted my attention when, early in my career, I read a now classic essay with a philological bent by José Juan Arrom. It discussed the origin and fluctuations of the term *criollo*, a label later associated almost exclusively with American-born children of Spaniards. Since then, researchers have turned their interest to colonial *criollismo* from a historiographic perspective. Beyond the ethnicity and place of birth of the varied people called criollos, these investigations have underscored the use of the term as an all-encompassing identity paradigm in the development of a national conscience.[2]

Considering the early origin of this term and its porous borders, it is not surprising to find it used by the author of *First New Chronicle and Good Government*. I will here bring to the fore questions about Guaman Poma's perception of the Spaniards and their offspring born in the New World, whom he called criollos. I contend that, when using this label, Guaman Poma goes beyond the traditional categories of origin and ethnicity to include conduct in his charac-

---

1. Guaman Poma apparently revised his chronicle in 1616. For details on these changes, see Rolena Adorno and Ivan Boserup, *New Studies of the Autograph Manuscript of Felipe Guaman Poma de Ayala's "Nueva Corónica y Buen Gobierno"* (Copenhagen, 2003), esp. chap. 3.

2. José Juan Arrom, "Criollo: definición y matices de un concepto," *Hispania*, XXXIV (1951), 172–176; a revised version appeared in Arrom, *Certidumbre de América: estudios de letras, folklore y cultura*, 2d ed. (Madrid, 1971), 11–26. On Peru in particular, see Bernard Lavallé, *Las promesas ambiguas: ensayos sobre el criollismo colonial en los Andes* (Lima, 1993). On New Spain, see D. A. Brading, *Orbe indiano: de la monarquía católica a la república criolla, 1492–1867*, trans. Juan José Utrilla (Mexico City, 1991); Solange Alberro, *Del gachupín al criollo: o de cómo los españoles de México dejaron de serlo* (Mexico City, 1992), and *El águila y la cruz: orígenes religiosos de la conciencia criolla: México, siglos XVI–XVII* (Mexico City, 1999).

terization of the criollos. He appears to transform the label into a cultural category associated with bad or good behavior. In addition, the Andean author takes advantage of the label to underscore the need to separate the different groups that form colonial society. Thus, my approach to the representation of the criollos in Guaman Poma's history takes into account the early article written by Arrom, the renewed interest in the origins of colonial criollismo as an identity paradigm, and my own concerns regarding the alternative view of colonial society proposed in documents written by Indians and *castas,* or racially mixed groups. In this context, and as an introduction to Guaman Poma's ideas on the topic, I will also comment briefly on how two seventeenth-century Peruvian writers, Inca Garcilaso de la Vega (1539–1616) and Juan de Espinosa Medrano (died 1688), known as El Lunarejo, understood and used this designation. Let us now turn to how the criollos were viewed during the colonial period.

Perceiving the Criollos

When studying how the term *criollo* was conceptualized and applied, it should be remembered that researchers have explored mainly Iberian sources. We, therefore, are more familiar with the European perception of the criollos, and less with the perception that the criollos had of themselves and their reaction to a label that early on could encompass many—from the children of African slaves born in the New World to the children of Spaniards born in America.[3]

With regard to the application of the term to the offspring of Spaniards, it is worth underscoring, as Bernard Lavallé has indicated, that the pejorative image of Spanish criollos was colored by the following perceptions: (1) their character was sleazy and their fidelity to the crown questionable, (2) they were close to mestizos and mulattoes, whose rebellious nature was often recorded and condemned in official documents, (3) they were intellectually inferior to the Europeans, (4) they were lazy, and (5) it was probable that they would eventually turn into Indians. For many observers, these traits and the ensuing poor conduct of the criollos were due to the influence of New World geography and climate, their contact with people of mixed blood, and even the milk from

3. It was noted, for example, by the Inca Garcilaso in *Royal Commentaries;* see Garcilaso de la Vega, el Inca, *Comentarios reales,* ed. Ángel Rosenblat, with a prologue by Ricardo Rojas (Buenos Aires, 1943), I, chap. 9, xxx.

black, Indian, and mestizo wet nurses who fed and raised the children of Spaniards.[4]

In order to better understand the fluctuations of the label *criollo* during the seventeenth century, it is instructive to note how the Inca Garcilaso, a mestizo writer, and Espinosa Medrano, of unknown background, used this term in their texts. In the prologue to the *Historia general del Perú*, completed in 1615, the same year that Guaman Poma concluded his *First New Chronicle*, Garcilaso addressed "los indios, mestizos y criollos de los reinos y provincias del grande y riquíssimo imperio del Perú" [the Indians, mestizos and criollos of the kingdom and provinces of the great and rich empire of Peru]. When so doing, the author, a mestizo, presents himself as their brother and compatriot and wishes everyone health and happiness. In addition, Garcilaso speaks of the intellectual abilities of the three groups (Indians, mestizos, and Spanish criollos) and emphasizes that the criollos are of Spanish descent, although born and raised in the New World—"nacidos y connaturalizados." The author exhorts members of these ethnic groups to live a pious life and to develop expertise in arms and letters. The pursuit of these activities, coupled with a virtuous way of life, will assure them eternal glory and earthly fame.[5]

With reference to Garcilaso's characterization of the criollos, I would like to underscore two words he used: "oriundos" and "connaturalizados." The first brings to the fore the Iberian origins of the criollos; the second emphasizes their acquiring "naturaleza," or "connaturalizarse," that is, the characteristics of a given place in order to enjoy its privileges and fruits.[6] It is evident that Garcilaso's address recognizes differences but minimizes them by pointing to the common Peruvian birth of these heterogeneous groups. Garcilaso attributes to all equal ability to be educated and to distinguish themselves in their chosen field. He is convinced that, perforce, the wealthy Peruvian empire produced intellectually gifted persons, be they criollos, Indians, or mestizos. In this manner Inca Garcilaso views all components of the Peruvian kingdom in a positive light; together they will build the fatherland, or *patria*. Such rhetoric brings to mind ideas about the negative influence of geography and climate on those born in America. However, Garcilaso cleverly inverts the proposition:

4. Lavallé, *Las promesas*, 19–21.

5. Garcilaso de la Vega, el Inca, *Historia general del Perú* (1617), ed. Ángel Rosenblat, introduction by José de la Riva Agüero (Buenos Aires, 1944), I, 9, 10. Translations into English of this and other texts are mine. About the date of this prologue, see the preliminary study by José Durand to his edition of *Historia general del Perú* (Lima, 1962) as well as n. 1.

6. "Gozar sus fueros, privilegios y utilidades," as defined in *Diccionario de Autoridades* (Madrid, 1990), I, 518 (*connaturalizarse*).

rich lands will, in turn, produce intelligent offspring, and their wealth will have a positive impact on all born and raised there. Inca Garcilaso uses *criollo* to label the children of Spaniards born in Peru. The novelty of his arguments, however, does not reside in this designation. He proposes a new paradigm: old and new natives of Peru—be they Indian, mestizos, or criollos—are capable individuals, able to positively contribute to building the Peruvian patria.

Similarly, Juan de Espinosa Medrano, in his *Apologético en favor de don Luis de Góngora* (1662), rejects the European vision of the criollos. In the dedication to readers ["Al letor"], the author comments ironically on the remote regions where criollos reside, and he identifies himself with this forgotten geography. El Lunarejo further states that, to these faraway regions, "las cosas de España" [matters from Spain] arrive very late. He goes on to add: "Pero ¿qué puede haber bueno en las Indias? ¿Qué puede haber que contente a los europeos, que desta suerte dudan? Sátiros nos juzgan, tritones nos presumen, que brutos de alma, en vano se alientan a desmentirnos máscaras de humanidad." [But, what good could the Indies have? What could they offer to please the doubting Europeans? They judge us to be satyrs; they believe we are Tritons, intrinsically dumb, with only a mask of humanity to disguise our animal-like nature.] This comment is significant for several reasons. The ancients associated the satyr with lust. It was a monstrous animal defined as a four-legged creature with the face of a man that ran on two feet and inhabited the plains of India. On the other hand, the Triton is characterized as a fish disguised as a man from the waist up. Generally, the Triton was depicted as playing big seashells as if they were trumpets.[7]

If we take into account these definitions, we can discern that the author was familiar, as Roberto González Echevarría has proposed, with the pejorative connotations associated with the word *criollo*. For the Iberians, the criollos were animals pretending to be men. They were controlled by lust (satyrs) and produced loud noises with primitive instruments (Tritons, seashells). It is not fortuitous that, when Espinosa Medrano addresses his readers, he mentions the

---

7. Juan de Espinosa Medrano, *Apologético en favor de Don Luis de Góngora* (1662), ed. Luis Jaime Cisneros (Lima, 2005), 127. On satyrs and Tritons *(sátiros* and *tritones),* see Sebastián de Covarrubias Orozco, *Tesoro de la lengua castellana o española* (1611) (Madrid, n.d.), 930; also *Diccionario de Autoridades,* III, 360–361. On Espinosa Medrano, see also Roberto González Echevarría, "Poetics and Modernity in Juan de Espinosa Medrano, Known as *Lunarejo,"* in González Echevarría, *Celestina's Brood: Continuities of the Baroque in Spanish and Latin American Literatures* (Durham, N.C., 1993), 149–169. Regarding the criollo theme in other works by El Lunarejo, see José Antonio Rodríguez Garrido, "Espinosa Medrano, la recepción del sermón barroco, y la defensa de los americanos," in Mabel Moraña, ed., *Relecturas del barroco de Indias* (Hanover, N.H., 1994), 149–172.

papagayo, one of the early symbols associated with the New World in European iconography. The singular beauty and flashy feathers of this tropical bird were linked to the criollo. His good looks and courteous demeanor hid the twin failings of his place of birth and his intellectual limitations. Like the papagallo, the criollo was condemned to show off, to imitate, and never to create. As did Garcilaso before him, Espinosa Medrano attempts to contradict this stereotype through his *Apologético,* an erudite literary contribution in which he displays his knowledge of the classics, of rhetoric, and of Luis de Góngora y Argote, the admired Spanish poet.

Thus, both Garcilaso and El Lunarejo take note of the ideas associated with the criollos and respond to them. The former attempts to integrate various ethnic groups—Indians, mestizos, Spanish criollos—and extols their virtues and wisdom. Their signal contribution will, in turn, create a Peruvian fatherland. The latter mockingly underscores the perception of the criollos and affirms their intellectual worth and his own through the *Apologético en favor de Don Luis de Góngora.* Both thereby enlarge upon the category *criollo* from distinct alternative perspectives.

Guaman Poma's Criollos

Let us examine how Guaman Poma incorporates this category into his discourse on good government. There are three iconic and linguistic representations labeled "criollos" in *First New Chronicle.* The first two separately portray a man and a woman, in the section devoted to "Españoles: de los talles, estatvras de los hombres y mugeres estados" [Spaniards: Of the Size and Height of Men and Women]. The third representation depicts a couple and is located in the subsection dedicated to Indians and labeled "Indios: criollos y criollas indios" [Indians: Indian Criollos and Criollas]. The heading of the illustration of the male criollo is "Españoles: soberbioso criollo o mestizo o mulato deste reyno en los pueblos" [Spaniards: Arrogant Criollo or Mestizo or Mulatto from This Kingdom in the Villages] (see Figure 7). Except for the difference in gender, the heading of the illustration of the female counterpart, or criolla, is identical (see Figure 8).[8]

Both drawings depict aggressive and abusive actions. In the first image, a

---

8. Felipe Guaman Poma de Ayala, *El primer nueva corónica y buen gobierno* (1615), ed. John V. Murra and Rolena Adorno, trans. Jorge L. Urioste (Mexico City, 1980), II, 552–554. Further references to this edition will appear parenthetically in the text. The complete text is available in a digital edition available on the Worldwide Web prepared under the supervision of Rolena Adorno and sponsored by the Royal Library, Copenhagen, Denmark.

FIGURE 7. A Spanish Criollo Abusing an Indian Male. From Felipe Guaman Poma de Ayala, *El primer nueva corónica y buen gobierno.* Courtesy the Royal Library, Copenhagen

FIGURE 8. A Spanish Criolla Abusing an Indian Female. From Felipe Guaman Poma de Ayala, *El primer nueva corónica y buen gobierno*. Courtesy the Royal Library, Copenhagen

man, dressed according to Spanish fashion, mistreats an Indian. He crushes his head with his left foot while threatening him with a dagger or knife held in his right hand. In the second drawing, a kneeling woman, also dressed in Spanish fashion, punishes a tearful Indian lady while pulling her hair. In the written description, the author points out that this type of behavior is shared equally by male and female criollos, mestizos, and mulattoes. However, he directs the thrust of his criticism against the Spanish criollo group:

> Cómo los dichos criollos que se crían con la leche de las yndias o de negras o los dichos mestizos, mulatos, son brabos y soberbioso, haraganes, mentirosos, jugadores, auarientos, de poco caridad, miserable, tranposos, enemigo de los pobres yndios y de españoles.
>
> Y ancí son los criollos como mestizos, peor que mestizos, porque de ellos no se a parecido seruicio ni se a escrito que aya seruido a Dios y a su Magestad que se pueda escriuirse de ellos en este rreyno ni en toda Castilla.
>
> De cómo los dichos criollos son peores que mestizos y mulatos y negros.

As the said criollos that are raised with the milk from Indian and black wet nurses, or the said mestizos, mulattoes, are quick to anger, arrogant, lazy, liars, given to gambling, greedy, of little charity, miserable, tricky, and enemies of the poor Indians and of Spaniards.

And thus the criollos are like the mestizos, [the criollos] are worse than mestizos, because they have not served the king. Nor has it been written that they have served God and his majesty, [nothing] has been written about them in this kingdom nor in all of Castile.

The said criollos are worse than mestizos, mulattoes, and blacks. (II, 553)

Similarly, Guaman Poma's description of the female criollas underscores their worst qualities, as does his drawing: "Criollas: cómo las dichas criollas que se crió con la leche de las yndias son peores que mestizas y mulatas, negras, haraganes, mentirosas, enbusteras, bachilleras, golozas y no dizen la uerdad, enemigo de los pobres yndios y no tiene caridad ni buena obra con los pobres." [Criollas: as the said criollas that were raised with the milk of Indian wet nurses are worse than mestizo, mulatto, and black women, they are lazy, lying, gossipy, talkative, greedy, and never telling the truth, enemies of the poor Indians; they lack charity; nor have they done good deeds on behalf of the poor] (II, 555). This harsh criticism leads to a number of questions. For example, the author mentions the milk of the Indian wet nurses on which the female criolla infants were raised; he also mentions the milk of Indians and blacks suckled by male criollo babies. In his desire to diminish the criollo Spaniards, be they male or female, Guaman Poma takes advantage of a controversial topic—the acquisition of bad traits through the milk of casta wet nurses—to establish his low regard for Spanish criollos who have turned out worse than any other group. Following his derogatory characterization of the criollos (and, surprisingly, of their Indian and black wet nurses), the Andean historian turns to underscoring their rebellious and untrustworthy nature. They are enemies of the Indians whose women fed them and of the Spaniards whose heritage they share (II, 553). Again, Guaman Poma situates Spanish criollos of both sexes below the mestizos, whom he detests. In addition, the record of the criollos, or lack of it, appears to confirm his suspicions. They have served neither God nor king, and nothing has been written about them. Thus, they should be condemned to oblivion.

This condemnatory judgment by Guaman Poma, who so desperately attempted to record events as well as his own deeds and service to king and country through text and image, can be better understood in the wider context of *First New Chronicle*. Displaying the flaws of the criollos fulfills a double purpose. On the one hand, it allows Guaman Poma to prevent their participation in the "buen gobierno"—that is to say, in the implementation of the colonial reforms he is proposing to the Spanish monarch. The criollos, abusive and aggressive in the iconic representation, their character tainted by milk of questionable provenance suckled as babies, and marked by a litany of defects that Guaman Poma takes great care in enumerating, provide every reason to suspect and isolate them. Since, at best, their conduct lacks virtue, they are incapable of governing. Inasmuch as their services to king and country are not recorded, or do not exist, what guarantees of their loyalty can they offer? The displacement of the criollos to the periphery of power through this criticism consequently leaves a void that only the author and traditional ethnic lords will be able to fill properly. In this regard, it is important to remember that in the section of *First New Chronicle* devoted to the civil wars of Peru the author takes great pains to display the loyalty and service of his family and other ethnic lords to the Spanish monarch.[9]

The third drawing is more complex, appearing in the section of Guaman

9. Guaman Poma repeatedly praises the skills and fidelity of the native population, comparing them to the ever-reliable Castilians. See, for example, *El primer nueva corónica*, II, 836.

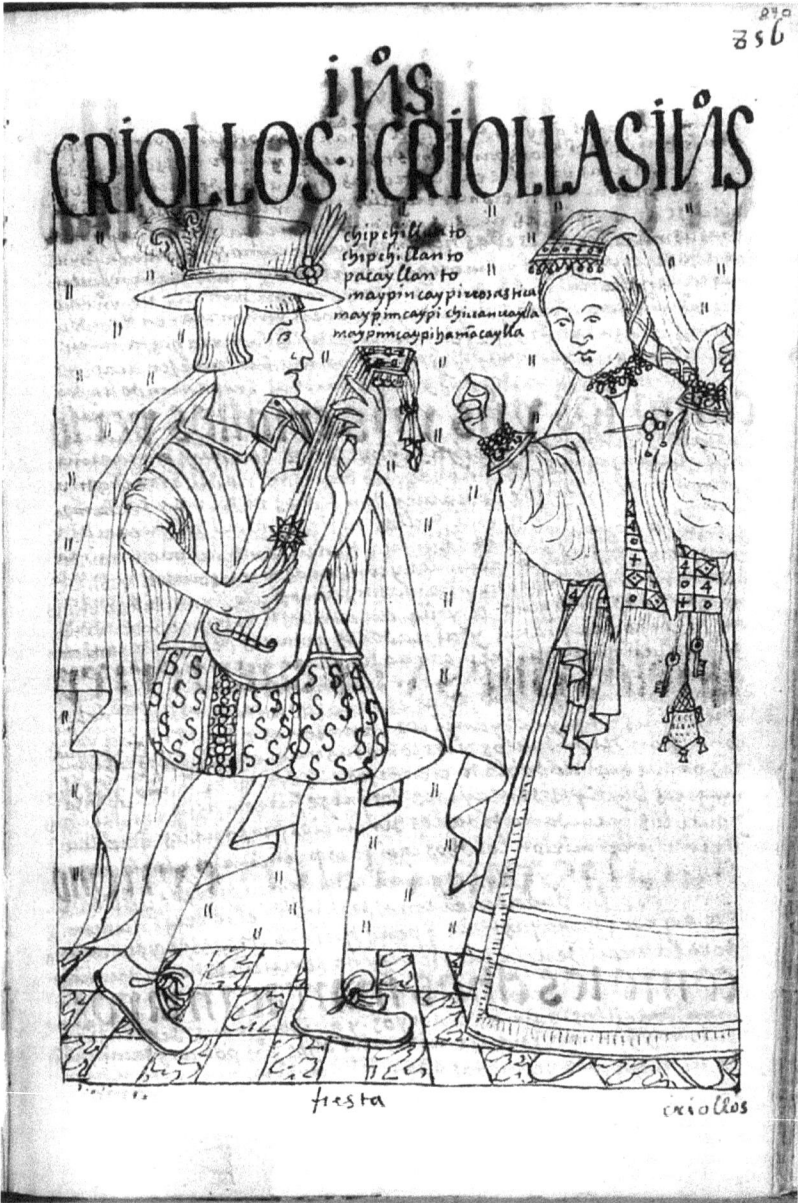

FIGURE 9. Indo-Criollo Couple. From Felipe Guaman Poma de Ayala, *El primer nueva corónica y buen gobierno.* Courtesy the Royal Library, Copenhagen

Poma's history in which native conversion to Christianity is discussed (see Figure 9). According to the author's introduction, the intellectual abilities and devotion of the Indians have been frustrated because of bad examples from priests, administrators, and *encomenderos* (land- and Indian-holders): "Ubiera sanctos o grandes letrados y cristianícimos. Todo lo estorua los dichos con sus tratos." [They would have been saints or great lawyers and very Christian. All was prevented by the aforementioned [priests, administrators, encomenderos] and their misdeeds] (II, 834). The behavior of the Indo-criollo couple points to the consequences of these bad examples. The man, dressed like a Spaniard, plays a string instrument and sings in Quechua; the woman, elegantly attired in Spanish and Andean clothing, looks down and seems ready to begin dancing. The label also indicates their background—"Indios: Criollos y criollas indios" [Indians: Indian criollos and criollas] (II, 870). However, beyond origin or ethnicity, this label forces us to reflect on a new cultural category: ethnically Indian subjects, born in "tienpo de cristianos españoles" [in the times of the Christian Spaniards] who have acquired the way of life and bad traits of Spaniards and their American offspring. In describing the image, the author takes behavior into account in order to categorize two types of conduct. The first includes Indians of both sexes who are Christians and follow the Ten Commandments. However, since the author uses the subjunctive mood to characterize this group, their deportment appears to be more utopian than real: "Cómo fuesen cristianos y guardasen los mandamientos . . . Fuera santa cosa." [If they were Christians and were to observe the [Ten] Commandments . . . It would be a holy thing] (II, 871). In the second category are found "yndios, yndias, criollos y criollas hechos yanaconas y hechas chinaconas" [criollo Indians of both sexes [who] have turned into servants]. Here Guaman Poma uses the qualifiers "hechos . . . hechas," making it appear that these actions correspond to reality (II, 871). He further describes members of this group as lazy, gambling, drunk, arrogant, and fond of partying. For Guaman, members of the last group do nothing but "borrachear y holgar, tañer y cantar, no se acuerdan de Dios ni del rrey ni de ningún seruicio" [get drunk and lazy, play and sing; they do not remember God or king or do any type of service]. In addition, they lack humility and charity and are arrogant, a major flaw that Guaman Poma criticizes frequently. He now adds an even more demeaning comparison. Since they are rogues and thieves, he compares the Indian criollos to the "getanos de Castilla" [Gypsies from Castile] (II, 871), a group that in the seventeenth century was despised in Spain. The comparison is surprising, as it shows that Guaman Poma was familiar with Spanish currents of thought about Gypsy otherness. At the same time, the Andean historian takes advantage of the comparison to place the Indo-criollos below the "criollos españoles" whom he has severely criticized and depicted in abusive postures. Like the mestizos and others of mixed blood, the Indo-criollos must be controlled. And, to do so, Guaman Poma recommends a curfew beginning at "las seys horas del nocheser" [at six hours in the evening] (II, 869).[10]

As noted before, the iconic representation shows an elegant Indo-criollo couple ready to party: the man is playing a string instrument while the lady is trying a dance step. But is the man playing? If we look closely, the instrument in his hand, a hybrid of guitar and lute, appears distorted and incapable of producing any melodious sound. But is the woman dancing? Her glance is sullen and gloomy. An analysis of the accompanying song could offer the clue to better understand the drawing:

Sombra de nuestros secretos,
sombra que nos ocultas,
¿dónde está la rosa?,—Aquí está.
¿Dónde están los verdes prados de Chiuana—Aquí están.
¿Dónde los de Amancay?—Aquí están.

Shadow of our secrets, shadow that hides us, where is the rose? Here you have it. Where are the green pastures of Chiuana.—Here they are. Where those of Amancay?—Here they are. (II, 869)[11]

---

10. Covarrubias characterizes the Gypsies as people "perdida y vagamunda, inquieta, engañadora, embustidora" [loose and lazy, restless, lying, deceitful]. He also reminds us that Charles V (I of Spain) expelled them from Germany in 1549 under suspicion of spying for his enemies; see *Tesoro de la lengua castellana, o española*, 642. In Spain, the idea of expelling the Gypsies was seriously discussed in the last decade of the sixteenth century. In 1594, for example, after attributing to the Gypsies a number of abnormalities, two deputies to the Cortes proposed that they be separated by gender to avoid procreation among them. See Bernard Leblon, *Los gitanos de España* (1985), trans. Irene Agoff (Barcelona, 1987), 30. I am grateful to José Luis Madrigal for this reference.

11. The translation from Quechua corresponds to Franklin Pease's edition of *El primer nueva corónica y buen gobierno* (Caracas, 1980), II, 870. Jorge Urioste offers the following translation:

Sombra del susurro.
Sombra del susurro.
Sombra de esconderse.
¿Dónde? Aquí están las rosas.
¿Dónde? Aquí están las grandes praderas.
¿Dónde? Aquí está la azucena.

Shadow of a whisper, shadow of a whisper, shadow of hidings. Where? Here are the roses. Where? Here are the great plains. Where? Here is the lily.

Guaman Poma, *El primer nueva corónica*, ed. Murra and Adorno, II, 870.

I will first comment on the woman's pose and later associate it with the song. Of particular interest is her gesture with the index finger and thumb forming a circle in each hand, or a *figa*. This gesture brings us to another one of Guaman Poma's drawings (whose sexual connotations were first revealed in a study by Mercedes López-Baralt). In that drawing (see Figure 10), a Spanish woman, in an identical gesture with her right hand, also holds a rose in her right hand while her left hand rests on her pubic area. She offers herself to an obese caballero who is making the sign of the figa with his right hand. As López-Baralt has pointed out in her analysis of this drawing, the rose symbolizes feminine sexuality, the garden of Eros. I propose now that the rose named in the song refers to the "india criolla" and her loose morals (a prostitute?)—she is the flower or rose that opens herself to carnal pleasures. Then, "sombra de nuestros secretos" [shadow of our secrets] could be interpreted as a reference to the questionable actions, the behavior of the couple. Following this line of interpretation, the reference to "los del Amancay" can be understood as a metaphor for the suitors of the woman.[12]

Let us further pursue this comparison. During the winter months (from June to August south of the equator), the *amancaes*, similar to lilies, bloom in yellow bulbs, giving out a pleasant scent. After establishing the link between "los de Amancay," or the place where the amancaes bloom, and the Peruvian bulbs, it is not difficult to relate this native plant to the traditional lilies, or "azucenas." In this regard, it is worth remembering that the latter were linked to forbidden love (Apollo and Hyacinth) and the temptation of the entrance to hell (Persephone and Hades). As we know, lilies, on account of their oversized pistils, are linked to Venus and the lusty satyrs; because of their enervating scent, lilies are also associated with aphrodisiac perfumes. In the Quechua song, these erotic associations are suggested by the amancaes—the Andean lilies. Is it possible that the secret solicitors of favors from the indigenous rose—the Indo-criolla woman—are from an area where the amancaes bloom? If so, the elegant appearance of the Indo-criollo couple and the joyful mood of the drawing cover up the questionable destiny of natives who have adopted the mores of the

12. Mercedes López-Baralt, *Guaman Poma, autor y artista* (Lima, 1993). The gesture has at least three meanings: protection against the evil eye, an insult, an impertinent invitation (often charged with sexual connotations). It is worth noting that *fica* is a vulgar term for the vulva and, by extension, is associated with women. In Naples during the nineteenth century and also among the ancients, using the index finger and thumb to form a circle, making the figa gesture with one's fingers, or using one's fingers to simulate the shape of a cylinder could mean an offense, an invitation, or a reference to a past deed; see Andrea de Jorio, *Gesture in Naples and Gesture in Classical Antiquity* (1832), trans. Adam Kendon (Bloomington, Ind., 2000), 91–93.

FIGURE 10. A Spanish Couple in a Provocative Posture. From Felipe Guaman Poma de Ayala, *El primer nueva corónica y buen gobierno.* Courtesy the Royal Library, Copenhagen

criollo Spaniards. The provocative gesture and grim glance of the woman, the forward posture of the man as well as the suggestive song, appear to point to the unfortunate role played by Indo-criollos in colonial society.[13]

Can it be that the sad countenance of the woman denotes the condemnatory character of her actions? Can it be that the hybrid string instrument, with its twisted handle, points to the dishonorable intentions of the man? The rose, absent in the iconic representation but mentioned in the lyrics of the song and symbolized by the body of the "criolla India," and the amancay, or native lily (absent from the drawing but mentioned in the lyrics of the song), strengthen the erotic charge of both the description and the drawing. One wonders whether the set of keys hanging from the waist of the "criolla India" might represent options for two paths to follow, two ways of life for the native population. Following both comportments outlined by the author in the text that introduces the section (II, 552), one option could be the entrance to the Garden of Eros and the condemnation to hell (for the "indios acriollados"), and the other, the entrance to the Garden of Eden through obedience to Christian law (for the Indians who reject the condemnatory behavior of Spaniards and their criollo offspring). The linguistic representation of this Indo-criollo couple brings to mind the worst characteristics and terrible conduct of the criollos of Spanish descent as well as its impact on the native population. Their behavior has been imitated by the criollos of Indian descent. In the same manner, the pictorial image of the couple points to the deceptiveness of appearances when denoting the tragic consequences of "acriollarse" for the Andean population. Criollo is thus understood by Guaman Poma as a cultural category in which conduct is the predominant vector.

CONTEMPORARY WRITERS held different views with respect to the criollos. Among them, Inca Garcilaso's and El Lunarejo's ideas were particularly important because they were born in America and expressed their concern for the designation *criollo*. Garcilaso felt that the rich Peruvian environment would produce a superior class of inhabitants regardless of ethnicity, and El Lunarejo also actively disavowed the perceived inferiority of the criollos. Guaman Poma takes a more complex approach to the question in his *First New Chronicle and Good Government*. He denounces those of Spanish lineage who, in his view, have been tainted by the milk of Indian and black wet nurses. Curiously, while aiming to criticize criollos, the author takes advantage of European ideas used

13. Jean Chevalier and Alain Gheerbrant, *Diccionario de los símbolos* (1969), trans. Manuel Silvar and Arturo Rodríguez (Barcelona, 1969), 651–652.

to demean the native Andeans that he extols in his illustrated chronicle. Guaman Poma also distances the criollos from the exemplary behavior of the "castellanos viejos" whom he has praised before (II, 557). Through the opposition Indian/criollo, the chronicler expands the meaning of the designation *criollo,* going beyond ethnicity and origin to include Indians that have acquired the mores of criollo Spaniards. By adding behavior and, particularly, deception to the traditional variables of nutrition, climate, geography, and ethnicity, he makes the designation even more problematic. In so doing, Guaman Poma relegates criollos of Spanish descent that look Spanish and Indians that behave and dress like criollos to the periphery of colonial power. Since neither group is suitable to govern, who can then administer the rich Peruvian lands?

The central role in administering the viceroyalty of Peru has to be played by those who, irrespective of their appearance or ethnicity, have behaved in a laudable fashion: those who, like the author, have remained loyal to traditional ways of life and have defended the natives. In other words, those who, like Guaman Poma, are exemplary Christians and have proved beyond any doubt their loyalty to the Spanish king are to be entrusted with the administration of the viceroyalty. By reviling all criollos and situating them on a lower social scale—together with the mestizos—the author presents himself as the perfect protector of the Andeans, and the ideal adviser to the Spanish monarch. Seen in this light, Guaman Poma's problematic approach to the designation *criollo* forces us to reconsider it beyond the traditional sense of identity or origin. Even with its contradictions, his premise is in harmony with the daring rhetoric and provocative pictorial challenge represented in *First New Chronicle and Good Government.*

JEFFREY H. RICHARDS

Barefoot Folks with Tawny Cheeks:
Creolism in the Literary Chesapeake, 1680–1750

The essential characteristics of European creolism in the Chesapeake, as observed by poets and other creative writers, include the following distinctions from practices in Britain: adaptation of new foodways (corn-based), clothing styles (radical simplicity), and expectations for household goods (spartan); centrality of alcohol to culture; exposure to the sun and consequent darkening of white skin; contact with other racial as well as culture groups in native peoples and Africans; altered vocabularies and linguistic patterns from those of the British Isles; freethinking; and political enfranchisement (of persons unable to exercise it at home). For the purposes of this essay, which is concerned primarily with colonial British-American literature during the eighteenth century, the term "creole"—still applied exclusively to the children of immigrants during the sixteenth and seventeenth centuries—will also include what is normally cast as "pidgin," that is, the cultural adjustments of the migrating generation. Unlike Africans, who were forcibly displaced and thrust amid an alien culture, British immigrants, even those transported, had opportunities to make rapid progress toward a new identity on the basis of some expected future liberty and prosperity. Those migrants who chose to remain or knew they would not leave the colonies were therefore capable of assuming an identity peculiar to the environment of the Chesapeake.[1]

I wish to thank Ralph Bauer and David Shields for the opportunity at the first Ibero/American Summit to rethink Ebenezer.

1. For a more traditional distinction between pidgin and creole, but with application to the colonial American context, see Richard Cullen Rath, "Drums and Power: Ways of Creolizing Music in Coastal South Carolina and Georgia, 1730–1790," in David Buisseret and Stephen G. Reinhardt, eds., *Creolization in the Americas* (College Station, Tex., 2000), 99–100. On the changing meaning of the term *creole* from the sixteenth and seventeenth centuries to the eighteenth century—to include also immigrants—see the Introduction to this volume.

The literary response to the experience of coming into the country and being something other than a Briton in Britain covers a range of expressed identities that indicates how much creole formation stimulated the act of writing about the Chesapeake. If at the beginning of the period writers pen texts that are largely occasional and practical, by the end, with printing presses and newspapers in both Virginia and Maryland, they participate in a literary culture that is conscious of itself as both like and unlike similar cultures across the Atlantic. At the same time, the fate of English migrants to the Chesapeake becomes also a staple of London publishing, with a variety of texts, from promotional tracts to imaginative renderings to antipromotional narratives, being offered for sale to British audiences. In many ways, the poets and other creative writers who wrote satirically about creoles and the response to them reinforce modern historians' understandings of life in the region; they also participate in what might be called a *creole imaginary*, a conversion of the colonizing experience into terms comprehensible to a European audience, yet deliberately alien from that audience as well. The creole imaginary is a conceptualization of the creole for the benefit of noncreole audiences, one that imagines for that audience what creoles might be like but also confounds expectations (particularly of degeneracy) by showing ways in which creoles resist their marginalization by the metropolis. In the works of four writers—James Revel, Aphra Behn, Ebenezer Cooke, and Thomas Cradock—I explore a variety of imaginative readings of creolism (that is, the enacting of the creole, rather than becoming creole, as in creolization) in the Chesapeake, from rejection to celebration to begrudging acceptance.[2]

The poem attributed to James Revel, *The Poor Unhappy Transported Felon's Sorrowful Account of His Fourteen Years Transportation at Virginia in America,* appears to be the product of a bound servant's experience in Virginia from around 1660 to sometime before 1676. Although not published until the mid-eighteenth century, and then for an English audience, the poem records what seems to be the authentic experience of a person who, for crimes committed in London, was sentenced to transportation and forced to serve a fourteen-year indenture in Virginia. References to Rappahannock County, a place-name that disappeared in 1692, indicate a seventeenth-century origin for the poem, and those to Jamestown suggest that events rendered in the poem took place before Bacon's Rebellion in 1676, in which rebels burned the entire town. This is a

2. I do not mean that these are the only four writers who deal with situations related to creolism in the Chesapeake; of course, William Byrd, Richard Lewis, James Sterling, Dr. Alexander Hamilton, and others show similarities and nuanced differences. On Byrd and creoles, see the essay by Susan Scott Parrish in this volume.

period, then, still relatively early in the colony's development. In the seventeenth century, many migrants to the Chesapeake were forced from the British Isles, often for economic reasons but also for legal ones. Although many, probably most, bound servant migrants remained in the Chesapeake, whether or not they preferred living at "home," Revel offers readers the voice of someone who expresses no desire to stay. His is the resistant experience, that of one who wishes no part in any creolizing process but intends to place himself back in the mainstream of English society, as the tearful reunion with his parents at the end of the poem indicates. Revel is but one of many "unhappy" colonists for whom the American experience was a kind of purgatory from which they learned no more than not to do whatever it was that got them there in the first place. In the 1620s, for example, the individual identified in anthologies as Richard Frethorne sent letters home describing in despairing terms the hunger, poverty, poor diet, and fear of Indians that constituted his indentured experience. The young man seems to have died in 1623 in Virginia, not living long enough even to have his letters acknowledged from his parents. In the eighteenth century, William Moraley arrived in the New World under articles of indenture and found quickly enough that his skill, clockmaking, was functionally worthless in the New Jersey and Pennsylvania communities in which he lived. Moraley's account lists his experiences in the mainland colonies, his getting free of his indenture, his attempt to make a living as an itinerant timepiece repairer, and, finally, his return home, with little to show except gratitude to be back in England. Revel's poem fits squarely between these other two chronologically and in severity of experience.[3]

3. James Revel, *The Poor Unhappy Transported Felon's Sorrowful Account of His Fourteen Years Transportation at Virginia in America* (London, [1780]); also in Paul Lauter et al., eds., *Heath Anthology of American Literature*, 4th ed. (Boston, 2002), I, 269–275. For background, see John Melville Jennings's introduction to the poem (as well as the poem) in *Virginia Magazine of History and Biography*, LVI (1948), 180–186; and Richard Beale Davis, *Intellectual Life in the Colonial South, 1585–1763* (Knoxville, Tenn., 1978), III, 1334. Jennings dates Revel's arrival between 1656 and 1671. As both Jennings and Davis point out, there is no certainty about the composition, authorship, or authenticity of the story, not to mention its original publication date or its possible circulation as an oral ballad, written down later. But, because it describes with some accuracy a probable experience for a transported felon, it is worth considering in this context. Although Revel decries his cruel treatment, he was fortunate to be in Rappahannock County, where malaria was not the significant problem it was elsewhere in the tidewater (Darrett B. Rutman and Anita H. Rutman, "Of Agues and Fevers: Malaria in the Early Chesapeake," *William and Mary Quarterly*, 3d Ser., XXXIII [1976], 44). See Richard Frethorne's letters in Lauter et al., eds. *Heath Anthology*, I, 257–260; and in Warren M. Billings, ed., *The Old Dominion in the Seventeenth Century: A Documentary History of Virginia, 1606–1700*, rev. ed. (Chapel Hill, N.C., 2007), 373–374 (Richard Frethorne to his parents, Mar. 20, Apr. 2, 3, 1623, from Susan Myra Kingsbury, ed., *The Records of the Virginia Company of London* [Washington, D.C., 1906–1935], IV, 58–59, 62). His

Despite Revel's return to England, he nevertheless describes a process whereby his original identity is stripped from him. Apprenticed to a tinsmith in England at thirteen, he gets into trouble, runs away, returns to his master, and then becomes involved with a gang of young thieves. Caught, he suddenly faces not just the displeasure of parents and master but also a possible death sentence—indeed, some of his accomplices are hanged. In the mildly religious tone of the poem, his being sentenced to transportation is a form of mercy. Even so, his voyage resembles depictions of the Middle Passage; all around him are cursing and smoking sailors, dead and dying felons, and in general a scene of misery. In the context of the poem, survival is no special opportunity, only a means to prolong the agony. Once in Virginia, he is gussied up for sale:

> The things were given that to each belong,
> And they that had clean linen put it on.
>   Our faces shav'd, comb'd our wigs and hair,
> That we in decent order might appear.

Exhibited in the manner of horses and slaves, his teeth and limbs examined, the temporarily well dressed Revel is finally sold off as a laborer, with the consequence that his European clothes and wig are confiscated, and his Americanization begins:

> Here my European clothes were took from me,
> Which never after I again could see.
>   A canvas shirt and trowsers me they gave,
> A hop sack frock in which I was a slave:
> No shoes nor stockings had I for to wear,
> Nor hat, nor cap, my head and feet were bare.

For the newly arrived person in servitude, the entry into life in the Chesapeake is a functional nakedness in which all the items of clothing that distinguish a person from a wretch in absolute poverty disappear to be replaced by minimal coverings, thus signifying one's status as someone's property. In Revel, as in other accounts, the most telling signs of this stripping down appear as uncovered head and feet; loss of hat and shoes exposes the individual both to the full force of the southern sun and to direct contact with the earth the laborer must hoe and turn. Baked on top, dirtied on the bottom, the bound laborer is

---

probable death is discussed in Ivor Noël Hume, *The Virginia Adventure, Roanoke to James Towne: An Archaeological and Historical Odyssey* (New York, 1994), 379–380. See also William Moraley, *The Infortunate: The Voyage and Adventures of William Moraley, an Indentured Servant,* ed. Susan E. Klepp and Billy G. Smith (University Park, Pa., 1992).

forcibly altered head to foot to accommodate to the specific physical conditions of the Virginia landscape. Revel's poem, written for an English audience of young men and boys who might be tempted to go astray, intends to stress the sort of threatening transformation wrought by servitude in the New World. The creole imaginary operates here to alienate English readers from the American experience by suggesting the terrors that loss of (English) identity creates in the hatless, shoeless Chesapeake.[4]

The poet makes clear that his daily routine for his first twelve years in Virginia is unredeemable toil, working among tobacco plants at the hoe from dawn to dusk, with occasional labor in the grain mill until midnight or later. One telling detail that helps date the poem is that Revel works alongside African slaves; in his work group are six transported felons and eighteen slaves, but the poem indicates little difference in the way all are treated. Such mingling of white and black characterized farm life in the early Chesapeake; in Maryland, a colony settled later than Virginia, that practice lasted nearly to the 1690s. But, as prices for tobacco rose and planters began to see slaves as a better economic investment than four- or five-year indentures (who were not as plentiful later in the century) or even fourteen-year transported convicts (the supply of which was cut off for a time by the General Court in Virginia), the Africans began to predominate in workforces and the number of white servants to go down. In Revel's poem, a mark of the poet's degradation is apparently this conjoined labor, because his final admonition to his countrymen includes the warning not to get in trouble at home as he did, then be forced "Among the negroes to work at the hoe." The punishments for miscarriage are the same for white and black, he seems to say, from adding time to the length of service for working time missed to hanging for more serious infractions. When he is sick, he must continue to work; the only compassion he receives is from the black slaves, not his white master—a trope (the abused but caring black) that would later appear in eighteenth-century drama, at least from the time of Isaac Bickerstaff's Mungo in the comedy *The Padlock* (1768). Made to work alongside blacks, with no compassion from his master, the poet turns to God to find comfort "in such a barbarous place."[5]

After his master dies, Revel is put up for sale by the widow along with the rest of the workers. Put into a "fold" like sheep, the laborers are once again examined, but this time Revel finds his market value lower than that of slaves. This

4. Revel, *The Poor Unhappy Transported Felon's Sorrowful Account*, 4, 5.
5. Ibid., 6, 8; Gloria L. Main, *Tobacco Colony: Life in Early Maryland, 1656–1720* (Princeton, N.J., 1982), 97–139.

devaluation reflects the circumstances in which planters in the Chesapeake found slaves to be a better investment than short-term white servants. Only after a cooper from Jamestown buys his remaining two years and puts him on a footing closer to that of the master does Revel experience anything like compassion from a white person and relief from the incessant drudgery of the tobacco fields. In this latter situation, he often travels with the cooper and sees much more of the countryside than he was able to on the plantation in Rappahannock:

> And in my heart I often griev'd to see,
> So many transport felons there to be,
> Some who in England have liv'd fine and brave,
> Were like old Horses forc'd to trudge and slave.

For Revel, the creole experience amounts to unwanted metamorphosis, from human to animal, and therefore remigration reverses the process. Despite the kindness of the cooper and the perspective wrought by his fourteen years (by the chronology suggested by the poem, Revel would have been in his early thirties at manumission) in Virginia, he expresses only gladness in deciding to return to England. Even though his current master seems to care about him and his previous master provided the example of a man who was himself a transported felon but had become a landowner, Revel indicates no internal debate about his choice. Unlike servants in Rappahannock County in the 1660s who staged an armed revolt to demand their freedom, the poet has complied meekly with his indenture only to depart. He has adapted physically, but not spiritually, and as resistant creole chooses to return to a place in which he had faced the possibility of execution. In this version of the creole imaginary, the migrant can successfully resist creolization, despite his long stay—nearly half his life—and his working side by side with Africans for most of the period, but at the same time express the more successful strategies of those who more willingly adapt. Whether Revel successfully reincorporated himself in England neither poem nor historical record can say, but the text in its multiple reprintings served as a warning to the young of Great Britain to avoid being forced into cultural nakedness, epidermal darkening, and dreaded creolism, even as it contained within it the seeds of another story, the young man redeemed and put on the road to American adaptation by the kindly creole cooper.[6]

Aphra Behn's *Widdow Ranter* (1689) offers another perspective on the creole

---

6. Revel, *The Poor Unhappy Transported Felon's Sorrowful Account*, 8; James Horn, *Adapting to a New World: English Society in the Seventeenth-Century Chesapeake* (Chapel Hill, N.C., 1994), 416.

experience in Virginia, this time from one with little direct knowledge of the Chesapeake but who might have spent at least a few years in the New World. The point of view is not that of the bound servant but that of the elite, a perspective that renders the experience of onetime servants in Virginia largely comic in comparison to the heroic sentiments of the wellborn characters. There are no Revels here, no sounds of suffering amid the insects, heat, and privations of a primitive plantation, but there is depicted a society composed of a mixture of moneyed elites and former farriers come to political power and preferment. Behn sets her play during Bacon's Rebellion, the 1676 revolt of English settlers on the frontier against the government of William Berkeley and his policy of nonviolence toward natives in the west. Nathaniel Bacon, the leader of the rebellion and brutal enemy of the Indians, died during the uprising, but his reputation, both in Virginia and in London, was very much a contemporary topic of debate. In Behn's drama, her Bacon character is set against the mob on one side and the heroic natives, Cavarnio and Semernia, on the other. Although the play bears the marks of many of her city comedies, with a clear Tory bias, Behn's Bacon cannot be made to stand for the traditional noble royalist without raising serious questions about what loyalty to king and country means. Bacon plays his role of high-sounding rebel as if he were a stage character, not a person in reality. His rebellion in the play against the council (rather than the governor and council, as in fact) simply maintains a London theatrical model of Restoration idealism on a Virginia stage set; Bacon the character shows he has learned nothing in particular from his Virginia experience and, like the resolute Cavarnio, dies fixed in his principles in a noble-seeming but lost cause. In that sense, he is not unlike Revel's transported felon as one who comes to the Chesapeake, resists change, and leaves the scene determined to cling to some original identity.[7]

But Behn's main title is *The Widdow Ranter*, not *Bacon's Rebellion*, and it is to that eponymous character that we turn for insights into Behn's understanding of Virginia creoles. Of most interest in this regard are the widow and the

7. Aphra Behn, *The Widdow Ranter; or, The History of Bacon in Virginia*, in Janet Todd, ed., *The Works of Aphra Benn*, VII, *The Plays, 1682–1696* (Columbus, Ohio, 1996), 292–354; as *The Widow Ranter . . .* also in Myra Jehlen and Michael Warner, eds., *The English Literatures of America, 1500–1800* (New York, 1997), 233–291. All subsequent citations are from the Todd edition. Most studies of the play focus more on Bacon than the council members. On problems posed by native-European miscegenation and its threat as a kind of creolism in the context of savagery and civilization, see Margo Hendricks, "Civility, Barbarism, and Aphra Behn's *The Widow Ranter*," in Hendricks and Patricia Parker, eds., *Women, "Race," and Writing in the Early Modern Period* (New York, 1994), 225–239. As Jenny Hale Pulsipher notes, which side one is on in the play matters less than who affirms royalist values: "*The Widow Ranter* and Royalist Culture in Colonial Virginia," *Early American Literature*, XXXIX (2004), 41–66.

lowborn council members, characters who have undergone some kind of transformation in the New World. In Behn's creole imaginary, stage Virginia is
ostensibly little different from stage London: love drives the high characters,
base impulses move the low, and the best outcome one can hope for is to pair
the right people, trim the mob, and restore the order predicated on an existing
hierarchy. At the same time, though, she plays to concerns in London about
what happens to persons who emigrate, against their will or voluntarily, to the
American colonies. The widow herself, we learn from the cavalier Friendly, first
arrives in Virginia as an indentured servant of Colonel Ranter, but, after only
"half a year," the master effectively buys off her remaining three and a half years
(assuming standard articles of indenture) by marrying her, then rewards her by
"dying in a year more" and making her a wealthy widow and independent to
boot. Because women in the Chesapeake were a relatively rare commodity—a
term chosen deliberately here—it was not unusual for indentured women to
find marriage partners very soon after serving their time. In addition, it occasionally happened that a lover would buy the remaining time from a master,
especially if the indentured woman became pregnant before her time was up.
Given also the shortened life spans for migrants in the seventeenth century (the
average age at death for men in the Chesapeake was early forties), Ranter's
reaching widowhood at a young middle age is highly likely. Although the
fortune Behn imagines for her widow, fifty thousand pounds, seems extravagant
by the standards of the 1670s in the Chesapeake, the playwright reflects with
some truth the condition for at least some women. In a world dominated
demographically by men, a woman, especially one with an estate, would have
been highly prized in historical Virginia. As Ranter herself says to Hazard, "We
rich Widdows are the best Commodity this Country affords."[8]

Beyond this demographic verification of the Widdow Ranter's status, Ranter
herself both betrays her English origins and shows some evidence of change
from her experience in Virginia. Unlike Revel's servant, who seeks no fortune in
America, the former servant widow fully intends to remain where she is rather
than return to a country that effectively expelled her for her poverty. Dramatically speaking, she is the tough-talking, hard-living antidote to the love
patter and more insipid lives of the citified elite to whom change comes slowly,

8. Behn, *The Widdow Ranter*, 299, 307. Supporting details on the situation faced by women in
the Chesapeake are from Lois Green Carr and Lorena S. Walsh, "The Planter's Wife: The
Experience of White Women in Seventeenth-Century Maryland," *WMQ*, 3d Ser., XXXIV (1977),
542–571. See also Janet Todd, "Aphra Behn: The 'Lewd Widow' and Her 'Masculine Part,'" in
Gender, Art, and Death (Cambridge, 1993), 11–31.

if at all. When offering a meal, for instance, Ranter serves a local favorite, buffalo, a dish unavailable in London. Although historically buffalo were fast disappearing from coastal areas, if they had been in the tidewater at all, Behn's use of the term suggests Ranter's adaptability to local foodways. American wood bison roamed the backcountry of Virginia well into the eighteenth century and as a sign of Ranter's adaptation to the Chesapeake would have fed the creole imaginary of London with an exotic and wild image of what colonists ate. When the city-comedy lover Friendly attempts to make some headway with the object of his affections, Chrisante, Ranter cuts him off: "Come, Come, a Pox of this whining Love, it spoyls good company." Some of her directness of speech may derive from her own working-class origins in England, but, as a widow in a country where status gives her power, it may also come from surviving the seasoning and accommodating to the more rough-and-tumble conditions of colonial gentry life. When new arrival Hazard hesitates to take a pipe of tobacco with her, she tells him straight up, "Oh fy upon't you must learn then, we all smoke here, 'tis a part of good breeding." Virginia is, after all, a tobacco colony; both Maryland and Virginia make their fortunes by sale of sotweed, as it came to be called, and it would be natural enough for residents to smoke a pipe. For a woman in England, such a practice might have been less thought of as "good breeding," but we know from Mary Rowlandson, for instance, that even a good Puritan minister's wife in New England liked a pipe on the porch when she could. In addition, Ranter enjoys her alcohol. This predilection again reflects the importance of alcoholic drinks, especially as punch, made from apple cider, brandy, rum, or some combination thereof. Reflecting the chronic use of punch among the planter class in the Chesapeake, Ranter calls the drink "my Mornings draught, my Table-drink, my Treat, my Regalio, my every thing." The combination of the pipe and the bowl marks Ranter as well adapted to Chesapeake culture. As Ranter tells the more genteel Crisante, "I must Smoke and Drink in a Morning, or I am Maukish all day." Pipe-smoking, hard-drinking, tough-talking, buffalo-eating, and independent, Ranter reflects possible adaptations for British women in seventeenth-century Chesapeake culture. Although historically there might not have been such a woman with such a fortune, Behn presciently reads into the record of the Virginia colony an amalgamation of creole characteristics that appears on stage as the Widdow Ranter.[9]

9. Behn, *The Widdow Ranter*, 306–308; Frank Gilbert Roe, *The North American Buffalo: A Critical Study of the Species in Its Wild State*, 2d ed. (Toronto, 1970), 213–217, 245–247; Mary Rowlandson, *The Soveraignty and Goodness of God . . .* (1682), in Jehlen and Warner, eds., *English*

Behn is less sympathetic to the other migrants who make up the bulk of the council and their associates. They, too, are of the widow's original English class status, but, in Behn's mind, they are only pretenders to advancement. In act 1, we learn all we need to know, from a royalist point of view, of the origins of Virginia's governing body. As Friendly acquaints the newly arrived Hazard, "We are Ruled by a Councill, some of which have been perhaps transported Criminals, who having Acquired great Estates are now become your Honour, and Right Worshipfull, and Possess all Places of Authority." And, although Friendly grants that a few are "honest Gentlemen" (he means Colonel Wellman and Colonel Downright, toward whom Behn is relatively sympathetic), the play makes much more of the origins and practices of the others. As with Ranter, the council members consider "Virginia Breeding" to include the drinking of punch and locally produced brandy, not the claret available at Downright's, and despise what they imagine to be the affectations of English manners simply translated to Virginia soil. Behn suggests that they can never attain to the niceties of British breeding, having themselves all come from base origins—and behaved basely to get to Virginia. Parson Dunce, for instance, was a farrier in England, but went bankrupt, faked a letter from the bishop, and came to Virginia as an ordained cleric. Mistress Flirt, though claiming noble birth, is the daughter of a tailor who trusted all in preparing goods for Oliver Cromwell's funeral, a poor choice, perhaps, both because the dead was a Puritan and the Restoration would soon put loyalties to the "good old cause" in the closet. Timerous in England was an embezzling excise man, forced to come to America as a servant. Dullman tries to put by the claim that he, like Revel, was a tinker who robbed back home and was transported. Boozer, for his part, appears to have been a pickpocket. The council members call themselves "Men of Honour," but Hazard labels them "Scoundrells." Although Behn likely intends that a London audience perceive them as poltroons, she uncannily exposes certain prejudices among the English who imagine fortunes are to be won in America without labor. Hazard tells the council, "I was not born to work"; he fully intends to make his mark by marrying well and settling down to the life of a gentleman squire. But Timerous is in truth the more realistic, thinking that Hazard's best road to success is to hire himself out "to make a Crop of Tobacco this year"—what he himself did when he arrived, "for all I am of the Honourable Councill." Indeed, the council members cannot believe that Hazard has no

Literatures, 361; Carr and Walsh, "Planter's Wife," *WMQ*, 3d Ser., XXXIV (1977), 557. For an intriguing reading of Ranter as reflecting Behn's own creolized identity, see Adam R. Beach, "Anti-Colonialist Discourse, Tragicomedy, and the 'American' Behn," *Comparative Drama*, XXXVIII (2004), 213–233.

rough patches in his history, that he is not "some broken Citizen turn'd Factor." Hazard throws his drink in Timerous's face, a nice theatrical touch to turn our sympathies to the gentleman, but in fact most British migrants to the Chesapeake in the early decades arrived as servants, a position that was a sign of their own failure to thrive in the competitive and restricted economic environment of the seventeenth-century British Isles.[10]

In the end, once Bacon dies and the wellborn rebels Dareing and Fearless return to civil government to join the council—a fantasy ending rather unlike the historical executions of the leaders of Bacon's Rebellion—many of the council realize they have overreached and step aside. Even so, Behn displays in their comic failure to show themselves as "betters" a successful adaptation to the Chesapeake world. Their speech may be a version of London stage language rather than a transcription of Virginia creole dialects, but, when Timerous says he will return to his "old Trade again," he means, not a "broken Exciseman," but a planter, someone who will "bask under the shade of my own Tobacco, and Drink my Punch in Peace." Ranter moves up the social scale through luck, sudden wealth, honesty, and bravery, but the council members sink a bit from cowardice and duplicity in handling the Bacon affair; in the end all have adapted to a new environment with a possibility of success unavailable to the lowborn characters in England. For being written by someone without perhaps more than a brief stop in Virginia to or from Suriname, *The Widdow Ranter* describes with surprising accuracy how English migrants became Chesapeake creoles. Although in her creole imaginary Behn might have sought to entertain through exotic location and imposition of Tory class politics on an alien landscape, she in fact inscribes the creole's resistance to metropolitan prejudice. Antagonistic as she is always in her plays to the mob, Behn nevertheless grants in this New World setting that creolism can have salutary effects on those persons otherwise doomed in English society to the lowest rungs without hope of climbing.[11]

The best-known literary work about "some broken Citizen turn'd Factor" is Ebenezer Cooke's poem, *The Sot-weed Factor* (1708). Cooke's Hudibrastic satire has much to say about the creole experience, written from the point of view of a stranger to Maryland but actually by someone who had lived and worked there off and on for many years. As with Revel and Behn, Cooke first published his

10. Behn, *The Widdow Ranter*, 299, 302; Lois Green Carr, "Emigration and the Standard of Living: The Seventeenth Century Chesapeake," *Journal of Economic History*, LII (1992), 272.

11. Behn, *The Widdow Ranter*, 301, 351. On British attitudes toward the council in this play, see Michal J. Rozbicki, "The Curse of Provincialism: Negative Perceptions of Colonial American Plantation Gentry," *Journal of Southern History*, XLIII (1997), 742.

work in England—there being no press in Maryland until the 1720s—and, consequently, like the earlier works, *The Sot-weed Factor* must also be considered in its context as a work disseminated first for an English reading audience. But, even more than the other two, Cooke beguiles his readers into potentially troubled readings of Chesapeake experience, exposing the altered landscape of English habitation in Maryland and the seductions of the creole identity that threaten to undermine London understandings of what it means to be British.[12]

As with Revel, Cooke portrays a temporary migrant, one who, outraged at the treatment he has received in the Chesapeake, eagerly retreats to England at poem's end, glad to be through with the American experience. In *The Sot-weed Factor,* however, the poet betrays his hybridity, his absorption of American words and scenes beyond his own ability to reflect on them. His vocabulary, for instance, is laced with New World words, many of native American origin: *"Canoo"* for the watercraft he attempts to negotiate standing up, or *"Succahana"* for water. Local foods have strange-sounding names and compositions: "Syderpap," "Pon," "Homine," "Mush." Frogs are called *"Virginea* bells"; the factor is terrorized by what he believes to be a "Rattle-Snake" and bothered by "Muskitoes," a word borrowed from a Spanish application to the New World insect; the tobacco is referred to as *"Oronooko,"* a term of uncertain origin but with possible analogies to the name of Aphra Behn's famous eponymous character in Guyana (spelled "Oroonoko") and by extension from that to the Orinoco River in South America. With all his explanatory notes, in fact, the factor betrays a pride in his knowledge of language and custom that belies the ignorance revealed in his actions and the curse he bestows on Maryland at poem's end.[13]

12. Ebenezer Cooke, *The Sot-weed Factor; or, A Voyage to Maryland, etc.,* in Lauter et al., eds., *Heath Anthology,* I, 697–715; *The Sot-weed Factor* first appeared anonymously in London, 1708. J. A. Leo Lemay, *Men of Letters in Colonial Maryland* (Knoxville, Tenn., 1972), 78–93; Robert D. Arner, "Ebenezer Cooke's *The Sot-Weed Factor:* The Structure of Satire," *Southern Literary Journal,* IV, no. 1 (Fall 1971), 33–47; Davis, *Intellectual Life,* III, 1357–1359. Rather than revisit the issue of what is being satirized—most commentators now accept some variant of the Leo Lemay and Robert Arner double-satire thesis—it seems more worthwhile to look at the peculiarities of creole life depicted in the poem as a reflection on the creation of new identities in the New World. I will not rehearse the litany of articles on *The Sot-weed Factor,* except to say that many critics stop well short—too short—of seeing in Cooke's Marylanders a real creolizing. For Cy Charles League, "The Process of Americanization as Portrayed in Ebenezer Cooke's *The Sot-Weed Factor,*" *Southern Literary Journal,* XXIX, no. 1 (Fall 1996), 22, for instance, the cockerouse only displays "the partial capitulation of British manners to American reality." But see other references below. Sarah Ford more closely approximates what I discuss here when she speaks of the Marylanders as "postcolonials": "Humor's Role in Imagining America: Ebenezer Cook's *The Sot-Weed Factor,*" *Southern Literary Journal,* XXV, no. 2 (2003), 1–12.

13. Cooke, *The Sot-weed Factor,* in Lauter et al., eds., *Heath Anthology,* I, 699, 700, 703, 709, 711.

Among the types of knowledge to which the factor fails ostensibly to attain is that connected to native Americans. Throughout the poem, the poet liberally bestows the word "Indian" on objects connected to the local landscape of Maryland: a tobacco pipe is an "*Indian* Gun"; the land is "*Indian* Country"; a sleeping place is an "*Indian* Bed"; the card-playing women are "*Indian* Froes"; a gourd is the product of an "*Indian* Vine." When he meets an actual native, he reacts with the characteristic fear and sense of threat of the "greenhorn," as Leo Lemay labels the factor, but he does repeat in the poem the Indian's greeting, "*Kekicknitop*," delivered to the first planter's son, who serves in the early part of the poem as the factor's Ralpho and guide. Importantly, the poem introduces a literal native to the mix, but of equal importance is that he sees only one indigenous person. Part of the lore of the Americas for Europeans rests on the fear of becoming the country, going native; thus, *American* as a noun originally referred to the native peoples, and from that by contemptuous extension it was applied by home-bound Europeans to whites who had lived on the other side of the Atlantic too long, who had become creoles. Cooke acknowledges the influence of Indian language and custom on the creation of English society in Maryland but also recognizes that Indians have little literal presence left, even at the end of the seventeenth century, in the tidewater region. Britons in America are, then, both more Indian than a reader in London might find acceptable and less, in the sense that culturally the native peoples are already headed for obliteration. Yet Cooke may also have one other feature in mind, the alleged origin of the Indians in the Welsh. In a note to *Hudibras,* a work Cooke surely knew, Samuel Butler glosses the word "Penguin" by saying both American Indians and the British use the same word for the same bird: "From whence (with other words of the same kind) some Authors have indeavour'd to prove, That the *Americans* are originally deriv'd from the *Brittains.*" Thus, to be *Indian* is to be *British,* and to be more Indian is, in a way, to be more original British, as in the ancient peoples of the Isles whose mythological past forms a good part of eighteenth-century British identity. Cooke's satire may include, then, the imputation that, the more Indian the creoles are, the more truly British they are. In this light, Cooke's satire is not merely on "greenhorns" but also on the complete scope of Anglo-American identity. What does it mean to admit "Indian" either to "British" or "American"? After all, he is not alone among Chesapeake colonials to make this link; as Ralph Bauer and José Antonio Mazzotti note in their Introduction to this volume, Robert Beverley has declared for his British reading audience in *The History and Present State of Virginia* (1705), "I am an *Indian.*" Cooke does not answer the national identity question—the factor would never make such a declaration as Beverley's—but he provides suggestive links that make the question a destabilizing one for colonial and British identity.[14]

The factor observes the transformation of English to creoles when he first arrives in Maryland. As he unloads the goods he has brought to sell for tobacco, he is soon surrounded by

> a numerous Crew
> In Shirts and Drawers of *Scotch-cloth* Blue.
> With neither Stockings, Hat, nor Shooe.

As with Revel, the ownership of hats and shoes defines the European; the absence of the same defines the American creoles, "These *Sot-weed* Planters." The university-educated Englishman (the factor suggests he has been to Cambridge) can hardly imagine such a radical simplicity of dress, but, for the planters, being hatless and shoeless in the Chesapeake climate defines the sensible man from the overcivilized fool. At the same time, the planters are dark-skinned, "tawny as a Moor," a likeness that suggests such a variety of racialized possibilities for Americans as to stupefy the factor. The creoles are of "Figure so strange, no God design'd, / To be a part of Humane Kind," even to the point of causing the factor to think he has been transported to some dreamland, or the "Land of Nod." Cooke plays to strong British prejudices about colonial gentry; as Michal J. Rozbicki observes for the British elite, "British American society was characterized as being made up of common-ers . . . with very limited title to the independence and liberties of the free, a view that proved to be a major obstacle for the legitimation of a colonial gentry." Like many Londoners, the factor believes, once his "Fancy" that Maryland was settled by Cain and his descendants has passed, that the planters are "a detested Race; / Who when they cou'd not live at Home, / For Refuge to these Worlds did roam" to escape the gallows in Europe. In other words, the factor imagines that, in a land composed of transported felons, he can have no hope of engaging in enlivening conversation or finding the tender manners of those "at Home." When the poet does encounter the native sometime after, he describes him as having "tawny Thighs, and Bosom bare," not so far removed from the

14. Ibid., 700, 701, 704, 708, 711, 712; Samuel Butler, *Hudibras*, ed. John Wilders (Oxford, 1967), 31n; Robert Beverley, *The History and Present State of Virginia*, ed. Louis B. Wright (Chapel Hill, N.C., 1947), 9. Jim Egan, "The Colonial English Body as Commodity in Ebenezer Cooke's *The Sot-Weed Factor*," *Criticism*, XLI (1999), 385–400, argues that the subtext of the poem focuses on the way in which the weakened body of the English factor (who is oblivious to "native" advantages) is shown as inferior to the hardened, Indianized bodies of the creoles.

planters as the factor is from his ostensible countrymen. Once again, the conflation of native and English produces a hybrid for which there is no equivalent in *contemporary* Britain.[15]

When the factor visits Battle-Town, the county seat, he finds that punch breaks down all social barriers; tipsy himself at the end of the day, he retires to a corn loft, only to wake without shoes, hat, wig, or stockings—all tossed in the fire. Now hatless and shoeless, if not yet tawny, like the Marylanders, the poet discovers the external signs of his distinction from the creoles reduced considerably. Whatever scorn the factor was able to reserve for the crude colonials, he loses in this functional nakedness; and, although not as literally naked as his poor companion, who has lost all of his clothes in a drunken fight, the factor's loss of hat is the more extreme sign, since the distinction between Indian and planter has already been observed as minimal, whereas the factor's sense of his own difference from the creoles has been extreme. As with Revel, the factor fears that loss of hat and shoes is the beginning of a threatening process of identity transformation, from English to creole. In the satire, Cooke mocks the British concern over external signs of distinction. To those who believe hat, stockings, shoes, and wig make the man, Cooke throws the whole issue of human nature on the table—and finds it bare. Not surprisingly, he even has his factor and his guide debate, in the style of a Virgilian bucolic, the origins of the native peoples, with each proposing an equally imaginative possibility. Cooke's point is, not to settle the question, but to call it, to make the issue of humanity, race, and sign one of endless deconstruction, visible in its indeterminacy in the figure of the tawny white, barefoot, bare-headed, and speaking something like English, something not.

The factor's own bias toward hat and shoes prevents him from taking the full measure of others that he meets. On two occasions, planters, one of modest means, another with a more substantial plantation, host him. In each case, however, he is treated with a hospitality and a diet befitting the country and unlike what he might find at home. At the first planter's, he eats the many corn-based foods that characterized the Chesapeake diet of the seventeenth century —pon, mush, hominy—a diet that, if not altered somewhat, leads potentially to pellagra, a niacin-deficiency disease. But even the few foods he mentions in-

15. Cooke, *The Sot-weed Factor*, in Lauter et al., eds., *Heath Anthology*, I, 698, 704; Rozbicki, "Curse of Provincialism," *Journal of Southern History*, XLIII (1997), 730. The clever, self-determining creole is the middle point between the Marylander and the Londoner as objects of satire; for the more bifurcated stance, see Armin Paul Frank, "Ebenezer Cook's *The Sot-Weed Factor*: An Intercultural Reading," in Carla Mulford and David S. Shields, eds., *Finding Colonial Americas: Essays Honoring J. A. Leo Lemay* (Newark, Del., 2001), 64–78.

clude milk, molasses, and bacon fat, which were the sort of extra ingredients that gave even poor residents of the Chesapeake a relatively hardy diet, one that ultimately led to the increased size of colonials over their European-bred colleagues. At the home of the second planter, whom the factor labels a "cockerouse" (spelled variously in this poem and in *Sotweed Redivivus*), the food is more varied: apple juice, wild fowl, fish, turkey, venison, Madeira. This meat-based diet suggests the cockerouse's larger estate; in fact, he could probably add beef, mutton, and pork to that as well, since even exclusive growers of tobacco diversified enough to raise domestic meat animals for plantation consumption. Whatever the factor's complaints about comfort—the bed linens at the second planter's have chinch bugs—he has none about the openness and largesse of the creoles to strangers.[16]

At each planter's, the factor encounters women who have made the adjustment to life in the Chesapeake. At the first, he meets one who, he dismissively remarks, "pass'd for [a] Chamber-Maid" and wore "loose and sluttish Dress." As with the men, so with the women: to accommodate both to the circumstances of material scarcity, especially of textiles, and to the climate, women of comparable station would have worn fewer and more comfortable clothes than their counterparts in England. What the factor thinks is "sluttish" may only be practical, given the woman's status as a servant in the early colonial Chesapeake. She has not, however, fully acclimated herself to her situation; like Revel, she complains that the nice clothes of her circumstances back home have been put aside for blue linen shifts, the female equivalent of male farm laborers' "*Scotch-cloth* Blue." Like the creole men, she is barefoot, and her "daily work" is spent "at the Hoe, . . . / In weeding Corn or feeding Swine." As Lois Green Carr and Lorena S. Walsh have observed, serving-class white women often had to labor outside, especially in the days before large-scale slavery, as well as at interior domestic chores. Cooke's factor does not believe her story, exactly, thinking that, as his own note puts it, she makes "Excuses" for being in America in the position of servant. In a sense, the factor appeals to the kinds of prejudices against a socially rising serving class that Behn assumes in *The Widdow Ranter*. More important, though, because we cannot trust the factor's own ability to understand his circumstances, her story comes to represent the new migrant, newly indentured, for whom the extreme physical labor expected of

16. The cockerouse is first mentioned in Cooke, *The Sot-weed Factor*, in Lauter et al., eds., *Heath Anthology*, I, 710. On comparative sizes of men, see Carr, "Emigration," *Journal of Economic History*, LII (1992), 273; on food, see 277–280, and Main, *Tobacco Colony*, 190–205, 208–211.

women in the Chesapeake was far more than even what serving women in Great Britain would have endured. In this fashion, then, the creole imaginary amounts to a double coding, both a resistant strain to the metropolis on the part of the creole and an equally resistant one to the creole experience from the perspective of the metropolitan. Whatever the truth of her origins, the facts of Maryland life dictated to white women of all classes long periods of hard, physical labor, but with the possibility that this labor might lead to great improvement in class position.[17]

If she survives the seasoning, however, and her four years' labor, she can look forward both to her freedom and to a likely and economically advantageous marriage. With women in short supply, a woman in England of low degree could in Maryland, as in Behn's Virginia, rise quickly in status, especially if she married an up-and-coming planter. At the home of the cockerouse, the factor meets a set of women who have passed their indenture and now live the somewhat more leisured lives of planters' wives. Again, though, the factor does not always see his subject clearly. Waking from a rest at the second planter's, he stumbles on a card game among several women. One wonders whether Alexander Pope had not read *The Sot-weed Factor* before constructing *The Rape of the Lock* (1712). For Pope, the ultracivilized card game Loo becomes the site of an epic battle, whereby all the niceties of English elite society are spoofed in the mock-language of a Homeric struggle. In Cooke's poem, the factor encounters women playing Loo, too, but he considers their game a performance, a sub-rosa mockery of a civilization to which the women could never attain. They are not ladies in the factor's eyes but "a jolly Female Crew" dressed "In Nightrails white, with dirty Mein," whom he likens to "Witches" and who have "nicely learn'd to Curse and Swear." As the factor listens to their conversation, he learns their origins—or at least divines competing tales of such. One of the "Indian Froes"—a phrase that betrays the factor's bias against both creoles and Dutch women—accuses another of having been an indentured servant, even though she is now a planter's wife: "Nature design'd you for the Hoe." The former servant retorts that her accuser was a prostitute in the old country who apparently granted favors to a sea captain in exchange for transportation. Unlike Pope's combatants, Cooke's "fairly fell to Blows," as perhaps his English reading audience might have expected from such lowborn women; but, on the other hand, no woman without some abilities to negotiate a tough physical environ-

17. Cooke, *The Sot-weed Factor*, in Lauter et al., eds., *Heath Anthology*, I, 701; Carr and Walsh, "Planter's Wife," *WMQ*, 3d Ser., XXXIV (1977), 547, 549.

ment will succeed in America. As the Marylanders would recognize, a woman of undue sensitivity would be destroyed or fade away in the Chesapeake.[18]

As the factor flees Maryland, following his fleecing there by the crafty Quaker, his parting words, including his curse, make little sense except to those readers who would cling to a British metropolitan identity rather than a creole one. In the creole imaginary, to be creole is to be outwardly deficient in home-country manners. The factor's calling Maryland "This Cruel, this Inhospitable Shoar" seems ludicrous given the creole capacity for entertainment of strangers and the many hearty meals he has had at others' expense, but it makes sense from the point of view of the English elite, who, as Trevor Burnard has noted, "considered all Chesapeake colonists to be worthless moneygrubbers." Perhaps from a sense that not everyone had understood the satire, Cooke revisited his factor in later life, publishing his sequel *Sotweed Redivivus* in 1730 and a slightly revised *Sotweed Factor* in 1731. The former has interest in this context as a poem told largely from the perspective of a colony that is settled and growing, where the issue is, not survival, but prosperity. The factor meets up with the cockerouse once again, they drink, and for most of the poem the planter discourses on specific remedies to lift Maryland out of its dependence on a crop, tobacco, that no longer provides the way to wealth in the colony. The details of his recommendations are less important here than that Cooke proposes a set of guidelines very specific to Maryland. They are not recommendations likely to sit well with the Board of Trade, for they presume a high degree of independence and self-determination on the part of Maryland, both seemingly against the interests of the proprietors and the government in London. If in *The Sotweed Factor* Cooke introduces the Maryland creoles to a skeptical and somewhat obtuse British reading public, in *Sotweed Redivivus* he in essence reinforces creole identity among the Marylanders as something worth cultivating more than tobacco for a depressed market. At the same time, he offers a warning to Britons about meddling in a colony's internal affairs without understanding precisely whom they are dealing with. In his own poem on Bacon's Rebellion, Cooke attacked Bacon as one who

O're the *Atlantick* Ocean came,
And put the People in a Flame;
Set Folks together by the Ears,
Who liv'd in Friendship many Years.

18. Alexander Pope, *The Rape of the Lock*, in Aubrey Williams, ed., *Poetry and Prose of Alexander Pope* (Boston, 1969), 78–100; Cooke, *The Sot-weed Factor*, in Lauter et al., eds., *Heath Anthology*, I, 711.

In acknowledging the strength of local identities and those bonds developed among Virginians and Marylanders, Cooke's oeuvre is a poetic tribute to the triumph of creolization in the Chesapeake and a critique of British understandings of the distinctiveness of Maryland's tawny white creoles.[19]

One aspect of Chesapeake life largely omitted by Cooke is the presence of African slaves. In *The Sot-weed Factor,* that omission is understandable because, in the early decades of Maryland history, whites dominated the labor market, with the relatively few blacks on Maryland plantations coming from Virginia or the West Indies. Only in the 1690s with the large-scale importation of slaves directly from Africa did the demographic composition of the colony change dramatically and plantations shift in proportion of whites to blacks toward more heavily black-dominated workforces. In *Sotweed Redivivus,* the cockerouse raises the problem more bluntly than the factor of the earlier poem but primarily as an economic rather than a social one: more slaves meant more tobacco meant an oversupplied market. A later poet, the Anglican parson Thomas Cradock, addresses the racialized dimension of creole life in Maryland more fully in his "Maryland Eclogues in Imitation of Virgil's," a set of nine poems written in the 1740s but left in manuscript until 1983. Alleged to be by "Jonathan Spritly, Esqr. Formerly a Worthy Member of the Assembly Revis'd and Corrected by his Friend Sly Boots," the "Maryland Eclogues" both recognize the peculiarity of Chesapeake identity and situate that identity in a social context where Africans more than natives dominate the nonwhite population. Cradock has a number of targets for his satire, most especially the low state of religion and the clergy in the region, but his poems build upon distinctive features of group identity in Maryland that, as with Cooke, separate the creoles from those back "home."[20]

19. Cooke, *The Sot-weed Factor,* in Lauter et al., eds., *Heath Anthology,* I, 715; Trevor Burnard, *Creole Gentlemen: The Maryland Elite, 1691–1776* (New York, 2002), 206; E[benezer] C[ooke], *Sotweed Redivivus; or, The Planters Looking-Glass . . . ,* in Bernard C. Steiner, ed., *Early Maryland Poetry* (Baltimore, 1900), 35–50; E[benezer] Cooke, "The History of Colonel Nathaniel Bacon's Rebellion in Virginia . . . ," in *The Maryland Muse . . . ,* 3d ed., corr. (Annapolis, Md., 1731), 1. On the "public spiritedness" of the cockerouse's proposals and the problems his proposals for Maryland entail, see David S. Shields, *Oracles of Empire: Poetry, Politics, and Commerce in British America, 1690–1750* (Chicago, 1990), 59–60. For the planters to succeed in Maryland, they must take upon themselves the development of their own economic sphere—also a creolizing gesture; see Chris Beyers, "Ebenezer Cooke's Satire, Calculated to the Meridian of Maryland," *EAL,* XXXIII (1998), 69. Race is a slipperier issue in *Sotweed Redivivus* than in *The Sot-weed Factor;* see Lemay, *Men of Letters,* 96; and Robert D. Arner, "Ebenezer Cooke's *Sotweed Redivivus:* Satire in the Horatian Mode," *Mississippi Quarterly,* XXVIII (1975), 495.

20. C[ooke], *Sotweed Redivivus,* in Steiner, ed., *Early Maryland Poetry,* 43; Main, *Tobacco Colony,* 127; Jonathan Spritly [Thomas Cradock], "Maryland Eclogues in Imitation of Virgil's," in

Whereas in Cooke the planter class dominates his *Sotweed* texts, in Cradock's eclogues it plays a somewhat reduced role. In number 5, two planters, Love-Rum and Ever-Drunk, meet to celebrate their late comrade, Toss-pot. As in the *Sotweed* poems, the planters remember great drinking bouts, especially those led by their friend, but here part of the amusement is that the survivors have stopped drinking—they simply cannot recreate the roistering fun at which Toss-pot excelled. In Cradock, chronic drunkenness remains a feature of Chesapeake life—the grounds by which Love-Rum and Ever-Drunk have gone to bed sober are rather flimsy—but it is not necessarily seen as an unmediated evil. As Love-Rum sings of the good old days,

> Our *Negroes* all their Hardships quite forgot,
> Our Overseers the *Seasons* heeded not;
> *Toss-pot* lov'd Ease and Indolence—So we
> To go the Road he led us, all agree.

The question remains: What happens to a plantation economy without alcohol? Will the overseers start to heed the seasons—and thus not drive the workers, particularly slaves, so hard in the hot summer? Will the *"Negroes"* remember the hardships of their incessant and permanently bound labor? Cradock refuses to go any further; after all, these poems are essentially a series of inconclusive pastoral debates. Nevertheless, he raises serious issues about the degree to which creole life, white and black, is made tolerable by drinking to oblivion.[21]

At the same time, Cradock also questions the social mobility of the plantation culture, whereby persons of low degree in Britain become persons of means in Maryland. Eclogue 10 (there is no number 7) features a lovelorn planter, Worthy, who lost his fiancée after she took a trip to England and found a better match. Following the failure of his neighbors, like Job's counselors, to give him solace, Worthy laments that he ever rose to the position of planter in the first place. Better that from his humble circumstances he had been content to remain an overseer; he would never have met such a catch as Flavia but would instead have married "Some Convict-Girl" or contented himself with "Black *Bess*," the sort of woman who, like a crab, has a forbidding exterior but whose "meat is good." Cradock no doubt is satirizing the propensity among

David Curtis Skaggs, ed., *The Poetic Writings of Thomas Cradock, 1718–1770* (Newark, Del., 1983), 138–200 (hereafter cited as Cradock, "Maryland Eclogues"). There has been relatively little criticism of Cradock's eclogues. The most complete treatment is Skaggs, ed., *Poetic Writings,* 63–71; see also Davis, *Intellectual Life,* III, 1393–1395.

21. Cradock, "Maryland Eclogues," 172.

Maryland whites either to wed transported servants or to turn to slave women for sexual satisfaction, but at the same time he charts a new direction in Chesapeake society: the elite planter's attempt to remake himself in the image of the mother country. Had Worthy been content to remain an overseer, he would have also been happily a creole, one whose mores accommodate to local conditions: a transported felon, a slave woman—either one would do in the conditions of low-planter society in Maryland. But to pursue a Flavia, and thus compete in a transatlantic marriage market against fortunes in England, means inevitably to lose not only to money but also to perceptions in Britain of Chesapeake gentry as no better than the picture of the overseer Worthy has just painted.[22]

In a parallel eclogue, number 8, Jemima (apparently a planter's daughter) has fallen in love with Crocus, a ship's surgeon, but, as with Flavia and Worthy, he has left Jemima for Dorinda, the wealthier woman. This and number 10 critique the instability of matchmaking in Maryland; Cradock portrays a society where love plays second fiddle to economics—and where the latter is as unstable as commodity prices. Jemima, we learn, is twenty-four, which, in a note from Sly Boots, the masked poet Cradock glosses as a great age for an unmarried woman in Maryland. This matches up with demographic data on women in the Chesapeake. The immigrating generation tended to be in their late twenties when they first married; the second generation, the creole daughters, often married in their early teens. By Cradock's time, the kind of marriage market that prevailed in Cooke's day, whereby a "Convict-Girl" could marry into the gentry as soon as her indenture was completed, no longer applied to the same degree; sex ratios began to even out, and a woman who was not affianced at fifteen or sixteen ran the risk of not being snapped up as quickly as fifty years before. Having attempted to make a match from someone of a notoriously peripatetic profession and one without a trace of "*Buckskin* blood" (that is, creole), country-born Jemima turns in desperation to Granny, an elderly herbalist who has learned her knowledge from "an old *Negro*."[23]

Thus, in all three of these planter eclogues, Cradock signifies that tawny white creole identity cannot be understood apart from its relation to African-American identity; the creoles may on the surface appear more parallel than intermixed, but, in the eclogues, almost regardless of subject, some element of racial contact and interaction clings to the construction of either creole iden-

---

22. Ibid., 199; Rozbicki, "Curse of Provincialism," *Journal of Southern History*, LXIII (1997), 752.
23. Carr and Walsh, "Planter's Wife," *WMQ*, 3d Ser., XXXIV (1977), 551–555, 564; Cradock, "Maryland Eclogues," 186, 188.

tity. Although Jemima's situation of the unrequited lover is fully in the European tradition, the outcome is not, at least in its details. Granny, for instance, likens Jemima's passion to that of sows wandering through the woods looking for boars, a homely metaphor to be sure, and a comic one, but also a trope taken directly from planter life, whereby hogs were allowed to forage in the woods without attendants, then were occasionally captured for butcher or sale. More important, the potion, a poison, that Granny prepares to bring Jemima love comes from the repertoire of an African: "Mighty his knowledge in them, tho' a Slave." As Sly Boots includes in a note, African herbalists were reputed masters of poisons, and slaves were sometimes accused of poisoning masters, with fatal results to both. Cradock has no trials or hangings; he suggests that knowledge in the Chesapeake is not simply European learning but a conglomeration of European, native, and African. In other words, the planter culture he portrays, no less than Cooke's, has its own rules and rites quite apart from those in Britain.[24]

In addition to planters, Cradock depicts in several eclogues various clergy, none of whom the poet offers as worthy of respect. Number 4, "The M[ary-lan]d D[ivin]e," and number 6, "Celsus," target deism and, for the most part, might be poems whose theme would find echoes in Britain. But Cradock has another critique in mind peculiar to Maryland: the many unqualified clergy or parsons who have come to religion from failure in other areas. A Maryland divine need not preach Christianity, as few of the planters anymore believe in the Anglican creed. The goal of clergy is to climb "to the Honours of the Forties," the forty pounds of tobacco per capita per annum that parsons are allotted for their labors, not to convert or to raise souls. In a somewhat more oblique criticism of his colleagues, eclogue 1, "Split-text," Cradock creates a dialogue between a defrocked Virginia cleric and his comfortable Maryland counterpart. His vestry has sent Crape packing—local expulsion of a parish priest was not allowed in Maryland—most likely for self-indulgence and failures to maintain his office. While he laments that he has lost his living, his friend Split-text expresses gratitude that in Maryland (where there are no punishments, it seems, for bad behavior), he can still "fill / My Pipe and Bowl, as often as I will." The problem, says Cradock, is that clergy came to the Chesapeake for the same reason as planters: economic advancement. Split-text tells Crape that, as a young man in England, "I quite grew weary of my country Fare. / Oatmeal

24. Cradock, "Maryland Eclogues," 188. On slave poisoning, see Philip D. Morgan, *Slave Counterpoint: Black Culture in the Eighteenth-Century Chesapeake and Lowcountry* (Chapel Hill, N.C., 1998), 612–619.

and Water was too thin a Diet, / To keep my grumbling Guts in peace and Quiet." As discussed above, the cuisine in Maryland, humble though it was, was a richer, more fulfilling one than could be got in Britain. Clearly envious of his colleague, Crape details Split-text's many pleasures, portrayed as a pastoral ideal, which include, interestingly, "Thy *Negros,* chanting forth their rustick Loves." When Crape complains that he can no more drink, smoke, and tell "a smutty joak" as was his wont while he still wore his robe, Split-text invites him to stay the night and enjoy Maryland hospitality, including the local drink, bumbo. In the last line, Split-text commands his slave, "Sambo, go, pen the Turkies, feed the Hogs." Thus, although the pastoral ideal may be the sounds of Africans singing, the reality is that clerical hedonism is supported by slavery. Perhaps the root of Chesapeake deism and loss of the old faith is the economic motivation for migration and the comforts in the position made possible by having slaves to command. In Cradock's view, creolism has done no favors for the established church, even though it is a reality that must be recognized in order to understand Maryland life.[25]

In two eclogues, Cradock imagines the voices of nonwhites, with some sympathy for their respective situations. In number 2, "Daphne," a slave, Pompey, is one more lamenting lover whose lady has been captivated by another—perhaps that African American chanting his "rustick Love." In the poems where white lovers abandon their betrothed for better offers, the loss for the unrequited is to a rival with a better fortune; here, Pompey must compete with his white master for Daphne's affections, an almost impossible task. The master successfully exploits his power advantage over Pompey, even though the latter tells Daphne all that he can do for her. Interestingly, Pompey rebukes Daphne's haughtiness in thinking she rates so highly as to be the master's favorite; he says that he is invited by his white mistress to her bed all the time. But I have resisted, he in essence tells Daphne, in hopes of your return. Cradock satirizes this kind of cross-racial exploitation, suggesting that the normal course of intraracial relationships becomes corrupted by white predatory practice. Cradock never intimates what he thinks about such cross-racial relationships pursued in the absence of slavery; his idealism is muted by what he takes to be overwhelming forces in Chesapeake society. Even further, there is nothing in the poem to suggest that whites are altered toward African traits or any new identity by having sex with slaves, but the poet does contend that the mere presence of an enslaved population turns English planters into creole voluptuaries, with all the attendant evils that befall the blacks. Yet, because he is writing pastoral, Cra-

25. Cradock, "Maryland Eclogues," 139, 140, 141, 142, 167.

dock cannot allow the full implications of the situation to play themselves out; there is no suggestion that Pompey will attempt to murder the master, even though Cradock hints in number 8 that African poisoners live in their midst. Instead, the poet has Pompey caution himself not to resist: "Make no more Rant, nor vex thyself about her." The poet offers no solution, only satirizes a corrupt behavior that has become part of creole daily life.[26]

A similar lesson adheres to number 9, "Gachradidow." The eponymous native and a friend, Tachanoontia (whose names derive from Iroquois participants at the 1744 Lancaster treaty negotiations), meet as Gachradidow travels to a white town to sell skins for trifles. As he has used Pompey to criticize white sexual exploitation of slaves, so Cradock employs his native dialogists to satirize the economic practices of the colonists and to emphasize that those who have pushed them from their traditional lands are nominally Christians. Tachanoontia, for example, mentions that a new treaty is in the works to prevent further conflicts with the colonists. Gachradidow replies that it is pointless to sign treaties with "*Christian-Whites,* whose Av'rice grasps at all." We, he continues, value liberty, which we maintain even though "Swarms of *Ch[ri]stian*-Scoundrels round us roam." Indeed, liberty is what defines America, Cradock avers, but that hardly seems to have motivated the settlers from Europe:

What Wonder that these Wretches seek our Shore,
Since Wealth, not Thee, O Freedom, they explore?
Nor wou'd they come, did not each fruitful Field
Large golden Crops of our *Tobacco* yield.

For the natives—in European eyes, a hatless, shoeless people—identity lies not in accommodations to whites, signified by Gachradidow's recognition of white economic hegemony in his trading with them; instead, the two men will seek out a third native, Shuncallamie, who makes no concessions to whites, who teaches the youths still to fight and resist settler encroachment, and "Whose stubborn Soul ne'er knew a Master yet." It may be, with Pompey, that such resistance is futile, and by Cradock's time, because natives posed a much-reduced threat to Chesapeake settlements than they had a half century before, the figure of the resisting native had more metaphorical than realistic power. Nevertheless, the poet posits a world whereby purer values rest, not in a land of assimilation to the corruptions of European creoles, but in a wilderness where noble, traditional values hold sway. What Cradock may suggest here is something of what Cooke implies in *The Sot-weed Factor:* to be more fully native

26. Ibid., 152.

American is to be more fully ancient British. Thus, the poet neither affirms the values of the home country nor celebrates the way Cooke does the development of a creole identity. The Maryland English creole is a half creature, neither Christian nor Indian, a being with tawny cheeks but the heart of a scoundrel.[27]

Cradock's eclogues recognize the reality of Chesapeake life; whites have firmly established their political, military, and economic power in the region, and, although they have developed a distinctive culture based on diet, economy, fashion, and other signs of difference, they have also magnified corruptions based on greed, license, and scorn for the liberty of those whose tawny color comes from nature. Curiously, Cradock anticipates the Crèvecoeur of Letter XII in *Letters from an American Farmer* (1782). In that letter, Farmer James, suddenly confronted with the violence of the American Revolution, must choose what to do with his family. He weighs leaving the farm, in a hostile zone, either for the city or the woods and decides for the latter as the less perverting to the virtuous ideal he has cultivated in the agricultural district. James's associates will no longer be Europeans but Indians, and, though he fears some of the effects of living among them on his children, he worries over the corruptions of the city more. In essence, James chooses a more radical creole existence than that lived on his prosperous Pennsylvania farm. In eclogue 10, Cradock's lovelorn planter, Worthy, having lost Flavia and lamented his own rise in station, likewise decides to depart from the agricultural area of the Chesapeake for the wilderness and to leave his English-ancestored neighbors behind, along with slavery:

> Meanwhile, *Scotch-Irish* shall my socials be,
> Wild as they are, quite good enough for me.
>
> . . . .
>
> The friendly *Indians* all my arms supply.

27. Ibid., 191, 192. According to Burnard, *Creole Gentlemen,* Cradock depicts the Maryland of the eclogues as a "haven . . . in which blasphemy, cruelty, greed, drunkenness, and contempt for religion and wanton display untempered by moderation flourished unchecked. . . . Cradock's vituperations against Marylanders' excess showed that he realized that Marylanders had a distinct identity that had both admirable and deplorable features" (226, 228). As Timothy Sweet points out, Robert Beverley (1705) views Indian attitudes toward tobacco from the perspective of the pastoral mode, whereby they plant at their leisure and for their leisure, not for the sake of economic gain. Sweet suggests that the distinction between the two Virgilian forms, eclogue, the pastoral mode that Cradock specifically imitates, and georgic, a mode that emphasizes labor, accounts for this rupture in Beverley between Euro-American and native attitudes. Thus, here, the Indians see all the ills of the whites foisted upon them as stemming from creole obsession with wealth obtained specifically through the "monoculture" of tobacco and their failure to obtain nobility through pastoral contemplation. See Sweet, *American Georgics: Economy and Environment in Early American Literature* (Philadelphia, 2002), 2, 86.

Sly Boots, in a note to the *"Scotch-Irish"* reference in Jonathan Spritly's poem, remarks that "tis hard to say whether the Indians or they are greater Savages." As with Crèvecoeur, Cradock presents the other side of creolizing, the frontier European savage, but, for the Maryland poet, the pioneers represent less of a moral threat than they do for the New York writer. Whereas Cradock's planters develop into their own character, a slightly Indianized, slightly Africanized version of a European, the poet implies here that the *"Scotch-Irish"* have undergone a more complete alteration, to the ways of the Indians. Yet Cradock in the previous eclogue has also portrayed Indians as noble and in many ways as embodying virtues seen as desirable in the English, notably the commitment to a natural liberty. Again, the poem provides no clear solution or perspective by which to adjudge Worthy's decision to flee to the woods; Cradock may mean it as no more than a fantasy. Nevertheless, the eclogues taken in total expose a complex process of creolizing, whereby various degrees of alteration produce a number of creole types—some amusing, some praiseworthy, some to be condemned. What the poet longs for, it seems, is a Christian version of the more radical creole imagined by Farmer James and the planter Worthy.[28]

THE DIFFERENCES contained within the creole imaginary between the British imperial center (that is, the metropolis) and the actual conditions of life in tidewater Maryland and Virginia produce disjunctions of identity that the Chesapeake writers themselves more often pose than resolve. Whether it is outright resistance to creolism, as in Revel; a grudging recognition of the process, as in Behn; a satiric affirmation of creolism, as in Cooke; or a lament for a process that has happened but lost its integrity, as in Cradock, the writers demonstrate their own conflicts of identity between home as Britain and home as found. All four writers, along with others writing about the region, suggest that the European American is a different kind of being; but whether that being deserves admiration, fear, or scorn is not always clear. For Susan Castillo, creole resistance to imperial authority "challenged . . . the legitimacy of imperial political hegemony and the pretended universality of European local narratives," but, at the same time, a figure like Robert Rogers, whom she labels "the embodiment of the English Creole in America," is a being "whose roots are in the new continent but whose cultural schemes of reference are based elsewhere." Nevertheless, even where creoles, like Cooke, express themselves with

28. [M. G. St. J. de Crèvecoeur] J. Hector St. John de Crèvecoeur, *Letters from an American Farmer and Sketches of Eighteenth-Century America*, ed. Albert E. Stone (New York, 1981), 200–227; Cradock, "Maryland Eclogues," 200.

reference to the imperial center, all of the writers discussed here demonstrate that the integrity of the metropolis itself is potentially undermined by the very persistence of creoles in the New World. Their conjoined English kinship and American otherness, the four writers suggest, offers a dark mirror for those gazing at the Chesapeake from London. Indeed, if, as David Armitage has argued, the British Empire before 1763 was an "ideology" whose grounds of unity were contested from the very beginnings of Atlantic colonization, and where resided unassimilatable others, the natives, then the flimsiness of such a conception of empire must have been present always in the metropolis in the vision of obstinate, degenerate, "American" creoles—a people whose hatless, shoeless being made them distinctly un-British, even as they were claimed by advocates of empire as part of the sphere of the mother country. Creolism threatened British identity taken as at the imperial center, and thus the recourse to the persistent mocking of creole manners by British elites has the hollow ring of a people who fear that at heart they are really Indians, tawny, natural, and naked.[29]

29. Susan Castillo, *Colonial Encounters in New World Writing, 1500–1786: Performing America* (London, 2006), 204, 223; David Armitage, *The Ideological Origins of the British Empire* (Cambridge, 2000).

YOLANDA MARTÍNEZ–SAN MIGUEL

Colonial Writings as Minority Discourse?

Almost the same but not white: *the visibility of mimicry is always produced at the site of interdiction.*—Homi Bhabha, "Of Mimicry and Man: The Ambivalence of Colonial Discourse"

Early, Trans, or Post? Paradigm Shifts in Colonial–Early Modern Studies

Criollismo has been one of the key discursive formations in the study of Latin American cultural and literary history for two main reasons. First, it has allowed scholars to focus on the articulation and emergence of a Euro-American discourse that is crucial for the constitution of a distinct Latin Americanist discourse. Second, in official history creoles were the leading social sector in the battles of independence, and their symbolic repertoire prevailed in most of the nineteenth- and twentieth-century nationalist discourses and imaginaries in the Americas. As a consequence, until the late 1990s, most of the hegemonic accounts of nationhood depended on the creole imaginary of an ethnic and racial synthesis in which Hispanic culture prevailed as the common denominator among most of the countries of Spanish America.

During the last three decades of the twentieth century, the study of nationalism as the master narrative of the collective sociopolitical identities of modernity reinforced and later interrogated the homogeneity of the hegemonic iden-

This essay summarizes the argument I develop further in *From Lack to Excess: Minor Readings of Latin American Colonial Discourse,* which analyzes the narrative and rhetorical structures of Latin American colonial texts by establishing a dialogue with contemporary studies on minority discourse, minor literatures, and colonial and postcolonial theory. Instead of focusing exclusively on a historical context to explain the thematic representation of the unequal relationships of power in the colonial period, or reading these texts as an extension of the ambiguous identity characteristic of a colonial subjectivity—as in the foundational work of Albert Memmi, Frantz Fanon, and Ashis Nandy, for example—this book studies how this "colonial" condition is incorporated into the verbal strategies of the chronicles and written texts of the sixteenth and seventeenth centuries in Latin America.

tity discourses in Latin America. One of the areas of inquiry that developed extensively during the 1990s was the exploration of the internal diversity and heterogeneity of the ethnic, linguistic, social, and political identities conforming modern nations. Mestizo, indigenous, African, and Asian identities became relevant cultural and ethnic sectors in studies that enrich and complicate our understanding of Euro-American creole identities. The other area of debate was the reemergence of colonial studies to identify and trace the specificity of identity formations that are not necessarily national or prenational and that are conceived within an imperial-colonial world-system. This other area of inquiry does not deny the importance of criollo identities but allows us to study criollismo in its specific colonial context in the Americas. Even though criollismo and modernity cannot encompass the whole complexity of coloniality in the Americas, we can explore some of the significant intersections between creole and colonial discourse to identify some common traits or strategies that are specific to the sixteenth and seventeenth centuries.

Therefore, I am proposing a new approach to analyzing the narrative and rhetorical structures of Latin American colonial texts by establishing a dialogue with contemporary studies on minority discourse and colonial and postcolonial theory. Instead of focusing exclusively on a historical context to explain the thematic representation of the unequal relationships of power in the colonial period, or reading these texts as an extension of the ambiguous identity characteristic of a colonial subjectivity, I would like to study how this "colonial" condition is incorporated into the verbal strategies of the chronicles and written texts of the sixteenth and seventeenth centuries in Latin America. I define a discursive spectrum, ranging from aphasia to redundancy, as a point of departure to describe and analyze a set of rhetorical strategies of this colonial discourse, which includes the use of different indigenous and metropolitan languages, the alternation of narrative and descriptive passages, and the use of silence, reticence, aphasia, hyperbole, repetition, amplification, intensification, and redundancy.[1]

I begin with a reflection on the 1980s crisis within the field of Colonial Studies and a review of emerging paradigms for the study of the cultural productions of the sixteenth through eighteenth centuries, such as Transatlantic, Early Modern, Imperial and Colonial Studies, Colonial and Postcolonial Theory, and Early Ibero/Anglo Studies. Discourse analysis and the constitu-

---

1. On the ambiguity of a colonial subjectivity, see Albert Memmi, *The Colonizer and the Colonized*, trans. Howard Greenfield (Boston, 1990); Ashis Nandy, *The Intimate Enemy: Loss and Recovery of Self under Colonialism* (Delhi, 1992).

tion of a colonial subjectivity were significant areas of emphasis and development after the reconfiguration of what is currently known as Latin American, American, and English Cultural Studies. Two questions were central in this debate: How can these texts be studied from a literary perspective? And, Why were these texts considered to be the origin of modern/national literary traditions? I focus on a third question, which has remained unexplored: What is the internal structure of colonial discourse?

As is already well known, Latin American colonial studies faced a significant crisis by the end of the 1980s due to the lack of specificity of its object of study and the problematic application of traditional theories of colonialism and postcolonialism to the context of Latin American history. Rolena Adorno proposed a solution to this crisis by focusing on discourse analysis as the object of study of Latin American colonial and cultural studies. A few years later, Walter Mignolo explored some of the limits of this new theoretical paradigm and coined another category that could include a wider variety of forms of verbal expression that are not necessarily alphabetical or written:

> When pushed to the limit, however, the concept of "colonial discourse," desirable and welcome as it is, is not the most comprehensive idea possible for understanding the diversity of semiotic interactions in colonial situations in the New World experience. . . .
>
> Because in the field of colonial literary studies, scholars must account for a complex system of semiotic interactions embodied in the discursive (oral) and the textual (material inscriptions in different writing systems), we need a concept such as *colonial semiosis*. This term escapes the tyranny of the alphabet-oriented notions of text and discourse, even though it adds to a large and already confusing vocabulary. On the positive side, *colonial semiosis* defines a field of study in a parallel and complementary fashion to existing terms such as *colonial history, colonial art,* and *colonial economy.* Furthermore, the concept of colonial semiosis includes the locus of enunciation, a dimension thus far absent from the current colonial fields of study.[2]

2. Walter Mignolo, "Colonial and Postcolonial Discourse: Cultural Critique or Academic Colonialism?" *Latin American Research Review,* XXVIII, no. 3 (1993), 120–134, esp. 125–126. A discussion of the initial crisis in the field of colonial studies can be found in Rolena Adorno, "Nuevas perspectivas en los estudios literarios coloniales hispanoamericanos," *Revista de crítica literaria latinoamericana,* XIV (1988), 11–28, esp. 11. J. Jorge Klor de Alva questions the use of colonial and postcolonial theory in a Latin American context in "Colonialism and Postcolonialism as (Latin) American Mirages," *Colonial Latin American Review,* I (1992), 3–23. In "Reconsidering Colonial Discourse for Sixteenth- and Seventeenth-Century Spanish America," *Latin Amer-*

Even though discourse and semiosis offer a broader perspective for the analysis of cultural production, it is my contention that it is precisely the intersection with a notion of "colonialism" that defines a specific area of interest that allows for the clear definition of a separate field of studies. It is in this context that the link with the colonial and postcolonial studies debate becomes relevant. As Ralph Bauer suggests, "Usually associated with the publication of Edward Said's *Orientalism* (1978), the beginnings of postcolonial theory within the Western academy originated in 'colonial discourse' criticism." Indebtedness to the work of Said, Homi Bhabha, and Gayatri Chakravorty Spivak was evident in the first articles published by Adorno and Mignolo on the crisis of colonial studies, but it was also evident that the theoretical appropriation of this paradigm was enmeshed with some contradictions or inherent differences between the colonial experience of the sixteenth through the eighteenth centuries in the Americas and the more recent experiences of Africa and India. This is precisely the moment in which the need for a specific definition of the time period—and an acknowledgment of the inapplicability of a nationalist paradigm—became a crucial element in the reconfiguration of colonial studies as a field: "However, the term 'post-colonial literatures' is finally to be preferred over the others because it points the way towards a possible study of the effects of colonialism in and between writing in english and writing in indigenous languages in such contexts as Africa and India, as well as writing in other language diasporas (French, Spanish, Portuguese)." How to reconstruct a colonial-imperial world before the emergence of modern nation-states became an issue resolved by redefinitions of time and space that can account for the experiences taking place in the Europe-Africa-America network.[3]

---

ican Research Review, XXVIII, no. 3 (1993), 135–145, Adorno accepts Mignolo's observation about the limitations of the term "discourse," and then she also questions her own use of the term "colonial discourse" (139). She understands "colonial discourse" as texts in which "discourses of domination"—defined as a "battleground . . . of racial and cultural differences"—can be identified (140, 144).

3. Ralph Bauer's discussion on postcolonial theory is developed in "Criticism on the Boundary: Postcoloniality and the 'Worlding' of Literature," *Centennial Review*, XL (1998), 401–416, esp. 401. The main texts cited in postcolonial Latin American studies are Edward Said, *Orientalism* (New York, 1978); Homi Bhabha, *The Location of Culture* (New York, 1994); Gayatri Chakravorty Spivak, *In Other Worlds: Essays in Cultural Politics* (New York, 1987). The redefinition of postcolonial literatures is taken from Bill Ashcroft, Gareth Griffiths, and Helen Tiffin, eds., *The Empire Writes Back: Theory and Practice in Postcolonial Literatures* (New York, 2003), 23–24. *The Empire Writes Back* proposes a distinction between "English"—as the standard code, or "the language of the erstwhile imperial centre"—and "english," "which has been transformed and subverted into several distinctive varieties throughout the world," particularly in postcolonial countries (8).

Colonial and postcolonial theory, transatlantic, and early modern studies share a concern with the recontextualization of *space* to incorporate existing economic and political networks during the colonial period. For example, one of the crucial contributions of the notion of the Black Atlantic set forth by Paul Gilroy is the redefinition of spaces that distinguishes the colonial context from a national paradigm. He proposes

> some new chronotopes that might fit with a theory that was less intimidated by and respectful of the boundaries and integrity of modern nation states than either English or African-American cultural studies have so far been. I have settled on the image of ships in motion across the spaces between Europe, America, Africa, and the Caribbean as a central organising symbol for this enterprise and as my starting point. The image of the ship—a living, micro-cultural, micro-political system in motion— is especially important for historical and theoretical reasons. . . . Ships immediately focus attention on the middle passage, on the various projects for redemptive return to an African homeland, on the circulation of ideas and activists as well as the movement of key cultural and political artefacts: tracts, books, gramophone records, and choirs.[4]

Although Gilroy is following Mikhail Bakhtin and his notions for text-analysis based on temporal and spatial categories, he also uses a concept very similar to Michel Foucault's definition of *heterotopia*. Both Gilroy and Foucault stress the importance of spatial conceptions to assist in understanding the political setting of social and cultural experiences that take place outside and before the existence of modern national boundaries. This same concern with "other" configurations of space is a central motive behind contemporary research and pedagogical projects, such as the one promoted by Susan Castillo and Ivy Schweitzer in *The Literatures of Colonial America,* which questions the fact that "American Studies has often been synonymous with the study of the United States," so it is time to "reconceptualize the object of our discipline with respect to other nations and groups outside the territorial boundaries of the US that have created their own vision of what it means to be American."[5]

4. Paul Gilroy, *The Black Atlantic: Modernity and Double Consciousness* (Cambridge, Mass., 1995), 4. M. M. Bakhtin defines *chronotope* as "the intrinsic connectedness of temporal and spatial relationships that are artistically expressed in literature"; "it expresses the inseparability of space and time." *The Dialogic Imagination: Four Essays,* ed. Michael Holquist, trans. Caryl Emerson and Holquist (Austin, Tex., 1983), 54.

5. Susan Castillo and Ivy Schweitzer, eds., *The Literatures of Colonial America: An Anthology*

Following the same interest in spatial reconfiguration, the Early Ibero / Anglo Studies Group thus presents its mission statement:

> Why American literature from a hemispheric perspective? Since 1985 a number of intellectual and cultural forces have moved scholars and teachers toward a more comprehensive, hemispheric understanding of American cultural legacies. The increasing number of Hispanic citizens in the United States inspired [a] search for Ibero-American artistic and cultural legacies. The tremendous archival recovery of British American literature during the last generation led to the recognition of an extensive British imperial tradition in the international context of the Spanish, French, Dutch, and Portuguese imperial projects of that era [that are] an anticipation of the mentality of the United States. The rise of Atlantic studies among historians promoted a scholarship that was international in scope and concerned with cultural exchange. A growing fascination with borderlands as zones of cultural mixing, creolization, and creation has led scholars interested in the question of what is distinctively American about life, art, and work in the New World to look beyond single national or cultural traditions. Furthermore, an awareness emerged of the anachronism of writing proto-nationalist literary and intellectual histories for a pre-national era.

Whether these fields adopt a hemispheric, transatlantic, or pan-American perspective, the fact is that it has become evident that to understand the colonial period it is important to conceive social, cultural, and political spaces in a way that captures the metropolitan and colonial networks of the period. One of the

---

(Malden, Mass., 2001), xvi; Bakhtin, *The Dialogic Imagination*. Foucault's notion of "heterotopia" is defined as follows:

> Brothels and colonies are two extreme types of heterotopia, and if we think, after all, that the boat is a floating piece of space, a place without a place, that exists by itself, that is closed in on itself, and at the same time is given over to the infinity of the sea and that, from port to port, from tack to tack, from brothel to brothel, it goes as far as the colonies in search of the most precious treasures they conceal in their gardens, you will understand why the boat has not only been for our civilization, from the sixteenth century until the present, the great instrument of economic development . . . , but has been simultaneously the greatest reserve of the imagination. The ship is the heterotopia *par excellence*.

See his essay "Of Other Spaces," *Diacritics*, XVI, no. 1 (1986), 22–27, esp. 27. Boats are also a crucial metaphor for contemporary postcolonial Caribbean imaginaries. See, for example Éduoard Glissant, *Poetics of Relation*, trans. Betty Wing (Ann Arbor, Mich., 1997); Silvio Torres-Saillant, *El retorno de las yolas: ensayos sobre diáspora, democracia, y dominicanidad* (Santo Domingo, 1999).

major contributions of these new conceptualizations of space has been the emergence of comparative studies to identify "a tradition of colonial discourse in the European language of history about America" for early American studies and to propose a "transatlantic perspective on early modern imperialism with an attention to the cultural and literary situation in the Mediterranean" for early European studies. Other excellent examples of the enrichment of Latin American colonial studies when reframed from a comparative perspective are Stephanie Merrim, *Early Modern Women's Writing and Sor Juana Inés de la Cruz,* which positions Sor Juana in a Euro-American context; Ralph Bauer, *The Cultural Geography of Colonial American Literatures: Empire, Travel, Modernity,* on early Iberian and Anglo texts. Some of these efforts, however, still contend with the conflict that arises between cultural specificity and intercultural contacts. Even though nations as such did not exist at the beginning of the colonial period, there are still certain historical and cultural traditions that inform each of the writers from the New World, and we are still facing many of the difficulties of how to study cultural intersections without losing the specificity of certain discursive expressions. Another area that still needs more development is the incorporation of the American indigenous cultures into the comparative paradigm informing some of these readings, so the local traditions and rhetorical strategies become visible in the discursive analysis of texts by canonical authors in the Latin American colonial corpus. Therefore, it could be said that the dilemma between what is local and what is global is a relevant area of discussion not only in contemporary societies but in understanding colonial and early modern cultures as well.[6]

6. Early Ibero/Anglo Studies Group Mission Statement, (http://www.mith2 .umd.edu/summit/mission.htm); Ralph Bauer, "Colonial Discourse and Early American Literary History: Ercilla, the Inca Garcilaso, and Joel Barlow's Conception of a New World Epic," *Early American Literature,* XXX (1995), 203–232, esp. 206; Barbara Fuchs, *Mimesis and Empire: The New World, Islam, and European Identities* (Cambridge, 2001), 3; Stephanie Merrim, *Early Modern Women's Writing and Sor Juana Inés de la Cruz* (Nashville, Tenn., 1999); Ralph Bauer, *The Cultural Geography of Colonial American Literatures: Empire, Travel, Modernity* (Cambridge, 2003). Serge Gruzinski uses current globalization as a point of departure to analyze the colonial experience in *The Mestizo Mind: The Intellectual Dynamics of Colonization and Globalization* (New York, 2002), 2–4. However, he also recognizes that these comparisons have significant limits, as the global village of the present does not function in the same way as the Atlantic and transatlantic networks of the sixteenth to eighteenth centuries. On the incorporation of American indigenous cultures into a colonial corpus, see José Antonio Mazzotti, *Coros mestizos del Inca Garcilaso: resonancias andinas* (Lima, 1996); Rolena Adorno, "Cultures in Contact: Mesoamerica, the Andes, and the European Written Tradition," in Roberto González Echevarría and Enrique Pupo-Walker, eds., *The Cambridge History of Latin American Literature* (New York, 1996), I, 33–57; Mignolo, "Colonial and Postcolonial Discourse," *Latin American Research Review,* XXVIII, no. 3 (1993), 120–133; Serge Gruzinski, *The Conquest of Mexico: The Incorporation of Indian Societies*

Another set of similar concerns has to do with the *temporal* redefinition of the period. This topic is central in the configuration of postcolonial and early modern studies. What happens before the constitution of the nation-states (early American, early Iberian) or after the end of colonialism (postcolonial) could become a theoretical framework to define the cultural productions of the sixteenth through the early nineteenth centuries. However, there has been some discussion about the problems that arise when a field or a period is defined by its limits or exclusions and not by its specific characteristics. Postcolonial studies, for example, dispelled the misconception of the field as the study of the development of communities or nations after the end of colonialism, by proposing: " 'Post-colonial' as we define it does not mean 'post-independence,' or 'after colonialism,' for this would be to falsely ascribe an end to the colonial process. Post-colonialism, rather, begins from the very first moment of colonial contact. It is the discourse of oppositionality which colonialism brings into being." However, the name of the field still carries with it a strong semantic emphasis on a period after colonialism that displaces the focus onto the specificity of the colonial period. Early (American, Iberian, or Anglo) modern studies, on the other hand, studies the beginnings of "modernity" and as such could be seen as a field that grants teleological privilege to an intellectual and cultural time period that is closely associated with the formation of Western nations, especially in the case of Latin America. In a sense, what is gained from the comparative and hemispheric perspective is somewhat lost in the dependency on an overarching Western category that displaces, but implicitly reaffirms, the centrality of nationalism or nation-states in our current paradigms of study. What does it mean to be premodern, and how can we conceive or study a mentality that is not yet modern and cannot even imagine what modernity could be? If globalization and transnationalism make it possible to question the national paradigms dominating our fields of inquiry, can we find a way of questioning and shifting the current dominance of the notion of modernity as an epistemological framework?[7]

into the Western World, Sixteenth–Eighteenth Centuries, trans. Eileen Corrigan (Cambridge, 1993). Raquel Chang-Rodríguez's and Carlos Jáuregui's essays in this collection offer an interesting approach, as they both emphasize the importance of including more indigenous and American texts and cultural practices in our study of definitions and perceptions of criollos.

7. Introduction, in Bill Ashcroft, Gareth Griffiths, and Helen Tiffin, eds., *The Post-Colonial Studies Reader* (New York, 1995), 117–118, esp. 117. On the relationship of early American studies and modernity, see William C. Spengemann, *A New World of Worlds: Redefining Early American Literature* (New Haven, Conn., 1994), 208–209; Bauer, "Colonial Discourse and Early American Literary History," *Early American Literature,* XXX (1995), 203–232, esp. 212–222. On the sociopolitical and epistemological meaning of the concept of modernity in Latin America, see Julio

One final area of debate, at least in Hispanic and Latin American studies, relates to the political dimension of the study of cultural productions within a colonial context. Identifying an area of study as colonial or early modern implicitly affiliates it with a very concrete political context, as well as a theoretical debate, for the colonial category, and a more abstract, or sometimes depoliticized, epistemological approach, for the early modern. Hernán Vidal addresses the applicability of colonial and postcolonial theory for the study of Latin American cultures: "Thus cycles of renewal of Latin American literary criticism were . . . based not on the social problems of the cultures being studied but rather on the new critical theories periodically introduced into the publishing market." Mignolo reflects on the historical and political relationship between colonial and early modern studies when he states that "colonial modernities, or 'subaltern modernities' as [Fernando] Coronil prefers to label it, a period expanding from the late fifteenth century to the current stage of globalization, has built a frame and a conception of knowledge based on the distinction between epistemology and hermeneutics and, by so doing, has subalternized other kinds of knowledge." His work points out that what Aníbal Quijano calls the "coloniality of power" affects not only political structures but also the ways in which knowledge is conceived, organized, and legitimized. As a very telling example, Mignolo reflects on the subalternity of Latin America and Latin American studies as producers of scholarship and argues, "From the epistemological perspective, European local knowledge and histories have been projected to global designs." He then redefines coloniality as "the reverse and unavoidable side of 'modernity'—its darker side, like the part of the moon we do not see when we observe it from earth." This opposition between modernity and coloniality illustrates some of the inner tensions that these new paradigms bring to this specific field of studies within Latin Americanism.[8]

Ramos, *Desencuentros de la modernidad en América Latina* (Mexico City, 1989); Carlos J. Alonso, *The Burden of Modernity: The Rhetoric of Cultural Discourse in Spanish America* (New York, 1998); Walter Mignolo, *Local Histories / Global Designs: Coloniality, Subaltern Knowledges, and Border Thinking* (Princeton, N.J., 2000); Francine Masiello, *Between Civilization and Barbarism: Women, Nation, and Literary Culture in Modern Argentina* (Lincoln, Nebr., 1992). Dalia Judovitz does an illuminating historical reconstruction of how the epistemological paradigm of modernity—centered in the rational subjectivity defined by Descartes—became hegemonic, by displacing other definitions of cognitive and intellectual subjectivies that were predominant during the Baroque. For more information on this topic, see her *Subjectivity and Representation in Descartes: The Origins of Modernity* (Cambridge, 1988).

8. Hernán Vidal, "The Concept of Colonial and Postcolonial Discourse: A Perspective from Literary Criticism," *Latin American Research Review*, XXVIII, no. 3 (1993), 113–119, esp. 115; Mignolo, *Local Histories*, 13, 17, 22, 263; Aníbal Quijano, "Coloniality of Power, Eurocentrism, and Latin America," *Nepantla: Views from the South*, I (2000), 533–580.

Beyond the various areas of debate and tension produced by these new paradigms for the study of colonial–early modern discourse, it is also evident that the transformation of cartographies and chronotopes as well as the questioning of the national paradigms and the emphasis on a comparative perspective can all be productive points of departure for the renovation and intellectual exchanges between American, Latin American, European, and cultural studies. However, the richness and complexity of modern scholarship calls for a clear delimitation of the areas of interest and "the locus of enunciation" of my research. I join the colonial–early modern studies scholarship as a literary critic trained in Latin American studies and as a reader committed to tracing the crucial political implications of coloniality for Latin American literary and cultural discourses and practices. I would like to refocus the debate from the temporal and spatial matrix previously discussed to analyze the internal structure of a discourse defined by the systems of domination specific to a metropolitan-colonial network. To accomplish this end, I would like to argue that the intersection between colonial and minority discourses could be a productive starting point in identifying a Colonial Rhetoric, or a set of discursive practices that are vital in the constitution of a colonial subjectivity.[9]

Colonialism and Minority Discourse

My combined study of colonial and minority discourses follows two observations made by Rolena Adorno in her reflections on the status of the field: (1) the link she establishes between the studies on minority discourse and new ways to approach the study of colonialism, and (2) her concern with the "dangers of calling every act of writing by sixteenth and seventeenth century authors . . . subversive." Adorno's scholarship suggests here the need to study voices that could be simultaneously marginal and central, subaltern and hegemonic. Her remarks also remind us of Serge Gruzinski's criticism of our incapacity to conceptualize in-between spaces and categories:

> Our confusion is not due solely to the complexity of the social and historical world. An understanding of mestizo processes runs up against intellectual habits which favor monolithic ensembles over "in-between" spaces. It is obviously simpler to identify solid blocks than nameless gaps. It is easier to think that "everything which appears ambiguous is only apparently so, that ambiguity does not exist." The simplicity of dualistic

9. I use Mignolo's notion of "locus of enunciation" as presented in "Colonial and Postcolonial Discourse," *Latin American Research Review,* XXVIII, no. 3 (1993), 123.

and Manichean approaches is appealing, and when they dress themselves in the rhetoric of otherness, they soothe our consciences even as they satisfy our thirst for purity, innocence, and archaism.[10]

Colonial and minority discourses share a major characteristic that could be useful in producing a reading that is sensitive to these contradictory impulses of coloniality described as in-betweenness, ambiguity, or ambivalence. According to Homi Bhabha, "The ambivalence of colonial authority repeatedly turns from *mimicry*—a difference that is almost nothing but not quite—to *menace*—a difference that is almost total but not quite." Bhabha centers his analysis on the ambivalence of the stereotype of the colonial subject:

> It is recognizably true that the chain of stereotypical signification is curiously mixed and split, polymorphous and perverse, an articulation of multiple belief. The black is both savage (cannibal) and yet the most obedient and dignified of servants (the bearer of food); he is the embodiment of rampant sexuality and yet innocent as a child; he is mystical, primitive, simple-minded and yet the most worldly and accomplished liar, and manipulator of social forces. In each case what is being dramatized is a separation—*between* races, cultures, histories, *within* histories—a separation between *before* and *after* that repeats obsessively the mythical moment or disjunction.

This ambiguous representation of the native could be translated discursively into a linguistic void: "Like the mirror phase 'the fullness' of the stereotype—its image *as* identity—is always threatened by 'lack.' " In the case of some colonial texts, the moment of recognition or subjectivation takes place in a space before or outside languages, in a parallel scene to the one described by Lacan as the mirror stage, so the lack of language is a significant experience in the articulation of difference in this discursive corpus.[11]

Raymond Grew, on the other hand, develops a theory of minority discourse that is also based on the notion of ambivalence:

> In its ambivalent contemporary usage, the concept of minority designates a weakness and affirms a strength. . . . Negative in the sense that it identifies a group in terms of its vulnerability to a majority that threatens

---

10. Adorno, "Nuevas perspectivas," *Revista de crítica literaria latinoamericana*, XIV (1988), 21–22, and "Reconsidering Colonial Discourse," *Latin American Research Review*, XXVIII, no. 3 (1993), 143; Gruzinski, *The Mestizo Mind*, 22.

11. Bhabha, *The Location of Culture*, 77, 82, 91.

to oppress or reject it, the concept is positive in its recognition of a group's cultural or moral value, which must be affirmed or recognized or protected.

Minorities are understood here as sectors of a population that are traditionally excluded from institutional or official forms of representation and power and as such are protected by law. Thus, a minority is simultaneously a disenfranchised collectivity and a politically visible entity. Both marginal and capable of exercising pressure, minorities have become one of democracy's most pressing aporias. Minority discourse presupposes a system of incorporation within the hegemonic discourse and official politics that parallels literary re-creation of marginal voices as a legitimate way of forging official and public spaces of representation. By focusing on minority discourse, I identify relevant and crucial differences between acquiring canonical status within the academic historical archive used to trace the formation of the subaltern subject and the reappropriation of this theorization in Latin American cultural and literary studies to study the creation of a collective imaginary. Finally, because ethnic minorities in the United States and Latin America are usually seen as a form of internal colonialism, I would like to use this shared notion of the episteme of ambivalence as a point of departure to explore some of the rhetorical strategies that could allow for a productive intersection of studies on internal and external colonialism.[12]

Ambivalence is a central category in Latin American colonial studies, used to deconstruct one of the main voices of the colonial period: creole discourse. For example, as Kathleen Ross points out:

> The criollos—some of whom were not totally pure-blooded Spaniards—remained identified with Europe, but as colonized Americans they lived a multifaceted reality ordered by hierarchies of race, class, gender, and

12. Raymond Grew, "Introduction," in André Burguière and Grew, eds., *The Construction of Minorities: Cases for Comparison across Time and around the World* (Ann Arbor, Mich., 2000), 1–14, esp. 1. For a detailed discussion of the history and emergence of the subaltern studies debate in Latin American studies, see Ileana Rodríguez, ed., *The Latin American Subaltern Studies Reader* (Durham, N.C., 2001); Alberto Moreiras, *The Exhaustion of Difference: The Politics of Latin American Cultural Studies* (Durham, N.C., 2001). On "internal colonialism" in the United States and Latin America, see Bob Blauner, *Still the Big News: Racial Oppression in America* (Philadelphia, 2001); Rodolfo Stavenhagen, "Classes, Colonialism, and Acculturation: Essay on a System of Interethnic Relations in Meso-America," *Studies in Comparative International Development*, I, no. 6 (1965); Elizabeth Burgos, "Prólogo," in *Me llamo Rigoberta Menchú y así me nació la conciencia* (Mexico City, 1985), 9–19, esp. 10.

religion. *Their literature shows a constant wavering of language from dominant to subordinate positions,* resulting in subversions of European models even when those models are consciously being imitated. And above all, the great preoccupation is history: rewriting it to include the New World. This foundation was made for themselves and their colonial reality, not for the modern nations of Spanish America that formed after independence; but it was American and not European, even though we cannot yet point to a nationalist impetus.

Antony Higgins, referring to the *Bibliotheca mexicana* (1755) by Eguiara y Eguren also refers to "la lógica contradictoria de la obra . . . que lo lleva a defender no sólo la Nueva España sino también la España misma frente a sus detractores de otras partes de Europa" [the contradictory logic of this text . . . that leads it to defend not only the New Spain, but also Spain itself, against its other detractors throughout Europe]. This ambivalence of a differentiated subjectivity, which is neither European nor American but simultaneously metropolitan and colonial, is also translated into an ambiguous discursive relationship with the indigenous cultures, praised as a local culture but excluded from the hegemonic sectors of the American society envisioned by creoles. Herman Bennett also points out that this ambiguity applies to the experiences of the persons of African descent who lived in colonial Latin America: "Becoming a creole literally involved navigating the judicial maze with the intent of exploiting the possibilities offered by legal obligations and rights." Ralph Bauer, following Bhabha, characterizes the "colonialist archive" as "the hybrid, ambivalent, indeterminate space of signification in which the subject splits and communication between colonizer and colonized is doubled." Finally, in his study of the *Naufragios* by Cabeza de Vaca, José Rabasa calls for a decolonization of Latin American colonial studies precisely by pointing out the "ambivalent" position of Alvar Núñez vis-à-vis the metropolitan centers of power and the indigenous cultures of the Americas. Therefore, it seems that ambivalence is a crucial notion in the conceptualization of the Latin American colonial subject, and as such it emerges as a more productive category if we explore it in the intersection between colonial studies and minority discourse.[13]

13. Kathleen Ross, *The Baroque Narrative of Carlos de Sigüenza y Góngora: A New World Paradise* (Cambridge, 1993), 7 (my emphasis); Anthony Higgins, "Sobre la construcción del archivo criollo: el *Aprilis Dialogus* y el proyecto de la *Bibliotheca Mexicana,*" *Revista iberoamericana,* LXI (1995), 573–589, esp. 574; Higgins, "La *Bibliotheca Mexicana*: hacia una poética de la legitimidad criolla," *Revista de crítica literaria latinoamericana,* XXII (1996), 77–87, esp. 80–81, 83, 85. In his work, Higgins develops further an idea already presented by José M. Gallegos Rocafull in *El pensamiento mexicano en los siglos XVI y XVII* (Mexico City, 1974). See

My main objective is to explore the broader colonial dimension of criollismo as an important element in our conceptualization of Euro-American identities in the sixteenth and seventeenth centuries. As Bauer and Mazzotti suggest in the Introduction, there seems to be a critical consensus about the complex position of criollos within the imperial-colonial world order established in the Americas; I would like to focus instead on the specific ambiguity produced by a colonial condition. My aim is not to devalue or dispose of the notion of criollismo for the study of the colonial period, but to interrogate binary simplifications of coloniality that tend to locate ambiguity in creole (and sometimes mulatto and mestizo) identities while conceiving European and indigenous subjectivities as monolithic, coherent, and sometimes even impervious to the colonial system of domination. Given that in colonial Latin American studies criollismo has been a privileged area of research and debate, I am interested in decentering and recontextualizing creole discourses and identities to explore their similarity with other forms of cultural and political practices within the framework of coloniality. My reflection would allow exploring the specific colonial and postcolonial dimensions of Euro-American discourses while insisting on the specific configuration of identities that are simultaneously imperial and colonial without yet being necessarily protonationalist, one of the main arguments developed in the study of criollismo in Latin America.

However, before I can analyze concrete examples of some of the discursive strategies common in the corpus of Latin American colonial texts, it is necessary to propose a working definition of a colonial subject as a minority. Following Gruzinski's reassessment of the conquest as a shocking process in which both the colonizers and the colonized lost their bearings, we can conceive colonialism as the context for the constitution of an identity that is characterized by an ambiguous relationship with an unequal and discontinuous structure of power between the metropolitan centers and the local governments in the Americas. Bill Ashcroft, Gareth Griffiths, and Helen Tiffin characterize this as a "double vision": "This vision is one in which identity is constituted by difference; intimately bound up in love or hate (or both) with a metropolis which exercises its hegemony over the immediate cultural world of the post-colonial." Thus, I define a colonial subject as *a position and a discourse produced*

also Herman L. Bennett, *Africans in Colonial Mexico: Absolutism, Christianity, and Afro-Creole Consciousness, 1570–1640* (Bloomington, Ind., 2003), 203; Bauer, "Criticism on the Boundary," *Centennial Review*, XLII (1998), 405; José Rabasa, *Writing Violence on the Northern Frontier: The Historiography of Sixteenth-Century Mexico and Florida and the Legacy of Conquest* (Durham, N.C., 2000), 78–83.

within that colonial context that is uncannily similar to the situation of minorities in a modern state. Therefore, for the sake of our analysis, a colonial discourse can be produced by Spanish conquistadors, indigenous narrators, and later by creole subjects. Colonialism produces a particular series of subject-positions that range from the European representative of the metropolitan power to indigenous and African populations. Along this spectrum of subject-positions, creoles are included as an intermediary social sector whose literary productions gradually develop an independent discourse.[14]

But in what sense can we define the colonial world as a space of minorities? First, we have to consider the Americas as the imperial border of Spain and Portugal, and later of other European metropolitan centers. As such, the individuals living in colonial society were continually struggling to become visible members—legally and socially—of these centers of metropolitan power. However, from very early on, the crown began a long struggle to control and regulate the powers of the *conquistadores* and *encomenderos*—conquistadors who were granted a plot of land and a group of natives—in the Americas. For example, the debate on the nature of the indigenous populations in which Bartolomé de las Casas was a prominent figure and the promulgation of the New Laws in 1542 to limit the assignment of *encomiendas* both illustrate the vulnerable position of many of the conquistadors vis-à-vis the European monarchies. (The encomienda system was supposed to be a way of evangelizing the native population of the Americas but soon became another way of using Indians as free labor.) We should also remember that both Columbus and Cortés lost the favor of the king and that their contribution to the expansion of the Iberian empire was questioned. The indigenous populations were also the center in a discussion about the extent of their spiritual and rational capabilities as well as of their very humanity, and they were themselves continually struggling to be recognized as the original inhabitants of the Americas, with the right to own their lands or to serve at least as intermediaries between the local governments and the centers of metropolitan power. We have visual and written accounts that illustrate the critical views and ambiguous forms of indigenous appropriation of European cultural referents and practices to survive within a colonial order. The African

14. Gruzinski, *The Mestizo Mind,* 45–47; Ashcroft, Griffiths, and Tiffin, eds., *The Empire Writes Back,* 25–26. Stephanie Merrim develops a similar definition of the colonial subject in her essay included below, defining *criollismo* "in the intertextual and positional senses," and she analyzes "Sor Juana's interactions with every aspect and with the full chronological sweep of Mexican discursive tradition, or what I will call the *Mexican Archive."* In both cases—her reading and mine—creole and colonial identities are conceptualized as the result of a particular context and a locus of enunciation, instead of as a direct consequence of the place of origin of the speaking subject.

population arrived in the Americas mostly as slaves and was in many cases officially excluded from civil society until the end of the eighteenth century and the beginning of the nineteenth century. Their participation in colonial society was characterized by what Herman Bennett describes as "social ambiguity and cultural dexterity." Africans and their descendants were slaves, free persons, and sometimes even soldiers and encomenderos, and as colonial subjects they used the existing institutions to gain access to a social and legal identity still understudied in the case of Latin America. Access to writing came late for these colonial subjects, and this tardiness was combined with a delayed institutional or individual interest in preserving any written accounts of their lives in the Americas. However, the scarcity of texts produced by Africans and their descendants cannot be equated with a lack of importance of these sectors in the economic, social, and cultural context of these societies. Their presence in historical documents and their significance in the configuration of Latin American *mestizaje* (miscegenation) has also been undervalued, especially in the case of the *Tierra Firme* (mainland) where African slaves and, later on, black maroons and *libertos* were also a crucial entity in the configuration of Latin American societies before and after independence.[15]

The creoles were also involved in a long discursive and political struggle to prove their rational and physical equality vis-à-vis the Spanish colonizers. Their desire for legitimation included a validation of their intellectual capabilities and a defense of their right to participate in the local governments established by the Spanish crown. Furthermore, there were many internal divisions between and within the groups of conquistadors and the indigenous and African communities as well as between the creoles and mestizos. Therefore, the colonial world comprised a variety of social and ethnic groups that continually tried to legitimize their right to participate fully in the civil life of the early modern world. Imperial powers were far from absolute. Hence, I would like to focus my reading on the internal fractures and tensions that characterize what Gruzinski

15. For a summary of the debate on the humanity of indigenous subjects, see Rolena Adorno, "La discusión sobre la naturaleza del indio," in Ana Pizarro, ed., *América Latina: palavra, literatura, e cultura*, I (Sao Paulo, 1993), 173–192. Among the best-known studies of indigenous cultural negotiations within the colonial order, see Martín Lienhard, *La voz y su huella* (Havana, 1989); Rolena Adorno, *Guamán Poma: Writing and Resistance in Colonial Peru*, 2d ed. (Austin, Tex., 2000); Mercedes López-Baralt, *Icono y conquista: Guamán Poma de Ayala* (Madrid, 1988); Mazzotti, *Coros mestizos*, on the Andean indigenous cultures. See also the work done by Elizabeth Hill Boone and Walter D. Mignolo, eds., *Writing without Words: Alternative Literacies in Mesoamerica and the Andes* (Durham, N.C., 1994); Miguel León Portilla, ed., *Visión de los vencidos: relaciones indígenas de la conquista* (Madrid, 1985); Ángel María Garibay K., *Historia de la literatura náhuatl* (Mexico City, 1953–1954); Gruzinski, *The Conquest of Mexico*, for the Mesoamerican region; Bennett, *Africans in Colonial Mexico*, 18.

called the "strange zones." This fragmentation within the colonial society translates into verbal narratives that are very often at odds with hegemonic and imperial discourses. In that sense, my reading of colonial texts follows Abdul JanMohamed and David Lloyd's definition of becoming minor: "[It] is not a question of essence (as the stereotypes of minorities in dominant ideology would want us to believe) but a question of position: a subject-position that in the final analysis can be defined only in 'political' terms." I propose a view of the struggles of these diverse social and ethnic entities in the context of minority discourses, because the Americas were conceived as an extension of the metropolitan world that occupied a secondary and sometimes peripheral place in the articulation of systems of knowledge and power. As a result, those living in the Americas became internal minorities in the discursive framing within the European order.[16]

My work also takes into account this complex process of intermediation that, according to Ross, resulted in the appropriation of the narratives of conquest and colonization during the seventeenth century, to use verbal discourse to represent a creole perspective. Even though each one of these subject-positions participated in and was excluded from the existing networks of imperial power in different degrees, the fact is that the colonial order functioned as a common context serving as the center of articulation for a wide range of ethnic, social, and political identities. In the same fashion that, later on, nation-states would configure a diverse array of identities, subject-positions, and degrees of subalternity and hegemony, colonialism functioned as a very specific articulating political, social, and cultural context. Minority discourse allows us to make the transition from the *ambivalence* of the colonial subject to the rhetorical *ambiguity* of a colonial discourse, without being trapped in the contradictions posed by the homogeneous-unitary nationalist agendas usually guiding literary analysis.[17]

The link between colonialism, minorities, and discourse analysis can be drawn out of Gilles Deleuze and Félix Guattari's "What Is a Minor Literature?": "A minor literature doesn't come from a minor language; it is rather that which a minority constructs within a major language." This foundational essay, central in the study of minority discourses, stresses the fact that a minor literature can

16. On creole discourse, see Ross, *The Baroque Narrative;* José Antonio Mazzotti, ed., *Agencias criollas: la ambigüedad "colonial" en las letras hispanoamericanas* (Pittsburgh, 2000); Antony Higgins, *Constructing the "Criollo" Archive: Subjects of Knowledge in the "Bibliotheca Mexicana" and the "Rusticatio Mexicana"* (West Lafayette, Ind., 2000); Gruzinski, *The Mestizo Mind*, 37–42, esp. 39; Abdul JanMohamed and David Lloyd, introduction, in JanMohamed and Lloyd, eds., *The Nature and Context of Minority Discourse* (New York, 1990), 1–16, esp. 9.

17. Ross, *The Baroque Narrative*, 7.

be identified by the context and dynamics of its production rather than by a set of intrinsic characteristics:

> The three characteristics of minor literature are the deterritorialization of language, the connection of the individual to a political immediacy, and the collective assemblage of enunciation. We might as well say that minor no longer designates specific literatures but the revolutionary conditions for every literature within the heart of what is called great (or established) literature.[18]

Colonial discourse becomes an excellent case to revisit Deleuze and Guattari's insight. First, given the marginal condition of its production and its double space of belonging, many of the texts included in this corpus could be read simultaneously as imperial and subaltern discourses. Furthermore, many of the texts that we currently analyze from a literary and cultural perspective were not intended as such, so in most of the cases we are dealing with legal and historical documents that constitute what has been redefined as colonial discourse. However, there are some texts—Cabeza de Vaca's *Naufragios* or Sor Juana's poetry and theater, for example—that can be easily classified as what we currently conceptualize as Literature, although their specific function and value during the colonial period is somewhat different from the place assigned to literature as a technology of social and cultural representation in contemporary societies. Finally, it is important to stress here that what defines a minor literature is not the presence of deterritorialization of language, a political dimension and a collective enunciation, but the conjunction of those three elements with the "revolutionary condition" of this discourse. Therefore, my reading of a Colonial Rhetoric is informed by this interest in perceiving and identifying the moments in which these texts become minor vis-à-vis the imperial literature to which they also belong.[19]

In the context of the early Americas, it is important to make a distinction between colonial and imperial discourses. I understand as colonial discourse those texts in which the project of colonization and conquest is depicted from an American perspective. Imperial discourses, on the other hand, are conceived

---

18. Gilles Deleuze and Félix Guattari, "What Is a Minor Literature?" in Russell Ferguson, ed., *Out There: Marginalization and Contemporary Cultures* (New York, 1990), 59–69, esp. 59, 61.

19. In my reading of a minority discourse, "revolutionary" does not mean subversive, but differentiated from hegemonic imperial discourses. For Deleuze and Guattari, "deterritorialization of language" is to appropriate a major language for strange and minor uses. The example they use is the transformation of a standard or official language through the linguistic transformations explored in ethnic and diasporic literatures.

from within a metropolitan perspective, and they endorse a European coloniz-ing project. Therefore, it is possible that one text could include colonial and imperial discourses in a process of interaction and negotiation. My reading of a Colonial Rhetoric, then, is an attempt to identify and deconstruct the discur-sive and narrative strategies used to constitute an American or mestizo per-spective that negotiates its place within or against metropolitan and imperial projects, in epistemological, political, or philosophical terms.[20]

From Lack to Excess: Defining a Discursive Matrix for a Colonial Rhetoric (Columbus, Cortés, and Las Casas)

My reading traces a discursive voyage from a rhetoric of lack to one of excess, using Columbus's foundational aphasia in his *Diarios de viaje* and Las Casas's excessive repetition and duplication of information in the *Brevísima relación de la destrucción de las Indias* as a defining paradigm to study the spectrum of verbal strategies of this colonial discourse. Foundational aphasia signals the failure of language to apprehend or grasp the complexity of the American reality as a discursive parallel to the lack of control over the newly discovered lands and subjects. Here is an example from Columbus's journal:

> Y así no surgí en aquella angla, y aun porque vide este cabo de allá tan verde y tan fermoso, así como todas las otras cosas y tierras d'estas islas que yo no sé adónde me vaya primero, ni se me cansan los ojos de ver tan fermosas verduras y tan diversas de las nuestras, y aun creo que a en ellas muchas yervas y mucho árboles que valen mucho en España para tinturas y para medicinas de especiería, mas yo no los cognozco, de que llevo grande pena.

> And so I did not anchor in that bay, seeing as I did this green and lovely cape in the distance. Everything on all these coasts is so green and lovely that I do not know where to go first, and my eyes never weary of looking on this fine vegetation, which is so different from that of our own lands. I

---

20. I still refer to the texts produced in the Americas before independence as "colonial," even though I make a distinction in terms of the different discourses and perspectives included in these pieces when I refer to colonial and imperial discourses. I use "American" as synonymous with "Americano(a)" as understood in a colonial–early modern framework. I refer to *mestizo* in the sense coined by Gruzinski: "to designate the mélanges that occurred in the Américas in the sixteenth century—mélanges between individuals, imaginative faculties, and lifestyles originating in four continents (América, Europe, Africa, Asia)" (*The Mestizo Mind*, 31).

think that many trees and plants grow there which will be highly valued in Spain for dyes and medicinal spices. And it saddens me to admit that I do not recognize them.[21]

This constant lack of words produces at some points of the Columbian discourse a form of linguistic erosion, since Columbus uses *maravilla* ("marvelous") and *disforme* ("amorphous") as empty signifiers to name the unrepresentable alterity of the New World:

Y vide muchos árboles muy disformes de los nuestros, d'ellos muchos que tenían los ramos de muchas maneras y todo en un pie, y un ramito es de una manera y otro de otra; y tan disforme, que es la mayor maravilla del mundo cuánta es la diversidad de la una manera de la otra. Verbigracia: un ramo tenía las fojas de manera de cañas y otro de manera de lantisco y así en un solo árbol de cinco o seis d'estas maneras, y todos tan diversos.

I saw many trees very unlike ours. Many of them had several branches of different kinds coming from one root, and one branch is of one kind and another of another; there is so much variation that it is quite marvellous to note how diverse is one form from the other. *Verbigracia:* one branch may have leaves like those of the cane and another like those of a mastic tree, and thus on a single tree there are five or six different kinds, all distinct from one another.[22]

Columbus uses the same words repeatedly to emphasize the evident difference of the natural setting he is traveling through in his account of the Indies. In this passage it is also noticeable that the narrator recognizes his struggle with language as a process of linguistic adaptation, or even creation, of the new

21. On Columbus's foundational aphasia, see Irlemar Chiampi, *Barroco y modernidad: ensayos sobre literatura latino-americana* (Mexico City, 2000), 113–114; Margarita Zamora, *Reading Columbus* (Berkeley, Calif., 1993), 158. Zamora points out the importance of taking into consideration the significant role played by Las Casas in the edition and manipulation of the currently existing version of the logbook of the "First Voyage" (39–94). Her interpretation tends to privilege Las Casas's voice and agenda, while it is evident that there is a conflict between two voices in the text to which we currently have access. I am using quotes that are supposed to be Columbus's "exact words" as stated by Las Casas, and I assume they preserve most of the rhetorical and linguistic strategies of the original text that is currently lost. Cristóbal Colón, *Los cuatro viajes: testamento*, ed. Consuelo Varela (Madrid, 1999), 75; Christopher Columbus, *The Four Voyages*, ed. and trans. J. M. Cohen (London, 1969), 69. I have included some revisions to the English translation.

22. Colón, *Cuatro viajes*, ed. Varela, 70–71; Columbus, *Four Voyages*, ed. and trans. Cohen, 64. In my use of this English translation here, I have made some minor corrections.

spaces described. The last sentence of this passage makes this relationship between language and apprehension of reality even more evident, as Columbus reiterates and summarizes his previous circumlocutory description of the trees as a result of verbal grace ("verbigracia"), understood here as the creating-originating power of language. Thus, "maravilla" and "disforme" function here as signifiers for the excess that the admiral cannot capture in his verbal account of the American landscape.

Columbus attempts to appropriate the New World by using comparisons and parallels, but his description also shows the predominance of alterity as an enigma that the text cannot resolve within the development of its internal subplots. Margarita Zamora has traced this same strategy in other texts written by Columbus and describes it in the following terms: "The exclamation may function as an attempt to disguise the narrator's aphasia in the face of difference, an aphasia that was not the result of some personal shortcoming, but of the essential incapacity of the discourses at his disposal adequately to express such difference. . . . The dissimilarity of the natural landscape is initially articulated as a semantic void, thinly veiled in a discourse of the ineffable." These passages also illustrate what Deleuze and Guattari classify as "intensive or tensors": " 'any linguistic tool that allows a move toward the limit of a notion or a surpassing of it,' marking a movement of language toward its extremes, toward a reversible beyond or before." Columbus could be read as a producer of a minor discourse because his narratives explore the limits of language to grasp the New World alterity, so the admiral becomes a "nomad and an immigrant" in the language he is using to convey his heroic deeds.[23]

At the other end of the spectrum we can identify the "redundant" descriptions and narrative techniques of Cortés and Las Casas. In these texts we notice that there is already a linguistic tradition used to depict the realities of the New World. In both cases, the political or ideological control over the New World is reflected through the way in which both of these authors represent the American setting. I begin with what I see as a redundant description that is central in Hernando Cortés's *Second Letter* to Charles V. *Italics* emphasize the use of the notion of totality in Cortés's text, and **bold** identifies the redundant lists included in this description:

Tiene esta ciudad muchas plazas donde hay contino mercado y trato de comprar y vender. Tiene otra plaza tan grande como dos veces la plaza de

23. Zamora, *Reading Columbus*, 158, 159; Deleuze and Guattari, "What Is a Minor Literature?" in Ferguson, ed., *Out There*, 62, 64.

la cibdad de Salamanca toda cercada de portales alrrededor donde hay cotidianamente arriba de setenta mil ánimas comprando y vendiendo, donde hay *todos los géneros de mercadurías que en todas las tierras se hallan* ansí de mantenimientos como de vestidos, joyas de oro y de plata y de plomo, de latón, de cobre, de estaño, de piedras, de huesos, de conchas, de caracoles, de plumas. Véndese cal, piedra labrada y por labrar, adobes, ladrillos, madera labrada y por labrar de diversas maneras. Hay calle de caza donde venden *todos los linajes de aves que hay en la tierra,* así como gallinas, perdices, codornices, lavancos, dorales, cerzatas, tórtolas, palomas, pajaritos en cañuela, papagayos, buharros, águilas, falcones, gavilanes y cernícalos. . . . Hay calle de herbolarios donde hay *todas las raíces y hierbas medecinales que en la tierra se hallan.* . . . Hay *todas las maneras de verduras que se fallan,* especialmente cebollas, puerros, ajos, mastuerzo, berros, borrajas, acederas y cardos y tagarninas. *Hay frutas de muchas maneras,* en que hay cerezas y ciruelas que son semejantes a las de España. . . . Finalmente, que en los dichos mercados se venden *todas las cosas cuantas se hallan en toda la tierra,* que además de las que he dicho son *tantas y de tantas calidades que por la prolijidad y por no me ocurrir tantas a la memoria* y aun por no saber poner los nombres no las expreso.

This city has many squares where trading is done and markets are held continuosly. There is also one square twice as big as that of Salamanca, with arcades all around, where more than sixty thousand people come each day to buy and sell, and where *every kind of merchandise produced in these lands is found;* provisions as well as ornaments of gold and silver, lead, brass, copper, tin, stones, shells, bones, and feathers. They also sell lime, hewn and unhewn stone, adobe bricks, tiles, and cut and uncut woods of various kinds. There is a street where they sell *game and birds of every species found in this land:* chickens, partridges and quails, wild ducks, flycatchers, widgeons, turtledoves, pigeons, cane birds, parrots, eagles and eagle owls, falcons, sparrow hawks and kestrels. . . .

There are streets of herbalists where *all the medicinal herbs and roots found in the land are sold.* . . . There is *every sort of vegetable,* especially onions, leeks, garlic, common cress and watercress, borage, sorrel, teasels and artichokes; and there are *many sorts of fruit,* among which are cherries and plums like those in Spain. . . .

Finally, besides those things which I have already mentioned, they sell in the market *everything else to be found in this land, but they are so many and so varied that because of their great number and because I cannot remember many of them nor do I know what they are called I shall not mention them.*[24]

This long description of the market in Tenochtitlán is an example of how Cortés literally takes control of the city, after Moctezuma designates him as his successor, by naming and describing the richness and variety of elements that compose the Aztec settlement. The distance from Columbus's aphasia is evident here, as Cortés describes the market hyperbolically as the place that contains "everything," proposing Tenochtitlán as a new totality once it becomes part of the Spanish kingdom. Furthermore, Cortés includes a detailed and redundant enumeration of what that *totality* means—expounded in the long lists of nouns that pretend to encompass all the known birds, vegetables, and spices found in the New World—in a discursive move opposite from the erosion of language that we noticed in some of Columbus's paradigmatic descriptions. In a gesture very similar to Columbus's aphasia, Cortés refers to his lack of knowledge or memory about the names of certain objects, but in this case his remark seems ironic, because his text has just exhibited an abundant and very specific and precise command of a broad lexicon in its long descriptions.[25]

A similar strategy is developed by Las Casas in his *Brevísima relación de la destrucción de las Indias*, when he uses narrative redundancy to intensify the ideological message of his text:

En estas ovejas mansas y de las calidades susodichas por su Hacedor y Criador así dotadas, entraron los españoles desde luego que las conocieron como lobos y tigres y leones crudelísimos de muchos días hambrientos. Y otra cosa no han hecho de cuarenta años a esta parte, hasta hoy, y hoy en día lo hacen, sino *despedazallas, matallas, angustiallas, afligillas, atormentallas y destruillas* por las estrañas y nuevas y varias y nunca otras tales ni leídas ni oídas maneras de crueldad, de las cuales algunas pocas abajo se dirán, en tanto grado que habiendo en la isla Española sobre *tres cuentos [millares, millones]* de ánimas que vimos, no hay hoy de los naturales della doscientas personas. *La isla de Cuba* es cuasi tan luenga como desde Valladolid a Roma: está hoy cuasi toda despoblada. *La isla de Sant Juan y la de Jamaica*, islas muy grandes y muy

---

24. Hernán Cortés, *Cartas de relación* (Madrid, 1993), 234–236; Hernán Cortés, *Letters from México*, ed. Anthony Pagden (New Haven, Conn., 1986), 103–104 (my emphases).

25. I develop further this idea in my essay "Poder y narración: representación y mediación de un deseo americano en la *Segunda carta de relación*," in Mazzotti, ed., *Agencias criollas*, 99–130.

felices y graciosas, ambas están asoladas. . . . Serán todas estas islas, de tierra, más de dos mil leguas, que todas están despobladas y desiertas de gente.

It was upon these gentle lambs, imbued by the Creator with all the qualities we have mentioned, that from the very first day they clapped eyes on them the Spanish fell like ravening wolves upon the fold, or like tigers and savage lions who have not eaten meat for days. The pattern established at the outset has remained unchanged to this day, and the Spaniards still do nothing save *tear the natives to shreds, murder them and inflict upon them untold misery, suffering and distress, tormenting, harrying and persecuting* them mercilessly. We shall in due course describe some of the many ingenious methods of torture they have invented and refined for this purpose, but one can get some idea of the effectiveness of their methods from the figures alone. When the Spanish first journeyed there, the indigenous population of the island of Hispaniola stood at some *three million;* today only two hundred survive. *The island of Cuba,* which extends for a distance almost as great as that separating Valladolid from Rome, is now to all intents and purposes uninhabited; and two other large, beautiful and fertile islands, *Puerto Rico and Jamaica,* have been similarly devastated. . . . All these islands, which together must run over two thousand leagues, are now abandoned and desolate.[26]

Las Casas constructs his narrative based on the repetition of certain thematic motives, such as (1) the description of the beauty and richness of a zone, (2) the praise of indigenous generosity and hospitality followed by Spanish destruction and barbarity, and (3) the metaphorical opposition of the indigenous people as innocent lambs and the Spanish as fierce wolves. This text is also structured with an accumulation of a diverse array of linguistic strategies, such as the lists of adjectives and verbs, the use of hyperboles, and the continual employment of the superlative. The redundancy in the narrative culminates in the cumulative repetition of the same miniplot, changing only the location in which the destruction takes place. In this sense, Las Casas travels throughout the Americas, but only to point out the superimposition of the same story of destruction and annihilation produced by the inhumanity of the Spanish conquest. Thus, this

26. Bartolomé de las Casas, *Brevísima relación de la destrucción de las Indias* (Mexico City, 1988), 72–73; Bartolomé de las Casas, *A Short Account of the Destruction of the Indies,* ed. and trans. Nigel Griffin (New York, 1992), 11–12 (my emphases).

narrative articulates verbal redundancy in a spatial context, and Cortés focuses on a linguistic duplication of information that enriches the description of one specific place.[27]

In these three texts, produced during the first sixty years of the conquest, Columbus, Cortés, and Las Casas use the absence of language to express a lack of control, but the excess of language represents the struggle for the ideological or political possession of the New World. Their texts are produced in the interstices of the colonial order, because they use the imperial languages and epistemes to represent a set of cultures, realities, and practices that were significantly different and virtually unknown for the individuals producing the verbal depictions of the New World as well as for the metropolitan officials and the members of the courts in Europe reading these accounts. At the same time, these three cases illustrate the paradoxical effects of the New World alterity on the European-metropolitan subjects that came to the Americas. Columbus, Las Casas, and Cortés were all colonial functionaries who were simultaneously representing and sometimes at odds with the interests of the crown. As a result, their narrative accounts are at once official reports of a service rendered by a loyal vassal to the crown and justifications of their particular agendas within an imperial project of colonization and conquest. Thus, power and language are inextricably linked in these narrations. These two extremes of linguistic expression—from aphasia to redundancy, or from lack to excess—become the framework from which I study the internal structure of a colonial discourse. I argue that colonial discourse in Latin America resignifies this rhetorical and verbal matrix through the reappropriation of this discourse by conquistadors, mestizos, and indigenous and creole subjects. The interplay between lack and excess is crucial in the definition of an ambivalent colonial subjectivity that wants to be like a metropolitan subject, "but not quite . . ."

The texts by Columbus, Cortés, and Las Casas could also be read as examples of a "minor" discourse, because all of them function as narratives in which a major or metropolitan language is deterritorialized or taken to its limits or extremes. Columbus's narrative is one of the most interesting examples, because his struggle with language goes beyond the well-known fact that he wrote in a hybrid Mediterranean Spanish that included lexicon and grammatical patterns from Portuguese, Italian, Spanish, and Catalan as well as an Atlantic perspective reflected in his use of African and Arawakan notions and vocabulary. In his *Diario*, the sailor illustrates the continual struggle of trying to convey

27. On the narrative structure of the *Brevísima*, see André Saint-Lu's introduction, in Las Casas, *Brevísima*, esp. 38–41.

to the crown a reality beyond verbalization, producing a narrative that exhibits the *negative* limits of language. Cortés and Las Casas also take their metropolitan language to its *excessive* extremes, but in a different way. Cortés wants to capture the richness and exuberance of the Aztec world to make it become an extension of the metropolitan possessions, trying at the same time to justify his unauthorized trip to Tierra Firme. Las Casas, on the other hand, portrays the destructive impact of colonization in the New World in his *Brevísima historia*, a brief yet redundant compendium. His narrative uses a metropolitan language to portray the darker side of the imperial project, and for that reason redundancy and linguistic excess become crucial strategies for the critical ideological project set forth by the Dominican friar. In all of these cases, language is deterritorialized (removed beyond its proper context), and the narratives produced in these texts can also be read as minor vis-à-vis the imperial context in which they are produced. Coloniality functions, then, as that negative dimension of the imperial project from which a minority discourse emerges.[28]

Complicating Criollismo

I would like to conclude by linking the rhetorical and discursive reading explored in the previous section with the ideological and political motives implied in the parallelisms between a Colonial Rhetoric and a minority discourse. In his book *Colonial Encounters*, Peter Hulme defines colonial discourse by linking a verbal and a political approach:

> The general area within which this study operates could then be named colonial discourse, meaning by that term an ensemble of linguistically-based practices unified by their common deployment in the management of colonial relationships, an ensemble that could combine the most formulaic and bureaucratic of official documents . . . with the most non-functional and unprepossessing of romantic novels. . . . Underlying the idea of colonial discourse, in other words, is the presumption that during the colonial period large parts of the non-European world were *produced* for Europe through a discourse that imbricated sets of questions and

28. On Columbus's hybrid Spanish, see Juan Gil, introduction, in Cristóbal Colón, *Textos y documentos completos* (Madrid, 1997), 15–79, esp. 31–63. The second chapter of Beatriz Pastor's *Discursos narrativos de la conquista: mitificación y emergencia* (Hanover, N.H., 1988) reconstructs the conflictive relationship between Cortés and Diego de Velázquez and traces the discursive strategies used by Cortés in the "Segunda carta" to legitimize his position as an ideal vassal of Carlos V.

assumptions, methods of procedure and analysis, and kinds of writing and imagery, normally separated out into the discrete areas of military strategy, political order, social reform, imaginative literature, personal memoir and so on.[29]

Hulme later points out, "The colonial discourse studied here cannot remain as a set of merely linguistic and rhetorical features, but must be related to its function within a broader set of socioeconomic and political practices: it must be read, that is to say, as an ideology." Deleuze and Guattari, Michel de Certeau, Adorno, Albert Memmi, and Bhabha all stress in their works the need to acknowledge the political and ideological specificities of the colonial context. Beatriz Pastor, in her foundational *Discursos narrativos de la conquista,* also establishes a crucial link between discursive and linguistic analysis and the ideological and political context of colonialism in Latin America. My reading is also informed by Zamora's linkage of the verbal paradigm of lack and excess with a political or ideological interpretation within a colonial context: "Difference could be represented as an absence, a lack or deficiency, but it could *not* be valueless or value-neutral." Although Zamora is referring here to the depiction of the Amerindians as inferior and lacking civilization, I would like to extend this strategy of her reading to the discursive and rhetorical analysis I am proposing here. Verbal lack and discursive excess become in this context the two extremes in a linguistic spectrum that implies an exercise of power over the Americas. As a result, verbal lack, or aphasia, represents a lack of control or comprehension of the American otherness that is usually portrayed as a deficiency or sign of inferiority of the colonial subject. Linguistic excess, in contrast, is an exercise of individual or collective power in which the narrative voice exhibits its control over the American reality represented. Between these two extremes, there is a diversity of verbal strategies that reveal the gradual appropriation of writing as a technology of representation, a process that includes what Ross conceives as the rewriting of narratives of conquest by creole subjects during the seventeenth century, and later on the emergence of differentiated identity discourses that will eventually become the foundation of the national identities in the Americas.[30]

In the theoretical model I propose here, colonial criollismo becomes another instance in a series of discursive and cultural practices in which the ambiguity

29. Peter Hulme, *Colonial Encounters: Europe and the Native Caribbean, 1492–1797* (New York, 1992), 2.

30. Ibid., 5; Zamora, *Reading Columbus,* 160; Ross, *The Baroque Narrative,* 7.

of coloniality is manifested. If the early texts produced by Spanish conquistadors and colonial functionaries share rhetorical strategies with indigenous, mestizo, and creole texts, the common denominator of all of these textual practices is the marginal and subordinate position of the Americas vis-à-vis the European epistemic and political world order. In this sense, the locus of enunciation within the colonial-imperial system becomes more important than the specific ethnic identity or place of origin of the speaking subject. In this approach, coloniality reemerges as a very crucial element for the constitution of an American identity. In the case of creole discourse this specific sociopolitical context produces a particular inflection of criollismo that must be clearly distinguished from the nationalist discourses that will emerge during the eighteenth and nineteenth centuries. Perhaps by exploring the shared rhetorical strategies we could deepen our knowledge of what is specifically colonial in indigenous, European, mestizo, mulatto, and creole discourses.

Minority discourse allows my analysis to focus on the internal ambiguity—both cultural and political—that is crucial in the definition of a colonial discourse. It also makes it possible for us to detect the varying degrees of subalternity and hegemony that characterize the perspectives of most of these texts. Columbus, Cortés, and Las Casas, but also el Inca Garcilaso, Sor Juana Inés de la Cruz, and Alonso Ramírez (the narrator of Carlos de Sigüenza y Góngora's *Infortunios de Alonso Ramírez*, 1690), are all subjects in between cultures, epistemological paradigms, and political centers of power. Their texts are simultaneously mimetic and disruptive of an imperial order at the same time they illustrate the paradoxical nature of otherness, so different yet so familiar. The colonial subject as a producer of a minority discourse becomes the source of an ambivalent perspective that desires, simultaneously, to be equated with a metropolitan subject while retaining some sort of local legitimacy. Finally, linking colonialism and minority discourses allows us to broaden Nathan Wachtel's and Miguel León Portilla's proposals to rescue the "vision of the vanquished" by including new dimensions of the indigenous and metropolitan voices that currently define the corpus of colonial writings. For example, this could be done by exploring the paradoxical subalternity of Las Casas, the Inca Garcilaso, or Alvar Núñez Cabeza de Vaca, given their complicity with local and metropolitan centers of power or their privileged condition vis-à-vis the majority of the indigenous populations that they were so invested in representing and defending. Perhaps one of the most important contributions of this link between colonial and minority discourses is the possibility of studying the multiple nuances of hegemony and subalternity, a central issue not only for the decolonization of our field of studies but also for the redefinition of our notions of identity, subjectivity, and their relationship to power, a topic so frequently essentialized in contemporary cultural and literary studies.[31]

31. For the theoretical elaboration of the "vision of the vanquished," see Nathan Wachtel, *La vision des vaincus: les Indiens du Pérou devant la conquête espagnole, 1530–1570* (Paris, 1971); Miguel León Portilla, ed., *Visión de los vencidos: crónicas indígenas* (Madrid, 1985).

PART II

The Cultural Geography of Creole Aesthetics

STEPHANIE MERRIM

Sor Juana Criolla and the Mexican Archive:
Public Performances

¿Quién pudiera poner en la memoria

. . . .

Solo un cuidado y una sola historia?

Who could place in memory a single concern and a single history?
—Bernardo de Balbuena, *Siglo de oro en las selvas de Erífile* (1608)

Sor Juana's World and the Mexican Archive

Saul Steinberg's pop classic 1976 print, *View of the World from Ninth Avenue,* gives us a witty, trenchant, conceptual map of the New Yorker's world-view. New York City and its towering buildings stand at the heart of that world, dominating it. The New Yorker's myopic view then leaps to New Jersey and from there telescopes immediately to the West Coast and, faintly, to the Orient and Siberia.

How might Sor Juana Inés de la Cruz's "View of the World" from seventeenth-century Mexico City look? We often train our sights on Sor Juana's literary panorama, so international and transhistorical; let us now situate her physically, contextually, locally. Cloistered as she was for more than half of her life (from 1669 to 1695) in the Mexico City Convent of San Jerónimo, a map of the world in which Sor Juana lived as she perceived it in her mind's eye would likely be even more schematic and conceptual than Steinberg's. Her inscape would not necessarily look much like the physical Mexico City of the seventeenth century. Rather, especially given the embattled circumstances of Sor Juana's life, it would comprise not only actual places but equally and indistinctively local force fields, the power brokers, hierarchies, and competing constituencies particular to her

Portions of this essay, especially those relating to *El Divino Narciso,* draw on my forthcoming book, *The Spectacular City, Mexico, and Colonial Hispanic Literary Culture.*

time and space. Beyond the obvious monoliths of church and state, a conjectural map or maps of Sor Juana's world would need to depict a broad, variegated landscape of interacting bodies—social, religious, civil, and geographical—each of which radiated very specific energies and connotations in the colonial milieu. These intensely politicized and nuanced entities, though almost invisible to us now or as opaque as hieroglyphs, were charged, palpitating, compelling bodies for Sor Juana. They conceivably pressed on almost her every move.

We can begin to envision Sor Juana's complex territory, with its bodies and their interactions. In proportions that shifted for the nun-writer throughout her life, the ethnic and *social bodies* of the map would include Indians, blacks, individuals of mixed race, creoles (Mexicans of European heritage), *gachupines* (Spaniards recently arrived in New Spain), *radicados* (Spaniards rooted in the New World), and viceregal Spanish personages. Hieronymites (Sor Juana's own order), Jesuits, and Franciscans would likely constitute the main *religious bodies* and the most powerful, conflicting entities of her map. Religion was politics, theology was ideology, as Octavio Paz observes. Hence, from the time that they burst onto the Mexican scene in 1572 onward, the worldly, wealthy, intellectually humanist Jesuits often clashed with the ascetic, orthodox Mendicant orders, principally with the founding Franciscans. Along the way, religious bodies formed alliances with social groups. Jesuits aligned themselves significantly with the creoles, Franciscans often with the Indians. The fact that Sor Juana's convent largely housed creole women, together with the leading role of the Society of Jesus in the intelligentsia, assigned Jesuit concerns a prominent place in her compass. *Civil bodies* had their own compasses, with the city council, or *cabildo,* from its beginnings run by the creoles and the *audiencia,* or high court, by Spaniards.[1]

Religious orders and their particular agendas inflected the *geographical bodies* that would figure prominently in Sor Juana's purview. Jesuits held much sway in Mexico City. On the other hand, Puebla de los Angeles, the second city of New Spain (founded in 1530 by the Franciscans), often pitted itself against Mexico City and the Jesuits. As treatises on the two cities by the Franciscan Augustín de Vetancurt in his *Teatro mexicano* [Mexican Treasury] (1697–1698) make clear, Puebla continued to view itself as the space of origins, pro-Indian evangelizing, and purity, versus the allegedly lapsed, decadent Mexico City. Sor Juana's geographical purview would also include her birthplace, Nepantla, and Oaxaca, where religious ceremonies of her composition were performed. Finally, and far

1. Octavio Paz, *Sor Juana; or, The Traps of Faith,* trans. Margaret Sayers Peden (Cambridge, Mass., 1988), 56.

more telescopically than the West Coast for the New Yorker, Spain loomed large on Sor Juana's horizon. Sometimes close by and sometimes distant, sometimes connected to viceregal Mexico in a direct line, and sometimes in a broken or intermittent one, Spain impinged on her daily, local reality.[2]

The foregoing map quite literally lays the groundwork for the present essay, which contends that Sor Juana bears both in her mind's eye and intensely in her literary mind the force fields just articulated and that she plays to them in her writings, especially in her work intended for Europe and for public performance. A cultural politics of this nature often undergirds Sor Juana's literary efforts, and we clearly need to read the nun-writer as a "reader" of her landscape in all its minute, politicized particularity. Sor Juana's literary production can take on a very new look, can become a fascinatingly different topography of agendas and ideologies and strategies, when viewed through the full grid of local pressures so present to her.

Although, when we project the map that I have tentatively sketched onto the vast map, or corpus of critical work on Sor Juana, a few of its signal bodies go missing or remain underinvestigated, modern approaches to Sor Juana have begun to flesh out the contextual terrain and hold great promise for the future. Some of the most lively studies to date, evolving from new archival work per se, attempt to untangle Sor Juana's relationship to then contemporary theological discourse, the Jesuits, and the Inquisition. Their findings remain open to debate, but they have dramatically refocused attention onto Sor Juana's cultural politics and local milieu. Other innovative studies deal with Sor Juana as a paradigmatic creole in a richly positional sense, that is, as a colonial subject divided between Mexico and Spain and as a broker of Indian, African, and feminine subalterns to the metropolis. Such studies have afforded us superb work on subjects like Sor Juana's representation of Indian and African voices in her religious ceremonies and theater.[3]

2. Agustín de Vetancurt, *Teatro mexicano: descripción breve de los sucessos exemplares dela Nueva-España en el Nuevo Mundo occidental de las Indias* (Madrid, 1960), II.

3. All citations in this essay to Sor Juana's works refer to Alfonso Méndez Plancarte's edition, Sor Juana Inés de la Cruz, *Obras completas*, 4 vols. (Mexico City, 1951–1957) (I: *Lírica personal;* III: *Autos y loas;* IV [ed. Alberto G. Salceda]: *Comedias, sainetes, y prosa*), cited hereafter as *Obras.* I have translated into English quotations from secondary sources in Spanish and provide the Spanish and English for primary sources. All translations are mine. The archival work to which I refer involves the magnificent flurry of activity around Sor Juana's sole explicit theological treatise, the *Carta atenagórica* (*Obras*, IV): its intertextuality, the debates that it provoked at the time, and its repercussions on her life—including, according to some, a possible secret Inquisition trial. For a summary and biting critique of these debates, see Antonio Alatorre and Martha Lilia Tenorio, *Serafina y Sor Juana* (Mexico City, 1998). As my text suggests, despite this reinvigoration of interest in Sor Juana's context, much work remains to be done in terms of her

Implicated in or incumbent upon this "creole" perspective is a perhaps less theoretical but no less gripping or theorizable construction of Sor Juana criolla: a consideration of her relationship to creole writers of her times (including, but extending far beyond her much-vaunted connections to Carlos de Sigüenza y Góngora). Similarly, and perhaps most important in that it subsumes all of the above considerations, one would want to attend to Sor Juana's interactions with every aspect and with the full chronological sweep of Mexican discursive tradition, or what I will call the *Mexican Archive*.

It is not simply logical but utterly inevitable that from her creole-dominated convent Sor Juana pored over works published in Mexico, for they were available and sanctioned. It is equally inevitable that Sor Juana's writing itself engaged not just with the theological but also with the literary and historiographic works most familiar to her milieu and that she deployed the Mexican Archive in toto both cannily and to advantage, as a locus of all sorts of fine, coded politics. In terms of Mexican authors, we know, for example, that Sor Juana directly cites in her work theologian and university chancellor Juan Díaz de Arce, Franciscan historian Juan de Torquemada, Jesuit poet Francisco de Castro, and, of course, Sigüenza y Góngora. However, more than to direct citation, Sor Juana tends to a diffuse intertextuality, to allusion and silent quotation. What other Mexican influences lurk in her works?[4]

Trying to answer the question brings us face-to-face with some seeming positives that turn into startling negatives. For, rather than deterring scholars, Sor Juana's elusive intertextual modus operandi has in fact provoked them. I refer, most notably, to Alfonso Méndez Plancarte, the editor in the 1950s of her *Obras completas* as well as of the fullest modern compendium of colonial poetry (the three-volume *Poetas novohispanos*), and to Octavio Paz, author of the encyclopedic *Sor Juana* (1981). The two Mexican scholars sleuth zealously for the nun's literary sources but not, counterintuitive as it seems, in the Mexican arena. Méndez Plancarte and Paz, propelled by their own set of nationalistic

---

literary criollismo. Works on the ambiguous identity of the creole to which I refer here include Yolanda Martínez–San Miguel, *Saberes americanos: subalternidad y epistemología en los escritos de Sor Juana* (Pittsburgh, 1999); José Antonio Mazzotti, ed., *Agencias criollas: la ambigüedad "colonial" en las letras hispanoamericanas* (Minneapolis, Minn., 2000); Mabel Moraña, *Viaje al silencio: exploraciones del discurso barroco* (Mexico City, 1998); Kathleen Ross, *The Baroque Narrative of Carlos de Sigüenza y Góngora: A New World Paradise* (New York, 1993); Georgina Sabat de Rivers, *En busca de Sor Juana* (Mexico City, 1998).

4. Juan Díaz de Arce figures prominently in the *Respuesta a Sor Filotea de la Cruz* (*Obras*, IV). Sor Juana refers to Juan de Torquemada in the *Neptuno* (*Obras*, IV, 385); dedicates her Guadalupan sonnet (*Obras*, I, no. 206) to Francisco de Castro; praises Sigüenza y Góngora's contribution to the 1680 festival in her Sonnet 204 (*Obras*, I). She dedicates other of her works to important viceregal figures, particularly to Jesuits.

concerns, have strived to establish Sor Juana as a world-class writer who wields the tabernacle of Western culture in defiance of colonialist intellectual oppression. Instead of Mexicanizing Sor Juana, they consequently and principally universalize her. With good reason, as we will see, the two scholars unearth European allusions in the nun's work, be they contemporary Spanish or classical, biblical, and patristic. Méndez Plancarte, for example, provides no New World references for the Eucharistic drama, *El Divino Narciso* [The Divine Narcissus] (subject of much of this essay) other than a couple of links to the Colombian colonial writers Hernando Domínguez Camargo and the Madre Castillo. Paz's universalizing agenda for Mexican culture in general and for Sor Juana in particular (he sees Sor Juana as moved by a "universalist esthetic") similarly short-shrifts the Mexican literary environment. Thus in the 1950s Méndez Plancarte set, and Paz ratified in the 1980s, an influential course that has guided and misguided Sor Juana scholarship. Oddly enough, contemporary Mexican cultural politics, as enacted by two authors uniquely qualified to establish Sor Juana as a Mexican or creole writer, have occluded her own conceivable Mexican cultural politics.[5]

In 1987, Rafael Catalá began in earnest to read the colonial Baroque against the universalizing grain. His *Para una lectura americana del barroco mexicano* [For an American Reading of the Mexican Baroque] claims that the preponderance of critical work on the subject has neglected to consider "the influence of Spanish-American writers on one another" and that the American Baroque, "itself hybrid, demands a reading from the viewpoint of hybridity [*mestizaje*]." Catalá's study, like a few others that surround it, performs an American reading of the Mexican Baroque that exposes reverberations of colonial writers, creole patriotism, and Aztec imagery in Sor Juana's work, primarily in her *Neptuno alegórico* [Allegorical Neptune] and *Primero sueño* [First Dream]. The intertextual approach that Catalá essays, his mining of the Mexican Archive, gains further dimension from Kathleen Ross's axiomatic assertion, "Baroque literature in Spanish America was the vehicle through which the criollos, or American-born Spaniards, engaged in an intertextual dialogue with the sixteenth century . . . with a literary history that had become their own as well as Europe's." As Ross intimates, intertextuality in a colonial milieu is rarely a mere formal exercise, for authors or critics. Colonial authors instrumentalize

<hr />

5. Alfonso Méndez Plancarte, ed., *Poetas novohispanos: primer siglo (1521–1621)*, 3 vols. (Mexico City, 1942–1945). On universalizing trends in modern Mexican criticism, see Deborah N. Cohn, "La construcción de la identidad cultural en México: nacionalismo, cosmopolitismo, e infraestructura intelectual, 1945–1968," *Foro hispánico*, XXII (2002), 89–103. The quote is from Paz, *Sor Juana*, 57–58.

intertexts, creating substrata teeming with political business and hidden polemics. In the case of Sor Juana and on the most overarching level, intertextual
relations with the Mexican Archive continually authorize her audacious, innovative writing in the volatile, orthodox, and misogynist environment of colonial New Spain.[6]

More specifically, not only does the Mexican Archive constitute an important
locus of Sor Juana's cultural politics, but her *criollismo*—in the intertextual and
positional senses—depends profoundly on it. The Mexican Archive affords her
creole texts past and present as well as the platform on which she builds bridges
between the New and Old Worlds. It allows her to exhibit, often to Spain,
representations of Mexican culture that in their sublimity and gravitas transcend the parodic, comical portrayal of Mexican diversity found in the nun's
carnivalesque religious festivals written for the colony. Sor Juana's relationship
to the Mexican Archive, I believe, proves to be just as enthralling and rich as her
engagement with Western culture at large, and a crucial piece of that engagement as well.

To put into meaningful action the array of issues raised up to this point, the
present essay examines works in which Sor Juan draws on the Mexican Archive
to perform her criollismo, her inscape, and Mexico itself—predominantly, texts
that she intended for public presentation. Before proceeding to the texts, however, an essential caveat is in order. The diffuse, elusive nature of Sor Juana's
intertextuality mentioned above requires acknowledgment of the fact that to
search for resonances of the Mexican Archive in her work is to enter a slippery,
unseizable territory.

Take, as a cardinal example and one relevant to the concerns of this study,
the enigmas surrounding the nun's involvement with the pivotal issue of
seventeenth-century Mexican creole patriotism, the Virgin of Guadalupe. Despite or perhaps because of her order's special relationship with the *Spanish*
Guadalupe, Sor Juana only once writes explicitly about the Mexican or any
Guadalupe, in Sonnet 206, to Jesuit Francisco de Castro. Nevertheless (in a rare
excursion into Sor Juana's Mexican Archive), scholars have asserted that Sor

---

6. Rafael Catalá, *Para una lectura americana del barroco mexicano: Sor Juana Inés de la Cruz y
Sigüenza y Góngora* (Minneapolis, Minn., 1987), 102, 123; Ross, *Baroque Narrative*, 7. Other
studies along the lines of Catalá's, in addition to the works on the creole Sor Juana already
mentioned, include Frederick Luciano, "The *Comedia de San Francisco de Borja* (1640): The
Mexican Jesuits and the 'Education of the Prince,'" *Colonial Latin American Review*, II (1993), 121–
141; María Esther Pérez, *Lo americano en el teatro de Sor Juana Inés de la Cruz* (New York, 1975).
Marie-Cécile Bénassy-Berling's superb and seminal *Humanisme et religion chez Sor Juana Inés de
la Cruz: la femme et la culture au XVIIe siècle* (Paris, 1982) is deeply contextual and remains an
indispensable source for the focus that I propose as well as for many others.

Juana draws on the Guadalupan work of creole Jesuit Miguel Sánchez, who once served as chaplain to the nuns of San Jerónimo. Sor Juana, they maintain, utilizes the connections that Sánchez's influential 1648 Guadalupan treatise establishes between the Mexican icon and the "black but beautiful" protagonist of the Song of Songs *and* the woman of the Apocalypse adorned with the sun, moon, and stars of Revelation 12:1–2. The myriad references in Sor Juana's writings to the preceding figures, therefore, may well allude to the Virgin of Guadalupe.[7]

That Sor Juana indeed fragments the Virgin of Guadalupe into her constituent attributes and scatters them throughout her works is eminently possible and even highly probable, yet impossible to determine absolutely. The same contingency holds for the subjects of the present essay. Sor Juana writes in a force field, the colonial arena, that warrants indirection, and in a literary mode, the Mexican Baroque, that is multiplicity incarnate. The Baroque Sor Juana, to use the words of my epigraph, no doubt endeavors to place in memory more than a single concern or a single history, but exactly how many or which stories is a matter of informed speculation and considered judgment, even for Méndez Plancarte. I leave the final judgment on my attempts to the reader.

Sor Juana: Mexican and Criolla

Particularly in view of the circumlocutions imputed to the nun vis-à-vis the Virgin of Guadalupe, one wonders how much, if left to her own devices, Sor Juana would have confronted head-on Mexican or New World issues. Her private work and her work intended for the Mexican court evince hardly any overt preoccupation with such matters. Conversely, her writings for public ceremonies, religious and civil, and for Europe throng with them. In other words, Sor Juana's American leanings come into clearest focus in public and/or in gestalt with Europe. There they often enter into concert with the author's literary self-fashioning, her self-presentation to powerful groups. Two such performances of and by the Mexican Sor Juana pulsate with creole texts and contexts that have not yet fully come to light: Romance 37, to the

7. Sonnet 206, *Obras*, I. In 1386, Alfonso XI entrusted to the Hieronymites the most important Marian shrine in Spain, the monastery of Our Lady of Guadalupe in Estremadura, which housed her image (D. A. Brading, *Mexican Phoenix: Our Lady of Guadalupe: Image and Tradition across Five Centuries* [Cambridge, 2001], 36–37; also the source for information on Sánchez and Sor Juana's convent [73]). On Sor Juana and the Virgin of Guadalupe, see George H. Tavard, *Juana Inés de la Cruz and the Theology of Beauty: The First Mexican Theology* (Notre Dame, Ind., 1991), chap. 3; Pamela Kirk, *Sor Juana Inés de la Cruz: Religion, Art, and Feminism* (New York, 1998), chap. 3; Bénassy-Berling, *Humanisme et religion*, part 3, chap. 4.

Portuguese María de Guadalupe Alencastre, duchess de Aveyro, and the *Neptuno alegórico.*[8]

Writing to the European duchess de Aveyro, cousin of the nun's patroness (the countess de Paredes, vicereine from 1680 to 1688) and a learned woman and benefactor of New World Jesuit orders, Sor Juana projects herself from America to Europe on "alas de papel frágil" [wings of fragile paper]. As if in a mystical bilocation, through her writing Sor Juana crosses the ocean to arrive at the feet of the powerful duchess. With Sor Juana arrives America. In the famous second movement of the romance that starts with line 81, the poet indulges in a self-stated digression on the New World. Sor Juana begins her riff by conflating herself with the New World, presenting herself as the best of it, in order to protest that neither she nor it requires the patronage of the duchess. (Sor Juana insinuates at the end of the poem that on her own, without the New World, she is "nadie," or no one, who must prostrate herself at the feet of the influential duchess.) From here, Sor Juana launches into the sole outright defense of the New World in all of her poetic works, punctuated by a profession of "dulce afición," or sweet affection, for her "Patria."[9]

Significantly enough, that defense replays several topics enshrined in the Mexican historiographic Archive, including the most consecrated topics of Mexican creole discourse or complaint as it had emerged from the late sixteenth century on. Sor Juana begins by invoking the myths of Latin American abundance and spontaneous generation of natural resources, with no need of labor. Colonial historiography particularly owed this styling of the New World to Pedro Mártir de Anglería's *Décadas del Nuevo Mundo* [Decades of the New World] (1530); Mexican radicado Bernardo de Balbuena had echoed it in his *La grandeza mexicana* [Grandeur of Mexico] (1604), a poem that creole discourse had adopted because of its hyperbolic encomium of Mexico City. From Mártir's and Balbuena's shared colonialist commodity fetishism, however, Sor Juana immediately segues to the heart of traditional creole discourse per se, creole complaint of Spanish abuses (which we glimpse in the Suárez de Peralta of Kathleen Ross's splendid contribution to this volume). An insatiable Europe, Sor Juana says, has bled the mines of Mexico dry. Moreover, Spaniards—she refers to the gachupines despised by the creoles for usurping their territory— have populated Mexico and appropriated its riches, forgetting their homeland in the process.[10]

---

8. Romance 37, *Obras,* I; *Neptuno alegórico, Obras,* IV.

9. Romance 37, *Obras,* I, ll. 125–126, 178.

10. Pedro Mártir de Anglería [Pietro Martire d'Anghiera], *Décadas del Nuevo Mundo,* trans.

As any member of the *ciudad letrada,* or educated community, of her milieu would know, Sor Juana's protests had a long and famous lineage in Mexican discourse. She speaks in absolute unison with the tirades of creole Baltasar Dorantes de Carranza, whose 1604 *Sumaria relación de las cosas de la Nueva España con noticia individual de los descendientes legítimos de los conquistadores y primeros pobladores españoles* [Summary Account of the Affairs of New Spain with Specific Information on the Legitimate Descendants of the Conquerors and First Spanish Settlers] bitterly argued for the rights of creoles to the *encomiendas,* or grants of Indian labor, of which the viceregal government was depriving them. Dorantes' summary account is an archive unto itself of texts supporting the creole position, including poems of the Spanish expatriate Mateo Rosas de Oquendo that acerbically satirize the very issues that Sor Juana mentions. Sor Juana's lines resonate equally with Arias de Villalobos's 1623 wild *Canto intitulado Mercurio* [Song Named after Mercury], influenced by the Jesuit Baroque aesthetic, which echoes Dorantes' complaints, *and* with a couple of lines of Sigüenza y Góngora's picaresque protonovel of 1690, *Infortunios de Alonso Ramírez* [Misfortunes of Alonso Ramírez], which continue to bemoan Europe's rape of its colonies. Given the association between the creoles and the Jesuits discussed above, that Sor Juana should present their Portuguese patroness with a microcosm of creole discourse that includes flecks of lay Jesuit Sigüenza's writings does not much surprise. More surprising is the familiarity with the Mexican creole archive of much earlier times that Sor Juana here reveals as she presents herself to a European personage. She evokes for a relative of the countess de Paredes, the nun's strongest supporter in her time of troubles, an originary, fractured, contentious moment in Mexico's past that bears a striking resemblance to the nun-writer's present.[11]

In 1680, before she wrote Romance 37, the actual arrival of European personages in New Spain and the presumably creole-dominated *cabildo* (chapter) of

Joaquín Torres Asensio (Buenos Aires, 1944); Bernardo de Balbuena, *La grandeza mexicana y compendio apologético en alabanza de la poesía,* ed. Luis Adolfo Domínguez (Mexico City, 1985). On the relationship between Balbuena's poem and creole discourse, see Merrim, "La grandeza mexicana en el contexto criollo," in Mabel Moraña and Yolanda Martínez–San Miguel, eds., *Nictimene . . . sacrílega: estudios coloniales en homenaje a Georgina Sabat-Rivers* (Mexico City, 2003), 81–100.

11. Baltasar Dorantes de Carranza, *Sumaria relación de las cosas de la Nueva España con noticia individual de los descendientes legítimos de los conquistadores y primeros pobladores españoles,* ed. José María de Agreda y Sánchez (1902; rpt. Mexico City, 1970); Arias de Villalobos, *Canto entitulado Mercurio,* in Genaro García and Carlos Pereyra, eds., *Documentos inéditos ó muy raros para la historia de México* (Mexico City, 1905–1911), XII; Carlos de Sigüenza y Góngora, *Infortunios que Alonso Ramírez: natural de ciudad de San Juan de Puerto Rico, padeció,* ed. J. S. Cummins and Alan Soons (London, 1984).

the city cathedral had provided Sor Juana with an early venue for a public, published performance. To celebrate the ceremonial entry into Mexico City of the new viceroy and vicereine, the count and countess de Paredes, the cathedral and city cabildos had, respectively, commissioned upcoming Mexican intellectuals Sor Juana and Sigüenza to design ephemeral triumphal arches and to compose explanatory texts to accompany the arches. The archbishop and incumbent viceroy confirmed the cabildo's decision (as Sor Juana herself tells us in a letter to her confessor). Sigüenza's arch stood at the traditional entry point for dignitaries, the Plaza de Santo Domingo. Sor Juana's arch occupied the sacred center of the city, across from the unfinished cathedral.[12]

The opportunities and perils of the supremely public situation did not escape the fledgling "Tenth Muse." In the prose explanation of her arch ("Razón de la fábrica") Sor Juana makes much of the cabildo's mandate and little of her person, formulaically debasing herself. She writes that she would have excused herself from so great an undertaking "a no haber intervenido insinuación que mi rendimiento venera con fuerza de mandato" from the "Venerable Cabildo" [had not the Venerable Cabildo intervened with a suggestion that my pliancy venerates as having the force of a mandate]. She says that the cabildo had apparently deemed the "blandura inculta de una mujer" [uncultivated gentleness of a woman] more effective for the occasion than the "elocuencia de tantas y tan doctas plumas" [eloquence of so many and so learned pens] of men. Sor Juana's radar for the fraught nature of the occasion and its political dynamics drives the prose and poetic texts written for the ceremony, her *Neptuno alegórico*. More than merely, as it were, assuming an abject position in the *Neptuno*, to legitimate and ingratiate herself Sor Juana trades on certain aspects of Jesuit discourse and on the Mexican Archive. The nun's tactics for her major public debut in Mexico, I should note before detailing them, proved both wholly warranted and insufficient. As Beatriz Mariscal Hay has argued, the fact that rising star Sor Juana and not her eminent Jesuit confessor, the severely orthodox Antonio Núñez de Miranda, was chosen as bard of the occasion catalyzed tensions between them that resulted in his slandering of her and her breaking with him not long after the 1680 ceremony.[13]

Sanctioned by the archbishop and the incumbent viceroy but caught in a minefield of Jesuit tensions, Sor Juana cautiously infuses her *Neptuno* with

12. Aureliano Tapia Méndez, *Carta de Sor Juana Inés de la Cruz a su confesor: autodefensa espirituel* (Monterrey, 1986), 15–17.

13. *Neptuno alegórico, Obras,* IV, 357–358; Beatriz Mariscal Hay, " 'Una mujer ignorante': Sor Juana, interlocutora de virreyes," in Sara Poot Herrera, ed., *Y diversa de mí misma entre vuestras plumas ando: homenaje internacional a Sor Juana Inés de la Cruz* (Mexico City, 1993), 91–99.

the Egyptology characteristic of the famed contemporary *German* Jesuit who wrote from the Vatican, Athanasius Kircher (1602–1680). The *Neptuno*'s central premise of praising the viceroy by extensively attributing to him the virtues of Neptune—whom the text posits as son of Isis, Egyptian goddess of wisdom— meshes with Kircher's concerns. It replicates Kircher's general fascination with Egypt as the cradle of civilization no less than his particular obsession with Isis. And Isis, the magnetic if not the ostensible center of the *Neptuno,* of course enables Sor Juana to showcase the learned woman and thus indirectly to promote herself.

The Egyptian leanings of Sor Juana's *Neptuno* deviated sharply from those of Sigüenza in his arch and text (*Teatro de virtudes políticos que constituyen a un príncipe* [Treasury of the Political Virtues That Constitute a Prince]). Sigüenza's *Teatro* places Neptune in service of creole patriotism by associating him with the Egyptian origins of Mexico alleged by Kircher. If not as radical as Sigüenza's Neptune, Sor Juana's makes an equally dramatic political statement. By invoking Kircher's Egyptology in a somewhat decorative but still deeply functional way, Sor Juana at once aligns herself with local Jesuits and transcends localisms. She tacitly, or maybe quite obviously for her milieu, pits the brilliant, universal, eclectic, but still Vatican-sanctioned Kircher, with his predilection for the female Isis, against the more constraining Núñez de Miranda and other Mexican Jesuits of his ilk. As the soul casts off the material body in the nun's *Primero sueño,* so does Sor Juana in the *Neptuno* subtly cast off repressive local Jesuits for the universal Kircher.[14]

At the same time as Sor Juana vaunts her ties in the *Neptuno* with Jesuits and their epistemology, she also activates entrenched pieces of the Mexican Archive for general consumption and effect. Where Sigüenza, outright creole patriot, provides a list in his *Teatro* of texts from the Mexican Archive that have sung the praises of the capital, Sor Juana quietly embodies fragments of her country's collective imaginary, starting with Neptune. Not at random do both Sor Juana and Sigüenza choose Neptune as the theme of their contribution to the festivities. God of the waters who carried a trident evocative of the Trinity, Neptune had a natural pertinence to the watery Mexico City originally built on canals and to the Spanish Christianizing mission. Neptune also had a literary genealogy in Mexico. In the late 1590s, at the time that the Jesuits were first introducing Mannerism to New Spain, *radicado* Eugenio de Salazar y Alarcón produced his outrageously avant-garde colonialist pastoral poem, "Bucólica:

14. Carlos de Sigüenza y Góngora, *Teatro de virtudes políticas que constituyen a un príncipe,* in William G. Bryant, ed., *Seis obras* (Caracas, 1984), 165–240.

descripción de la laguna de Méjico" [Bucolic: Description of Mexico's Lagoon], in which Neptune figures prominently. Salazar's mythological and metaphorical version of the conquest, a portrayal of Viceroy Alvaro Manrique de Zúñiga and his wife, has Neptune riding triumphantly into Mexico City atop a huge whale, attired in shining pearls and holding a trident as his standard. The Jesuit-influenced, Mannerist, avant-garde audacity of the "Bucólica," a precedent for Sor Juana's, together with the fashion in which Neptune's whale ride tropes both the conquest and the ceremonial entry of a viceroy into Mexico City, might well have appealed to the nun-writer. For, unlike Sigüenza's *Teatro*, her *Neptuno* places the sea god–viceroy at the helm of a ship in an allegory of the viceroy's ruling Mexico according to God's law. The later paean of the "Bucólica" to the "whiteness" and fidelity of the vicereine finds its match (though without the disturbing racial overtones) in Sor Juana's unusual and prescient inclusion of the vicereine in her text as a "refulgente estrella" [refulgent star] and "fidelísima esposa" [most faithful wife]. Sigüenza, we see, is not Sor Juana's only Mexican conversation partner in the *Neptuno*. Once again she reaches out to the beginning of the century, now to its aesthetic as well as its political agenda.[15]

An analogous Mexican dynamic obtains in Sor Juana's inscribing of her *Neptuno* in the genre of Mirror for Princes, or *de regimine principum*. Both Sor Juana and Sigüenza utilize the genre, which allows subjects to offer advice to rulers, and both tender similar recommendations for the viceroy. More, and more precise, aspects of the local Mexican reality than found elsewhere in Sor Juana's works make their way into the *Neptuno* under the aegis of the Mirror for Princes. So, too, does the Mexican Archive. The Mirror of Princes had already entered Mexico in several prestigious works, including but not limited to the *Túmulo imperial* [Imperial Tomb] (1560) by Francisco Cervantes de Salazar, first professor of rhetoric at the Mexican university; in the ponderous prefatory materials of Balbuena's *La grandeza mexicana,* the very second work published in seventeenth-century Mexico (the first is lost); and in the *Historia real sagrada, luz de príncipes y súbditos* [Royal Sacred History, Light of Princes and Subjects] (1643) by Juan de Palafox y Mendoza, briefly the viceroy and then famed pro-Indian, anti-Jesuit bishop of Puebla. While conceivably bearing in

15. Ibid., 203. On Mexican Mannerism, see Jorge Alberto Manrique, *Manierismo en México* (Mexico City, 1993); Eugenio de Salazar y Alarcón, "Bucólica: descripción de la laguna de Méjico," in Bartolomé José Gallardo and Marcelino Menéndez y Pelayo, eds., *Ensayo de una biblioteca española de libros raros y curiosos* (Madrid, 1889), IV, 362–370; *Neptuno alegórico, Obras,* IV, 398, 401.

mind various branches of the illustrious tradition, Sor Juana ostentatiously reenacts the extravagant etymological wordplay with the dignitary's name that Balbuena had executed in *La grandeza mexicana*. In taking Balbuena's verbal gymnastics as the modus operandi for several key pages of the *Neptuno*'s counsel to the viceroy, Sor Juana steps into the literary politics of *Grandeza*, often viewed as constituting the origins of a Mexican Baroque *before* the literary mode was significantly imported from the metropolis, Spain. The *Neptuno* has thus stealthily staged for the incoming viceroy a veritable retrospective of Mexican concerns, creole-Jesuit and literary. Only *El Divino Narciso*, the genuine theatrical performance to which we now turn, would rival or outdo the Mexican energies of the *Neptuno*.[16]

El Divino Narciso: Spain, Mexico, and the Mexican Archive

The *Neptuno* evidences the alacrity and expertness with which Sor Juana wielded Baroque public statecraft, skewing it toward Mexico and into the service of her personal interests. With fierce storm clouds gathering around her in Mexico by 1688, a unique opportunity arose for the nun to present herself and her writings to Europe. The count and countess de Paredes were in that year called back to Spain, leaving Sor Juana bereft of her greatest allies. In consolation, they carried with them her complete works, the first installment of which the countess would have published in 1689 as the *Inundación castálida* [Overflowing of the Castalian Spring]. Sor Juana's oeuvre transported to Spain included *El Divino Narciso*, a dramatic work comprising a *loa* (short introductory play) and an *auto sacramental* (Eucharistic drama). As the subtitle of one edition of the work tells us, Sor Juana wrote *El Divino Narciso* at the behest of the vicereine shortly before she left Mexico "to be taken to the court in Madrid so that it could be performed there," presumably in the Madrid feast of Corpus Christi in 1689. *El Divino Narciso* did not find publication in the initial edition of the *Inundación*, reaching print only in subsequent Spanish tomes of Sor Juana's works and as a volume unto itself in Mexico in 1690. Nevertheless, the play emits strong signals indicating that Sor Juana intended it as her debut in Spain, arguably as a trailer, or advertisement, for the publication of her complete works shortly to follow.[17]

16. For echoes of *Grandeza*'s wordplay, see *Neptuno*, *Obras*, IV, 369–372, 378.
17. Sor Juana Inés de la Cruz, *Inundación castálida*, ed. Georgina Sabat de Rivers (Madrid, 1982); *El Divino Narciso* and its loa, in *Obras*, III, and subtitle, *Obras*, III, 513. *El Divino Narciso*

With the stakes imponderably high, the three staples that had previously galvanized Sor Juana's recourse to the Mexican Archive—public performance, European audience, self-presentation—now converge. And in *El Divino Narciso,* as I want to argue, Sor Juana works them for all they are worth. She works them flamboyantly and mutely, for a Spanish and a Mexican milieu, as a Mexican and as a transatlantic, or creole, writer. In so doing, Sor Juana draws deeply and more broadly than before on the Mexican Archive, and more than in her other Eucharistic dramas or their loas. Critical studies have well investigated many Mexican aspects and polemics of the famous loa to *El Divino Narciso.* I aim to demonstrate that the exacerbated, high stakes of *El Divino Narciso's* praxis catapult *both* of its components, the loa and the auto sacramental, into sinuous, loaded performances of the Mexican Archive. Always with an eye to the organic relationship between its two components, my discussion of the important *El Divino Narciso* will focus successively on (1) the work as a whole, (2) the loa, (3) the auto sacramental. From all of this it will emerge that in *El Divino Narciso* Sor Juana stages a thesaurus of indigenous and creole concerns, truly a theatrical revue of the state of Mexican culture just as the bicentennial of Columbus's European discovery of the New World is coming onto the horizon.[18]

In both parts of *El Divino Narciso,* eager to make a mark, Sor Juana positions herself on the European horizon as a flaming, iconoclastic, distinctively Latin American "Phoenix." Assuming the role of rara avis from the colonies that Europe itself had exoticized, Sor Juana most flagrantly makes her mark by taking outrageous positions. In other of her works, partaking of New World writers' characteristic contestatory *self*-exoticizing and attuning it to her own circumstances, Sor Juana develops an iconography of anomaly that exploits rather than sidesteps her gender. Here (although, as we will see, she attaches some self-referentiality to the plays' female characters), the nun-writer plays extreme games that rely more heavily on literary and ideological moves than on gender. The extreme games of *El Divino Narciso* involve a "shock and awe" campaign in which Sor Juana brandishes her, and (by extension or explicitly) Mexico's, cultural originality or differential edge vis-à-vis Spain. They foreshadow Jorge Luis Borges' assertion in "The Argentine Writer and Tradition"

---

was first published in the third, or Barcelona, edition of vol. I of Sor Juana's complete works (1691) and again, with her other Eucharistic plays and their loas, in the second Spanish volume of Sor Juana's works in Seville, 1692 (Sabat de Rivers, *En busca de Sor Juana,* 266). See Martínez–San Miguel, *Saberes americanos,* chap. 5, for copious bibliography on *El Divino Narciso* (and p. 175 for a review of that bibliography).

18. The important loa to Sor Juana's Eucharistic play, *El mártir del Sacramento, San Hermenegildo* (*Obras,* III), also written for Spain, features Columbus himself and addresses New World issues. The auto itself, however, treats a chapter in the history of early Christian Spain.

that the Latin American writer can essay all received European themes, wield-
ing them with skill and with impunity.[19]

Consequently, the prime weapon in *El Divino Narciso's* extreme arsenal is
catachresis, first the catachrestic rendition in the auto sacramental of the then
popular classical myth of Narcissus. Sor Juana boldly projects the myth onto
the Eucharistic drama as follows in brief. Her *Kontrafaktur*, or spiritual rewriting of a secular work, makes Eco, conventionally a beautiful nymph whom Juno
punished for her loquacity, the devil. Devil-Eco and Naturaleza Humana [Hu-
man Nature] vie for the affections of Narciso, who in Sor Juana's bold version
represents Christ himself. Narciso-Christ arrives at a fountain that symbolizes
the Virgin Mary, redeemer of sinners. Eco has toiled mightily to cloud the
waters of the fountain in order to keep Narciso from seeing therein the image of
Naturaleza Humana. Yet, when Grace clears the waters, Christ-Narciso becomes enamored with that mirror image of himself and dies for love of her.
Narciso punishes Eco for her transgressions by depriving her of an autonomous
voice and by consigning her to a death-in-life of suffering. Naturaleza Humana,
on the other hand, finds herself redeemed and compensated for the loss of Narciso by his ever-renewable presence in the Eucharist, the triumphant appearance of which wraps up the play and confirms its nature as an auto sacramental.

Even the preceding schematic account of the play makes it clear that Sor
Juana has done extreme, if purposeful, violence to both the myth of Narcissus
and the Eucharistic drama. Though authorized by connections to plays by the
Spanish Pedro Calderón de la Barca and to other works of the period, Sor
Juana's drama remains jarringly catachrestic, to great effect and equally pur-
posefully. The auto gains riveting suspense and dramatic force from the myth
that it so radically disturbs. For an auto sacramental, in fact, it is a real cliff-

19. The epithet Phoenix of America was often applied to Sor Juana. On her iconography of
anomaly and early modern women writers' extreme games, see chaps. 1 and 2, respectively, of
Stephanie Merrim, *Early Modern Women's Writing and Sor Juana Inés de la Cruz* (Nashville, Tenn.,
1999). On colonial self-exoticizing in Latin America, Paz well notes: "To the baroque sensibility
the American world was marvelous. . . . Among all these American marvels there is one that from
the beginning, from the writings of Terrazas and Balbuena, was glorified by the criollo: his own
being. In the seventeenth century the aesthetic of the strange expressed with rapture the strange-
ness of the criollo" (*Sor Juana*, 58). On the same subject also see Roberto González Echevarría,
Celestina's Brood: Continuities of the Baroque in Spanish and Latin American Literatures (Durham,
N.C., 1993), chap. 6; Paz, *Sor Juana*, chap. 4; Stephanie Merrim, "Wonder and the Wounds of
'Southern' Histories," in Jon Smith and Deborah Cohn, eds., *Look Away! The U.S. South in New
World Studies* (Durham, N.C., 2004), 311–332; and Merrim, "Spectacular Cityscapes of Baroque
Spanish America," in Mario J. Valdés and Djelal Kadir, eds., *Literary Cultures of Latin America: A
Comparative History* (New York, 2004), III, 31–57. Jorge Luis Borges, "The Argentine Writer and
Tradition," *Labyrinths: Selected Stories and Other Writings*, trans. Donald A. Yates and James E.
Irby (New York, 1962), 177–185.

hanger, a truly virtuoso performance by an appropriately reverent and irreverent colonial Mexican "Phoenix." To promote herself as such, Sor Juana has taken calculated risks: however orthodox the denouement of the play, echoes of the myth's prideful, self-involved Narcissus could easily infiltrate and destabilize the auto. She both contains the danger and flaunts her originality by repeatedly explaining the overwrought allegorical mechanisms of the play. The female Religión (in the loa), Naturaleza Humana, and the Devil-Eco successively introduce and didactically elucidate the mix of pagan and sacred scripts in the auto. With the floating mistresses of ceremony, we see, Sor Juana serves up a complex composite portrait of (her) authorship in which the divine, the human, and the diabolical all meet. This new female trinity indexes the category-crossings bound up in the "Tenth Muse" herself, colonial supplement to the nine consecrated muses.[20]

For its part, the daring loa to *El Divino Narciso* exerts its extreme maneuvers directly on the colonial world and strikes at the heart of the Spanish colonial mission. The loa depicts Spanish efforts to convert the Aztecs to Christianity. Its second scene cuts right to a nerve as it dramatizes an internecine conflict about methods of conversion. Spanish Religión argues for peaceful evangelizing, and Spanish Celo (Zeal, in the form of a *conquistador*) for a violent approach. Celo initially has his brutal way. In a scene, or "scenario," remarkably akin to Pedro de Alvarado's massacre of the Aztecs, Celo attacks the Indians as they celebrate their God of the Seeds. Religión accuses him of effecting an offensive of punishment, terror, and revenge on America. The allegorical character América verbally assaults Celo as well, calling him a "barbarian" and a "madman" who has disrupted the calm that the Indians enjoy in "serena paz" [serene peace].[21]

---

20. Méndez Plancarte, in the introduction to *Obras*, III, and the notes to *El Divino Narciso* contained in that volume, provides a great sweep of Spanish sources for the auto. Bénassy-Berling, in *Humanisme et religion*, part 6, chap. 1, does the same, with an explicit focus on Sor Juana's anomalous rendition of the myth. Both scholars note that Sor Juana draws heavily not only on Calderón's *Eco y Narciso* but also on his *El Divino Orfeo*. That Sor Juana gives Narciso-Christ an orphic voice exalts poetry and by extension the author of *El Divino Narciso*. Yet, to read the female characters of the loa and the auto as figurations of Sor Juana is also to encounter in them, not the heroic Isis of the *Neptuno*, but Sor Juana's more characteristic refraction of the self into "dark" and "light" avatars.

21. Loa to *El Divino Narciso*, *Obras*, III, 9. In *The Archive and the Repertoire: Performing Cultural Memory in the Americas* (Durham, N.C., 2003), performance studies scholar Diana Taylor views "scenarios" as "culturally specific imaginaries—sets of possibilities, ways of conceiving conflict, crisis, or resolution—activated with more or less theatricality" (13) and as "meaning-making paradigms that structure social environments, behaviors, and potential outcomes," whose "portable framework bears the weight of accumulative repeats" (28). The conquest paradigm that Sor

Celo's aggression only occasions Indian resistance to Christianity. Hence, in its second movement the loa counters aggression with an intellectual, theological form of conquest that successfully persuades by bringing to light similarities between the Eucharist and Indian sacrifice (here, the ritual of *teocualo* that Juan de Torquemada described as the consumption of an image of Huitzilopochtli devised of seeds and blood). Such efforts on the part of Religión allow "divine inspiration" to enter the Indians and to sway them toward Christianity. Concomitantly, they bring the Spaniards into an understanding and appreciation of Indian religion as a meaningful system in its own right. Hence all, Spaniards and Indians alike, implausibly exit singing, "¡Dichoso el día / que conocí al gran Dios de las Semillas!" [Blessed was that day that I encountered the great God of the Seeds!][22]

Mexican scholar José Blanco considers the loa to have broached "the most scandalous theme imaginable." No less emphatically have other scholars noted the ways in which Sor Juana takes Spain to task for its violence, legitimates Aztec religious practices, and, all told, reverses the customary flow of knowledge by teaching the conquerors about the conquered. In her loa Sor Juana has instrumentalized the Eucharistic theme of the festival efficaciously, creatively, and just as catachrestically as she had the Narcissus myth of the auto. From the first part of the dramatic work on to its end, in her desire to have an impact on the Spanish literary scene the emphatically Mexican Sor Juana has assumed the role of the upstart Eco (*"Reprobate* angelic nature"), agent of diabolical differentiation and dissimilation. Sor Juana's agency as Eco, aggregate of her extreme games, of her "shock and awe" campaign, certainly produced a dramatic effect, though perhaps not the desired one. For reasons unknown but not hard to imagine, it appears that neither part of *El Divino Narciso* reached the stage in seventeenth-century Spain or in colonial Mexico.[23]

Juana here depicts and then disrupts would constitute one such "scenario." Taylor's framing of the "Archive" as composed of written texts also coincides with mine (which aligns with that of Roberto González Echevarría, *Myth and Archive: A Theory of Latin American Narrative* [Durham, N.C., 1998], and Antony Higgins, *Constructing the "Criollo" Archive: Subjects of Knowledge in the "Biblioteca Mexicana" and the "Rusticatio Mexicana"* [West Lafayette, Ind., 2000]). However, Taylor associates the archival with government power: "We might conclude that the archival, from the beginning, sustains power" (19). As my essay should bear out, the Archive need not necessarily sustain the hegemony.

22. Loa to *El Divino Narciso, Obras*, III, 17, 21; Juan de Torquemada, *Monarquía indiana*, ed. Miguel León-Portilla (Mexico City, 1969), II, 71–73.

23. José Joaquín Blanco, *Esplendores y miserias de los criollos: la literatura en la Nueva España* (Mexico City, 1989), II, 49. Treatments of the loa include Bénassy-Berling, *Humanisme et religion*, part 5, chap. 2; the two essays on the subject by Sabat de Rivers, *En busca de Sor Juana*, 263–331; Martínez–San Miguel, *Saberes americanos*, chap. 5; also Carmela Zanelli, "La loa de 'El Divino

The auto nonetheless allows the Devil-Eco a duet with Narciso-Christ, which obliquely, only too obliquely, sanctions her. To a similar end, Sor Juana joins forces in *El Divino Narciso* with venerable European knowledge. *El Divino Narciso,* especially the auto, boasts the greatest erudition, the most intense intertextual connections with Western culture of any of the nun's works except her masterpiece, the *Primero sueño.* A breathtaking range of reference configures *El Divino Narciso.* The play encompasses classical mythmakers, patristic sources, Spanish Renaissance and Baroque masters, and the Old and New Testaments. In terms of the Bible, the auto displays a notable predilection for the Song of Songs and the prophets Isaiah and Ezekiel. Sor Juana's first comedia, *Los empeños de una casa* [The Trials of a Noble House], fitfully gestures to Spanish sources but ends up as a sort of Möbius strip, all surface and no depth; *El Divino Narciso* in contrast plunges its audience into a labyrinth of references that vastly enhance the reaches of the work, invoking Western cultural capital meaningfully and organically. With this, Sor Juana parades before the Spanish court and literati her intellectual credentials, the extreme and deep erudition that qualifies her for any quarter as a Baroque intellectual.

In *El Divino Narciso,* her most transatlantic work, Sor Juana thereby assumes the quintessential creole position. She brokers Indian cultural practices and herself as a distinctively Mexican writer (together, as we will soon see, with the Mexican Archive) to Spain. Simultaneously she displays, as Yolanda Martínez-San Miguel puts it, "official Eurocentric and Metropolitan knowledge" in a work that posits "the specificity of an American identity, yet does not break with Metropolitan paradigms of cultural and subject formation."[24]

As a builder of bridges between the New and the Old Worlds, Sor Juana would naturally turn her thoughts to the syncretism that enjoyed enormous currency in seventeenth-century European and Latin American historiography and that labored to link the two continents. Seventeenth-century official syncretism was the last dream of similitude, a final, sometimes hallucinated effort to unify the world under the aegis of Christianity in face of the threatening plurality that the New World and the Orient had introduced. Luis Harss elegantly characterizes the thrust of syncretism: "The key factor was the humanist

---

Narciso' de Sor Juana Inés de la Cruz y la doble recuperación de la cultura indígena mexicana," in José Pascual Boixó and Arnulfo Herrera, eds., *La literatura novohispana: revisión crítica y propuestas metodológicas* (Mexico City, 1994), 183–200. I discuss Eco and dissimilation in my "Narciso *desdoblado*: Narcissistic Stratagems in *El Divino Narciso* and the *Respuesta a sor Filotea de la Cruz,*" *Bulletin of Hispanic Studies,* XLIV (1987), 111–117. On *El Divino Narciso*'s not reaching the stage, see Sabat de Rivers, *En busca de Sor Juana,* 266.

24. *Los empeños de una casa, Obras,* III; Martínez–San Miguel, *Saberes americanos,* 140, 214.

sense of an expanding world that required a new unifying scheme capable of accounting for cultural diversity." Historiographic syncretisms of various breeds had in common the attempt to rescue the Christian world from a dangerous pluralism or heterodoxy by placing all known societies on a continuum and by coordinating them teleologically with Christianity, as forerunners of it. The lures of syncretism for the creole, or transatlantic, Sor Juana should be apparent. And avail herself of syncretism she did. In political ways that held coded messages for the Mexican milieu in the loa, and in literary ways in the auto, Sor Juana dramatizes for Spain its own technology for managing the catachrestic New World.[25]

The loa exercises its politics and poetics on the syncretist historiography of Mexico, a tangled territory that requires a short introduction. By Sor Juana's time, for more than one hundred years historiographers affiliated with various religious bodies had taken a syncretic approach to New World history. Landmark syncretist historiographers of New Spain include, in chronological order, Franciscan Bernardino de Sahagún, Dominican Bartolomé de las Casas, Jesuit José de Acosta, Franciscan Gerónimo de Mendieta, Franciscan Juan de Torquemada, Augustinian Antonio de la Calancha, and Sor Juana's contemporaries, the Jesuit-allied Sigüenza y Góngora and his friend, the Franciscan Agustín de Vetancurt. Each and every one of the preceding authors occupies a common territory. They all compose comparative histories that equate Indian and Western civilizations, therein rescuing precontact Indian history from oblivion and exalting the secular achievements of Indian civilization. At the same time, they condemn Indian religious practices, attributing the marked similarities between Christian and Indian religions to the devil whom they believed to have ruled the New World. Always taunting God, the devil allegedly shaped New World religions into parodic copies of Christianity, with diabolical equivalents of such Christian rituals as baptism and communion.

Invested in the universalizing project described in the first section of this essay, Octavio Paz places enormous weight on Sor Juana's involvement with the outreaching *Jesuit* brand of syncretism. Jesuit syncretism was associated with Italian Renaissance Neoplatonic hermeticism and shared hermeticism's Egyptian leanings. As enacted by Kircher and Sigüenza with reference to Mexico, Jesuit syncretic historiography partook of the common territory just outlined but moved in more radical directions. In his *Oedipus Aegiptiacus*, Kircher endowed Mexico with Egyptian origins, as established by similarities between Mexican and Egyptian pyramids and hieroglyphs. So, in his *Teatro* and citing

25. Luis Harss, ed. and trans., *Sor Juana's Dream* (New York, 1986), 15.

Kircher, does a Sigüenza proud of the association of his homeland with the Egyptian *prisca theologia*. Sigüenza skews syncretism in other directions that reflect his creole patriotism. We know that in his now lost *Fénix del oeste* [Phoenix of the West], following predecessors of varying provenance including Calancha, Sigüenza maintains that the apostle Thomas in fact preached in Mexico under the guise of no other than Indian deity Quetzalcóatl. Sigüenza's assertion fully dovetails with the spirit if not the letter of mainstream syncretism, as does the extraordinary use to which he turned the Aztec leaders in *Teatro*'s Mirror for Princes. There, like other of his compatriots, Sigüenza utilizes Indian history as an expression of creole patriotism and brashly proposes the indigenous monarchs as models for the Spanish viceroy himself.[26]

We now have the principal tools necessary to identify the terms of engagement of Sor Juana's syncretic loa with the Mexican historiographic Archive, tools that gainsay Paz's wholesale claims of her Jesuit syncretism. For the loa, like the *Neptuno,* eschews the radical leanings of Jesuit discourse. It brooks no mention of Thomas, Quetzalcóatl, or Egypt. Instead, the loa aims for the common denominator of official syncretism in general. As it lays out the parallels between Indian and Christian religions, sacrifice and Eucharist, the play emphasizes that the devil has implanted the correspondences. Religión articulates the heart of the matter, saying,

¡Válgame Dios! ¿Qué dibujos,
qué remedos o qué cifras
de nuestras sacras Verdades
quieren ser estas mentiras?
¡Oh cautelosa Serpiente!
Oh Aspid venenosa!

.   .   .   .

¿Hasta dónde tu malicia
quiere remedar de Dios
las sagradas Maravillas?

Heaven help me! What kind of outlines, imitations, or ciphers of our sacred truths do these lies purport to be? O cautious Serpent! O poisonous Asp! How far will you go to imitate the sacred Marvels of God?

---

26. Sigüenza y Góngora citing Kircher, in *Teatro,* 181. On Sigüenza and Thomas, see D. A. Brading, *The First America: The Spanish Monarchy, Creole Patriots, and the Liberal State, 1492–1867* (Cambridge, 1991), chap. 17.

Together with the Jesuit Acosta and subsequent historians of other orders, the loa invokes Paul's words to the Athenians on the "Unknown God" whom heathens worship in the form of their own gods from Acts 17:22–23. Moreover, while it features traces of Franciscan Mendieta, the loa appears to depend most heavily on Franciscan Torquemada's 1615 *Monarquía indiana*.[27]

Juan de Torquemada's tremendously influential history itself effected syntheses and incited polemics. The multivolume *Monarquía* is a historiographic archive, a compendium that Benjamin Keen calls the "capstone and epitome of the Franciscan scholarly enterprise in New Spain" for the fact that it assembles writings of Sahagún and the unpublished work of Mendieta. The *Monarquía* also reproduces, among others, works of Dominican Bartolomé de las Casas and Jesuit Acosta without full attribution. In his bulky *Teatro mexicano* published in 1697–1698, several years in the making and thus likely to have circulated earlier in some form, Vetancurt accused Torquemada of plagiarism. His accusations drew attention in Sor Juana's milieu to the profoundly synthetic nature of the *Monarquía*. Vetancurt's friend Sigüenza took issue with Torquemada on different fronts. Anathema to Sigüenza was the Franciscan author's attribution of Mexico's origin to savage peoples rather than to the Egyptians as well as Torquemada's failure to subscribe to the Thomas-Quetzalcóatl theory.[28]

Archive and lightning rod, the *Monarquía* provides Sor Juana with a platform that enables and certifies the coded goals of her syncretic loa. In opting for reliance on Torquemada, she confirms the moderate, synthetic nature of her syncretism. Sor Juana draws a line in the sand between herself and certain Jesuits while still, in her pro-Indian stance, aligning herself with the Jesuit-influenced creoles who exploited Indian history to patriotic ends *and* with the pro-Indian Franciscans. The nun-writer follows in Torquemada's footsteps as she discursively coordinates sometimes adversarial constituencies, seizing on the aspects of syncretism that they hold in common. True to the very spirit of syncretism, the loa therefore mediates currents within Mexico (including tensions between Mexico City and Puebla?) and unites the New with the Old

27. Loa to *El Divino Narciso, Obras*, III, 13–14. I am simply suggesting that Paz's treatment of Jesuit syncretism in *El Divino Narciso*'s loa would profit from more depth and nuance. Far from denying the influence of Jesuit syncretism on Sor Juana, I believe that the matter is even vaster than Paz believes, and of crucial importance. For example, we might consider Sor Juana's conceivable desire to curry favor with the Jesuits by employing Kircherian syncretism in the *Respuesta* or in the *Sueño*. I leave that task to another writing.

28. Benjamin Keen, *The Aztec Image in Western Thought* (New Brunswick, N.J., 1971), 180. On Vetancurt's accusations of Torquemada's plagiarism, see Blanco, *Esplendores*, 158.

World. In this primordial aspect of the loa, as in her universalizing intertextuality, Sor Juana abjures the role of dissimilating Devil-Eco and finesses herself into a Narciso, her deity of reflection and harmony.[29]

Predictably, Narciso's divine energies prevail in the loa and the auto, uniting them as well. That is to say, although the loa situates itself in history and the auto in an allegorical atemporality, although the loa addresses American issues and the auto universal ones, the harmonizing force of syncretism pervades both works. For the auto, as my earlier discussions of its plot and extensive intertextuality will have suggested, both thematizes and textualizes the mechanisms of mirroring and harmonizing that underpin syncretism. Traces of New World historiographic syncretism per se also make their way into the auto. Naturaleza Humana proposes that God often places signs of his highest mysteries in pagan works; Eco, like the devil to whom historians ascribe dominion over the New World, tempts Narciso with the beauties and abundance of her vast lands. In both cases, the auto presents us with diffuse, hypostatic reenactments of the loa's syncretic apologetics (together, it should be said, with a "black but beautiful" Eco who retains some resemblance to Christ and who thus indirectly brings the dark-skinned Virgin of Guadalupe into the mix). The theme of the Eucharist, with the poetics of transubstantiation that it invites, also perforce unites the loa with the auto and unites them both under the rhetorical auspices of metaphor, harmony.[30]

Now, at the end of the loa, Religión promises that the auto will introduce Mexico to Spain in the abstract, essentialized form of allegorical ideas that can pass easily between worlds. The foregoing examples of diffuse carryovers of syncretism from the loa to the auto indicate that the auto keeps Religión's promise. Such carryovers begin to dissolve the patent disjunctions between the two parts of El Divino Narciso. They nonetheless keep one opposition standing, that of the loa as local or Mexican versus the auto as universal. My last foray into El Divino Narciso assails that opposition by examining the imprint of the Mexican Archive, specifically the Mexican pastoral novel, on the auto sacramental.[31]

The stunningly lush, erotic, natural sensuousness of El Divino Narciso's auto strikes readers as a major departure from the usual geometrical disposition of Sor Juana's works. Grappling with nature for one of the few times in her career

---

29. On Narciso as deity of reflection, see my "Narciso *desdoblado*," *Bulletin of Hispanic Studies,* XLIV (1987), 112–113.

30. Martínez–San Miguel, *Saberes americanos,* chap. 5, presents an excellent treatment of carryovers between the loa and the auto; particularly interesting is her assertion that Naturaleza Humana represents the New World.

31. Loa to *El Divino Narciso, Obras,* III, 20.

yet revealing herself as an instant past master of the subject, Sor Juana installs her auto squarely in the territory of the pastoral lyric and novel. The question therefore arises of *why* Sor Juana might have chosen this occasion so singularly and fully to perform the pastoral. A two-pronged answer comes to mind. On the one hand, the pastoral novel had extraordinary cachet in seventeenth-century Spain. Considered sublime, just one step removed from the biblical Song of Songs (which Jerome, patron saint of Sor Juana's order, had translated into Latin), the pastoral had become the genre of choice and preponderance, the sine qua non for authors wishing to establish themselves on the Spanish literary scene. Both Lope de Vega and Cervantes, for example, had inaugurated their literary careers with pastoral novels. On the other hand but still analogously, the pastoral had made determining inroads into New World discourse. Following the lead of Columbus and Pedro Mártir, innumerable colonial writers had purveyed the New World as a utopic and paradisiacal space of abundance, a bucolic locus amoenus.

So great was the purchase of the pastoral on the discourse of the New World that, as Mexican literature began to take shape, radicado and creole authors availed themselves of the bucolic mode to represent the *city*. Salazar y Alarcón's "Bucólica" manifests this oxymoronic combination, which persisted all the way to Sigüenza y Góngora's portrayal of a city convent as a paradisiacal garden in his *Parayso occidental* [Western Paradise] (1684). The pastoral acquired further new valences in Mexico owing to the mission of the original Franciscans to recreate in New Spain the unsullied purity of the primitive church, to return to an idyllic Golden Age. Invocations of the pastoral in Mexico could therefore be construed as alluding to the Franciscan project. Given, too, the obvious congruence between bucolic literature and the Spanish pastoral, or religious, enterprise in the colonies, examples of pastoral literature *a lo divino* [in a divine mode] abound in colonial Mexico. Finally, by Sor Juana's era, the pastoral had linked up with Guadalupan narratives like that of Miguel Sánchez, who in 1648 portrayed the site of the apparition as an earthly paradise, the Promised Land, a land of milk and honey.[32]

Hence, we begin to gather that it was not by chance or without significance for both Spain and Mexico that Sor Juana stages a pastoral for Madrid. Overtly,

32. On the Franciscan project for Mexico, see John Leddy Phelan, *The Millennial Kingdom of the Franciscans in the New World*, 2d ed., rev. (Berkeley, Calif., 1970), especially part 2; Miguel Sánchez, "Imagen de la virgen María, Madre de Dios de Guadalupe: milagrosamente aparecida en a ciudad de México, celebrada en su historia, con la profecía del capítulo doce del Apocalipsis," in Ernesto de la Torre Villar and Ramiro Navarro de Anda, eds., *Testimonios historicos guadalupanos* (Mexico City, 1981), 152–281.

she plays out for an elite audience an elite Spanish genre, brandishing her mastery of it. Covertly—perhaps as a matter of personal national pride, or perhaps hoping that the literati of the Spanish audience or *expecting* that a potential Mexican audience will grasp her allusions—Sor Juana brings into play the most ingrained and one of the most defining aspects of the Mexican literary Archive. With her sortie into the pastoral mode, the creole Sor Juana reifies the point of greatest convergence between Mexican and Spanish literature. She exhibits one of Mexico's principal claims to Spanish literary fame. And, as Sor Juana infuses the Eucharistic drama with vivid, manifold echoes of two specific Mexican pastoral novels, she further Mexicanizes the auto, binding it to the patently Mexican loa and rendering both pieces performances of the Mexican literary Archive.

By cleaving to the universal Sor Juana, the source-sleuthing that has been brought to bear on the auto has captured only the European half of the creole writer's transatlantic agenda. It has neglected two Mexican works that contain several of the play's signature elements. I refer to Bernardo de Balbuena's wholly secular pastoral novel, *Siglo de oro en las selvas de Erífile* [Golden Age in the Forest of Erífile] (his first work, written in Jalisco but published in Spain in 1608), and to creole Francisco de Bramón's pastoral novel a lo divino, *Los sirgueros de la Virgen sin original pecado* [Heralds of the Virgin Who Is Exempt from Original Sin] (Mexico, 1620), created for an occasion most dear to the Jesuits, the Feast of the Immaculate Conception. Bramón's novel interacts with Balbuena's. Together, they constitute the first novels written in and about Mexico, which fact consolidates the import of the pastoral for New World discourse.[33]

Separately and conjointly, Balbuena and Bramón claim and reinvigorate the pastoral for Mexico. They do so in ways that would appeal to Sor Juana as important for her auto to carry in its wake or with moves that directly enter her play. Both male authors reterritorialize the pastoral novel by inserting pieces of Mexican reality into their works, be it a dream vision of Mexico City in the case of Balbuena or references to the University of Mexico in the instance of Bramón. Bramón in fact concludes his novel with a "Gozo mexicano," or "Mexican rejoicing," that stages the Aztec dance known as a *tocotín*. The tocotín contains quite specific kinships with *El Divino Narciso*'s loa, which both corroborates Sor Juana's knowledge of *Sirgueros* and sets up another tie between

33. All of the sources that Méndez Plancarte lists for the pastoral aspects of *El Divino Narciso* are biblical and Spanish, not New World or Mexican. Bernardo de Balbuena, *Siglo de oro en las selvas de Erífile* (Jalisco, 1989); Francisco Bramón, *Los sirgueros de la Virgen,* ed. Agustín Yáñez, 2d ed. (Mexico City, 1994).

the loa and the auto. Equally arresting is the hyperliterary, hyperintellectual, literarily innovative cast of the two pastoral novels, so akin to Sor Juana's own predilections. The shepherds of both novels and, notably, the shepherdesses of Bramón's, live to discourse upon and write poetry. Balbuena, author of the first New World treatise on poetry ("Compendio apologético en alabanza de la poesía" [Apologetic Compendium in Praise of Poetry], published with *Grandeza*), engineers his pastoral novel into a meditation on the genre that contemplates the assimilation of new literary currents into the pastoral forest of Erífile, archetypal poetic space. His *Siglo de oro,* as avant-garde as *Grandeza,* effects a quintessential Mannerism. Bramón's Jesuit-influenced work constitutes an early yet full-blown example of the Baroque that still reigned in Mexico at the end of the seventeenth century.[34]

Together, additionally, the two novels introduce Ovid to the New World, setting the course that Sor Juana epitomizes in her metamorphosis-ridden *Primero sueño.* Most vitally arguing for influence of the two texts on Sor Juana's auto, their Ovidian inclinations lead them to showcase the myth of Echo and Narcissus and to pay special attention to the fountain that plays a crucial role in the myth. The title of Balbuena's work refers to the fountain of Erífile, source of poetry, something of a Castalian fount. Bramón's interpolation of a Marian fountain into the myth directly portends Sor Juana's and authorizes her seemingly catachrestic deployment of the myth.[35]

The emphasis that, beginning with the title of his work, Bramón places on portents themselves likewise dovetails with the prophetic, syncretic motor of *El Divino Narciso*'s auto. Balbuena's novel culminates in the cosmic mourning for shepherdess Augusta and the reconsecration of Erífile as a poetic space, both of which matters coincide with the Eucharistic ending of Sor Juana's auto. Many other aspects large and small implicate the early-seventeenth-century pastoral novels in the weave of the nun's 1688 auto. It would be tedious and probably superfluous to lay them out exhaustively. More interesting, I suspect, are the conclusions to which the presence of Balbuena and Bramón's work in the auto leads, conclusions that will bring this essay to a close.

At more than one juncture in the preceding pages we have witnessed Sor Juana looking back in her dense cultural politics to the beginning of the seven-

34. Luis Leal, "El hechizo derramado: elementos mestizos en Sor Juana," in Herrera, ed., *Y diversa de mí misma* (Mexico City, 1993), 196–197, relates Sor Juana's to Bramón's tocotín.

35. Important instances of the fountain: in *Siglo de oro,* 102; in *Sirgueros,* 30. Bénassy-Berling, *Humanisme et religion,* 386, 404, 407, views the fountain as one of the most significant connections between the myth and the religious play, and as a main impetus for Sor Juana to rewrite the myth a lo divino.

teenth century in New Spain, a time of foundations at once literary (Mannerism, the Baroque), religious (consolidation of Jesuit activity), political (emerging tensions between creoles and Spaniards), and historiographic (Torquemada)— and hence a rich period for the Mexican Archive and for creoles. Scholars have repeatedly noted and lamented that the subsequent heart of the century, though a crucial time for Guadalupan works like Miguel Sánchez's, proved far less literarily dynamic, as countless second-rate poets lapsed into an epigonic and static Gongorism. The end of the seventeenth century, on the other hand, presents a new burgeoning of Mexican literature, largely in the hands of the creole Sor Juana herself.

When Sor Juana gazes backward in *El Divino Narciso,* she chiefly encompasses the bookends of the century in her literary glance. The imprint on the auto of Balbuena and Bramón, as authors who inaugurated the currents that Sor Juana herself conceivably epitomizes and brings to Spain, coordinates the beginning with the end of the century. At the same time and significantly, Balbuena's and Bramón's presence in the auto again ramifies the two parts of *El Divino Narciso.* It bifurcates them, *not* into the Mexican loa versus the Spanish or universal auto, but into mis-en-scènes of two phases of colonial New Spain's cultural history. First, we have the loa, which affords a microcosmic representation of the conquest shot through with Torquemada's famous beginning-of-the-century syncretism. Second, we have the auto: by recouping in 1688 the early pastoral novels of the Mexican Archive, the play emerges as a gestural portrait of the colonial, largely creole Mexican culture that ensued from the initial clash of the conquest, an elite culture that first flowered at the turn of the seventeenth century and reached fruition at its end. The pastoral and syncretism in this scenario furnish threads of continuity that join the two stages and place them on a continuum as constituent elements of the Mexican Archive.

Hence it becomes clear that at the moment of her debut for Madrid, with the bicentennial of the discovery fast approaching, the creole Sor Juana has mounted an (almost) fin de siècle retrospective of Mexican colonial culture that embodies myriad and diverse entities of her inscape as well as their interactions. In view of the philosophically recapitulatory nature of her *Primero sueño,* one might even venture to say that Sor Juana has continuously strived to produce a literary fin de siècle. It also becomes clear that on what she envisioned as a singular public stage, like Balbuena in his inaugural *Siglo de oro,* the "Tenth Muse" calls for a renewal of the original (metropolitan) poetic space. Sor Juana brings the Mexican Archive home, as it were, to Spain, but makes it patent and palpable that, like her own exemplary oeuvre, European cultural memory must now accommodate more than a single concern, more than a single history.

Creole Bradstreet: Philip Sidney, Alexander the Great, and English Identities

Was Anne Bradstreet born of noble blood? Bradstreet scholars have long wondered. What, after all, could she have meant in 1650 when she claimed in "An Elegie upon That Honourable and Renowned Knight, Sir *Philip Sidney*" to share "the self-same blood" as the famous poet whose noble lineage was beyond dispute? If the substitution of "English" for "self-same" in the 1678 Boston edition of her poetry was meant to clarify the issue, it has had precisely the opposite effect. Scholars have been led to wonder whether she revised those lines to clarify what a first-time poet had left ambiguous, or altered them, as most critics now argue, in a bow "to decorum" that was also a concession to the "outright criticism" she received after making such a boastful claim. While no one has yet solved the mystery, critics do agree that, whatever the truth of the matter may be, the Bradstreet-Dudley families of colonial New England believed they were of finer stock than most colonists, a belief the family seem to have kept largely to themselves.[1]

I do not intend to solve the mystery surrounding Bradstreet's bloodlines

---

1. Ann Stanford, "Anne Bradstreet's Portrait of Sir Philip Sidney," in Pattie Cowell and Ann Stanford, eds., *Critical Essays on Anne Bradstreet* (Boston, 1983), 97–100, esp. 98; Stanford, *Anne Bradstreet: The Worldly Puritan* (New York, 1974), 110. The most comprehensive discussion of the case for a familial link between Bradstreet and Sidney can be found in Elizabeth Wade White, *Anne Bradstreet: The Tenth Muse* (New York, 1971), 12–17. Stanford provides further evidence in "Anne Bradstreet's Portrait of Sir Philip Sidney."

Relevant editions are [Anne Bradstreet], *The Tenth Muse, Lately Sprung up in America; or, Severall Poems . . .* (London, 1650); [Anne Bradstreet], *Several Poems, Compiled with Great Variety of Wit and Learning, Full of Delight . . .* (Boston, 1678). Probably the best modern accessible edition of the 1650 edition is Joseph R. McElrath, Jr., and Allan P. Robb, eds., *The Complete Works of Anne Brastreet* (Boston, 1981); probably the best modern accessible edition of the 1678 edition is Jeanine Hensley, ed., *The Works of Anne Bradstreet* (Cambridge, Mass., 1967), which has line numbers. Quotations in the text follow the 1650 edition unless the 1678 is specifically cited; parenthetical references in the text to "The Four Monarchies" are by page number to the 1650 edition and by line number to the Hensley (1678 / 1967) edition (e.g., p. 136 / l. 2143).

here. I do want, however, to join those who have sought to understand the significance of the revision in what would seem to be two simple lines of poetry. For these two lines of poetry raise issues that have been at the center of scholarship on colonial British-American literature since the field's beginnings. How did British-American colonists see themselves, scholars have long wondered, in relation to the English community they had left behind? How were the ways of figuring identity that dominated English discourse, such as the notion that blood determined status, transformed in New England, Virginia, and the various other outposts of British America? What, if anything, was distinctive about the colonial British-American identities that developed in the New World in the first place but especially in relation to the ways in which identity was understood by the people the colonists left behind across the Atlantic? In order to pursue these kinds of questions, I want to turn our attention away from biographical matters to figurative ones by interrogating these lines in relation not only to the other lines in her poetry but also where those lines were published in the first place. What significance can be made, I want to ask, of the indisputable fact that these lines were printed on different sides of the Atlantic? I wonder what work a claim to nobility would do for a colonial British-American writer in the world of 1650 London publishing. I wonder, too, what work the seemingly self-evident claim by a colonial English writer to English identity would be doing in a work from 1678 Boston. Aside from the useful information these lines might provide us about the biography of an important American writer, I would like to ask, What might these lines tell us about the ways in which colonial British-American writers negotiated the problem of being an English person who lived outside England?

I am referring here, of course, to the problem of demonstrating to those they left behind in England—and perhaps to themselves—that they had avoided what later English colonists would refer to as "creolian degeneracy." The problem creolization posed for English colonists is now so well known among scholars as to require little explanation. Suffice it to say that early modern theories of identity formation held that the colonists put their very identities at risk when they chose to live in the supposedly degenerate New World climate adjacent to if not among native people who would only hasten the colonists descent into savagery. The identity of those people who lived outside England proper but wanted to retain their Englishness thus posed a grave conceptual problem for the European inhabitants of Massachusetts Bay.[2]

2. The scholarship on the significance of humoral theory and its interaction with environmentalist theories of identity in the early modern period is now quite extensive. I discuss this issue in

Bradstreet's poetry subtly engages the threat of degeneration she and her fellow colonists faced in living so far removed from the supposedly civilized environment of England. It is not that Bradstreet directly addresses the problem of creolization, though. Instead, her poetry engages with the problem of who and what counts as English in the first place. Englishness itself was hardly a static concept in the seventeenth century. Bradstreet in particular and the colonists in general, in other words, were not writing about identity in relation to an agreed-upon notion of Englishness that existed at home in England, but were, instead, entering a fiercely contested debate over just what constituted true Englishness. Barbara Fuchs, in fact, speaks of the "fragility of English identity" in the early seventeenth century, and Richard Helgerson writes that just what counted as English during the very period in which Bradstreet wrote was the subject of "a continuing struggle between conflicting interests and conflicting discursive shapings."[3]

Authorizing Experience: Refigurations of the Body Politic in Seventeenth-Century New England Writing (Princeton, N.J., 1999), esp. 14–31. For alternate readings of the significance of environmentalist theories of identity as they relate to early American literature and culture, see Joyce E. Chaplin, *Subject Matter: Technology, the Body, and Science on the Anglo-American Frontier, 1500–1676* (Cambridge, Mass., 2001); Trudy Eden, "Food, Assimilation, and the Malleability of the Human Body in Early Virginia," in Janet Moore Lindman and Michele Lise Tarter, eds., *A Centre of Wonders: The Body in Early America* (Ithaca, N.Y., 2001), 29–42, and Martha L. Finch, "'Civilized' Bodies and the 'Savage' Environment of Early New Plymouth," 43–60. For the perspective on these issues from scholars of British literature, see Jean Feerick, "Spenser, Race, and Ire-land," *English Literary Renaissance*, XXXII (2002), 85–117; Mary Floyd-Wilson, *English Ethnicity and Race in Early Modern Drama* (Cambridge, 2003), esp. 1–86; Roxanne Wheeler, *The Complexion of Race: Categories of Difference in Eighteenth-Century British Culture* (Philadelphia, 2000), esp. 2–48.

3. Barbara Fuchs, *Mimesis and Empire: The New World, Islam, and European Identities* (New York, 2001), 2; Richard Helgerson, *Forms of Nationhood: The Elizabethan Writing of England* (Chicago, 1992), 301. Again, the scholarship on the debates over just what counted as Englishness in the sixteenth and seventeenth centuries is extensive, though I think it is safe to say that Helgerson's has become the standard treatment. I have also learned a great deal on this subject from David J. Baker, *Between Nations: Shakespeare, Spenser, Marvell, and the Question of Britain* (Stanford, Calif., 1997). I speak of the problems of English identity throughout this essay, but the relation of just what counted as English in relation to what counted as British during the same period was of great importance. For an interesting treatment of this problem that "national consciousness in Tudor England was largely 'British' rather than narrowly 'English'" in content and character, see Philip Schwyzer, *Literature, Nationalism, and Memory in Early Modern England and Wales* (Cambridge, 2004), 3. For an alternative reading of Bradstreet's attempts to "articulate . . . her communal and national identity," especially in her Sidney poems, see Christopher Ivic, "'Our British Land': Anne Bradstreet's Atlantic Perspective," in Philip Schwyzer and Simon Mealor, eds., *Archipelagic Identities: Literature and Identity in the Atlantic Archipelago, 1550–1800* (Aldershot, 2004), 195–204. I should also add that I have chosen not to interrogate how the printing and public distribution of verse by a New Engand "Gentlewoman" might itself serve as ammunition in the rhetorical battles waged over the colony's claims to be as English as England

In order to investigate Bradstreet's contribution to these debates, I focus on the two versions of "An Elegie upon That Honourable and Renowned Knight, Sir *Philip Sidney*." More specifically, I want to investigate how the two versions of this poem figure English identity. The London and Boston editions of what would seem to be the same elegy by what is indisputably the very same poet offer two fundamentally different and perhaps incompatible versions of Englishness. One poet, in other words, figures English identity in what seems to be the very same poem differently in the version published on American soil than in the one published across the Atlantic in London. In spite of the differences between the two versions of this poem, though, one figure serves as the pivot point in both figurations of Englishness. Alexander the Great plays a key role in Englishness on both sides of the Atlantic. In what follows I would like to suggest that using Alexander to set the terms of true Englishness necessitates, at least in the way Bradstreet frames him, an understanding of Englishness in relation, not to what the colonists saw before them, but, instead, to figures from classical literature with which they had no physical contact. Another way to put this might be that Bradstreet suggests that Englishness depends more on things to her east than to her and the colonists' west. Bradstreet accomplishes this geographic sleight of hand through a kind of imaginary grave robbery, where colonial corpses can be confused for classical ones. Such morbid imaginings present a challenge to dominant theories of identity formation. For how could members of the colonial New England elite be considered degenerate if their very bodies were interchangeable with the body of an icon of classical culture, an icon who formed part of the foundation of what early modern English writers considered civilized culture in the first place? Bradstreet's version of colonial British-American identity, in other words, grounds itself on classical figures, on bodies foreign to the American environment, rather than on the land in front of them or encounters with Indians or any distinctly New World object or idea.[4]

_____

herself. The mere appearance of these volumes might work on its own, before one even read the poetry, to silence those who would cast doubt on the Englishness of the colonists by showing that, at least among the colonial elite, inhabitants of the colonies could produce verse of obvious learning that adheres to the most exacting standards of European high culture. The 1678 *Several Poems* might also work to challenge environmentalist theory, but, given its imagined audience of colonial British-American readers, I would suspect, as I argue below, it would do so in a fundamentally different way than *The Tenth Muse* would have worked in London.

4. The problem of gender no doubt also plays a role in the representation of identity in Bradstreet's poetry. I have avoided engaging in detail with gender in these poems, not because I believe it is unimportant, but rather because I believe gender in Bradstreet's poetry has already received considerable attention, which has produced a wealth of important and impressive

BEFORE I begin examining Bradstreet's Sidney poems, I want to look very briefly at how *The Tenth Muse* (1650) frames the problem of the relation between space and identity. The very title page of the London edition defines the book in explicitly geographic terms: *The Tenth Muse, Lately Sprung up in America*. Geography differentiates this book from the many other works of poetry or works relating to America coming out of the press during the 1630s, 1640s, and early 1650s. This is not, in other words, just another book, but one whose distinctive characteristics have to do with the geographic location of its production. This is true at the quantitative level. Of the approximately forty works printed in the British Isles from 1640 to 1655 that make mention of America on the title page, Bradstreet's is the *only* book of poetry. It is also true at the discursive level. Since geographic spaces were already invested with moral and cultural meanings, to indicate where a book's poems were produced was to ask that those poems be read, at least in part, in relation to the systems of meaning associated with those places on a globe. But, if the reader had any doubts about the significance of place of production to his or her understanding of these poems, then the title page removes all doubt when it announces at the bottom of the page that the poems are "By a Gentlewoman of those parts." "Those parts" simply makes crystal clear what the top of the page only intimates. Whoever wrote these poems, we are told here, was not, strictly speaking, of *these* parts but of some *other* parts.[5]

In specifying America as the Other location from which the poems spring, the title combines two seemingly incompatible cultural categories, colonial America and classical figures. In saying, no doubt with tongue firmly in cheek, that the Tenth Muse has sprung up in America, the title page aims to play on the seventeenth-century English reader's sense of America's alterity. The juxtaposition of a mythical figure from classical culture with the supposedly degenerate New World populated by savages would, I suspect, appeal to the book's

---

scholarship. I want to focus attention here on geography, blood, and classical and Eastern figures as they relate to colonial British-American identity, which, I believe, has been less closely analyzed in Bradstreet's poetry. In future work on Bradstreet I hope to investigate the ways in which gender is relevant to the problems of identity I explore in this essay.

5. [Bradstreet], *The Tenth Muse, Lately Sprung up in America*. I am hardly the first person to discuss the importance of a geographic spatial economy in early modern writing in English. For a discussion of the significance of space in early modern literature, particularly as it relates to geographic space and the concepts and assumptions that provide the underlying logic of such ways of thinking, see John Gillies's discussion of the "poetic geographic economy" of early modern English literature in *Shakespeare and the Geography of Difference* (Cambridge, 1994), esp. 1–39. See also Edward Said's discussions in *Orientalism* (New York, 1979) of the significance of what he calls "geographic imagination" for literary study in general and studies of orientalism in particular.

publisher, since such seeming incongruities might work to sell the book. After all, in the discursive system of seventeenth-century England, classical figures signify the ideal of cultural achievement while the colonial American environment represents precisely the absence of such achievement. The Muses would never lower themselves to inspire those who lived in the savage world of America. The inhabitants of America were not worthy of such enrichment, and so they would they not be able to produce great poetry even with assistance from the Muses. The sense of estrangement between the author and the book's potential audience is only heightened on the title page by the use of what was most commonly a metaphor for the rapid growth of vegetation, the claim, that is, that the Muse has "sprung up," thus suggesting a kind of growth of that classical figure in the decidedly unclassical environment of the New World. And, if all these conceptual contradictions were not enough to intrigue potential readers, the title page adds one final conundrum by calling the poet "a Gentlewoman." The word "Gentlewoman" was sure to raise some eyebrows, given that the colonists were not generally imagined to be of sufficient rank to be afforded such social distinctions.[6]

The commendatory poetry subtly challenges the global spatial economy on which the 1650 title page relies. Where geography differentiates potential readers from the work's author by suggesting America's distance and difference from England, the commendatory poetry works to show the author's ties to prospective readers. Take, for instance, "In Praise of the Author, Mistris *Anne Bradstreet,* Vertue's True and Lively Patterne, Wife of the Worshipfull *Simon Bradstreet* Esquire," probably by Nathaniel Holmes. The poem quite literally refuses to let America stand as the place-name to describe the place of production. Instead, Holmes tells us she lives "in *America,* alias nov-anglia." Readers who expect to find an American poet will, the poem suggests, be only half right. They will find an English poet living in an America whose Latin renaming works to connect that land to the classical culture to which England aspires. This is not, the poem tells us, the America of the savages but the America transformed by English people into a new England.[7]

---

6. For an illuminating discussion of the print market of 1650s London, see Nigel Smith, *Literature and Revolution in England, 1640–1660* (New Haven, Conn., 1994).

7. White identifies Holmes as the probable author of this verse. See White, *Anne Bradstreet,* 264. For a discussion of the commendatory poetry as a whole, see Phillip H. Round, *By Nature and by Custom Cursed: Transatlantic Civil Discourse and New England Cultural Production, 1620–1660* (Hanover, N.H., 1999), 189–200; Kathryn Zabelle Derounian-Stodola, "'The Excellency of the Inferior Sex': The Commendatory Writings on Anne Bradstreet," *Studies in Puritan American Spirituality,* I (1990), 129–147.

"In Praise of the Author, Mistris *Anne Bradstreet*" challenges the primacy of place in determining a culture's characteristics by moving England to the East. This sardonic geographic shift draws on two contemporaneous theories of identity formation that cast identity in terms of geography. When Holmes figures Bradstreet as a "splendent STAR . . . (From th' Orient first sprung)" who has moved so far that she now shines in the "West," he invokes the theory of translatio studii that early modern European writers in general and English writers in particular used to bolster their claims of the value of England's cultural products. The theory of translatio studii held that the center of knowledge and culture moved westward, like the sun, traveling from Eden to Jerusalem to Babylon to Athens to Rome to, at long last, London. Holmes playfully suggests here that learning is on the move again—but now out of England to the supposedly "degenerate climes" of America. This newfound muse in America, in other words, might be a signal that the geographic center of culture has moved out of London into the New World. According to the spatial economy of the title page, the poet puts her very identity at risk in producing poetry outside the bounds of civilization. According to the spatial logic of the commendatory poems, all those in England risk being left behind as civilization continues its march west across the globe.

As if a threat to the theory of translatio studii were not enough, the very same language of geographic space that is simultaneously to be read as an indicator of cultural worth is used to challenge environmentalist theories of identity formation. For, in producing such excellent poetry while living for twenty years in the wild climate of America, Bradstreet has put the lie to those theories that held that all things degenerate when they move out of their natural climates. After all, while the poetry is said to have "sprung" in an "Oriental England," it is "the West" of America where the poetry itself gains its life so that it "shines" forth. The truths the poetry brings to light, at least according to Holmes, were going "to die" rather than be revealed had Bradstreet not come to live in New England. In this way, the commendatory poetry twists to its own advantage the language of generation found on the title page that subtly casts doubt on the Englishness of the poet. The parody of casting England as Orient challenges the spatial economy on which the title page depends by suggesting that points on the compass be understood as directional signals rather than makers of culture. The poem engages with environmentalist logic with an implied question: If English people degenerate in America because of its place on the globe, then what happens to England when we realize that the discovery of America makes England part of the East? What the writer hopes will have to be dismissed by English readers as absurd for England to be itself will leave those readers with no choice but to reimagine the relationship of English subjects in America to England herself.[8]

The poem does not so much intend for us to take these threats to the supremacy of English culture seriously, then, as use them to discredit those who would denigrate the poetic production of an English woman simply because she produced the poetry in the wilds of America. I say this because the poem does not make America Bradstreet's permanent residence. For, if all these rhetorical ploys are not enough to convince those who might wonder whether an English writer in America could produce poetry worthy of being classified as English, the poem simply reconnects Bradstreet with England by insisting on the impermanence of Bradstreet's residence in America. She is, after all, only living there "at present." The phrase suggests that she will be somewhere else sometime soon, and, given Bradstreet's history and the imagined readership, where else could this somewhere be but England? Of course, in suggesting that Bradstreet will return to England, the poem slyly undercuts its point that civilization has left England behind. At the same time, the poet's return to England presents a problem for those who would insist that England's American colonies should not be grouped in the same geographical category as England. Holmes presents the reader with the same geographic choice I mentioned above by locating her "present" residence as in the "Occidentall parts of the World." When she returns to England, she will be leaving the Occident for, the poet suggests, the Orient. But the advancement of learning, like the sun, does not move west to east. As for the environmentalist theory of identity, one does not regenerate when one returns home. Stop denigrating America as a site that inevitably produces savagery, the poem tries at every stage to persuade its readers, or give up England's place in the West.[9]

THIS VERY same symbolic spatial economy I have suggested *The Tenth Muse* challenges defines the figure of Alexander as well. To understand this, we need

8. For a thorough and illuminating discussion of the significance of the theory that the cultural center of civilization moves west, as it applies to early modern British-American literature, see John C. Shields, *The American Aeneas: Classical Origins of the American Self* (Knoxville, Tenn., 2001), 3–37. Shields argues that, rather than referring to this theory as "translatio studii," it should, more appropriately, be labeled "translatio cultus."

9. Round offers a provocative reading of this poem in *By Nature and by Custom Cursed:* that by positioning Bradstreet in the West in this poem Holmes grants Bradstreet "the surprising ability to reverse the geographic logic of the trope of the *translatio studii*" (197). Round goes on to to argue, "In this one gesture, Holmes suggests that there is not only cultural continuity between old England and New England, but that Bradstreet's verse has in fact come to 'revive' English cultural norms annihilated by civil war and social disorder" (197).

to look beyond Bradstreet's poems on Sidney. When we do so, we see that it is hard to exaggerate the importance of Alexander to Bradstreet's poetry. Anne Bradstreet wrote far more poetry concerning Alexander the Great, more than one thousand lines, than on any other topic or person. To put this another way: Bradstreet devoted more poetry to Alexander than to her husband, her children, her grandchildren, her father, or her mother, either individually or combined. She devoted more lines of poetry to Alexander than to one of the most important icons of her age, Elizabeth I, or to one of the most important political events of her time, the English Civil War. She wrote more poetry about Alexander than she did about the New England Way or her life in the New World. She wrote more about Alexander than she wrote about her experiences as a woman, and she wrote more poetry about Alexander than she wrote about native Americans. In fact, we might never have had a published work from her in the first place had Bradstreet not been quite so fascinated with Alexander. Virtually all of the material on Alexander appears in "The Four Monarchies," and this poem alone, as Jane D. Eberwein points out, "takes up more than half of *The Tenth Muse.*" "Without its sheer mass," Eberwein continues, "it is improbable there ever would have been such a book."[10]

In "The Four Monarchies," Bradstreet uses the figure of Alexander to define geographic space itself, by linking geographic space with the very body of the great conqueror. The poem makes sure we understand the importance of this connection between world geography and Alexander's body right from the start by figuring the parts of his body in terms of geography in the very opening lines of "The Third Monarchy." From the moment Alexander appears in her poetry, in other words, his body is inextricably linked with geographic space. It's not just, Bradstreet insists, that Alexander wants to extend his dominion beyond his home country. It's not just, in other words, that he "scorn'd" being "confin'd" to *"Greece"* alone (p. 119 / ll. 1621–1623). No, all of geographic space is barely able to contain Alexander's body parts. "The universe scarce bounds his large vast minde" (p. 119 / ll. 1621–1622). Bradstreet associates not only his body but his very identity with geographic space. His fame will "last . . . whilst there is Land" (p. 148 / ll. 2577–2578). At the very height of his power, when he has brought "All Kingdoms, Countries, Provinces . . . From *Hellispont* to th' furthest Ocean" under his control, Alexander is made to "oft lament" the fact that "there was no worlds, more, to be conquered" (pp. 147, 148 / ll. 2508–2509, 2601–2602).

10. Jane D. Eberwein, "Civil War and Bradstreet's 'Monarchies,'" *Early American Literature,* XXVI (1991), 119–144, esp. 140.

Given that Alexander's very body tests the limits of geographic space, it should come as no surprise that Bradstreet highlights Alexander's constant motion over such space in this section of "The Four Monarchies." Indeed, the emphasis on geographic movement suggests that this is as much a poem about space itself as about Alexander. In this sense, she distinguishes herself from her sources. Whereas Sir Walter Ralegh, for instance, spent a good deal of time in his treatments of Alexander discussing his political and personal entanglements, or broke up the narrative of Alexander's movements for digressions on Alexander's relevance to English politics and culture, Bradstreet omits such material entirely. To be sure, Bradstreet supplies the names of rivers and mountains. She speaks of the River Granicus (p. 121 / l. 1675) and the Black Sea (p. 122 / l. 1691). She even speaks of steep banks that prevent Alexander's men from ascending quickly (p. 121 / l. 1679). In line 1914 (p. 128), she speaks of an "eeven plain." When drawing near to Persia, Alexander is said to have his ships sailing by the mouth of the Indus flood where the boats are stuck upon the flats and mud (pp. 142–143 / ll. 2360–2375). Instead of providing the details of the particular place Alexander has conquered, Bradstreet fixes our attention on which parts of the globe Alexander goes to. Scanning the lines of poetry on any page from "The Third Monarchy" takes us in a matter of seconds across hundreds of miles of often rugged, mountainous territory. So it is that in fewer than one hundred lines Alexander moves from Gaza to Jerusalem to Egypt to Syria, then back to Egypt, until he finally ends up in Phoenicia. As if to leave no doubt what the poem is really about, Alexander continues his journey even after he dies (p. 154 / l. 2775). His dead body travels for two years before being laid to rest in Macedonia. Even death, it seems, cannot control this body's geographic motion.

Death does not stop Alexander; the "East" does. For it is only trying to extend his empire ever further into the "East" that puts an end to Alexander's geographic journey. We can see how Bradstreet aims to naturalize what is ultimately a cultural distinction between East and West in the way she describes Alexander's military decisions and asks us to interpret his ultimate demise. So, for instance, when Alexander decides he should turn his attention "to the East" (p. 135 / l. 2141) once he has defeated his great rival, Darius, Bradstreet casts what might be seen as a strategic decision in cultural terms. She tells us his decision to move toward "the East" is a sign of Alexander's inability to heed the "bounds" set up by the "world" itself (p. 136 / l. 2143). Indeed, the desire to transgress this particular boundary between East and West is used as evidence of Alexander's "boundlesse, fond ambition," which refuses to recognize any of the "bounds" set up by nature (p. 136 / l. 2144). Bradstreet suggests that Alexander stops his unnatural move "East-ward" only when "his Souldiers had no will" to "further extend" his dominion, leaving Alexander no wiser in regard to the sanctity of natural boundaries but without the force necessary to continue his transgressions (p. 141 / ll. 2324–2330).[11]

The corruption and moral degradation Bradstreet and her sources ascribe to Alexander derive, in Bradstreet's version of world history, from his efforts to demolish these boundaries that separate East from West. Geography gets linked to body, which, in turn, gets associated with cultural practices. Alexander's transgression of the natural geographic boundaries that separate one cultural construct, the West, from its supposed opposite, the East, leads to a similar transgression of other supposedly natural boundaries. In other words, the refusal to obey the geographic boundaries that separate East from West produces an Alexander who is unable to maintain cultural boundaries. Once he has extended "his empire" not only to "th' furthest ocean" but even more crucially "to the furthest bounds of th' orient," once the extension of his empire has created an army defined by its "monstrous bulk," Alexander no longer behaves within the moral boundaries set by God (pp. 147, 150 / ll. 2508, 2512, 2626). So, for instance, when his wealth has grown "boundless" by the extraordinary breadth of his rule, "Him boundlesse made, in vice, and cruelty" (p. 129 / ll. 1945–1946). He sets fire to whole towns, puts to death former allies for no discernible reason, and pursues power for power's sake alone.

Alexander's most egregious acts of cruelty grow directly, Bradstreet suggests, from his efforts not only to conquer the East but also to adopt eastern forms. His very death might be taken in this poem to signify the dangers of trying to consume the East in the first place. For, once he heads east, Alexander not only dresses "with *Persian* robes" but insists that "his Nobility" do the same. Indeed, he suddenly and without warning adopts the "manners, habit, gestures" of "that conquered, and luxurious Nation" of Persia (p. 136 / ll. 2166–2170). Lest we miss the implication of his turning Turk, as the early moderns would have said, his "Captains" were "griev'd" at the transformation these seemingly stylistic changes produce: they lament the change they see in his very "minde" that these new "manners" bring about (p. 136 / ll. 2171–2172). It should not surprise

11. Helena Maragou, "The Portrait of Alexander the Great in Anne Bradstreet's 'The Third Monarchy,'" *Early American Literature*, XXIII (1988), 78. Maragou provides the only detailed analysis of the figure of Alexander in "The Foure Monarchies." Eberwein offers a brief though illuminating reading of him in relation to the poem as a whole in "Civil War and Bradstreet's 'Monarchies,'" *Early American Literature*, XXVI (1991), 119–144.

us, then, that his corruption becomes so unmanageable in the East that his subordinates can overtake him as he drinks himself to death.

WHEN BRADSTREET compares Sidney to Alexander in "An Elegie upon That Honourable and Renowned Knight, Sir *Philip Sidney*, Who Was Untimely Slaine at the Seige of *Zutphon*, Anno 1586," she calls on the image of Alexander I have been discussing as well as a long tradition of elegizing Sidney and, within that tradition, a rather conventional comparison in linking Sidney with Alexander. In writing of Sidney at all, in fact, Bradstreet chose to resurrect a poetic tradition that had long been dead. Sidney died in Holland in October 1586, and the elegies began flooding what would pass for a print market in 1587, only to peter out a few years later. Bradstreet tells us she composed her Sidney poem in 1638. This would mean that Sidney had been dead almost fifty years, and the elegiac tradition that memorialized him almost as long. Alexander offered no more original an image. For, by the time Bradstreet wrote her elegy on Sidney, the figure of Alexander the Great had been used so often by other Renaissance writers as to have become a cliché. The figure of Sidney as a modern Alexander was just as conventional. Indeed, "Sidney's earlier elegists," as Raphael Falco points out, "again and again compare the dead hero to Alexander." Bradstreet even co-opts one of the most common themes among those elegists when she claims that both men combined qualities of the poet with those of a warrior, or were, in her words, "Heire to the Muses, the Son of *Mars* in truth." In short, Bradstreet chooses a defunct subgenre to honor a long-dead poet in terms that only replicate the praise the subject had already received.[12]

Such unoriginal poetry can be and has been seen as an indication of the limits of Bradstreet's poetic imagination, but such dismissals miss the role such repetitions function as in Bradstreet's poetry. First, repetition of praise by writers from England performs a kind of cultural work in itself for the colonial writer. In repeating what has become a convention in the homeland, Bradstreet's poem on Sidney serves as a way of demonstrating the Englishness of the colonists. Her praise of Sidney shows that she—and, as a representative for all

12. The date of the Sidney poem is listed in *The Tenth Muse* immediately after the poem's title with the line, "By A. B. . . . . 1638." For a discussion of the many elegies about Sidney as well as the use of Alexander the Great in those elegies, see Rachel Falco, *Conceived Presences: Literary Genealogy in Renaissance England* (Amherst, Mass., 1994), esp. 52–94, 120. Stanford argues in "Bradstreet's Portrait" that "the elegy is modelled upon Joshua Sylvester's elegy on the death of William Sidney, the nephew of Sir Philip," in Cowell and Stanford, eds., *Critical Essays*, 97.

those English people living in America, the colonists in general—has not degenerated though she lives outside England.[13]

If her comparison was conventional, the relationships she posits between colonial, English, and Greek bodies offer a radically different spatial economy that aims at nothing less than to transform conventional notions of identity. In this way, she puts a rather tired comparison in a stale genre to work by using it to sneak a new theory of identity into English discursive systems. To do this, she first casts Sidney in relation to geographic space just as she had cast Alexander. Indeed, she figures Sidney's value to England in terms of geographic space. His worthiness grows out of actions performed, Bradstreet is careful to tell us, outside England. We can see this most prominently, perhaps, in the fact that the poem identifies the place of Sidney's death in the title. What is perhaps most striking about this is that in no other published poem does Bradstreet call our attention in a poem's title to a specific geographic space. But Bradstreet does not stop there. She mentions where he died again in the poem itself, spending several lines telling us how Sidney's death here makes known what would otherwise be an obscure point on a map. Place seems to outshine any other detail of his death, for it is the only detail she deems worthy to mention. In both the 1650 and the 1678 versions of the poem, Bradstreet specifies the precise location of Sidney's decaying body. "His bones do lie interr'd in stately *Pauls.*" Geographic space even serves as the figure for what the nation gains from Sidney's heroic, noble behavior: Sidney brings "Honour to our *British* Land." I take Bradstreet here to be using "Land" as a figure for the English nation, both the political entity of England and the cultural products created by her members. The logic in the Sidney poem seems to be, then, that his death

---

13. I am not claiming here that Bradstreet is representative of colonial New England society in the sociological sense. She is a member of an elite group of New Englanders, separated in many ways by her wealth and status, and for this reason her beliefs and opinions should not be used as an indicator or representative of all the various categories of people in seventeenth-century New England. I do want to argue, though, that *The Tenth Muse* casts Bradstreet as representative in several ways, for instance, as a representative colonist, a representative New England woman, and a representative Puritan mourner. The book's framing material and Bradstreet's poetry frequently want us to understand her as a type, and as such she stands as a representative figure for, sometimes, all of New England or, at other times, part of New England. It is the way in which Bradstreet's poetry works to produce a set of meanings (including its own representativeness or typology status) in particular English and New English discursive systems even as it claims to be only reflecting those systems that I take her as "representative" of colonial identity. I would add only that I think such rhetorical maneuvers and the effects they have on the ways in which discursive systems organize the world have a profound, and perhaps even constitutive, effect on what I called the "sociological" above.

outside England earns him burial on hallowed English ground, which, in turn, makes England itself healthier.

Bradstreet uses Sidney's death outside England as a way of demonstrating England's greater glory during Elizabeth's reign. Bradstreet frames her elegy on Sidney as a meditation on an ideal English identity set during "her Halsion dayes." She casts Sidney not simply as exemplary of this period but as a "Patterne" that all those who reside on "*British* Land" should follow. In calling him a "Patterne" she draws on the meaning of the term at the time as, in the words of the *Oxford English Dictionary*, "anything fashioned, shaped, or designed to serve as a model from which something is to be made." In this way Bradstreet makes Sidney a potentially productive figure who serves not only as a representative of an ideal Englishness but also as a force whose very image will reproduce itself and, thereby, continually reproduce the halcyon days in which he lived. Those halcyon days, we should remember, come when English nobility die outside England.

Sidney's ideal Englishness is insufficient, though. For Sidney to be a pattern worthy of emulation, he must be something more than merely an ideal Englishman. No matter how much praise sixteenth- and seventeenth-century English writers lavished on their storied island home, they inevitably authorized that greatness through a comparison with classical culture. England was great because, for instance, it measured up to ancient Greece. Bradstreet adopts the same rhetorical strategy here. Bradstreet establishes Sidney's ultimate value by obliterating the bodily distinction between this figure of ideal Englishness and the Greek figure of conquest and monarchy. In the very section of the poem, the "Epitaph," meant to give us the essence of the elegy's subject, when she conjures up for her readers the figure of Sidney's "bones . . . interr'd in stately *Pauls*," we read, "*Philip* and *Alexander* both in one."[14] Through Bradstreet's figurative sleight of hand, one dead body becomes indistinguishable from another. English bones become Greek bones. And not just any bones. The very

14. In her extremely insightful essay "Epitaphic Conventions and the Reception of Anne Bradstreet's Public Voice," *Early American Literature*, XXXI (1996), 243–263, Nancy E. Wright argues that the "Epitaph" should be considered a "discrete poem" of its own. While her point that the epitaph has distinctly different generic conventions from the elegy is accurate, I believe the elegy and epitaph are meant to be read as a single unit. Bradstreet uses the same structure, for instance, in her poem on Elizabeth. Indeed, Wright herself notes that the epitaph's "rhyming couplets and the theme of fame . . . relate it to the elegy" (249). For her informative discussion of the concluding lines of the Sidney poem, including a discussion of the epitaph, see 249–250. For another interesting reading of the 1650 version of the Sidney poem that differs from mine in concentrating more on the importance of gender and the role of manuscript culture in the production of the poem's meaning, see Round, *By Nature and by Custom Cursed*, 176–179.

bones of the pattern of ideal Englishness merge their identity with the figure of classical leadership: the figure of classical leadership who Bradstreet has cast in relation to the struggle between East and West and who was widely viewed, as Shankar Raman has noted, as "the one exceptional individual who had apparently embarked upon that terrifying journey to the eastern limits of the world."[15]

The conflation of Sidney's identity with Alexander's works a figurative magic on the struggles over English identity as well; it resolves the tension within English identity that the poem itself enacts. What are we to make, after all, of the fact that Bradstreet identifies as "British" the land to which Sidney brings "Honour" but calls the "Rolls" which authorize his fame as *"Englands"*? What logic underlies her classification of the "tongue" that Sidney's writing helps "refine" as "British," but the "blood that runs within" the author's "veines" as "English"? It is precisely these identity categories, in fact, that caused such heated debate in the years immediately before *The Tenth Muse* and would continue to provide fodder for the London presses for many years to come. Bradstreet consolidates the categories into one when she robs Alexander's figurative body to make it Sidney's own. The poem effectively silences any dispute over what the relation is between English and British identities by saying that, in the end, they are neither English nor British but Greek and English and British simultaneously.[16]

But the poem does not rest at transforming English identities into Greek ones. Or, perhaps, it does not let those identity categories remain unsettled by its figurative attack on the spatial economy that would relegate the colonial English poet to a mere sideshow freak. Bradstreet uses the figure of blood to link her own body with the great Alexander and, by extension, the colonists

15. Shankar Raman, *Framing "India": The Colonial Imaginary in Early Modern Culture* (Stanford, Calif., 2002), 91. The national identity of Alexander's bones raises a host of problems. Neither the modern nation of Greece nor the collection of associations that Alexander helped forge into something known as "Greece" in the ancient world existed when Bradstreet wrote her poem, nor did it exist in 1678, when her poetry was published in New England. Nonetheless, when Bradstreet refers to Alexander and the entity for which he fights in "The Four Monarchies," she refers to him as "Greek."

16. Timothy Sweet offers a very different reading in his provocative and powerful "Gender, Genre, and Subjectivity in Anne Bradstreet's Early Elegies," *Early American Literature*, XXIII (1988), 152–174. Sweet argues that the poem should be read as "an exploration of [English Renaissance] discourse itself" regarding gender and how this discourse works as a "pre-scription of subjectivity" (160). Ivic provides an insightful reading of the reference to "British Land" and "British tongue" in " 'Our British Land,' " in Schwzyer and Mealor, eds., *Archipelagic Identities*. He argues that Bradstreet "performs a Briticization of Sidney that allows her to disarticulate and redefine Englishness. . . . that opens a space for a women writer to inscribe herself into discourse on the nation" (201).

with classical culture. Sidney serves as the pivot point in this link. In order to see how she uses Sidney, we must now consider the differences in the two versions of the Sidney poem as we analyze the way in which Bradstreet connects the colonists to Alexander. When the poem was republished in *Several Poems* twenty-eight years after *Tenth Muse*, it lost almost 50 lines, going from a poem of approximately 145 lines in 1650 to 95 lines in 1678. As I noted at the beginning of this essay, the changes in two lines have generated the most critical interest and bear the most relevance here. In the 1650 version, the speaker of the poem asks potential critics not to dismiss her praise of Sidney simply because she shared with the famous poet "the self-same blood." The 1678 Boston edition of this very same poem substitutes "English" for "self-same."

In both 1650 and 1678, blood serves as the figure that connects Bradstreet with Sidney. In 1650, the phrase "self-same" implies a familial relation, whereas the allusion to "English" in 1678 imagines the more distant connection as members of the same national community. This blood, familial or national, links her own body with the great Alexander. She links classical bodies with colonial ones, then, by linking the blood that flows through a noble British body with the blood that flows through hers. The logic is simple: if Alexander and Sidney are one and Sidney's body is of a piece with Bradstreet's, then Bradstreet and Alexander must be one. [17]

But the 1650 poem relies on precisely the opposite rhetorical strategy to make its point in this passage from what the 1678 version uses. In 1650, Bradstreet asks that readers take her praise of Sidney as motivated by his qualities rather than by her familial connections. In so doing, though, the poet tells us something we simply don't need to know. If the family relation is a closely kept secret, then how would anyone except members of her family even think to disallow her verse for reasons they could not possibly have known? The 1650 poem thus works to contain the very criticisms it alone has made possible and, in so doing,

---

17. For a very different reading of the significance of Bradstreet's invocation of her kinship to the Sidney family, see Ivy Schweitzer, "Anne Bradstreet Wrestles with the Renaissance," *Early American Literature*, XXIII (1988), 291–312. Schweitzer argues, "By invoking a blood relationship to Sidney . . . Bradstreet casts herself as male, son and heir" (299). In so doing, Bradstreet makes herself "an English son," but "her blood connection and writing, contaminated and contaminating because of her sex, are 'strains,' which, as the poem suggests, test her limits" (300). Schweitzer argues that Bradstreet "manages" in the Sidney poem "to transform the potentially paralyzing presence of Sidney into a productive aggression on the cultural constraints on her voice" (300). In "Epitaphic Conventions," *Early American Literature*, XXXI (1996), Wright argues that Bradstreet "explores" in this elegy and her elegy to the French poet, Guillaume Du Bartas, "how the conventions of an epitaph that articulates the name and fame of her precursors authorize and endow her voice with the poetic agency customarily denied to women" (244, and see esp. 244–246).

grant credit to the criticisms themselves. If one accepts Bradstreet's claim to nobility only in order to dismiss her praise of Sidney, then Bradstreet has succeeded in producing at least a small community of the English public who concedes a colonial woman's claim to noble birth. If they, on the other hand, dispute the claim because they do not believe any right-minded English person of noble birth would live in the wilds of America, the very claim of English nobility works to limit the terms of the rejection. Her readers, in other words, are led to deny her status as a member of *English* nobility but, therewith, concede her English identity, however low in rank.

In setting itself up to be criticized for claiming to be of English nobility, then, the poem tries to get its detractors to deny the author's nobility while conceding her a place in the larger English community, even if that place is in the wilds of America. Of course, one logical extension of theories of identity at the time would exclude Bradstreet from Englishness while she lived in the colonies, but it is a reading that would leave the reader in a difficult position. If the English-born poet of this English-language elegy on an undisputed figure of English identity does not belong to this country, to what country does she belong? Or perhaps it should be put more pragmatically: if the country cannot claim Bradstreet as one of its own, on what basis does it claim to rule the colonists in the manner that it does? To disallow Bradstreet's inclusion in the category, then, is to disallow all those whom she represents as well, and to disallow them is to disallow the legitimacy of English practice in the colonies and throughout the world in a burgeoning expansion of English activities across the globe. Either of these readers grants a status to the provincial British-American colonial writer that theories of identity formation cast in doubt. Either conclusion is a rhetorical victory for Bradstreet and, by extension, for all those who live in the colonies.

Of course, this reading assumes an English audience for the poem. I have done so, at least in part, because the title page frames the work with an English audience in mind. It would be hard to imagine British-Americans in the 1650s reading the poem with the same suspicions about one of their own. The 1650 London poem, then, speaks from "over there" to back "here," as the title page implies, where "there" signifies the very edge of England's empire and "here" the imagined homeland of England. The revisions made to the title page of the 1678 collection suggest that John Foster, the publisher of the Boston edition, notices the significance of geography to his readers. The change in place of publication produces a different spatial economy, for Foster changes precisely those lines referring to geography I mentioned above. He drops entirely the reference to the muse growing in America so that the title of this second edition becomes precisely what had, in London 1650, been an alternate title, "Several Poems." This is no longer a work that challenges the distinction between classical and colonial cultures—it simply does not mention such a distinction. And when Foster does locate the poet, he refers to her residence as *"New-England"* rather than "America." The poet transforms into "a Gentlewoman in *New-England"* where before she had been "A Gentlewoman in those parts." Where the 1650 title page, in other words, estranged the book's prospective readers on the basis of a spatial economy that traded on a notion of America and its inhabitants as different from where, and which, readers would consume the book, the 1678 title page uses geography to link its readers to the work's producer.[18]

Indeed, far from representing an alien figure whose geographic location cast doubt on her character, the name "Bradstreet" would have signified social distinction to New Englander readers. For, if colonial New England had had a nobility, the Bradstreet family would have been among it. In addition to blood itself, as I mentioned above, the Bradstreets occupied numerous positions of political and social power within the colony from its very beginnings. Thomas Dudley, Bradstreet's father, was one of five officers of the Massachusetts Bay Company chosen to travel to New England in 1629. Once in the colonies, Dudley quickly became a fixture atop colonial New England society. He served four terms as governor and several more as deputy governor, "second only to Winthrop among the leaders of the colony." Bradstreet's husband, Simon, occupied a position of equal esteem. For instance, in 1661, Bradstreet and John Norton were sent to England as colonial envoys to the court of Charles II, where they persuaded the king to restore the colony's charter. Bradstreet the widower became deputy governor of the colony the same year *Several Poems* was published.[19]

Bradstreet's distinguished pedigree allows us to see how the change from "self-same" to "English" relies on a very different rhetorical strategy from what she used for London readers in 1650. Where the 1650 poem asks its readers not to dismiss her praise of Sidney because she is a member of his family, the 1678 version provides no invitation to dismiss her claims. Indeed, in calling herself English, Bradstreet drapes herself in a category that would be hard to challenge. To suggest otherwise is to imagine a reader in late-seventeenth-century Massachusetts Bay who would deny the Englishness of an esteemed member of the colonial English community who had only recently died. The poem casts the

18. [Bradstreet], *Several Poems.*
19. White, *Anne Bradstreet,* 158.

disallowal of the poet's praise here as a disallowal of Sidney's merits, which every *English* person must concede, rather than as a disallowal of the poet's "blood" connection to Sidney. "Please do not dismiss my praise of Sidney because I am a member of his family" becomes, in 1678, "All those of truly English blood sing the same praises of Sidney, and those who fail to are clearly not English." The poem thus casts the poet's praise of Sidney as a duty all members of the "country" of England owe Sidney. True English people, the poem suggests, praise Sidney. Of course, her readership in late-seventeenth-century New England would be limited almost exclusively—if not entirely—to readers who would identify themselves as English. In agreeing that Sidney's merits should be praised, the Boston reader, it would seem, confirms his or her own status as a member of the English community in the very act of affirming the merits of a member of English nobility who died outside Europe a century before fighting a religious war for England's survival as a Protestant nation.

This notion of Englishness imagined by *Several Poems* has fundamentally changed since *The Tenth Muse* some twenty-eight years earlier. The Boston Englishness of 1678 is a more inclusive figuration of Englishness than its 1650 London counterpart—or at least it includes more colonists in the figure of identity the poem presents. We can see this greater inclusiveness if we look again at the merging of Sidney's bones with Alexander's. Alexander and Sidney remain "both in one" in Boston as they were in London, but their bones bear a different relation to the world from what they did less than thirty years earlier. Sidney himself suffers a decline. Sidney dies in 1650 as "the quintessence of men," whereas in 1678 he "dy'd 'mong most renown'd of men." He goes, in other words, from being a figure for the purest qualities of all humanity to being one member of the category of people who have gained high esteem among their peers. Bradstreet does not take away Sidney's representative status completely, though. He remains in Boston as he was in London the "Patterne" for England's "Halsion dayes." When we put these changes together, we see that in 1650 the "Patterne" for ideal Englishness managed to rise above the very model of classical greatness to define humanity itself. The pattern for the English nation, in other words, bests the pattern for antiquity and, in so doing, suggests that England itself might be better at its very best than even the most storied classical figures. The England of 1678 Boston achieves no such heights. This England can claim only to be among Alexander's—and therefore, classical antiquity's—peers.

What it loses in status it gains in numbers. While Boston's England falls from its perch atop all nations, that very same England can lay claim to a more inclusive body politic. For Bradstreet's London poem sought entry into the

English nation on behalf of her fellow colonists by claiming noble birth, a move that might have won her entry into those English circles but would have excluded the vast majority of her fellow New Englanders. Boston's Englishness, on the other hand, does not depend on noble birth, but imagines a national blood that runs through all those English peoples scattered across the globe. Boston's Englishness is both more and less nationalist. It is less nationalist in that it deflates England's status among the civilized nations of history. It is more nationalist in that it sweeps more peoples in more places into its not-always-so-loving family.

I want to be clear about what I am trying to argue here. I am not claiming that Bradstreet changes this figure to argue for a creole identity. Quite the contrary. I believe Bradstreet alters the way in which she figures her ties to England from nobility to nation in the hopes that this will allow her and her fellow colonists to claim what might be called an unqualified English identity. She and her fellow colonists, I maintain, want to avoid being labeled "creoles." In 1650, she sought to avoid this label by claiming ties to English nobility. In 1678, she sought to avoid this label by claiming ties to the English nation and culture. In both cases, though, Bradstreet wants us to understand these ties as untainted by where she is on the globe. Place, she insists, does not make person.

The shift from claiming to be a member of Sidney's family to being a member of a community of English subjects might have as much to do with audience as with modesty. We should remember that just one year before the 1678 publication of *Several Poems* the very same publisher printed Increase Mather's *Relation of the Troubles Which Have Hapned in New-England, by Reason of the Indians There,* and William Hubbard's *Narrative of the Troubles with the Indians in New-England.* Only four years later Samuel Green in Cambridge would print Mary Rowlandson's *Soveraignty and Goodness of God.* The specter of Indianization haunts New England readers of 1678 in a way that it certainly did not haunt 1650 London readers. The almost total annihilation at the hands of the Indians in the recent wars described by Mather and Hubbard would have brought the question of one's relation to one's colleagues across the Atlantic into violent relief. The change from "self-same" to "English" directly addresses such a concern by providing a way for its readers to establish their membership in a transatlantic English community through simple affirmation of Sidney's greatness. In so doing, they also link themselves—for themselves, rather than for an English audience—to a classical figure of unchallenged status. Bradstreet's poems engage the threat of degeneration, then, by use of classical figures, that is, figures from the past, whose identity derives from their battles with what Bradstreet refers to as the "East." The figuration of English identity by a colonial writer threatened by the specter of degeneration looks as much to the corrupted yet powerful conqueror of the East for its sense of itself as it does to the supposedly savage lands and peoples imagined to be—perhaps hoped to be—somewhere to its west.[20]

IF THE analysis above has any validity, it raises, I believe, more questions about English creole identity than it answers. Benedict Anderson's notion of "creole pioneers" remains the most dominant force behind our understanding of the way in which creole identity functions in the colonial Americas. In his now famous formulation, Anderson suggests that the colonists developed a distinct identity as a result of defining themselves against the indigenous populations and as still a part of the communities they left behind in Europe. The colonists became both European in relation to other New World peoples and American in relation to old Europe. Anderson's argument (as others have pointed out) relies on, even if it does not explicitly analyze as such, early modern theories of identity formation that depend on spatial figures as much as they do on the figure of pure blood. After all, creoles are excluded from certain positions of power solely on the basis of where on the globe they were born. Bradstreet's poetry adds another spatial as well as a temporal dimension. Bradstreet's poems engage the problem of creolization by use of classical figures, that is, figures from the past, whose identities derive from their battles with the "East." The indigenous peoples of the New World are mentioned only once in her poetry, and even then they are mentioned in relation to "the Indians of the East." How, I would ask, do we fit Bradstreet's specifically colonial refiguration of English identity into a theory of creolization when her work seems to offer a way of positioning the colonial subject that stands outside the theories we have at hand? What role, in other words, might the use of classical figures have in the development of specifically colonial identities? After all, Alexander can only be a figure for Bradstreet in the sense that, unlike native Americans, he not only does not but cannot present himself to her in the same way as the indigenous peoples of North America. I ask this since, after all, Bradstreet would have known of the people and places of what she refers to as "the East" only through

<hr />

20. Ivic, " 'Our British Land,' " in Schwyzer and Mealor, eds., *Archipelagic Identities,* provides the most provocative and compelling analysis that I have seen on the revision of "self-same" to "English" that has been my focus in this essay. Ivic asks whether Bradstreet can "be heard" in this change "to proclaim her 'English blood,' to reclaim an English identity." He goes on to point out that an ambiguity exists in how one reads "yet" in the line. After all, Ivic reminds us, we can read "yet" "as implying continuity. . . . But 'yet' can also mean 'still,' " which, in turn, "can . . . be read as expressing a deep anxiety about degeneracy, a decaying of identity" (202). In certain ways, my essay as a whole stands as an attempt to respond to these very important questions.

writing, whereas her knowledge of native peoples would have almost certainly been more immediate.[21]

In this, Bradstreet appears to offer a challenge to the assumption that underlies much analysis of creole identity formation, namely, what Mary Louise Pratt has called the model of the "contact zone." The Englishness that Bradstreet offers her readers from the wilds of America emerges from the zone of reading that occurs in the midst of colonial encounters. This zone of reading that is composed of figures of speech might very well lead us to ask about the very terms we use to categorize Bradstreet's contributions to early modern debates over identity formation. Indeed, in paying close attention to the figures of Bradstreet's rather bookish Englishness I think it is fair to ask whether we do not risk fundamentally misconstruing her contribution by using a Spanish model to understand an English discursive system. I say this because, as scholars before me have pointed out, English writers in both the colonies and England only rarely before the eighteenth century used "creole" to refer to the English people living in America, even though the word was readily available to them.[22] As noted above, Bradstreet herself uses her poetry in part in order to show that she is just as English as anyone who lives in the British Isles. She seems, in other words, to reject the label "creole." I worry, then, that, if we ask how British-American colonial writers represent creolization, we might already have resolved the problem that drove us to the archive before we have even looked at the texts. Is there an alternate set of figures that writers in English on either side of the Atlantic used to classify themselves that gives us a different— even if related—picture of colonial identity from what we find in Spanish writers? What figures do the English colonists turn to in the hope of showing they have lost none of their Englishness while living outside England?

21. Benedict Anderson's classic formulation of the importance of what he calls "creole pioneers" can be found in the chapter of the same name in *Imagined Communities: Reflections on the Origin and Spread of Nationalism*, rev. ed. (London, 1991), 47–65. For an analysis of the "spatial dialectics" as they relate to the theory of creolization, see Ralph Bauer, *The Cultural Geography of Colonial American Literatures: Empire, Travel, Modernity* (Cambridge, 2003), esp. 12–14.

22. Mary Louise Pratt elaborates on the significance of what she calls writing that emerges out of a "contact zone" in *Imperial Eyes: Travel Writing and Transculturation* (London, 1992), 6. John Canup mentions the problem of the infrequency of the use of the word "creole" in English in the seventeenth century for any study of creolization, in the final chapter of *Out of the Wilderness: The Emergence of an American Identity in Colonial New England* (Middletown, Conn., 1990), and in "Cotton Mather and "Criolian Degeneracy," *Early American Literature,* XXIV (1989), 20–34.

LÚCIA HELENA COSTIGAN

Self- and Collective Identity among New Christians in the Periphery of the Iberian Empires: Bento Teixeira, Ambrósio Fernandes Brandão, and Manuel Beckman

In the Introduction to *Colonial Identity in the Atlantic World, 1500–1800,* John H. Elliott observes that the tendency to study areas of the colonial Atlantic world as compartmentalized societies has led to a narrowing focus and a great divide even among "specialists, working on the same empire." The narrowing focus and the "great divide" underlined by Elliott can be seen in the historiography that constitutes the canon known as colonial Latin American studies. Using as an example the colonial period, one can see that, despite the inclusion of the experiences of indigenous subjects, the canon is still very restricted in its approach to minorities that played a major role in the development of the Atlantic colonial world, such as blacks and individuals of Jewish heritage that during the rise of the Spanish and the Portuguese Empires were forced to convert to Christianity and were called *conversos,* or *cristãos novos,* or New Christians. Another limitation of the colonial Latin American canon has to do with the fact that it centers primarily on the viceroyalties of Mexico and Peru and excludes less central Spanish areas as well as the Brazilian and Caribbean regions.[1]

A preliminary version of this essay was read at Purdue University; I would like to thank Professor Paul B. Dixon and the faculty members of the Department of Foreign Languages and Literatures for the invitation. I also would like to thank Ralph Bauer, José Antonio Mazzotti, Derek Petrey, Thomas Stovicek, and, particularly, Gil Kelly for reading the text and helping polish some of the translations from Portuguese.

1. In Elliott's words: "Regions have been broken up into subregions and colonial empires have been fragmented into a congeries of individual historical units, leaving a great divide even between specialists working on the same empire." John H. Elliott, "Introduction: Colonial Identity in the Atlantic World," in Nicholas Canny and Anthony Pagden, eds., *Colonial Identity in the Atlantic World, 1500–1800* (Princeton, N.J., 1987), 3–13, esp. 2–3.

Creole identity or consciousness is one of the topics in colonial studies where one can very clearly detect the overemphasis on New Spain and Peru. Anthony Pagden and Solange Alberro are among the critics who portray Spanish settlers from Mexico and Lima as the first colonists to reveal in their writings self-awareness, or "criollo consciousness." In his essay "Identity Formation in Spanish America," Pagden states that, compared to the English, the Portuguese, and the French, the Spanish settlers "possessed a distinctive set of political aspirations." By the middle of the seventeenth century, he argues, the native-born creole elite from Mexico and Peru had already acquired "a clear sense of belonging to a culture that in many, if not yet all, respects was independent of the 'mother country.'" "In most other areas, economically more dependent upon the metropolis, such self-awareness came much later." Following in Pagden's footsteps, Alberro defends a similar point of view. In her essay "La emergencia de la conciencia criolla: el caso novohispano," she asserts that mainly the viceroyalties of Peru and New Spain displayed a clear sense of collective identity among Spanish creoles. She also highlights Mexico City and Lima, urban centers with solid economic and institutional organizations, as the only places able to promote the development of a distinct identity among the Spanish ruling elite and their descendants.[2]

In contrast with Pagden's and Alberro's point of view, Stuart B. Schwartz suggests that a feeling of distinctiveness, a lack of identification with Europe, and a profound realization of the colonial reality existed precociously among the mestizo and mulatto populations who lived in different parts of the New World. I agree with Schwartz. In the particular case of Brazil, the existence of Quilombo dos Palmares, the settlement of runaway and freeborn African slaves,

2. Anthony Pagden, "Identity Formation in Spanish America," ibid., 51–93, esp. 52; Solange Alberro, "La emergencia de la conciencia criolla: el caso novohispano," in José Antonio Mazzotti, ed., *Agencias criollas: la ambigüedad "colonial" en las letras hispanoamericanas* (Pittsburgh, 2000), 55–71, esp. 69. For the purpose of the present essay, the expression "criollo consciousness" refers to the process of accommodation and self-affirmation by the individuals who lived in the New World. The New Christian subjects analyzed in this text were also known in Portuguese as "gente da nação," an expression that can be associated with the negative meaning of the word "damnation." This expression finds correspondence in José Antonio Mazzotti's ethnic characterization of the concept of "nación criolla" as a group of people who shared among them "fuertes rasgos de unidad racial, cultural y lingüística, muchas veces coincidente con el concepto de 'casta,' y casi siempre identificable por la aceptación común de una dinastía fundadora" [strong characteristics of racial, cultural, and linguistic unity, often coinciding with the concept of "caste," and almost always identifiable by the common acceptance of a founding dynasty]. See Mazzotti, "Resentimiento criollo y nación étnica: el papel de la épica novohispana," in Mazzotti, ed., *Agencias criollas*, 143–160, esp. 144. In this essay I avoid the use of the Portuguese word *crioulo* because of its pejorative meaning. In colonial Brazil individuals born from white Portuguese parents were called *mazombos*.

founded in the Serra da Barriga hills in the 1600s as a center of resistance for thousands of runaway slaves and lasting for almost a century, clearly exemplifies a sense of collective identity among Africans and their descendants. Resistance to slavery by blacks, mulattos, and mestizos who lived in Quilombo dos Palmares during the sixteenth and seventeenth centuries not only corroborates Schwartz's thesis but also puts into question Pagden's and Alberro's view that only among members of the criollo elite from Mexico and Peru does one detect distinctive political aspirations by the middle of the seventeenth century. Palmares also challenges the idea, dating back to colonial times, of harmonious racial relations in Brazil. While focusing on colonial Brazil, Schwartz also detected two major groups of white colonizers who, similar to the mulattoes and mestizos, revealed a strong attachment to the New World. These two white groups were formed by the Jesuits and the New Christians (a term in popular usage often extended to Jewish descendants over several generations).[3]

Members of the Society of Jesus and the descendants of Jews who came to Brazil in the second half of the sixteenth century distinguished themselves from other white settlers, arguably, because the followers of Ignatius of Loyola, as an emergent religious order, and the New Christians, who were then regarded as a despised ethnic and religious minority, did not find space in sixteenth-century Spanish society. Different from the traditional Iberian and criollo elite who saw the New World as a point of departure for recognition in Spain and Portugal, the Jesuits and the New Christians saw the Americas as a place where they could start a new life without the limitations that they faced in the Iberian Peninsula during the sixteenth and seventeenth centuries. Another aspect that connects the Jesuits and the descendants of Jews, which distinguishes them from traditional Catholics, is the fact that both the Jesuits and the New Christians did not believe that, in order to gain eternal life, a person had to renounce this world. These facts, combined with the personal and the commercial connections that existed among the Jesuits and the Portuguese New Christians

3. Although written before Solange Alberro's essay, Stuart B. Schwartz's "Formation of a Colonial Identity in Brazil" shares with Elliott the concern related to the "great divide" in colonial studies, particularly those dealing with criollo consciousness. The cultural historian observes that criollo self-identity has been treated in isolation from the social and political contexts within the colonies that formed the New World; see Schwartz, "The Formation of a Colonial Identity in Brazil," in Canny and Pagden, eds., *Colonial Identity in the Atlantic World*, 15–50. In his essay "Palmares: An African State in Brazil," *Journal of African History*, VI (1965), 161–175, R. K. Kent portrays Palmares as a kind of harmonious African state in Brazil. Because of the lack of supporting documentation, Kent's essay has been contested by Brazilian historians. However, as one can see in Ronaldo Vainfas, ed., *Dicionário do Brasil colonial, 1500–1808* (Rio de Janeiro, 2000), Brazilian historians also admit that the resistance by those who lived in Palmares threatened the economy of the Brazilian society that so heavily depended on slave labor.

who lived in Africa and in the Americas, contributed to creating among these two groups of white colonizers early manifestations of a collective sense of a distinct identity.[4]

In this essay, I focus on three Portuguese New Christian colonists who lived in the northern regions of Brazil in the sixteenth and the seventeenth centuries, who from very early on revealed political, religious, and social ideas that distinguished them from other colonists, including some Spaniards who lived in Mexico City and Lima. To better exemplify the development of a distinct criollo consciousness in Brazil, I center my analysis on Bento Teixeira (1561–1600), Ambrósio Fernandes Brandão (1555–1618?) and Manuel Beckman (1630–1685). The period covered extends from August 5, 1580, the date of the recognition of Philip II of Spain as Philip I of Portugal, to November 2, 1685, when a popular revolt in the northern part of Brazil, known as the Levante do Maranhão, ended with the death of Manuel Beckman.

Bento Teixeira and His *Prosopopéia*

Bento Teixeira was a New Christian born in Porto, Portugal, around 1561 who moved to Brazil when he was five years old. He studied with the Jesuits in the Salvador da Bahia and became a man of letters who knew Latin

4. The thesis that the Jesuits planned, not to stop the religious reform started by Martin Luther, but to surpass it, is defended by Bolívar Echeverría, who explains that for the members of the Jesuit order truly Christian behavior consisted, not in renouncing the world, but in fighting in it and for it, in order to conquer evil. ("Para la Compañía de Jesús, el comportamiento verdaderamente cristiano no consiste en renunciar al mundo, . . . sino en luchar en él y por él, para ganárselo a las tinieblas, al mal, al diablo.") He also underlines the fact that the followers of Ignatius of Loyola succeeded in cultivating the criollo elite and in building a solid economic enterprise in early modern times. ("En América, la actividad de la Compañía de Jesús en los centros citadinos tuvo gran amplitud e intensidad. . . . Desde el cultivo de la élite criolla hasta el manejo de la primera version histórica del capital financiero, pasando por los multiples mecanismos de organización de la vida social.") See Bolívar Echeverría, "La Compañía de Jesús y la primera modernidad de América Latina," in Petra Schumm, ed., *Barrocos y modernos: nuevos caminos en la investigación del barroco iberoamericano* (Frankfort on the Main, 1989), 49–65, esp. 55, 58. Luiz Felipe de Alencastro documents the commercial and personal connections among New Christians and Jesuits from Brazil and Africa. In his opinion, the Atlantic-African conditionings—distinct from the European connections—mark the originality of the Brazilian historical formation: "Os condicionamentos atlânticos, africanos—distintos dos vínculos europeus—, . . . marcam a originalidade da formação histórica brasileira"(21). [The Atlantic, African conditionings—distinct from the European connections—mark the originality of the Brazilian historical formation.] Because of the monsoon winds and the seasonal storms that made it very difficult for vessels to sail from Bahia or Recife directly to Lisbon after April, many ships sailed to Angola, and from there to Lisbon. As a result of the trade connection between Portuguese America and the west coast of Africa, people in Lisbon considered Angola an extension of Brazil. See Luiz Felipe de Alencastro, *O trato dos viventes: formação do Brasil no Atlântico sul* (São Paulo, 2000).

and Hebrew and was very familiar with mythology, Cabala, and classical as well as Renaissance texts. Upon completing his education he married Filipa Raposa, a woman considered an Old Christian, who lived in the Bahian town of Ilhéus. To cope with the economic responsibilities of marriage, Bento moved to Pernambuco, where, in addition to being a teacher, he found time to write, to translate the Old Testament from Hebrew into Portuguese, and to act as a counselor for other descendants of Jews who lived in the region. During the first visitation of the Inquisition on the northeast of Brazil (1591–1595), Bento had an entanglement with the Holy Office. In 1593, perhaps from fear of being accused of Judaism, he killed Filipa Raposa, giving as justification that she had betrayed him with other men, including the local priest. Apparently, while the death of his wife caused him no problems, his religious inclination did. Denounced before the representative of the Holy Office as a heretic, Bento Teixeira was jailed in 1595 in Recife and in 1596 was transferred to the Inquisition's cells in Lisbon. He remained there until January 31, 1599, when he participated in an auto-da-fé and apparently abjured Judaism. As a result, Bento, instead of burning at the stake, received the penitential garment (called *sambenito*) and was sentenced to spend the rest of his life in Lisbon under the eyes and care of a Catholic priest. However, shortly after his release from the Inquisition jails, he died of tuberculosis in July 1600. Bento Teixeira's story did not have any impact on Brazilian literature, because most of the nineteenth- and twentieth-century critics who wrote about the epic poem *Prosopopéia* did not know exactly who the author of the poem was. Nor did they know that Bento Teixeira had been a victim of the Inquisition.

It is clear from a reading of Bento Teixeira's *Prosopopéia,* the first epic written in Portuguese in the New World, that Pernambuco was to him not only a place to rise within the traditional social order but also a safe haven for all those who were seeking to escape persecution in Europe. The encomiastic poem, written during the last decade of the sixteenth century, when Portugal and all its lands were under the domain of Philip II of Spain, was dedicated to Jorge de Albuquerque Coelho, governor of Pernambuco. Perhaps in order to be read and published, Bento Teixeira chose to model his poem after *Os Lusíadas,* by Luís de Camões (1524–1580). It is relevant to note that Camões's epic was published for the first time in 1572, just eight years before Dom Sebastião, the unmarried Portuguese king, disappeared in the Battle of Alcacer Kibir in 1578, leaving Portugal without an heir to the throne.

Because *Prosopopéia* was modeled after the most famous Lusitanian epic and because of a critical preoccupation with questions of aesthetics, Portuguese and Brazilian critics, by failing to see how its aesthetics engage with its content, have usually regarded Bento Teixeira as a cheap imitator of Camões. Thus, they saw the first epic written in Pernambuco as a poem without merit of its own. By considering solely the aesthetic aspect of the epic, these critics failed to see the subtle critique of Spanish domination in *Prosopopéia*. As the verses that follow suggest, the poet seemed to be encouraging the Portuguese people who were suffering persecution to find the strength to face the difficulties that they experienced after the disappearance of King Dom Sebastião:[5]

Neste tempo Sebasto Lusitano

Da fome, e da sêde o rigor passando,
E outras faltas em fim dificultosas,
Convém-vos aquirir ūa força nova
Que o fim as cousas examina e prova.

In this Sebastian Lusitane time, facing hunger, thirst, and other hardships even worse, you should acquire a new power that examines and tries things at the final hour.[6]

The verses above allude to the intensification of sufferings of the Portuguese people after the death of Dom Sebastião. In the face of the many adversities that they are experiencing, the poetic voice urges them to acquire a new strength and power. The hardships that the Portuguese people, and particularly the New Christians, faced after 1580, can be documented in the passages of Bento Teixeira's trial. Also, the findings of historians like João Lúcio de Azevedo, David M. Gitlitz, and Gordon M. Weiner, among others, point to the intensification of

---

5. Sônia Aparecida Siqueira and Luiz Roberto Alves each analyze Bento's poem and also his Inquisition trial in order to underline the presence of crypto-Judaism in the poet. Nelson Vieira and Kênia Maria de Almeida Pereira rely primarily on the title, on the emphasis on Proteus, and on other aspects of the *Prosopopéia* to refer to the poet's crypto-Judaic attitude. See Sônia Aparecida Siqueira, "O cristão-novo Bento Teixeira: cripto-judaísmo no Brasil Colônia," *Revista de Historia*, XC (1972), 395–476; Luiz Roberto Alves, *Confissão, poesia, e Inquisição* (São Paulo, 1983); Nelson H. Vieira, "Simulation and Dissimulation: An Expression of Crypto-Judaism in the Literature of Colonial Brazil," *Colonial Latin American Review*, II (1993), 143–164; Kênia Maria de Almeida Pereira, *A poética da resistência em Bento Teixeira e Antônio José da Silva, o judeu* (São Paulo, 1998). For a more detailed study of the reception of Bento Teixeira's epic poem by nineteenth- and twentieth-century critics, see my "Épica e Inquisição no novo mundo: a *Prosopopéia* segundo o processo 5.206 da Inquisição de Lisboa," in Karl Kohut and Sonia V. Rose, eds., *La formación de la cultura virreinal* (Madrid, 2000), 161–180.

6. Bento Teixeira, *Prosopopéia* (1601), ed. Celso Cunha and Carlos Duval (Rio de Janeiro, 1972), 59, 65. Further references to this edition will appear parenthetically in the text. English translations are mine.

persecution of Portuguese New Christians after the coronation of Philip II as king of Portugal in 1580.[7]

It is possible to argue for an intertextual relationship between the *Prosopopéia* and Camões's *Os Lusíadas* in communicating messages of hope and resistance to other Portuguese New Christians who were forced into diaspora after the imposed conversions in the Iberian Peninsula in the last decade of the fifteenth century, and particularly after 1580, with Philip II's coronation. The following lines illustrate this argument:

Companheiros leais, a quem no Côro
Das Musas tem a fama entronizado,
Não deveis ignorar, que não ignoro,
Os trabalhos que haveis no Mar passado.
Respondestes 'té 'gora com o fôro,
Devido a nosso Luso celebrado,
Mostrando-vos mais firmes contra a sorte
Do que ela contra nós se mostra forte. (59)

Loyal companions, whom the choir of Muses has enthroned to fame, ignore not (as I do not) the labor you have spent at sea. Until now you have responded with the forum, owing to our celebrated Luso, showing yourselves firm against fate, which, arrayed against us, is shown to be great.

Verses that allude to collective sufferings and resistance such as those function as a reference to the persecution suffered by Lusitanians of Jewish origin. They could also be seen as a manifestation of the Lurianic Cabala movement that spread throughout the Old and the New World in the sixteenth and the seventeenth centuries as a response to the calamitous times experienced by Jewish exiles from the Iberian Peninsula that started in the last decade of the

7. João Lúcio de Azevedo explains that in order to get rid of the New Christians who lived in Portugal Philip II obtained a special permission from the pope that limited their benefits. In his words: "Interveio Filipe II, alcançando de Xisto V a proibição de serem providos em benefícios indivíduos de linhagem hebraica." [Philip II intervened, coercing Pope Sixtus V to prohibit special benefits to those of Hebrew heritage.] David M. Gitlitz documents that in the last twenty years of the sixteenth century "more than fifty autos-da-fé" took place in Portugal. Gordon M. Weiner affirms, "After the Inquisition began in earnest in Portugal in 1536, and especially after the unification of the Spanish and Portuguese crowns in 1580, there was a dramatic increase in Sephardic migrations." See Azevedo, *História dos cristãos-novos portugueses*, 2d ed. (1921; Lisbon, 1975), 151; Gitlitz, *Secrecy and Deceit: The Religion of the Crypto-Jews* (Philadelphia, 1996), 52; Weiner, "Sephardic Philo and anti-Semitism in the Early Modern Era: The Jewish Adoption of Christian Attitudes," in Richard H. Popkin and Gordon M. Weiner, eds., *Jewish Christians and Christian Jews: From the Renaissance to the Enlightenment* (Dordrecht, 1994), 189–214, esp. 190.

fifteenth century. After the disappearance of Dom Sebastião in 1578 and the annexation of Portugal by the Spanish Empire in 1580, the cataclysmic experiences felt by the Portuguese people in general and the New Christians in particular gave origin to Sebastianism, a popular messianic movement that spread throughout Portugal and its colonies. Taking advantage of topoi of Renaissance and Baroque poetry that emphasize the instability of life, such as one sees in the verses, "O sorte tão cruel, como mudável" [O fate so cruel, so changing] (43) and "Neste tempo Sebasto Lusitano" (65), the poet seems to be allegorically referring to the uncertainty of the lives of New Christians who lived in the Portuguese Empire at that time. Going against the norm of ancient epic tradition that attributed justice and other virtues to the king, the poetic voice does exactly the contrary. It denounces the king's injustice and lack of sincerity with his subjects:

Mas quem por seus serviços bons não herda
Desgosta de fazer cousa lustrosa,
Que a condição do Rei que não é franco
O vassalo faz ser nas obras manco. (33)

But those who are not rewarded for their efforts give up doing good deeds because the lack of honesty of the king will result in the lack of honorable work from the vassals.

In stanza 34 the poetic voice again seems to be criticizing the king. This time it is the despotism and the ingratitude of the monarch that the poet attacks:

Mas, quando virem que do Rei potente
O pai por seus serviços não alcança
O galardão devido e glória digna,
Ficarão nos alpendres da Piscina. (43)

But, if they see that, from the mighty king, the father receives for his work neither due reward nor glory dignified, they will remain waiting forever for the king's promises.[8]

---

8. In note 8 of stanza 34 in their edition of *Prosopopéia,* Cunha and Duval explain that the verse "Ficarão nos alpendres da Piscina" corresponds to "Ficarão à espera das mercês reais" (117). This expression puts in evidence the power of the king. They also explain that the word *piscina* ("fish pond," "altar basin"), derived from the Latin term *piscis,* corresponds to the Hebrew term *Bethsaida,* or Bethesda, a biblical word that means lake, fountain, and place of healing. The Hebrew meaning of this word (which appears in capital letters) reinforces the idea of crypto-Jewish and messianic messages encoded in Bento Teixeira's poem.

Silvio Romero, the scholar who first introduced sociopolitical orientation into Brazilian literary criticism, detected a gesture of colonial resistance in these verses when he affirms in his *História da literatura brasileira* that the poem displays "uma certa dose de humor satírico,—uma censura aos reis descuidados e inúteis" [a certain dose of satirical humor and criticism against the careless and good-for-nothing kings]. More specifically, I would argue, the poet from Pernambuco penned his verses as a criticism directed at Philip II, a king known among Spaniards by the nickname "the Prudent" but who was regarded by the Portuguese people in general and the descendants of Jews in particular as an overbearing ruler who was engaged in an attempt to purge Portugal of its New Christian population.[9]

As I have attempted to prove elsewhere, based on passages of Bento Teixeira's Inquisition trial, the poet seemed to have regarded Philip II and his political and religious zeal as a threat to all the descendants of Jews who lived under the Spanish Empire. A passage from his trial clearly shows the poet's opposition to the policies of the monarch regarding New Christians. In one of the statements written in the Inquisition jails the poet explains that he and other Portuguese New Christians caught by the Inquisition had to pay large sums of money for forgiveness of their sins and that, even after the payment, they did not obtain the pardon promised by the royal highness, and the social stigma linked to their ethnic and religious past was never lifted:[10]

> Mostrem este capítulo aos que vão para Madri, e digam-lhes que não reparem com sua real Magestade em dinheiro inda que seja dar-lhe um milhão e meio d'ouro, porque pelo capítulo desta me obrigo a dar eu só 30.000 cruzados de letras passadas à vista e mais me obrigo só no Brasil tirar 400.000 cruzados.

> Show this chapter to those who are going to Madrid, and tell them not to dispute matters of money with his royal majesty, even if to give him one and a half million in gold. By this chapter, I commit myself to give 30,000 cruzados in promissory letters passed before my eyes, and, furthermore, I also obligate myself, in Brazil alone, to raise 400,000 cruzados.[11]

9. Sílvio Romero, *História da literatura brasileira* (1888), 6th ed. (Rio de Janeiro, 1960), II, 362.

10. See Lúcia Helena Costigan, "A experiência do converso letrado Bento Teixeira: um *missing link* na história intelectual e literária do Brasil-colônia," *Revista de crítica literaria latinoamericana*, XL (1994), 77–92, and "Empreendimento e resistência do cristão-novo face à política de Filipe II: o processo inquisitorial de Bento Teixeira," *Colonial Latin American Review*, XII (2003), 37–61.

11. Cf. "Quinto Aviso," Processo 5.206 da Inquisição de Lisboa (microfilm 633), Arquivo Nacional da Torre do Tombo, Lisbon.

Another passage of the trial proceeding makes clear that the policies of the Spanish emperor hurt New Christians:

> Estes anos atrás mandou El-Rei Filipe visitar as inquisições deste reino . . . as quais visitou Martin Gonçalves da Câmara, que em tempo del Rei Sebastião governou o reino todo. E tal seja a sua saúde e vida, qual foi a visita que ele fez, que se antes disto prendiam muita gente da nação mais prendem agora e penitenciam.[12]

> Some years ago King Philip ordered the Inquisitions to come to this kingdom . . . Martin Gonçalves da Camara went to see them, he who in the time of King Sebastian governed the whole kingdom. And long be his health and life, which was the visit he made, that if they previously seized many people from the land, now they seize and punish them even more.

Here the poet makes it clear that the Inquisition became harsher toward New Christians during the rule of Philip II. This fact can be confirmed with letters written to the Spanish king by his nephew the Archduke Albert of Austria, found in the Archivo General de Simancas. In a gesture that reveals suspicion and hostility toward the Portuguese people of Jewish origin, the Archduke Albert—who occupied simultaneously the roles of viceroy and chief inquisitor of Portugal—replies to his uncle in a letter dated August 9, 1586: "Por muitas vezes tratei a importancia de que he irem-se desta Cidade [Lisboa] os judeus que nella andão. E VMe. o tem assi mandado, E por mais diligências que nisso se fizerão, até agora não foi possível acabarem de se ir." [Many times I have noted how important it is that the Jews of this City [Lisbon] leave. And your royal majesty has so ordered. However, despite all the efforts made toward this end, until now it has not been possible to succeed in getting all of them to leave.][13]

The passage reveals that Philip II of Spain was behind the dispersal of the many Portuguese of Jewish origin who left the Lusitanian nation in the last decades of the sixteenth century. Bento Teixeira's suggestion in his trial that,

---

12. See "Título das palavras que usam a gente da nação . . . ," Processo 5.206 da Inquisição de Lisboa.

13. Secretarías provinciales, libro 1550, Archivo General de Simancas (microfilm). Similar to *Os Lusíadas* of Camoës and *La Araucana* of Alfonso de Ercilla y Zúñiga, the *Prosopopéia* breaks away from the rules of the ancient epic tradition by incorporating autobiographical elements. However, different from the previous poems, Teixeira does not dedicate his poem to the king, as was the general norm at the time, but dedicates it to Jorge Coelho de Albuquerque, governor of Pernambuco, then a marginal area of the Spanish Empire.

after the death of Dom Sebastião and the coronation of the Hapsburg monarch as king of Portugal, New Christians were persecuted by the Inquisition more than before provides a context for understanding the political message of the *Prosopopéia* as an address to other New Christians and Sephardic Jews who were active in the imperial rivalries involving Portuguese, Spanish, and Dutch interests during the sixteenth and the seventeenth centuries. It is thus similar to *Os Lusíadas* of Camões and *La Araucana* of Alonso de Ercilla y Zúñiga (1533–1594), in which, as James Nicolopulos has observed, "the hallowed occidental practice of *imitatio*. . . . [or] poetic imitation, far from serving as mere digressive ornament . . . played a key role in the construction of a new 'poetics' of imperialist expansion." Different from Camões's and Ercilla's epics, however, both of which share "vital rivalry and dialogue," Bento Teixeira's *Prosopopéia* does not defend the transatlantic expansion as a messianic mission reserved for the Christians of Portugal and Spain. Beneath the epic imitation of Camões's *Os Lusíadas* we find in *Prosopopéia* a poetic, messianic, and religious program that assigns a central role to the descendants of Sephardic Jews in the imperial expansion to the west.[14]

Because of the praises that the poet directs to Pernambuco, *Prosopopéia* could be compared to Bernardo de Balbuena's *Grandeza mexicana*, a poem written in 1604, considered by some critics an early manifestation of criollo consciousness in New Spain. However, one major difference between these two early poems rests in the fact that, while *Grandeza mexicana* emphasizes Spanish institutions such as the Inquisition, the churches, the convents, and above all the power of the ruling elite from the city of Mexico, the *Prosopopéia* praises Pernambuco for the generosity of its fauna and flora, for the courage of its people, and for its port, which functioned as a safe haven for those seeking refuge and a better life in the New World:[15]

14. James Nicolopulos, *The Poetics of Empire in the Indies: Prophecy and Imitation in "La Araucana" and "Os Lusíadas"* (University Park, Pa., 2000), ix, xi.

15. Despite the ambiguities that Georgina Sabat-Rivers sees in *Grandeza mexicana*, she recognizes Balbuena's poem as an early manifestation of criollo consciousness. She bases her argument on the fact that, different from his poem *Siglo de oro en las selvas de Erífile*, where praises are reserved solely to Spain, *Grandeza mexicana* lauds Mexico for its flora, fauna, inhabitants, and its religious and political institutions. In her words: "La gran ambigüedad que presenta *El Bernardo* (1624), puesto que se trata de un poema épico de tema español, se acerca más a *Grandeza Mexicana* que al *Siglo de Oro*, donde apenas hay oportunidades de alabanzas a España" (67). [The great ambiguity presented by *El Bernardo* (1624), given that it is about a Spanish-themed epic poem, more closely approximates *Grandeza mexicana* than it does *Siglo de oro*, where there are merely opportunities to praise Spain.] See Sabat-Rivers, "El barroco de la contraconquista: primicias de conciencia criolla en Balbuena y Domínguez Camargo," in Mabel Moraña, ed., *Relecturas del barroco de Indias* (Hanover, N.H., 1994), 59–95.

Pera a parte do Sul, onde a pequena
Ursa se vê de guardas rodeada,
Onde o Ceo luminoso mais serena
Tem sua influïção, e temperada;
Junto da Nova Lusitânia ordena
A natureza, mãe bem atentada,
Um pôrto tão quieto e tão seguro,
Que para as curvas Naus serve de Muro. (31)

For the southern part, where the Ursa Minor sees itself surrounded by guards, where the luminous heavens most serene have influence and temperance; next to New Lusitania Nature, a caring mother, arrays a port so quiet and safe that it serves as a wall for ships within its curves.

Contrary to the general assumption by those historians who have posited the viceregal centers as the prime locations in which a criollo consciousness emerged in the New World, Pernambuco, the place that Bento praises in his epic, is not a center with strong institutional organizations, nor one that exhibits the glamour of viceregal cities such as Mexico City and Lima; rather, it is a colonial region that in the last part of the sixteenth century attracted many outcasts who were seeking a better life in the Indies. In the verses above, the poet depicts Nova Lusitania, today Pernambuco, as a kind of locus amoenus where one could find security. Recife, capital of Nova Lusitania, is transformed in Bento Teixeira's epic into a kind of earthly paradise, or Promised Land, where anyone could find peace and prosperity. In this, and in other aspects, *Prosopopéia* shares commonalities with documents written in the last quarter of the sixteenth century by those who rebelled against Philip II. Similar to the images that emerge from William of Orange's *Apologie, or Defence . . . against the Proclamation and Edict Published by the King of Spaine,* published in 1581, a sense of empathy with the Portuguese people and a distinct idea of the New World appear in Bento Teixeira's poem. The subtle but strong criticism against Philip II's politics, the empathy with the Lusitanian people, and the view of northern Brazil as a place of hope and salvation coincide with the following attitude that emerges from the words of William:

. . . if in all Spaine they had bin able to have founde a tyraunt, more fit to exercise tyrannie upon the poore Portugales then he [Philip II].

. . . for amongst the Indies and in other places, where they [Spaniards] commaunded absolutely, they yeelded to evident a proofe, of their perverse, naturall disposition, and tyrannous affection and will.

Benjamin Schmidt's study of the impact of the Dutch Revolt against Spain (1568–1648) and the ferocious war of words waged by the rebel party concludes that, as a result of the work of the polemicists close to William, "from this assumption of mutual suffering [between the Dutch and the inhabitants of the New World] evolved a more ambitious notion of a tactical alliance between those two 'nations' that most intimately knew the misrule of Spain."[16]

Bento Teixeira and other Portuguese New Christians who lived in the New World and in the Netherlands showed the same hostility toward the Hapsburgs. Therefore, the depiction of the northern regions of Brazil as a place of promise and salvation that emerges in *Prosopopéia* fits the imperial rivalries that helped to broaden the geography of the Netherlands during the late sixteenth century. The messianic role of Pernambuco envisaged by Bento Teixeira was fulfilled when, after the Dutch invasion of Pernambuco in 1630, the grandson of William's brother transformed Recife and the region described in the *Prosopopéia* into a place where people from different religious, social, and ethnic backgrounds experienced prosperity and harmony.[17]

Although scholars such as Antonio Candido generally regard the *Prosopopéia* as a minor literary work, they have also celebrated it as an early expression of nativism. However, it is in the writings of the New Christian Ambrósio Fernandes Brandão, a contemporary of Bento Teixeira, that nativism is most widely recognized by the critics.[18]

Ambrósio Fernandes Brandão and His *Diálogos das grandezas do Brasil*

Ambrósio Fernandes Brandão was born in Portugal around 1555 but lived in Pernambuco and in Paraíba most of his life. He was twice denounced before the Inquisition. Upon being cleared of the charges of Judaism, he returned to Brazil, where he wrote the *Diálogos das grandezas do Brasil*. It is not

16. H. Wansink, ed., *The Apologie of Prince William of Orange against the Proclamation of the King of Spaine* (1581) (Leiden, 1969), 53, 90; Benjamin Schmidt, "The Hope of the Netherlands: Menasseh ben Israel and the Dutch Idea of America," in Paolo Bernardini and Norman Fiering, eds., *The Jews and the Expansion of Europe to the West, 1450–1800* (New York, 2001), 86–106, esp. 93.

17. Arnold Wiznitzer explains that from 1630 until 1654 Recife, the capital of Pernambuco, became the first vibrant center for Jewish life in the New World. In the Sephardic congregation Zur Israel in Recife "all Jews were considered citizens of the Jewish community, enjoying equal rights." See Wiznitzer, *The Records of the Earliest Jewish Community in the New World* (New York, 1959), 11.

18. Antonio Cândido and Aderaldo Castello recognize the historic significance of the poem when they state that Bento Teixeira was the precursor of Brazilian nativism in poetry; see their *Presença da literatura brasileira*, I, *Das origens ao romantismo*, 5th ed., rev. (São Paulo, 1973), 29.

known when Brandão died, but he was no longer alive when the Dutch colonizers who had invaded Pernambuco in 1630 arrived in Paraíba in 1634.

Written around 1618, during the rule of Philip III of Spain (II of Portugal), a complete version of the manuscript was discovered in Leiden by Francisco Adolfo de Varnhagen (1816–1878), a nineteenth-century historiographer who, along with João Capistrano de Abreu (1853–1927), searched for archival documents that shed new light on the colonial past. For almost a century after its discovery, many critics believed that the author of the manuscript was Bento Teixeira. Only with the critical edition published by José Antonio Gonsalves de Mello, in 1962, did it become clear that Ambrósio Fernandes Brandão was the author of the *Diálogos*.[19]

The text consists of six dialogues between Brandônio, a Portuguese man who had settled in Pernambuco, and Alviano, a newcomer from the Iberian Peninsula full of misconceptions about Brazil. The names of the protagonists and autobiographical elements in the text played a major role in the identification of its author. Brandônio and Alviano are a Latinization of the names of the writer and of his friend and fellow tax collector Nuno Alvares. Unlike Bento Teixeira, who chose the epic as the generic vehicle for his political critique, Brandão chose the dialogue form, a rhetorical device based on exposition and argumentation that had been widely used by both classical and medieval writers. Despite the pragmatic tone of the dialogue form, in many passages the writer rises to poetic heights as he lauds the beauty and grandeur of the new land. The text starts with a conversation between Brandônio, a tax collector and longtime resident, and Alviano, a skeptical newcomer.[20]

Alviano:—Que bisalho é êsse, Sr. Brandônio, que estais revolvendo dentro nesse papel? Porque, segundo o considerais com atenção, tenho para mim que deve ser de diamantes ou rubis.

19. In addition to José Antonio Gonsalves de Mello's edition of *Diálogos do Brasil* (Recife, 1962), which elaborates on the differences and similarities between the manuscript found in Lisbon and the one found in Leiden, other sources for the study of Brandão include Frederick Holden Hall, William F. Harrison, and Dorothy Winters Welker, Introduction, in Ambrósio Fernandes Brandão, *Dialogues of the Great Things of Brazil,* ed. and trans. Hall, Harrison, and Welker (Albuquerque, N.Mex., 1987); and *Diálogos das grandezas do Brasil* (1618) (Rio de Janeiro, 1968), following the edition of the Academia Brasileira de Letras of 1923, the first edition published. In this study I rely on information found in these editions.

20. Hall, Harrison, and Welker explain that "Brandão's models were . . . most likely contemporary works that used the dialogue to extol the glories of favored lands, especially the newly-discovered ones," such as "Garcia d'Orta's *Colóquios dos simples e drogas da India* (1563) and Luiz Mendes de Vasconcellos's *Diálogos do sítio de Lisboa* (1608)." See Hall, Harrison, and Welker, Introduction, in Brandão, *Dialogues of the Great Things of Brazil,* 11.

Brandônio: Nenhuma coisa dessas é, senão uma lanugem que produz aquela árvore fronteira de nós em um fruto que dá do tamanho de um pêssego, que semelha pròpriamente ã la. . . . A umidade de que gozam tôdas as terras do Brazil a faz ser tão frutífera no produzir que infinidade de estacas de diversos paus metidos na terra, cobram e em breve tempo chegam a dar fruto; e esta árvore, que vos parece nascer de dentro desta casa, foi um esteio que se meteu na terra, sôbre o qual, com outras mais, se sustenta este edifício, que por pender, veio a criar essa árvore, que demonstra estar unida com a parede. (21–22)[21]

Alviano: What is that little trinket, Senhor Brandônio, that you are turning over on that piece of paper? From the way you are looking at it so carefully, I should think that it must be made of diamonds or rubies.

Brandônio: It is nothing like that, but just a bit of fluff that looks rather like wool. That tree right there in front of us has a fruit about the size of a peach, and the fluff grows inside it. . . . The humidity that all the soils of Brazil enjoy makes them produce so abundantly that any kind of stick thrust into the earth will send forth roots and soon bear fruit. This tree, which looks to you as if it is growing out of the house, was a pile driven into the ground—one of several that support the house. The pile took root, and from it grew the tree that seems to be part of the wall. (15–16)

The dialogue between Brandônio and Alviano portrays Brazil as a kind of earthly paradise that had much to offer to the settlers from the Old World. The editors of the English translation correctly observe that "the fluff both illustrates and symbolizes the fertility of Brazil and its yet untapped natural resources." Brandônio is the curious and knowledgeable observer of the Brazilian scene. Alviano, on the other hand, reveals himself as "a heretic in things Brazilian," as Brandonio calls him later. As the editors suggest, "The episode is a happy introduction to Brandônio's grand plan: to describe the 'great things of Brazil' so convincingly that even a skeptic like Alviano will become better informed and able to change [his] opinion." This task is successfully accomplished. The sixth and last Dialogue ends with a persuaded Alviano, who, overwhelmed by Brandônio's arguments, no longer has doubts about Brazil, even offering to spread the word about the greatness of the land: "You have me

21. Brandão, *Diálogos das grandezas do Brazil*, 41–42; for the English translations of the passages therefrom I relied on Brandão, *Dialogues of the Great Things of Brazil*, ed. and trans. Hall, Harrison, and Welker. Paginal citations from these editions will appear parenthetically in the text.

so converted to your sect that everywhere, wherever I may be, I shall proclaim of Brazil and its great things the praises they merit" (326).[22]

With expertise from his long and successful experience in trade and industry, Brandônio showed how the riches of the new land could be turned to the advantage of the metropolis—or, more properly (as Hall points out), of Spain, since Portugal was part of the Spanish Empire, though it retained certain rights regarding the administration of its overseas lands. But it is primarily in defense of the commonwealth of Brazil and of its permanent settlers that Brandonio engages in the dialogue with Alviano. Besides the literary, cultural, historic, ethnographic, and cosmographic value of Brandão's work, one very particular novelty of the *Diálogos* is the way the writer describes the settlers. Diverging from the majority of the chroniclers who lived in other areas of the New World, the main interlocutor criticizes the European colonizers who came to Brazil with the purpose of becoming rich and returning to their mother country. He blamed the greedy and the lazy Europeans, including the representative of the court, for their selfish intent on enriching themselves to the detriment of the land and its permanent residents. In a gesture of collective identity, the writer argues that the richness of Brazil should favor the settlers who remained on the land. He continually praises the local residents for their good and polite manners. According to Brandonio, Brazil was superior to any kingdom or city. Even the *degredados,* or outcasts from Portugal, transformed themselves into better people because of the opportunities found in Brazil, seen by the writer as "a crossroads of the world":

> *Alviano:* . . . Sabemos que o Brasil se povoou primeiramente por degredados e gente de mau viver, e pelo conseguinte pouco política; pois bastava carecerem de nobreza para lhes faltar a polícia.
>
> *Brandônio:* Nisso não há dúvida. Mas deveis de saber que esses povoadores, que primeiramente vieram a povoar o Brasil, a poucos lanços, pela larqueza da terra deram em ser ricos, e com a riqueza foram largando de si a ruim natureza, de que as necessidades e pobrezas que padeciam no Reino os faziam usar. E os filhos dos tais, já entronizados com a mesma riqueza e govêrno da terra despiram a pele velha, como cobra, usando em tudo de honradíssimos têrmos, com se ajuntar a isto o haverem vindo depois a êste Estado muitos homens nobilíssimos e

---

22. Hall, Harrison, and Welker, Introduction, in Brandão, *Dialogues of the Great Things of Brazil,* 15. The argument between the two interlocutors typifies a conflict that extended over several centuries between those who saw the New World as a land of either innocence or promise and those who condemned it out of hand as savage or degenerate.

fidalgos, os quais casaram nêle, e se liaram em parentesco com os da terra, em forma que se há feito entre todos uma mistura de sangue assaz nobre. (184–185)

Alviano: . . . We know that Brazil was settled first of all by persons of evil ways and men who had been banished from Portugal for their crimes, and therefore persons of scant civility. Their not being of gentle birth surely was enough for them to lack all refinement.

Brandonio: There is no doubt of that. But you must realize that the first settlers who came to Brazil had many opportunities to get rich in a hurry on account of the liberality of the land. As they prospered, they promptly shed their evil nature, which the necessity and poverty they had suffered in the Kingdom had brought out. And the children of those men, having those riches and enthroned as rulers of the land, sloughed off their old skin just the way a snake does, and adopted in everything the most polished manners. I must add that later on many gentlemen and persons of noble birth came out to this state. They married here and became attached to the colonists by family ties. Thus there was developed among them a mixture of fairly gentle blood. (147–148)[23]

Contradicting the hierarchical thinking prevalent in the European society of early modern times, Brandão discards the assumption that evil nature was inherent in people outside the nobility when he states that it resulted from "necessity and poverty they had suffered in the Kingdom." In statements such as this one, the *Diálogos* appears surprisingly modern for the early seventeenth century.

In Dialogue 6 Brandão also describes some of the customs of the country, both European and native. He regards the local residents as more elegant than the people who live in Madrid, then the center of the Spanish and the Portuguese court: "E eu vi já afirmar a homens muy experimentados na corte de Madri que se não traja melhor nela do que se trajam no Brasil os senhores de engenhos, suas mulheres e filhas, e outros homens afazendados e mercadores" (181). [And I have heard men who have had much experience at the Court in Madrid say that even there they do not dress better than the mill owners, their wives and daughters, other rich men, and the merchants of Brazil] (146). Contrary to the "indio feo" [ugly Indian], "abominable . . . de mala cara y de

23. The assumption that New Christians and Portuguese minorities found in Brazil opportunities to integrate into the majority and ascended the social ladder is demonstrated in Ernst Pijning, "New Christians as Sugar Cultivators and Traders in the Portuguese Atlantic, 1450–1800," in Bernardini and Fiering, eds., *The Jews and the Expansion of Europe*, 485–500.

peores fueros" [abominable . . . of a bad appearance and a worse heart] that Bernardo de Balbuena portrays in his *Grandeza mexicana,* the natives described by Brandônio are healthy, handsome, and intelligent.[24]

> *Alviano:* Não pode haver mais bárbaro costume dêsse que me tendes referido; e creio que por todo o mundo se não achara seu semelhante, nem era lícito que o houvesse senão entre êstes índios, que não faço diferença deles às brutas feras.
>
> *Brandônio:* Enganai-vos grandemente nisso; que posto que usam deste e de outros semelhantes costumes que aprenderam, . . . todavia se acha neles bons discursos e agudas respostas, e não se deixam enganar de ninguém. (336)

> *Alviano:* There can be no more barbarous custom than that which you have described [the couvade]. It is unthinkable that it should be found anywhere except among these Indians, whom I hold to be no different from brute beasts.[25]
>
> *Brandônio:* Now there you are greatly mistaken, for though they follow this and other customs that they learned and inherited from their ancestors, still one meets among them people who can reason a thing out and give you a shrewd answer. They do not allow themselves to be deceived by anyone. (309)

Because of the natives' unselfishness, Brandônio even sees them as superior to the people of Spain:

> *Brandônio:* . . . Se não enxerga entre êles, rosto nenhum de ambição.
> *Alviano:* Disso se lhe pode ter grandes invejas, por ser coisa de que a nossa Espanha anda muito desviada. (334)

> *Brandonio:* One cannot discern in them even a trace of covetousness.
> *Alviano:* One might envy them greatly for that, which is a trait not often to be met with in our Spain. (308)

As one can see in those passages, for its fertile lands, for the wealth and generosity of its inhabitants, and for its rich and abundant fauna and flora,

---

24. Bernardo de Balbuena, *Grandeza mexicana* (1604), ed. José Carlos González Boixo (Rome, 1988), 70, 122. Despite trying to defend the reputation of the natives from the misconceptions and prejudices that Alviano and other settlers had about the Tupinambá Indians, Brandão also repeats some of the erroneous beliefs, like the one that stated that the spiritual guide of the Indians was the devil. However, he does not fail to present the Indians as handsome and intelligent people.

25. The couvade is the practice where at birth the father mimics the mother, taking to bed.

Brazil is portrayed as a Promised Land for any European, including outcasts such as the descendants of Sephardic Jews who were facing discrimination in the Iberian Peninsula. Compared to Bento Teixeira's poem, in the *Diálogos* one can also detect signs of crypto-Judaism in the references to the Old Testament and to Jewish figures such as David, Solomon, Jacob, and Habakkuk. What is notable as well, however, is the omission of the names of Jesus, the Virgin Mary, and other Christian references that were so plentiful in the literature of the discovery and conquest. The omission of the name of Christ and the lack of reference to the expansion of Christianity in the New World suggest Brandão's Judaic faith. But above all what is evident in *Diálogos* is the fact that the writer loved Brazil, the country that he adopted with both heart and mind. If as a tax collector he served the crown, as a writer he defended above all the interests of the permanent settlers of Brazil.[26]

Manuel Beckman and the Levante do Maranhão

Manuel Beckman was another Portuguese New Christian who loved Brazil and who distanced himself from the Europeans who came to the New World to exploit the land and its people. Born in Lisbon in 1630 of a German father and a Portuguese mother, Manuel came to Brazil in 1662, when Portugal was facing serious economic problems, the consequences of Spanish rule for more than half a century. After declaring independence from Spain in 1640, Portugal was engaged in several wars against its powerful neighbor to regain its continental territory. During this period, known as the Restoration, which lasted until 1668, many Portuguese people migrated to Brazil looking for a better life. However, since during the Restoration Brazil was seen as "the milk cow of Portugal," some of the settlers, upon arriving in the new land, discovered that the burden of heavy taxation imposed by the

26. Based on the fact that Brandão was twice denounced to the Inquisition, and also on the writer's omission of Christian names and praises to the expansion of Christianity, it is safe to assume that he was a crypto-Jew. Käthe Windmüller arrives at exactly this conclusion when she says that one thing that the critics did not notice in Brandão's text is the lack of mention about the Christianization and conversion of the Indians. Gitlitz also noticed that "for many *conversos* who struggled to remain Judaizers in the fear of rapidly eroding Jewish knowledge, the essence of the Jewish identity was a strong affirmation of not being Catholic." The absence of Christian references in the writings of Brandão, Teixeira, and Beckman functions as affirmation of their Jewish identity. See Windmüller, "Omissão como confissão: os *Diálogos das grandezas do Brasil*, de Ambrósio Fernandes Brandão," in Anita Novinsky and Maria Luiza Tucci Carneiro, eds., *Inquisição: ensaios sobre mentalidade, heresias, e arte* (Rio de Janeiro, 1992), 416; Gitlitz, *Secrecy and Deceit*, 137.

king to pay for the wars and restore the economy of the kingdom was too much for them.[27]

This was the situation that Beckman faced when he settled in Maranhão, a colony in the north of Brazil established in 1618. In 1664 he married Maria Helena de Cáceres, a woman of Jewish heritage. Starting in 1670, Beckman played an active role in regional politics. As an elected councillor, he defended the interests of the permanent settlers before the representatives of the Portuguese crown when he opposed the policies of the governor Inácio Coelho da Silva, which were perceived as contrary to the interests of the local people. The confrontation with the governor led to Beckman's incarceration in 1679.[28]

While in jail Beckman wrote "Representação a S.M. de hũ home culpado nũa morte com a rellação do succedido e alguas noticias do Maranhão" [Representation to Your Majesty of a Man Blamed in a Death with a Relation of the Happenings in and Some News from Maranhão], a letter addressed to Dom Pedro II, a sovereign who ruled Portugal and its domains as prince regent from 1668 until 1682 and as king from 1683 until 1706. Confirming one of the arguments made previously by Brandão, Beckman blamed the greed of people who came from Europe only to seek fortunes in the land as the cause of the problems in Maranhão. However, according to his letter, the despotism of the governors and ministers of Portugal was the major obstacle to the prosperity of Maranhão and its permanent settlers: "Os governadores chegam pobres ao Maranhão e usando o seu poder e despotismo regressam a Portugal com enormes fortunas." [Governors arrive at Maranhão poor, and using their power and despotism, return to Portugal with enormous fortunes.][29]

Beckman's letter to the king describes the difficulties experienced by the local

27. Luiz Felipe de Alencastro states that during the Portuguese restoration Brazil was the primary economic support of the crown, or as a milk cow ("vaca de leite") of Portugal, according to an expression used by John IV in a conversation with a French diplomat in 1655. See Alencastro, *O trato dos viventes*, 247.

28. Pedro César de Menezes governed Maranhão between 1671 and 1678. Starting with him, the residence of the governors was established in Belém, a town far from Maranhão. The discontent of the settlers of Maranhão was in part motivated by the absence of the governor. In 1678, a popular unrest by the people of Maranhão resulted in the replacement of Menezes by Inácio Coelho da Silva, who governed from 1678 until 1682. It was during the government of Coelho da Silva that the conflict between Beckman and the governors started. During the government of Francisco Sá e Menezes (1682–1688) the frustration of the residents of Maranhão led to the popular revolt that resulted in the death of Beckman.

29. Maria Liberman, *O levante do Maranhão, "judeu cabeça de motim": Manoel Beckman* (São Paulo, 1983), 73. Further citations from Beckman's "Reprezentação a S.M. de hũ home culpado nũa morte com a rellação do succedido e alguas noticias do Maranhão," the only document signed by him found in the Arquivo da Biblioteca da Ajuda in Lisbon, follow this edition and will appear parenthetically in the text. English translations are mine.

residents, emphasizing particularly "as miseráveis condições de vida da população e a exploração a que estava sujeita" (71), the miserable living conditions of the population, and the exploitation imposed on them by the incompetent, greedy, and corrupt governors. Similar to the self-educated Andean Indian Guamán Poma de Ayala's denunciations of the ruling Spaniards and Peruvian criollos in his *Nueva corónica y buen gobierno* (discussed by Raquel Chang-Rodríguez in her essay above), Beckman argues that the governors who came to Maranhão "did not love the king" (72), because they betrayed his rules and his cause. He reports on the risks that the fortress of the region, abandoned by the governors, posed to the people and to the Portuguese Empire. He also believed that, if not for the dedication and love of the permanent settlers, "the real defenders of the frontiers" (73), the northern lands of Brazil would have fallen into the hands of the Spaniards. Although not a skillful writer like Bento Teixeira and Brandão, the self-educated Beckman was successful in the use of metaphors to convince the king. In the following passage, he compares Maranhão to a healthy body that became crippled with the abuses, the exploitation, and the disregard of the representatives of the crown. Beckman also explains that, using the excuse of serving the king, the governors spent most of their time in the city of Belém, coming to Maranhão only to exploit its land and its people:[30]

> Os governadores e mais ministros de Vossa Alteza todos acistem no Pará, por servirem a V[ossa] M[agestade] mas por se aproveitarem assy, por do Maranhão já não terem que tirar porque o que avia lhe tirarão e de cabeça do estado o tornaram em pés e o puzeram em moletas. (73)

> The governors and other ministers of your highness, they all remain in Pará, so as to better serve your majesty, but they come to Maranhão for profit, even though there is nothing left to take, since what there was, they have already taken, turning the state [Maranhão] upside down by twisting its feet and putting it on crutches.

Before signing the letter Beckman also states that he was "willing to give his life to the people of Maranhão" (73), a sacrifice that, in his opinion, no governor was willing to make.

30. D. A. Brading shows how Guamán Poma de Ayala contrasted "the relative virtues of Europeans and Africans with the absolute vices of the Spaniards and blacks born in Peru, describing the Creoles as fierce, proud, lazy, liars, gamblers, avaricious, of little charity, miserable tricksters, enemies of the poor Indians and of the Spaniards, thus are the Creoles, just like the mestizos, only worse than the mestizos." See Brading, *The First America: The Spanish Monarchy, Creole Patriots, and the Liberal State, 1492–1867* (Cambridge, 1991), 158.

Perhaps because the king was moved by Beckman's argument, or because he feared a major popular revolt in Maranhão, Dom Pedro II of Portugal, in a letter dated September 22, 1679, ordered the immediate replacement of the governor and the release of Beckman from jail. Unfortunately, despite the steps taken by the king, the conflicts between the local people and the government did not end. In 1684, the imposition of new taxes by the government upon the residents of Maranhão resulted in a major popular uprising. The revolt that erupted on February 24 became known as the Levante do Maranhão.

According to archival documents and chroniclers that describe the event, the participants of the mutiny comprised hundreds of local residents, including priests, owners of sugar plantations, humble workers, mulattoes, mestizos, and free blacks as well as Old and New Christians. The popular revolt forced the new governor, Francisco de Sá e Menezes, and also the members of the Jesuit order, who had control over the Indians, to leave the region. A collective letter addressed to the king dated the day of the revolt, signed by sixty representatives of the participants in the Levante, explained that the popular revolt was motivated by the oppressive regime and the lack of assistance from the government (89). The document also clarifies how the oppression from the government forced the people of Maranhão to change the situation with their own hands.

This time the reply that the people of Maranhão received from the king of Portugal was very different. On May 15, 1685, Gomes Freire de Andrade was sent to Maranhão as a new governor with the special mission of punishing the rebels and establishing peace in the region. Involved in accusations that portrayed Manuel Beckman as a criminal, a traitor, and a Jew, the new governor charged him as the "cabeça do levante" [leader of the revolt] and sent him to prison. Fearing a new revolt from the people who tried to break into the prison and set their leader free, the new governor sent Beckman to Pará, where he was hanged on November 2, 1685. The Levante do Maranhão, considered by historians such as Anita Novinsky "the first organized explosion that took place in Brazil," can be compared to the revolt that agitated Mexico City in 1692, which was described by the well-known criollo Carlos de Sigüenza y Góngora in his *Alboroto y motín de los indios de México.* However, in contrast to the position taken by Manuel Beckman, Sigüenza y Góngora did not identify himself with the Mexican people in the rebellion. The word "alboroto" chosen by the writer to describe the popular uprising is associated with disorderly, confused, noisy, and boisterous gathering, conveying therefore the idea that those who participated in it were far from humans. By presenting only the Indians as the participants of the revolt, Sigüenza y Góngora distanced himself from the popular movement that involved people from different social, racial, and economic backgrounds. The praises that he directed to the viceroy Count Galvez and the meaning of the word *alboroto* suggest that the criollo from Mexico was a faithful servant of the Spanish crown, for which reason the Indians and other people considered inferior castes had to be contained by and lawfully subjugated to the Spaniards and Spanish criollos. The position taken by Sigüenza y Góngora also contrasts with that of Beckman, who, in his letter to the king as well as before being hanged, not only defended the rebellion but also offered his life for the betterment of the people of Maranhão. Based on archival sources and on the descriptions of the scene of Beckman's hanging by the historian João Francisco Lisboa, Maria Liberman writes: "A cena do enforcamento de Beckman foi comovente, e tocou os que conheceram seus últimos atos. A dignidade e a grandeza de sua pessoa impressionam, ainda hoje, os que lêem os cronistas do tempo. Antes de subir ao patíbulo, pediu perdão se por acaso havia ofendido a algum seu próximo e declarou que 'pelo povo do Maranhão morria contente.'" [Beckman's hanging scene was moving and affected those who attended. The dignity and grandeur of his person impress, even today, those who read the chroniclers of the time. Before going up to the platform he asked for forgiveness if he had offended any of his neighbors, and declared that "for the people of Maranhão he was dying happily."][31]

AS ONE can see from the writings of the New Christians Bento Teixeira, Ambrósio Fernandes Brandão, and Manuel Beckman, a sense of collective identity emerged in the Americas, and not exclusively in the urban centers with courts, cathedrals, universities, and other European institutions. Possibly because as descendants of Jews they had been banished from the centers of imperial power, writers such as Teixeira, Brandão, and Beckman asserted their criollo consciousness in faraway lands of the New World that did not receive much attention from the kings. The places where they lived were distant not only from Lisbon and Madrid but also from Bahia, the capital of Brazil. However, possibly also because of the awareness of their subaltern condition, their writings do not display the antiplebeian attitudes, the preoccupation with

31. On the Levante do Maranhão, see Novinsky's introduction in Novinsky and Carneiro, eds., *Inquisição: ensaios*, 4. On Sigüenza y Góngora's *Alboroto y motín*, see Sam Cogdell, "Criollos, gachupines, y 'plebe tan en extremo plebe': retórica e ideología criollas en *Alboroto y motín de México* de Sigüenza y Góngora," in Mabel Moraña, ed., *Relecturas del barroco de Indias*, 245–280, esp. 265. See also Moraña, "'El tumulto de indios' de 1692 en los pliegues de la fiesta barroca: historiografía, subversion popular, y agencia criolla en el México colonial," in Mazzotti, ed., *Agencias criollas*, 161–175, esp. 163; José Rabasa, "Pre-Columbian Pasts and Indian Presents in Mexican History," *Dispositio/n: American Journal of Cultural Histories and Theories*, XIX (1994), 245–270, esp. 259. On Beckman, see Liberman, *O Levante do Maranhão*, 98.

courtly values, the attachment to the metropolis, or the ideology of the dominant sector of society that is evident in much of the creole discourse in the vice-regal centers of power, such as Balbuena's *Grandeza mexicana,* and in Sigüenza y Góngora's *Alboroto y motín* in the case of New Spain.

I would like now to return to Pagden's insights. Before focusing on Spanish and creoles from Mexico and Peru as a homogenous group who surpassed other colonists in the manifestation of criollo consciousness, Pagden stated, "Self-identity in the Spanish American world developed in different ways, in different periods, and in response to different contingencies throughout the various colonies." One such contingency was the forced conversions imposed upon the Iberian Jewish population by the end of the fifteenth century, when many Spanish conversos and Portuguese New Christians became crypto-Jews, practicing in secret the religion that persecution had forced them, or their ancestors, to renounce. The social, economic, and religious constraints that the descendants of Sephardic Jews faced in the Iberian Peninsula during the sixteenth and seventeenth centuries led them to find self- and collective identity, not only in the colonial cities with strong institutional organizations but also in towns located in marginal areas of the Iberian empires. I agree with Pagden, but I would broaden his statement to encompass the entire New World.[32]

32. Pagden, "Identity Formation in Spanish America," in Canny and Pagden, eds., *Colonial Identity in the Atlantic World,* 51.

LISA VOIGT

Spectacular Wealth: Baroque Festivals and Creole Consciousness in Colonial Mining Towns of Brazil and Peru

In studying the emergence of a creole consciousness among New World inhabitants of Iberian ancestry, critics have traditionally focused on texts produced in and about Mexico City and Lima, as Lúcia Helena Costigan has pointed out. She cites the example of Solange Alberro's essay "La emergencia de la conciencia criolla: el caso novohispano" [The Emergence of Creole Consciousness: The Case of New Spain], which argues that only the viceregal centers of New Spain and Peru, with their strong economic and institutional structures—court, administration, cathedral, inquisition, universities, academies, convents, guilds, brotherhoods, printing presses, bookstores, theaters—were able to promote the development of a distinct identity among creole elites. The present essay broadens the scope of inquiry to several mining boomtowns of South America—Potosí, in the viceroyalty of Peru, and Vila Rica and Mariana, in the province of Minas Gerais—to ask whether and how one can trace a discrete creole identity in these areas, distant from the political and intellectual centers of their respective empires (Madrid and Lisbon as well as the coastal colonial capitals of Lima and Bahia) and without such important cultural institutions as universities, printing presses, or, in the Brazilian case, religious orders. Whereas José Antonio Mazzotti will analyze below the creole manipulation of the legend of El Dorado to extol the cultural and spiritual wealth of Lima and the Peruvian viceroyalty as a whole, I investigate here how writers transpose the celebration of tangible riches into a defense of mining boomtowns and their creole inhabitants.[1]

1. Solange Alberro, "La emergencia de la conciencia criolla: el caso novohispano," in José Antonio Mazzotti, ed., *Agencias criollas: la ambigüedad "colonial" en las letras hispanoamericanas* (Pittsburgh, 2000), 55–71, esp. 68–69. Throughout this essay, I have modernized my citations from primary sources only with respect to accent marks and the letters *f/s* and *y/i*. All

Their remote locations, of course, did not prevent Potosí and Minas Gerais from becoming centers in their own right. In both cases, the discovery of substantial mineral reserves led to the creation of towns that quickly exploded in population through the arrival of a heterogeneous array of immigrants, from the Iberians and other Europeans lured by the prospect of quick riches to the Africans and Amerindians forcibly brought to serve as labor in the mines. The rich silver deposits of the Cerro de Potosí [Mountain of Potosí] were discovered in 1545, and the subsequent rush led to Potosí's status as one of the world's most populous cities, at as many as 120,000 inhabitants, by 1580. Portuguese knowledge of Potosí's treasures led to numerous expeditions searching for another silver mountain in the interior of Brazil as well as to extensive illegal trade via Río de la Plata. The Brazilian *sertão* [backlands] eventually did yield comparable riches, but only after the first significant gold strikes in the 1690s and the discovery of diamonds in the 1720s. Gold production in Minas Gerais [General Mines] reached its peak around 1750, about a century after silver production in Potosí had begun to decline. Despite the chronological lag in their development, both areas came to represent—and quite literally provide for—the jewels in the crowns of their respective empires.[2]

---

translations are my own unless otherwise noted. Lewis Hanke gives an overview of Potosí's history as "boom town supreme" in Hanke, *The Imperial City of Potosí: An Unwritten Chapter in the History of Spanish America* (The Hague, 1956), 1–6. James Lockhart and Stuart B. Schwartz indicate Potosí's political marginality by pointing out that it "always remained a *villa*, or 'town,' whereas La Plata (Sucre) was a *ciudad*, or 'city,' and the seat of the Charcas Audiencia, even though Potosí came to be by far the larger and more active center," in Lockhart and Schwartz, *Early Latin America: A History of Colonial Spanish America and Brazil* (New York, 1983), 102. Charles R. Boxer recounts the history of the gold and diamond rush in Minas Gerais and its principal town, Vila Rica, in Boxer, *The Golden Age of Brazil, 1695–1750* (Berkeley, Calif., 1962), 30–60, 204–225. A. J. R. Russell-Wood describes Vila Rica's brief period as a "core" town of the Brazilian colony owing to its role in gold production but emphasizes the long-standing demographic, political, and commercial centrality of coastal cities (particularly Salvador de Bahia and Rio de Janeiro, which replaced Salvador as the colonial capital in 1763); see Russell-Wood, "Centers and Peripheries in the Luso-Brazilian World, 1500–1808," in Christine Daniels and Michael V. Kennedy, eds., *Negotiated Empires: Centers and Peripheries in the Americas, 1500–1820* (New York, 2002), 105–152, esp. 128–129.

2. On the Portuguese presence in Potosí and the city's economic ties to Brazil through the illegal silver trade, see Lewis Hanke, *The Portuguese in Spanish America, with Special Reference to the Villa Imperial de Potosí* (n.p., 1962), esp. 15–29. Like Hanke, Boxer characterizes the Portuguese search for mineral wealth in the Brazilian interior as partially inspired by "the (misconceived) geographical propinquity of silver-bearing Potosí," in *Golden Age of Brazil*, 30. Regarding Potosí's population, Bartolomé Arzáns de Orsúa y Vela cites a census taken in 1580 of 120,000 and another in 1610 of 160,000; see his *Historia de la Villa Imperial de Potosí*, ed. Lewis Hanke and Gunnar Mendoza (Providence, R.I., 1965), I, 10, 286. Peter Bakewell compares these figures to those of contemporary European cities in Bakewell, *Silver and Entrepreneurship in Seventeenth-Century Potosí: The Life and Times of Antonio López de Quiroga* (Albuquerque, N.Mex., 1988),

Although the Iberian courts and their European lenders rapidly exhausted the gold and silver reserves, the abundant mineral wealth of both regions still permitted, for a time, the staging of dazzling and costly festivals. Public celebrations of both religious and secular events—Corpus Christi and other holidays; the arrival of government officials and ecclesiastical authorities; royal births, marriages, deaths, and coronations—ostensibly replicated the festivals' Peninsular counterparts in the display of the supremacy and magnificence of the crown and church. Whether of a sacred, official, or popular nature, festivals involved the participation of not only creole elites and visiting authorities but all members of the diverse population of mining boomtowns, including mestizos, Amerindians, and Africans. More than mere spectators, the latter groups joined in the processions and pageantry with indigenous and African costumes, music, dances, and rituals. The various meanings that the festivals had for such participants—certainly not limited to the veneration of the power and splendor of the institutions of colonial authority—have been the subject of increasing critical attention. This essay focuses on creole appropriations and uses of the festival, particularly their manifestations in the archive (of "enduring materials" like texts) rather than the repertoire (of "embodied practice"), in Diana Taylor's terminology.[3]

As Taylor points out, the notions of archive and repertoire do not correspond neatly to a binary of (writerly) domination and (performative) subversion: if much of the colonial festival's repertoire seeks to constitute or preserve hegemonic power, the archival response, as with some of the texts analyzed in this

---

19[1]n. 45. The population of Vila Rica, the capital of Minas Gerais, reached 20,000 at the peak of its gold production in the 1740s but dropped to around 7,000 by 1804; see Russell-Wood, "Centers and Peripheries," in Daniels and Kennedy, eds., *Negotiated Empires*, 128.

3. Diana Taylor, *The Archive and the Repertoire: Performing Cultural Memory in the Americas* (Durham, N.C., 2003), 19. It bears pointing out that the participation of Amerindians and Africans in colonial festivals was not limited to the "repertoire" of embodied practice but extended to the "archive" as well; for example, the "Irmãos Pretos da Irmandade do Rosario" [Black Brethren of the Brotherhood of the Rosary] sponsored the publication of one of the texts discussed in this essay, *Triunfo eucharístico* (1734). On Amerindian participation in colonial Andean festivals, see Carolyn Dean, *Inka Bodies and the Body of Christ: Corpus Christi in Colonial Cuzco, Peru* (Durham, N.C., 1999); Leonardo García Pabón, "Indios, criollos, y fiesta barroca en la 'Historia de Potosí' de Bartolomé Arzáns," *Revista iberoamericana*, LXI (1995), 423–439; Teresa Gisbert, "Art and Resistance in the Andean World," in René Jara and Nicholas Spadaccini, eds., *Amerindian Images and the Legacy of Columbus* (Minneapolis, Minn., 1992), 629–671; and Luis Millones, "Las ropas del Inca: desfiles y disfraces indígenas coloniales," *Revista de crítica literaria latinoamericana*, XXI (1995), 51–66. Many of the essays in István Janscó and Iris Kantor, eds., *Festa: cultura e sociabilidade na América portuguesa*, 2 vols. (São Paulo, 2001), address the African participation in Brazilian colonial festivals; see also Marina de Mello e Souza, *Reis negros no Brasil escravista: história da festa de coroação de Rei Congo* (Belo Horizonte, 2002); and José Ramos Tinhorão, *As festas no Brasil colonial* (São Paulo, 2000), esp. 87–102.

essay, may endeavor to challenge that power. As we will see, accounts often claim that festivals in mining boomtowns actually surpass those of the mother country or the viceregal capitals in both piety and grandeur. Whereas the festivals' organizers and participants exploit the regions' mineral riches to spectacular effect, the texts themselves are signs of the regions' cultural and intellectual wealth. Narratives of festivals intended to exalt religious or political authority thus come instead to celebrate a specific American locale and, in particular, its creole residents.[4]

What follows elaborates upon the rhetorical reorientation of the spectacular wealth of mining town festivals—from an instrument of imperial power to a platform for creole identity—in four texts. Two pertain to Potosí: Diego Mexía de Fernangil's *El Dios Pan* [The God Pan / The God of Bread] (written 1617), a pastoral eclogue describing a Corpus Christi celebration in Potosí, and Bartolomé Arzáns de Orsúa y Vela's *Historia de la Villa Imperial de Potosí* [History of the Imperial Town of Potosí] (completed 1737), which includes numerous festivals in its chronicle of nearly two centuries of the city's history. The other two texts feature festivities in Minas Gerais: Simão Ferreira Machado's *Triunfo eucharístico* [Eucharistic Triumph] (1734), describing the celebrations surrounding the transfer of the Holy Sacrament to a new church in Vila Rica in 1733, and the anonymous *Áureo throno episcopal* [Golden Episcopal Throne] (1749), which relates the 1748 entry of the first bishop into Mariana, the seat of a newly created diocese in Minas Gerais. I structure my analysis according to the celebratory aims of the festivals and the rhetorical strategies of the texts rather than adhere to the geographic and linguistic borders that traditionally separate the study of colonial Spanish America and Brazil, or, more appropriately, the Spanish and Portuguese Empires. The comparative perspective, focused on geographically, politically, and culturally peripheral spaces of both empires, seeks to recognize local specificities as well as the affinities that are so often obscured by modern national and linguistic boundaries.[5]

---

4. Taylor, *Archive and the Repertoire,* 22. I am deeply indebted to Stephanie Merrim's discussion of how writers instrumentalized the "aesthetic of amazement" proper to Baroque festivals—an aesthetic designed to "manage modernity" but that also "contained the seeds of its own implosion"—in their construction of creole identity; see her "Spectacular Cityscapes of Baroque Spanish America," in Mario J. Valdés and Djelal Kadir, eds., *Literary Cultures of Latin America: A Comparative History* (New York, 2004), III, 31–57. Merrim examines texts from not only Mexico City and Lima but also Santafé de Bogotá and Potosí, whose "muse" she locates "in the spectacle"; see 49–50.

5. Although comparative Luso-Hispanic studies have become more common (see, for example, the issues dedicated to comparative studies in *Revista de crítica literaria latinoamericana,* XXIII [1997], and *Revista iberoamericana,* LXIV [1998]), they are usually centered on modern,

Eucharistic Triumphs

"Inefable, / grandioso, y admirable es el Dios vuestro" [Ineffable, grandiose, and admirable is your God], declares the "gentile" Damón in Diego Mexía de Fernangil's *El Dios Pan*, after merely hearing an oral description of his interlocutor Melibeo's God. But when Melibeo responds, "Y mucho más os muestro" [And I will show you much more], he alludes to the even more powerful rhetorical sway of the urban Corpus Christi festival to which he takes his shepherd companion. The public celebration of the Eucharist in Potosí, Melibeo knows, will overwhelm all Damón's senses and thus persuade him to abandon his pagan deity, Pan, for the one who manifests himself in *pan* [bread], according to Catholic doctrine. Indeed, Damón's reaction to the lavish display of wealth in the plaza is nothing less than incredulity:

Suspenso y asombrado, o Melibeo,
estoy, pues lo que veo, con mis ojos
me parecen antojos o ilusiones;
. . . tanto veo
que se ahita el deseo; pues el oro,
perlas, plata, y tesoro que esparcido
columbro y repartido en la ancha plaza,
me ofusca, turba, embaza.

I am astonished and filled with wonder, o Melibeo, because what my eyes behold seem like fancies or illusions. . . . I see so much that I am bursting with desire, for the pearls, silver, and treasure that I glimpse spread about the wide square blinds, bewilders, and confuses me.

---

national literatures rather than the colonial period, in which such an approach is perhaps most viable and productive: not just because of the empires' common sovereign from 1580 to 1640 but also because of shared literary and artistic influences, particularly the Baroque. The Cuban author José Lezama Lima compares the sculptures of the Andean Indian Kondori and those of the Brazilian mulatto Aleijadinho as two paramount expressions of the *barroco americano* [Latin American Baroque] in Lezama Lima, *La expresión americana* (Mexico City, 1993), 103–106. Working in Potosí and Minas Gerais, respectively, these artists turned the mineral wealth of their hometowns into artistic splendor. The Brazilian critic Haroldo de Campos affirms that "the Latin American writers of the Baroque evolved among themselves a dialogue which has only now begun to be re-established," in Campos, "The Rule of Anthropophagy: Europe under the Sign of Devoration," *Latin American Literary Review*, XV (1986), 42–60, esp. 49. Hanke points to concrete manifestations of this "dialogue" in terms of the "Portuguese contribution to the history of Spanish America," paying particular attention to Portuguese writers active in Potosí; see *Portuguese in Spanish America*, 3, 18–35.

The marvelous sights of the procession and the adornment of the city itself are complemented by the music and aromas that Damón encounters in the festival, all of which lead to his ultimate conversion. In particular, the gold and silver, pearls and treasure that fill Damón with wonder and desire suggest that a spectacular display of wealth plays a role in Melibeo's spiritual victory over his pagan companion.[6]

Clearly a foil for indigenous Andeans, whose idolatry the colonial authorities were more aggressively attempting to stamp out through campaigns of extirpation, Damón's conversion points to the propagandistic and evangelistic aims of religious festivals throughout the Iberian empires. Corpus Christi would serve such aims particularly well, since it already takes the "form of a triumph, a celebration heralding a victor," as Carolyn Dean points out in her study of the festival in colonial Cuzco: the triumph of Christ over sin and death, of the Catholic Church over heresy (with respect to the doctrine of transubstantiation), and, finally, of the Spanish crown over non-Christian peoples in the New World. Indeed, after Melibeo's explanation of a motto dedicated to Charles V, Damón's response confirms the emperor's success at gaining new subjects and converts in "Hemisferio más remoto" [the most remote hemisphere]:

¡Ay Melibeo,
y cómo, a lo que veo, algún influjo
del gran Dios Pan me trujo a esta su fiesta,
ya el alma va dispuesta y convencida
a buscar Pan de vida, pues mi suerte
me ha dado Pan de muerte hasta ahora!

Oh, Melibeo, and how, from what I can see, some influence of the great God of Bread brought me to this festival of his, and how my soul is already disposed and convinced to seek the bread of life, for my luck has given me the bread of death until now![7]

More broadly, Damón's amazement and ensuing conversion point to the Baroque aesthetic principles that informed such spectacles in the religious as

6. Diego Mexía de Fernangil, *El Dios Pan*, in Rubén Vargas Ugarte, ed., *De nuestro antiguo teatro* (Lima, 1943), 1–26, esp. 6. Dean describes the main elements of the Corpus Christi festival and outlines its history in Spain and introduction in the Andes in *Inka Bodies*, 7–22. Whereas *El Dios Pan* represents a pagan's conversion to Christianity through his observation of a Corpus Christi festival, Dean contends that native participation in the festivities was essential to the Spaniards as evidence of successful evangelization.

7. Dean, *Inka Bodies*, 7–8; Mexía de Fernangil, *El Dios Pan*, in Vargas Ugarte, ed., *De nuestro antiguo teatro*, 8.

well as the political realm. As José Antonio Maravall explains, "The obscure and the difficult, the new and the unknown, the rare and the extravagant, the exotic, all these were effective means in the Baroque precepts that sought to move the will, leaving it in suspense, provoking its admiration, and impassioning it through what had never been seen before." According to Maravall, the extravagance and ostentation of urban festivals are an integral part of the Baroque culture of seventeenth-century Spain, serving the goals of absolutist power and Counter-Reformation ideology: to impress the masses with the power and splendor of the court and church, to attract their political loyalty or religious devotion, and to distract them from their material needs and social concerns. Many critics have made similar claims about festivals in the American colonies, where geographic distance and cultural heterogeneity heightened the urgency for the imperial state to ensure the submission and indoctrination of conquered Amerindians, enslaved Africans, and even Euramericans with suspect allegiance to the mother country. In this sense, festivals represent an instrument in the arsenal of cultural and spiritual conquest, a tool of "political acculturation and ideological Castilian-ization of this society in construction."[8]

8. José Antonio Maravall, *La cultura del barroco: análisis de una estructura histórica* (Madrid, 1975), 453–498, esp. 467. For similar readings of Spanish Baroque festivals, see Maravall, "Teatro, fiesta, e ideología en el Barroco," in José María Díez Borque, ed., *Teatro y fiesta en el Barroco: España e Iberoamérica* ([Barcelona], 1986), 71–95, and Díez Borque, "Relaciones de teatro y fiesta en el Barroco español," 11–40; Antonio Bonet Correa, "La fiesta barroco como práctica del poder," in *El arte efímero en el mundo hispánico* (Mexico, 1983), 45–78. Roy Strong emphasizes the political instrumentality of Renaissance festivals but distinguishes their "represen[tation of] an aspiration towards political order" from the celebration of the absolutist monarch characteristic of Baroque festivities; see his *Art and Power: Renaissance Festivals, 1450–1650* (Berkeley, Calif., 1973), esp. 19, 171. The final quote is from Víctor Mínguez, "Los 'Reyes de las Américas': presencia y propaganda de la monarquía hispánica en el Nuevo Mundo," in Agustín González Enciso and Jesús María Usunáriz Garayoa, *Imagen del rey, imagen de los reinos: las ceremonias públicas en la España moderna (1500–1814)* (Pamplona, 1999), 231–257, esp. 235. For similar interpretations of colonial Spanish-American festivals, see Ángel López Cantos, *Juegos, fiestas, y diversiones en la América española* (Madrid, 1992), 20; Rafael Ramos Sosa, *Arte festivo en Lima virreinal (siglos XVI–XVII)* (Andalusia, 1992), 19; and Rosa María Acosta de Arias Schreiber, *Fiestas coloniales urbanas (Lima-Cuzco-Potosí)* (Lima, 1997), 37–38. On festivals as conservative political instruments in Portugal and colonial Brazil, see José Pedro Paiva, "Etiqueta e cerimônias públicas na esfera da Igreja (séculos XVII–XVIII)," and Laura de Mello e Souza, "Festas barrocas e vida cotidiana em Minas Gerais," in Jancsó and Kantor, eds., *Festa*, I, 75–96, 183–195. In the same volume, Pedro Cardim, "Entradas solenes: rituais comunitários e festas politicas, Portugal e Brasil, séculos XVI e XVII," and Iris Kantor, "Entradas episcopais na capitania de Minas Gerais (1743 e 1748): a transgressão formalizada" (97–124, 169–180), point out the more transgressive potential of festivals. Stephanie Merrim discusses both of these dimensions of festivals in "Spectacular Cityscapes," in Valdés and Kadir, eds., *Literary Cultures of Latin America*, III, 33–37. In her essay in this volume (above), Merrim examines Sor Juana Inés de la Cruz's use of a triumphal arch and its explanatory text, *Neptuno alegórico*, to stage creole Mexican concerns.

Through Damón's response, *El Dios Pan* suggests the fiesta's success at achieving the political and religious ends attributed by Maravall and other critics to Baroque festivals. However, the text itself reveals rhetorical goals and objects of celebration beyond those of affirming church and state power. In his first reaction to the bustling, festooned city, Damón vacillates in his admiration:

Admírame el concierto que ay en todo;
ay tanto y de tal modo compartido
que se pasma el sentido y no se sabe
la lengua aquí qué alabe: si las cosas
vanas, ricas, grandiosas: o si el arte
con que pone y reparte lo dispuesto.

I admire the harmony found in everything; there is so much and it is so well divided, that the senses are stunned and the tongue does not know which to praise: whether the vain, rich, and grandiose things or the art which distributes and arranges them.

Although the "rich and grandiose things" provoke his astonishment and contribute to his conversion, his allusion to their vanity suggests that "art"—the talent and ingenuity of Potosí's residents—has more to do with the festival's spectacular dimensions and spiritual efficacy.[9]

As a Spaniard who resided in Potosí for only a dozen years (1608–1620), although he arrived in the New World some twenty-five years earlier, Diego Mexía de Fernangil perhaps had less at stake in vindicating the artistic and intellectual prowess of the city's inhabitants than some of the other authors that we will discuss. Yet this author of a translation of Ovid's *Heroides* and more than two hundred sonnets on the life of Christ, among other works, certainly had reason to defend the value and power of art. Indeed, Melibeo responds to Damón's decision to get baptized at the end of eclogue by redirecting the festival's capacity to amaze to the text itself: "Asombre a todo el mundo; / hecho tan sin segundo." [Let the whole world be astonished by such an extraordinary act.] The readers, in other words, are encouraged to share in Damón's sense of wonder by marveling at the "extraordinary act" represented in the text and by admiring the portrait of the festival that so moved the pagan shepherd. These final, self-reflexive lines revise Damón's earlier affirmation of the incapacity of art to capture Potosí's grandeur. After enumerating the classical artists and writers who he wishes could depict the city (Apelles, Quintilian, Homer), the supposedly uncultured shepherd expresses his doubt that "riqueza tan

9. Mexía de Fernangil, *El Dios Pan,* in Vargas Ugarte, ed., *De nuestro antiguo teatro,* 7.

grandiosa / pincel verso, ni prosa la pintaran" [such grandiose wealth could be painted by brush, verse, or prose]. By the end of the eclogue's representation of "such grandiose wealth," the "astonished" readers might be led to believe that Mexía de Fernangil has surpassed his classical forbears, as much as Potosí itself has exceeded Lima, and even Rome, in its spectacular adornment.[10]

Whether or not *El Dios Pan* was intended for the stage, the dialogic form of the work and its incorporation of *villancicos* [carols] sung at the festival grant the work a performative quality, making the readers virtual spectators of the Corpus Christi procession alongside Damón and Melibeo. Of course, *El Dios Pan* depicts, not a historical, but a model fiesta, capable of inspiring the ideal response in its heathen observer. Resembling the eclogue in the attention to every sensorial detail, narratives of actual festivals also constituted a popular European genre by the seventeenth century. With respect to Renaissance court festivals and royal entries, Roy Strong characterizes the "vast corpus of literature printed to commemorate these events" thus:

> These describe to us, in minute detail, what might at first glance seem essentially trivia: the architecture, paintings and decorations, the sculptures, allegorical devices, scenery and costumes that made up such occasions. These descriptions and their commentaries were to enable those who were not there to savour the transitory wonder and to grasp its import from afar. Commemorative books, with their elaborate illustrations printed under official auspices, were designed to pass to posterity as monuments of princely magnificence.

Although rarely printed with elaborate illustrations or under official auspices, accounts of New World festivals abound in both printed and manuscript form, offering full descriptions of the elements identified by Strong as well as the poetry, sermons, and songs recited on the occasion. Like *El Dios Pan*, these

---

10. Ibid., 6–7, 26. José Toribio Medina, *Biblioteca hispano-americana (1493–1810)*, II (Santiago de Chile, 1900), 88–91, describes Mexía's literary works, including his translation of Ovid: *Primera parte del Parnaso antártico, de obras amatorias* [First Part of the Antarctic Parnassus, of Amatory Works], published in Seville in 1608, and the unpublished "La segunda parte del Parnaso antártico de divinos poemas" [The Second Part of the Antarctic Parnassus, of Religious Poems]. In the latter, Mexía describes his literary activity in Potosí: "He desenvuelto muchos autores latinos, y he frecuentado los umbrales del templo de las sagradas musas." [I have deciphered many Latin authors, and I have frequented the threshold of the temple of the sacred muses.] See Toribio Medina, *Biblioteca hispano-americana*, II, 90. Comparisons to classical Rome, as well as to modern European or viceregal capitals, are frequent in festival accounts. Damón affirms that the beautiful cloths decorating the church "ni las ha visto Lima, ni vió Roma" [have not been seen by Lima, nor were they seen by Rome] (Mexía de Fernangil, *El Dios Pan*, in Vargas Ugarte, ed., *De nuestro antiguo teatro*, 18).

narratives preserved and extended the "transitory wonder" of American festivals to readers not present at the events. Such accounts are no less performative than *El Dios Pan,* for they employ rhetoric of persuasion and glorification that exceeds their putatively mimetic, documentary function as written records of public events. And this "performance" is not limited to the celebration of the power and magnificence of the crown and church, as has often been argued with respect to colonial festival accounts.[11]

The creole *potosino* Bartolomé Arzáns de Orsúa y Vela (1676–1736) drew on numerous such accounts in his *Historia de la Villa Imperial de Potosí* to incorporate elaborate descriptions of festivals that occurred long before his birth. In his narrative of the Corpus Christi festival of 1608, Arzáns demonstrates how New World fiestas and their accounts can transform the commemoration of the Eucharist into an act of self-celebration. He opens part I, book 6, chapter 9 by affirming that, since histories are written not only to delight and please but also to instruct, he will tell of the "famosas fiestas que en este año de 1608 celebró la nobleza, y juventud criolla de esta Imperial Villa de Potosí, motivándolas solamente el pundonor y vanidad, en que no falta que reprender, porque la vana ostentación de los hombres enfada mucho a Dios, aunque sean señores y reyes" [famous fiestas celebrated by the creole youth and nobility of the Imperial Town of Potosí in this year of 1608, being motivated only by honor and vanity, in which there is much to reprehend, because the vain ostentation of men angers God a great deal, even though they be lords and kings]. As he explains, the creole youth wanted to remedy an injury to their honor by disproving the rumors that had been spread about them by various Spanish "nations," as Arzáns refers to the different ethnic groups that reside in Potosí. Hostility between these nations— creoles, Estremadurans, Andalusians, Castilians, Basques, Portuguese—seethes throughout Arzáns's colorful history, sometimes erupting in violence. In this case, the Spanish nations had apparently ridiculed the creoles' lack of dexterity, gallantry, and inventiveness in a previous festival, and the latter sought to use the Corpus Christi festival to improve their reputation.[12]

11. Strong, *Art and Power,* 21–22. Kathleen Shelly and Grínor Rojo affirm that *El Dios Pan* is "unrepresentable" and that, rather than a dramatic work, it is a "type of 'meta-theater' which depicts an ideal religious festival"; see their "El teatro hispanoamericano colonial," in Luis Íñigo Madrigal, ed., *Historia de la literatura hispanoamericana,* I, *época colonial* (Madrid, 1982), 319–352, esp. 334. López Cantos emphasizes the laudatory dimensions of colonial Spanish American festival accounts in similar terms to Strong, affirming that they were written "more as a panegyric to the monarch who was being celebrated than as popular chronicles for the memory of the community. In the mind of the authors it was always present that the one to whom homage was being paid was the king, or, in default, the metropolitan authority" (*Juegos, fiestas, y diversiones,* 25).

12. Arzáns de Orsúa y Vela, *Historia de la Villa Imperial,* ed. Hanke and Mendoza, I, 267.

Since Arzáns was a creole himself, it is hardly surprising to see with whom his loyalties lie and how quickly—in the following paragraph—he turns a condemnation of the creoles' "vain ostentation" into a critique of the other nations' "gossip born of envy or ill will." The moral lesson of the opening paragraph is eventually forgotten in the painstaking, laudatory description of the participants' costumes and their horses' livery (laden with gold, silver, pearls, precious stones, and rich brocades), their performances and prizes won in the festive competitions, and their "invenciones," elaborate floats and sculptures including a gigantic, silver wheel of fortune (with the Cerro de Potosí at the top) and a massive, enameled pyramid containing the seven wonders of the world (dwarfed by another artificial Cerro de Potosí, made of the finest silver, of course). Although Arzáns affirms that Corpus Christi itself was celebrated "con el mayor culto, veneración y grandeza que hasta allí se había visto en Potosí" [with the greatest worship, veneration, and grandeur that had ever been seen in Potosí], he quickly turns his attention to the "regocijos humanos" [human rejoicings] that followed the religious holiday. Thus his references to the more traditional elements of a Corpus Christi celebration—songs in praise of the Holy Sacrament, a mock battle between Spaniards and Indians, who here participate in the traditional role of defeated pagans—are overwhelmed by the lengthy depictions of a very worldly display of wealth and artifice. Arzáns insistently highlights the audience's admiring response to the spectacle as much as Mexía does through the character of Damón in *El Dios Pan*, but the effect is clearly to convince onlookers—and readers—of creole merit rather than the superiority of the Catholic religion.[13]

Just as the creoles substitute the spiritual intent of the festival with the self-aggrandizing demonstration of material and intellectual riches, Arzáns displaces his originally declared motive for writing about the festival. The goal of offering moral instruction about the sin of vanity is overshadowed by the narrative's attempt to delight and awe its readers with the ingenuity and grandeur of the creole festival—and, by extension, with the author's own ingenious and grandiose depiction of such splendor. In this sense, Arzáns follows the Baroque precepts outlined in his prologue: "Todo será para deleite y provecho del ánimo, atendiendo también a que lo narrativo agrade por nuevo, admire por extraño, suspenda por prodigioso, por ejemplar exhorte." [Everything will be for the delight and benefit of the soul, also making sure that the narrative

13. Ibid., 267–277, esp. 270, 274–276. In "Indios, criollos, y fiesta barroca," *Revista iberoamericana*, LXI (1995), 423–439, García Pabón also reads this narrative as an example of the way in which New World festivals permit the expression of a creole "subject in formation."

pleases through novelty, provokes admiration through strangeness, astonishes through prodigiousness, exhorts through exemplarity.] The spectacular character of the festival is thus reflected in the historical narrative itself, which also seeks to provoke admiration. As Lewis Hanke points out in an extended footnote to the chapter, the wealth and extravagance described by Arzáns are difficult to reconcile with what we know about Potosí from contemporary documents, which suggest a serious economic crisis at the time. Nevertheless, it would be wrong to seek in accounts like Arzáns's an accurate picture of the city or the festival. Instead, his description extends and amplifies the creoles' own intentions in offering the festival, which already reorient Corpus Christi's primary purpose of celebrating the Eucharist.[14]

The commemoration of spiritual triumph represented by the Eucharist also becomes the triumphant celebration of an American boomtown and its inhabitants in Simão Ferreira Machado's *Triunfo eucharístico, exemplar da Christandade lusitana em pública exaltação da fé na solemne trasladação do diviníssimo Sacramento . . . em Villa Rica, corte da capitania das Minas* [Eucharistic Triumph, Example of Lusitanian Christianity in Public Exaltation of the Faith in the Solemn Transfer of the Divine Sacrament . . . in Vila Rica, Court of the Captaincy of Minas]. The author identifies himself, not as a creole, but as a "native of Lisbon, and resident of Minas Gerais" on the title page of the work, which was published in Lisbon in 1734. Yet his narrative of the festivities surrounding the transfer of the Sacred Host to a new and larger church in Vila Rica also represents another "transfer," one that, like Arzáns's narrative of the 1608 Corpus Christi festival, displaces the glory and grandeur of the Eucharist onto the mining town and its inhabitants.[15]

As in the case narrated by Arzáns, as well, *Triunfo eucharístico* responds to negative perceptions of the boomtown and its residents. Despite the ostentatious name with which it would come to be known, Vila Rica de Ouro Preto [Rich Town of Black Gold] had only been established as a township in 1711; one of the inquisitorial licenses to the volume affirms that the residents deserve great praise for their demonstration of religious fervor, "sendo habitadores de terras tão longínquas, como incultas" [since they are inhabitants of lands as distant as they are uncivilized]. Machado's account works as hard as the creoles

14. Hanke's footnote is found in Arzáns de Orsúa y Vela, *Historia de la Villa Imperial,* ed. Hanke and Mendoza, I, 274n. 7; for Arzáns's discussion of the goals of instruction and entertainment in historical writing, see I, clxxxv, 267.

15. Simão Ferreira Machado, *Triunfo eucharístico,* in Affonso Ávila, ed., *Resíduos seiscentistas em Minas: textos do século do ouro e as projeções do mundo barroco* (Belo Horizonte, 1967), I, 131–283, esp. 135.

of Potosí to disprove such a reputation of cultural backwardness and isolation. If the title page presents Vila Rica as the "court" of the captaincy of Minas Gerais, the "prévia allocutória" [preliminary address], which offers a brief overview of Brazilian history, describes the "Rich Town" in even more magnificent terms:

> Nesta villa habitão os homens de maior comércio, cujo trafego, e importância excede sem comparação o maior dos maiores homens de Portugal: . . . nella residem os homens de maiores letras, seculares, e Ecclesiásticos: nella tem assento toda a nobreza, e força da milicia: he por situação da natureza cabeça de toda a America, pela opulência das riquezas a pérola preciosa do Brasil.

> In this town live the chief merchants, whose trade and importance incomparably exceed the most thriving of the leading merchants of Portugal. . . . Here dwell the best educated men, both lay and ecclesiastic. Here is the seat of all the nobility and the strength of the military. It is, by virtue of its natural position, the head of the whole of America; and by the wealth of its riches it is the precious pearl of Brazil.

Like Arzáns, Machado highlights not only the town's mineral but also its cultural and intellectual wealth, both of which are put on display in the festival as well as in its written account.[16]

As Charles R. Boxer points out with respect to the above citation, "The citizens of Mexico City or of Lima would certainly not have agreed that Vila Rica de Ouro Preto was the chief city in all America; but they would not have disputed another contemporary writer's description of this Brazilian mining town as a 'golden Potosí.'" Indeed, Machado's Vila Rica bears some resemblance to Arzáns's Villa Imperial. Mindful of his metropolitan readership, Machado highlights the primacy of Vila Rica not only within the Americas but in the Portuguese Empire, stressing how it provides "grandiosos auxílios, e quantiosos rédditos; sem dúvida os maiores à Coroa do Monarcha" [great assistance and copious incomes, without doubt the greatest to the crown]. If America and Portugal owe their glory to Vila Rica, "the whole world" is indebted to it for the "copioso, e fino ouro, que recebe em seus Reynos" [copious and fine gold that is received in its kingdoms]. The assertion of American primacy and worldwide renown evokes the opening lines of Arzáns's history, which calls the Villa Imperial the "honor y gloria de la América; centro del Perú; emperatriz de las

16. Machado, *Triunfo eucharístico*, in Ávila, ed., *Resíduos seiscentistas*, I, 152, 180–181; in the second quotation, I use Boxer's translation, cited in *Golden Age of Brazil*, 163.

villas y lugares de este Nuevo Mundo" [honor and glory of America, center of Peru, empress of the towns and cities of this New World]. Throughout several paragraphs of similar laudatory epithets, Arzáns describes the Cerro de Potosí as celebrated, envied, and sought after by nations from the "four parts of the world."[17]

Machado's subsequent narration of the spectacular festivities confirms the extravagant presentation of Vila Rica in the introductory remarks. Preceded by six days of fireworks, music, dances, and masquerades, the transfer of the Holy Sacrament to its new dwelling incorporates all the elements of a traditional Corpus Christi celebration: "dances of Turks and Christians," triumphal floats and arches, elaborately costumed allegorical figures adorned with gold and diamonds, and a procession incorporating the religious brotherhoods, clergy, government officials, and "toda a Nobreza militar, e literária da Villa" [all the military and literary nobility of the town]. Following the procession are three days each of masses, tournaments, theatrical performances, and bullfights, all accompanied by splendid banquets for the local nobility and distinguished clergy.[18]

Despite Machado's invocation of the insufficiency of language to capture the magnificence of the celebrations—a standard trope of festival accounts— *Triunfo eucharístico* manages to transform the "glorioso triunfo do Eucharístico Sacramento" [glorious triumph of the Eucharistic Sacrament] into a glorious image of the city and its residents. As we have seen, however, Machado's concern is not merely to celebrate Vila Rica's material riches. He concludes by affirming that, although this was the greatest religious festival ever celebrated in America, he would have liked to describe individually

> os festivos applausos que em diversos tempos nesta parte da América se tem visto; e então ficaria manifesta a grande piedade, e religião, com que os seus moradores resplandecem; e entre as demais nações com singular ventagem se fazem conhecidos, desmentindo a maldicência daquelles, que os pretendem infamar de ambiciosos.

> the festive applauses that at different times have been seen in this part of America; for then the great piety and religion with which the inhabitants shine would be made manifest, and they would be recognized for their

17. Machado, *Triunfo eucharístico,* in Ávila, ed., *Resíduos seiscentistas,* I, 183. Arzáns de Orsúa y Vela, *Historia de la Villa Imperial,* ed. Hanke and Mendoza, I, 3; Boxer, *Golden Age of Brazil,* 163. The "contemporary writer" Boxer cites is Francisco Tavares de Brito, *Itinerário geográfico . . . do Rio de Janeiro: até as Minas do Ouro* (Seville, 1732), 19.

18. Machado, *Triunfo eucharístico,* in Ávila, ed., *Resíduos seiscentistas,* I, 37–121, esp. 110, 116, 121.

singular advantage among other nations, disproving the slander of those who try to defame them as ambitious.

The reference to "slander" alludes to exactly the same moral flaw that Arzáns— as we will see in the following section—insistently attributes to foreigners in Potosí, in contrast to the creoles. Although Arzáns is more careful than Machado, a native of Portugal, to distinguish creoles from the other ethnic groups residing in the mining town, both authors use festival accounts to challenge accusations of the spiritual, moral, cultural, and intellectual inferiority of the boomtown inhabitants.[19]

Similar to Arzáns's account, then, the characterization of the residents of Minas Gerais as a discrete "nation"—that is, a locally based ethnic or social group, not a wider entity seeking independence from the metropolis—emerges both from the slander of outsiders and the assertion of a distinctive superiority. Machado goes on to affirm that, if the Portuguese exceed all other nations in the world in religious fervor, "agora se vem gloriosamente excedidos dos sempre memoráveis habitadores da Parróquia do Ouro Preto" [they are now gloriously exceeded by the forever memorable inhabitants of the parish of Ouro Preto]. And the author stresses that Vila Rica's "Catholic zeal," evident in the construction of sumptuous churches and altars as well as in the "majestic pomp" of its festivals, is even more admirable given the town's distance from civilization:

> Se fizerão tão superiores a todas as naçoens do Mundo os moradores do Ouro Preto, que só com pasmos, e admiraçoens se podem dignamente applaudir; pois estes fidelíssimos Cathólicos vivendo tão apartados da communicação dos povos, e no mais recôndito do sertão, se empregão com tanto disvelo . . . em festejar a Divina Magestade Sacramentada . . . fazendo assim mais conhecida, e dilatada na terra do Soberano Senhor Sacramentado a devida veneração, e eterna gloria.

The residents of Ouro Preto have shown themselves to be so superior to all the nations of the world, that only with astonishment and admiration

---

19. Ibid., 278–279. Arzáns points out the foreigners' avarice when he describes the creoles' "joyas, preciosas perlas y piedras de sumo valor, que dieron mucho que mirar y mucho más que notar a los forasteros, que con nueva codicia encendió los deseos que en algunos había de las riquezas de Potosí" [jewels, valuable pearls, and precious stones, which gave the foreigners much to look at and even more to admire, for the desire that some had for the riches of Potosí was incited with new greed], in *Historia de la Villa Imperial*, ed. Hanke and Mendoza, I, 268. On the "charges of physical degeneracy and moral turpitude" leveled at the inhabitants of Brazil, see Russell-Wood, "Centers and Peripheries," in Daniels and Kennedy, eds., *Negotiated Empires*, 109–110.

can they be justly applauded; for these devout Catholics, living so far from the communication of people, in the most hidden corner of the backlands, dedicate themselves with such zeal . . . to celebrating the Divine Majestic Sacrament . . . , thus making the proper veneration and eternal glory of the sovereign Holy Sacrament better known and spread throughout the land.

Triunfo eucharístico recalls the festive spirituality of *El Dios Pan,* in which the spectators' amazement at the extravagant display of religious fervor can be matched only by the readers' admiration. Yet *Triunfo eucharístico* more closely resembles Arzáns's account of the creoles' Corpus Christi festivities by explicitly celebrating the town and its residents as much as the Eucharist itself. Whereas the Potosí festival is aimed at Spanish maligners as evidence of creole wealth, nobility, and ingenuity, in *Triunfo eucharístico,* the propagandistic intent of the festival's narration targets the European reader, whom it seeks to convince of Vila Rica's grandeur as well as piety in spite of its remoteness from even the colonial centers of culture. All three texts do more than propagate the "proper veneration and eternal glory" of the Holy Sacrament; they also attempt to make the mining towns' material and cultural splendor "better known and spread throughout the land."[20]

Episcopal Entries

When the festival centers on a human rather than a divine figure, the textual reorientation of the event's original intent becomes even more evident. Two narratives of newly appointed authorities' triumphal entries in Potosí and Mariana, Minas Gerais, exemplify this transformation. In the first, Arzáns de Orsúa y Vela recounts the festivities surrounding the visit to Potosí of an archbishop appointed viceroy; in the latter, the anonymous author of *Áureo throno episcopal* describes the laudatory reception of the first bishop in Mariana, the seat of a newly formed diocese in Minas Gerais. The festivals occur during or after the peak of mineral production in each region and, thus, at a time when the boomtowns' decline is already in evidence. If the accounts

20. Machado, *Triunfo eucharístico,* in Ávila, ed., *Resíduos seiscentistas,* I, 280–281. Laura de Mello e Souza similarly argues that what is being celebrated in the festival is not the Holy Sacrament but the mining community itself; see *Desclassificados do ouro: a pobreza mineira no século XVIII* (Rio de Janeiro, 1982), 21. On the early modern understanding of "nations" as "human groups within a larger kingdom who had their own distinct racial and cultural characteristics," see José Antonio Mazzotti's essay in this volume.

FIGURE 11. *Entrada del Arzobispo Virrey Morcillo en Potosí*. By Melchor Pérez Holguín. Circa 1716. Courtesy Museo de América, Madrid

present the extravagant wealth on display in the festival as particularly extraordinary given the current economic woes, they are even more concerned with extolling the moral, intellectual, and cultural wealth of the inhabitants.

Although he was surely a witness to the events, Arzáns claims to have based his description on Fray Juan de la Torre's official account of the "entry, reception and fiestas" of Diego Morcillo Rubio de Auñón, archbishop of La Plata. The archbishop was designated interim viceroy of Peru in 1716 and stopped in Potosí on his way to Lima to assume the office. There, he was greeted with eight days of magnificent festivities celebrating what would turn out to be a short-lived appointment. Besides de la Torre's official written account, a visual record of the entry was created by the mestizo artist and Arzáns's contemporary Melchor Pérez Holguín. Although Arzáns does not refer to the painting, he describes many of the same elements as those depicted in Holguín's *Entrada del Arzobispo Virrey Morcillo en Potosí* [Entry of the Archbishop Viceroy Morcillo] (see Figure 11).[21]

On the far right of the canvas, we see one of the two triumphal arches constructed for the occasion; this one features a folded "cloud" hanging from its first tier, which Arzáns describes as opening up just as the archbishop passed underneath, dropping a tiara over his head while beaten silver and gold show-

21. Arzáns de Orsúa y Vela, *Historia de la Villa Imperial*, ed. Hanke and Mendoza, III, 46–53, esp. 48. Holguín was active in Potosí from 1693 to 1724; see José de Mesa and Teresa Gisbert, *Holguín y la pintura altoperuana del virreinato* (La Paz, 1956), esp. 61–72.

ered down from above. In the procession, the archbishop is led under a canopy before balconies adorned with paintings, tapestries, and admiring observers and accompanied by richly attired officials, musicians, and infantry. In the foreground, to the right of the painter's self-portrait, two elderly onlookers marvel at the spectacle; the speech scroll emerging from the woman's mouth states, "En cientoitantos años no e bisto grandeza tamaña." [In one hundred and some years I have not seen such grandeur.] In the upper left inset, Holguín portrays the procession's entry into the town's main plaza; to the right, we see the same plaza at night, teeming with a lively masquerade. Corroborating the details of the painting, Arzáns explains that the masquerade, presented by the city's mining engineers on the following day, featured a procession of costumed historical and mythological figures, Turks, Ethiopians, and Inca nobility as well as a float with a miniature Cerro de Potosí and children representing the archbishop, angels, an Inca princess, an Indian miner, and—although they are not visible on the painting—two children symbolizing Europe and America: "La una manifestaba haberle sido su oriente y dádole su cuna, y la otra sus dignidades episcopales y gobierno." [Europe spoke of how she had provided his ancestry and been his cradle, America of how she had given him his episcopal honors and government post.] Indeed, the archbishop's debts to "America" and to Potosí specifically, rather than the other way around, figure prominently in Arzáns's written representation of the festival, providing a narrative frame that renders a more complex picture than the snapshots of festive splendor offered in the painting.[22]

Despite the opulence and solemnity with which Arzáns portrays the festival, he is also careful to point out the city's present financial difficulties. If Potosí's material decline is inextricably linked to moral decadence in Arzáns's Baroque worldview, in this chapter he impugns the virtue of royal administrators, and even the archbishop himself, more than the town's residents. Arzáns alludes to the economic crisis when he praises the *cabildo* [town council] for taking responsibility (together with "some of the wealthier guilds") for the festival's expense instead of raising the money through collections, "considerando la fatiga en que se hallaban los oficiales y demás pobres" [taking into consideration the hardship to artisans and other poor folk]. Later, he indicates one culprit for the town's material woes when he explains, "Aunque los españoles han cargado con infinidad de aquella riqueza y la han dado a los franceses,

22. Arzáns de Orsúa y Vela, *Historia de la Villa Imperial,* ed. Hanke and Mendoza, III, 50; the English translation is from R. C. Padden, ed., Frances M. López-Morillas, trans., *Tales of Potosí* (Providence, R.I., 1975), 193.

con todo eso no faltó para continuación de la grandeza de esta Villa." [Although the Spaniards have made away with an enormous amount of wealth and have given it to the French, yet enough is left to maintain the grandeur of this city.][23]

The critique of Spanish appropriation of Potosí's wealth—with a jab at French influence in Spain under the Bourbon dynasty—is complemented by a more explicit condemnation of court-appointed local administrators. Arzáns opens the chapter describing the entry by discussing one of the reasons behind Potosí's continuing crisis: the sins of its inhabitants. But even worse, he quickly adds, is that "los mayores pecados se hallan en las mayores cabezas" [the greatest sins are found in the highest leaders]. More specifically, he complains of the greed and poor administration of the *corregidores* [royal magistrates], for Potosí "no se experimenta otra cosa sino la peoría en la sucesión de los unos a los otros . . . porque sólo se hallan enfrascados en la codicia de riquezas, de suerte que si no administraran los alcaldes ordinarios de la manera que se puede acabara de perecer de una vez esta Villa" [experiences nothing but deterioration from one to the next . . . because they are only caught up with the desire for riches, such that, if the *alcaldes ordinarios* did not administer things as best they could, this town would have perished once and for all]. Indeed, it is these same alcaldes ordinarios [senior members of the town council] who bear the enormous expense of the archbishop's entry, which, as Arzáns points out, is usually the responsibility of the corregidor. In this case, he complains, the corregidor Don Francisco Tirado shrewdly fled to La Plata when he learned of the archbishop's appointment instead of staying to receive him, "[no ignorando] que de irse allá podría mucho más medrar, que estándose acá no podía sino experimentar algún menoscabo su riqueza" [not unmindful of the fact that by going to La Plata he could improve his position considerably, whereas if he remained in Potosí he would only have experienced a diminution of his wealth]. Arzáns's critique of the corregidor's behavior, reinforced by the subsequent soliloquy on the evils of ambition and greed, is a stark contrast to his praise of the generosity and nobility of the cabildo throughout the chapter.[24]

23. Arzáns de Orsúa y Vela, *Historia de la Villa Imperial,* ed. Hanke and Mendoza, III, 47, 48; Padden, ed., López-Morillas, trans., *Tales of Potosí,* 185, 189. As Hanke and Mendoza explain, Arzáns traces Potosí's decline beginning in the mid-seventeenth century to three principal causes: the civil wars, the collapse of a dam and subsequent flood, and the debasement of the coinage. The quality of the silver also began to deteriorate at this time, and output dropped to 1570s levels around 1710. See Lewis Hanke and Gunnar Mendoza, "Bartolomé Arzáns de Orsúa y Vela: su vida y su obra," in Arzáns de Orsúa y Vela, *Historia de la Villa Imperial,* ed. Hanke and Mendoza, I, xxvii–cxxxi, esp. cxxiv–cxxv; and Bakewell, *Silver and Entrepreneurship,* 16–17.

24. Arzáns de Orsúa y Vela, *Historia de la Villa Imperial,* ed. Hanke and Mendoza, III, 42–43,

The sin of ambition is eventually attributed to Archbishop Morcillo as well, who by the end of the chapter becomes an object of criticism rather than one of celebration. Apparently not content with the extraordinary sum spent on the festivities and the lavish gifts bestowed upon him—some 150,000 pesos total—the archbishop also leaves with 100,000 pesos from the royal treasury. The sum had been earmarked to pay back part of the amalgamator guild's debt, incurred through restoring the mercury mines of Huancavelica (themselves lost "through the neglect of those who govern"). Although the amalgamators warn the archbishop that mercury supplies will cease if the debt is not paid, thus contributing to the crisis in silver production, he takes it anyway, claiming that he will resolve the problem later—which, Arzáns points out, he never does. Arzáns concludes, "Por varias maneras fue su venida de gravísimo daño a esta Villa" [In many ways his coming was of great damage to this town], and affirms that the 150,000 pesos spent on the celebrations and gifts "fuera mejor gastarlo en otras buenas obras" [would have been better spent on other good works].[25]

The archbishop himself had refused an opportunity to spend money on "good works," in another instance of frankly unchristian comportment that distinguishes him from the generous and pious residents of Potosí. At the beginning of the chapter, Arzáns had described how an Augustinian missionary came to town with five recent Chiriguano Indian converts, requesting alms for the construction of a church in order to better propagate the faith among the remote tribe. Whereas the "caritativa Villa" [charitable town] liberally gave everything necessary for "tan buena ocasíon" [such a good work], the missionary's request was surprisingly rebuffed by the archbishop: "Quién dijera que petición tan santa había de merecer desabridas respuestas, y nuevas instancias un 'No se puede'?" [Who could say that such a saintly petition would warrant rude responses, and new requests [would earn] the reply, "It cannot be done"?]

46; Padden, ed., López-Morillas, trans., *Tales of Potosí*, 184. Arzáns dedicates a paragraph to Potosí and its cabildo's merit in *Historia de la Villa Imperial*, III, 45:

> Hónrelos mucho el rey nuestro señor porque ellos [los senadores del cabildo] son los atlantes de república que tiene por suya. . . . El rey es el que lo hace todo, pero ellos tienen en los hombros al rey, a que también podemos añadir que un monte de plata como el de Potosí, si no tiene en sus hombros al cielo tiene en ellos a toda la tierra, y así merece esta ilustre Villa y su cabildo toda estimación.

> May the king our lord honor the town council members, for they are the Atlases of their republic. . . . The king is the one who does everything, but they have the king on their shoulders, to which we could add that a mountain of silver like this one of Potosí, if it does not have the sky on its shoulders it has the whole world, and so this illustrious town and its council deserve the greatest esteem.

25. Arzáns de Orsúa y Vela, *Historia de la Villa Imperial*, ed. Hanke and Mendoza, III, 52.

Arzáns condemns the response in no uncertain terms, invoking his earlier diatribe against the ambition of corregidores: "No se puede dudar que siendo esta tan fea mancha entre los seglares, es infamia vilísima que deslustra y obscurece el honor de los eclesiásticos, y mucho más de las altas dignidades." [One cannot doubt that, since this is such an ugly stain among lay people, it is a vile infamy that tarnishes and obscures ecclesiastical honor, and especially that of high posts.][26]

The archbishop's blatant disregard for both the spiritual and material welfare of his subjects makes him an unfit object of adulation and his appointment as viceroy a cause for consternation rather than celebration. (He would, however, barely enjoy the position, since the more permanent appointee would arrive only a few months later.) What Arzáns's narrative displays and celebrates is, not the power, authority, and virtues of this representative of the Catholic Church and the Spanish crown, but the nobility and generosity of the residents of Potosí, who are capable of putting on such a spectacular festival even in times of economic woe. Thus the extravagant celebration of the archbishop's entry becomes a sign less of material riches than of the spiritual and cultural wealth of the Villa Imperial that put it on a par with any European city. Arzáns is careful to note the viceroy's admiring response to the miner's masque:

Alegre y admirado su excelencia ilustrísima dijo haber visto en la corte de Madrid varias máscaras de caballeros, pero que ninguna de semejante riqueza, curiosidad y propiedad de papeles, y del mismo modo la engrandecieron y alabaron todos los de Europa, y la verdad fue cosa admirable que tan en breve se dispusiese en tiempo tan calamitoso.

Much pleased and impressed, His Excellency remarked that he had seen a number of masques performed by gentlemen of the court at Madrid but that none had equaled this one in sumptuousness, ingenuity, and appropriateness of roles; and all the other Europeans were equally complimentary. Indeed, it was a most remarkable thing that it had all been accomplished so quickly and in a time of economic distress.

The affirmation of not just the equality but the superiority of a festival in a colonial mining town with respect to the metropolis reflects Arzáns's concern with defending his compatriots against accusations like the ones to which the creoles responded in the 1608 Corpus Christi festivities. If Arzáns here places the archbishop in the role of admiring observer rather than the venerated object

26. Ibid., 43–44, 51–52.

of observation, the narration of the festival is framed in such a way that the Potosinos are the only possible targets of the readers' admiration, in contrast to the morally suspect representatives of the church and crown. In fact, the careful structure and consistent themes of the chapter—most notably, the opposition between Christian generosity and sinful avarice and between local government and royal appointees—suggest that our admiration might also be directed to the writer, whose rhetorical skills have far exceeded a simple transcription of events.[27]

Some twenty-two years later, Bishop Frei Manoel da Cruz made his triumphal entry into the gold-mining town of Vila do Carmo, which had just been renamed the city of Mariana and elevated to the capital of a newly formed diocese in Minas Gerais, Brazil. The events surrounding the bishop's arrival are narrated in an anonymous work entitled *Áureo throno episcopal, collocado nas minas do ouro; ou, notícia breve da creação do novo bispado marianense, da sua felicíssima posse, e pomposa entrada do seu meritíssimo, primeiro bispo, e da jornada, que fez do Maranhão, o excellentíssimo, e reverendíssimo Senhor D. Frei Manoel da Cruz* [Golden Episcopal Throne Established in the Gold Mines; or, Brief Notice of the Creation of the New Bishopric of Mariana, of the Most Joyful Investiture and Pompous Entrance of the Worthiest First Bishop, and of the Journey from Maranhão Made by the Most Excellent and Most Reverend Lord Father Manoel da Cruz]. If the title seems to direct its verbal pomposity toward the figure of authority in whose honor the festivities were organized, the rhetorical force of this narrative, like that of Arzáns, lies more in the glorification of an American city and its inhabitants than in the adulation of the European institution represented by the bishop.[28]

Frei Manoel da Cruz's arrival to assume his post as the region's first bishop was greeted with all of the splendor that might be expected from a boomtown at the height of its gold production. If Potosí's reception of Archbishop Morcillo lasted a generous eight days, Mariana's celebrations were preceded by eight days of masques announcing the future festivities. Highlighting the ephemeral architecture constructed for the occasion was an elevated garden on the city's main street, replete with native flora as well as twenty-two sculpted nymphs and a multijet fountain. In the procession and ceremony marking the bishop's entry, magnificent triumphal floats alternated with allegorical figures, mulatto children dressed as Amerindians and performing indigenous dances, and, of course, the members of the local brotherhoods, clergy, and nobility. During the

27. Ibid., 50; Padden, ed., López-Morillas, trans., *Tales of Potosí*, 194.
28. *Áureo throno episcopal*, in Ávila, ed., *Resíduos seiscentistas*, II, 335–592.

following days, the celebrations continued with musical performances, dances, masques, fireworks, and, significantly, poetic competitions.

Although Potosí and Minas Gerais experienced very different levels of mineral production in the first half of the eighteenth century, the narratives of both episcopal entries coincide in pointing out present material decadence—a circumstance that would seem to be contradicted by the spectacular wealth they describe. The narration of the bishop's entry into Mariana is preceded by an account of his travels from his former post in Maranhão, in which we read that the bishop's plan was to conceal his arrival

> para não dar lugar aos excessivos gastos da pompa, e lustre, com que os habitadores daquelle dourado Empório da America costumão ostentar-se em semelhantes funções, sem embargo de ser tanta a decadência do mesmo paiz, que por acaso se acha nelle quem possa com o dispêndio necessário para a conservação da sua pessoa, e fábricas.

> so as not to allow the excessive expenses of pomp and glory with which the inhabitants of that golden emporium of America usually show off in such functions, despite the same country's decadence, to the point where you can hardly find someone with enough resources to support himself and his industry.

Under these circumstances, the abundance of precious stones, silver, and gold adorning the costumes and triumphal floats is even more worthy of the astonishment that it provoked among the spectators. However, *Áureo throno* also draws attention to the spiritual and intellectual wealth on display in the festival.[29]

Fifteen years after Simão Ferreira Machado's *Triunfo eucharístico*, Minas Gerais continues to be depicted in terms of its distance from civilization, as *Áureo throno* announces in its opening lines:

> O paiz das Minas, que he o mais util à Lusitania entre os vastos domínios da sua Coroa, não só se acha falto das utilidades temporaes, que convidavão aos Portuguezes a soffrer hum desterro voluntário naquelles sertões, mas não tinha ainda toda a cultura espiritual necessária para a salvação das almas.

> The country of the mines, which is the most useful to Lusitania among the vast dominions of its crown, is not only lacking in useful temporal

29. Ibid., 381. On the actual poverty of Minas Gerais during the gold rush, particularly in contrast to the wealth depicted in the 1733 and 1748 festival accounts, see Mello e Souza, *Desclassificados do ouro: a pobreza mineira no século XVIII* (Rio de Janeiro, 1982), esp. 19–42.

things, which invited the Portuguese to suffer a voluntary exile in those backlands, but it also did not yet have all the spiritual culture necessary for the salvation of souls.

The narrator refers to the region's remoteness while under the jurisdiction of the Rio de Janeiro bishopric; the creation of the new diocese and the bishop's entry would thus represent the extension of ecclesiastical power into uncivilized and unchristian lands. Yet the work's conclusion testifies to the festival's successful demonstration of an already prevalent piety:

> Assim se celebrou a solemne entrada de S. Excêllencia; e no desvelo daquelle glorioso triunfo, para que [o qual] privativamente concorrerão os moradores seculares desta povoação, se veio no conhecimiento da Christiandade, e veneração com que elles costumão receber os Prelados da Igreja, desvanecendo o diverso, e injusto conceito, que em outro tempo os pertendeo desluzir.

> In this way the solemn entrance of His Excellency was celebrated; and in the zeal of that glorious triumph, to which the secular inhabitants of this village privately contributed, the Christianity and veneration with which they usually receive the prelates of the church were revealed, thus dispelling the different and unjust concept with which they used to be denigrated.

As in *Triunfo eucharístico,* the festival account serves to disprove false assumptions about the mining region's lack of "spiritual culture."[30]

The lack that the narration most conspicuously fills, however, is that of intellectual culture. If the text describes in overabundant detail all the gold, silver, diamonds, plumes, and rich cloths that embellish the costumes and triumphal floats, it also transcribes the Latin emblems and mottoes that serve as further adornment. The narrative is frequently interrupted, as well, by the poetry that was recited and sung during the processions and ceremonies; the author expresses regret, for the sake of brevity, at not being able to include all those that are "merecedores de estampa" [worthy of print]. Furthermore, the work appends to the description of the celebrations the text of the *Oração académica e congratulatória* [Academic and Congratulatory Oration], pronounced by the president of the local academy, José de Andrade e Moraes, a sermon celebrating the dedication of the new cathedral by the same author, and much of the verse that was recited at the poetic competition. Perhaps more

---

30. *Áureo throno episcopal,* in Ávila, ed., *Resíduos seiscentistas* II, 347, 461–462.

important than evaluating each of the (frequently mediocre) poems is considering how the narrative includes and highlights so many different manifestations of textual as well as visual culture. The products of diverse hands and voices, they contribute to an image of a society that is just as rich and vibrant in intellectual and artistic culture as it is in mineral wealth. One of the licenses preceding the work highlights this very aspect, in praise as Baroque as the poetry recited in the competition:

> Assim nas obras, que neste livro se achão escritas em prosa, como nas que nelle se contém em verso, mostrarão os seus Authores a agudeza dos seus engenhos, subtileza de seus conceitos, e elegância de seus discursos, porque compoz cada hum delles huma harmoniosa música de diversas figuras rhetóricas, e fabricarão todos juntos hum delicioso savo de erudição tão deliciosa, que ministra com doçura huma grande affluência de sublimes ideas.

> In the works of prose that are found in this book, as well as those of poetry, the authors have displayed the sharpness of their wits, the subtlety of their conceits, and the elegance of their discourse, because each one of them composed a harmonious music of diverse rhetorical figures, and together they created a delicious honeycomb of erudition so delightful that it sweetly ministers a great affluence of sublime ideas.

What the creoles of Potosí demonstrate through their spectacular invenciones, the "authors" of Mariana display in their literary creations. The academy president's comparison of these "sublime authors" to Pindar, Cicero, and Demosthenes echoes El Dios Pan's enumeration of the classical writers and artists who would be unable to capture the grandeur of the Corpus Christi festival in Potosí. Local authors are surely necessary to render effectively—and to represent themselves—the city's splendor.[31]

Indeed, it is intellectual and literary "affluence," celebrated throughout the text, that Áureo throno itself seeks to display with its own spectacular Baroque prose. As in Arzáns's descriptions of festivals in Potosí, Áureo throno offers more than an "exacta narração" [exact narration] of the reception of the bishop, as another license refers to it. The work is ultimately more performative than documentary, but it diverts the festival's rhetorical aims by celebrating the city's

---

31. Ibid., II, 342, 410, 466–467. Ávila offers an analysis of the Baroque stylistics of the sermon and the poetry of several authors and affirms, "What effectively stands out in the diverse program, more than the mere objective of public diversion and religious celebration, is a noticeable preoccupation with intellectual splendor, with the introduction of erudite elements and forms in the various solemnities"; see I, 25–60, esp. 31.

grandiose reception of the bishop rather than the triumphal entry of ecclesiastical authority into Brazilian backlands. In so doing, the narrative adds to, if not alters, where Mariana's true wealth lies.[32]

In these accounts of Eucharistic triumphs and episcopal entries, the Andean and Brazilian texts alternate in the local, creole virtues that they extol. If Arzáns's narrative of the 1608 Corpus Christi festival focuses on the intellectual inventiveness of the creoles of Potosí—a self-celebration of artistic skill already suggested in *El Dios Pan*—*Triunfo eucharístico* celebrates the religious piety of Vila Rica's inhabitants. On the other hand, whereas Arzáns uses the entry of Archbishop Morcillo to proclaim the Potosinos' Christianly virtue in contrast to the greed of the archbishop and other officials, the episcopal entry narrated in *Áureo throno episcopal* highlights both the spiritual and the intellectual culture of Mariana. In all cases, however, far from a simple documentary record of the festivals, the accounts themselves constitute rhetorical performances that magnify and reorient the spectacular wealth that they describe. The authors of the narratives replace the original propagandistic intent of such festivals—to celebrate the triumph and the power of the church and crown in these distant boomtowns—with the goal of attesting to American, and even more local, grandeur.

The self-celebration traps the texts in their own mirror of reflexivity as well, as when we read the motto adorning a miniature Cerro de Potosí in Arzáns's narrative of the 1608 Corpus Christi festival: "Yo sí maravillo al mundo." [I do marvel the world.] Does this "marvelous I" refer to the mountain, to the model of the mountain, to the text of the motto, or to Arzáns's writing itself? The latter three are testaments to creole ingenuity. But the presence of the silver mountain as the source of the marvel suggests a distinctive feature of the production of creole identity in mining boomtowns: the importance of negotiating the concept of wealth, whether it is celebrated, exaggerated, elided, or redefined. And perhaps this insight can point us to a veritable gold mine of comparative possibilities for the analysis of creole identity formation in the Americas: an approach that can excavate the mountains of nation-states and empires, to strike at veins of connections and correspondences that lie beneath.

32. Ibid., II, 343.

PART III

Creole Bodies: Race, Gender, Ethnicity

KATHLEEN ROSS

Gender and Gossip in Criollo Historiography: Juan Suárez de Peralta's *Tratado del descubrimiento de las Indias y su conquista* (1589)

In discovering America Europe had discovered itself.—J. H. Elliott

In the end, let's face it, white or not, practicing homosexuals or liberal straights, . . . colonial creoles felt royally screwed by imperial Spain.
—José Piedra

The present essay grows from a larger project concerning American-born historians writing in colonial Mexico around the turn of the seventeenth century; it examines their complexities and positionalities as colonial subjects and the role of their narratives in a larger colonial and historiographical discourse. This corpus of texts includes the work of criollo, mestizo, and indigenous historiographers and epic poets such as Francisco de Terrazas, Baltasar Dorantes de Carranza, Antonio de Saavedra Guzmán, Alvarado Tezozomoc, and others. These are not works with which many readers, even scholars in the field, are immediately familiar; in fact, these texts have received very little critical attention, either in the United States or in Mexico. To put them in context, what have been better studied during this time period are the classical natural histories of the New World by clerics such as the Jesuit Joseph de

Preliminary versions of sections of this paper have been published in Spanish in Kathleen Ross, "Chisme, exceso, y agencia criolla: *Tratado del descubrimiento de las Indias y su conquista* (1589) de Juan Suárez de Peralta," in José Antonio Mazzotti, ed., *Agencias criollas: la ambigüedad "colonial" en las letras hispanoamericanas* (Pittsburgh, 2000), 131–141; and Ross, "Sigüenza y Góngora y Súarez de Peralta: dos lecturas de Cortés," in Alicia Mayer, ed., *Carlos de Sigüenza y Góngora: homenaje, 1700–2000*, II (Mexico City, 2002), 139–149. All English translations, except where noted, are my own.

Acosta, or certain first-person chronicles, like those of Bernal Díaz del Castillo or Inca Garcilaso de la Vega in Peru, which lend themselves to a more literary analysis.

What characterizes the group as a whole is a second-generation writing that follows the original narratives and epics of conquest written by Spaniards up to the mid-sixteenth century, that is, the works of Columbus, Cortés, Bartolomé de las Casas, Gonzalo Fernández de Oviedo, Pedro Cieza de León, Alonso de Ercilla, and others. If the dreams of those Spaniards revolved around the twin desires for gold and souls, for material and spiritual conquest, and their memories were of the Spain of the *Reconquista* (the Reconquest) that had expelled the Jews and triumphed over Islam, what were the dreams and memories of the writers who, born in America, narrated the consolidation of empire, with all its cruel triumphs and losses, through prose and poetry? This is the key question I seek to explore.

My group of texts is a heterogeneous one, including writers representing some of the different ethnicities that resulted from the arrival of Spain in the New World. As Walter Mignolo has demonstrated so convincingly in *The Darker Side of the Renaissance,* the destruction of Amerindian memory in Spanish America took many forms, and, while none of them succeeded entirely in their devastation, the damage done was violent, ravaging, and lasting. The dreams of Europe—the invention of America—displaced the memories of the peoples and cultures encountered in conquest and colonization. And that basic truth, as has been so well pointed out by other critics also, is what students of the colonial period always confront. Any analysis of colonial Spanish-American discourse, of the dreams and memories of empire and subjection to empire, must include the Amerindian presence. Without it, our work is but a Western monologue.[1]

My project, however, is circumscribed within the bounds of Western literacy, of the written word rather than the pictorial or oral text. And within it the largest group of writers is the criollos, the American-born Spaniards whose identification with both New and Old Worlds continues to pose many unanswered questions. Within this group, Juan Suárez de Peralta's 1589 *Tratado del descubrimiento de las Indias y su conquista* [Treatise on the Discovery of the Indies and Their Conquest] stands as one of the most elusive and intriguing, and also one of the least read.

Most work on Suárez has been carried out in Mexico by literary historians

---

1. Walter Mignolo, *The Darker Side of the Renaissance: Literacy, Territoriality, and Colonization* (Ann Arbor, Mich., 1995).

seeking to place New Spain's sixteenth-century writing in a national context, or looking for literary antecedents to what comes later in modern Mexico. As I have wrestled with Suárez's text, I have drawn on my own prior work on Carlos de Sigüenza y Góngora's seventeenth-century criollo historiography and Baroque rewriting of the foundational chronicles of discovery and conquest, in the process considering the implications of the one-hundred-year gap between these two historians. In many ways the Spanish-American Baroque of the late seventeenth century, despite its complexities and excess, represents firm ground compared to a narrative such as Suárez's. Later I will return to this point through the example of Sigüenza y Góngora's *Piedad heroyca de don Fernando Cortés* (1693?).[2]

Many, including myself, have located the beginnings of American writing in the celebration and originality of its Baroque, in the affinity of the criollos for a metropolitan style that reflected their own complex selves back to them within a constantly changing but highly developed colonial society. With Suárez's generation—the sons of the first Spanish conquerors and settlers—we confront instead the resentment of shattered dreams and the glorious memories of an American home that evaporated all too quickly, a moment between the fanatical ideologies of conquest and the structured spectacle of Baroque culture. In this essay, then, I hope to offer some new possibilities for grasping this rather slippery chronicle.

As with all the American-born historians who concern me, Juan Suárez de Peralta's identity, or lack thereof, remains a key issue when considering his writing. I mean "lack thereof" in several senses, the first being the most simple and basic: we know very little about this man besides what he himself tells us. Born in Mexico City sometime between 1535 and 1540, as the son of Juan Suárez de Avila, a close friend and brother-in-law of Hernán Cortés, this future chronicler belonged to the small circle of criollo aristocracy who very quickly came to feel a proprietary interest in the colonial capital. It is evident from the *Tratado* that Suárez de Peralta had no elaborate education, but rather was a dilettante who considered himself one of "los que no somos letrados y como yo, que no tengo sino una poca de gramática, aunque muncha afición de ler historias y tratar com personas doctas" [those like myself who are not men of letters, who have only a little education, but a great enthusiasm for reading histories and for talking with learned people]. As the second son, he inherited no part of the family *encomienda*—that is, the land and indigenous forced labor granted to

2. Kathleen Ross, *The Baroque Narrative of Carlos de Sigüenza y Góngora: A New World Paradise* (Cambridge, 1994).

them by the crown as colonizers—and found few paths for self-support; he held low-level bureaucratic posts and joined his older brother in business, principally running gristmills. The upper-class pursuits of raising horses and falcons occupied a substantial part of their time as well; besides the *Tratado del descubrimiento,* the only other texts of Suárez that we know are the *Tractado de la cavallería de la gineta y brida* (a manual for horseback riding published in Seville, 1580) and the *Libro de albeitería* (a book of equine veterinary medicine written sometime in the 1570s). Juan Suárez de Peralta married within his class but apparently had no children. In 1579 he left Mexico for Spain; we have no evidence that he returned to America and know nothing about his life in Europe or the date or circumstance of his death.[3]

Regarding the *Tratado del descubrimiento,* as with so many chronicles, the text never saw print in Suárez's lifetime, but it was published in Madrid in 1878 by Justo Zaragoza, who had found it in the archives of Toledo, under the title *Noticias históricas de la Nueva España.* Giorgio Perissinotto published a new edition in Spain in 1990, finally making the text readily accessible. The full title reads *Tratado del descubrimiento de las Yndias y su conquista y los ritos y sacrificios y costumbres de los indios; y de los virreyes y gobernadores, especialmente en la Nueva España y del suceso del marqués del Valle, segundo, Don Martín Cortés; de la rebelión que se le imputó y de las justicias y muertes que hicieron en México los jueces comisarios que para ello fueron por Su Majestad; y del rompimiento de los ingleses, y del principio que tuvo Francisco Drake para ser declarado enemigo* [Treatise on the Discovery of the Indies and Their Conquest, and the Rites and Sacrifices and Customs of the Indians; and on the Viceroys and Governors, Especially in New Spain, and the Incident of the Second Marqués del Valle, Don Martín Cortés; on the Revolt That Was Imputed to Him and the Judgments and Deaths Decided in Mexico City by the Judges of the Commission Sent for That Purpose by His Majesty; and on the Defeat of the English, and the Beginning of Francis Drake as a Declared Enemy].

To narrate this multitude of topics, Suárez divides the text into forty-four chapters, some very brief, ending with the ascension to power of the viceroy Don Luis de Velasco in 1589. I mentioned above this text's elusive and slippery character; much of that has to do with the apparent lack of focus in the narrative, as demonstrated in the title. But even more vexing, no indication

3. Juan Suárez de Peralta, *Tratado del descubrimiento de las Yndias y su conquista* [1589], ed. Giorgio Perissinotto (Madrid, 1990), 71. My source for this biographical information is Giorgio Perissinotto, "Estudio preliminar," in Suárez de Peralta, *Tratado,* 11–36. All quotes from Suárez's text also come from this edition.

of an intended reader or of any intended motive is given in the *Tratado*. Perissinotto opines,

> Si sus otras dos obras son la manifestación literaria de la gran afición que tenía por los caballos, el *Tratado del descubrimiento*, me atrevería a decir, obedece al impulso de explicar su país natal a una sociedad que, es sabido, ignoraba en gran parte los usos y costumbres de esa tierra que tanto contribuyó a la grandeza imperial.

> If his other two works are the literary manifestation of the great enthusiasm he had for horses, the *Tratado del descubrimiento*, I would dare say, follows the impulse to explain his native country to a society that, as is known, in large part was ignorant of the customs and ways of that land that contributed so much to imperial greatness.

Fernando Benítez, whose *Los primeros mexicanos* (1953; published in 1965 in English as *The Century after Cortés*) can be read as a gloss of Suárez's *Tratado*, takes a more Romantic view of the author:

> Empujado por la nostalgia, inició la redacción de su *Tratado de las Indias* que terminó en 1589. Oía sonar del otro lado del Atlántico un pretal de cascabeles y su imaginación le representaba animadamente los sucesos alegres o trágicos de su juventud a medida que los años lo inclinaban a la melancolía. El hecho de que se desterrara voluntariamente de México no significa que hubiera dejado de amarlo.

> Inspired by nostalgia, he began work on his *Tratado de las Indias*, which he completed in 1589. The chime of harness bells rang in his ears from across the Atlantic, and as the years brought their tinge of melancholy he kept seeing a lively picture of the gay or tragic events of his youth with the eyes of imagination. He had gone into voluntary exile from Mexico, but that did not mean he had ceased to love it.[4]

Whatever their ideas of the motive for writing the *Tratado*, these two critics agree with the assessment of others that the only sections of the book of real interest for the modern reader are those narrating events in New Spain to which Suárez himself was eyewitness, these being the chapters where "su estilo se hace visual y vivaz" [his style becomes visual and vivid]. Since the chapters dealing

---

4. Perissinotto, "Estudio," ibid., 23; Fernando Benítez, *Los primeros mexicanos: la vida criolla en el siglo XVI* (1953; Mexico City, 1962), 238; Benítez, *The Century after Cortés*, trans. Joan MacLean (Chicago, 1965), 238 (English translation).

with the Spanish discovery and conquest, as is characteristic of this generation of chroniclers, rewrite the texts of Cortés, López de Gómara, Las Casas, Sahagún, Motolinía, and others, according to this formulation Suárez can offer nothing new until he tells what he knows, and one might just as well skip to the juicy parts straightaway. Perissinotto notes in his introduction to the text:

> Y si el Peralta historiador sigue muy de cerca sus pocas lecturas . . . no es menos cierto que su narración se eleva notablemente al disponerse a tratar temas netamente criollos: la vida cotidiana, las costumbres y convivencia con los indios, los acontecimientos políticos de los que fue testigo.

> And if Peralta, as a historian, follows the few texts he has read closely . . . it is no less true that his narration becomes notably better as he addresses purely criollo topics: daily life and customs, shared life with the Indians, the political events to which he was a witness.

The value of these eyewitness accounts, beyond their colorful, entertaining, and even novelesque descriptions, rests in what they tell us about the formation of a criollo mentality. To quote Perissonotto once more, "El cronista vive— como todos los criollos—en un continuo debate interno entre su ascendencia peninsular y su amor por América." [The chronicler lives—like all criollos— in a continuous debate between his Peninsular background and his love for America.][5]

However, unless we read the whole text, we can go no further than mere appreciation for the anecdotal. Suárez's criollo search for identity reduces to a nostalgic gesture, and his writing on the Indians, on repression by the imperial state, and on criollo culture suggest only a tired wish for the golden age of encomienda. Moreover, we can no more speak of "all criollos" as an undifferentiated class than we can perform the same homogeneizing operation on Amerindian groups. The *Tratado* offers a vehicle through which we can begin to define some of the earliest criollo production and positionality and, eventually, to contrast it with the better-known work of a century later. There is one complex area, though, where I believe we can read this text, in its entirety, anew: its markedly oral nature, characterized by gossip, and the relation of this orality to questions of gender.

By the oral nature of the narrative, I mean its informal, talkative tone, its first-person narrative voice, and its digressive tendencies. Here I return to the issue

5. Enrique Anderson Imbert, *Historia de la literatura hispanoamericana* (Mexico City, 1957), 45; Perissinotto, "Estudio," in Suárez de Peralta, *Tratado,* ed. Perissinotto, 24, 27.

of lack of identity that I mentioned earlier and another of its manifestations: neither Suárez nor his text reveals an identity immediately to the reader. This is not a legal account, or *relación,* with its standard autobiographical beginning, nor an authoritative history with the weight of rhetoric behind it. The relatively long first chapter, in fact, begins all in a rush, as if propelled by great anxiety:

Las Yndias son tierra la más fertilísima que deve aber oy descubierta en el mundo, y más llena de todas aquellas cosas que en él son menester para el serviçio del ombre y aprovechamiento del. Que tratar em particular es proçeder en ymfinito, y así, para berificación desto y calidad della, considérese la riqueza que an tenido y tienen de oro y plata y muncha suma de ganados, especialmente en la isla Española de Santo Domingo, Cuba y su distrito, y Nueba España. Quel ganado bacuno y iehuas son ya tantas que se crían en los campos y montes bravos, que llaman çimarrones, ques sin dueño, ni se puede conocer cuyo es. No se aprovechan del sino es del cuero y sebo, que la carne se queda perdida en los campos donde la comem perros bravos, que son çimarrones que se crían en los montes, los cuales son tantos ya que hazen muncho daño en las jentes. Cómense esta carne unos pájaros grandes, negros, a manera de gallinas de la tierra que en España llaman pabas. Son de peor talle y feos y de malísima carne, que no sirven ni son para otra cosa, sino es para limpiar los campos donde ay cosas muertas. Estos pájaros y perros comem la carne del ganado que matan para el cuero y sebo. Y si por ellos no fuese, abría muncha peste a causa de la carne que se pudriría, y el mal olor haría munchísimo daño.[6]

The Indies are the most very fertile lands that have been discovered in the world today, and the ones most full of all those things necessary for man's use and advantage. To address this in detail is to go on to infinity, and so, to prove this, consider the wealth they have had and do have in gold and silver and many head of cattle, especially on the island Hispaniola of Santo Domingo, Cuba and its environs, and New Spain. The cattle and the mares are now so many that they grow up in the countryside and the wild forests, and are called cimarrons, that is, without an owner, nor can it be known whose they are. Only their hides and tallow are used, but the meat is left there in the countryside, where wild dogs that are cimarrons that grow up in the forests eat it, and they are now so many that they do much harm to people. This meat is eaten by large black birds, like the

6. Suárez de Peralta, *Tratado,* ed. Perissinotto, 39–40.

chickens that are called *pavas* in Spain. These look worse and are ugly and have very bad meat, and aren't good for anything except cleaning the countryside of dead things. These birds and dogs eat the meat of the cattle that are killed for their hides and tallow. And if it weren't for them, there would be much illness because of the meat that would rot, and the bad odor would cause much harm.

I have quoted this entire long paragraph to show the strange, rather wild progression of ideas with which Suárez initiates his narration, proceeding rapidly from a Columbus-like paradise to a nightmarish world of rotting meat. There follows a brief, controlled interlude of rumination on the biblical origins of the Indians and their rituals, but in less than a page, after stating that "esto de la ydolatría lo mejor es procurar se acabe y no tratar dello em particular" [the best thing in this matter of idolatry is to try to end it and not go into detail], Suárez yields to the force of memory and first-person narration: "Aunque trataré de una manera de ydolatrar, que yo bí los ystrumentos con los que la hazían." [Although I will treat a kind of idolatry, as I saw the instruments that they use for it.] A long passage then takes us inside a prohibited Amerindian temple, hidden in the sierras, where a group of men were taken prisoner in 1573. With great detail Suárez describes the temple decorations crafted in jade, feathers, and gold—some of which, he says, he himself brought to Spain and gave to his relative the duke of Medina-Sidonia—and the rites of human sacrifice performed by the idolaters. Eventually the narrative returns to the authoritative sources of the Bible, Sahagún, and Aristotle to concur with the standard thinking of the era on the question of Indian origins.[7]

The text moves forward in this lurching manner, following Suárez's train of thought, alternating religious and secular matters until, finally, now in chapter 5, the author makes the statement of his lack of formal training quoted earlier and protests: "Me quiero retirar de tratar cosas que son para teólogos y bolver a mi propósito, ques tratar de las Yndias." [I want to stop treating matters for theologians and return to my purpose, which is to treat the Indies.] Trying to corral his wayward text into submission, albeit with notable digressions on African cannibalism and native weaving techniques, he does tell the story of discovery and conquest. Reaching chapter 7, and by now relating Cortés's biography, Suárez reveals a new source: his own father. Referring to Cortés's adventures in the New World, he holds back from divulging all: "No quiero tratar de todas las cosas que le sucedieron en este discurso, por no ser prolijo,

---

7. Ibid., 41.

aunque sé munchas porque se las oy dezir a mi padre, que fue uno de los mayores amigos de Cortés tubo, a quien él lo contó." [I do not want to treat all the things that happened to him, so as not to go on too long, although I know of many, because I heard my father talk about them; he was one of the best friends Cortés had, and Cortés told him.][8]

And here a mystery noted by all who have read this text since the nineteenth century unfolds: while "mi padre" remains nameless, a man named Juan Suárez de Avila becomes an important presence in the history as Cortés's brother-in-law and close friend. Reading the *Tratado,* "mi padre" and "Juan Suárez de Avila" seem to be two separate people, in contrast to Suárez de Peralta's older brother Luis and his father-in-law, specifically named in later chapters, and identified by their family relationship. Perhaps, as some have hypothesized, this has to do with the legal case made by Juan Suárez de Avila in 1529, accusing Cortés of causing the death of his sister Catalina, Cortés's first wife; Juan Suárez de Peralta, who staunchly defends Cortés's innocence, here is disloyal to his own family. Or perhaps the (also unnamed) intended audience of the *Tratado* would be expected to know these genealogical details without being told, unlike a modern reader.[9]

In any case, what interests me more than solving this enigma is the presence of the father as a source of oral history. Much like Inca Garcilaso de la Vega's mining of his uncle's preconquest memory in Peru, Suárez de Peralta relies on his father's experience to narrate, with authority, the chapters of New World history he has not lived himself. But, unlike Garcilaso, or Bernal Díaz, Suárez does not write against anyone in particular or correct other chroniclers; there is no underlying text for Suárez to gloss or comment on. Thus the disorganization of the *Tratado,* which reflects the bits and pieces of knowledge as they surface. These include, prominently, gossip: oral sources that remain uncited.

One of many examples: comparing the religious observance of converted Indians with that of Spaniards, Suárez reports:

> Lo que diré es berdad, que lo oí en España, a un cavallero, ques más
> delito: yrse a comulgar y topar una mujer y parlar con ella, y conçertar
> que después se berían, porque yba a comulgar, y era día de jubileo. Cierto
> que mescandalizé. Luego se me bino a la memoria lo que los yndios

8. Ibid., 72, 82.

9. One hypothesis is that of Giorgio Perissinotto in his "Estudio preliminar": "Al encontrarse en la intrincada posición de tomar partido entre su padre y Cortés, opta por exculpar a este y enjuiciar a los acusadores sin identificarlos como parientes suyos." [Finding himself in the delicate position of having to take sides between his father and Cortés, he decides to exculpate the latter and to judge his accusers without identifying them as his own relatives.] Ibid., 17.

*hazen de bentaja en esto. Pues en el oyr misa, luego los berán estar
parlando a ellos ni a ellas, y faltar destar hincadas ambas rodillas rezando.*

What I will say is the truth, I heard it in Spain from a gentleman, which is
even a worse sin; to go to take Communion and come across a woman
and talk with her, and agree to meet afterwards, because she was going to
take Communion and it was a feast day. Of course I was shocked. Then I
remembered what the Indians do worse than this. When they go to hear
Mass, they can be seen talking, men and women, and not kneeling on
both knees while they pray.

The double experience of living in the Old World and the New, this gesture of
cultural translation whereby the gossipy news heard in the present forces a
reconsideration of the past, brings Suárez to a middle, criollo ground. The freedom that gossip affords the historian allows his own comparative response.[10]

Here that response, although scandalized, is moderate. But, as the *Tratado*
progresses into its second half, excess becomes the rule, and gossip and rumor
turn deadly as names are named. The first half covers the period up to the
arrival of the viceroy Antonio de Mendoza in 1535, approximately the time of
Suárez's birth. As the narrative enters his lifetime and he replaces his father's
American experience with his own, the criollo takes more control of his oral
history through greater detail. Critics and literary historians have not been in
error, of course, when observing the vivacity and compelling quality of these
chapters; what I submit is that only after writing the first anxious half of the
Tratado, after bowing to and then betraying the combined weight of both
written and paternal authority, can Suárez allow his criollo memories primacy.

A peak is reached with the narration of the intrigue and aftermath of the
conspiracy to unseat the viceroy in favor of Martín Cortés, the second marqués
del Valle, who returned triumphantly to New Spain from Europe in 1562.
Suárez, of course, knew everyone involved and refers to his own participation at
some crucial moments. When the Avila brothers, condemned as the main
plotters, are publicly beheaded, he rides alongside them in the procession to the
platform and thus becomes privy to the confession Alonso de Avila makes: "Lo
oy io, porquestaba tan cerca del tablado que tenía mi caballo la frente pegada a
él, y lo bí y oí todo." [I heard it, because I was so close to the platform that my
horse had his head up against it, and I saw and heard it all.] Clearly Suárez was
not among those implicated in the plot, for he has lived to tell the tale, but how
the tale was told to the authorities is another matter. The small-town reality of

10. Suárez de Peralta, *Tratado,* ed. Perissinotto, 62–63.

the mid-sixteenth-century criollo aristocracy, living its fleeting moment of feudal glory, crystallizes in passages like the following:

> Baltasar de Aguilar Cerbantes . . . descubrió todo lo que abía del alçamiento. . . . No lo dijo a sordo, sino a un cuñado suyo y primo ermano . . . y éste le dijo: "Pues hermano, asigurá vuestra onrra y hazienda y luego yd a denunciar de bos y de los que más savéys están en esa conjuración." Y es berdad, por lo que bí, que fue lleballe como por los cabellos. . . . Luego fueron con él Alonso de Villanueva Cerbantes, hermano del cavallero que avía sido primero abisado, que se llamaba Agustín de Billanueva Cerbantes. Este dio parte a unos amigos suyos, entre los quales fue uno don Luis de Belasco, hijo del buen birrey don Luis, y él y los demás que lo savían acudieron a la justicia a dalles parte.

> Baltasar de Aguilar Cervantes . . . revealed everything about the uprising. . . . He didn't keep it to himself, but told his brother-in-law and first cousin . . . and the latter told him, "Well, brother, keep your honor and property safe and go denounce yourself and the others you know are in this plot." And this is the truth, from what I saw, which was that he took him by the hair. . . . Then Alonso de Villanueva Cervantes went with him, the brother of the gentleman who was first told about it, who was named Agustín de Villanueva Cervantes. The latter told some friends of his, among whom was Don Luis de Velasco, the son of the viceroy Don Luis, and he and the others who knew went to the authorities to inform them.[11]

Names are named, and criollo heads will roll, as the crackdown on the conspiracy expands into a period of state terror. Suárez's sensuous descriptions of criollo masquerades and drunken revelry, of fabulous wealth and constant pleasure, give way to detailed, repeated accounts of the executions and their victims and incomprehension in the face of imperial power. Certainly, Alonso de Avila was guilty. Yet: "Si algo fue causa de su perdición o a lo menos ayudó, fue que era tocado de la banidad, mas sin perjuizio de nayde, sin estimación que tenía en sí, por ser, como era, tan rico y tan jentil ombre y emparentado con todo lo bueno del lugar." [If anything was the cause of his perdition, or at least aided in it, it was that he had a touch of vanity, but without being hurtful to anyone, without thinking too much of himself for being, as he was, so rich and

11. Ibid., 196, 215.

such a gentleman and related to all the best people there.] How could such a gentleman hurt anyone? How could anyone want to hurt him?[12]

According to José Piedra's provocative essay "Nationalizing Sissies," in which a section on Suárez de Peralta represents the most challenging reading of the *Tratado* to date, this author's narrative, in confronting "the traumatic primal scene of his mixed heritage," moves him toward a balancing of polarities such as male/female or civilization/barbarity, as he recognizes the hybrid nation that is New Spain. To quote Piedra: "The creole coming to grips with the Spanish abuses of power, property, and propriety brings to the surface a creole consciousness in cahoots with the true native values of America and of the Americans." In this gendered formulation, Suárez's highly detailed and sentimental narration of the criollo conspiracy to put Martín Cortés in power and of the bloody repression that put it down becomes a "sissy nationalist trick" where the weak, feminized, and colonized win out in the end against imperial machismo: "Nation in Suárez de Peralta's text, and more covertly in those of his contemporaries, is in the hands of the apparently submissive, ladylike martyrs of European civilization."[13]

Piedra's argument compels, and yet I am not entirely convinced of the ultimate outcome of this narration. Does apparent submission lead to a criollo win, in the text or otherwise? To venture some possible conclusions, I will consider one more aspect of the *Tratado:* its positioning as a narrative composed by a criollo subject writing from the metropolis. "In discovering America Europe had discovered itself," J. H. Elliott tells us. What does Suárez discover in Spain, writing a decade after his emigration to the motherland, the *madre patria?* If he does not yet have the Baroque language through which Sigüenza y Góngora and Sor Juana Inés de la Cruz would affirm their criollo selves a century later, how does he write the hybrid nation, the American home, that according to Piedra takes shape in this text? Does a gendered reading of balanced polarities do enough to explain the criollo dreams and memories captured here?

The narrative of the *Tratado,* leaving the emotionality of the Martín Cortés episode behind, devotes its last twenty-five pages to three other topics: the 1568 incursion of a boat captained by the Englishman John Hawkins into the harbor of San Juan de Ulúa in Veracruz, the establishment of the Inquisition in New

12. Ibid., 208.
13. José Piedra, "Nationalizing Sissies," in Emilie L. Bergmann and Paul Julian Smith, eds., *¿Entiendes? Queer Readings, Spanish Writings* (Durham, N.C., 1995), 401, 403, 405–406.

Spain, and, finally, the history of the viceroys governing up to 1589. Of the very interesting chapters on the English, I note here Suárez's sympathetic, firsthand portrayal of their gentlemanly conduct and noble bearing: "Entrellos conoçí yo dos, el uno sobrino de un señor de Yngalaterra pariente del conde de Yorc, y otro muy deudo de la reyna." [Among them I met two, one a nephew of a noble Englishman related to the count of York and the other very close to the queen.] The ultimate Spanish defense of the harbor causes no special joy for Suárez and, indeed, is blamed for causing the later, destructive actions of Francis Drake in America.[14]

The institutions of church and state, however, receive his wholehearted approval. Discussing the punishment of idolaters before the Holy Office of the Inquisition arrived in New Spain, Suárez returns to his earlier pattern of digression with another anecdote of ritual human sacrifice and contemporary superstitious practices. Now, he declares, with the ascension of Archbishop Moya de Contreras, the Inquisition does its work for a grateful criollo population: "Siendo ynquisidor onraba a todos los cavalleros muncho y los tratava como padre y señor." [As inquisitor he did much honor to all the gentlemen and treated them as a father and lord.] In like manner, the viceroy Luis de Velasco, beginning his reign in 1589, is in fact welcomed in New Spain as one of its own, since as the son of the previous viceroy of the same name he had lived many years and married there.[15]

In these later pages of Juan Suárez de Peralta's text there surface not only a criollo consciousness but solidarity with an international aristocracy and its apparatus. Future chances for Suárez's prosperity depend on the favor of the viceroy and his own powerful Spanish relatives; perhaps, at the age of fifty or so, he writes hoping to return to the court. For this criollo historian, writing from the metropolis with tales of home, the indignation of his youth yields to acceptance of and identification with imperial power and its macho ways. If we consider the trajectory of the entire *Tratado*, then, and not just the description of the rebellion, it is hard to take the "tricks of the weak" that Piedra sees here as a strategy of power for Suárez de Peralta's multiple positioning as both colonial subject and colonizing aristocrat.

While Suárez does indeed tell the story of repressed rebellion with a tone of hurt and bewilderment that may mask a more angry resistance and while the loving description of the beauty of other men here is unmistakable, I must

14. Suárez de Peralta, *Tratado*, ed. Perissinotto, 244.
15. Ibid., 257.

venture another reading less provocative than Piedra's. The work of historians of the early colonial period, including Anthony Pagden, Bernard Lavallé, and others, consistently shows a dual mentality among the criollos that allowed them to identify with the factors differentiating them as a group while continuing to fully support the imperial project of the crown. Indeed, during the sixteenth century, this group of descendants of *encomenderos* (those granted an encomienda) did not think of themselves as colonials at all, but rather just another part of the empire that should be granted certain privileges of self-administration. Work by James Nicolopulos and José Antonio Mazzotti concerning epic poets who followed the great model of Alonso de Ercilla's *La Araucana* points in this direction of bipolarity, rather than balance, as the various divisions within the ruling class of Spaniards and criollos are teased out through the texts.[16]

Here, as promised earlier, I contrast this situation with that of Baroque writers, who had many more tools at their disposal to express the rarity of the American situation. José Lezama Lima made famous the figure of the "señor barroco," comfortable with his urban life in a colonial city whose luxuries and celebrations overflowed and surpassed those of a metropolis in decline and economic depression. For such writers, a kind of balance of polarities was indeed possible, built in large part on their distance from the actual events of the conquest. Both conquerors and conquered, for the Baroque subject, had become memories known only through the chronicles of more than a century before, chronicles to be rewritten with Baroque language. Thus for Sigüenza y Góngora, both Cortés and the preconquest Amerindians were sources of pride and identification, whereas the indigenous people of his own time received only scorn.[17]

This can be seen with great clarity in Sigüenza's *Piedad heroyca de don Fernando Cortés* (1693?), considered by historians such as Elías Trabulse to be one of the author's most important texts, principally for its chapter on the apparition of the Virgin of Guadalupe. However, *Piedad heroyca* offers as well a reading of Cortés that we may productively contrast with that of Suárez de Peralta. Alicia Mayer, comparing the figures of Sigüenza y Góngora and Cotton

16. Anthony Pagden, "Identity Formation in Spanish America," in Pagden and Nicholas Canny, eds., *Colonial Identity in the Atlantic World, 1500–1800* (Princeton, N.J., 1987), 51–93; Bernard Lavallé, *Las promesas ambiguas: ensayos sobre el criollismo colonial en los Andes* (Lima, 1993); James Nicolopulos, "Pedro de Oña and Bernardo de Balbuena Read Ercilla's Fitón," *Latin American Literary Review*, no. 52 (July–December 1998), 100–119; José Antonio Mazzotti, "Resentimiento criollo y nación étnica: el papel de la épica novohispana," in Mazzotti, ed., *Agencias Criollas*, 143–160.

17. José Lezama Lima, *La expresión americana* (Havana, 1957).

Mather, places the composition of *Piedad heroyca* at a complex moment juxtaposing imperial decadence and an ascendant criollo culture:

> No resulta ilógico que por esas fechas, en que el peligro francés resultaba amenazador y cuando, por otro lado, se abría una nueva frontera contra indios hostiles hacia Nuevo México y Texas, Sigüenza rescatara la figura de Hernán Cortés, el gran conquistador, el que había puesto los cimientos de la colonización española en América.

> It seems not illogical that at that time, when danger from the French threatened and when, in addition, a new frontier against hostile Indians was being opened with New Mexico and Texas, Sigüenza would reclaim the figure of Hernán Cortés, the great conquistador, the one who had placed the foundations for Spanish colonization in America.

Mayer goes on to explain that, while it is Cortés's role as the generous and pious founder of a charitable institution (the Hospital de la Inmaculada) on which Sigüenza dwells, it is, at the same time, impossible for the criollo to separate this religious aspect from that of Cortés's military and strategic genius as a conqueror.[18]

The section of *Piedad heroyca* where we can see precisely how Sigüenza managed to characterize both of Cortés's facets, the military and the pious, is chapter 6, entitled "Pondérase la insigne piedad de don Fernando Cortés, y se desvanece lo que acerca deste Hospital y otras memorias suyas, por personas poco noticiosas se afirmó hasta ahora." [Wherein is considered the famous piety of Don Fernando Cortés, and what has been claimed up to now by poorly informed persons regarding this hospital and other memoirs of his is dispelled.] In this chapter, as contrasted with others where the author cites various sixteenth- and seventeenth-century historians, the written source upon which this essentially corrective history is based is Cortés's own text, his 1547 last will and testament.[19]

The text of the will is first cited at the end of chapter 2, in which Sigüenza proves the antiquity of the Hospital de la Inmaculada by quoting a clause ordering that the hospital and its chapel be finished. Cortés instructs that the building "se acabe á mi costa, segun y de la manera, que está trazado: y la Capilla mayor de él se acabe conforme a la muestra de madera que está hecha é

18. Elías Trabulse, *Los manuscritos perdidos de Sigüenza y Góngora* (Mexico City, 1988); Alicia Mayer, *Dos americanos, dos pensamientos: Carlos de Sigüenza y Góngora y Cotton Mather* (Mexico City, 1998), 90.

19. Carlos de Sigüenza y Góngora, *Piedad heroyca de don Fernando Cortés* [1693?], ed. Jaime Delgado (Madrid, 1960).

hizo *Pedro Vasquez Geometrico,* ú a la traza que diere el Escultor que yo embié a la Nueva-España este presente año de 1547" [be finished at my expense, in the manner in which it has been drawn up, and that its principal chapel be finished according to the wooden model made by the geometrician Pedro Vásquez, or the drawing to be done by the sculptor whom I sent to New Spain in this same year of 1547]. This citation leads into chapters 3, 4, and 5, where the hospital's site, architecture, and income are discussed and Sigüenza, not incidentally, is able to demonstrate his own erudition in the fields of urban archeology and indigenous history.[20]

The fact that the site of the hospital before was

el lugar donde por arte diabolica (según lo persuaden las circunstancias) rebozó hasta anegar la Ciudad con lamentable estrago de sus edificios y habitadores la no caudalosa agua, que del manantial de *Acuecuexco,* que brota junto á la villa de *Coyuhuacan,* para abastecer su Ciudad de Mexico trahia por una atargea (cuyas ruynas perseveran hasta estos tiempos) el Emperador *Ahuitzotl*

the site where, through diabolical arts (as circumstances persuade us), the low-level water fron the spring at Acuecuexco that rises alongside the town of Coyuhuacan (brought by the Emperor Ahuitzotl to supply Mexico City through a pipeline whose ruins last to this day) overflowed and flooded the city, with a lamentable ravaging of its buildings and inhabitants

allows the criollo to give praise that, "donde experimentó México en su gentilidad tan dolorosa ruina halle ahora para los Catholicos que la habitan providencia caritativa" [where Mexico in its pagan times experienced such painful ruin, today is found providential charity for its Catholic inhabitants]. Then, describing the building itself, Sigüenza gives himself up to excess:

Media entre estos dos patios la mas hermosa escalera que tiene Mexico. Confieso, que no se me ofrece modo para describirla, de forma que se haga pleno concepto de su estructura. Excede (dizenlo los que las han visto) no solo á la que adorna las casas del Conde de Benavente en Valladolid de España, sino á la del Real Palacio de Madrid.

Between these two patios is the most beautiful staircase in Mexico City. I confess that no manner of describing it that would give a full idea of its structure occurs to me. It exceeds (according to those who have seen

20. Ibid., 10.

them) not only the one adorning the house of the Conde de Benavente in Valladolid, Spain, but also that of the Royal Palace in Madrid.

And in this way, after laying down a foundation superior to the house of the king himself, we come to chapter 6.[21]

Here, Sigüenza takes up the question of the relative importance of piety and valor, religion and effort, with the classical Aeneas as his example. With a deft handling of terminology, he says:

> Pero desde aqui abrá de darle su valor (siendo tan grande) á su piedad religiosa el lugar primero, no tanto por lo que tengo dicho . . . quanto por lo que de las clausulas de su testamento (que por necessarias para mi asunto fue necesario leer) deducirá por consequencia legítima quien las ponderare.

> But from here on, his valor (being so great) will have to give first place to his religious piety, not so much for what I have already said . . . as for what, from the clauses of his will (that I had to read as necessary to my subject), anyone who ponders will deduce as a legitimate result.

The text of the will, then, is worth more than Sigüenza's text, and even more than Cortés's own actions: "Y aunque los positivos actos de su piedad (como ya se ha escrito) han dado materia inacabable para formarle elogios, quales se contrapesarán a los que el mismo se formó en esta propria clausula." [And although his positive acts of piety (as has already been noted) have given inexhaustible material with which to compose his praises, none of them outweigh the ones he himself composed in this very clause.][22]

The clauses he goes on to cite demonstrate an unaggressive Cortés, ordering restitution for anyone who might own part of the land designated for the hospital, "por manera que mi conciencia quede descargada" [so that my conscience will be clear]. Sigüenza is amazed that a man of such great actions, upon dying, would pay attention "en cosas (comparandolas a quantas otras suyas vocean las historias) tan en estremo leves" [to things (compared to so many others of his that histories shout about) so extremely slight]. That is to say that, when contemplating what the man of valor did and what he wrote in his last, pious testimony, the text clearly should be cause that

> encoja los hombros la admiracion, calle la invidia, y aunque no necessita de ello para su credito, pregone la Fama de gente en gente, lo que por

21. Ibid., 13, 17.
22. Ibid., 27.

digno de eterna memoria, me parecio aqui expressar, como en lugar conveniente, para añadir á los elogios de su piedad y justificacion, tan relevante testimonio.

surprise shrugs its shoulders, envy goes silent, and, although his credit does not require it, Fame proclaims among the people that which I have thought to express here in an appropriate place as worthy of eternal memory, in order to add such relevant testimony to the praise of his piety and his justification.[23]

Clearly, for Sigüenza, Cortés the conqueror of Tenochtitlan and Cortés the founder of a charitable institution are one person, impossible to separate into two. But what makes it possible for the criollo to reconcile each with the other is his text. This is what gives him the distance needed to historicize events, as he crafts them into his own Baroque text, *Piedad heroyca*. Sigüenza takes hold of Cortés's testimony and makes it his own, through commentary, erudition, and praise.

This becomes even more evident at the end of chapter 6, when Sigüenza uses Cortés's testimony in order to "desvanecer las vulgaridades, que á cerca de este Hospital, entre personas que discurren poco, ha tiempo que corren como si fueran oráculos" [dispel the vulgarities about this hospital among people of little reflection, which have been going around as if they were oracles for some time]. The historian fulminates against colleagues who badly interpret the document, or have not read it, or say that it has codicils that, according to Sigüenza, do not exist. This will, besides serving as the basis for the religious homage that the criollo wants to make to the pious conquistador, is evidence for laying severe criticism against his contemporaries. Like any modern historian, Sigüenza claims as his the documents with which he arms himself for intellectual battle. But, given the marginal situation of a colonial historian, to arm himself with the conquistador's will takes on another resonance. Ultimately, what permits Sigüenza to do so is Baroque language. Through its celebration of the strange and monstrous, its embrace of polarities, valor and piety combine as opposites in a trope that only makes the criollo historian's writing greater.[24]

Such a solution was not available to Suárez de Peralta; for him there was no equilibrium to be found in duality, no historical distance. The memory of

23. Ibid., 28, 29.
24. Ibid., 29–30.

conquest of which he availed himself was that of his own father, and recently conquered Indians and their immediate descendants were part of his family's own inheritance. If we recall Suárez's hesitation to describe rites of idolatry, his protestations that such matters were better left to theologians, alongside the obvious fears of censure we can also see an anxiety generated precisely by a lack of distance from the actual conquest. Moreover, his fascination with forbidden rites and sacrifices, with the beautiful decorations of jade and gold, finds no relief in the Baroque language of exoticism or excess. At such moments of anxiety, when there is no recourse to literary language, the chronicle can only return to paternal authority, to the memory of the father he dares not name and to praise of the punishing arm of the Inquisition. With dreams of criollo autonomy finally dashed, Suárez's narrative of necessity circles back to the allegiance he never lost in the first place, of identification with the crown and with empire. Despite the royal screwing, then, the dream and the memory of privilege remain, and power attracts more than the "true native values of America."

We know, of course, that everything was not perfectly ordered in Sigüenza's life either, especially at the end, when he suffered from physical pain and the loss of loved ones. Sigüenza, like Suárez, wrote *Piedad heroyca* around the age of fifty, with dreams broken and the end of a century in sight. Like Suárez, he was a member of the first generation of his family born in America, although he received a rich intellectual and urban legacy from his father, rather than horses, land, and memories of glory in conquest. But Sigüenza writes from a consolidated, Baroque New Spain that provides him with the tools necessary to feel at home, in both his life and his work.

If in the end we could say that Suárez's *Tratado* is the inverse of Elliott's formula—that here, in discovering Europe it is America that discovers itself— what implications does this hold for the agency of sixteenth-century criollos? Just that the only way out at this point is negotiation, the hallmark of criollo discourse and its challenges to Peninsular authority. Suárez travels to Spain bearing gifts of confiscated Amerindian objects, things that signify barbarism to his Peninsular relatives and lived personal experience to him. These objects will buy him favor, perhaps, and allow him to live off the wealth of others who may regard him with suspicion. He must trade on his own difference to survive, to negotiate a deal that will give him the time and space to write this memoir of an inherited, rather than earned, criollo glory. The language does not yet exist for a memoir like this one to declare its own agency without such negotiation.

For that agency, American writers would have to wait until the next century.

Sigüenza collects those same objects, studies them, and Americanizes them; they are part of a remote past no longer threatening. And neither does Hernán Cortés threaten to take away what now is his. The Cortés of *Piedad heroyca,* finally, is worth more dead than alive, when his pious last words outweigh his conquering deeds, when his text too becomes a part of an American history begun a century earlier by the first criollo writers.

TERESA A. TOULOUSE

Female Captivity and "Creole" Male Identity in the Narratives of Mary Rowlandson and Hannah Swarton

In 1697, the third-generation New England minister Cotton Mather transcribed or, more probably, ghostwrote the narrative of a Casco Bay woman, Hannah Swarton, who had been held captive first by Indians and later by French Canadians from 1690 until 1695. In supporting, appropriating, and even writing the story of a woman taken captive, Mather follows in the footsteps of his father, Puritan minister Increase Mather, who, some fifteen years before, had possibly written and certainly supported the preface to a wildly popular text preceding and influencing that of Swarton, the 1682 narrative of Mary Rowlandson, wife of Increase Mather's friend and ministerial colleague, Joseph Rowlandson of Lancaster, Massachusetts. Why, over two generations, did powerful male elites like the Mathers seize upon representations of orthodox women taken captive?[1]

Versions of this essay, which expands on and differs from arguments in *The Captive's Position*, were delivered before audiences at the University of Colorado in 2006 and at the joint conference in 2007 of the Omohundro Institute of Early American History and Culture and the Society of Early Americanists. I thank these audiences for their comments. I also particularly thank Fredrika J. Teute, Ralph Bauer, and José Antonio Mazzotti for their early support for this project.

1. For one claim of Mather's authorship, see Lorrayne Carroll, " 'My Outward Man': The Curious Case of Hannah Swarton," *Early American Literature*, XXXI (1996), 45–73. The initial ascription of Swarton's narrative to Cotton Mather was made by Thomas James Holmes, *Cotton Mather: A Bibliography of His Works*, 3 vols. (Cambridge, Mass., 1940), I, 210. Mary Rowlandson's narrative was reprinted four times in 1682. The text used here is Mary Rowlandson, *The Sovereraignty and Goodness of God, Together, with the Faithfulness of His Promises Displayed; Being a Narrative of the Captivity and Restauration of Mrs. Mary Rowlandson; Commended by Her, to All That Desires to Know the Lords Doings to, and Dealings with Her; Especially to Her Dear Children and Relations*, 2d ed. (Cambridge, Mass., 1682), rpt. in Richard Slotkin and James K. Folsom, eds., *So Dreadfull a Judgment: Puritan Responses to King Philip's War, 1676–1677* (Middletown, Conn., 1978), 301–369. See also Kathryn Zabelle Derounian, "The Publication, Promotion, and Distribution of Mary Rowlandson's Indian Captivity Narrative in the Seventeenth Century," *EAL*, XXIII (1988), 239–261.

Although historical studies of captivity narratives like Swarton's and Row-landson's have considered their transformation from religious to political texts, from theological to sentimental and sensational uses, and from high cultural to popular cultural dominance, they have often neglected the relationship be-tween support for these texts and the specific moments of their publication. Similarly, those interested in questions of female authority and agency in these narratives have not addressed the possible male identification with representa-tions of female captivity at the end of the seventeenth century. Examining cap-tivity narratives as orthodox religious interpretations of wars with the Indians (particularly King Philip's War, 1675–1676) or with French Canadians or as accounts of female resistance, scholars have overlooked the ways in which these narratives by or about women captives respond to profound shifts in colonial political and cultural authority during the period in which they appeared.[2]

For Massachusetts was not only torn by intermittent Indian wars between 1676 and 1697; it was concurrently engaged in continuing political and social in-fighting. Between 1686 and 1697, for example, the colony experienced seven changes in government, each administration highly criticized by competing colonials as lacking legitimate grounds of authority. Deprived of political power with the 1685 erosion of local control over the Massachusetts charter and the embarrassing failures of Sir William Phips, the first imperial governor appointed

2. Roy Harvey Pearce's essay "The Significances of the Captivity Narrative," *American Litera-ture*, XIX (1947), 1–20, provides the locus classicus for this reading. Another key point of reference for any study of the cultural continuities and transfiguration in captivity narratives is Richard Slotkin, *Regeneration through Violence: The Mythology of the American Frontier, 1600–1860* (Middletown, Conn., 1973). On female authority and agency in Puritan captivity narratives, see Mitchell Robert Breitwieser, *American Puritanism and the Defense of Mourning: Religion, Grief, and Ethnology in Mary White Rowlandson's Captivity Narrative* (Madison, Wis., 1990); Michelle Burn-ham, *Captivity and Sentiment: Captivity and Cultural Exchange in American Literature, 1682–1861* (Hanover, N.H., 1997); Christopher Castiglia, *Bound and Determined: Captivity, Culturehood, and White Womanhood from Mary Rowlandson to Patty Hearst* (Chicago, 1996); and William J. Scheick, *Authority and Female Authorship in Colonial America* (Lexington, Ky., 1990). Essays dealing with Rowlandson in particular and questions of agency in general include Kathryn Zabelle Derounian, "Puritan Orthodoxy and the 'Survivor Syndrome' in Mary Rowlandson's Indian Captivity Narrative," *EAL*, XXII (1987), 82–93; Tara Fitzpatrick, "The Figure of Captivity: The Cultural Work of the Puritan Captivity Narrative," *American Literary History*, III (1991), 1–26; Teresa A. Toulouse, "'My Own Credit': Strategies of (E)Valuation in Mary Rowlandson's Cap-tivity Narrative," *American Literature*, LXVIII (1992), 655–676; Lisa Logan, "Mary Rowlandson's Captivity and the 'Place' of the Woman Subject," *EAL*, XXVIII (1993), 255–277. Many of these studies do not explicitly address the way passivity allows for movement, but each is concerned with the ways in which, while claiming orthodoxy, Rowlandson's captivity narrative allows for some change in literal or psychological positioning.

under the new charter that Increase Mather had negotiated in 1691, prominent ministers like Increase and Cotton Mather also experienced a diminution in their cultural and religious dominance during this period. Unable to explain and contain crises such as the Salem witch "outbreak," they were also increasingly incapable of managing threats from other religious groups, like the Quakers, or from competing colonial insiders, such as William Hubbard and, later, Solomon Stoddard. Clearly, the world of the first-generation Puritan fathers, especially as these second- and third-generation sons were re/constructing the memory of the "fathers" during this time period, seemed at the point of disintegration.[3]

This broad context of the breakdown of older forms of cultural and political authority and the emergence of newer ones informs the brief reading of female captivity offered here. In what follows, I explore how historical issues of authority and continuity over two Puritan generations are expressed in the structure of captivity narratives and in the representation of the captive orthodox woman. My analysis derives from a key assumption about the connection of literary features to the moments of their appearance. Like a number of essays in this collection, I am assuming here that choices of form represent not only generic choices; they also register responses to history. Formal choices are thus never simply formal. In the narratives at hand, formal choices do not express a univocal response to historical shifts in authority. Late-seventeenth-century captivity narratives by and about women gesture two ways—toward the desire to contain meaning in a given shape and toward the in/adequacy of that shape fully to contain or circumscribe what is desired by those who employ it. The responses to historical change that are shaped in and by female captivity narratives are what I call ambivalent responses—they tend simultaneously in two directions.

Although, as argued below, the structure of the narrative and the representation of the captive woman serve to defend the authority and legitimacy of the first-generation Puritan fathers, they at the same time also draw such authority into question by revealing alternative desires from which the form is ostensibly

3. For varying general accounts of political, social, and economic contexts informing the publication of late-seventeenth-century captivity narratives, see Perry Miller, *The New England Mind: From Colony to Province* (Cambridge, Mass., 1953); Bernard Bailyn, *The New England Merchants in the Seventeenth Century* (New York, 1964); Richard R. Johnson, *Adjustment to Empire: The New England Colonies, 1675–1715* (New Brunswick, N.J., 1981); William Pencak, *War, Politics, and Revolution in Provincial Massachusetts* (Boston, 1981); Stephen Saunders Webb, *1676: The End of American Independence* (1984; rpt. Syracuse, N.Y., 1995). See also Michael G. Hall, *The Last American Puritan: The Life of Increase Mather, 1639–1723* (Middletown, Conn., 1988); and Kenneth Silverman, *The Life and Times of Cotton Mather* (New York, 1984).

to defend. In the language of two commentators on ambivalence, captivity narratives thus reveal an "emotional attitude" in which "the positive and negative components . . . are simultaneously in evidence and inseparable, and where they constitute a non-dialectical opposition which the subject, saying 'yes' and 'no' at the same time, is incapable of transcending."[4]

In some current accounts on captivity, the concept of ambivalence has been used to argue that these narratives break down the possibility of any exceptionalist colonial identity. My reading of the ambivalence of these texts suggests instead that they perform a different kind of cultural work for the male ministerial elites who appropriated, supported, and wrote them: at certain determinate historical moments, popular narratives of female captivity helped not merely to express but also to produce an exceptional form of creole male identity. This case is made, in large part, by a reading of Mary Rowlandson's 1682 narrative. Equally significant, however, is Cotton Mather's failed attempt, some fifteen years after the publication of Mary Rowlandson's text, to himself write a narrative of female captivity that would ideally repeat the female text appropriated by his father and his supporters. Expressing a continuing desire by certain elite colonial men to inhabit an ambivalent identity position vis-à-vis fatherly authority, formal features of Cotton's third-generation narrative reveal how both this authority and this position were, almost unwittingly, transformed by 1697.[5]

4. J. Laplanche and J.-B. Pontalis, *The Language of Psycho-analysis*, trans. Donald Nicholson-Smith (New York, 1973), 28. For a similar view, though directed to a different form and a different generation, see David Leverenz, *The Language of Puritan Feeling: An Exploration in Literature, Psychology, and Social History* (New Brunswick, N.J., 1980), 18.

5. On ambivalence in captivity narratives, see, for example, Burnham, *Captivity and Sentiment*, 1–9. Burnham is drawing on two early and influential studies by Homi K. Bhabha, "Of Mimicry and Man: The Ambivalence of Colonial Discourse," and "Signs Taken for Wonders: Questions of Ambivalence and Authority under a Tree outside Delhi, May, 1817," which are reprinted in Bhabha, *The Location of Culture* (London, 1994), 85–92, 102–122. For two different critiques of aspects of Bhabha's claims about ambivalence and cultural hybridity, see Patrick Colm Hogan, *Colonialism and Cultural Identity: Crises of Tradition in the Anglophone Literatures of India, Africa, and the Caribbean* (Albany, N.Y., 2000), 24–43; and Anne McClintock, *Imperial Leather: Race, Gender, and Sexuality in the Colonial Contest* (London, 1995), 61–69. In engaging the generational dimensions of New England creoles' use of particular forms here, I share a mode of inquiry with Kathleen Ross's essay, above, on colonial Mexican histories. Both essays address how to read and historically situate specifically formal disjunctions in creole texts. They also draw attention to the differences as well as the similarities among texts written in or in response to differing institutional matrices, whether political or religious. More broadly, each of the essays in this section engages the intriguing comparative question of how colonial New England and Hispanic elites negotiate and rewrite creole identity not only through thematic choices but also through formal and generic choices made at determinate historical moments.

Rereading Rowlandson

Bracketing much-explored questions about the historical Mary Rowlandson herself and focusing instead on Increase Mather's almost certain support for her text, let us examine two related questions. What is the relationship to authority being expressed in the overarching structure of her narrative? What seems at stake in certain colonial men's identification with the position of the female captive?

Most generally, we can argue that the structure of Rowlandson's captivity narrative expresses an attitude toward a providential authority, the divine, fatherly "Sovereignty" referenced in the American title of her text, *The Soveraignty and Goodness of God, Together, with the Faithfulness of His Promises Displayed*. Although the structure of the Rowlandson captivity inscribes movement —a going out and a return—it does so under the aegis of what is already providentially decreed. Captivity, like other Puritan forms, expresses relationships to two types of time—distinguishing between what Sacvan Bercovitch, drawing on Herman Melville, has called "Horologicals" and "Chronometricals" —human time and divine time. Although the narrative structure of Rowlandson's captivity seems to move, the point of this movement is only to return to where, in some sense, she who is elect has never left. If, in the captive's eyes, such movement *seems* temporal and contingent, in divine terms this temporality is spatial. Divine authority has already decreed what will happen.[6]

As she is moved, or in the text's terms "removed," from Indian encampment to encampment (her text is broken into segments entitled "removes"), Rowlandson is famously represented as becoming aware of this overarching plan through a series of "special providences." From register to register, whether through dispensations to her health (her feet are kept dry), answers to her prayers (that her son might appear) or, perhaps most strikingly, Indian victories (proof that "we" are not yet ready for redemption), Rowlandson's captivity ostensibly unfolds in the context of an authority that is always already present. Even at the most trying moment in her text, when external signs no longer seem to signify at all, Rowlandson resolutely claims that God leaves us "in the dark" just when the exercise of his delivering power is nearest.[7]

The captive who undergoes such movement must ideally remain humble, obedient, and passive to God's will. Though taken captive, coerced into pas-

---

6. See Sacvan Bercovitch, *The American Jeremiad* (Madison, Wis., 1978), 28.
7. Rowlandson, *The Soveraignty and Goodness of God*, in Slotkin and Folsom, eds., *So Dreadfull a Judgment*, 329–330, 333, 334, 357.

sivity, she must also demonstrate her acquiescence in the divine plan by simultaneously choosing such passivity as her aim. In the captive's willed passivity lies the proof of her belief in and her loyalty to God's plan rather than to human desires.

That actively accepting passivity is key to this text is indicated not only by the narrative action but also by anecdotes that stop such action. At the beginning of the Rowlandson text, for example, when the narrator is describing the horrifying immediacy of the bloody raid on herself, her family, and her town, the text suddenly stops to register an anecdote about the difficulty her elder sister had confronted years before in fully accepting the belief that God's grace alone could save her: "In her younger years she lay under much trouble upon spiritual accounts, till it pleased God to make that precious scripture take hold of her heart, 2 Corinthians 12.9. *And he said unto me, my grace is sufficient for thee.* More than twenty years after I have heard her tell how sweet and comfortable that place was to her. But to return . . ." In contrast to this sister who accepts the necessity of her passivity before God's authority is the woeful tale of one Mrs. Joslin from the Fourth Remove. Actively importuning the Indians to go home— and thereby revealing her unwillingness to wait on God's will—the pregnant Joslin is burned at the stake with her two-year-old in her arms. At the end of the Fourth Remove, Rowlandson marks her difference from the weeping and complaining Joslin, quoting Jeremiah 31:16: "*Thus saith the Lord, refrain thy voice from weeping, and thine eyes from tears, for thy work shall be rewarded, and they shall come again from the land of the Enemy.*"[8]

Through its particular scriptural choices, its "special providences," and its anecdotes, the Rowlandson narrative is bent on establishing a relationship between the position of the passive woman and the divine plan whose claims to authority she acknowledges in her very acceptance of this position. Although Rowlandson's narrative uses what I call an A-B-A pattern—Rowlandson is taken from the Puritan community, experiences captivity, and is restored—the narrative seeks to encourage belief that B is only the occasion of realizing that A, the state of being "justified" by God, is and has been present all along.

This particular configuration has been recognized in religious terms, but it has never been specifically related to the broad historical conflicts over authority sketched above. So read, it becomes clear, the stance toward divine fatherly authority and the representation of the passive female captive should no longer be interpreted solely in terms of King Philip's War but must also be read as taking on a specific valence in the contexts of threats to the Massachusetts

8. Ibid., 324, 331–332.

charter, debates over which occur both before and after the charter's eventual abrogation in 1685.

As I have argued elsewhere, there is direct and implied commentary about the possibility of English intervention in matters of colonial sovereignty after King Philip's War. The religious and political "independency" of Massacusetts is challenged, both directly and indirectly, by visiting Englishmen like Edward Randolph, and events in England and France point not only to the suppression of Dissenters but also to the almost certain ascension of a Catholic to the English throne. Central to this discussion are the two main *rhetorical* tactics for addressing such challenges that emerged in the early 1680s. First, there was an intense revival of interest in divine providence. In 1681, for example, Increase Mather issued a call to ministers throughout New England to contribute to a planned collection of providences. In 1682, Mary Rowlandson's narrative was published, and the recently deceased Urian Oakes's sermon, *The Soveraign Efficacy of Divine Providence,* was republished. In 1684, following a series of sermons examining the providential meanings of comets, Increase Mather published both his own sermons on providence, *The Doctrine of Divine Providence Opened and Applyed,* and the results of his 1681 call, *An Essay for the Recording of Illustrious Providences.* Clearly, in the face of political threats to Massachusetts after King Philip's War, Mather and his cohort were promoting massive textual support for a providential reading of both past and coming events in New England.[9]

Given this concerted turn to such themes and such rhetoric, the second tactic to which the ministers turned is not unexpected. As Sacvan Bercovitch has astutely noted, jeremiads of the post–King Philip's War period increasingly take passivity as their aim. Sermon after sermon, they urge that all colonials, male and female alike, take a humble, obedient, passive position in the face of divine sovereignty. In Mary Rowlandson's 1682 account, both tactics come to intersect as providential history enacts its ends in the "narrative" of a passive, humble, justified captive who is restored to the divinely justified state she has never really left. Loyalty to the ways of the first-generation fathers— theologically, politically—is at once tested and affirmed as the passive female captive performs their belief in the authority of the sovereign God to "restore" and "redeem" them to their place in the eternally authorized plan.[10]

---

9. Teresa A. Toulouse, "The Sovereignty and Goodness of God in 1682: Royal Authority, Female Captivity, and 'Creole' Male Identity," *English Literary History,* LXVII (2000), 925–949. For a classic description of late-seventeenth-century debates over the New England charter from 1684 onward, see James Truslow Adams, *The Founding of New England* (Boston, 1921), 364–460.

10. Bercovitch, *The American Jeremiad,* 81–83.

Situating Rowlandson's captivity in the midst of other 1680s texts suggests the concerted effort certain second-generation ministers initially made to unify community response to royal threats to the Massachusetts charter. It also indicates the important role the representation of a woman taken captive, afflicted, and restored was to play both in the ideological defense of the first generation and in the second-generation sons' construction of their own loyal identification with the politics and theology of their fathers. It does not, however, address why a woman's text was to perform this work.

The Female Position

New England ministers preferred to appropriate women's rather than men's captivities, as Annette Kolodny long ago pointed out, because women as examples of vulnerability provided more compelling object lessons than men. And, after all, Mary Rowlandson's captivity had literally happened to her, not to her husband. Still, it is telling that, in this instance, the Rowlandson family, especially Joseph, had connections with Increase Mather. Important as Rowlandson's support for Increase's position on matters like the Halfway Covenant might have been, however, even more important for Mather's purposes was the stress put on a feminized passivity, humility, and obedience in Puritan theology.[11]

Amanda Porterfield and Ivy Schweitzer have examined how, in the spiritual realm, all the "saints" exhibit similar qualities that draw on the representation of the pious woman. In a position of power and authority over women, children, and servants in the secular world, men thus are in the position of the woman in the realm of the spirit. The representation of the humble female captive is an old religious means, both in the history of Christianity and in the history of Puritanism, of displaying the spiritual stance a whole people should take in the face of natural and social disasters. What seems unusual in the Rowlandson narrative is its elision of the spiritually feminized position with a secular male

11. Annette Kolodny, *The Lay of the Land: Metaphor as Experience and History in American Life and Letters* (Chapel Hill, N.C., 1975), 21. Joseph Rowlandson apparently served as one of the mediators in the bitter Third Church dispute, a conflict that involved one group (the Third Church) separating from another (the First Church) over the Halfway Covenant. The Third Church supported the new rules for church membership; the more traditional First Church did not. See Robert K. Diebold, "Mary Rowlandson," in *American Writers before 1800: A Biographical and Critical Dictionary*, ed. James A. Levernier and Douglas R. Wilmes, 3 vols. (Westport, Conn., 1983), III, 1244. Michael Hall notes how Mather stayed with the Rowlandsons in 1665 during a brief vacation. See Hall, *The Last American Puritan*, 75.

political position. The female passivity shared in the face of sovereignty in the spiritual world here becomes a means of actively confronting perceived threats to the first-generation fathers' authority in the political as well as the religious realm.[12]

That certain ministers were uncomfortably aware of a possible problem in this elision of religious passivity and secular activity is indicated by a well-known comment in the anonymous preface to Mary Rowlandson's narrative, which is often attributed to Increase Mather. Seeking to dispel any notion that Rowlandson is seizing upon an authority outside the traditional cultural roles ascribed to women, the writer notes: "Though this gentlewoman's modesty would not thrust it into the press, yet her gratitude unto God made her not hardly persuadable to let it pass. . . . I hope by this time none will cast any reflection upon this gentlewoman, on the score of this publication of her affliction and deliverance." Besides, reasons the author, "let such further know that this was a dispensation of public note, and of universal concernment, and so much the more, by how much the nearer this gentlewoman stood related to that faithful servant of God"—Joseph Rowlandson. If Mary Rowlandson can be representative of the humble position *all* must inhabit on a spiritual level, her self-authorizing act of writing and publishing must not be seen as replicable by *women* in the secular world. Hers is a special "dispensation."[13]

Cultural assumptions about women in the secular world also inform Joseph Rowlandson's final sermon, *The Possibility of God's Forsaking a People,* which is also published jointly with his wife's narrative. Those who retain trust in God, even when he is absent, are like the spouse in Canticles; those who do not are like "the Adultress in her Husbands absence, [who] will seek after other Lovers." If Mary Rowlandson is, by implication, to be seen as the spouse, local gossip

12. Amanda Porterfield, *Female Piety in Puritan New England: The Emergence of Religious Humanism* (New York, 1992), 3–13; Ivy Schweitzer, *The Work of Self-Representation: Lyric Poetry in Colonial New England* (Chapel Hill, N.C., 1991), 5–35. Schweitzer is more particularly interested in the lack of authority granted to real women in the secular world by the Puritan men who identified with women's culturally constructed position in the spiritual world.

13. Ter Amicam [Increase Mather?], "The Preface to the Reader," in Rowlandson, *The Sovraignty and Goodness of God,* in Slotkin and Folsom, eds., *So Dreadfull a Judgment,* 320. Commentators have often used David Richards's 1967 unpublished Yale College honors thesis, " 'The Memorable Preservations': Narratives of Indian Captivity in the Literature and Politics of Colonial New England, 1675–1725," to make the claim for Mather's authorship of the preface. But Richards nowhere makes this claim; he does point out that the arguments advanced in the preface were certainly shared and disseminated by Mather (20–30). Given Mather's stature at this point and given his relationship with the Rowlandson family, it seems clear that the text would not have been published without his support.

apparently saw her more like the adultress. According to Nathaniel Saltonstall, it was rumored that she had married an Indian chief![14]

Seeking to defend the fathers, a supporter of Increase Mather or Increase Mather himself seized on a representation of female captivity that confirmed colonial sons' loyalty to the authority of their fathers and their fathers' God. At the same time, implying the political as well as the spiritual meanings of this representation, advocates of Mather's position also opened up issues involving the culturally constructed doubleness of the woman's position—loyal, humble, obedient spouse on the one hand, duplicitous usurper of authority and idolatrous adultress on the other.

Two arguments have addressed this cultural doubleness of the female captive's position. One maintains that its ministerial supporters, especially Increase Mather, were aware of it but sought to contain and to circumscribe its meanings in the preface that framed the narrative. The other argues that Rowlandson herself, both directly and inadvertently, nonetheless expresses anger at, if not a repudiation of, traditional Puritan readings or understandings of her experience. Here, returning to the representation of the captive woman and the structure of captivity narratives addressed above, I suggest a third approach to this doubleness, one that will specifically relate it to second-generation men's identification with the position of the captive woman.[15]

On the one hand, the loyal female captive clearly represents such men's claim to their first-generation fathers' connection to the sovereign God. She proves or maintains this relationship through her performance of a theologically mandated passivity. The female position so demonstrated supports a traditional vision of colonial identity and continuity with the first generation. On the other hand, the vulnerable female captive expresses this relationship through representations of separation. Taken captive she is separated and separate from her community and thereby open to acculturation (as gossip about Rowlandson expressed) by other groups. As many have noted, for example, Mary Rowlandson, while claiming to be unchanged by her experience, demonstrates in her actions—how she eats, dresses, behaves toward her captors—that she has, in fact, adapted and transformed herself in this new situation.

The doubleness of female passivity—its expression of loyalty as well as its expression of separation—can be read at the level of structure as well. As argued

14. Joseph Rowlandson, *The Possibility of God's Forsaking a People* . . . (Boston, 1682), 16; N[athaniel] S[altonstall], *A New and Further Narrative of the State of New England* (London, 1676), in Charles H. Lincoln, ed., *Narratives of the Indian Wars* (New York, 1913), 112–167.

15. For the first reading see Breitwieser, *American Puritanism*, 101–102; for the second reading, see note 2, above.

earlier, the experience of captivity, B, occurs only within the frame of A, God's overarching plan that is present both at the beginning and at the end of the narrative. In this reading, Rowlandson is restored to a justified state she has to recognize she has never really left. But could not this structure also be read otherwise? Shifting our attention to B, the narration of the experience of captivity itself, we could argue, obviously, that there would be no narrative—and no revealing of the eternal divine plan, A—without it. To what extent does A, in fact, *depend* on B, rather than vice versa? Viewed in this light, it is not only Rowlandson but also divine authority itself that is being tested in a series of narrative "removes" (B).

From another angle, B appears even more subversive of A. Under the aegis of its description of affliction or test, it is B that, like female passivity, *allows* for an experience of separation from A. Although this experience can be represented as terrible—for Rowlandson it literally involves the death of loved ones and extraordinary physical and psychological deprivation—it also represents the captive's resourcefulness and her competence in new situations. Telling here is the Rowlandson text's use of the prodigal son. The son ostensibly represents the captive's humbling and the father's forgiveness, but his story suggests other meanings. Even though he returns home destitute to sleep among the swine, for example, the prodigal son has nonetheless claimed his birthright and enjoyed it on his own before he is forced to return.[16]

To reread the structure of Rowlandson's captivity in these terms is not to repudiate the logic of providentialism that fuels the narrative. It is crucial for second-generation male identity that the representative captive woman be restored to her previous state as justified saint. Only in her return can the sons' political and theological loyalty to the authority of their fathers, and their fathers' God, be proved and sustained. At the same time, however, as I have just suggested, both the representation of the passive captive and the structure of captivity also allow for the expression of other kinds of feelings—the wish to separate from the fathers, the wish to experience new situations, the wish to test one's own competence away from traditional authority. As Jay Fliegelman points out in reference to Hannah Dustan's captivity, these texts early on point to a nascent frontier self-reliance, but this move is neither contemplated nor completed in the Rowlandson text. For, whatever the Rowlandson narrator may describe the female captive as doing, the narrator interprets her actions within

16. For a major use of the prodigal son in Rowlandson's narrative, see the end of the Thirteenth Remove (Rowlandson, *The Soveraignty and Goodness of God*, in Slotkin and Folsom, eds., *So Dreadfull a Judgment*, 346–347). Prominent minister Samuel Willard published a sermon, *Mercy Magnified on a Penitent Prodigal . . .* , in Boston in 1684.

the frame of a passive subject waiting for providential action. That is, whatever her experience of B, Mary Rowlandson must be returned to A—the point from which, on a higher level, she has never really departed.[17]

Ambivalence

The renewal of threats to colonial political and cultural authority in the post–King Philip's War period leads, as we have seen, to a heightened concern with the nature of the providential plan for New England and with the proper position to inhabit in the face of this plan. Powerful second-generation male elites like Increase Mather and Samuel Willard respond to these threats not only in sermons and treatises but also in their support for what became an extremely popular narrative of female captivity. In Mary Rowlandson's narrative, the interlinked theology and authority of the New England fathers could be defended as the representative captive woman maintained the appropriately humbled and passive position toward divine, not kingly, sovereignty.

At the same time, far beyond the level of local gossip about Mary Rowlandson, the susceptibility of the representation of the captive woman and of the structure of her captivity account to cultural readings about the doubleness of the woman's position suggests that other desires are at stake in second-generation ministerial support for this narrative. For all that it demonstrates loyalty to the fathers, captivity also represents a separation and hence a possible difference from them as well. If the authority of the first generation is defended in this narrative, it is equally drawn into question.

Using the term introduced earlier in this essay, Rowlandson's captivity, in its narrative structure and in its representation of the female captive, may be described as ambivalent. Historians of American Puritanism have used the concept of ambivalence to explore how diverse social practice of first- and some second-generation Puritans—from child rearing to marriage and inheritance customs—could have encouraged mixed feelings in their sons. Indebted to such insights, the analysis here explores how the appropriation and publication of female captivity narratives coincides with and responds to the breakdown of the traditional political and cultural authority of the first-generation fathers. The sources of ambivalence are less of a concern than why, at a moment of exacer-

17. Jay Fliegelman, *Prodigals and Pilgrims: The American Revolution against Patriarchal Authority, 1750–1800* (Cambridge, 1984), 145–146.

bated threat to colonial legitimacy, an ambivalent form like the female captivity narrative is chosen to represent the position of particular colonial men.[18]

In an earlier reading of Rowlandson's narrative, I concluded that her text ended in an impasse—an incapacity to choose one position with which to identify over another. Michelle Burnham has since argued that the text's ambivalence in fact proves destructive of any fixed or essential identity position. Although both readings usefully shift attention from whether the text is complicit or resistant to orthodoxy—it is both—neither addresses the possible *function* that the text's ambivalence served for those colonial men who supported it. In reading ambivalence solely as prohibitive or destructive of identity, we have neglected to consider how it might have, at determinate historical moments, helped to create identity.[19]

What does the ambivalence of female captivity allow? As the doubleness in structure and representation in Rowlandson's text indicates, it allows for a going out from, even a testing of, the fathers' legitimacy that nonetheless eventuates in a safe return to their authority. It allows for an experience of the new—however horribly construed or warned against—that challenges traditional authority structures at the same time that it also confirms them. It permits those sons identifying with the passive female captive's position to persist in their belief in absolute obedience to the fathers in the face of external threats at the same time that it permits them to experience other desires. The paradox here is that the desire for different connections, however painfully represented in Rowlandson's narrative, has, in many instances, already been realized.

The Synod of 1679–1680, officiated by Increase Mather, admits as much in its attack on what it viewed as the rampant materialism—and concomitant breakdown of traditional social hierarchies that seemed to be invading New

18. As I read them, Laplanche and Pontalis, *The Language of Psycho-analysis,* trans. Nicholson-Smith, particularly urge the importance of historicizing ambivalence (28). Whereas their stress falls on individual histories, I am here suggesting the equal importance of historicizing the concept for certain members of a generational group. For a comprehensive discussion of the tensions between first-generation fathers and second- and third-generation sons, see Emory Elliott, *Power and the Pulpit in Puritan New England* (Princeton, N.J., 1975), 16–62. Elliott draws on Philip J. Greven, Jr., *Four Generations: Population, Land, and Family in Colonial Andover, Massachusetts* (Ithaca, N.Y., 1970). For a well-known treatment of Puritan child-rearing practices, see Greven, *The Protestant Temperament: Patterns of Child-Rearing, Religious Experience, and the Self in Early America* (New York, 1977). See also John Demos, *A Little Commonwealth: Family Life in Plymouth Colony* (New York, 1970).

19. See Toulouse, "'My Own Credit,'" *American Literature,* LXVIII (1992), 672; Burnham, *Captivity and Sentiment,* 1–9.

England—provoked not only by more colonials seeking "Land, and worldly accommodations" on the frontier but also by renewed economic and cultural ties with England after the Restoration. Increase Mather himself had once desired to return to England, and his original disagreement with his father, Richard, over the Halfway Covenant had eventuated from his own concern for retaining a sense of what he believed to be an international, as opposed to a more localized, form of Protestant church organization. In spite of his apparent resignation to his father's views on church organization in New England, Mather would soon spend two heady years in London negotiating a new charter and, as a recent biographer argues, he never quite lost his passion for returning to England to argue New England's "cause." That a separation from the first generation was not only desired but had, in many ways, been enacted, is also represented in the Synod's focus on "Indianized" colonials. According to the Synod, colonials had been afflicted by Indians because they had become like them; they had turned to other cultural mores and other gods. What was supposedly most valued—to remain like the fathers—had in fact not occurred. The sons had changed and now were being punished for it, by Anglican English and French men as well as by Indian wars.[20]

In spite of second-generation men's awareness of such literal and metaphoric strains on traditional political and religious authority, however, the structure of captivity narratives and the representative position of the captive woman also served to sustain their reliance on the continuing presence and validity of the divine law they sought to transgress. Uncannily prefiguring the structure of Nathaniel Hawthorne's "Young Goodman Brown," Rowlandson's captivity account permitted those sons who identified with it to sustain the fantasy

20. [Increase Mather], *The Necessity of Reformation with the Expedients Subservient Thereunto, Asserted* . . . (Boston, 1679). For varying readings of continuing and new English economic connections, see Bailyn, *The New England Merchants;* Christine Leigh Heyrman, *Commerce and Culture: The Maritime Communities of Colonial Massachusetts, 1690–1750* (New York, 1984); Stephen Innes, *Creating the Commonwealth: The Economic Culture of Puritan New England* (New York, 1995); and John Frederick Martin, *Profits in the Wilderness: Entrepreneurship and the Founding of New England Towns in the Seventeenth Century* (Chapel Hill, N.C., 1991). Critically summarizing these differing positions, Mark A. Peterson suggests that the discourse of declension should be read as rhetorical rather than real and describes how, in fact, certain ostensibly orthodox New England churches religiously as well as economically benefited from their members' transatlantic connections (*The Price of Redemption: The Spiritual Economy of Puritan New England* [Stanford, Calif., 1997], 1–22). Nonetheless, what variable purposes the fathers' continuing rhetoric of declension was meant to serve remains unclear. For discussions of Mather's intermittent plans to emigrate to Barbados or to England, see Hall, *The Last American Puritan,* 48–49, 61–62, 65, 280–282. Hall suggests that, although some of Mather's reasons might have been economic, others involved both his anger at theological or political decisions made against his will and his continuing belief in his role in a larger international Puritan movement.

of going out to experience the new while retaining the ability to return—unchanged—to the old. In the early 1680s, at a time of profound crisis over colonial legitimacy and continuity, a representation of female captivity clearly allowed certain elite men to keep a number of relational possibilities to authority in motion, while removing the need, for a particular moment, to choose absolutely among them. In so doing, Mary Rowlandson's ambivalent narrative of female captivity limned the contours of a distinctive male identity.

Continuity and Transformation

In 1697, Cotton Mather largely wrote his own captivity narrative of a Casco, Maine, woman, Hannah Swarton, who was taken captive in 1690 and released in 1697. Mather returned to the representation of a female captive ostensibly to perform a balancing act similar to his father's. Mary Rowlandson had been moved from home to captivity among Indians to home in order to prove the political and theological embeddedness of the New England she represented in providential history. Hannah Swarton is moved not only to Indian captivity but also to what is represented as an even more horrific captivity among French Catholics, only to return to "publish" God's goodness to her. Given Cotton Mather's humiliating failure to justify his interpretation of the witchcraft controversy, it was undeniably useful for him to publish the dramatic narrative of a female captive that could unproblematically serve as a focus of community identification and sympathy. In using Hannah Swarton's narrative for such unifying purposes, Mather, like his father, could also have been levying implicit political commentary on the current New England situation.[21]

Swarton was taken captive in 1690 as the result of an Indian raid some blamed on then royal governor, Edmond Andros, appointed by James II. Her captivity might thus be viewed as an effect not only of French and Indian warfare but also of treasonous behavior by the colonists' own governor. (As rumors of the ascendancy of William and Mary to the English throne arrived in New England, Andros was overthrown in a bloodless revolt in 1689.) Although the narrative of Swarton's captivity was not published until 1697, it can be read as commenting on the dangers of English royal governorship. In 1691, Increase Mather had returned with a new royal charter for Massachusetts and a commission for a new colonial-born governor selected by Mather, Sir William Phips. In spite of Increase and Cotton Mather's great expectations, however, Phips

---

21. Information on Swarton can be found in Carroll, "'My Outward Man,'" *EAL*, XXXI (1996), 45–73; and in Alden T. Vaughan and Edward W. Clark, eds., *Puritans among the Indians: Accounts of Captivity and Redemption, 1676–1724* (Cambridge, Mass., 1981), 147–148.

proved a spectacular failure and was recalled to London only to die unexpect-
edly in 1695. By 1697, as Cotton Mather was deciding to write and publish a
narrative associated with the Andros regime, many New Englanders were waiting, some with immense trepidation, for a new royal governor, not of their own
choosing. If Swarton's narrative was intended to bolster Cotton Mather's falter-
ing religious authority as loyal grandson and son of Puritan fathers, it was also,
implicitly, meant to express certain colonials' continuing attitudes toward the
imposition of royal governance. Although the captive Swarton would be used to
show third-generation colonial loyalty to England in the face of continuing
European and colonial war with France, she would at the same time demonstrate their loyalty to a New England version of Protestantism against all
challengers.[22]

Even though Swarton's captivity is clearly moved to a new arena, it seems to
share similar aims with Mary Rowlandson's narrative—the defense of a traditional New England orthodoxy and polity against external threats. When we
look at the structure of Swarton's captivity account and the representation of
the female captive, however, there are certain striking differences. Structurally,
Swarton's narrative represents two captivities—one among the Indians and one
among the French. Swarton is thus at a double remove from her New England
"home." This split makes her captivity not only about physical deprivation
among cultural others but also—and more importantly—about spiritual threats
among those who differ largely in religion. Accordingly, the narrative fulfills the
older fear that French Catholics and English Catholic sympathizers will replace
the Indians as captors of New England. In contrast to Rowlandson's text, the
specific question of *why* New England has fallen captive is crucial. In Hannah Swarton's case, it is because she has not remained within the Puritan
community:

> And as I desired to consider of all my sins for which the Lord did punish me,
> so this lay very heavy upon my spirit many a time that I had left the public
> worship and ordinances of God where I formerly lived (*viz.* at Beverley)
> to remove to the north part of Casco Bay where there was no church or
> minister of the Gospel. And this we did for large accommodations in the
> world, thereby exposing our children to be bred ignorantly like Indians and

22. For commentary on the Andros administration, see Johnson, *Adjustment to Empire,* 73–91;
See also Hall, *The Last American Puritan,* 206–211; and Silverman, *The Life and Times of Cotton
Mather,* 55–82. See, more generally, David S. Lovejoy, *The Glorious Revolution in America* (New
York, 1972).

ourselves to forget what we had been formerly instructed in, and so we turned our backs upon God's ordinances to get this world's goods.

What is different here from Rowlandson's text is perhaps not evident at first glance. Mary Rowlandson comes from a settled town with a settled minister, her own husband. As the story of her sister and her own admission during captivity that she has sinned in no externals suggests, Rowlandson is also one of those already justified—she is a "saint." It is her spiritual complacency as Puritan insider, not her status as frontier outsider, that is used to explain her captivity. The structural point is that Rowlandson, although she does not go back to destroyed Lancaster, does return home in a religious sense, to an awareness of her role as representative saint in a divine providential plan for New England.[23]

Swarton's narrative, in contrast, does not follow the A-B-A sequence of Mary Rowlandson's text. She begins already outside A, say in B; undergoes two captivities, say C (among the Indians) and D (among the French); before being taken to Boston, A. What is most evident about this sequence is the explanatory apparatus about it that is lacking in the narrative. The Swarton narrator certainly uses scriptural voices to call on God in her narrative. They focus, for example, on her humiliation, her prayers for deliverance, and her vows to publish his glory when she is saved:

> I sometimes bemoaned myself as Job, chapter 19:9, 10, "He hath stripped me of my glory and taken my crown from my head; He hath destroyed me on every side, and I am gone, and my hope hath He removed like a tree." Yet sometimes encouraged from Job 22:27, "Thou shalt make thy prayer to Him, and He shall hear thee, and thou shalt pay thy vows." I made vows to the Lord that I would give up myself to Him if He would accept me in Jesus Christ."

Orthodox as they may be, however, these citations do not make reference to God's overarching providence. Unlike the Rowlandson narrative, the Swarton text neither appeals to such providence nor offers numerous examples of "special" providences to the captive herself. At the level of scriptural citation and, perhaps more significantly, at the level of its overall structure, the sense of a divine plan always already realized has dropped out of the Swarton narrative.[24]

---

23. "A Narrative of Hannah Swarton Containing Wonderful Passages Relating to Her Captivity and Deliverance," related by Cotton Mather, in Vaughan and Clark, eds., *Puritans among the Indians*, 150–151.
24. Ibid., 151–152.

In Rowlandson's narrative, we noted the relationship between references to providence and the passive position assumed by the female captive. Although Swarton may be read as passive in the face of her initial captivity and physical deprivations among the Indians, her text makes no use of Scriptures dealing with passivity, with waiting on God to act, and so forth, even though her own captivity lasted years longer than Rowlandson's. The real aims of the narrative seem to be, first, to maneuver the female captive into debate with French clerics over theological issues, and, second, to represent her experience of conversion while she is in Catholic captivity. In fact, Swarton is represented as an active defender of the faith even before her conversion. Although, as Lorrayne Carroll notes, the narrator modestly pulls back from such debate—admitting her status as a "poor woman"—she is nonetheless shown as more than intellectually capable of confounding her French captors:

> For their praying to angels they brought the history of the angel that was sent to the Virgin Mary in the first of Luke. I answered them from Rev. 19:10 and 22:9. They brought Exod. 17:11 of Israel's prevailing while Moses held up his hands. I told them we must come to God only by Christ, John 6:37, 44. For purgatory they brought Matthew 5:25. I told them to agree with God while here on earth was to agree with our adversary in the way, and if we did not, we should be cast into hell.

It is in thus debating the nature of faith that Swarton discovers how "I could not be of a false religion to please men, for it was against my conscience." With her awareness of this inner voice comes her conversion—to traditional New England Congregationalism! After agonies of self-doubt, she proclaims, "I thought it was good for me to be here, and I was so full of comfort and joy I even wished I could be so always and never sleep or else die in that rapture of joy and never live to sin any more against the Lord."[25]

Crucially, inner conscience, not outer providence in conjunction with it, guides Swarton's actions. The interplay between an overarching providence and human narrative in Rowlandson's text breaks down in Hannah Swarton's narrative because what is learned is from the experience offered at the level of the narrative alone. The female captive appears not as passive, but as actively debating (and thereby learning) the nature of the inner state that will ripen into her conversion.

Hannah Swarton's orthodox narrative has been contrasted to the violent narrative of Hannah Dustan, another unconverted frontier woman seized by

25. Ibid., 154, 155.

Indians. Cotton Mather himself juxtaposed the two texts when he published his sermon, *Humiliations Follow'd with Deliverances,* in 1697. Although Dustan's narrative had originally appeared at the end of the sermon, Mather added the narrative of Swarton to the published version. Unlike Swarton, Dustan does not travel to Canada. Rather, famously, she and two accomplices murder ten of her captors (largely women and children) while they slept, and return to Boston with their scalps to claim a bounty for them. Carroll has persuasively argued that Swarton's more orthodox text could have been used by Mather rhetorically to compete for authority with Dustan. In Jay Fliegelman's terms, Hannah Dustan, rather than the converted Hannah Swarton, provides an initial image of frontier self-reliance. What I am arguing about the Swarton text's representation of an active orthodox woman suggests something slightly different. For, what seems to be happening in Dustan's text—its move to self-authorization—is also occurring in Swarton's captivity, but at the level of orthodoxy itself. Swarton's narrative places an equal focus on the self's active realization of its inner capacities, without acknowledging a providential frame of reference. Although Tara Fitzpatrick has linked this focus on inner experience to the growing interest in Pietism in general on the part of Cotton Mather and later third- and fourth-generation preachers of the Awakening, there are two other dimensions to this transformation that bear on the type of colonial male identity explored here.[26]

First, in dramatizing a conflict between Protestant and Catholic belief systems, the female captive must be represented as active, not passive. What had been feared and condemned in 1636, when Ann Hutchinson claimed the similar authority of an inner voice, is both valorized and celebrated in the context of a renewed political competition that is also staged as a religious competition between English Protestantism and French Catholicism. Even Swarton's very New England conversion narrative, in which she admits her doubt and inadequacy only to experience a sense of being justified by God's grace, is placed in the context of an active Scripture-laden debate over the nature of the "true" religion.

The feminized position made active allows for an equally active male identi-

---

26. See Carroll, " 'My Outward Man,' " *EAL,* XXXI (1996), 45–73; and Fliegelman, *Prodigals and Pilgrims,* 145–146. Tara Fitzpatrick makes a similar argument about how Puritan ministers at the end of the seventeenth century, in order to retain some cultural authority, come to valorize individual conversion in the wilderness instead of in the community. Crucially, for Fitzpatrick, such a move admits the redemptive rather than the demonic possibilities of the wilderness (Fitzpatrick, "The Figure of Captivity," *American Literary History,* III [1991], 18–21). In my own study of these narratives, I read wilderness as equally metaphorical, referring as much to colonial or metropolitan cityscapes as to "real" landscapes *(The Captive's Position).*

fication with her defense of the faith, an identification confirmed by Cotton Mather's heavy emendation of her text at this point and his pulling back only at the end of her (his) high-level scriptural debate with male clerics when Swarton acknowledges her status as a "poor woman." In fact, rather than representing Swarton as passively waiting for an overarching fatherly authority to manifest itself on her behalf, the narrative presents the active woman as *the* explicit savior of the Protestant cause. What authorizes her is no longer related to external signs of a providential plan, however; it is solely her own active conscience.

Second, there is the issue of the context in which this arousal of individual conscience occurs. Scholars have focused on the ways an incipient form of individual self-authorization arises on the frontier, but Swarton's narrative suggests something rather different. Instead of taking place in the wilderness, Swarton's conversion occurs within the diverse social context of a colonial *city*. Following her conversion, Hannah Swarton is represented as joining a small church group composed of other captives. In doing so, she is following the New England tradition in which a conversion narrative precedes full church membership. Here, however, her joining occurs in the context of other available religious options.

Unlike Rowlandson's narrative, Swarton's text thus does not confirm the existence of a pure community from which an already converted captive is taken and to which she returns. If, as some have argued, captivities like Swarton's suggest that conversion can happen anywhere—it is not limited to a bounded pure community—her captivity also indicates that the notion of community itself has changed. Just as Quebec is represented as diversely filled with Indians, loyal captives, French Catholics, and even converted English men and women, so is colonial Boston now irremediably filled with diverse and competing religious and social groups. Swarton's church group does not represent the entire community, whether in Quebec or in Boston. Cut off from the exemplarity of the providential worldview, her little group seems only one among many competing for a modicum of cultural authority.[27]

What becomes of the productive ambivalence I have claimed for female captivity when both its form and its representation of the female captive are so altered? One answer is obvious: as much as Hannah Swarton seems to replicate Mary Rowlandson, she does not. Directed to a new generation and a new audience under new historical conditions, her text reveals what had been gradually, if unconsciously, recognized by certain elite men who still claimed to be

27. In contrast, Fitzpatrick argues that Swarton found her "illumination in the wilderness"; see "The Figure of Captivity," *American Literary History*, III (1991), 17.

loyal to their fathers and their fathers' God: conceptions of the nature of authority had changed. If the interrelation of female passivity to providence is altered, the fantasy of experiencing change without really changing can no longer be maintained. Even passionately orthodox third-generation men can neither sustain nor produce the same ambivalent identity position as their second-generation fathers.

This response, given in terms of what is no longer possible, however, does not address another interesting question arising from the comparison of these narratives: Where was authority now to be located? Swarton's captivity, like Dustan's, suggests the fascinating new role to be played by quasi-fictive active women in representing attitudes toward individual male competition, so one answer is, authority will be located in competition among diverse "sons" rather than adjudicated by "fathers," whether they are saving or damning. But there is another possibility as well, suggested by the absence of an overarching providential frame in Swarton's narrative. As providential history waned as the frame for fatherly authority, a new kind of imperial authority that equally, if differently, affected the actions, identities, and popular representations of competing colonial men began to emerge.[28]

28. A variety of literary studies consider the intersections of early capitalism, the novel, and representations of women. See, for example, Michael McKeon, *The Origins of the English Novel, 1600–1740* (Baltimore, 1987); Sandra Sherman, *Finance and Fictionality in the Early Eighteenth Century: Accounting for Defoe* (Cambridge, 1996); and Catherine Ingrassia, *Authorship, Commerce, and Gender in Early Eighteenth-Century England: A Culture of Paper Credit* (New York, 1998).

LUIS FERNANDO RESTREPO

The Ambivalent Nativism of Lucas Fernández de Piedrahita's *Historia general de las conquistas del Nuevo Reyno de Granada* (1688)

In 1663, the vicar general of the archbishopric of New Granada, Lucas Fernández de Piedrahita (Santa Fe de Bogotá, 1624–Panamá, 1688), had to travel to Spain to defend himself against the accusations of the *visitador* (royal inspector) Don Juan Cornejo. The indictment touched a sensitive point for colonial Spanish American society: Piedrahita's mother was a mestiza, grand-daughter of Inca princess Francisca Coya, and his father was reportedly a carpenter. Could this accusation damage irreparably the reputation of an other-wise highly successful ecclesiastical official?[1]

Throughout Spanish America, preoccupations with purity of blood and a contempt for manual labor made part of a code of social differentiation that placed Iberian-born Spaniards at the apex of colonial society and most often barred someone like Piedrahita from achieving any high post. Mestizos were, for the most part, considered troublemakers and inferior to Spaniards and criollos. But still, a small number of mestizos like Piedrahita were able to move up the social ladder in numerous ways and achieve the same status as criollos,

---

I am indebted to the late Alvaro Félix Bolaños for his careful reading of this essay. Any errors, of course, are my own responsibility. My work is greatly indebted to Joanne Rappaport's seminal work on the politics of memory in Colombia and José Rabasa's suggestive essay "Pre-Columbian Pasts and Indian Presents in Mexican History," included in Alvaro Félix Bolaños and Gustavo Verdesio, eds., *Colonialism Past and Present: Reading and Writing about Colonial Latin America Today* (Albany, N.Y., 2002).

1. The visitador resented the president of New Granada's request to attend the funeral of Piedrahita's mother: "Hizo ir (al Real acuerdo) al entierro y honras de Catalina de Collantes, madre del doctor Piedrahita, provisor que era 'in sede vacante,' siendo la dicha difunta mujer humilde y mestiza, y mujer de un oficial de carpintería" (cited in Gustavo Otero Muñoz, ed., *Historia general de las conquistas del Nuevo Reino de Granada* [Bogotá, 1942], I, viii). [He made (the royal council) attend the funeral of Catalina Collantes, mother of Doctor Piedrahita, interim vicar general, even though she was a humble mestiza woman, married to a carpenter.]

through marriage, military service, religious orders, education, and even the legal purchase of official posts or titles of nobility. Upward mobility was not impossible, as Piedrahita's case illustrates. However, for Indians, blacks, and poor mestizos, the opportunities were clearly limited. Mestizos with some affluence gained social recognition by concealing their mixed origin and stressing their Peninsular heritage, articulating their social status through a relation of continuity with Spanish society. In this case, the mestizos' and criollos' social standing depended on the Spanish symbolic economy.[2]

There was, however, an emerging space first claimed by the conquistadors and later by their criollo and mestizo heirs that expressed an identity based on a relationship of rupture with Spanish society. Their social recognition depended on the value of their experiences in the Indies. In other words, it was a matter of extracting symbolic capital *(honra)* from their American exploits or origin. As we will see, to sustain their hegemonic position in colonial society and to claim a space for themselves in history, the seventeenth-century New Granadine elite had to juggle continually between these two poles, a Peninsularism and a nativism. Piedrahita's case suggests that the Neogranadine elite, excluded from high administrative positions in the colonial bureaucracy, sought alternative pockets of power and prestige, such as the religious orders and the intellectual field. However, to fully see the dimensions of what that undertaking involved, it is not that some preconceived criollo subject occupies a position in certain colonial institutions. Rather, it is a discourse-mediated process, as Anthony Higgins suggests: "A *criollo* subject-in-process unfolds in, and between, the spaces of educational institutions and civil society, in both written culture and economic production."[3]

Under indictment, Piedrahita had to defend himself. It was precisely during

2. The Spanish words *español, criollo, mestizo, zambo* (mixed Indian and black), *indio,* and *cholo* (acculturated Indian) are used in the sense they conveyed in seventeenth-century New Granada. They were legal and social categories based on the Castilian notion of purity of blood. A classic study on the topic is Magnus Mörner, *Race Mixture in the History of Latin America* (Boston, 1967). Two modern studies on criollos and mestizos in the viceroyalty of Peru, of which New Granada was part until the eighteenth century, are Bernard Lavallé, *Las promesas ambiguas: ensayos sobre el criollismo colonial en los Andes* (Lima, 1993); and Berta Ares Queija, "El papel de mediadores y la construcción de un discurso sobre la identidad de los mestizos peruanos, siglo XVI," in Ares Queija and Serge Gruzinski, *Entre dos mundos: fronteras culturales y agentes mediadores* (Seville, 1997), 37–59. For the particularities of Neogranadine society, see Jaime Jaramillo Uribe, *La sociedad neogranadina* (Bogotá, 1989); Guiomar Dueñas Vargas, *Los hijos del pecado: ilegitimidad y vida familiar en la Santafé de Bogotá colonial* (Bogotá, 1997); Virginia Gutiérrez de Pineda and Roberto Pineda Giraldo, *Miscegenación y cultura en la Colombia colonial, 1750–1810*, 2 vols. (Bogotá, 1999).

3. Anthony Higgins, *Constructing the Criollo Archive: Subjects of Knowledge in the "Bibliotheca Mexicana" and the "Rusticatio Mexicana"* (West Lafayette, Ind., 2000), 6.

the six years that he had to remain in Spain, clearing up his record, that he wrote the *Historia general de las conquistas del Nuevo Reyno de Granada,* published in 1688 in Antwerp. The *Historia* could be thus considered part of Piedrahita's defense in a debate that, although it touched him personally, had broader dimensions, and for this reason it is a debate that sheds light on the cultural politics of the seventeenth-century Neogranadine elite.[4]

It is important to note that it was far from a homogeneous elite, as it was composed of Spaniards, criollos, and mestizos. There were also significant regional differences within the district of the Audiencia del Nuevo Reino de Granada, which included, in the seventeenth century, the provinces of Santa Marta, Cartagena, Popayán, and Antioquia. In the mining regions of Antioquia and Zaragoza, for example, the dominant group was much more mestizo than the one in Santa Fe or Tunja. Although far from being an egalitarian society, the mining districts of New Granada were for the most part precarious small towns where poor whites, African slaves, and runaway Amerindians lived and worked side by side. Throughout the region, however, the Neogranadine elite most often kept their mestizo origin in the closet and were frequently described as "whites" in most censuses. It is crucial, then, to pay attention to how a hetero-geneous elite constructs a common culture, of which Piedrahita's *Historia* is a part. His educational and ecclesiastical experiences also reveal the role of colo-nial institutions in producing a corporate identity that delimited and founded a criollo consciousness that expressed a sense of pride for their American home-land. Unlike the nineteenth-century criollo desire for political and territorial independence, the colonial sense of pride for the homeland was not necessarily an anticolonial sentiment. It could be quite the opposite, and Piedrahita's case is illustrative in this respect. His text is a univocal affirmation of New Granada

---

4. I cite throughout from the two-volume facsimile edition of *Historia general de las conquistas del Nuevo Reyno de Granada,* ed. Juan Bautista Verdussen (Amsterdam, 1688). This facsimile edition is derived from one of the copies now held by the Biblioteca Nacional de Colombia, Bogotá, and was republished by Carvajal S.A. (Santander del Quilchao, Cauca, 1986). All further references to this edition will appear parenthetically in the text. There are three additional editions of Piedrahita's text. One, edited by Sergio Elías Ortiz (Bogotá, 1973), gives a wrong title and date to Piedrahita's text. He renames it *Noticia historial de las conquistas del Nuevo Reino de Granada* and gives as publication date the year 1668, reproducing the error of the previous edition. Gustavo Otero Muñoz's four-volume edition of Piedrahita's text was published in Bogotá in 1942. Both of these two modern editions omit the notes in the margin that appear in the princeps and facsimile editions. There is also a nineteenth-century edition by Medrardo Rivas (Bogotá, 1881). The facsimile edition comes from a copy that has three engraved plates depicting Muisca lords and conquistadors (see Figure 12). Of the three princeps editions that I consulted in the Biblioteca Nacional de Colombia, only one had the three plates.

as part of the Spanish Empire. The explicit addressees of his *Historia* are Spaniards who have not heard or do not know about the wonders and the history of New Granada.

In this essay I discuss Piedrahita's exaltation of the culture of his place of origin, understood here as a nativism. After briefly discussing Piedrahita's embellished image of New Granada, I examine how Piedrahita draws from previous histories of the region in a narrative that revamps the image of the Muisca and rearranges Andean and Spanish histories into one continuous chronology. I then discuss how Piedrahita' effort to preserve the status quo is expressed through a preoccupation with purity of blood. In the final section, based on Piedrahita's lifelong relationship with the Jesuits, I highlight the importance of schooling in forging an elitist criollo consciousness. My interest in Piedrahita is part of a larger project on the Muisca experience of modernity under colonialism and the ethnopolitics of memory in present-day Colombia.

Written almost two centuries after Columbus's first voyage, Piedrahita's *Historia* is part of a long tradition of writings about American landscape as a land of abundance. The *Historia* begins with a bird's-eye view of New Granada with the typical laudatory tone, describing the climate, rivers, mines, and wealth of the region. From the beginning, Piedrahita's text validates the colonial appropriation of the land and the exploitation of Amerindian communities. Turning the American territories into awe-inspiring landscapes, however, suppresses the violence of everyday colonialism from view.[5]

In his prologue to the reader of his *Historia,* Piedrahita noted that, because most histories of the Indies had paid so little attention to New Granada, he decided to write a clear, well-ordered, more readable and useful history of the region. Thus, Piedrahita's *Historia* places a local history next to other American histories. But, as we will see, the *Historia* is also integrated into the universal Christian history. All these different elements are apparently well integrated. Looking closer, however, the *Historia* is much more ambiguous if we consider who writes the story, the sources it employs, where it is written, and whom it addresses.

Let us start by looking at one of the most significant features of Piedrahita's *Historia,* its organization of the historical narrative. The *Historia* recounts the history of the region occupied today by the Republic of Colombia from roughly a century before the Spanish invasion until 1564. The text is divided into twelve

---

5. As Raymond Williams argues in *The Country and the City* (Oxford, 1973), landscapes are artistic representations that tend to erase the social relationships of a given land.

books, each divided into five to eleven chapters. At the end of the *Historia,* Piedrahita promised a second part covering the history of the region until 1630, which he never wrote. The first two books are dedicated to the "first inhabitants." Piedrahita describes briefly several indigenous groups that are found in the region. The main focus of these first two books, however, is the Muisca (also known as the Chibcha). For Piedrahita, the Muisca were the most civilized indigenous group in the region: "son los naturales mas politicos, y andan todos vestidos" (15) [the natives most civilized and well-dressed]. Muisca people are handsome and well proportioned: "Son todos estos naturales, assi hombres, como mugeres, por la mayor parte de hermosos rostros, y buena disposicion" (15). [All these natives, men and women alike, have, for the most part, beautiful faces and good disposition.]

Piedrahita is the first historian of the region to identify the Muisca as the origin of New Granada. His historical project even includes reordering chronologically Muisca narratives about their past, as he affirms in the "Prologue":

> Mas viendo, que los acaecimientos Politicos y Militares, que avian tenido
> los Reyes Indios entre si, corrian mezclados con los que despues tuvieron
> con los Españoles, con la nota de no asignar tiempo a sus operaciones, y
> que la relacion de las costumbres, ritos, y ceremonias de su gentilidad,
> confundia muchas vezes la de los progressos de la conquista . . . me
> resolví a poner separadamente aquellas noticias, que mezcladas quitaban
> la claridad de la Historia.

> But noticing that the military and political actions of the Indian kings
> before the Spaniards were mixed with those that happened afterwards,
> because the natives did not assign a specific time to the events in
> question and also because the accounts of their pagan costumes, rites,
> and ceremonies were often confused with events that happened after the
> conquest . . . I decided to put separately those mixed events that
> diminished the clearness of [this] History.

Piedrahita's reworking of Muisca memory involved making Andean cosmology compatible with the Christian Bible. First he tackled the issue of how there could be people and animals in the Indies that antiquity had not heard of. He briefly commented on what others had written on the topic, including Fray Antonio Calancha, Fray Pedro Simón, and José de Acosta (2). They discussed how Noah could not have transported so many beasts in one ship and how the people from antiquity could not have reached the Indies without a compass. Piedrahita did not take much time to cut through the debate in a dogmatic way:

If God needed to transport people and animals to the Indies, he had the means and people to do it (3). So, in chapter 2 Piedrahita affirmed as a matter of fact that the people of the Indies are descendants of Noah's son Japhet (8).

Piedrahita's project involved more than imposing a foreign story on a tabula rasa. He also sought to transform Muisca memory from within. Piedrahita claimed that a civilizing Muisca deity known as Nemquetheba or Bochica was in fact the apostle Saint Bartholomew (19). For a doctor in theology and a well-reputed orator, Piedrahita does not put much effort in supporting his claims. He mentions that Bochica was dressed in a Nazarene tunic and that in Ubaque there was a footprint left by the apostle. Piedrahita affirms that Bochica was a white man because the Muisca referred to him with the same epithet that they used to call the Spaniards, *Zuhé* (sun, in Muisca).

The main proof that Piedrahita offered, however, was that Muisca beliefs were somehow similar to the Christian dogma. According to Piedrahita, the Muisca believed in the immortality of the soul, the Final Judgment, and Resurrection. Their notions of good and evil were similar to the Christian beliefs, and they venerated the cross (19). However, Piedrahita notes that these beliefs were accompanied by numerous errors.

In a few strokes, Piedrahita had integrated Muisca past with a universal Christian narrative. This was not completely new in the historiography of the Indies. What seems important here is not the originality of any particular author but rather that, in contexts of colonization where multiple temporalities collided, the unity and continuity of Christian teleology had to be continually reaffirmed. Including Muisca past in the universal Christian narrative justified the subordination of postconquest Amerindian societies. This integration of Muisca and Spanish histories had inherent tensions that could not be ironed out. Whereas the nativist project highlighted the Muisca's ethnic specificity, the universal narrative emptied it. In the end, the *Historia's* narrative continuity of Muisca past and colonial order ruptures in the references to the contemporary Muisca, who are referred to as *indios*. Paradoxically, Piedrahita's nativist project needed both, the culturally specific Muisca and the generic Indians, as we will see below.

If one compares the previous colonial texts about the Muisca and the *Historia,* in the latter there is a noticeable boosting of the Muisca's positive image. Writing almost a century and a half after the invasion, Piedrahita does not offer much new information on the Muisca, but I contend that there is a significant recasting of that image. As a result, Piedrahita turned Muisca memory into a useful past for the Neogranadine elite. However, in order to convert Muisca past into symbolic capital of New Granada's hegemonic society, he had to face two tasks. First, Piedrahita had to doctor the image of the Muisca from savage

FIGURE 12. *Muisca Lords and Spanish Conquistadors.* Details from plates added to Lucas Fernández de Piedrahita, *Historia general de las conquistas del Nuevo Reyno de Granada* (Amsterdam, 1688). © Biblioteca Nacional de Colombia, Bogotá

to hero. The freely composed illustrations added to the 1688 edition of the *Historia* by the Flemish editor seem to strengthen Piedrahita's project. If the purpose was to produce a visually captivating edition, Antwerp was not a random choice. Flemish printers were highly regarded by Spanish authors, and the Verdussens in particular published well-known titles, such as an edition of Antonio de Herrera y Tordesillas's *Decadas,* two illustrated editions of *El Quixote* (1697, 1716), and also illustrated editions of Spanish kings such as *Corona gothica castellana austriaca* (1678). In Piedrahita's *Historia,* two plates depict several grandiose Muisca lords and some battles with the Spaniards. Another plate depicts some of the conquistadors of New Granada in a similar manner. The symmetry of the plates suggests that both camps have heroes of equal stature.

In New Granada, Franciscan historians provided the amplest corpus of knowledge on Muisca culture. Fray Pedro de Aguado's *Recopilación historial* (circa 1570) and Fray Pedro Simón's *Noticias historiales de las conquistas de Tierra Firme en las Indias occidentales* (1627) were two sources that Piedrahita consulted. By far, the Franciscan histories offer a much more detailed and comprehensive view of the Muisca than Piedrahita's text. In the Franciscan texts, however, the Muisca did not occupy the same symbolic space as in Piedrahita's *Historia,* the beginning of the narrative. In both Aguado and Simón, the Muisca are described among numerous native groups. Aguado, for example, dedicates book 5 to the Muisca. This book was completely suppressed by the censors, but, based on the table of contents (which survived), it discussed Muisca culture in detail. Simón discussed Muisca culture in the second part of his *Noticias historiales.* The main thread of the second part, however, is the narrative of conquest, which Simón tries not to interrupt with information on native practices. In the first chapter of the second noticia, Simón explains "why the myths and costumes of these Indians are not discussed here." Therefore, in the first three noticias, or books, Simón narrates the Spaniards arrival in Muisca territory, and it is only in the fourth noticia that he starts discussing Muisca culture. Both Franciscan historians are focused mainly on idolatry, cannibalism, sodomy, and other practices that inscribed the Muisca and other indigenous groups such as the Pijao and the Panches as savages, as Alvaro Félix Bolaños and Jaime Humberto Borja have argued. For example, in the first chapters to his *Noticias* Simón described the Indians as cannibals, drunks, traitors, lazy, sorcerers, vengeful, liars, thieves, adulterers, and so on.[6]

Another important history of the region is Juan de Castellanos's epic poem *Elegías de varones ilustres de Indias* (1589–1601), a text cited often by Piedrahita.

6. Fray Pedro de Aguado, *Recopilación historial,* ed. Juan Friede (Bogotá, 1957); Fray Pedro Simón, *Noticias historiales de las conquistas de Tierra Firme en las Indias occidentales,* ed. Juan Friede (Bogotá, 1981), III, 113, 155 (quote); Alvaro Félix Bolaños, *Barbarie y canibalismo en la retórica colonial: los indios Pijaos de Fray Pedro Simón* (Bogotá, 1994); Jaime Humberto Borja Gómez, *Los indios medievales de Fray Pedro de Aguado: construccíon del idólatra y escritura de la historia en una crónica del siglo XVI* (Bogotá, 2002).

Castellanos dedicated the fourth part of the *Elegías* to New Granada, the *Historia del Nuevo Reino de Granada*. In Castellanos's *Historia,* the Muisca are given considerable attention, but the main focus of this epic text is the military achievements of the conquistadors. To a lesser extent, Castellanos narrates a few heroic deeds of some Muisca lords. But, in the end, in Castellanos's *Historia* Muisca warriors are included precisely because they were defeated by his "illustrious" Spanish men, dutifully individualized by name and title, in a narrative that celebrates the massacring of numerous nameless Amerindian warriors. For Castellanos, the wars against the Indians were legitimate, and the conquistadors and their heirs deserved to occupy a privileged place in society (as I have argued in my work on the *Elegías*). To some extent, Piedrahita distances himself from Castellanos's vision. He condones the violence of the colonization, expressly inscribing himself within a century-old critical tradition that began with figures like Fray Bartolomé de las Casas. Like Las Casas, Piedrahita advocated a gentler, Christian colonialism. Piedrahita, for example, condemns Fernán Pérez de Quesada's public execution of the Tunja lord Aquiminzaque: "¡Lastimoso espectaculo!, donde mas se necessitaba de halagos para imponer el yugo suave del Evangelio, que de rigores, para que por tantos años se aya dudado, si fue verdadera la conversion de aquellas almas" (347). [A painful spectacle! It would have been better to follow gentler ways to impose the soft yoke of the Gospel, instead of rigid measures that never proved that those souls truly converted.][7]

There is an empathy for Muisca culture that is absent in Castellanos as well as in the first criollo chronicler of New Granada, Juan Rodríguez Freyle. In *El carnero* (1639) Freyle dedicated some of the initial chapters (2–6) to Muisca culture. Freyle's contempt for the indigenous peoples, however, is impossible to miss, as Alvaro Félix Bolaños has pointed out: the Indians are described as thieves, drunks, murderers, and the like. In chapter 5, for example, Freyle suggests that Muisca people are stupid. Freyle tells the story of a native priest that was easily tricked by a Spanish cleric. The Spaniard robs the native priest of the gold he kept in his secret Muisca shrine. Freyle's interest in Muisca past is muddled by his preoccupations with economic gain from Muisca labor. Recounting the battle between the Muisca lords Bogotá and Guatavita, Freyle laments the death of more than ten thousand Indians. Freyle asserts: their

7. Juan de Castellanos, *Elegías de varones ilustres de Indias* (Bogotá, 1997); Luis Fernando Restrepo, *Un nuevo reino imaginado: las elegías de varones ilustres de Indias de Juan de Castellanos* (Bogotá, 1999).

harvest "la tomara yo este año de 1636 de fanegas de trigo, y aun el que viene también" [would have given me plenty of bushels of wheat this year of 1636, and next year too].[8]

Although not expressing any personal interest, Piedrahita is also concerned with Muisca labor. In book 11, he regrets the abuse of the Indians in the mines, the *obrajes* (textile mills), and the fields (457–461). The New Laws (1542) were ineffective because the well-being of New Granada depended upon gold and silver (460). Piedrahita eventually suggests that moderate work is just and necessary and that it should be well compensated, not turned into the compulsory and "tyrannical" personal services that the crown had outlawed in the sixteenth century. This common preoccupation of Freyle and Piedrahita (also present in Castellanos) is due, in part, to the Spanish and creole dependence on Muisca labor in the cities, mines, food supply, transportation, firewood, and other services that sustained colonial society. Through the encomienda system (tribute system), the *mita* (rotating, compulsory work in the mines or cities), and later with the *concertaje* (work for hire) the Muisca territory had become the breadbasket of New Granada, producing wheat and corn for the interior cities and the gold mines in Antioquia and even feeding the Caribbean port of Cartagena de Indias. In this context, Piedrahita's revalorization of Muisca culture may not be as spontaneous as it appears at first hand but may have to do with the continuous exploitation of Muisca communities under colonial rule.

Colombian historiography has documented well how Indians were turned into peasants. From a cultural perspective, the process is much more complex and less unidirectional: Indians, Muiscas, laborers. These three words are articulated in various ways and given different content during the colonial period itself in a process that continued after independence until today. The point I am trying to stress is that there is a significant discursive production that would give the Muisca its central, symbolic place in the memory of the region, which involves doctoring that image to fit the different politics of memory.[9]

The first accounts describing Muisca culture were primarily concerned with

8. Juan Rodríguez Freyle, *El carnero,* ed. Dario Achury Valenzuela, 2d ed. (Caracas, 1992), 31, 38–40; Alvaro Félix Bolaños, "History and Plunder in *El carnero:* Writing, among Indians, a History of Spaniards and Euro-Americans in Colonial Spanish America," in Bolaños and Gustavo Verdesio, eds., *Colonialism Past and Present* (Albany, N.Y., 2002), 215–237.

9. Germán Colmenares, *Historia económica y social de Colombia, 1537–1719* (Bogotá, 1975); Silvia M. Broadbent, "The Formation of Peasant Society in Central Colombia," *Ethnohistory,* XXVIII (1981), 259–277; Jesús Antonio Bejarano, "Campesinado, luchas agrarias, e historia social en Colombia," in Pablo González Casanova, ed., *Historia política de os campesinos latino-americanos* (Mexico City, 1984–1985), III, 9–72.

the territorial colonization: access to precious metals and natural wealth. In the *relación* (official report) of Juan de San Martín and Antonio Nebrija as well as the anonymous *Epítome de la conquista del Nuevo Reino de Granada* (circa 1550), Muisca culture appears within the narrative of exploration and colonization, providing an inventory of Muisca wealth (gold, emeralds, salt), military practices, beliefs, and other tactical information. In contrast, in the seventeenth century that information was not as crucial as the labor that made possible the extraction of natural wealth. In this context, Las Casas's critique of the colonization and the abuses of the encomenderos becomes a key subtext of the *Historia*. However, the Lascasian critique tended to grasp the Muisca mainly through the universalizing discourse that emerged in the laws of the Indies: Indians were rational beings, free vassals of the crown, whose property rights and right over their own bodies *(dominium)* were inalienable, as Anthony Pagden has shown. As a result, there is an overlapping construction of the Muisca in Piedrahita's *Historia* as ethnic subjects and as modern colonial subjects. Historically, the colonization turned the Muisca and other indigenous groups into generic indios, in a process that tended to erase their particularities. Nonetheless, Piedrahita's *Historia* did not let go of the cultural specificity of the Muisca. Why? Perhaps because he needed something to define his homeland in a sense that generic Indians could not. The *Historia* was, after all, a project Piedrahita initiated far from his homeland, inspired by reading the histories of Joseph Acosta, Antonio de Herrera y Tordesillas, El Inca Garcilaso and other histories that spoke wonders about Andean and Mesoamerican cultures. In this context, Piedrahita was not inventing a new historiographic model, but rather he was basically adapting the organizing scheme of other histories of the Indies. One such model was the *Comentarios reales,* a text that provided a rich and awe-inspiring history of past Amerindian societies before the invasion. In other words, Piedrahita seems to be stating that the Muisca were as great as the Aztecs and the Incas. The production of the *Historia* reveals the contexts that frame historiographic writing about America: Piedrahita's case illustrates how the colonial archive produced by the metropolis makes it possible to write local American histories. The key question is whether, ultimately, local histories such as Piedrahita's fragment the homogenizing imperial narrative we find in texts such as Herrera y Tordesillas's multivolume work *Historia general de los hechos de los castellanos en las islas y tierra firme del mar océano* (1601–1615). It seems that the metropolis itself, with its material accumulation of knowledge, created the conditions of possibility of a fruitful transatlantic dialogue that ultimately produced a criollo sense of homeland. However, access to that metropolitan archive was clearly restricted to a privileged elite. A criollo's way to such archive was literally paid with the wealth derived from colonial plunder and exploitation.[10]

Piedrahita's nativist project is crisscrossed by ambivalences originating from numerous factors, including his own mestizo background and his privileged position in colonial society. To examine these ambivalences it is important to recount some aspects of Piedrahita's life.[11]

Piedrahita was born in Santa Fe de Bogotá in 1624, the legitimate son of Domingo Hernández de Soto Piedrahita and Catalina de Collantes. Catalina was the grandaughter of Juan Muñoz de Collantes, one of the conquistadors of Santa Marta and Peru, and Doña Francisca Coya, an Inca princess from Cuzco. This information is also provided by Piedrahita himself in the *Historia:*

> Y el Juan Muñoz fuera de matrimonio, y estando en Cusco, tuvo por hija en Doña Francisca Coya a doña Menzia de Collantes, que casó con el Capitán Alonso de Soto, natural de Valladolid . . . de quienes por línea materna desciende el Autor de esta historia. (210–211)

> In Cuzco Juan Muñoz and Doña Francisca Coya had a daughter out of wedlock named Doña Mencia de Collantes, who married Captain Alonso de Soto, born in Valladolid. From this maternal lineage descends the author of this history.

Far from admitting he is a mestizo, this disclosure of Andean origins is ambiguous. If Piedrahita wanted to stress his noble Andean lineage, as El Inca Garcilaso did, why reveal an ancestor born out of wedlock? I still have no answer to

10. Joan de Sanct Martín y Antonio de Lebrija, "Relación," reproduced in Gonzalo Fernández de Oviedo y Valdés, *Historia general y natural de las Indias* (Madrid, 1959), III, 83–92; Carmen Millán de Benavides, ed., *Epítome de la conquista del Nuevo Reyno de Granada* (Bogotá, 2001); Anthony Pagden, "Dispossessing the Barbarian," in Pagden, ed., *The Languages of Political Theory in Early-Modern Europe* (Cambridge, 1987), 79–98; Inca Garcilaso de la Vega, *Comentarios reales de los incas* (Lima, 1991); Antonio Herrera y Tordesillas, *Historia general de los hechos de los castellanos en las islas y tierrafirme del mar océano* (Madrid, 1934), 14 vols.

11. Juan Flórez de Ocáriz, *Genealogías del Nuevo Reino de Granada*, facs. ed. (Bogotá, 1990), I, 141; Joaquín Acosta, *Historia de la Nueva Granada* (Medellín, 1971); José María Vergara y Vergara, *Historia de la literatura en la Nueva Granada, desde la conquista hasta la indepenencia, 1538–1820* (Bogotá, 1958); Vicente Restrepo, "Vida del ilustrísimo señor doctor D. Lucas Fernández de Piedrahita," in *Apuntes para la biografía del fundador del Nuevo Reino de Granada y vidas de dos ilustres prelados . . .* (Bogotá, 1897), 185–210.

There is no updated, well-researched biography of Piedrahita; most of the information we have was provided in 1674 by Juan Flórez de Ocáriz in his *Genealogías del Nuevo Reino de Granada* and by nineteenth-century historians such as Joaquín Acosta, José María Vergara y Vergara, and Vicente Restrepo.

this question. The comparison to the writer of the *Comentarios reales* is important because in the first edition of Piedrahita's *Historia* there is a note (omitted in the modern editions) in the margin in which the Neogranadine writer cites El Inca Garcilaso to document his own lineage (210). As is well known, Garcilaso, who was born of a conquistador and an Inca princess, stated that his noble status came from both sides of his family. However, in New Granada, it seems that such identity politics was not common, perhaps because, as Piedrahita notes in the last chapter of the *Historia,* there were not as many marriages between Muisca nobles and Spaniards. In his comments, there is a tacit desire that such integration had happened:

> Aviendo en el Nuevo Reyno tantas mugeres nobles, hijas, y hermanas de Reyes, Caziques y Vzaques, que sin menoscabo de su lustre pudieran recibir por esposas los mas nobles, que passaron a su conquista, como se practicó en las demás partes de la America, no se hallará que alguno de todos ellos casasse con India, por más calificada que fuesse. (599)

> Even though there are many noble Indian women, daughters and sisters of kings, lords, and nobles, that those Spaniards of noble origin could have married without losing status, as happened in other parts of America, none of them has married any Indian woman, even if she was highly qualified.

According to Piedrahita, it is not that the Neogranadine elite did not accept that there were noble Andean women. He states that in New Granada, the Spaniards did not marry noble Muisca women, because they already had the means to abuse them "en la sujeción de prisioneras" [held as prisoners] (816). As Piedrahita suggests, there were in fact many unions considered illicit, a point corroborated by Dueñas Vargas in *Los hijos del pecado,* a well-documented history of interracial sexual relationships in New Granada.[12]

There is a recurrent preoccupation with chastity and purity of blood in Piedrahita. Although not unusual to find such concern in a religious historian, it is important to examine how it affects his nativist project. Discussing the exploitation of the Indians in the mines, fields, and textile mills, Piedrahita singles out the main cause for the diminishing Indian population, unrestrained sexual desire:

> La principal, y que sobresale entre todas, nace del desenfrenamiento, con que los Españoles, mestizos, y negros, se han mezclado con las Indias,

12. Dueñas Vargas, *Los hijos del pecado,* 54–59.

sacandolas muchas vezes de sus pueblos, de que se sigue, y ha seguido la muchedumbre de mestizos, zambos y cholos que ay. (459)

The main cause, which exceeds all the others, is the unrestrained relationships of the Spaniards, mestizos, and blacks with Indian women, often taking them away from their Indian towns, from which a multitude of mestizos, zambos [mixed Indians and blacks] and cholos [acculturated Indians] has resulted.

Here Piedrahita refers respectively to the *castas,* or "impure" and "vulgar" people *(muchedumbre),* from which he seems to distance himself. As a result, Piedrahita states that, "regrettably," there are only a few "indios apurados" [pure Indians] left (459). Comparing the few remaining pure Moors in Granada, Spain, after the Reconquest, Piedrahita asks in a tone that echoes Las Casas: "¿Qué podrá esperarse brevemente, sino la total destrucción de los indios puros, en quienes carga todo el peso de los tributos?" (459). [What can we expect in the near future but the total destruction of the pure Indians, who must bear all the burden of tribute?] The crown's ethnopolitics sought to maintain the Indians separate from the rest of colonial society. Piedrahita raises a concern that also preoccupied many New Granada officials in the seventeenth century. Under unbearable demands, Indians defected from their native towns and mixed with the general population to avoid paying tribute, creating a shortage of labor. Therefore, for the Neogranadine elite, a Muisca-less New Granada seemed unbearable. It is in the fear of this absence that Piedrahita's nativism emerges. His preoccupation with pure Indians reveals other concern: The emerging heterogeneous social groups (castas) were a threat to a colonial order based on the subordination of an identifiable, fixed other.[13]

Denouncing others' unrestrained sexual and economic desires—luxury and greed, to put it in more contemporary terms—the narrator of the *Historia* appears as a moral authority detached from the violent colonial order. This distanced subject is quite problematic. The *Historia* has numerous moral and philosophical reflections that frame the events narrated, making the *Historia* a manual of virtues and prudence in personal and public matters. This edifying element is quite common in the historiography of the period. Histories as manuals of virtues may have quite specific goals in terms of the elite's projects

13. Spaniards, criollos, mestizos, and other castas were forbidden from living in Indian towns, although over the years numerous non-Indians moved into native towns displacing the indigenous residents. Geographer Martha Angel Herrera has studied this process in detail in New Granada, in *Poder local, población, y ordenamiento territorial en la Nueva Granada, siglo XVIII* (Bogotá, 1996).

of social engineering. Examining the Jesuit manuals of virtues in New Granada and Quito, Valeria Coronel suggests that these manuals sought to regulate and maintain control over subaltern populations in the context of an expanding colonial market. The manuals defining obligations and social conduct can be seen as the fundamental codes of an emerging contractual society. In this context, the subaltern groups' access to the money economy and thus to social mobility was quite troubling for the Neogranadine elite. For this elite, conceiving the subaltern groups as undisciplined and unruly justified placing them under their tutelage and restricting their access to the market as well as regulating the accumulation and redistribution of wealth.[14]

Piedrahita's view of colonial society is molded in part by his affiliation with the church, and to the Jesuits in particular. Bernard Lavallé and Solange Alberro have argued that the different religious orders were a catalyst for an emerging criollo conscience in Peru and New Spain. At varying degrees, some orders placed restrictions on criollos and mestizos. The Jesuits, in particular, sought to limit the number and power of the American-born members of the order, according to Lavallé. Piedrahita's case may not be the most representative of what occurred in New Granada. His is a successful story of integration into the establishment, where we don't find the tension between creole and Peninsular priests described by Lavallé and Alberro. The important issue that problematically tends to be excluded in this debate is the relationship of both the Peninsular and creole clerical elite to the subaltern colonial populations. From this point of view the wedge between creole and Peninsular members of the religious orders seems to provide no significant alternative structural conceptions of the colonial social order.[15]

Let us look at Piedrahita's long and close relationship with the Jesuits. Piedrahita studied in the Jesuit Seminario de San Bartolomé in Santa Fe de Bogotá, from which he graduated as master of arts. Afterward he pursued a doctorate in theology at the Universidad de Santo Tomás also in Santa Fe. Throughout his life, Piedrahita kept close contacts with the Society of Jesus, not surprisingly, considering the strong corporate identity that the Jesuits instilled. In 1662, for example, he donated a house for the order's *noviciado* (seminary), together with

14. Valeria Coronel, "Santuarios y mercados coloniales: lecciones jesuíticas de contrato y subordinación para el colonialismo interno criollo," MS. The philosophical foundations of this contractual society come from the Scholastic tradition of Salamanca, including the works of Jesuit Francisco Suárez, who was studied at the Jesuit Colegio de San Bartolomé in New Granada. Based on Thomas Aquinas and Aristotle, society as conceived by Suárez was a voluntary association of free wills.

15. Lavallé, *Las promesas ambiguas*, 198–201; Solange Alberro, *El águila y la cruz: orígenes religiosos de la conciencia criolla, México, siglos XVI–XVII* (Mexico, 1999).

a "miraculous cross" that had belonged to San Francisco de Borja, as noted by Piedrahita himself in the *Historia* (217). When he had to travel to Spain to defend himself against the charges of the visitador Cornejo, Piedrahita was also accompanied by the *provisor* (head) of the Jesuit order in New Granada. Piedrahita died in Panama in 1688 and was buried in the church of the Jesuit school, as he had instructed.

It is not clear how Piedrahita got the initial support of the Jesuits. Apparently, he received partial support from Cristóbal de Araque throughout his studies, according to Elias Ortiz. Piedrahita might have been one of the ten to twelve students of San Bartolomé who received financial aid *(beca)*, which scholarships were generally given to the criollos from Santa Fe and the provinces. The applicants to San Bartolomé and other schools in the city like El Colegio del Rosario had to submit sworn testimonies attesting to the purity of blood and high social standing of their families, known as *el procesillo* (background check), which was similar to the petitions for nobility. The applicant had to come from a legitimate family and prove the purity of blood of at least three generations. The occupation of the father was also crucial. Applicants whose parents had jobs considered low or vile ("oficios viles y mecánicos") were rejected.[16]

Taking into consideration the discriminatory admission policies, one wonders how Piedrahita, a mestizo and son of a carpenter, entered the Jesuit school. In fact, some mestizos did enter the school, especially in the early years, because there was a limited number of qualified applicants. However, these mestizos, who were called *donatarios,* often ended up as "brothers," occupying low positions in the hierarchy of the order. The criollos too had limited opportunities to occupy high posts in the Catholic Church in general. Of the 475 ecclesiastical officials that studied in San Bartolomé between 1605 and 1719, only 6 became bishops. In this context, Piedrahita, who became bishop of Santa Marta and later Panama, is an exceptional case. Many of San Bartolomé students pursued a doctorate, as Piedrahita did, but achieving a higher degree in itself did not open the doors to the highest posts. About 15 percent of the 475 students were able to secure middle-range ecclesiastical offices such as *prebendados* (prebendary). A large number of them (300 of 475) would become parish priests *(párrocos)*. Not surprisingly, Piedrahita started as parish priest of Fusagasugá and then Paipa before being transferred to the Metropolitan Cathe-

16. Sergio Elías Ortiz, prologue, in Lúcas Fernándes de Piedrahita, *Noticia historial de las conquistas del Nuevo Reino de Granada* (Bogotá, 1973), 11. In the prologue to the 1973 edition of the *Historia*, Elias Ortiz does not provide any specific documentation to confirm Araque's support. Renán Silva, *Universidad y sociedad en el Nuevo Reino de Granada . . .* (Bogotá, 1993), has studied the awarding of scholarships in detail.

dral in Bogota, where he rapidly won several posts, including, from 1653 to 1658, *racionero, canónigo, tesorero, maestrescuela* and *chantre* (food keeper, prebendary, treasurer, teacher, and preceptor). My main concern here, however, is not to stress the personal success story, nor to deny it. More important is how this mestizo elaborated a local history that made sense only from a point of view of an emerging sector in colonial society, the criollos.[17]

Piedrahita's identification with the criollo elite is evident in his description of Santa Fe de Bogotá, as Rodolfo Guzmán has shown. Piedrahita proudly describes his native city, and he draws attention to the impressive altars, chapels, and convents in the city. Neogranadine space is codified through the religious discourse, and in Piedrahita these architectural forms are the embodiments of a virtuous Christian creole elite that rightfully and diligently rules over the land.[18]

The grandiose city that Piedrahita describes is the product of forced Amerindian labor and is sustained by Amerindian workers: there are three thousand Spaniards living in the city and ten thousand Indians in the surrounding area. Piedrahita dedicates a few lines to proudly characterize the people of Santa Fe, their intelligence, language, religious fervor, bravery, and festive spirit:

> Ylos que vulgarmente se llaman Criollos son de vivos ingenios: hablan el idioma español con mas pureza castellana que todos los demás de las Indias; inclínanse poco al estudio de las leyes y medicina, que sobresale en Lima y Méjico; y mucho al de la Sagrada Theología, filosofía y letras humanas; extrémanse en la celebración ostentosa del culto divino, y en agasajar forasteros; son generalmente famosos hombres de a caballos, buenos toreadores y diestros en la esgrima y la danza. (214)

> And those regularly called criollos are quite intelligent. They speak pure Castilian Spanish better than the rest of the Indies. They do not prefer to

---

17. Silva, *Universidad*, 62, 175, 208, 294. Doctor Cristóbal de Araque y Ponce de León (Pamplona, New Granada–Madrid, 1667) was also implicated in the charges raised by the visitador Cornejo. Araque traveled to Spain with Piedrahita. He was also a student of San Bartolomé, where he earned a doctorate in theology in 1639, according to José Restrepo Posada, *Arquidiócesis de Bogota* (Bogotá, 1971), IV, 59–60. Although mestizos were barred from being ordained, in sixteenth-century New Granada there were numerous mestizo priests who worked mainly in the encomiendas, because a high number of them spoke Muisca. Among the mestizo priests were Juan de Figueredo, Juan García de Matamoros, Martín Gaytán, Hernán Gómez de la Cruz, Sebastián López, and Gonzalo García Zorro (Alberto Lee-López, *Clero indígena en el arzobispado de Santa Fé de Bogotá, siglo XVI* [Bogotá, 1986]). Although Lee-López documents which priests were Spanish, criollos, or mestizos, he uses the term *indígena* to designate any resident of New Granada. There were, however, no indigenous Catholic priests.

18. Rodolfo Guzmán, "La representación de la ciudad en Lucas Fernández de Piedrahita como expresión de identidad y transformación sociocultural en el criollo preilustrado de la Nueva Granada," *Cuadernos de literatura*, VI (2000–2001), 42–70.

study law or medicine as in Lima and Mexico. They prefer theology, philosophy, and literature. Their Christian celebrations are passionate and pompous. They are also great hosts. They are famous horse riders, good bullfighters, and skillful fencers and dancers.[19]

This description presents the criollos of Santa Fe as a homogeneous group with a set of positive, common characteristics. They are "good," civil subjects, a fact that is also suggested by Piedrahita when he notes that the city was given the title of most noble and loyal in 1565 (220). Here we have a criollo consciousness that is quite different from the antagonistic, political, and territorial creole texts of the independence movements. In Piedrahita's *Historia*, Santa Fe and its people are compared favorably to the cities and the people of Spain. This description seems to emphasize that Santa Fe is one important city among the other Spanish cities. This transatlantic bond is stressed by Piedrahita himself, who says that he offers the description of Santa Fe for those Spaniards interested in going to New Granada (214).

Piedrahita's description of Santa Fe, however, only mentions briefly the Muisca. The contemporary Andean people are denied the thick ethnic specificity granted in the first parts of the *Historia*: the contemporary Muisca are only described as Indians. There is no pride here. In addition, no mestizos, zambos, or cholos are mentioned. Therefore, Piedrahita's nativism was a strategic composition of inclusion and exclusion of Andean elements. The description of the subaltern groups as unruly and undisciplined is suppressed here, providing an image of a peaceful colonial order.

I have shown that in the *Historia* Piedrahita's inscription of the Muisca as the origin of New Granada created an imagined community different from other regions in the Indies and from Peninsular society, but one where the region was still conceived as an integral part of the Spanish Empire. This local history assumed a paternalistic view of Andean society. The writer of the *Historia* presented himself as the preserver of Muisca memory and the benevolent protector of contemporary Andean workers, when in fact his privileges rested upon the exploitation of the Amerindians. This paternalistic view attempted to legitimize the violent social order that made possible Piedrahita's own success. In the first place, Silva reminds us, the schools were sustained in part by Indian labor and tribute, as were the scholarships of San Bartolomé. In the Jesuit annual letters we see that the order soon was assigned important encomiendas like Cajicá and Fontibón to support the school in Santa Fe. The school's

19. Ibid.

restrictions on admissions made possible the concentration of knowledge and power of only a few like Piedrahita in a scheme parallel to the persecution of native priests (*chuques*) and the suppression of Muisca knowledge (a topic that has been well documented by Carl Langebaek). Thus we come to see the limits and contradictions of Piedrahita's nativism. It incorporated Muisca past, but it did not give contemporary Andean societies the same recognition. In the history of New Granada, Piedrahita's adherence to the Neogranadine elite contrasts with the story of another well-known mestizo, Don Diego de Torres, the cacique of Turmequé. Don Diego, the son of a conquistador and a Muisca princess, risked his life defending Indian rights. For this reason, he was persecuted, incarcerated, and eventually banned from New Granada. Almost one century later, Piedrahita's text provided a nostalgic and tamed view of the Muisca that exalted the criollos' pride of their native land. Don Diego, in constrast, inspired fear: there were numerous rumors of a Muisca revolt commanded by Don Diego.[20]

However, the comparison of Piedrahita and Don Diego de Torres is somehow unfair to the story of uprootedness of Piedrahita's Andean family. Was Francisca Coya's relationship with Diego Muñoz de Collantes consensual? Was it the will of their daughter (Doña Mencia Collantes) to relocate to New Granada after marrying Alonso de Soto? How much Quechua did Piedrahita's mother, Catalina Collantes, speak? What links did she have with her Cuzco relatives? We know that most of what Piedrahita mentions about Inca culture (Tawantinsuyo) comes from El Inca Garcilaso's *Comentarios reales*. Clearly Piedrahita did not have the experience or the contacts to elaborate a history comparable to Garcilaso's. In relation to the Andean peoples in New Granada, Piedrahita did not have the family ties to Muisca communities that Don Diego did. After all, Piedrahita (according to Vicente Restrepo) did not even know Muisca.[21]

Nonetheless, the opportunities to learn about and dialogue with the Muisca were there. The Jesuits in New Granada produced Muisca grammars, vocabularies, and confession books and regularly taught Muisca in San Bartolomé. In addition, Piedrahita's first assignments were in two small towns, Fusagasugá and Paipa, where Muisca most likely was still the dominant language. Piedra-

20. Silva, *Universidad*, 55; Archivum Romanum Societatis Iesu, Novi Regni et Quitensis, Rome, XII–XV; Carl Langebaek, "Resistencia indígena y transformaciones ideológicas entre los muiscas del los siglos XVI y XVII," in Felipe Castañeda and Matthias Vollet, eds., *Concepciones de la conquista: aproximaciones interdisciplinarias* (Bogotá, 2001), 281–328; Luis Fernando Restrepo, "Narrating Colonial Interventions: Don Diego de Torres, Cacique of Turmequé in the New Kingdom of Granada," in Bolaños and Verdesio, eds., *Colonialism Past and Present*, 97–117.

21. Vicente Restrepo, "Vida del ilustrísimo señor doctor D. Lucas Fernández de Piedrahita," in *Apuntes para la biografía*, 194.

hita's nativist project, however, did not originate from a dialogue with Andean communities. As he declares in his prologue, while in Spain he decided to write the *Historia* after noticing that most historians of the Indies had paid so little attention to New Granada. It is precisely in dialogue with this transatlantic intellectual tradition that his project takes form. In this dialogue, the Muisca were a passive referent that could be remembered, praised, and protected. This tamed image of the Muisca would prove quite useful to the criollos in the following centuries and is still being showcased by the Republic of Colombia in its ostentatious Gold Museum in Bogota.

THE STORY of the Muisca is still unfolding today, and their struggles with the now transnational hegemonic society and the neoliberal state are far from settled. I am not a distant, detached observer, since I come from a relatively well-to-do Colombian family, who for generations thought of themselves mostly as whites, despite the fact that my national identity card *(cédula)* seems to tell another story: color: *trigueño* (tan). Mestizo or criollo, for me as an intellectual there are two important points here. (1) I recognize that the privileged position I have is related to the colonial history of exclusions and repression of the Muisca and other indigenous groups. In one way or another my family's preoccupation to be part of good and decent society was in fact owing to exclusionary practices that justified exploitation and allowed the accumulation and reproduction of material and symbolic capital from one generation to another that ultimately gave me access to higher education and a position at a research institution. (2) My intellectual project is ultimately an act that seeks to break with such history and to create the conditions needed to work in solidarity with the indigenous intellectuals and peoples to salvage a country torn by violence, where the state itself has been an agent of terror. Ultimately this is a struggle to create a postcolonial space for all or for no one, where the multicultural policies of liberal democracy may prove to be insufficient to radically break with the colonial legacies.

Thus, unraveling the ambivalent nativism of Piedrahita's *Historia* confronts me with my own privileged position in the teaching machine as well as the multilayered implications of my own intellectual project on the Muisca developed from United States academia. A reflexive approach allows me to question the epistemological, institutional, and geopolitical frameworks that inform my own work, but it does not cancel them. The fundamental question remains open: how to work through the violence ingrained in the academic reading and writing about Amerindian peoples. This question may be problematic if it assumes that the centrality of academic knowledge is due, not to its historically produced hegemony, but to a purportedly intrinsic, scientific value, and if it conceives indigenous intellectuals as outsiders to the academic world. Thus, as heirs of a brutal epistemic machine, can we academics engage in a substantial dialogue with the indigenous intellectuals and peoples of today, both inside and outside academia?

A starting point could be a settling of accounts with the past that was repressed by the creole-mestizo clerical intellectuals like Piedrahita. Such opening to the past allows us to return to a forbidden dialogue whose ethical dimensions and epistemological possibilities were shut down too soon, as revealed by this seventeenth-century Muisca confession manual question: "Suetyba chequy bohza umcubunuoa nga ys acubun ocasac umguaquyoa?" [Have you spoken with any shaman and given credit to what he said?][22]

22. María Stella González de Pérez, ed., *Diccionario y gramática chibcha: manuscrito anonimo de la Biblioteca Nacional de Colombia* (Bogotá, 1987), 351.

SUSAN SCOTT PARRISH

William Byrd II and the Crossed Languages of Science, Satire, and Empire in British America

Cultural historians of the colonization of America have repeatedly emphasized European languages' role in mitigating the strangeness of the New World. From Columbus's renaming of western islands after Christian holy figures and monarchs to the projection of biblical and classical narratives to the imposition of Linnaeus's universal taxonomies in the mid-eighteenth century, colonials pasted single words, plots, clusters of metaphors, and nomenclatural systems on American matter to claim literal or intellectual possession over it. Anthony Pagden, focusing on Ibero-America, calls this process of assimilation and possession "attachment"; Robert Lawson-Peebles, focusing on British America, dubs this cognitive projection "redcoatism"; and Mary Louise Pratt argues that "travel and exploration writing *produced* 'the rest of the world' for European readerships at particular points in Europe's expansionist trajectory."[1]

Each author, moreover, describes the point at which this phenomenon began to break down. For Pagden, it was when travelers to the New World became migrants: for the migrant, "recognition was a more complex business for which attachment was an inadequate strategy, since any prolonged exposure immediately raised the difficulty of context"—the difficulty of maintaining the familiarity of a home culture—so that the migrant began to mix "memories of a 'mother-country'" with "fragments of the indigenous cultures." For Lawson-Peebles, it was the Anglo-American encounter with the unanticipated and

I would like to thank Ralph Bauer for his continuing encouragement regarding this work on William Byrd, which I first delivered at an American Studies Association conference at Montreal in 1999 on a panel with Professor Bauer.

1. Anthony Pagden, *European Encounters with the New World: From Renaissance to Romanticism* (New Haven, Conn., 1993), chap. 1, esp. 21; Robert Lawson-Peebles, *Landscape and Written Expression in Revolutionary America: The World Turned Upside Down* (Cambridge, 1988), 22–62, esp. 22; Mary Louise Pratt, *Imperial Eyes: Travel Writing and Transculturation* (New York, 1992), 5.

decidedly unpastoral Rocky Mountains that demanded a new, national idiom of grand but alarming fragmentation in the early nineteenth century. For Pratt, "acculturation," whereby the indigenous culture begins to use the colonial culture's idioms to its own ends and actually changes the colonial culture, gave to travelers' accounts a "heteroglossic dimension." What each of these studies assumes is that a given European language practice was relatively stable until forced into contact with starkly alien physical forms and cultural patterns; it was the indigenous plants, rocks, or peoples that introduced the rupture into the Old World, begetting mixture and heteroglossia. Such a working assumption needs revision. In order to make a more complicated model of the varying modes of representation colonials brought to their New World experience, we must add nuance to our sense of the multiple cultural affiliations elite colonials felt vis-à-vis their European nation. If we understand the European languages and identities arriving in the New World to be already heterogeneous (even within one nation's elite or within a given individual), then we can more faithfully describe and theorize the processes of attachment and acculturation, the expressions of individual colonials, and indeed the various discourses of empire.[2]

The Anglo-American figure William Byrd II (1674–1744) and his now-canonical narratives that recount the expeditions undertaken in 1728 to settle the disputed boundary between Virginia and North Carolina, *The History of the Dividing Line* and *The Secret History of the Line* (circa 1730s), will provide a test case of just such a method. Byrd felt contradictory allegiances to a variety of practices and factions: to the science of the "Moderns," the wit of the "Ancients," the interests of the Augustan Empire and those of the colony of Virginia, and—something yet more nebulous—the uncharted and ultimately unchartable ground itself. This essay contends that, in his histories, Byrd poised the various claims, projects, and representational practices emerging out of these sites against each other. If, in his imperial virtuoso mode, Byrd attaches British verbal and material signs to New World nature in a "ceremony of possession" (to use Patricia Seed's phrase), then, in his transatlantic wit mode, he draws attention to the makeshift, endlessly compromising, and agonistic nature of this process. Though his own self-interest prevents him from plainly critiquing the enterprises of science and empire yoked together in the fron-

2. Pagden, *European Encounters*, 37–38; Lawson-Peebles, *Landscape and Written Expression*, 204–230; Pratt, *Imperial Eyes*, 135. It is unlikely that any of these critics would deny internal cultural differences within a given European elite, but, it being their main objective to point up dissonance produced within the traveler by contact, none applied the complexity of travelers' home cultures to this question of contact.

tier mapping expedition, he situates his wit at a kind of ground's-eye view and, from there, mimics those marks that attempt to designate the land as British property.[3]

For a sketch of the disparate types of elite subjectivity in early-eighteenth-century London, an apt, if slightly caricaturish, text is Susanna Centlivre's satire *A Bold Stroke for a Wife* (1718). A young unmarried woman (of thirty thousand pounds), Ann Lovely, has been left by her deceased father under the care of four male guardians "as opposite to each other as the four elements," all of whom must approve of her suitor before she can be married.

> One [Mr. Periwinkle] is a kind of Virtuoso, a silly half-witted Fellow, but positive and surly, fond of every thing antique and foreign, and wears his Cloaths of the Fashion of the last Century; doats upon Travellers, and believes more of Sir *John Mandeville* than he does of the Bible. . . .
> Another [Mr. Trade Love] is a Change Broker; a Fellow that will out-lie the Devil for the Advantage of Stock, and cheat his Father that got him, in a Bargain; He is a great Stickler for Trade, and hates every Man that wears a Sword. . . . The Third [Sir Philip Modelove] is an old Beau, that has *May* in his Fancy and Dress, but December in his Face and his Heels; He admires all the new Fashions, and those must be French; loves Operas, Balls, Masquerades, and is always the most tawdry of the whole Company on a Birth-Day. . . . [And the fourth, Obadiah Prim, is] a very rigid Quaker.

It is the job of the suitor, Mr. Fainwell, to assimilate his dress, carriage, language, conversational topics, and professed beliefs to each of these four guardians. The

3. Patricia Seed, *Ceremonies of Possession in Europe's Conquest of the New World, 1492–1640* (Cambridge, 1995). In *Wilderness and the American Mind*, 3d ed. (New Haven, Conn., 1982), Roderick Nash isolates Byrd as one of the few colonial figures who "appreciated" nature, against a more typical frontier attitude of agonism (51–52). What I am arguing, though, is not just that Byrd was tapped into the emerging discourse of metropolitan Augustan pastoral and was in the vanguard of bringing such an attitude to the American wilderness; I am arguing for his ventriloquism, through wit, of something more subversive in the ground's resistance to the mapping hubris of both science and empire, even if this critical sense did not impede his acquisitive behavior. As such, I propose to ecologically minded critics, or ecocritics, the inclusion of the usually unexplored genre of satire in their American canon. In his excellent essay, "Plotting William Byrd," *William and Mary Quarterly*, 3d Ser., LVI (1999), 701–722, Douglas Anderson argues for Byrd's continuous alternation between "containment and resistance—between an appetite for order and the irrepressible mutability of experience" (709) and "the tendency of events to take shape as an intersection of many plots"(717); whereas Anderson is mainly interested in Byrd's crisscrossed plotting of behavioral ethics on his journey, I am interested in various land ethics, if you will, that Byrd deploys depending on whether he is in his imperial or Scriblerian mode.

allure of the play is in both the satirization of these male types as well as in the positing of cultural identity as inherently scripted.[4]

Among others, all four of these cultural "elements" of London's elite world carried over to British America, and colonials capitalized on them: orthodox religiosity, self-fashioning as a "beau," New Scientific curiosity, and satire of provincial bumpkins were cultural modes brought to and developed in the periphery that played well in the Metropolis during the seventeenth and early eighteenth centuries. Because especially relevant for Byrd's *Histories of the Dividing Line betwixt Virginia and North Carolina,* the discourses of the New Science and satire need to be explained here. Although both of these discourses offered ways for the colonial to distinguish him- or herself from negative creolization by proving his or her retained capacity for an urbane curiosity— whether about the natural world or human "naturals"—each mode bore within it contrasting uses and theories of language. If the language of the New Science aspired to the perfect linkage between a verbal signifier and its material referent (such that the signifier would effectively disappear), satire, by contrast, often worked through drawing attention to the misconnection between the signifier and its referent and then by playing within and hence exaggerating the waywardness of signification.

John Wilkins, the first secretary of the Royal Society of London (England's central scientific institution), in his 1668 project for linguistic reform titled *An Essay towards a Real Character, and a Philosophical Language,* attempted to reverse what he termed *"the Curse of the Confusion"* that befell at Babel "the first Language [that] was *con-created* with our first Parents." This confusion seems best exemplified in America, where, Wilkins notes, an observer found "more than a thousand different languages" among the native inhabitants. Wilkins is then driven to a recollection of the Greek experience of colonialism, "by which dispersion and mixture with other people [their language] did degenerate into several Dialects." Presumably the English language would be at particular risk in a time of imperial expansion into territories already beset by a swarming of tongues. What Wilkins proposed as a remedy to this modern linguistic crisis was "a *Real universal Character,* that should not signifie *words,* but *things* and *notions.*" And one of the especially troublesome foibles of language that he hoped to eliminate was what he called *"Equivocals,"* that is, words of "several significations . . . [that] must needs render speech doubtful and obscure"; he gives as an example the word "Bill," which "signifies both a *Weapon,* a Bird's

4. Susanna Centlivre, *A Bold Stroke for a Wife,* in *The Dramatic Works of the Celebrated Mrs. Centlivre,* III (London, 1872; rpt. New York, 1968), 209–210.

Beak, and a written *Scroul."* Wilkins concludes, "Though the varieties of Phrases in Language may seem to contribute to the elegance and ornament of Speech; yet, like other affected ornaments, they prejudice the native simplicity of it, and contribute to the disguising of it with false appearances." Such universal and transparent signifiers were meant to work in tandem with empiricism's rejection of ancient book- and Mediterranean-bound authority and its promotion of firsthand inspection of species around the globe.[5]

Restoration and Augustan satirists espoused a different creed when it came to how language and curiosity ought to work. From Thomas Shadwell's *Virtuoso* (1676) to the Scriblerus Club's *Memoirs . . . of Martinus Scriblerus* (1741, but begun in 1714), satirists—variously dubbed "Ancients" and "Scriblerians"—had made fun of the attempts by naturalists, or "Moderns," to pass off their degrading immersion in material triviality as "useful knowledge." But it was especially William King in *The Transactioneer* (1700) who forwarded the contention that writers at the Royal Society of London (and especially the then-editor of the society's *Philosophical Transactions,* Sir Hans Sloane) never achieved anything like the "Real Characters" of Wilkins's devising. According to Roger Lund, the accusation was that "Sloane had offered his readers tautology in the place of definition, mere nomenclature and neologism where explanation and identification ought to stand. . . . Scientific reporting had become a kind of arcane game played by a small coterie for their own obscure purposes." In one of King's dialogues between a "Virtuoso" defending Sloane and an ingenuous "Gentleman" trying to master Sloane's modern style and mode of knowledge, the Virtuoso quotes Sloane's account of a botanic specimen: "The Bark consists of two parts one outward, and another inward."

> *Gent.* That's common to all Barks, for I know none but it hath an outside
>   and an inside.
> *Virtuos.* But you misapprehend; this Bark is different from all others, for
>   'tis Two Barks; our Author uses Parts and Barks as synonymous Terms.
> *Gent.* But how will your Author make *the Bark,* Two Barks?
> *Virtuos.* This he does by dividing the word Bark in Two Parts, and then
>   calling each of those Parts a Bark.

5. John Wilkins, *An Essay towards a Real Character, and a Philosophical Language* (London, 1668), epistle dedicatory, 2, 3, 13, 17, 18. See also Thomas Sprat, *The History of the Royal-Society of London, for the Improving of Natural Knowledge* (London, 1667), 111–113; and see Bacon's damning of the Scholastics' love of syllogisms, because they are only a play about words and "never take hold of the thing," and his calls for a language that could work with the inductive method in the *Novum organum* (1620), trans. R. Ellis and James Spedding (London, 1922), 62–63, which he writes exclusively in the form of listed aphorisms.

If scientific language was meant to make itself invisible as it provided a perfect medium for encountering the material world—Nehemiah Grew had promised in his *Anatomy of Plants* (1682), "Yet not I, but Nature speaketh these things"— the satirists contended that the Moderns were merely in the business of inventing and multiplying the terms of an areferential language. The satirists asked readers to watch areferentiality at work; King advised that one not forget language in favor of "things" but rather notice how referents, or words, get knotted in themselves and disconnected from the realm of things. His satire's "aesthetic play" is to be found in these knots. In Restoration and Augustan England, the language practices of the elites were by no means unitary.[6]

William Byrd II, never one to be shut out from an opportunity for performance, positioned himself at many places on this field of transatlantic cultural debate. Born in Virginia into the local elite, he was sent at the age of seven to receive a genteel education at the Felsted School in Essex—where he learned, in the absence of a close father figure, how to be a gentleman through such manuals as Henry Peacham's *Compleat Gentleman* (1634)—and stayed on to be trained in business at Rotterdam and in law at the Middle Temple. As a colonial cut off from his family and place of birth, he no doubt experienced the Lockean premise that identity is something acquired. He thus familiarized himself with all the disparate but still overlapping spheres of elite English society: he played the beau, the wit, the merchant, the public servant, and the virtuoso at court circles, spas, and coffeehouses. Byrd was elected to the Royal Society, brought to their meetings live New World specimens such as the rattlesnake and the female opossum, and published in its *Transactions* "An Account of a Negro-Boy That Is Dappel'd in Several Places of His Body with White Spots" (1697). While at a Tunbridge Wells spa, he wrote flattering verse sketches that were printed in *Tunbrigalia* (1719). He displayed his bookish knowledge of the healing arts in *A*

6. Roger D. Lund, "'More Strange than True': Sir Hans Sloane, King's *Transactioneer*, and the Deformation of English Prose," *Studies in Eighteenth-Century Culture*, XIV (1985), 221–222; for more on Augustan scientific satire, see Charles Kerby-Miller's lengthy preface to Alexander Pope et al., *The Memoirs . . . of Martinus Scriblerus* (New York, 1966); William King, *The Transactioneer* (1700; Los Angeles, 1988), 10; Nehemiah Grew, epistle dedicatory, in Grew, *The Anatomy of Plants* (1682; New York, 1965). I am borrowing the term "aesthetic play" from David S. Shields, who used it to describe Augustan clubical humor that was summarized in the third earl of Shaftesbury's philosophy of sociability; Shields elaborates, "Social clubs . . . constituted havens of aesthetic play and free conversation in which the most troublesome sorts of expressions to church and state could be voiced as burlesque or travesty" ("Anglo-American Clubs: Their Wit, Their Heterodoxy, Their Sedition," *WMQ*, 3d Ser., LI [1994], 293–294). For the full treatment, see Shields, *Civil Tongues and Polite Letters in British America* (Chapel Hill, N.C., 1997). Anglo-American satire, whether of the Scriblerian, Grub Street, clubical, or other sort, assaulted the authority and pretenses of religion, the state, modern science, and polite society.

Discourse concerning the Plague (1721), and mocked women's superstitions in a scatological lampoon, "The Female Creed" (1725). Byrd returned to Virginia to inherit his father's estate, his lucrative post as receiver general of the quitrents, and to be elected to the Executive Council of the colony between 1705 and 1715; otherwise, he was in London until his final return to Virginia in 1726, arguing colonial causes before the Board of Trade, disputing with Virginia's lieutenant governor Alexander Spotswood, amassing one of the largest book collections in the colonies, accosting maidservants, and courting English heiresses, who rejected him largely because of his colonial status. After 1726, he acquired thousands of acres of land in frontier territory (increasing the Byrd possessions from 26,231 acres to 179,440) and tried (unsuccessfully) to establish a colony of Swiss immigrants there; he rebuilt his father's estate, entertained and wrote to important naturalists, and founded the future cities of Richmond and Petersburg.[7]

Byrd was, in his savvy adoption of the epistemological decorum and rhetorical style of a number of different social spheres in Augustan England, a kind of colonial Fainwell. In the precarious position of being a semioutsider as a native-born Virginian and subject to anxieties about what Cotton Mather termed "criolian degeneracy," as many elite colonials were, he worked hard at disciplining his body (through a devoutly followed exercise regime and careful food consumption) as well as mastering the varying codes of the metropolis. Not only did Byrd exhibit this feigning-well in adopting a range of prose forms—the scatological satire, the New Scientific description, the learned discourse, the panegyric—but, in his most inventive and comprehensive works, *History of the Dividing Line* and *Secret History of the Line,* he collates all these forms. This matters to a discussion of colonialism and creolity because these two texts enact imperial land possession as a disinterested, improving, and chivalric rite, showing how science and empire worked in tandem. At the same time, driven by the satiric tendency to sabotage hubris of any sort, Byrd detonates the

7. On Byrd's life, see Kenneth A. Lockridge, *The Diary, and Life, of William Byrd II of Virginia, 1674–1744* (Chapel Hill, N.C., 1987), which makes the argument that Byrd assembled his identity through texts during his education in Europe because he was so isolated and because his father was so astringent (14–26). It also discusses Byrd's troubles with courtships because of his colonial status (84–94) and explains the context of the dividing line expedition (128–143). On Byrd's library and its stages of acquisition, see Kevin J. Hayes, *The Library of William Byrd of Westover* (Madison, Wis., 1997); on land acquisition, see William K. Boyd, "Introduction to the First Edition" (1929), rpt. in Byrd, *William Byrd's Histories of the Dividing Line betwixt Virginia and North Carolina* (New York, 1967), xxxvii–xxxviii. On Byrd's involvement with the Royal Society, see Maude H. Woodfin, "William Byrd and the Royal Society," *Virginia Magazine of History and Biography,* XL (1932), 23–34, 111–123. On Byrd the scatological satirist, see Peter Wagner, " 'The Female Creed': A New Reading of William Byrd's Ribald Parody," *Early American Literature,* XIX (1984), 122–137.

ceremonial line all along the way with explosions of language, enacting a kind of automimicry. In trying to show his readers that he can be curious in both a New Scientific and satirical mode, doubly ridding himself of any imputation of peripheral degradation, he outwits himself—or, to put it differently, allows his wit to repudiate the alleged "disinterest" and "honour" of science and empire. Alternatively, it should be said that Byrd, as a member of the creole elite, understood how the empire and its English-born agents curtailed his and other Virginia planters' authority in their home territory. His identification with the ground also comes out of that local sense of resentment at distant measures.[8]

The Histories

Much like Ebenezer Cooke (as well as fellow early-eighteenth-century satirists of creolity Ned Ward, Sarah Kemble Knight, and Alexander Hamilton), Byrd in his *Histories* attributes the symptoms of climatically induced creolean degeneracy to other people's bodies while his own discerning eye and lashing tongue prove his maintenance of a metropolitan standard. In particular, Byrd attempts to construct the boundary line as an environmental seam separating physical decency (in Virginia) from deformity or indecency (in North Carolina). At the coastal place appointed for the beginning of their line, Byrd encounters—on the southern side of the line, importantly—a human pair who show that allowing American nature and native mores to condition your body and behavior does not promise Adamic renovation, Crusoean reclamation, or Odyssean repose but instead leaves you in "a dirty state of Nature." Byrd finds

a Marooner, that Modestly call'd himself a Hermit, tho' he forfeited that Name by Suffering a wanton Female to cohabit with Him.
His Habitation was a Bower, cover'd with Bark after the Indian

8. Cotton Mather's term "Criolian Degeneracy" comes from his first election sermon, *The Way to Prosperity* . . . (Boston, 1690); see also Mather's *Things for a Distressed People to Think Upon* (Boston, 1696); and John Canup, "Cotton Mather and 'Criolian Degeneracy,'" *Early American Literature,* XXIV (1989), 20–34. The term and the notion of the "mimicry" of the colonized was introduced by Homi Bhabha in his "Of Mimicry and Man: The Ambivalence of Colonial Discourse," *October,* XXVIII, no. 1 (Spring 1984), 125–133. Bhabha uses this term to describe the many ways in which colonized people did not merely absorb and replicate European culture, but, instead, manipulating the ways in which European culture could not perfectly copy itself onto the colonial sphere, the colonized resisted and hybridized colonial culture as they appeared to be absorbing it. English colonials like Byrd were not "the colonized" in the same way as were the subjugated non-English of the "second" British Empire whom Bhabha is describing; thus Byrd's automimicry was an ambivalent gesture in which he acted as an agent of a distant power while critiquing the legitimacy of such a process through satire.

Fashion, which in that mild Situation protected him pretty well from the Weather. Like the Ravens, he neither plow'd nor sow'd, but Subsisted chiefly upon Oysters, which his Handmaid made a Shift to gather from the Adjacent Rocks. Sometimes, too, for Change of Dyet, he sent her to drive up the Neighbour's Cows, to moisten their Mouths with a little Milk. But as for raiment, he depended mostly upon his Length of Beard, and She upon her Length of Hair, part of which she brought decently forward, and the rest dangled behind quite down to her Rump, like one of Herodotus's East Indian Pigmies.

Here was one version of the Englishman's naturalization to the New World; it involved nakedness, "wanton" and indolent behavior, Indianization, animaliza-tion, and regression from an agrarian state to a barbarism that typified the eastern periphery of ancient civilization. Farther inland and a number of days later, Byrd remarks, "The only Business here is raising of Hogs, which is manag'd with the least Trouble, and affords the Diet they are most fond of. The Truth of it is the Inhabitants of N Carolina devour so much Swine's flesh, that it fills them full of gross Humours," bringing upon them "the Yaws, called there very justly the country-Distemper. This has all the Symptoms of the Pox, with this Aggravation, that no Preparation of Mercury will touch it."[9]

Having countered his spatial proximity to such figures with his cultural distantiation from them (camouflaging his voyeurism in a superior erudition and his own liability to physical decline in a physician's language of diag-nosis), Byrd goes on to establish his expedition as a chivalric act of fealty to the crown: he describes his fellow Virginian commissioners as so many "Knights Templars," carrying out "His Majesty's gracious Intention" with "Vigour" and "Industry"—wresting the westward lands from the "Infidels" (or "Lazy In-dians") but also prohibiting the "borderers," who live in the undetermined territory between Virginia and North Carolina, from "mak[ing] bold with the King's Land there abouts, without the least Ceremony." Byrd, hailing from the royally owned and administered colony of Virginia, posits his own role as outraged agent of the king witnessing various miscarriages of justice in the proprietary colony of North Carolina, where "the Government . . . is so Loose, and the Laws so feebly executed, that, like those in the Neighborhood of Sydon formerly, every one does just what seems good in his own Eyes." Byrd also claims for himself the role of Defoean "projector," remarking on ways the land

9. William Byrd, *History of the Dividing Line Run in the Year 1728*, coll. in Byrd, *Histories*, 46, 54. All subsequent references will be to this edition; I will differentiate, though, between the *History* and *The Secret History of the Line*, both printed in that edition.

could be "improved": for example, by draining the Great Dismal Swamp and thereby "render[ing] so great a Tract of Swamp very Profitable."[10]

He makes use of the discourse of natural history; against the interested, merely land-hungry bellies and false witnessing of the Carolinians, he posits his disinterested role in the expansion of scientific knowledge into previously "hidden" territory, his Baconian experimentalism, and his transparent language:

> I found near our Camp some Plants of that kind of Rattle-Snake Root, called Star-grass. The leaves shoot out circularly, and grow Horizontally and near the Ground. The Root is in Shape not unlike the Rattle of that Serpent, and is a Strong Antidote against the bite of it. . . . Thus much I can say of my own Experience, that once in July, when these Snakes are in their greatest Vigour, I besmear'd a Dog's Nose with the Powder of this Root, and made him trample on the large Snake Several times, which, however, was so far from biting him, that it perfectly Sicken'd at the Dog's Approach, and turn'd its Head from him with the Utmost Aversion.

Extending the promise displayed here of correct observation, direct experience, and plain representation to his commission's larger act of boundary determination, Byrd explains that his men, though deserted by the North Carolina commissioners, "extended the Dividing Line so far West, as to leave the Mountains on each Hand to the Eastward of us." "This we have done with the same Fidelity and Exactness, as if those Gentlemen had continu'd with us. Our surveyors acted under the same Oath which they had taken in the Beginning, and were Persons whose Integrity will not be call'd in Question." The Carolinians, to the contrary, "Execute[d] the orders of their Superiors by halves," ignoring these orders' "plain meaning"; moreover, they and their sympathizers proceeded "to disguise and falsify the Truth," indeed "cooking the Story" to their patrons.[11]

These aspects of the text, along with the many scenes of sexual predation (which Byrd bemusedly relates but shows himself abstaining from), provide

---

10. Byrd, *History*, 36, 44, 54, 74, 84, 104, 120. Daniel Defoe's *Essay upon Projects* (London, 1697) described (in the words of its 1702 longer title) "effectual ways for advancing the interest of the nation." On Byrd's plans to drain the Dismal, see his *Description of the Dismal Swamp and a Proposal to Drain the Swamp*, ed. Earl G. Swem, Heartman's Historical Series, no. 38 (1922); and Boyd's introduction to the *Histories*, xxxviii. In the *History*, he wrote: "It wou'd require a great Sum of Money to drain it, but the Publick Treasure cou'd not be better bestow'd than to preserve the Lives of his Majesty's Liege People, and at the same time render so great a Tract of Swamp very Profitable" (84).

11. Byrd, *History*, 152; Byrd, *Secret History*, 183, 185, 333. Though Byrd is actually confusing two separate species here, he is right in assessing the metropolitan New Scientific fascination with poisons and antidotes, a frequent topic in the *Transactions*.

plenty of fuel for a reading of his expedition and his *Histories* as imperial ceremonies of possession, establishing the mastery of the English crown or the lords proprietors over the land and various liege peoples (both native and Anglo-American), the mastery of English scientific prose over exotic flora and fauna, the mastery of the straight line of measurement and division over a naturally perplexing territory, and the mastery of the male over the female body, all the while establishing Virginia as that colony before all others that represented a retention of English civility. This reading, moreover, is substantiated by historical events. Byrd did purchase approximately 140,000 acres of land westward of his Westover plantation during and after his expedition, and the era of relative power for native American southeastern tribes who could play the French and British Empires against each other during the "Long Peace" was soon to come to an end: 1763 marked the replacement of complex multinational tensions with a "racially defined frontier line" of "Reds defending the West, Whites pushing relentlessly across it from the East." What makes it difficult, however, to read Byrd's *Histories* as perfectly enacting ceremonial possession is that, in many textual moments, he sabotages the very ceremony, rhetoric, and system of signs he elsewhere works so assiduously to establish.[12]

Because Byrd's expedition is involved with the measurement of land for division between the king and the lords proprietors and for their respective colonial grantees—because his commission is measuring on behalf of absent and interested parties—there is a necessity that the various signs of the commissioners are based on authentic forensic discovery (asking: What land did the old grants actually refer to?) and accurate measurement and that they legibly adhere to the land. The planted poles, blazed trees, maps, and journal all need to conform in a perfect semiology with the political and geographical

12. For historiographic and literary critical treatment of the sexual scenes in the *Histories*, southern patriarchal ideology more generally, and masculinist allegories in descriptions of American land, see Myra Jehlen, "The Literature of Colonization," in Sacvan Bercovitch, ed., *The Cambridge History of American Literature*, I, *1590–1820* (Cambridge, 1994), 107–108; Kathleen M. Brown, *Good Wives, Nasty Wenches, and Anxious Patriarchs: Gender, Race, and Power in Colonial Virginia* (Chapel Hill, N.C., 1996); Richard Slotkin, *Regeneration through Violence: The Mythology of the American Frontier, 1600–1860* (Middletown, Conn., 1973), 218–222; Annette Kolodny, *The Lay of the Land: Metaphor as Experience and History in American Life and Letters* (Chapel Hill, N.C., 1975), 3–25; and Susan Scott Parrish, "The Female Opossum and the Nature of the New World," *WMQ*, 3d Ser., LIV (1997), 475–514. Lockridge reads the *Histories* as "a minor epic of mastery" (*Diary, and Life*, 132). Rhys Isaac shows how Byrd's walking the boundary line conformed to English land practices of ceremoniously circumambulating property in Isaac, *The Transformation of Virginia, 1740–1790* (Chapel Hill, N.C., 1982), 19–20. On the impact of the Treaty of Paris on native peoples, see Daniel K. Richter, *Facing East from Indian Country: A Native History of Early America* (Cambridge, Mass., 2001), 187.

territory of their findings and of their making. Yet Byrd's *Histories* call into question, in a number of crucial moments, the unnatural or discursively constructed nature of the commission's work of binding signs to places. Importantly, this revelation of referential fabrication makes Byrd's texts unique in the pervasive genre of the colonial travel narrative–cum–natural history in British America. Though his *Histories* are about settlement—about settling a controversy so that Europeans can settle in a frontier territory—Byrd unsettles the new scientific assumptions about the epistemic refinement and value of curiosity and about the purity of language in its reference to nature.

Explaining in detail the severance of land from Virginia's southern region that created North Carolina in the first place, Byrd writes that Charles II "granted it away to the earl of Clarendon and others, by His Royal Charter, dated March the 24th, 1663." "The Boundary of that Grant towards Virginia was a due West Line from Luck-Island, (the same as Colleton Island), lying in 36 degrees N. Latitude, quite to the South Sea." William Berkeley, then governor of Virginia as well as a grantee of Carolina, advised Lord Clarendon that there was a space of thirty-one miles between the settled southern border of Virginia and the northern boundary of Carolina. "His Lordp [Clarendon] had Interest enough with the King to obtain a Second Patent to include [this thirty-one-mile space], dated June the 30th, 1665." This 1665 patent described the bounds "to run from the North End of Corotuck-Inlet, due West to Weyanoke Creek . . . and from thence West, in a direct Line, as far as the South Sea." However, "in a long Course of years Weynoke Creek lost its name, so that it became a controversy where it lay." As settlers of this border zone began to take out patents "by Guess," not knowing who the rightful grantor was, the two governments decided to "enter into Measures . . . to terminate the Dispute, and settle a Certain Boundary between the two colonies." "All the difficulty," concludes Byrd, "was to find out which was truly Weyanoke Creek."[13]

When Byrd writes, "Weynoke Creek lost its name," he is beginning to sound like the Scriblerian virtuoso, who said: "This he does by dividing the word Bark in Two Parts, and then calling each of those Parts a Bark." Byrd means to say that the words "Weynoke Creek" no longer name a known body of water, that signifier and signified have become severed; yet, in making the name the subject of the sentence, he gives to the word a putative material reality as if the words refer to a thing rather than act merely as a floating name; he treats the signifier wishfully, as if it were the signified itself. Moreover, when Byrd writes, "It became a controversy where it lay," the creek, because it has lost its name,

13. Byrd, *History,* 10, 11.

seems to have lost its fixed place in nature; it appears dystopically to hover away from any creek bed or meaningful matrix. What this obfuscated history of reference involves is the history of Indian removals. Was "Weynoke" a name given this creek by native American speakers and adopted by the English or given by English colonists to indicate a native presence? If the original naming or named people have been moved from their territory, the lost historical context of the word—brought about by colonial westward expansion—makes it unintelligible. The evisceration of this aboriginal sign (or sign of aboriginal life) ironically calls into question the bounds of the English entitlement to land. In order to recover the lost history of the word—"to find out which was truly Weyanoke Creek"—Byrd, who cannot recover knowledge of the place's human history, must attempt instead, through mathematical measures, to reattach a name to a location. That Byrd is both interested in reattaching language to land as well as in satirically anatomizing, in a Scriblerian mode, his and his commission's fraught labors of attachment becomes increasingly clear.

Byrd tells us that, once all the commissioners were finally assembled at Corotuck Inlet to commence the acts of land measurement and division,

> the first Question was, where the Dividing Line was to begin. This begat
> a Warm debate; the Virginia Commissioners contending, with a great
> deal of Reason, to begin at the End of the Spitt of Sand, which was
> undoubtedly the North Shore of Coratuck Inlet. But those of Carolina
> insisted Strenuously, that the Point of High Land ought rather to be the
> Place of Beginning, because that was fixt and certain, whereas the Spitt of
> Sand was ever Shifting, and did actually run out farther now than
> formerly. The Contest lasted some Hours, with great Vehemence, neither
> Party receding from their Opinion that Night.
> . . . Nevertheless, because positive proof was made by the Oaths of two
> Credible Witnesses, that the Spitt of Sand had advanced 200 Yards
> towards the Inlet since the Controversy first began, we were willing for
> Peace-sake to make them that allowance. Accordingly we fixed our
> Beginning about that Distance North of the Inlet, and there Ordered a
> Cedar-Post to be driven deep into the Sand for our beginning.

One could say that, for the history of a dividing line, such is not a very auspicious "Place of Beginning." Just as "Weynoke Creek" had lost its referent, the words "North Shore of Coratuck Inlet" cannot be attached to a certain spot of land. Is the north shore the end of that spit of sand whose naturally enlarging accretions make it slide ever southward? Within this literal definition of a northern point, the agitated quality of the sand and the water has made the language that attempts to fix its terminus into an image of itself: shifting, restless, forgetful. On the other hand, the "fixt and certain" high point of land, although geographically stable, misses the mark of the title's designation. So, although the literal north shore is continually altering its location, the nearest fixed ground does not conform to the designation of a northern shore. As "neither party reced[es] from their opinion" of how to affix language to place, the men come to be engulfed in a stubborn tidal metaphor.[14]

Never able to resolve what the "North Shore of Coratuck Inlet" actually designates through observation, tools of measurement, or the land's self-evidence, the commissioners must rely instead on "the Oaths of two Credible Witnesses" about the words' buried history. As the commissioners in this final decision about the "Place of Beginning" do not rely on language's observable adherence to land but rather on a juridical compact about their language's prior but lost referent, these men acknowledge that the semiology that guides their line is not founded in present nature but in the subjective discourse of humans. Each party thus "recedes" a bit from his opinion as they make a compromise about what words mean.

On March 14, the surveyors for both Virginia and Carolina, along with twelve men to assist them, entered the Great Dismal Swamp to measure and lay the dividing line approximately fifteen miles through its perplexing and secreted morass. Describing the small "pocosons" along the line that leads to the Great Dismal, Byrd demonstrates that the physical ground of the swamp is resistant to human inscription and to linear penetration. In this "filthy Bogg," the ground was "full of Sunken Holes and Slashes"; "we found the Ground moist and trembling under our feet like a Quagmire"; and "every Step made a deep Impression, which was instantly fill'd with Water." Byrd continues: "To their sorrow, too, they found the Reeds and Bryars . . . firmly interwoven. . . . But the greatest Grievance was from large Cypresses, which the Wind had blown down and heap'd upon one another. On the Limbs of most of them grew Sharp Snags, Pointing every way like so many Pikes." What was more,

> the Eternal Shade that broods over this mighty Bog, and hinders the sun-beams from blessing the Ground, makes it an uncomfortable Habitation for any thing that has life. Not so much as a Zealand Frog cou'd endure so Aguish a Situation. . . . Not even a Turkey-Buzzard will venture to fly over it, no more than . . . the Birds in the Holy-Land [would] over the Salt Sea, where Sodom and Gomorrah formerly stood.

14. Ibid., 44, 46.

Contrary to his indication that the smaller swamps are full of amphibious life, the Great Dismal is apparently so obscure and damned a location that not even repugnant scavengers dare traverse it. The erasure, perplexity, and obscurity endemic to the Dismal thus make it the most challenging of grounds for human investigation and for inscribing signs of possession.[15]

Given such natural resistance to human curiosity, it is not surprising that Byrd was foiled from gaining any knowledge of the Great Dismal from the locals:

> Tis hardly credible how little the Bordering inhabitants were acquainted with this mighty Swamp. . . . Yet . . . they pretended to be very exact in their Account of its Dimensions . . . but knew no more of the Matter than Star-gazers know of the Distance of Fixt Stars. . . . We saw plainly there was no Intelligence of this Terra Incognita to be got, but from our own Experience.

Byrd later refers to the swamp as a "Terra Australis Incognita" that "no body before ever had either the Courage or Curiosity to pass." Because of this, the men believed they "shou'd gain immortal Honour by going thro' the Dismal." Though a damned and misbegotten site, the Dismal's resistance to human knowledge gathering made it an ideal stage for the trial of empirical inquiry.[16]

Byrd tells the readers of his *History*, "Altho' there was no need for Example to inflame Persons already so cheerful, yet to enter the People with better grace, the Author and two more of the Commissioners accompanied them half a Mile into the Dismal." Byrd also sanctified their rite of discovery with a sample of public oratory:

> Here Steddy [Byrd's pseudonym] thought proper to encourage the Men by a short harangue to this effect. "Gentlemen, we are at last arriv'd at this dreadfull place, which til now has been thought unpassable. Tho' I make no doubt but you will convince every Body, that there is no difficulty which may not be conquer'd by Spirit and constancy. You have hitherto behaved with so much vigour, that the most I can desire of you, is to persevere unto the End. . . . I shall say no more, but only pray the Almighty to prosper your Undertaking, and grant we may meet on the

15. Ibid., 60, 62, 64, 66, 70. For an ecological / historical treatment of the swamp, see Jack Temple Kirby, *Poquosin: A Study of Rural Landscape and Society* (Chapel Hill, N.C., 1995); and, for a history of the swamp as a symbol in American culture, see David C. Miller, *Dark Eden: The Swamp in Nineteenth-Century American Culture* (New York, 1989).

16. Byrd, *History*, 60, 64; Byrd, *Secret History*, 61, 63.

other Side in perfect Health and Safety." The men took this Speech very kindly, and answer'd it in the most cheerful manner, with 3 Huzzas.

After Mr. Swan, one of the Carolina surveyors, emerged eight days later from the Dismal, "We got about him as if He had been a Hottentot, and began to Inquire into his Adventures." The rest of the party also "recovered firm Land, which they embraced with as much Pleasure as Shipwreckt Wretches do the shoar"; all the Dismalites "lookt very thin, and as ragged as the Gibeonite Ambassadors did in the days of Yore."[17]

Byrd stages this dismal experience as a heroic "discovery" or "adventure" by invoking biblical and medieval quests and early modern maritime voyages. He also represents the journey as a valiant Baconian moment in which intelligence is wrought through direct experience, in which credulous narrative is replaced by eyewitness and measurement, and in which an obscure perplexity gives way to linear penetration. In a sense, these objectives have been fulfilled: despite the water's transforming their footsteps into small, illegible pools, and despite the impeding fabric of briars and uprooted trees, the troop has cut through the Dismal, laid down chains, and measured the swamp. Both colonies have left marks of possession, and a first move of reconnaissance has been made in Byrd's grand scheme to raise funds to drain the Great Dismal. Moreover, Byrd has offered scenes of the physical agon of the swamp as proof of the expedition's right of possession: the men's unprecedented "courage and curiosity" in the face of topographical resistance seems to entitle their colonies to ownership.

Yet what type of curiosity did these men exhibit? Did they encounter the Herodotean monsters that would mark their journey with narrative trophies of outlandishness? Did they cross over into abnormality and return intact with specimens and tales? Did they discover any new species of plant or animal life to add to the European catalog of nature? In fact, the only discovery that the surveyors and their aides made in the Dismal was that of distance. What is more, though they measured and marked the first ten miles, they then, fearing starvation, left off measurement and simply "made" the total breadth of the line through the swamp to be fifteen miles. In this site that Byrd has constructed as the most pronounced moral and physical topos of the curious trial and of empirical heroism, the only knowledge gathered is that of an approximate number. Byrd displays, in these instances and many others, that the language of the line is not transcendent, immanent in royal power or in nature, or even,

17. Byrd, *History,* 62, 82; Byrd, *Secret History,* 63.

once the North Carolinians split off and return home, bound within a consensual system of signs.[18]

Byrd's texts are both possessive and dispossessive. The expedition along the line lays imperial claim to land through measurement and sign making. Within this model, Byrd's *History* is the official record of legitimate possession, and his natural historical descriptions function as an inventory of royal property. Yet, in Byrd's revelation of the difficulty of reading and naming the land, of making the official signs and documents adhere to their referents, he calls into question the legal and rhetorical legitimacy of imperial possession. In both histories, Byrd does deploy the imperial claims of curiosity—namely, that genteel and disinterested knowledge can redeem wild places and peoples from obscurity and enfold them in an emporium of sacred facts. At the same time, in answering the generic demands of the "secret history"—to reveal lapses in civil codes of behavior, whether sexual misdeeds, internecine squabbling, factionalism, or the fabrication of "facts"—Byrd allows "secrets" to undermine New Scientific and imperial curiosity. He did this emphatically in his manuscript for coterie circulation, *The Secret History of the Line,* but did not fully excise the discourse of secrecy and satire when he revised his account for publication as *The History of the Dividing Line.* Byrd's access to and transmission of both secrets and curiosities proved to his readers his virtuosic capacity for both Ancient wit and Modern knowledge. Though a creole compromised by distance from London and proximity to an infectious climate, he mobilized a number of competing elite Augustan discourses to show his civility. Because the discourse of satire often targeted those of empire and the New Science, Byrd, in attempting (as a Virginia creole) to play to as many audiences as he could and feeling ambivalent about his role as the executor of an imperial mandate, undermined his colonial ceremony of possession.

Roland Greene has identified for Ibero-America a similar process in which colonial subjects participated in both "constructional" and "critical" writing; he calls this "thinking alongside the colonial enterprise." Indeed, a thorough analysis of colonial culture must reckon with just such mobility of identification among the most self-conscious colonials. What I am claiming for Byrd is something like an environmental identification that ripples the surface of his narrative. Literary critics and environmental historians have identified imperial administrators and scientific figures who observed the natural thresholds of certain tropical island and coastal environments in the seventeenth and eigh-

18. Byrd, *History,* 82.

teenth centuries, situating the roots of a modern ecological awareness in the colonial space. Roderick Nash has pointed to Byrd as one of the first Anglo-American figures who "appreciated" nature. Slightly different from these claims, this essay has argued that Byrd, tutored in and by the satirical practices of the wits in London and in the colonies, was able to see and record the makeshift quality of his expedition's attempt to reduce nature to an imperial/scientific construct (of measurement, naming, and graphic representation) on the southern frontier. In his texts, the ground speaks as a subversive wit.[19]

19. Roland Greene, "Comparative Semantics in the Colonial World," paper presented at "In Comparable Americas: Colonial Studies after the Hemispheric Turn," conference sponsored by the University of Chicago and the Newberry Library, April 30–May 1, 2004; Richard H. Grove, *Green Imperialism: Colonial Expansion, Tropical Island Edens, and the Origins of Environmentalism, 1600–1860* (Cambridge, 1996); Timothy Sweet, "Economy, Ecology, and Utopia in Early Colonial Promotional Literature," *American Literature,* LXXI (1999), 399–427.

PART IV

Creole Politics of Memory and Knowledge

JOSÉ ANTONIO MAZZOTTI

El Dorado, Paradise, and Supreme
Sanctity in Seventeenth-Century Peru:
A Creole Agenda

The legend of a land of gold accompanied the history of the Spanish conquest from its very beginning. Even as the earliest settlements of La Española (present-day Dominican Republic and Haiti) were being established in the late 1400s, numerous stories had begun to circulate about the great wealth of the newly discovered islands. Columbus was the first to mention the abundance of gold in the New World, although his observation was largely wishful thinking, used to lure support from the Spanish monarchs. In the third of his *Diaries,* Columbus actually claims that the Garden of Eden must have been located in the New World; after carefully examining the stars' positions and measuring the land distances—assuming, as he did, the eastern location of "the Indies"—Columbus identified the Orinoco River as one the four rivers of paradise described by Moses in the first book of the Pentateuch. This idea of paradise's being located in the New World, with its bountiful gold and teeming water supplies, recurred throughout Columbus's writings. Likewise, and not long afterward, both Américo Vespucio (in his *Mundus novus* of 1503) and Pedro Mártir of Anghiera (in *De orbe novo* of 1516) would also extol the plentiful stores of gold and the multitude of naturally good souls found in the fertile lands of the newly discovered territories.[1]

---

1. On Columbus's paradise, see Cristóbal Colón, *Los cuatro viajes del almirante y su testamento* (1946; Madrid, 1980), 184. On the abundance of gold, see his First Diary, where Columbus states: "Allí afirman que [en Cibao] hay gran cantidad de oro, y que el cacique trae las banderas de oro de martillo" (106). [They claim there that a great amount of gold exists [in Cibao] and that the cacique uses banners of hammered gold.] (The translations here and in all other quotes from the Spanish are mine.) The image of infinite gold appears again in the Fourth Diary: "Allí [en la provincia de Ciguare] dicen que hay infinito oro y que traen corales en las cabezas" (191). [There [in the province of Ciguare] they say that there is infinite gold and that the people wear corals on their heads.] Further examples abound. For other sources on the plenty of gold and good souls,

This essay examines the origin and development of El Dorado and other legends in colonial Spanish writings, paying close attention to the ways that creoles in the Peruvian viceroyalty made use of those legends to consolidate their own discursive identity and stake out their particular political claims. Although most studies envision El Dorado as a phenomenon of the mid-sixteenth century, the emphasis here will be on the seventeenth. This was the period when creoles emerged as protagonists in viceregal economic and intellectual life. We will also explore the early construction of a form of creole ethnic nationhood, based, not in the modern, enlightened definition of "nation," but in the primordialist and archaic meaning of the term. Originally referring to slaves of African descent who were born in the New World, the term *creole* (*criollo* in Spanish) also came to refer—originally in a derogatory way—to white, neo-Europeans born in the Americas. In this essay, *creoles* designates those of Spanish descent born in the New World. Despite their many collaborative ventures, the creoles and Peninsular Spaniards experienced an intense rivalry that dated back at least to the late 1560s.[2]

In economic terms, creole merchants of the seventeenth century began to exercise greater control over Peru's extensive commercial networks—the most active and lucrative in all of the Americas at the time. In particular, the merchants of Lima enjoyed tremendous commercial autonomy vis-à-vis the Spanish crown, largely because of their ability to control local financial operations through the Tribunal del Consulado. By the 1600s, this regulating mercantile body was mainly composed of wealthy creoles and their financial allies, including, most importantly, the owners of Lima's seven banks. Within this locally based system, the Catholic Church and the various creole-dominated religious orders also played important roles as bankers and creditors. As a result, the Consulado was able to regularly offer large amounts of money to the crown in exchange for the privilege of administrating viceregal commercial operations.

---

see Américo Vespucio, *El Nuevo Mundo: cartas relativas a sus viajes y descubrimientos* (Buenos Aires, 1951), 181–187; and Pedro Mártir de Anglería, *Décadas del Nuevo Mundo,* 2 vols. (Santo Domingo, 1989), decade 3, book 10, chaps. 1, 2. David Brading also refers to this topic extensively in his *Orbe indiano: de la monarquía criolla a la república criolla, 1492–1867* (Mexico City, 1991), 29–33 (translation by Juan José Utrilla of *The First America: The Spanish Monarchy, Creole Patriots, and the Liberal State*).

2. On the origins of this rivalry, see Bernard Lavallé, *Las promesas ambiguas: ensayos sobre el criollismo colonial en los Andes* (Lima, 1993), 15–25. Other scholars have argued in favor of the alliances and commonalities between elite creoles and Spaniards, especially during the eighteenth century. See Guillermo Villena Lohmann, *Los ministros de la audiencia de Lima bajo el reinado de los Borbones* (Seville, 1974); and Ruth Hill, *Hierarchy, Commerce, and Fraud in Bourbon Spanish America: A Postal Inspector's Exposé* (Nashville, Tenn., 2005).

According to Margarita Suárez, "Bastaba una contribución pecuniaria para que el rey permitiese que sus leyes fueran burladas." [A monetary loan was all that was needed for the king to allow his laws to be ignored.][3]

Despite the Spanish crown's obvious and desperate need for specie and precious metals to meet its many imperial obligations, it seemed incapable of creating or sustaining any effective economic administration. In this context, New World chroniclers and poets repeatedly called attention to the wealth and luxury of Lima and to its many ornate churches. Guillermo Lohmann Villena explains the source of this wealth in his scholarly introduction to the *Noticia general del Perú*, a seventeenth-century text written by viceregal treasurer Francisco López de Caravantes. According to Lohmann Villena, the accelerated extraction of silver from Potosí after 1570 began to greatly enrich the city of Lima, creating a vigorous commercial economy and a steady flow of precious metals. Luis Miguel Glave, too, points to the abundant wealth within the seventeenth-century City of Kings (Lima) and argues that the distributive patterns of this wealth began to restructure relationships between the city's various social sectors. A creole elite thus emerged in Lima, largely driven by its merchant houses. For young creole men without access to commercial capital or to a lucrative post within the viceregal bureaucracy, the priesthood became the preferred career choice. It should come as no surprise, then, that the creole intellectual elite that began to emerge in Peru's seventeenth century was formed within the viceroyalty's various religious orders.[4]

There is an extensive body of creole writings from this period that somehow incorporates the legend of El Dorado, or at least that part of it that suggests a place of inexhaustible richness in the South American territory. This essay argues that this seventeenth-century textual production had an important role in the formation of an early type of ethnic creole nationhood in Lima. What we find in these texts are creole intellectuals within the capital city of Spanish

3. Margarita Suárez, *Desafíos transatlánticos: mercaderes, banqueros, y el estado en el Perú virreinal, 1600–1700* (Lima, 2001), 397.

4. Although the Spaniards discovered the Potosí silver mines in 1545, it was not until the administration of Viceroy Toledo (1569–1581) that a massive labor force was mobilized to work these mines through the manipulation of the ancient Inca system of the *mit'a*. See Guillermo Lohmann Villena, "Estudio preliminar," in Antonio de León Pinelo, *El gran canciller de Indias* (Seville, 1953), 7–186; Guillermo Lohmann Villena, "Noticia preliminar," in Franciso López de Cervantes, *Noticia general del Perú*, 2 vols. (Madrid, 1985). By the early seventeenth century, Lima had a population of approximately twenty-five thousand; of these, ten thousand or so were of European descent, ten thousand were of African descent, and five thousand or so were Indian. See Luis Miguel Glave, *De rosa y espinas: economía, sociedad, y mentalidades andinas, siglo XVII* (Lima, 1998), 163.

South America strategically carving out their own identity. While always insisting upon their loyalty to the Spanish dominion, they proclaim the superiority both of their native Peru and of their particular ancestral lines (that is, their descent from the original conquerors). This essay's argument must, of course, be understood in relation to the particulars of sixteenth- and seventeenth-century terminology and not in relation to the modern era. During those centuries, the word "nation" still referred to a group whose common ancestry, language, religion, territorial origins, and, most important, cultural ties defined its members as being born (literally, *natio*) of a central matrix. "Nation" generally referred to those groups within a larger kingdom who had their own distinct racial and cultural characteristics. Examples from the Peruvian viceroyalty include terms such as "the Indian nation" (with its many peoples, including the Cañaris, Huancas, and Collas), "the African nation" (with its Lucumí, Angolese, Carabalíes, and others), and "the Spanish nation" (among them its Castilians, Andalusians, and Catalans). Creoles in the New World who wished to differentiate themselves from the Peninsular-born members of the "Spanish nation" began to emphasize their particular origins by using the term "creole nation." By the second half of the seventeenth century, this term had become commonplace and expressed a clear sense of an early form of nationhood. Carlos de Sigüenza y Góngora, the Mexican savant, used it in his *Theatro de virtudes políticas* in 1680, as would Bartolomé Arzáns de Orsúa y Vela, the creole historian of Potosí, in his early-eighteenth-century *Historia de la villa imperial de Potosí*. Surely, then, "nation" in the seventeenth century meant a series of subjective commonalities within and among human groupings, and, as I shall show, it was during that century that the term "creole nation" began to be expressed with great form and eloquence.[5]

---

5. Both Carlos de Sigüenza y Góngora, *Theatro de virtudes políticas* (1680), fol. 17; and Bartolomé Arzáns de Orsúa y Vela, *Historia de la villa imperial de Potosí*, 3 vols. (Providence, R.I., 1965), book 9, chap. 18, use the term "creole nation." For a detailed discussion of the term's ambiguity, multiple meanings, and different uses during the colonial period, see Luis Monguió, "Palabras e ideas: 'patria' y 'nación' en el virreinato del Perú," *Revista iberoamericana*, XLIV (1978), 453–470. The concept of a "form of nationhood" is drawn from Richard Helgerson's illuminating study *Forms of Nationhood: The Elizabethan Writing of England* (Chicago, 1992). Obviously, however, there are substantial differences between the "pluralist communal base of the early modern nation-state" (Helgerson, 5) and the situation of the creole group at issue in this essay. The particularities of the issues in Spanish America—regarding religion, plurilingual social subjects, racial "essences," border conflicts, and other questions—forged a different form of articulation among creoles who were expressing their collective identities and negotiating with the Spanish crown and its New World officials. The concept of "nation" that I utilize here has more to do with ethnic background than with specific language uses. However, even in terms of the role of language in articulating claims and a discourse of collective identity, the creole elite of

Before focusing on these issues, let us begin with a brief review of the origins of the El Dorado legend in important sixteenth-century expeditions and chronicles. After this, the focus will turn to five seventeenth-century authors who are closely identified with the city of Lima, either through birth or extended residence: Buenaventura de Salinas, Antonio de la Calancha, Antonio de León Pinelo, Juan Meléndez, and Francisco de Montalvo, all of whom wrote about the incredible wealth and gold and the insuperable sanctity to be found in Peru and the New World. Although each of these authors' writings differ in style and in purpose, they all coincide in their glorification of Lima and of Peru in general. Furthermore, all five agreed that more important still than the great wealth of El Dorado was the equivalent richness to be found in the natural and spiritual qualities of Peru's neo-European inhabitants. Just as the sixteenth-century chroniclers attributed the highest grade to the gold of El Dorado, so, too, did these five seventeenth-century authors attribute the loftiest spiritual qualities to the creoles. By thus infusing the legend of El Dorado with new meanings, the creole writers served their own political purposes very well.[6]

First Expeditions and Texts

When tracing the origins of El Dorado, one must return to Diego de Ordás's 1529 expedition to the Orinoco River. As Demetrio Ramos Pérez has pointed out, Ordás was the first to make references (albeit very vague ones) to a rich, New World kingdom lying beyond the jungle and the mountains of the coast. His comments were based on feeble bits of information and a few pieces of gold worn by some Indians, according to Enrique de Gandía. Ordás referred to this imagined South American kingdom as "el país de Meta," or "the country of Meta," and hoped it would equal in size and splendor the Aztec capital of Tenochtitlán (which Ordás was familiar with, having served under Cortés

---

Lima and other Spanish-American cities all seemed to take pride in their particular use of the Castilian language, which they considered far superior to the Castilian spoken by their Peninsular counterparts. See also Anthony Pagden, "Identity Formation in Spanish America," in Nicholas Canny and Pagden, eds., *Colonial Identity in the Atlantic World, 1500–1800* (Princeton, N.J., 1987), 51–93, esp. 91, for a discussion of the term "creole nation."

6. However, it is worth noting that not all authors had such a positive idea of Lima. The City of Kings was also depicted as an emporium of lust and frivolity. See, for example, Juan Antonio Suardo's *Diario de Lima (1629–1634)* (Lima, 1935), and Josephe de Mugaburu and Francisco de Mugaburu's *Diario de Lima (1640–1694): crónica de la época colonial*, 2 vols. (Lima, 1917–1918) for numerous entries about passional crimes in the city during the seventeenth century. More recently, María Emma Mannarelli proposes that half of the population of Lima in the same century was born outside of legal marriage relations; see her *Pecados públicos: la ilegitimidad en Lima, siglo XVII* (Lima, 1993).

during the 1521 conquest of Mexico). There is no way of knowing whether the vagaries Ordás heard about a fabulous kingdom to the west were simply references to one of the Chibcha or Muisca settlements of present-day Colombia or were actually references to the great Inca Empire.[7]

In the aftermath of the 1534 occupation of Quito by Sebastián de Benalcázar, a lieutenant of Francisco Pizarro's who had been ordered to secure the northern borders of the Inca Empire after the 1532–1533 capture and execution of the Inca ruler Atahualpa, Spanish soldiers began to hear and recollect more detailed accounts of this marvelous golden place. In these stories, one finds the first appearance of the figure known as El Dorado, a *cacique* who supposedly covered himself with gold dust in order to perform certain rituals and ceremonies. A key component of this El Dorado story was the proximity of the cacique's community to a lake, identified as Lake Guatavitá. The cacique would throw pieces of gold and other precious stones into the waters of the lake, both as an offering to his gods and in memory of his dead wife. Benalcázar himself referred to these indigenous tales to justify new incursions into uncharted territory.[8]

Many subsequent expeditions into the South American hinterland were to follow. Among these were the 1541 expedition led by Gonzalo Pizarro and Francisco de Orellana, resulting in the "discovery" of the Amazon, and the 1559 expedition by Pedro de Ursúa, which ended in the disastrous episode of Lope de Aguirre. These are just two of the better-known attempts to conquer the jungle and find El Dorado and the imaginary "country of cinnamon," a city said to be surrounded by brave female warriors whom the conquerors referred to as Amazons. Both of these expeditions produced written accounts, namely Gaspar de Carvajal's *Descubrimiento del Río de las Amazonas* and Francisco Vázquez's *Relación de Omagua y Dorado,* respectively. Other writings from the mid-to-late sixteenth century, including chronicles by Cieza de León, Fernández de

7. See Demetrio Ramos Pérez, *El mito del Dorado: su génesis y su proceso* . . . (Caracas, 1973), 28, 38; Enrique de Gandía, *Historia crítica de los mitos de la conquista americana* (Madrid, 1929), 125–126.

8. For more information on Benalcázar's expedition, see Juan de Castellanos, *Primera parte, de las elegías de varones illustres de Indias* (Madrid, 1589), part 3, chant 2; Pedro Simón, *Noticias historiales de las conquistas de Tierra Firme en las Indias occidentales,* 9 vols. (Bogota, 1953), II, 163–164; Constantino Bayle, *El Dorado fantasma* (Madrid, 1943), 16; Ladislao Gil Munilla, *Descubrimiento del Marañón* (Seville, 1954), 173; Gandía, *Historia crítica,* chap. 7; and, for a summary of sixteenth- and seventeenth-century indigenous accounts, Ramos, *El mito del Dorado,* 293–304. V. S. Naipaul has also recounted the history of the legend beginning from the late sixteenth century and mainly focusing on the southern Caribbean scenario in his *Loss of El Dorado: A History* (Harmondsworth, 1973).

Oviedo, and Juan de Castellanos, also mentioned El Dorado and elaborated upon its image.[9]

Despite evidence of the legend's indigenous origins, scholars have emphasized the possible European origins of El Dorado, noting the importance of certain classical myths and topics to the imaginary of the conquering Spanish soldiers. The most notable of these myths had to do with the Amazons, the kingdom of California, the Golden Age, the Ophir, or golden mines of King Solomon, and the existence of giants—all commonplaces of European popular culture at that time. Another classical myth circulating among Spanish soldiers was the tale of the Argonauts, including its references to the golden apples and Golden Fleece that existed along the shores of the Black Sea in a country called "Colquide," or "the country of the Sun." Clearly, an exhaustive discussion of the origin and development of the legend of El Dorado is beyond the scope of this essay. For our purposes, what is essential to recognize are some of the constituent elements of the legend: pure gold, abundant water, hidden treasures, and a fabulous city (called Manoa, in some versions). With these factors in mind, one can reach a greater appreciation for the discursive strategies of seventeenth-century Peruvian creoles as they appropriated the El Dorado legend for their own purposes.[10]

In terms of myths that circulated in sixteenth-century writings imaging Peru as a land of infinite richness, El Dorado was not without its parallels. An analogous legend surrounded the Jauja Valley of the central Peruvian Andes, which chroniclers described as a Golden Age land of plenty. The first to write

9. Lope de Aguirre rebelled against Ursúa and declared his anger against Philip II while claiming his own right to the newly discovered territories. After navigating on the Amazon River and the surrounding coast of South America, he was killed on the island of Margarita, north of Venezuela. References to a legendary "country of cinnamon" are frequent in Vázquez's and Carvajal's chronicles.

10. See Irving Albert Leonard, *Los libros del conquistador* (Mexico, 1953). In his analysis of the myth of the Amazons in America, Gandía (*Historia crítica*, 90) suggests that the name "Manoa" or "Manua" is a derivation of the Quechua word "manu," or debt, understood in this case to be the tribute payment from the Amazonian tribes to the Inca emissaries. To corroborate this definition, see also Diego González Holguín's *Vocabulario de la lengua general de todo el Perú llamada lengua Qquichua o del Inca* (1608) (Lima, 1989), 229. With the 1476 publication, in Bologna, of an edition of *La Argonautica* by first-century C.E. Roman poet Gaius Valerius Flaccus which had itself been based upon a third-century B.C.E. poem by Apollonius of Rhodes, all of Europe became awash in rumors and narratives about the mythical "country of the sun." Ramos (*El mito del Dorado*, 404) states that the image of a country of gold lying on the shores of a lake (the Black Sea in the myth) would have been a familiar reference among the conquering soldiers of the sixteenth century, who fully expected to find a corresponding reality in the newly discovered lands of South America. For further discussion on this topic, see Gil Munilla (*Descubrimiento*, 175), and Manuel Ferrandis Torres's *El mito del oro en la conquista de América* (Valladolid, 1933), 158–170. For a well-documented, critical history of myths in the Americas, see Gandía's *Historia crítica*.

about the richness of this highland valley were the Spaniards Francisco de Jerez and Pedro de Cieza. Nestled within their accounts of the Spanish conquest of Peru, the descriptions of this Peruvian land of bounty stirred the imagination of the Spanish public. Seville playwright Lope de Rueda went on to fictionalize this setting in a play entitled *The Land of Jauja*. Although probably composed in the mid-1550s, the play later appeared as the fifth "paso," or short play, in Juan de Timoneda's 1567 compilation entitled *El deleitoso*. One of the characters from Rueda's play, a man called Honziguera, boasted of the abundance of food in the highland Peruvian valley, going so far as to claim, "En la tierra de Xauxa hay un río de miel; y junto a él, otro de leche; y entre río y río, hay una puente de mantequillas encadenada de requesones, y caen en aquel río de la miel, que no paresce sino que están diciendo: 'Cómeme, cómeme.'" [In the land of Xauxa there is a river of honey; and alongside it, another one of milk; and between the two rivers stretches a bridge of butter chained together with cheese curds that fall into the river of milk as if to say: "Eat me, eat me."][11]

Two other contemporary legends analogous to El Dorado were the Mountain of Silver and *El Paititi*. Both of these images carried the resonance of indigenous tales regarding the grandeur and legendary wealth of the Inca Empire. Certainly the Chiriguana and Guaraní from the eastern lowlands of the Andes and the Chaco Desert told stories about a faraway and magnificent empire in the mountains to their west and northwest. However, even before encountering these peoples, Spanish and Portuguese explorers along the eastern coasts of South America had begun to hear such tales. The earliest expeditions to coastal Brazil, including one in 1508 led by Nuño and Cristóbal de Haro and one in the early 1520s led by Alejo García, were motivated to explore farther inland by indigenous stories—however vague—about a golden kingdom to the far west. Alejo García actually traveled inland to meet with the indigenous Caracara people of Charcas (in present-day Bolivia), who were under Incan dominion at the time and who were able to provide García with numerous samples of silver. García would be killed during his return trip to Puerto de los Patos on the shores of the Paraná River, ironically in the same general area where he had been shipwrecked years before during the 1516 Juan de Solís expedition. In any case, García was the first European to ever set foot in Incan territory, sometime around 1525. Shortly thereafter, expeditions led by Sebastián Cabot and Diego García (in 1526 and 1527, respectively) also attempted to reach the legendary

11. Lope de Rueda, *Pasos,* ed. Fernando Gonzáles Ollé and Vincente Tusón (Madrid, 1981). For more discussion of the topic of Jauja, and in particular an analysis that traces the ramifications of this theme in the popular sixteenth-century *romancero* genre, see Miguel Herrero, "Jauja," *Revista de Indias,* V (1941), 151–159.

kingdom, but to no avail. Both men returned to Spain in 1529 with nothing but more exorbitant stories about a country of gold and silver that lay to the west. That same year, however, Francisco Pizarro signed a royal contract known as the capitulaciones allowing him to attempt the conquest of Peru from the shores of the Pacific. Although his first two expeditions failed, the third was more successful. On November 16, 1532, Pizarro managed to capture Atahualpa, the reigning Incan emperor. A few years later, the Spanish were able to occupy the Charcas territory, where, in 1545, they discovered the silver mines of Potosí (which the Incas had already been exploiting, but only on a moderate scale). The "discovery" of Potosí seemed to confirm the many indigenous stories about a country with copious supplies of precious metals. Of course, the colonizers of eastern South America would have very little access to this wealth.[12]

However, just at the time the Mountain of Silver became unattainable for such men, another tale of bounty—the legend of El Paititi—began to circulate. The 1535 expeditions of Pedro de Mendoza and Juan de Ayola might have been personally disastrous for their commanders (Mendoza died on the journey back to Spain in 1537, and Ayola died only a few years after his return), but the ventures resulted in yet more extraordinary tales of lands of abundant wealth. The Mendoza expedition led to the 1536 founding of Buenos Aires and, shortly thereafter, to the founding of the inland Spanish fort at Asunción (site of the present-day capital of Paraguay). Surrounded by native communities, the Spanish soldiers at Asunción heard many ancient tales about the existence of a powerful empire steeped in infinite richness and a lake with a golden house where the sun would go to sleep. Enrique de Gandía has suggested that this Guaraní image of the golden house of the setting sun, or El Paititi, was an echo or symbolic rendering of the defeated Incan Empire. Studies by Hélène Clastres and Lucía Gálvez of ancient indigenous accounts of the "Land without Evil" suggest that the localization of this mythical place is consistent with that of the legendary El Paititi. In any case, for Spanish colonizers, the mere suggestion of such a place became a convenient means of justifying further exploratory incursions and garnering support for the necessary troops and supplies.[13]

12. On Alejo García, see Gandía, Historia crítica, 157–159; John V. Murra, " 'Nos Hazen Mucha Ventaja': The Early European Perception of Andean Achievement," in Kenneth J. Andrien and Rolena Adorno, eds., Transatlantic Encounters: Europeans and Andeans in the Sixteenth Century (Berkeley, Calif., 1991), 73–89; Manuel Domínguez, La Sierra de la Plata y otros ensayos (Asunción, 1996), 101–109; and Charles E. Nowell, "Aleixo García and the White King," Hispanic American Historial Review, XXVI (1946), 450–466. On the prediscovery of the mines of Potosí by the Incas, see Domínguez, El Chaco boreal . . . (Asunción, 1925), 14.

13. On El Paititi and its resemblance to the Inca Empire, see Gandía, Historia crítica, 192–193. On the Land without Evil, see Hélène Clastres, La Tierra sin Mal: el profetismo tupí-guaraní

As mentioned earlier, the name of the lake originally associated with El Dorado was Lake Guatavitá. Over time, however, the legend would become associated with many different lakes, including Xayares, Parime, and Titicaca. Through some apparent semantic slippage, the name "El Dorado" also came to be identified with the Guaraní image of El Paititi. In fact, writings from the late sixteenth and early seventeenth centuries show a blurring of the borders between these legendary places, and eventually both become identified with the whole or portions of the Peruvian territory. For example, in chant 5 from *La Argentina* (1602), Martín del Barco Centenera's description of the "Gran Moxo del Paitite" evokes not only the golden temple of the sun that once graced the shores of Lake Titicaca but also the entire Inca Empire.[14]

In a thorough recompilation of Europe's imaginary vicissitudes regarding Peru as a gold-rich emporium and a new utopia, the illustrious Antonello Gerbi also noted: "Inevitabilmente, l'Eldorado si trasformava in una proiezione ideale del Perú, in suo 'dopio' astrale e mitologico. Il desiderio di trovare un *altro* Perú si espresse in quella designazione tanto sicura quanto irreale." [Unavoidably, El Dorado became an ideal projection of Peru, its astrological and mythological "double." The desire to find other Peru is expressed in such a certain as unreal designation.] The semantic coupling of El Dorado / Peru functioned for a long time as the signifier of one cultural entity. Which denomination was used depended upon the particular emphasis of an author at any given moment: the jungles of the Amazon, the territory of the Peruvian viceroyalty, the totality of the New World. As Gerbi himself has pointed out, Peru was often used to represent the New World, since that viceroyalty was considered "the best in the Indies."[15]

(Buenos Aires, 1989), 34–36; and Lucía Gálvez, *Guaraníes y jesuitas: de la Tierra sin Mal al paraíso* (Buenos Aires, 1995), 15–19. Because of its imaginary and religious character, this mythical place within Tupi-Guaraní beliefs does not seem to have had any one fixed location. Clastres cites testimonies that described the Land without Evil as a place of incredible wealth "beyond the mountains" where warrior souls went to dance with their ancestors. According to Clastres, "The Tupí Guaraní situated the Land without Evil in real space, whether to the east or to the west. It seems that most times it was to the west, at least for the Tupí of the coastal regions" (35). Gálvez suggests that the expedition of Alejo García toward the Inca Empire could well have motivated the indigenous to "envision the Land without Evil, this time, in the direction of the west" (88).

14. Martín del Barco Centenera, *Argentina y conquista del Río de la Plata, con otros acaecimientos de los reynos del Peru, Tucumán, y el estado del Brasil* (Lisbon, 1602). On El Paititi as an image of the Inca Empire, see Gandía, *Historia crítica*, 216–217; see also 201.

15. See Antonello Gerbi, *Il mito del Peru* (Milan, 1988), 50, 52. The phrase "the best in the Indies" to refer to Peru was uttered by Mateo Vázquez de Leca, secretary to Philip II, as part of the advice he offered the Spanish king in 1584 regarding the appointment of Don García Hurtado de Mendoza to a post as viceroy in the New World. Vázquez de Leca argued that Hurtado be given the Mexican post, since offering him the viceroyalty of Peru would mean too rapid an

In general, then, sixteenth-century chronicles of Spanish expeditionary ventures are permeated by images of Peru's abundant richness and glories. Creoles in the seventeenth century would go on to use these many images of goodness and plenty to reflect upon the spiritual characteristics of the New World and its occupants. As Jorge Cañizares Esguerra has shown, many creoles also began to link the richness of the New World and its inhabitants to the configuration of stars in the Southern Hemisphere. Before and after the discovery of the New World, theories had been circulating within Europe about the relationship between the stars and the particular characteristics of a land and its people. Texts by Marsilio Ficino, Girolamo Cardano, and other Renaissance scientists, physicians, and philosophers had speculated at length about the influence of the stars on the human body. They argued that the configuration of stars above a particular territory somehow determined the personal and psychological features of the cities and inhabitants of that land. As one might expect, creole observations of New World astronomy served much the same purpose as their reworking of the golden images of the El Dorado legend: as a means to posit their own spiritual grandeur. Thus seventeenth-century Peruvian creoles were able to stake a claim for greater political rights within the viceregal system. At the same time, the discourse of plenty became a powerful weapon in the creoles' struggle to consolidate a local—albeit still Spanish—form of collective identity.

Salinas and the Agenda for Peruvian Sanctity

Creole writers' use of the El Dorado legend to suggest creole spiritual grandeur ran parallel to the dynamic social and political situation experienced by creoles during the seventeenth century. Specifically, their efforts to glorify creole religiosity (and thus affirm their biological and cultural superiority over Peninsular Spaniards—not to mention Indians and Africans) must be under-

---

ascent through the tiers of royal administration. The quote appears in a document cited in Teodoro Hampe's "Esbozo de una transferencia política: asistentes de Sevilla en el gobierno virreinal de México y Perú," *Historia mexicana*, XLI (1991), 49–81, esp. 53. In this article, Hampe shows that, of the twenty-four viceroys that served in Mexico and Peru during the sixteenth and seventeenth centuries, ten served as viceroys in both territories; and, of these ten, all served first in Mexico and were then "promoted" to Peru (in some cases with two times the salary). Aurelio Miró Quesada confirms this fact in the case of the viceroy Marqués de Montesclaros, who first served as the Mexican viceroy (with a twenty thousand ducat salary) before becoming Viceroy of Peru (with a forty thousand ducat salary); see Aurelio Miró Quesada, *El primer virrey-poeta en América (Don Juan de Mendoza y Luna, Marqués de Montesclaros)* (Madrid, 1962), 67.

stood in relation to the creole-led campaign to secure the canonization of Rose of Lima, Francisco Solano, Toribio de Mogrovejo, and Martín de Porras.[16]

All of these historical figures lived in Peru during the early seventeenth century and enjoyed great popularity, both because of their exemplary lives and the miracles with which they were credited. Rosa de Santa María (1584–1617), or Rose of Lima, as she became known, was the most prominent of the four and a native of the City of Kings. She received widespread recognition during her lifetime because of certain miracles (including her ability to converse with mosquitoes) and prophecies (especially the one foretelling that Lima would be swallowed by the waters of the Pacific for its sins). The power of Rose's prayer was also credited with preventing the Dutch corsair Joris Van Spielbergen from disembarking on Peruvian soil in 1615. Although Francisco Solano (1549–1610) was born in Montilla near the city of Córdoba in southern Spain, he lived most of his adult life in Peru, where he was said to have floated on the air while praying. Toribio de Mogrovejo, who served as the archbishop of Lima from 1581 to 1606 and led the influential Third Council of Lima, was instrumental in setting up many of the policies regarding the education and conversion of the indigenous peoples of the Andes. Fray Martín de Porras (1579–1639) was a lowly mulatto who worked as an aide in the Dominican convent of Lima and who was credited with several miracles, including making a dog, cat, and mouse share the same plate. These four personages were the objects of cult worship in Lima even before their death. The creole-driven agenda to get them canonized was successful: Saint Rose was canonized in 1671; Mogrovejo and Solano in 1729; and Martín de Porras, finally, in 1962. The campaign for Saint Rose's

16. Antonio de la Calancha argued in favor of creole biological and intellectual superiority in his *Crónica moralizada . . .* (Barcelona, 1638), fol. 68, which will be discussed in the following pages. In an earlier article, José Antonio Mazzotti, "La heterogeneidad colonial peruana y la construcción del discurso criollo en el siglo XVII," in Mazzotti and U. Juan Zevallos Aguilar, eds., *Asedios a la heterogeneidad cultural: libro de homenaje a Antonio Cornejo Polar* (Philadelphia, 1996), 173–196, I made note of a passage from Calancha that posits the racial superiority of Spaniards born in Peru. Calancha mainly staked his claim upon the aristocratic quality of the creoles' ancestry and upon the temperate climate of Peru, which he believed would eventually produce more and better individuals of the "right" bloodline. Jorge Cañizares Esguerra has examined the astrological explanations that Spaniards and creoles offered for colonial racial distinctions, finding that Indian, creole, and black bodies were each said to have been composed of particular combinations of "matter," thus explaining why three very different types could emerge from the same "universal causes" (position of the stars, weather, food, and so forth). Cañizares Esguerra traces Calancha's sources to the German physician Heinrich Martins and to the writings of Juan de Cárdenas in Mexico, where a similar discourse of patriotic exaltation was occurring. Jorge Cañizares Esguerra, "New World, New Stars: Patriotic Astrology and the Invention of Indian and Creole Bodies in Colonial Spanish America, 1600–1650," *American Historical Review,* CIV (1999), 33–68.

canonization, which was handled by Dominican officials and backed by creole advocates and the general public, demonstrated the impressive power that the creole elite could muster in their effort to gain spiritual and ecclesiastic legitimacy. In addition to defending their saints, creoles also pointed to the large number of *alumbradas* (women who claimed to have direct communication from God), *beatas* (religious women with no formal ties to the church), and other mystics who populated the nine convents, six monasteries, and many churches of Peru's viceregal city.[17]

In 1630, the distinguished Lima creole Fray Buenaventura de Salinas published a treatise entitled *Memorial de las historias del Nuevo Mundo Pirú,* in which he argued that Francisco Solano deserved to be canonized. In the first of its three parts, or "discourses," Salinas insists that Lima (Peru, more generally) is a holy place that exhibits just as much sanctity as any European city. Salinas then devotes much of the rest of his text to extolling the superiority of Lima and its creole inhabitants. The third part centers on Peru's Indian population and the living conditions they endured; this discourse forms part of a larger argument that claims that only people born and raised in Peru or who have resided for many years in the Andean region can fully appreciate the value of the indigenous population. Of vital importance is that the third part of the *Memorial* flows logically from the first two parts and reflects—but also reinforces—the text's underlying purpose of defending the honor of the Peruvian homeland.[18]

---

17. On the number of monasteries and convents in seventeenth-century Lima, see Bernabé Cobo, *Historia de la fundación de Lima* (1650), ed. Manuel Gonzales de la Rosa (Lima, 1882), chap. 3. On the alumbradas, see Fernando Iwasaki Cauti, "Mujeres al borde de la perfección: Rosa de Santa María y las alumbradas de Lima," *Hispanic American Historical Review,* LXXIII (1993), 581–614. Studies by Teodoro Hampe Martínez and Ramón Mujica Pinilla have explored the political motivations behind the creole campaign to canonize Saint Rose. See Hampe Martínez, *Santidad e identidad criolla: estudio del proceso de canonización de Santa Rosa* (Cuzco, 1998); and Mujica Pinilla, *Rosa limensis: mística, polítca, e iconografía en torno a la patrona América* (Lima, 2001).

18. See Buenaventura de Salinas y Córdova, *Memorial de las historias del Nuevo Mundo Pirú* (Lima, 1630), where he asks: "¿Es posible, que todos quantos tienen ojos, y coraçon humano, no se abrassan para clamar, y reclamar por lo passado, y para pedir el remedio de los pocos que an quedado, y no gritan por la honra de la Patria, que tales hijos crió; y por la honra de Dios, que es la suma, y que mas obliga a dolor?" (fol. 270). [Can it be possible that anyone with eyes and a human heart does not burn with the desire to denounce and reclaim the past, to seek remedies for the few [Indians] who are left, and to cry aloud for the honor of the fatherland that raised him, and for the honor of God, who is the almighty and who obliges us to feel compassion?] The love for the "fatherland" expressed in this quote has led some historians (for example, Brading, *Orbe indiano,* 353) to posit the existence of a local, class-based patriotism but not yet a form of nationalism. It is possible to discern a form of creole nationhood in quotations such as this, but only if one assumes a seventeenth-century understanding of the word "nation," that is, as a specifically ethnic and cultural construct.

Parts 1 and 2 enable the subsequent vindication of the Andean indigenous population by establishing the uniqueness of Peru and its peoples. The first discourse offers a detailed exaltation of Pizarro and the conquest, of Incan architectonic and material grandeur, and of the richness of the Peruvian territory; the second is dedicated to praising the "merits and excellent qualities of the City of Lima." Although he makes no explicit mention of either El Dorado or El Paititi, Salinas constructs the hyperbolic praise of his native kingdom through an identification of the land with its gold. According to him, Peru is synonymous with gold; and its best inhabitants—the white creoles—are the incarnation of that richness.[19]

In a representative passage, Salinas presents Peru as the maternal breast from which the entire world sucks its gold and silver milk:

> Porque si Roma es la cabeça del mundo, y Castilla la de sus Reynos, y Señorios; el Pirú es el pecho donde Roma, Castilla, Italia, Flandes, Napoles, Milan, Mexico, Portugal, la China, el Japon, las Filipinas, y todas las demas Provincias del mundo estan mamando, y sustentandose de su sangre convertida en leche de oro, y plata, con que los alimenta a dos carrillos.[20]

> If Rome is the head of the world, and Castile the head of her kingdoms and lordships; then Peru is the breast where Rome, Castile, Italy, Flanders, Naples, Milan, Mexico, Portugal, China, Japan, the Philippines, and all the other provinces of the world are sucking, sustaining themselves on [Peru's] blood converted into the milk of gold and silver which stuffs the mouths of those provinces with nourishment.

The use of this kind of maternal image to describe a territory that feeds the world and is therefore pivotal to the empowerment of Spain vis-à-vis her enemies was a common creole gesture that feminized Peru in order to stake out its place within the hierarchy of the Spanish Empire.[21]

---

19. Salinas y Córdova, *Memorial de historias,* discurso 2, unnumbered folio.

20. Ibid., discurso 1, unnumbered folio.

21. The feminization of the viceroyalty was a gesture that many creoles of the late seventeenth century continued to endorse. This was the case with Rodrigo de Valdés, for example, who claimed in 1687, "Lima haze lo mismo que hizo Ariadna con Theseo, con los Españoles, dandoles las hebras de oro de las ricas Minas del Perù, mugeres honrosas, estado, honor, y estimacion. O! no quiera Dios, que sean tan ingratos los Españoles, con Lima, como lo fuè Theseo con Ariadna, dexandola acabar, y consumir en lo retirado de este nuevo mundo." [Lima does with the Spaniards just as Ariadna did with Theseus, giving them threads of gold from the rich mines of Peru, honest women, status, honor, and respect. Oh, God forbid that the Spaniards would be as ungrateful to Lima as Theseus was to Ariadne, leaving her to rot and die in the remoteness of this

At the same time, however, this dominated, yet prideful, creole subjectivity insisted that Lima was the very center of the civilized world and no mere appendix of European culture and power:

Reconozca [mi estilo] en este nuevo mundo la Roma santa en los Templos, Ornamentos, y divino Culto de Lima; la Genoua soberuia en el Garvo, y brio de los que en ella nacen; Florencia hermosa, por la apacibilidad de los Temples; Milan populosa, por el concurso de tantas gentes como acuden de todas partes; Venecia rica, por las riquezas que produce para España, y prodigamente las reparte a todas, quedandose tan rica como siempre; Bolonia pingue por la abundancia de sustento; y Salamanca por su florida Universidad, y Colegios; pues quien nace en ella no tiene que embidiar meritos, pues sus padres, y abuelos se los dexaron.[22]

In this new world, let [my style] recognize holy Rome in the churches, statues, and divine religion of Lima; proud Genoa in the grace and bravery of those who are born in her; beautiful Florence in the peace of her valleys; populous Milan in the abundance of her people who come from everywhere; rich Venice in the richness she produces for Spain and that she generously distributes to all the other provinces, remaining [herself] as rich as always; plentiful Bologna in the abundance of her foods; and Salamanca in her flourishing university and colleges. For he who is born in [Lima] need not envy any such merits because his parents and grandparents bequeathed them to him.

The idea that Lima encapsulated all the virtues and comforts of Europe's most important cities implied not only the place of a dominated subject but also the place occupied by the best member of the Spanish family. By virtue of Salinas's exaltation, Lima becomes the logical place from which to best administer the empire or, at least, the place to enjoy and value as the most important city of Christendom. In a later work entitled *Memorial, informe, y manifiesto* (1646), Salinas would even declare that Europe seemed almost nonexistent in comparison to the richness and grandeur of the New World:

La America lo hace todo; quando de su estomago robusto, por tantos hilos y arterias de Oro, y Plata reparte, y deriva su substancia a todos los

---

New World.] See Rodrigo de Valdés, *Fundación y grandezas de Lima* (Madrid, 1687), fol. 2. As a modern Ariadne, Lima depended upon the Spanish Theseus, but she was also indispensable in his struggle to defeat the enemy.

22. Salinas y Córdova, *Memorial de historias,* discurso 1, unnumbered folio.

terminos del Orbe. Que mucho si es mundo Carolino, y Emisferio nuevo.
Tan grande, que a juizio de varones cuerdos si comparamos à Europa con
el Mundo antiguo, que antes estaba descubierto, parece un rincon
pequeño: pero si se compara con el Mundo Nuevo Carolino, que despuès
se hallò; es tanto menos, que parece nada.[23]

America does it all, when she spreads and diffuses her substance to every
corner of the globe through the countless veins and arteries of gold and
silver that extend out from her robust belly. It matters little that she is a
Caroline world and a new hemisphere. [She is] so great that, in the
judgment of sensible men, if we compare Europe to the Old World that
was known before, Europe appears as a small corner; but if we compare
Europe to the Caroline New World, discovered later, Europe diminishes
so much that it practically disappears.

A natural consequence of this kind of discursive premise was the positive
characterization of the neo-European inhabitants of Lima and of Peru in general. In his 1630 *Memorial de historias,* Salinas flatly affirmed that creoles were an
improved version of the Spanish nobility:

[Los criollos] son con todo estremo agudos, vivos, sutiles, y profundos en
todo genero de ciencias [porque] este cielo y clima del Pirú los levanta, y
ennoblece en animos.[24]

Creoles are extremely intelligent, lively, subtle, and well versed in all
genres of science [for] the skies and climate of Peru elevate them and
ennoble their spirit.

It should be noted that Salinas's gesture was not completely original. As early
as 1620, Francisco Fernández de Córdoba, a prestigious creole scholar from
Huánuco, described a similar image of the noble creole:

Los Criollos son hijos de la nobleza mejorada con su valor, . . . siendo más
aventajados en esta transplantación, [de lo] que fueron en su nativo
plantel.[25]

---

23. Buenaventura de Salinas y Córdova, *Memorial, informe, y manifiesto . . . al Rey Nuestro
Señor . . .* (Madrid, 1646), fol. 16.

24. Salinas y Córdova, *Memorial de historias,* 246. On the precocity of creoles, testimonies
abound. See a few examples in Cañizares Esguerra, "New World, New Stars," *American Historical
Review,* CIV (1999), 61–65.

25. Francisco Fernández de Córdoba, "Prólogo al lector" (Sept. 9, 1620), in Alonso Ramos
Gavilán, *Historia de nuestra señora de Copacabana* (1621) (La Paz, 1976), 8.

Creoles are children of the nobility, [but] improved by bravery . . .
becoming more advantaged when transplanted here than [their parents]
had been in their native land.

In any case, Salinas's influential description of the creoles would be paraphrased
and further developed by his brother, the Fray Diego de Córdoba Salinas, in
1651:

Los que nacen acá son por extremo agudos, vivos y profundos en todo
género de ciencias, y lo que más admira es ver cuán temprano amanece a
los niños el uso de la razón y que todos en general salgan de ánimos tan
levantados que son pocos los que se inclinan a las artes y los oficios
mecánicos, que sus padres les trajeron de España; porque el cielo, el
clima, la abundancia y riqueza los levanta y ennoblece en ánimos y
pensamientos.[26]

Those who are born here are extremely intelligent, lively, and well versed
in all genres of science, and what is most admirable to see is how soon the
use of reason is awakened in the children and how in general they are all
of such elevated spirits that few are inclined to the arts and mechanic
trades that their parents brought with them from Spain; for the sky, the
climate, the abundance, and the richness [here] elevates them and
ennobles their spirits and minds.

From such positive portrayals, it becomes apparent that seventeenth-century
creole discourse articulated social, political, and spiritual concerns that reached
far beyond the question of whether El Dorado actually existed. Indeed, Salinas's
text represents the kind of "militant Creolism" that Bernard Lavallé finds within
the colonial religious orders or an early example of the kind of "creole patriotism" that David Brading locates in the eighteenth century. Certainly the
exaggerated defense of the indigenous population and the stinging criticism of
the Spanish authorities for their "bad government" and neglect of the common
good were characteristic of the genre of *arbitrista* tracts that became common
on both sides of the Atlantic by the seventeenth century. At the same time, it
deserves underscoring that Salinas's metaphor linking the New World's abundance of gold to the matchless qualities of its creole subjects might well be an
indirect derivation of the El Dorado legend of the sixteenth century; for, by
the seventeenth century, creole writers had reinvested the key elements of

26. Diego de Córdoba Salinas, *Coronica de la religiossisima provincia de los doze apostoles del
Peru: de la orden de nuestro Serafico P. S. Francisco de la regular observancia* . . . (1651), ed. Lino E.
Canedo (Washington, D.C., 1957), 479.

that legend with discursive and spiritual meanings more favorable to a creole agenda.[27]

Calancha and Ralegh: A Golden Dispute

Another prominent creole writer from the seventeenth century who devoted attention to the idea of El Dorado was Fray Antonio de la Calancha. In many ways, Calancha's 1638 *Chronica moralizada del Orden de San Agustín en el Perú* can be read as a response to the 1596 publication of Sir Walter Ralegh's famous *Account of the Discovery of Guyana*, which had first disseminated the El Dorado legend on an international scale. Because Ralegh's text had been immediately translated into both Latin and Dutch, the idea of South America's infinite richness spread quickly throughout Europe and took hold on imaginations there. Although Calancha agreed with Ralegh on the existence of an El Dorado in Peru, the creole writer diminished the importance of the site in an attempt to thwart any possible British plans to invade Peru and claim El Dorado as its own. Instead, Calancha envisioned El Dorado as just one manifestation of the larger phenomenon of Peruvian wealth, a richness and a purity best exemplified in Peru's white creole population.

To better appreciate Calancha's discursive strategy, it makes sense to first examine the Ralegh text against which Calancha was writing. Ralegh's is a complex narration of his South American expedition, seasoned with colorful descriptions of monstrous creatures, inexhaustible wealth, and the magnificent beauty of South America. William Wirt Henry, a nineteenth-century British historian and one of Ralegh's many readers, summed up the author's intention as follows: "[Ralegh] had already discovered that the power of Spain was due to

27. Brading, *Orbe indiano*, trans. Utrilla, chaps. 14, 15. See Sara Almarza, *Pensamiento crítico hispanoamericano: arbitristas del siglo XVIII* (Madrid, 1990), for a discussion of the genre of arbitrista writing in the New World. Almarza suggests an eighteenth-century origin for this genre when she posits Pedro de Peralta's *Lima inexpugnable: discurso hercotectonico, o de defensa, por medio de la fortificación de este grande emporio* (Lima, 1740) as the first example of this kind of systematic claim. However, one could argue that arbitrista texts had existed in Peru from at least the mid-sixteenth century. Even before Guaman Poma and Buenaventura de Salinas, authors such as Luis de Morales, Miguel de Agia, and others had clearly presented some features of the *arbitrista* genre. Specifically, they criticized the deplorable situation of the indigenous populations and proposed some immediate remedies to improve their lives. Both the criticisms and the proposals were part of an overall desire to promote the "common good" of the entire kingdom. See José Antonio Mazzotti, "Indigenismos de ayer: prototipos perdurables del discurso criollo," in Mabel Moraña, ed., *Indigenismo hacia el fin de milenio: homenaje a Antonio Cornejo Polar* (Pittsburgh, 1998), 77–102, esp. 81–87.

the wealth she derived from her American possessions, and he earnestly desired to secure for England the same source of power."[28]

According to Ralegh, Queen Elizabeth of England had a legitimate right to possess the South American lands and all their riches; after all, was there not a prophecy foretelling that the British were to liberate the Incas, and was not the queen herself a kind of Amazon, a brave virgin warrior? Ralegh concluded that the Amazon jungle should be Britain's next logical conquest:

> And where the South Border of *Guiana* reacheth to the Dominion and Empire of the *Amazons,* those Women shall hereby hear the Name of a Virgin, which is not only able to defend her own Territories and her Neighbors, but also to invade and conquer so many great Empires, and so far removed.[29]

Ralegh was one of the first writers in a non-Spanish language to claim that the Incas had built El Dorado. According to him, in the face of the Spanish invasion of Cuzco, one of Huayna Capac's sons fled eastward into the jungle and there erected the splendid city. Although Ralegh fails to mention the name of the son, he does refer to him as "The Powerful Young One" and the twelfth ruling Inca. These details suggest that Ralegh was referring to the rebel Manco Inca, who escaped from the Spaniards in 1536 and went on to conquer and renovate a pre-existing city in the jungle:

> I had knowledge, by Relation, of that mighty, rich, and beautiful Empire of *Guiana,* and of that great and golden City, which the Spaniards call *El Dorado,* and the Naturals *Manoa,* which City was conquered, reedified, and enlarged by a younger Son of *Guainacapa* Emperor of Peru, at such

28. William Wirt Henry, "Sir Walter Ralegh: The Settlements at Roanoke and Voyages to Guiana," in Justin Windsor, ed., *Narrative and Critical History of America,* III (Cambridge, Mass., 1884), 105–126, esp. 106.

29. Sir Walter Ralegh, "A Voyage to the Discovery of Guiana," in Thomas Birch, ed., *The Works of Sir Walter Ralegh, Kt., Political, Commercial and Philosophical, Together with His Letters and Poems* (1596), 2 vols. (London, 1751), II, 235. Ralegh claims that he learned of the alleged prophecy from Antonio de Berrío, the Spanish governor of Margarita Island: "And I farther remember that Berreo confessed to me and others (which I protest before the Majesty of God to be true) that there was found among Prophecies in *Peru,* (at such time as the Empire was reduced to the *Spanish* Obedience) in their chiefest Temples, amongst divers others which foreshewed the Loss of the said Empire, that from *Inglatierra* those *Ingas* should be again in Time to come restored, and delivered from the Servitude of the said Conquerors." See José Antonio Mazzotti, "The Dragon and the Seashell: British Corsairs, Epic Poetry, and Creole Nation in Viceregal Peru," in Alvaro Félix Bolaños and Gustavo Verdesio, eds., *Colonialism Past and Present: Reading and Writing about Colonial Latin America Today* (New York, 2001), 197–214, for more details about the argument regarding the nominal possession of the land of the *Ingas* (or Incas) by "Inga-la-tierra."

Time as *Francisco Pazaro [sic]*, and others, conquered the said Empire, from his two elder Brethren *Guascar and Atabalipa*, both then contended for the same, the one being favoured by the *Orciones* of *Cuzco*, the other by the People of *Caximalca*.[30]

It bears mentioning that El Dorado's translation, or relocation, from the highlands of central Colombia to the Amazonian jungle of Peru had taken place a few decades earlier. Back in the 1550s, Pedro de Cieza de León presented the story of a Chanca warrior named Ancoallu, who led a group of his people into the Amazon jungle sometime in the mid-fifteenth century after the Incas defeated the Chancas in the great war between the two nations. Chroniclers generally recognized this legendary battle as the trigger for Incan imperial expansion, but Cieza was the first to note that some Andean peoples actually migrated into the jungle rather than live under the centralizing, dominant order of the Incas. The Inca-fication of the El Dorado myth would become widespread only with the emergence of the clandestine rebel city of Vilcabamba, constructed in the jungle by Manco Inca after his unsuccessful 1536 rebellion against the Spaniards. This Incan government in exile was finally dismantled by Viceroy Toledo in 1572, the same year that Toledo executed Tupac Amaru I, Manco Inca's last surviving son, in Cuzco's central plaza.[31]

Ralegh's account of the Amazonian city of El Dorado begins with a description of the surrounding countryside: "On both Sides of this River [Orinoco], we passed the most beautiful Country that ever mine Eyes beheld." Then, after traveling four hundred miles "into the said Country, by Land and River," he adds:

> The Country had more Quantity of Gold, by manifold, then the best Parts of the *Indies*, or *Peru*; all or most of the Kings of the Borders are already become her Majesty's Vassals, and seem to desire nothing more than her Majesty's Protection, and the Return of the *English* Nation.[32]

Although Antonio de la Calancha's *Chronica* was written a few decades after Ralegh's narrative, one finds echoes of the same images of El Dorado that had been presented by the famous British corsair. Indeed, when recounting the

30. Ralegh, "A Voyage," in Birch, ed., *Works of Sir Walter Ralegh*, II, 141.

31. On the relocation of El Dorado, see Pedro Cieza de León, *La crónica del Perú: primera parte* (1553) (Lima, 1984), 192, 211, where he referred to Ancoallu and his descendants and to their escape into the jungle. Cieza further states that Ancoallu founded a colony on the shores of a lake in the province of Chachapoyas. Ramos (*El mito del Dorado*, 460–461) mistakenly identifies Ancoallu as an Incan captain.

32. Ralegh, "A Voyage," in Birch, ed., *Works of Sir Walter Ralegh*, II, 141–142, 191.

founding of the magnificent jungle city, Calancha actually relies upon Ralegh's text as an authoritative voice:

> Uno de los ijos de Guaynacapac ermano de Guascar i de Atagualpa (como dice Gualtero Raleg) se fue con millares de Indios Orejones, que eran los mas valientes, i pobló aquella parte de tierra, que està entre el rio grade de las Amaçonas, i el Baracoa, que se llama Orenòque.[33]

> One of the sons of Guaynacapac, a brother of Guascar and Atahualpa (as Walter Ralegh said), fled from the battle with thousands of Indian *Orejones* ["Big Ears," or noble Incan warriors], who were the bravest of all, and they populated the land lying between the great river of the Amazon and the river of Baracoa, also called the Orinoco.

Calancha also echoed Ralegh in claiming that the surviving Incas would likely become collaborators in any future British invasion into South America. Ralegh had expressed great optimism about this idea; Calancha expressed great horror. Clearly, the legend of El Dorado was still very much alive in the seventeenth century, and it remained of great importance to both Peninsular Spaniards and creoles in Peru.

What is most interesting to note, in terms of El Dorado and creole nationhood, is that Calancha elaborates upon Ralegh's image of El Dorado in such a way as to privilege the creole community of Peru:

> Si el Peru es la tierra en que mas igualdad tienen los dias, mas tenplança los tienpos, mas benignidad los ayres i las aguas, el suelo fertil, i el cielo amigable; luego criarà las cosas mas ermosas, i las gentes mas benignas i afables, que Asia i Europa.[34]

> Since Peru is the land where the days are the most similar, the climate most temperate, the winds and waters most beneficial, and with fertile soils and a favorable sky, then it must raise the most beautiful things, and people much kinder and more affable than in Asia and Europe.[35]

Years earlier, Salinas had used metaphor to liken the spiritual purity of creoles to the quality of New World gold. Calancha took another step, arguing that New World gold and the white creoles of Peru were both a reflection of the superiority of the New World's natural resources. In this way, he took the

33. Calancha, *Crónica moralizada*, fol. 115.
34. Ibid., fol. 68.
35. For the idea of creole superiority based on the position of the stars, see Cañizares Esguerra, "New World, New Stars," *American Historical Review*, CIV (1999), 33–68.

remaking of the El Dorado legend to another level, further consolidating creole efforts to purify themselves through a new construction of El Dorado.

León Pinelo and Gold Abundance in the New World Paradise

Antonio de León Pinelo, an intellectual living in Lima at the same time as Calancha, is another principal figure in the history of the El Dorado and paradise myths. Originally born in Spain sometime in the 1590s, the young Pinelo first arrived in Buenos Aires in 1604, then moved to Lima in 1612, where he lived for the next nine years. Upon his return to Spain in 1621, León Pinelo wrote several important works, many of them dealing with his seventeen years of experience in the Americas. Included among his texts is one of the most important seventeenth-century treatises on the wealth and significance of the New World. *El paraíso en el Nuevo Mundo* [Paradise in the New World] was written in Spain between 1645 and 1650, although it was not actually published until 1943. This text has received very little scholarly attention; however, its argument is central to an understanding of creole discourse on the uniqueness of the New World and on the overall material superiority of the New World in relation to the Old World (Europe, Asia, and Africa).[36]

Like Salinas before him, León Pinelo does not mention El Dorado specifically; however, he locates his image of the New World paradise in the jungles of Peru, somewhere near the Amazon River. And although his lengthy argument is largely based on biblical, mythological, and historical texts from the Old World, he also incorporates personal testimony based on his own experiences in Peru, including the nine years he spent studying law and participating in the intellectual life of what was South America's greatest capital city.[37]

36. Regarding Antonio León de Pinelo's biography, Raúl Porras Barrenechea states that the author was born in Valladolid in 1595 or 1596. See Porras Barrenechea, "Prólogo," in León Pinelo, *El paraíso en el Nuevo Mundo: comentario apologético, historia natural, y peregrina de las Indias occidentales, islas de Tierra Firme del Mar Océano* (Lima, 1943), iii–xlv, esp. vi. Guillermo Lohann Villena claims that he was born a few years earlier, in 1590 or 1591 (24); see Lohmann Villena, "Estudio preliminar," in León Pinelo, *El gran canciller de Indias* (Seville, 1953), vii–clxxxvi, esp. xxiv. Regarding the text of *El paraíso en el Nuevo Mundo*, the 1943 Porras edition is based upon a 1780 copy of the original seventeenth-century manuscript. The copy was completed by José Sobrino Manxón and is currently housed in the Biblioteca Real de Palacio in Madrid. León Pinelo's original seventeenth-century manuscript is lost. However, the author did manage to publish a small pamphlet in 1656 that contained an *aparato*, or table of contents, heralding the existence of the much longer text (Porras, "Prologo," in Léon Pinelo, *El Paraíso en el Nuevo Mundo*, xix, xxiii–xxiv).

37. León Pinelo writes: "Caminado he por el Perú muchas leguas sabido de lo que otros han

Unlike Calancha, who expressly referred to El Dorado as an Incan city founded by one of the last surviving Incan rulers, León Pinelo identifies the vast natural and handcrafted treasures of the New World paradise with the South American continent as a whole. Notably, his work forges a subtle connection between the richness of the land and all the hidden treasures found among South America's various indigenous groups, including the Indians of Puná, the Incan coastal settlements at Pachacamac, and all the descendants of Huayna Capac (the eleventh royal Inca) who placed valuable treasures in the Inca's tomb under the Coricancha temple of Cuzco. Indeed, after listing several more examples of gold caches found throughout Spain's newfound territories, León Pinelo goes on to underscore the practical impossibility of calculating the exact quantities of precious metals and pearls that the New World had sent to Spain. Following an example set by the Inca Garcilaso de la Vega's *Historia general del Perú* (the second part of the *Royal Commentaries* [1617]), in which the author attempted to calculate the amount of gold and silver sent from Peru to Spain, León Pinelo opens book 4, chapter 25 of his *El paraíso* by noting how difficult it would be to calculate the exact number of pesos that Spain had received during the period from the conquest to 1650. Although León Pinelo adopts a humble tone by claiming that no human language would be equipped to express such an astronomical number, he attempts an approximation anyway. After reviewing his calculations, he arrives at the astronomical figure of 56,250,000,000,000 pesos.[38]

---

visto en sus provincias." [I have walked many leagues in Peru experiencing what others have seen in their provinces] (*El paraíso en el Nuevo Mundo*, 13). His journey from Buenos Aires to Lima in 1612 and his privileged position as a law student certainly gave him firsthand experience and direct social contact that could have been drawn upon in his later descriptions of South American geography. In *El gran canciller de Indias*, 18, he also confesses, "Navegué sus mares [del Nuevo Mundo], atravessé mucho de sus Provincias sin cargos y con ellos, haziendo notas y juntando papeles i advertencias, poniendo estudio muy particular en entender sus materias." [I navigated the New World seas and crisscrossed many of its provinces, sometimes in the capacity of an administrator, sometimes not; but always taking notes and gathering papers and notices, putting special care in understanding its issues.]

38. See León Pinelo, *El paraíso en el Nuevo Mundo*, II, 372. Gonzalo Fernández de Oviedo claims that the 1533 ransom for Atahualpa alone produced some two million pesos of gold for the Spaniards. See Gonzalo Fernández de Oviedo y Valdés, *Historia general y natural de las Indias* (1535), ed. Juan Pérez de Tudela Bueso, 5 vols. (Madrid, 1992), I, 157. On the incredible quantities of precious metals sent from Peru to Spain by the conquerors and other viceregal authorities between 1534 and 1538 alone, see José Toribio Medina's *La imprenta en Lima* (Amsterdam, 1965), II, 163–176. Medina's study includes long lists of the objects of gold and silver received by the crown. The lists that León Pinelo includes in his own work show an equal abundance of precious metals. In terms of what these values would equal today, if one peso contained 8 *tomines* (approximately 48 decigrams, or 4.8 grams of gold) as Fernández de Oviedo claimed (see *Historia general*, I, 165), then León Pinelo's quantity of 56,250,000,000,000 pesos of gold mea-

León Pinelo then turns to several passages from Genesis to help describe the New World paradise. In this way, he sets up a parallel between the newly discovered paradise and the one outlined within the sacred text. Included in his description is the Fison, one of the four rivers that departs from the biblical paradise, representing the place "en que nace el Oro, y es el que allí se cria purisimo y azendrado" [where gold is born, and where it grows highly pure and shiny]. Just as in the sixteenth century, images of El Dorado, water, and gold appear together. Most likely, León Pinelo himself dismissed—even scorned— the actual legend of El Dorado, for the myth is nowhere mentioned in his text. Yet he subtly transforms the legendary idea of an incredibly rich place into an exaltation of the entire South American territory—identifying the Amazon, Orinoco, Magdalena, and Plate rivers with the four rivers of paradise.[39]

Apparently, León Pinelo never forgot his youth in South America; indeed, he makes repeated reference within his works to his years there. He even refers to Lima at one point as his adopted "fatherland." It would hardly be far-fetched, then, to suggest that León Pinelo experienced a sentimental alliance of sorts with his peers in the New World, with whom he had gone to law school and shared in many youthful adventures. A powerful monument to his fascination and love for the New World was his compilation of the legislation of the Indies, entitled *Recopilación de las leyes de Indias*. With this work, León Pinelo seems to have been following in the footsteps of his mentor, Justice Juan de Solórzano, whose famous *Política indiana* (1628 in Latin, 1647 in Spanish) also defended the rights and privileges of creoles in the New World. In the opening discourse of his *Recopilación*, León Pinelo declares that the compilation is dedicated "a todas las Indias que con veinte años de existencia tengo por patria" [to all of the Indies, which after twenty years of residence, have become my fatherland].[40]

Meléndez and Creole Moral Superiority

A few decades after León Pinelo penned his work on the New World paradise, a creole Dominican friar from Lima named Juan Meléndez carried out one of the most eloquent defenses of creole superiority to that date. His 1681

---

sured in pieces of gold and silver would equal approximately 270 million tons of pure gold today. From there, one would need to factor in the price of gold on the contemporary market and then convert this value into dollars, euros, or another kind of currency. Keep in mind that the figure proposed by León Pinelo only corresponded to the treasures sent before 1650.

39. León Pinelo, *El paraíso en el Nuevo Mundo*, book 5, chap. 1.

40. Porras, "Prologo," ibid., xxii. According to Porras, "Solórzano es el más profundo y solvente de los comentadores del derecho colonial" (viii). [Solórzano is the most comprehensive and best-informed commentator on colonial laws.]

Tesoros verdaderos de las Yndias [True Treasures of the Indies] powerfully posits the spiritual as well as material predominance of the New World over the Old. In an introductory essay evaluating Meléndez's work, Francisco Antonio de Montalvo concludes that the "tesoros verdaderos de las Yndias [son] los muchos hijos de Santo Domingo" [true treasures of the Indies [are] the many sons of Saint Dominic]. Montalvo's statement was based on Meléndez's portrayal of Dominican friars (most of whom were creole) who staunchly maintained their vows of humility and poverty in the face of the opulence and greed characterizing Spanish society in Peru at the time. Melendez's work bases its exaltation of the religiosity of Lima on two important premises: the friars' resistance to powerful temptation and the spiritual qualities of the city's white creoles.[41]

High praise for the native white population of Lima characterizes Meléndez's writing as a whole. In addition to their spiritual grandeur, creoles are described as having a precocious ability to learn and a complete mastery of the Spanish language. Meléndez proceeds to trace the lineages of Lima's leading creole families, demonstrating that their noble ancestries were, for the most part, far most prestigious than those of most Peninsular Spaniards. In defending his conationals, Meléndez defiantly uses the term "creoles" and criticizes those Peninsular Spaniards who cannot grasp the meaning of the term. He refers to such ignorant Peninsulars as *safios,* or stupid ones, and goes so far as to suggest that their ignorance has rendered them inhuman:

> Para distinguirnos de los mismos Españoles que nacieron en España, nos llamamos allà Criollos, voz que de cierto en España se ríen mucho: pero con la razón con que se ríen algunos de todo lo que no entienden: propiedad de gente safia indigna de tener figura de hombres.[42]

> In order to distinguish ourselves from the Spaniards born in Spain, we call ourselves creoles, a term that, certainly, Spaniards laugh at very much; but they laugh for the same reason that some people laugh at the things they do not understand. Such is the behavior of stupid people who are unworthy of being called men.

Such a strong statement could hardly have been an isolated or spontaneous gesture. After all, Meléndez was a member of the upper echelons of the Domini-

---

41. Francisco Antonio de Montalvo, *El sol del Nuevo Mundo: ideado y compuesto en las esclarecidas operaciones del Bienaventurado Toribio arçobispo de Lima* (Rome, 1683).

42. Juan Meléndez, *Tesoros verdaderos de las Yndias en la historia de la gran provincia de San Juan Bautista de el Perú de el orden de predicadores,* 3 vols. (Rome, 1681), I, fol. 353.

can order, and his *Tesoros verdaderos* must have been subject to several administrative and inquisitorial filters. In truth, the insult was not a blanket condemnation of all Peninsular Spaniards; rather, it was aimed at only those incapable of recognizing the superlative qualities of the Spanish kingdoms lying on the other side of the Atlantic. Meléndez's ontological degradation of certain Spaniards to the level of subhumans is reminiscent of the language that some European writers would later use to depict the New World's cultural "other." For example, in the eighteenth-century "dispute over the New World" (as Gerbi has called it), Buffon and De Pauw would use the same scornful language to describe creoles. In response, creole writers such as Francisco Javier Clavijero and Pablo Viscardo y Guzmán would hurl the same derogatory terms back at the Europeans. Given a seventeenth-century context in which the American-born subjects of the Spanish crown were also conceived of, and treated, as simple animals or less than white, it makes sense that Meléndez and other creole writers prefigured the better-known responses of their eighteenth-century counterparts. In the text in question here, Meléndez turns the Spanish insult ("criollo") on its head, appropriating the term for his own uses and wrapping it in a long text full of examples of self-proclaimed spiritual grandeur.[43]

In a parallel move, Meléndez underscores the importance of blood purity—that ever-present obsession of Spaniards—and claims that it is actually better preserved in Peru than in Spain:

> Hacemos pues mucho aprecio los Criollos de las Yndias de ser Españoles, y de que nos llamen assi, y nos tengan por tales, y en orden à conseruar esta sangre Española pura, y limpia se pone tanto cuydado, que no tiene ponderacion: Quien da en el Peru una hija, que no sepa primero si es Español, de que Reyno, y de que pueblo el marido a quien la das. Muy al revez de lo que passa en España con arta lastima de los que saben sentir con razon y entendimiento estas cosas, pues ven casarse Españoles con hijas de Estrangeros, y Estrangeros con hijas de Españoles, y aun salirse ellas mismas de las recamaras de sus Madres a casarse con hombres de otras naciones.[44]

> We, the creoles of the Indies, very much appreciate being Spanish and being recognized that way and considered as such; and in order to maintain the cleanliness and purity of this Spanish blood, we take great care and go to any length. Who in Peru gives a daughter to someone

43. Antonello Gerbi, *La disputa del Nuevo Mundo: historia de una pólemica, 1750–1900* (Mexico, 1982).

44. Meléndez, *Tesoros verdaderos*, I, fols. 353–354.

without first finding out if the future husband is Spanish, and if so, of what kingdom and what town? This is totally opposite from what happens in Spain, much to the dismay of all those who think about this issue with reason and understanding; for now they see Spaniards getting married to the daughters of foreigners, and foreigners getting married to the daughters of Spaniards, and they even see daughters leaving their mothers' chambers on their own to marry men from other nations.

In Meléndez's text, then, creoles are portrayed as the most genuine and valuable human capital within the entire Spanish Empire. The text assumes, of course, that superior religious values result from greater purity of blood. A Spanish woman who marries a "foreigner" (possibly a Lutheran or a *converso*, a New Christian of Jewish origin) would potentially spread a bad seed and cause the ruin of the crown and the church. From at least the sixteenth century, it was believed that the intermingling of Spanish and non-Spanish blood brought about the transmission of idolatry and heresy.[45]

Having thus established creole superiority on multiple grounds, Meléndez devotes volume II of his *Tesoros verdaderos* to a narration of the life of Saint Rose of Lima. According to Meléndez, the cradle that gave birth to this lofty figure in the Catholic pantheon of saints had to have been equally important and saintly. He thus likens Lima to the holy city of Jerusalem, that is, a place especially designed by God:

> Y pues se parecen [Jerusalén y Lima] en la forma, bien puede presumirse piadosamente, que la diseñò Dios, para que la fundassen los Españoles, por caueza de las nueuas tierras,y nueuos Cielos, que se descubrieron, y conquistaron. Es pues la planta de la Ciudad de Lima perfectissima.[46]

> And since Jerusalem and Lima are similar in form, it can be assumed in all piousness that God designed Lima so the Spaniards could establish it as the head of the new lands and new skies that they discovered and conquered. After all, the design of the City of Lima is absolutely perfect.

The comparison of Lima to heaven or to the earthly paradise provides Meléndez with the means to purify and lift the city to heroic heights. The suggestion that Lima was actually designed by God implied a divine plan to relocate the center of the Catholic faith to the New World, thus displacing the Old World paradigm of European cultural and spiritual superiority over other

45. Cañizares Esguerra, "New World, New Stars," *American Historical Review*, CIV (1999), 67.
46. Meléndez, *Tesoros verdaderos*, II, fol. 155.

parts of the world. Not only does Meléndez's text question the reasoning ability of Peninsular Spaniards; it also presents a renewed Christian space, where the purest Spanish bloodlines could be developed and the most elevated spiritual life achieved. With this holy context established, Meléndez proceeds in the rest of volume II to narrate the life of Saint Rose.

Volume III is dedicated to biographies of other saintly figures from Lima's history, including Martín de Porras and Juan Masías. Here, Meléndez resorts to biblical sources to bolster his discursive authority. In the opening pages of this volume, Meléndez directly addresses his European readers:

> Sino te lleno las manos de Pesos de Potosi, te lleno el coraçon del Peso inmmarcesible de la gloria . . . que es la verdadera riqueza del Cielo, en las vidas admirables de los Siervos de Dios, que te presento, en cuya comparacion, es vil arena el oro mas subido de quilates, que tambien dijo el Espiritu Sancto.[47]

> If I don't satisfy your hands with pesos from Potosi, I will fill your heart with the indestructible peso [weight] of glory . . . which is the true richness of heaven, through the lives of God's admirable servants which I present to you here. In comparison to these lives, the best quality gold is but vulgar sand, to echo the words of the Holy Spirit.

By resting his argument on words from sacred texts ("to echo the words of the Holy Spirit," from the Gospels), Meléndez bestows a discursive authority upon his text that surpasses that of a straightforward historical narrative. In no way does he deny the material superiority of the New World; however, he does remove his account from the genre of natural history by stating that even the purest gold has little value when compared to the worth of Lima's saintly figures. His volume then concludes with another remark beseeching his European readers to appreciate the true gold of Peruvian spiritual sanctity. Only by denouncing greed, Meléndez implies, can Spain's true mission in the New World be realized:

> Lee mis libros (bueluo a decir) con piedad, y hallaràs mucho oro, y purissimo, entre sus desaliños, y mucha plata, y finissima, entre sus escorias; y haste rico de vna vez de lo que truxo vn Indiano, si para poderlo ser en tantos años no te han bastado las Yndias.[48]

47. Ibid., III, unnumbered folio.
48. Ibid.

Read my books (I repeat) with piety, and you will find plenty of gold, and of the purest grade, among their disorder, as well as plenty of silver, and of the very finest, among their defects. Make yourself rich with what someone from the Indies has shown you, if all your years in the New World have not yet provided you with enough riches.

In this passage, "someone from the Indies" manages to overturn the terms of domination. Here the European reader is questioned in a quasi-inquisitorial way, challenging his/her reliability as an ethical subject. Inasmuch as Meléndez dangerously transfers the long-standing accusations of idolatry among native peoples into the realm of Peninsular religiosity, his text demonstrates a very compelling example of the uses of the "lettered city" in colonial Latin America. Meléndez is able to attribute greed and potential idolatry to the Spaniards by means of a communicative form (alphabetical writing) that had initially been used by Spaniards to diminish the capacity and legitimacy of New World peoples to govern themselves.[49]

In the case of Meléndez's text, then, the myth of El Dorado is recentered in the realm of written discourse. Writing itself has become the treasure, symbolizing the incomparable value of the subject who aligns himself with the creole agenda.

Francisco de Montalvo and Spiritual Wealth

Francisco Antonio de Montalvo was a Spanish priest of the Order of Saint Anthony of Vienna. Although born in Seville, Montalvo lived in Peru for several years and wrote at length about his experiences there. His main work, *El Sol del Nuevo Mundo* [The Sun of the New World] was published in Rome in 1683 and dedicated to the viceroy Melchor de Navarra y Rocafull, duke of La Palata. This same viceroy would, two years later, order a series of protective adobe walls to be built around the city of Lima—walls that actually remained in place until the late nineteenth century. Just as Salinas had devoted his 1630 *Memorial* to canonization for Francisco Solano, Montalvo's work sets out to persuade crown and church authorities to support the canonization of another pious figure: Toribio de Mogrovejo, archbishop of Lima from the late sixteenth to the early seventeenth centuries. Like Rose of Lima, Fray Martín de Porras, and

49. For the concept of "lettered city" in modern colonial studies, see Angel Rama, *La ciudad letrada* (Hanover, N.H., 1984).

Francisco Solano, Mogrovejo was an important local religious figure, credited with several miracles by the inhabitants of Lima and surrounding communities.

In order to establish the sanctity of Mogrovejo and of Peru's inhabitants in general, Montalvo resorts to the familiar strategy of exalting the richness of the land and the benignity of the weather. Just like Salinas and Meléndez before him, Montalvo uses the terms "New World" and "Indies" as synonyms for Peru. When describing the New World, he makes note of its privileged natural location: "Es tan afortunado por naturaleza . . . que no tiene cosa mala, porque su cielo es veneuolo, su aire apacible, su agua saludable, y su tierra fertil." [It is very fortunate by nature . . . for it has nothing wrong with it; its sky is benevolent, its air peaceful, its water healthy, and its land fertile.][50]

In further praise of its climate, Montalvo observes that Peru's days and nights are roughly equal in length because of the territory's location in the Torrid Zone. Moreover, the winters are not "tan elados como en España, ni los veranos tan ardientes como en Africa, debiendo esta fertil tierra a sus vientos australes la continua y apacible primavera de que goza" [as frigid as they are in Spain, nor are summers as hot as they are in Africa; and this is owing to the southern winds that allow this fertile land to enjoy an eternal and peaceful springtime]. As was pointed out earlier, such prominent creole intellectuals as Salinas and Calancha had made similar arguments. Furthermore, the notion of eternal springtime was also a commonplace in descriptions of that other important Spanish capital in the New World: Mexico City. In 1604, to cite just one notable example, Bernardo de Balbuena had praised Mexico's calm weather, describing it as the "immortal spring" in his *Grandeza mexicana*.[51]

Closely related to such images are Montalvo's descriptions of the material superiority of the Peruvian land. Both of these "natural" conditions lay the groundwork for Montalvo's ultimate argument about the spiritual elevation of the New World's inhabitants.

La tierra del Perù es la mas rica, y feliz que conoce el mundo, de sus fertilidades se satisfacen sus naturales, de su riqueza nunca se hartò nuestra codicia, porque ellos toman lo que les vasta, y nosotros anhelamos por lo que nos sobra. Produce el mejor oro del universo en distancia de mas de mil leguas, desde Castilla del Oro al estrecho de

50. Montalvo, *El sol del Nuevo Mundo*, fol. 6.

51. Ibid., fol. 9; Bernardo de Balbuena, *Grandeza mexicana* (1604) (Mexico, 1992), 47. For the Mexican cases, see Jacques Lafaye's reference to this phenomenon in Lafaye, *Quetzalcoatl y Guadalupe: la formación de la conciencia nacional en México, 1531–1813* (1974) (Mexico City, 1995), 102–123.

Magallanes ... en los parajes de Quito ... en Carabaya cerca del Cusco el
Rey del oro y desprecio del Arauia, y del Ofir, en todo el reyno de
Chile.... Dase en unas regiones el oro en minas, y en otras entre las
arenas de los rios, excediendo en quilates, y cantidad a quanto crian todas
demas tierras del orbe.[52]

Peru is the richest and happiest known land in all the world. While its
fertileness satisfies its native inhabitants, our greed has never been
satiated by its richness; for [the natives] just take what they need, yet we
desire more of what we already have in excess. Peru produces the best
gold in the universe, over a distance of more than one thousand leagues
from Castilla del Oro [in Panama] to the Strait of Magellan ..., in the
hinterlands of Quito ... in Carabaya, near Cuzco (the King of Gold and
the enemy of Arabia and Ophir) and throughout the kingdom of
Chile.... In some regions, gold is found in mines; in others, it is found
among the sands of the rivers, exceeding in quantity and in carats all that
the other lands of the world produce.

Like his predecessors, Montalvo makes no explicit mention of El Dorado.
However, he does differentiate Peru from the kingdoms of Ophir and Arabia
and declare that Peru yields the purest gold in all the world. He even refers to
Cuzco as the "King of Gold." This "golden" reference carries an implicit resonance of the El Dorado legend, for the passage also includes mention of Peru's
"fertileness," suggesting abundant supplies of water. Montalvo further emphasizes the presence of water by noting the coastal boundaries that enclose this
"golden" land ("from Castilla del Oro to the Strait of Magellan").

Although Montalvo identifies himself with a "we" that refers to the Spaniards, he nonetheless sympathizes with the creoles; he claims that they are
satisfied with the fruits of their land and not prone to the kind of greed that
characterizes Peninsular Spaniards. Along with his praise of creole generosity
and high moral standards, Montalvo establishes a subtle link between the purity
of the gold that emerges from the New World and human and intellectual
superiority.

Los hombres y mugeres que cria este nuevo Mundo, por mas
proporcionados a la participacion de los benevolos influjos de sus astros
gozan de excelentes calidades, y de todos aquellos dones con que la
naturaleza ilustra a sus muy favorecidos, los cuerpos de las mugeres
tienen mucha alma, las almas de los hombres mucho entendimiento, y

52. Montalvo, *El sol del Nuevo Mundo,* fol. 9.

todos en comun, buenos talles, hermosas caras, afables condiciones, y liberales animos. Aun donde la agudeza es muy natural se gastan seys y ocho años para estudiar la grammatica, y los criollos del Perù en menos tiempo acaban todos sus estudios, de que se infiere no ser inferiores à otras algunas naciones en la habilidad, y que exceden à muchas en la aplicación.[53]

Because they are more adapted to partake in the benevolent influences of their stars, the men and women of this New World enjoy excellent qualities; and as a result of all the gifts with which nature has favored them, women's bodies have plenty of soul, men's souls are filled with understanding, and everyone has nice figures, beautiful faces, kind manners, and generous spirits. Even in those parts of the world where intelligence comes naturally, people spend six or eight years studying grammar; however, since the creoles of Peru finish all their studies in less time, it can be inferred that Peruvian creoles are not inferior to other nations in their abilities, and that they surpass many others in their diligence.

Here again, one finds no direct mention of El Dorado. However, the legend's meaning seems to have been displaced from its emphasis on a golden land to an emphasis on the people of that land. In any case, the argument insists upon the privileged position of the creoles and their right to be more fully recognized and empowered within the imperial order; that is, to attain a political status that would parallel and supplement the commercial protagonism they already enjoyed. Like León Pinelo, Montalvo was a Peninsular subject who nonetheless established a sentimental alliance with creoles after spending significant time in the New World. Creoles usually referred to this more sympathetic version of the dominant colonial subject as a *baqueano* (a Spaniard with long experience in the New World) in contrast to the more derogatory *chapetón* or *gachupín* (used as insults to the Spaniards in Peru and Mexico, respectively). The latter two terms referred to Peninsular Spaniards who lived in the New World for only a few years and who contributed nothing to the welfare of the viceregal societies. In fact, these two terms were synonymous with Spaniards who did nothing but take advantage of both the Indians and the creoles. This exploitation on the part of Peninsular Spaniards would only intensify during the second half of the eighteenth century with the implementation of the Bourbon reforms.

53. Ibid., fol. 16.

Conclusions

To the list of the authors examined in this article, one could add the names of Gregorio Casasola, Francisco de Echave y Assu, Fernando de Valverde, and Rodrigo de Valdés. All of these seventeenth-century writers coincided in their exaltation of the Peruvian landscape and of the superior quality of its native, white inhabitants. The same discursive strategy also appears in a variety of other writings on Peru—both by Peruvian creoles and by "naturalized" Spaniards. Although, by the eighteenth century, El Dorado was beginning to disappear from the imaginary of many Spaniards and creoles, as late as 1776 the governor of Guayana sent out a search party to locate the mysterious city. Furthermore, both José Oricaín in 1790 and the historian Jacob A. Van Heuvel in 1844 still referred to El Dorado as a real place in South America. Even in our own twenty-first century, Polish archaeologist Jacek Palkewitz claims to have discovered El Dorado under the waters of a lake in the Madre de Dios province of Peru.[54]

Truth or myth, El Dorado and other legends have been pivotal to the construction of an ethnic form of nationhood in Peru. The most articulate expression of this can be found in the writings of the seventeenth-century authors examined in this essay and in the writings of other prominent creole intellectuals from the eighteennth century, including Pedro de Peralta, Pedro José Bermúdez, José Llano y Zapata, and Juan Pablo Viscardo y Guzmán. The identifications of paradise, El Paititi, El Dorado, and other myths with Peru, of Peru with gold, and of gold with the neo-European New World inhabitants resulted in cultural constructions that creoles used in defending and enhancing their position within the viceregal order. The importance of this early form of ethnic nationalist discourse becomes especially clear when conceptualized within the axiological and ontological paradigms of its own time.[55]

In defining this early form of creole nationhood, it makes sense to examine Benedict Anderson's influential argument about modern nationalism's forming as a "cultural artifact" of enlightened bourgeoisies who imagined their respective national collectivities through periodical print and travel narratives. However, given that the authors examined here wrote during the pre-Enlightenment

54. See Ramos, *El mito del Dorado*, 462; Bayle, *El Dorado fantasma*, 42–43; Ricardo Ramírez, "El Dorado no era un sueño," *Diario Ojo* (Lima), Aug. 4, 2003, 20–21, and "Tesoros bajo las aguas," Aug. 5, 2003, 7.

55. The following paragraphs reproduce some of the ideas already laid out in Mazzotti, "Epic, Creoles, and Nation in Spanish America," in Susan Castillo and Ivy Schweitzer, eds., *A Companion to the Literatures of Colonial America* (Malden, Mass., 2005).

era, Anderson's illuminating proposal must be complemented by notions about the forms of collective identity that existed before the eighteenth century. Indeed, in his *Nations before Nationalism,* John Armstrong insists that "an extended temporal perspective is especially important as a means of perceiving modern nationalism as part of a cycle of ethnic consciousness." In modern nationalism, Armstrong critically observes, ethnicity manifests itself through the search for "permanent 'essences' of national character instead of recognizing the fundamental but shifting significance of boundaries of human identity." To support this, Armstrong points to the important work of Norwegian anthropologist Fredrik Barth, whose more dynamic approach sets forth "a social interaction model of ethnic identity that does not posit a fixed 'character' or 'essence' for the group, but examines the perceptions of its members which distinguish them from other groups." In such a model, ethnicity is defined by its borders and not by its contents. In early forms of ethnic nationalism, Armstrong finds that collective identity is more the product of exclusions and oppositions than the result of nontemporal features. Given the nature of such changing interactions and the constant redefinition of borders and group limits, the lower classes of a particular society can easily be manipulated by the dominant elite if there is no counterelite able to lend legitimacy to a separate, lower-class sense of identity.[56]

In the case of the Peruvian viceroyalty, one may assume that the Spanish officials were not as effective as the creole elite in attracting the support of poor creoles. Furthermore, the existence of a neo-Incan elite in Cuzco posed a different set of challenges to the assumptions of Spanish imperial discourse. Under these conditions, one may also assume that the sentiments of militant Creolism reached far beyond the writings of a few lettered men and expressed the sense of community shared by many other subjects of Spanish origin who happened to have been born in Peru. I do not mean to imply that either the creole or the neo-Incan protohegemonic elites of viceregal Peru would have been considering "an autonomous political structure" as the means of defining their different collective identities. As far as the white creoles were concerned, this possibility was not envisioned until at least the second half of the eighteenth century. Instead, the kind of militant creolism in question here could be seen as falling within the category of "lateral ethnies" that Anthony Smith establishes in his examination of ethnic nationalisms in the Old World context.[57]

56. John A. Armstrong, *Nations before Nationalism* (Chapel Hill, N.C., 1982), 4–7.
57. Anthony D. Smith, *The Ethnic Origins of Nations* (London, 1986), 147. The Great Rebellion, led by Tupac Amaru II in 1780, was the final, and most important, attempt to realize the dream of

Also relevant is Paul R. Brass's work on the formation of ethnic identities. In studying the formation of political structures among ethnic groups in the South Asian context, Brass underscores the value of both the primordialist and the circumstantialist approaches. In terms of the former, he acknowledges that language, extended kinship groups, one or more common founders, and the construction of categories of racial inclusion and exclusion are all important elements in the formation of collective identities. However, Brass also sees the aforementioned elements as changing and changeable, that is, capable of being manipulated by an elite. Although specifically used to discuss the Muslim-Hindu conflicts in India and Pakistan, Brass's multifaceted approach to the issue of religious difference can be most valuable in examining the case of seventeenth-century ethnic creolism. Of course, one must first acknowledge that the Spanish Empire was distinguished by constant internal power struggles, with each of its many individual kingdoms exalting its own character and superiority. Beyond this Peninsular competition, many differences were also widely noted between the most powerful kingdoms of the Iberian Peninsula and the viceroyalties of "the Indies." Even today, the variety of languages and cultural features among the Spanish regions has led to the division of "autonomias," or local semiautonomous forms of government. Within both Peru and Mexico, the descendants—both real and alleged—of the original conquerors developed their own, very ample set of themes and primordial references that could serve as symbolic fodder in the struggle to expand the dominion of their self-perceived superiority. Furthermore, in the face of blatant discrimination based on place of birth, the creoles discovered the usefulness and the importance of a territorial argument in establishing the validity of their ethnic claims.[58]

The need for New World creoles to insist upon their worth was apparent from the earliest decades after the conquest. In 1574, Juan López de Velasco, an official cosmographer and chronicler of the Spanish crown, characterized both creoles and Spanish *baqueanos* in the following scornful terms:

---

an autonomous government in the hands of a neo-Incan elite. The rebellion was plagued by internal contradictions and was literally decapitated in 1781 with the execution of Tupac Amaru II and his family in the main square of Cuzco; see Scarlett O'Phelan Godoy, "Repensando el movimiento nacional inca del Siglo XVIII," in O'Phelan Godoy, comp., *El Perú en el siglo XVIII: la era borbónica* (Lima, 1999), 263–278.

58. Paul R. Brass, "Élite Groups, Symbol Manipulation, and Ethnic Identity among the Muslims of South Asia," in David Taylor and Malcolm Yappe, eds., *Political Identity in South Asia* (London, 1979), 35–43, included in Brass, *Ethnicity and Nationalism: Theory and Comparison* (New Delhi, 1991), 69–108.

Los españoles que pasan a aquellas partes y están en ellas mucho tiempo, con la mutación del cielo y el temperamento de las regiones aun no dejan de recibir alguna diferencia en la color y calidad de sus personas; pero los que nacen dellos, que llaman criollos, y en todo son tenidos y habidos por españoles, conocidamente salen ya diferenciados en la color y tamaño, porque todos son grandes y la color algo baja declinando a la disposición de la tierra; de donde se toma argumento, que en muchos años, aunque los españoles no se hubiesen mezclado con los naturales, volverían a ser como son ellos: y no solamente en las calidades corporales se mudan, pero en las del ánimo suelen seguir las del cuerpo, . . . porque por haber pasado aquellas provincias tantos espíritus inquietos y perdidos, el trato y conversación ordinaria se ha depravado.[59]

Because of the mutation they experience in the stars and the climate, Spaniards who travel to those [New World] lands and remain there for a long time cannot but experience changes in their color and the quality of their persons; but it is well known that their children, who are called creoles and who are looked upon and treated as Spaniards, are differentiated at birth by both their color and size. They are all large and of a lowly color, descending to the color of the land. This is the basis for the argument that the Spaniards who live there will, after many years, become just like the Indians, even if they do not actually mix with them; transformed not only in the quality of their bodies but in the quality of their souls, which tend to reflect the [condition of] the bodies . . . for because so many lost and rebel souls have gone on to live in those provinces, ordinary manners and conversation have become depraved.

This ontological degradation of baqueanos and creoles turned all the white residents of the New World into potential Indians in the eyes of the Spaniards. Within a few decades, as I have shown, the creoles' reaction against this bias is nothing short of patriotic. Indeed, much more was at stake in the Peruvian viceroyalty than just simple pride or the problem of identity. The creoles of seventeenth-century Peru would appropriate the golden image of El Dorado and paradise and transform them into images of the superiority—moral, religious, and cultural—of the white people of the New World. This discursive strategy constituted just one of the myriad ways that these ambiguous subjects would formulate a defense of their right to participate in the imperial project.

59. Juan López de Velasco, *Geografía y descripción universal de las Indias* (1571–1574) (Madrid, 1971), 37–38.

The synecdochal flux in the meaning of El Dorado and paradise appears to have been the result of decades of material progress, combined with corresponding developments in astrological, biological, religious, and political discourse. And, although this particular aspect of colonial discourse could be contrasted with many examples of loyalist writing, the fact remains that elite creole intellectuals in Lima insisted upon certain "essential" differences between their land and the other nations of the Spanish Empire. At the same time, the forms of racism that took root in the New World constituted the external face of creole self-definition; the same discourse that exalted the white inhabitants of the New World achieved its effectiveness through the constant exclusion of other racial groups, Indians and blacks in particular. This practice would remain squarely in place well after the initial creation of the Spanish American republics. However, like the legend of El Dorado, the characteristics of that early creole racism would also begin to change and be remade, transformed into more modern forms of cultural, economic, and social discrimination.

JERRY M. WILLIAMS

Popularizing the Ethic of Conquest:
Peralta Barnuevo's *Historia de España vindicada*

HISTORIA, *es una narracion, y exposicion de acontecimientos*
pasados: y en rigor es de aquellas cosas que el Autor de la
historia vio por sus propios ojos, y dà fee dellas, como testigo de
vista. . . . Pero basta que el historiador tenga buenos originales, y
Autores fidedignos de aquello que narra, y escribe, y que de
industria no miente, ó sea floxo en averiguar la verdad, antes
que la assegure como tal.

History is a narration and exposition of past events, and—
strictly speaking—of those happenings that the history's author
saw with his own eyes and so testifies as an eyewitness. . . . But
sometimes it is sufficient for the historian to have good original
sources and trustworthy authors for what he writes and
narrates and does not lie intentionally or be remiss in finding the
truth before he declares it so.
—Sebastian de Covarrubias, *Tesasurus de la lengua castellana*

Lima's Pedro Peralta Barnuevo (1664–1743), along with Mexico's Carlos Sigüenza y Góngora, has been called one of the few geniuses that America produced; he inherited many of the sobriquets last applied to Peninsular
writers such as Cervantes, Lope de Vega, and Calderón de la Barca: "fénix de los
ingenios" [phoenix of creative persons] and "monstruo de naturaleza" [prodigy
of nature]. Born almost one hundred years after Lope de Vega, he came to be

I acknowledge with gratitude the support and encouragement received from David Geis, Ruth
Hill, Neal A. Messer, David F. Slade, the Ibero-American division of the Society for Eighteenth-
Century Studies, and West Chester University's College of Arts and Sciences Development
Awards Program.

known as "el gran Peralta" [the great Peralta], "monstruo de erudición" [prodigy of erudition], "fénix americano" [the American phoenix], and the "Pico della Mirandola peruano" [Peruvian Pico della Mirandola], among other flattering titles. During his lifetime, Peralta wrote more than sixty-four works on subjects that range from astronomy and history to engineering and opera. The majority of his writings remain obscure, archived in rare book libraries and private collections. Indeed, Peralta is seldom studied in graduate programs, where he is often a parenthetical note to Peruvian letters. As a reflection of his vast talents, he served as the first professor of mathematics at the University of San Marcos, was the official cosmographer and chief engineer commissioned to draft and superintend military engineering projects and general public works, was the nation's poet laureate, operated his own Academy of Mathematics and Elocution, maintained a thriving practice as a lawyer and accountant, was a tax collector for the Royal Tribunal of Accounts, and was an intimate of viceroys, politicians, and the aristocracy. Peralta achieved recognition in Europe and America for his vast talents. Although he never traveled beyond the confines of his native Peru, he attracted the attention of the European scientific community when in 1717 the Royal Academy of Sciences in Paris, of which he was a member, published his *Observationes astromomicae, habitae Limae, totius Americae Australis emporii celeberrim*. French and Spanish scientists, such as Charles Marie La Condamine, Jorge Juan y Santicilia, and Antonio de Ulloa, traveled to Peru to seek his counsel.[1]

Historia de España vindicada (Lima, 1730) is one of Peralta's two major works that have yet to be fully appreciated by critics, who have failed to recognize its intimate conceptual link with *Lima fundada* (1732) as a history of conquest. The historical-scientific course that Peralta espoused in *Historia* gave rise to the poetic notion of conquest found in *Lima fundada*. The ambitious plan for *Historia*, frustrated by a number of factors, prepared the ground for a more successful and fundamentally poetic account of conquest in *Lima fundada*, an epic that affirms creole identity through an examination of the history of New World cultural and political formations. In *Historia* Peralta champions history

---

1. See my *Peralta Barnuevo and the Art of Propaganda: Politics, Poetry, and Religion in Eighteenth-Century Peru* (Newark, Del., 2001), 4. Among other laudations that Peralta garnered from academy colleagues we find "el Virgilio español" (the Spanish Virgil), "la honra del Perú" (the pride of Peru), "el primer poeta de América" (America's foremost poet), and "una enciclopedia viviente" (a living encyclopedia). Peralta's early poetic works are archived in the proceedings of the literary academy that Viceroy Castell-dos-Rius operated from September 23, 1709, until his death at age seventy on April 24, 1710. Ricardo Palma edited the proceedings and published them, along with a work by Juan del Valle y Caviedes, as *Flor de academias y diente del Parnasso* (Lima, 1899). In editing the volume, Palma did not include musical compositions.

as an art, expounds his "historical method," and attempts to chronicle and interpret the complex history of Spain's conquest of Old and New World lands. His cast of nations, empires, rulers, and diverse peoples—with their attendant ambitions, triumphs, and losses in war and genealogy—participates to create the modern Spain responsible for discovering and conquering the New World.[2]

In *Historia* Peralta does not base history on the themes of adventure and glory, nor does he limit himself to the territorial notion of conquest. His goals are to consider ways of rewriting and revisiting conquest and to render these criteria intelligible to a readership. Peralta's unique view of history and conquest is shaped by the French influences that accompany the Bourbon ascendancy to the throne in 1700. That political change ushered into the empire Cartesian thought and French neoclassical philosophy and poetics and led to a restructuring of the bureaucracy as part of a plan to resuscitate the crown and its faded empire. The remaining constituents of Peralta's revision of conquest are divine Providence, tradition, geography, climate, and human will. Through a didactic and moral concept of conquest, Peralta—within his creole situation and contradictory modernity vis-à-vis French aesthetics—acknowledges epic models of conquerors but shifts emphasis from a European notion of conquest to a creole interpretation of it as applied to Peru. The latter is delimited by governance, service, development over arms, and the interplay of political and religious discourses (conquest of providentialism and an invitation to conquest). Peralta views conquest, achieved by military means in order to affirm imperialism, to be of no less consequence than conquest occasioned by love of liberty and peace: a nation's tranquility is achieved through its ability to resist configuring peace in the face of ambition and by allowing itself to be disarmed by nature. In *Historia* nationhood that reflects imperial ties is linked to bloodlines, or *privilegios de la sangre,* whereas Peruvian nationhood is defined by the soil: *nuestro suelo, patrio suelo, la nobleza del primitivo suelo* [our soil, homeland, the nobility of the native earth].[3]

By targeting *Historia* to a Peninsular and Peruvian audience that, by inference, would come to understand Spain's complicated conquest of Peru,

2. Pedro de Peralta Barnuevo, *Historia de España vindicada* (Lima, 1730) (hereafter cited as *Historia*).

3. José Antonio Mazzotti avers that "ideas about creoles, epic, and ethnic nationhood were mutually constructed and nearly always articulated—albeit in a veiled fashion—in relation to the other social subjects of the Viceroyalties"; see "Epic, Creoles, and Nation in Spanish America," in Susan Castillo and Ivy Schweitzer, eds., *A Companion to the Literatures of Colonial America* (Malden, Mass., 2005), 496. In his essay above, Mazzotti analyzes how the word "nation" was employed and identifies the body of writings that helped to articulate the concept of creole nationhood.

Peralta sees himself as serving both the monarchy and its American colony and defending the political and religious entity of nation *(nación)*, or group identification. At the time of Spain's patent military decline, when "sceptres and sciences" had displaced arms, Peralta asserts, as he had done in 1714 in *Imagen política del gobierno*, that letters form an integral presence in the tripartite relationship of sceptres, sciences, and letters. As Ruth Hill has stated, the rise of men of letters and the decline of men of arms led Hispanic humanists to promote physical atomism and a dynamic interpretation of heroism and conquest, which helped to maintain political and religious institutions and defend a stratified society. Peralta conceives of himself as a modern warrior of the state, whose weapon—the pen—defends the nación as valiantly as had any soldier. In the words of his brother José, Peralta's

> arte para persuadir ... es una fortaleza y vivacidad de entendimiento que, aunque pacífica, no es menor y puede ser más útil al público que la fuerza de los espíritus guerreros; y la posteridad conocerá que sirvió a la gloria de la nación con la pluma, como los valerosos capitanes con la espada.

> art of persuasion ... is a strength and vivacity of understanding that, though peaceful, is no less so, and can be more useful to the public than the strength of warlike spirits; and posterity will know that he brought glory to his country with the pen as much as brave captains did with the sword.[4]

Within Peralta's conceptualization of history, he is a literary conqueror now forced to wage war and investigate truth on the battlefield of history, to which Peninsular historians had laid waste and left the origin of Spain's language, towns, rulers, saints, and triumphs and losses confused and injured. Spain, its provinces, and colonies were to find vindication in *Historia*. References abound in the text to the fertility and force of the pen and its ability to persuade,

---

4. José Peralta, "Carta," in *Historia*, unpaginated front matter. Luis Monguió affirms that the definition of *nación* as race or caste is prevalent in viceregal Peru, in "Palabras e ideas: 'Patria' y 'Nación' en el virreinato del Perú," *Revista iberoamericana*, XLIV (1978), 451–470. In positing that a reconceptualization of late Baroque and Enlightenment culture is required because we lack a viable scholarly archetype, Ruth Hill postulates a series of three developments that are key to disentangling the modern legacy of humanists, who smoothed a middle ground between scholastics and moderns in Spain and Spanish America: "Hispanic humanists participated in the inventing of traditions and historical continuity, a process which entailed Visigothic and Castilian customs and the imperial traditions, at the same time that they confronted them." Her analysis of Peralta's notion of group identification is crucial to contextualizing his defense of Roman versus Visigoth ethnic, political, and religious origins of the Spanish nation, a cause that the Bourbon regime promoted. See Ruth Hill, *Sceptres and Sciences in the Spains: Four Humanists and the New Philosophy (ca. 1680–1740)* (Liverpool, 2000), 14.

influence, injure, redress, beautify, and serve: "Por esto podré decir que si he acertado a consagrar mi anhelo, la mayor parte de las provincias de España quedarán gloriosamente servidas de mi pluma" (*Historia,* Prologue, unnumbered folio). [This is why I will be able to state that, if I have succeeded in consecrating my desire, the majority of Spain's provinces will be served gloriously by my pen.] *Historia* filled a void in Spain's history at a time when the Peninsula was in transition from practicing the sword and the art of war to defending its colonial situation through the efforts of men and women of letters.[5]

The trajectory of the notion of the pen as a weapon—first introduced in *Imagen política*—culminates in *Historia,* which, when compared to other contemporary histories, begins with the earliest origins of Spain. In *Imagen política* Peralta discourses on the importance of arms and letters flourishing together and how, without science, neither could exist:

> No sólo se defienden con las armas y se mantienen con [las] del despacho y la abundancia los imperios. Son necesarias las letras para su buen gobierno. Sin las ciencias no hay armas ni política: son débiles las fuerzas sin orden y bárbaras las repúblicas sin arte. Caminan tan a un paso armas y letras que jamás han estado en un reino triunfantes las unas que no vean florecientes las otras.

> Without sciences, there are no arms or politics: forces without order are weak, and republics without art are barbarian. Arms and letters walk hand in hand, so much so that we have never seen in a kingdom the former triumph without the latter flourishing.

Where Antonio de Nebrija in 1492, on the heels of the reconquest of Spain, had called for the Peninsula to be united by arms and letters, as were the church and state, Peralta centuries later—after the Golden Age was but a memory, and at a time when the colonies were menaced by piracy and political and economic hardship—renews the call in *Historia.*[6]

The discourse on arms and letters takes on a moral tone when it refers to the dangers that surround regents. Exposed kingdoms similar to Spain, although favored by God, can be led into decline and ruin by political errors and violation of principles of governance, which precipitate rapid decay of power.

5. A fine example of the debate over the decline and defense of men-of-arms is Pedro José Bermúdez de la Torre y Solier, *Ilustración de la destreza Indiana* (Lima, 1712), written under the pseudonym Francisco Santos de la Paz.

6. Pedro de Peralta Barnuevo, *Imagen política del gobierno* . . . (Lima, 1714), fols. 79–81.

La extensión de los dominios no produce el aumento de las fuerzas: antes
las diminuye. En los mayores imperios la cumbre de la grandeza ha sido
abismo de la profanidad, y como todo lo que subieron de escasos se
despeñaron de abundantes. Por cuya falta ha sido la España un imperio
universal de frutos que se han tenido todas las naciones para alistarlo
contra ella. (Angel Ventura Calderón y Cevallos, front matter to *Historia*)

The expansion of territories does not produce an increase in strength; on
the contrary, it diminishes it. In the greatest empires the height of their
greatness has become an abyss of profanity, and, as with everything, those
who climbed the highest when poor fell to the lowest when rich. Because
of this shortcoming, Spain has been a universal empire of production that
all nations have held to levy against her.

Spain's population and culture are not only its greatest capital but also its most
vital asset. In *Imagen política* Peralta had sounded a similar moral admonition to
the monarchy.[7]

Historia consists of 72 unnumbered pages of front matter printed on both
sides, followed by 822 numbered pages, each divided into two columns, and 144
unnumbered pages, among which are bound 24 engraved portraits within
decorated borders of rulers such as the Egyptian Hercules, Hispano, Hannibal,
Scipio, Viriathus, Sertorius, Julius Cesar, Trajan, Theodosius, and Wallia. The
72 pages of front matter begin with an explanation of the frontispiece, followed
by licenses, approval letters, the author's Prologue, and a genealogical overview
of illustrious Roman families cited in each of the five books. The front matter
concludes with an index to the 68 chapters and a table of errata. Book 1 covers
the geography and natural riches of Spain, the languages and religions of early
settlers, the arrival of the Greeks, the power of Carthage, and the ruin of
Sagunto. It offers provocative commentary on the decadence of Spain's monarchy. Book 2 examines Roman rule in Spain, the campaigns of Gnaeus Scipio
Cornelius, Scipio Africanus, Viriathus, Sertorius, Julius Caesar, and Augustus; it
also discusses the ruin of Numantia and numerous battles. Book 3 is devoted to

7. Ibid., fols. 83–87. In *De rege et regis institutione* (1598) the controversial Jesuit historian Juan
de Mariana postured in favor of the notion that the state and, in rare cases and under special
circumstances, the individual are justified in removing a tyrant from office (chap. 6). Mariana's
treatise was thought to be a considerable motivating factor that led to the assassination in 1610 of
Henry IV of France. Its three books treat the function of the king and the scope of royal authority,
the education of princes, and the ways of governing one's subjects. Mariana's point of view
upheld doctrinal Catholic philosophy with respect to rule: true authority originated in God, who
conferred that faculty to nations that make collective judgments about its ruler. (Mariana did not
clarify how God conferred his authority to nations.)

FIGURE 13. Frontispiece. Pedro Peralta Barnuevo, *Historia de España vindicada*. 1730. Courtesy The John Carter Brown Library

the preaching of James the apostle and the apparition of Nuestra Señora del Pilar at Zaragoza, and the subsequent martyrdom of James. Book 4 is a protracted treatment of the deeds of various emperors and celebrated Spaniards and treats the origins of the Christian Church and its ecclesiastical hierarchy, the German invasion, the Council at Illiberis (Elne), and the tyranny of Eugene. It ends with the councils at Zaragoza and Toledo. Book 5 inquires into the invasions of the fifth century by the Alans, the Suevi, and the Vandals, the last days of Roman Spain, and the origin, rule, and settlements of the Visigoths; it concludes with the death of Leovigild and the end of Arian domination.

The engraved copper frontispiece (see Figure 13), explained in the first pages of *Historia,* illustrates the physical-geographical and philosophic-religious notion of conquest reflected in Peralta's historical method. Ascending gradations of Religione (firm religious piety) and Constantia (perseverance) lead to the goddess, Queen Spain, who is seated atop the gradation of Fortitudini as testimony to the natural quality of strength that marks her people. Bearing a sceptre in her left hand and a portrait of Fernando VI, she presides over arms, letters, and sciences. A laurel-crowned muse, kneeling on a globe that displays only the names of South America and Lima, extends to Queen Spain a copy of *Historia.*

Historia is designed to model a scientific inquiry in which fiction, myth, and legend have no place. Peralta's objective is to reprove historians who "angered truth" by stretching it with digressions into fabulous accounts. The motives for writing the history were many but were guided by a search for truth and a desire to see Spain reflected in a clearer light by which she could be defended for the good of the nación.

> Ver padecer a España unos despojos de historia y unos atentados de discursos; el derecho de su primera población quitado a Tubal; su originaria lengua a fuerza de disputarla, oscurecida; sus antiguos reyes, por quererlos verificados, confundidos; las primitivas glorias de sus patronos y sus santos, destruidas; . . . y, lo que es más doloroso, ver mucho de esto ejecutado por mano de los más obligados a su culto; la firmeza de las épocas y los tiempos vacilantes; la pérdida y recuperación de España tan confusas que parece quedó más arruinada a la memoria que al dominio; y en fin la fijeza de muchos sucesos desquiciada: han sido todos poderosos impulsos que, haciéndoseme compasión en la noticia, se me formaron violencia en el trabajo. (*Historia,* Prologue)

> To see Spain suffer some plundering of her history and attacked in speeches; the right of her first population taken away from Thubal; her

original language obscured by dint of so much arguing about it; her ancient kings confused because of oververification; the primitive glories of her patrons and saints destroyed; . . . and what is more painful, to see most of the firmness of the times and periods in doubt; the loss and recovery of Spain so confused that it seems it was ruined much more by memory than by occupation; and finally the certainty of many events unhinged. All these have become powerful impulses that, although they moved me to compassion when I discerned them, made me outraged in my work.

Unlike other modern historians, Peralta cites the necessity of begining *Historia* with the origins of Peninsular Spain in order to cleanse the inaccuracies of early works and to compare Spain's origins with those of Peru. His task is facilitated by cartographic and narrative models that range from New World chroniclers such as José de Acosta, Bartolomé de las Casas, and Gerónimo de Mendieta to diverse European writers such as Jean Bodin and René Rapin. As an example, Peralta cites as one of his models Lucas Fernández de Piedrahita's *Historia general de las conquistas del Nuevo Reyno de Granada* (which Luis Fernando Restrepo studies above). Both writers intend for their histories—a product of the colonial archive of the metropolis and a reflection of Christian history—to find acceptance locally and nationally. Since Peralta's stated desire is to avoid the errors other historians had committed, he would comment less on the ancient centuries in favor of modern times, thus focusing on emperors whose governments were connected to Spain in some meaningful way.[8]

History, in its broadest application, is to be measured by its excellence as a moralizing, didactic teacher who furthers the cause of learning. In judging his style to be unaffected, unlike that of his contemporaries, Peralta reasoned that the purity of history resided in the particular style of historians, their choice of

8. Peralta cites the stylistic reasons he esteems selected Peninsular authors: "Y en cuanto al modo universal añadiré en el juicio a Morales, a Zurita y al marqués de Mondéjar; en la elegancia a Saavedra, en la suavidad a Solís, y a Abarca en la hermosura" (Prologue). [With respect to universal style I will add to this judgment Morales, Zurita, and the marquis of Mondéjar; in elegance, Saavedra, in gentleness, Solís, and in beauty, Abarca.] In the text and marginal notes of *Historia* are found the numerous primary and seconday writers whose life or works had an impact on Spain's political and intellectual development, and by inference on Peru's literary and cultural history as well.

The two works by Rapin that Peralta cites in *Historia* are *Réflexions sur l'usage de l'éloquence de ce temps* (1672) and *Instruction por l'histoire* (1677). In the former Rapin defines art as "good sense reduced to method," contends that pleasing the rules is a bad principle, and laments the lack of a natural style found in Spanish and Italian bucolic poetry; in the latter eloquence (rhetoric)—as a teacher unbound by technical dictates, who pleases while instructing, and appeals to the temperament and discretion of an audience—is to be found in all disciplines.

words, clarity of narration, the brilliance of their aphorisms, the force of their clauses, their sense of judgment or definition of a character's dilemma, and the discernment of their praise. A well-composed history based on truth would inspire or persuade readers to action, for they would see in it models of conduct and a variety of human experiences. Peralta specifies that the design of history is to aid the memory in serving comprehension. An expert writer's appeal lay in the ability to rework history for mass consumption by making it more palatable, as evidenced in the successes enjoyed by ancient authors, namely Cicero, Sallust, and Livy, whose style approaches that of Virgil. Rewriting history, Peralta instructs, is akin to seeing better in adjusted lighting or making sweeter music on a different lyre: "¿Por qué la historia no ha de ilustrar, y no se ha de oir más atractiva en mejor pluma? No es esto defender mi estilo (que eso sería presumir), sino mi deseo, que es sólo aspirarlo. . . . ¿Dónde han de ir a buscarse las noticias si no puede haber quien las escriba ciertas?" (*Historia,* Prologue). [Why should not history enlighten, and why should it not be heard in a more attractive way written by a better pen? It is not a question of defending my style (for that would be presumptuous of me), but rather my wish, which is the only thing I aspire to. . . . Where is one supposed to find reports if there is no one who can write them accurately?] He sees himself engaged in a collective task that will result in a collective good. This political philosophy regarding history and the historian's role broke with the classical tradition, which it used as a point of departure and anchor; it embraced the critical methods of Bodin's *Methodus ad facilem historiarum cognitionem* (1566) but fell short of reflecting Voltaire's concern with the moral and social aspects of history.[9]

Peralta believes that his job as historian is to avoid dissipating a reader's animus with confused narratives and antiquated words and to facilitate understanding. He makes a case for supplementing Thucydides' prose in the incomplete *History of the Peloponnesian War:* "Sé lo que se ha notado de las digresiones de Tucídides, derivado de la crisis que de él hizo Dionisio Halicarnaso. Pero fue merecida censura de su confusión, de que sirve de ejemplo el modo con que procedió en el libro tercero de su *Historia*" (*Historia,* Prologue). [I know what has been remarked about Thucydides' digressions, which derived from the analysis that Dionysius of Halicarnassus made of his work. But it was a deserved criticism of his confusion, as exemplified by the way in which he

---

9. Jean Bodin's *Methodus ad facilem historiarum cognitionem* (1566) laid the groundwork for his philosophy of history (later published in *La république,* 1579) and posed his theory about the influence of climate over society, government, and progress. Peralta admired Bodin's concept of sovereignty (where the monarch is absolute with powers that derive both from magistracy and the law) and the nation-state.

proceeded in the third book of his *History*.] He argues that, before Thucydides finished writing about the Mytilenes, he started to narrate the events at Lacedaemon (Laconia), the story of which he also left unfinished, because he diverted his attention to the siege at Plataea, which he interrupted in order to return to the war at Mytilene (Lesbos); from there he jumped to the sedition of the inhabitants of Corcyra (Corfu, or Kérkira) and their war with Corinth and went on to discuss the first expedition of the Athenians in Sicily and other accounts. The end result was a deformed tree whose trunk and branches had been cut. *Historia,* boasts Peralta, is neither truncated nor confused. The lack of confusion is due more to his marginalia than to simplicity and tight organization of his material, for digressions abound, as do factual errors. This critical appraisal is indicative of how Peralta employs classical authors to both support his claim of producing a modern history more free of errors than others and how his style is superior to that of accepted authors, such as Livy. In a letter that precedes the Prologue, his brother José, a member of the Convent of Preachers and later bishop of La Paz and Buenos Aires, found:

> En Tito Livio también hallaron qué notar, aunque defectos más ligeros; habiendo sido más feliz por no haber caído entre las manos de un crítico tan acre como Dionisio, y por el gran respeto que ha tenido la antigüedad a su mérito. Pero con todo se le nota el estilo muy difuso, con que queriéndolo amplificar todo, carece de la fuerza y vigor que se admira en el otro. . . . Que afecta servirse de términos muy antiguos que no están de uso, y que tiene modos de hablar incógnitos a los demás autores; y otros varios, aunque siempre ligeros, como he dicho. (*Historia,* Prologue)

> In Titus Livy the critics also found something to reprove, although they were minor defects; and that was because he was fortunate enough not to fall under the scrutiny of such a harsh critic as Dionysius and because of the great respect that antiquity had for his merit. But, after all, it is obvious that he possessed a very diffuse style, because—in his effort to dissect everything—he lacks the force and vigor that are admired in Dionysius. . . . His affected use of very old terms, now obsolete; his way of writing, unknown to other authors; and several other examples, although, as I have said, very minor ones.

For Peralta, history is the essential element that links different epochs of human experiences. Its three qualities are truth (a mirror of existence), elegance (a lighted candle of the soul), and instruction (the impulse to imitate): "El alma de ella es la verdad, el cuerpo el orden, el traje la elocuencia, la reflexión la voz, y la acción el fruto" (*Historia,* Prologue). [Its soul is truth; its body, order; its clothes, eloquence; its reflexion, voice; and its action, growth.] History and poetry are distinguished by their elegance and can be understood once the reader takes note of their beauty:

> En fin un poema de la verdad sin metro; pues dejando a lo poético la fábula, la invención, la figura y el ritmo, se tiene toda el alma de la poesía en su elegancia. . . . Solamente ha de tener la historia la forma, no la materia, de la poesía; y el estilo del pensar, no del decir. (*Historia,* Prologue)

> In short it is a poem of beauty, but without verses; in fact, leaving poetry to fiction, invention, form and rhythm, its elegance holds all the soul of poetry. . . . History needs to possess only the form, not the matter, of poetry; and the style of thinking, not of speaking.

In his estimation, what was called history in his day was confused with relations, memories, and annals. It should appear that poets imitate the style of historians, and not vice versa.[10]

The Prologue underscores this charge. It sets forth the models and rules Peralta uses in dividing *Historia* chronologically into episodes, or *estados,* the first of which corresponds to the period of Liberty, from the founding of Spain to the invasion of the Carthaginians and Romans. The second period is of wars and conquests that conditioned the Roman Empire, "que es el tiempo de la más triste sujeción, es el de la más clara memoria" (*Historia,* Prologue) [which is the time of the most sorrowful domination and the clearest memory], for which he relies on Livy. Peninsular and Roman sources inform Peralta's assessment of the period of monarchy founded under the Visigoths, where the blood of conquerors and conquered mix to form a dominant lineage. The third is the modern era, which comprises ten centuries, starting with the loss of Spain under the Moors up to the eighteenth century. For the fourth period, he adjudges that official documentation is wanting because Spain was engaged more in exercising "la espada y las artes de la guerra" [the sword and arts of war] than in providing accurate and reliable historical accounts.

Peralta adheres to Rapin's historical model and straddles a middle ground between extremes, which allows his providential view of history to accommodate the radical empiricism or Cartesian spirit represented by modern historians:

10. The extent to which Peralta recognizes that *Historia* courses a new direction in historiography is the subject of Guillermo Lohmann Villena, "Concepto de la historia en Peralta Barnuevo," *Revista Histórica,* XXVII (1964), 31–41.

Nota el amenísimo Rapín en aquella su admirable reflexión sobre la historia porque ella es la que forma el más vasto plano del entendimiento, del juicio, de la despasión y de aquella nobleza de expresiones que, sin caer a las humildades del bajo estilo, trepe al sublime y pomposo fausto de moda levantada, de suerte que tomar el medio en estos dos extremos ha sido el más crítico punto de este género de estudio. (Juan de Gazitúa, "Approval" letter in *Historia*)

Witty Rapin observes in his admirable reflexion on history that history forms the highest plane of understanding, judgment, dispassion and that nobility of expression that, without falling into the humblest realm of low style, climbs to the sublime and pompous splendour of high fashion, so that taking the middle road between these two extremes has been the most critical point of this kind of study.

The middle ground makes possible an embrace of modern historians whose texts reflect Cartesian influences. In accordance with French neoclassical norms, Peralta's style was not only natural but was also clear, orderly, sublime, and restrained—yet florid—in the way he applied Rapin's concept of history

Inasmuch as Peralta writes for the general public, reading *Historia* does not presuppose knowledge of the complex history of Spain's origins. In retelling history, his job is to personalize it, as in narrating the collective suicide of the inhabitants of Sagunto against the impulses of Hannibal (book 1, cols. 285– 295), or the sacrifice of the inhabitants of Numantia (book 2). By seducing the imagination, establishing an affinity between the readership and the text, and observing the Cartesian model of making unencumbered transitions from one narration to the next, he seeks to have readers invest in the foundation of their own history. History profits from adornment and embellishment as "un animado viviente de razón. . . . El fin de ésta es la instrucción y así fue preciso que en ella sirviese al entendimiento la memoria" (Prologue) [an animated living being with reason. . . . The latter's goal is education, and it was thus necessary that—to this end—memory would aid understanding]. Yet Peralta owns that, in exceeding the limits of historian to become an apologist, his zeal exposes him to censorship.

Si se juzgaze que he excedido en estos capítulos los términos de historiador y he pasado a los de apologista, perdónese esto a la naturaleza de un asunto en que va el celo de la verdad histórica tan al lado del de la nación, considerando que cuando la sinrazón discurre ofensas, es preciso

que la razón pronuncie desagravios. En lo demás, . . . créase la defensa y
sufro la censura. (Book 3, cols. 799–800)

If one were to judge that in these chapters I have overstepped the
boundaries of a historian and have become an apologist, attribute it to
the nature of a matter in which zeal for historical truth goes together
with the zeal for the country, considering that, when foolishness incurs
offenses, it is necessary for reason to provide disclaimers. For the rest . . .
accept my defense, and I will accept your criticism.

To controvert the authority of Peninsular historians was considered unpatriotic
and a transgression against truth and verisimilitude, because it too diminished
the "paradoja de historia" (book 1, col. 27) [paradox of history] of those who
stated, for example, that Spain was the cradle of humanity and the seat of Eden.
When Peralta refutes ancient and modern historians, he acknowledges the
difficulty in remaining unbiased: "Bien quisiera mi genio poder aplicarse al
partido de los modernos bien afectos, pero esto sería no ser historiador sino
abogado, y hacer sospechoso lo ínclito justamente alabado con lo perverso
falsamente defendido" (book 5, col. 1544). [My mind would very much like to
side with the well-intentioned modern historians. However, in that case I would
not be a historian but, rather, an apologist, and I would render suspect the
illustrious that is so highly praised as well as the perverse, so falsely defended.]
In the Prologue to *Historia,* he chastises Florián de Ocampo for his shortcomings in documenting Spain's history only up to the death of the two
Scipios; Ambrosio de Morales for chronicling only up to King Bermudo el Tercero; Alfonso Núñez de Castro, who pursuing Saavedra, stopped with Henry II;
and, others who, like José Pellicer de Ossáu Salas y Tovar, began their history by
recounting Spain's losses but quickly fell into digressions and violated the
Spanish language. Hence, Peralta justifies his mission in writing still another
traditional yet corrective history:

Y así me pareció que haría un singular servicio a la nación y al orbe
político si acertase a escribir una historia de España comprehensiva,
corregida y corriente, en la cual sola tuviese cualquiera las de todos, y en
fin una historia vindicada de aquellos agravios que hace el amor tan bien
como la emulación.

And so it seemed to me that I would perform a distinct service to the
nation and the political sphere if I managed to write a comprehensive,
amended, and current history of Spain, so that anyone could find in just

this book everything in all of those others, and in short a history
vindicated of those mistakes that love, as well as emulation, creates.

The rationale for going against the grain of historiography and writing a history
that begins with Spain's earliest origins is that it will redress the egregious errors
of past historians, strengthen the nation-state, and furnish both Peninsular and
Peruvian subjects alike with an account of the past both share.[11]

In outlining his historical method, or "order," Peralta accuses Peninsular
historians of presenting historical facts as if they were anecdotes, and not upholding the commendable models of Sallust, Livy, and Lucius Annaeus Florus.
The historical-scientific method of *Historia* entails studying in detail the physical and political geography of the Iberian Peninsula; establishing and measuring positions, longitude, and latitude by using procedures agreed on by the
Royal Academy of Paris; consulting ancient and modern maps published in
Paris and Amsterdam; and following observations and tables from the royal
Spanish observatory. Those modern instruments allow him to challenge historians, theologians, and astronomical calculations in order to pinpoint, for example, the exact date, hour, and age of Christ at the time of his death (book 3, cols.
869–675), to favor Cassiodorus's over Idacio's calculation for computing the
beginning of Thurismundo's reign and the death of Theodoric (book 5, col.
1378), and to reject speculative conclusions and errors advanced by Tertullian
and Giovanni Battista Riccioli, among others, regarding the coming of the

---

11. *Los quatro libros primeros de la Crónica general de España* (1543) of Florián Ocampo, royal
chronicler in 1539, was the unreliable source on which other historians (notably Ambrosio de
Morales) based their faulty history by following Ocampo's falsehoods, which were a reflection of
his patriotism. Morales's *Descripción de España* (1574) (also known as *Crónica general de España*)
was a continuation of Ocampo's history. The contribution of Morales was to describe his method
of writing history. He produced a second volume in 1577 entitled *Las antigüedades de las ciudades
de España que van nombradas en la Corónica*. Diego de Saavedra Fajardo, Spanish diplomat, wrote
Corona gothica, castellana, y austriaca, políticamente ilustrada (1646), which emphasizes the vital
role the Visigoths played in furthering the Spanish political state, which Peralta uses to prove
Spain's religious and political continuity. Peralta identified with Saavedra Fajardo's assessment of
Spain's decadence, his concise style, pleasingly quaint knowledge of historical data, and uncon-
tested patriotism. As the official chronicler of Castile (1629) and Aragon (1637), José Pellicer de
Ossáu Salas y Tovar, poet and historian, authored more than two hundred works, two of which
Peralta cites in *Historia: Aparato a la monarquía antigua de las Españas, en los tiempos del mundo, el
adelón, el míthico, y el histórico* (1671) and *Anales de la monarquía de España después de su pérdida*
(1681), completed after his death by his son Miguel. A copy of the *Anales* was listed in the
inventory of Peralta's library. Alonso Núñez de Castro's pedestrian history entitled *Coronica de los
señores reyes de Castilla, Don Sancho el Deseado, Don Alonso el Octauo, y Don Enrique el Primero*
(1665) was a continuation of Saavedra Fajardo's *Corona gothica*. As Núñez de Castro drew on
multiple sources, he was able to span the years A.D. 716 to the rule of Henry II of Castile in the
fourteenth century.

apostle James to Spain. In the nomenclature of cities and places, Peralta surpasses Ambrosio de Morales and Jean Moret by employing Pliny, Ptolemy, Strabo, Pomponius Mela, Livy, and Polybius.[12]

The principal fault of Peralta's retrospective patriotism is his insistence on a pious adherence to the glories that false traditions and ecclesiastical history promoted within the Spanish church: chimerical bishops, saints, and martyrs and a credulous attitude toward legends and myths. In his religious zeal he accepts without questioning the tenet held by Isidore of Seville, Ocampo, Juan de Ferreras, and Juan de Mariana that Tubal, son of Japheth and grandson of Noah, was a primitive inhabitant of Spain. Against Pellicer, he recreates the travels of Bacchus and Pan throughout Spain; he accords recognition to the travels of the apostle James and the transfer of his body from Jerusalem to Galicia (book 3, chaps. 1–4, 8); he accedes to the miraculous apparition of the Virgin in the Pilar de Zaragoza (book 3, chaps. 5–7); he makes a case for the monotheism of ancient Iberians (Galicians, Asturians, Cantabrians); and, against Ferreras and Pellicer he avows the presence in Spain of the warrior-legislator Egyptian Hercules during the struggle of the Tartessians against the Phoenicians (book 1, chap. 8). In addition, he distorts the history of Hermenegild and accepts Leovigild's public retraction of Arianism (book 5, chap. 19); he rejects that the Arian Visigoths, as Spain's enemy, could have ever received divine intervention in battle against Chlodoveoch (Clovis II), king of the Franks (book 5, chap. 12). He applauds the arrival and the havoc of the Berbers as a providential salvation; and, in accepting Spain as a Visigothic monarchy, he excuses the Goths of all errors, namely the sacking of Rome. Last, his credulity leads him to see the fall of imperial Rome only as divine retribution for ancient persecutions against Christianity.[13]

---

12. *Investigaciones históricas de las antigüedades del reino de Navarra* (1655) by José de Moret later served as a preface to *Anales del reino de Navarra* (1684–1704), continued by Francisco de Aleson.

13. In its treatment and use of historical data, *Historia* shows strong influences of Juan de Mariana's 1592 masterpiece, *Historiae de rebus Hispaniae libri XXX* (the first part of which was translated into Spanish in 1601 as *Historia general de España*), dedicated to Philip III. Of greater literary than historic value, it traces the founding of Spain by Tubal, son of Japheth, up to the court of Charles V (Charles I of Spain). He modeled the austere style of the work after the histories of Livy and Sallust, but its principal defect was Mariana's credulous reliance on the fabulous sources he employed and the severity with which he reprehended the vices of princes. Peralta identified with Mariana's declaration that his role was not to write history but rather to "poner en orden y estilo lo que otros habían recogido . . . sin obligarme a averiguar todos los particulares. . . . Ninguno se atreve a decir a los reyes la verdad; todos ponen la mira en sus particulares: miseria grande, y que de ninguna cosa se padece mayor mengua que en las casas reales" (*Historia*, lii) [put in order and style what other [historians] have gathered . . . without obligating

Nearly forty years after its publication, *Historia* was considered a scarce book and unavailable for purchase. In 1769 Ignacio de Escandón, in a letter to José Eusebio de Llano Zapata, lamented that it was one of many books that could not be found in Lima. In 1874, Juan María Gutiérrez remarked that the book rarely appeared for sale in European book catalogs, despite its importance as a provocative affront to the Spanish crown on the part of a creole whose erudition represented a contradictory modernity in philosophy, style, and politics.[14]

Peralta undertook the burden of writing *Historia* without the financial backing required to see the entire project to completion. Economic constraints were a factor when he published only one of four volumes of this magnum opus. The first volume chronicled up to and including the end of the sixth century; the last of the four volumes would have concluded with the death of Carlos II and the end of the Austrian empire. A catalog in *Lima fundada* of unpublished works overoptimistically stated: "Se está imprimiendo el segundo [tomo]." [The second volume is at press.][15]

Although Peralta dedicated *Historia* to Fernando VI (1713–1759), prince of

---

myself to verify the details. . . . No one dares to tell kings the truth; everyone minds his personal affairs, of which nothing suffers greater shame in royal houses]. Juan de Ferreras, theologian and historian, served as chief librarian in 1716 at the Academia Real Española and contributor to its *Diccionario de autoridades*. His *Synópsis histórica chonológica de España* (17 vols., 1700–1727) earned him fame as a modern historian, as did *Dissertatio de praedictione evangelii in Hispania per s. apostolum Jacobum Zebedaeum* (1705). Peralta cites both works in *Historia*. José de la Riva Agüero adjudges *Historia* a provincial publication, whose lacunae reflect a systematic or apologetical defense and indicates a backward spirit; see "Don Pedro Peralta (fragmento de un ensayo sobre los historiadores nacidos en el Perú)," *Revista histórica*, IV (1909), 104–157, esp. 147.

14. Juan María Gutiérrez, "Doctor Don Pedro de Peralta-peruano," *Revista del Río de la Plata*, VIII (1874), 441. Llano Zapata echoed a similar complaint: "Tanto más necesitamos este socorro como que en España son bien raros los libros de autores americanos, ya sean de los impresos allá, ya de los que se imprimieron acá." "Prueba clara de esta verdad es que no hemos podido aún encontrar con toda nuestra diligencia la *Historia* del Padre Acosta, la *Bibliotheca* de Antonio de León Pinelo, la *Historia de España* de D. Pedro Peralta y Barnuevo, ni aún completas las *Décadas de Herrera*" (José Toribio Medina, *La imprenta en Lima* [Santiago de Chile, 1904], 3, 18). [We need this request so much since it seems that in Spain books by American authors are quite rare, be they printed over there or here. . . . Clear proof of this truth is that despite our diligence we have not been able to find Father Acosta's *History*, Antonio de León Pinelo's *Bibliotheca*, don Pedro Peralta y Barnuevo's *History of Spain*, nor even a complete set of Herrera's *Decades*.]

15. Pedro de Peralta Barnuevo, *Lima fundada, o, conquista del Peru* (Lima, 1732). In a letter dated April 19, 1733, Peralta requested a royal subvention for three thousand reals annually for a six-year period to complete the remaining three volumes. The solicitation was unsuccessful, despite the lobbying of prestigious supporters. Peralta made the initial request to Pardo de Figueroa in a letter that is of singular importance in tracing the composition and publication of *Historia*. The letter, written after the first volume was published, calls into question both the mention of the second volume and the physical and economic plight of its author. The full text of the letter is in Jerry M. Williams, "Feijoo and Peralta Barnuevo: Two Letters," *Dieciocho: Hispanic Enlightenment*, XXI (1998), 237–246.

Asturias, it was Felipe V and the Spanish court that he sought to impress. Felipe V never acknowledged *Historia,* and there is no evidence that he ever knew about this demonstration of Peralta's devotion as a loyal subject. Peralta's discourse of loyalty is a continuation of the discourse of commentary found in the body of sixteenth- and seventeenth-century chronicles of South America and in histories of Spain by Peninsular authors. Peralta's design is similar in nature to the work of his compatriot, Inca Garcilaso de la Vega, who preceded him by two centuries and disputed conventional historiography by writing a reclaimed history of the Inca empire. In his role as spokesperson and chronicler, on whom viceroys and dignitaries relied for inditing the official view of history, and in deference to the Spanish crown, Peralta asks that the history of Spain be shaped by the uniqueness of his mature creole voice. On repeated occasions he had proven himself adept at using the written discourse of loyalty to control, order, and influence public opinion, as reflected in his festive, religious, and political writings. At the forefront of Peralta's discourse of loyalty to the Bourbon monarchy is the ever-present image of Peru and his beloved Lima.

Spain's decline as a world power and its moral and economic bankruptcy are among the issues that Peralta addresses in an attempt to vindicate her honor. In a hierarchical structure, where the monarch was absolute, Peralta considers the viceroys to be ministers or extensions of the crown in the New World, servants to be guided by principles of loyalty and servitude, as would be expected of national subjects: "Es el príncipe una deidad ante la cual no tiene la lengua otra misión que el himno o el ruego." [The prince is a god before whom speech's only mission is a hymn or entreaty.] Peralta regards America as prospering from its relationship with Spain. Peru was better off than other Spanish colonies because it thrived under the largesse of the Bourbon era. In effect, he accepts that Spain, as head of an American empire, had inherited not only the history of Rome but also its majesty and power. This scheme promotes monarchical sovereignty over territorial possessions as justifiable within the framework of history and *Historia.* In supporting monarchical absolutism with his pen, Peralta supports the case for Spain's colonies' constituting, if not the head of the Spanish government, at least the heart of its wealth.[16]

Historia is as much a tribute to the glory of Spain and the Bourbon dynasty as it is to the role that Peru had played in furthering Spain's greatness. Com-

16. Pedro de Barnuevo Peralta, *El templo de la fama vindicado* (Lima, 1720), 15. According to Luis Martín, Peralta is a "staunch defender of the *real patronato,* the authority of the crown over ecclesiastical matters, and he saw the king as a quasi-divine figure to whom absolute obedience and respect were always due." Luis Martín, *The Kingdom of the Sun: A Short History of Peru* (New York, 1974), 108.

parisons between Spain and America (and, by extension, Peru) exist in three basic areas: (1) Spain's and America's shared circumstances as former and present colonies, (2) linguistic dominance, and (3) the early religious systems of each country. America's relationship to Spain is a mirror image of the close ties that had existed between Spain and Rome, a political affiliation that had produced distinguished literary figures.

> No hay duda que el América ha dado a España y a sí misma grandes varones que la han ilustrado, y que cada día la ilustran caminando por aquellas dos grandes calles de la gloria que han formado a un nivel armas y letras. No digo esto por blasonar la paridad sino por defender absoluta la aptitud con que debe cesar cualquiera preocupación, quedándonos sin diferencia alguna, y como a un plan de honor en ambos mundos. (Prologue)

> There is no doubt about America's having produced for Spain and for itself great men that have enlightened it and that each day enlighten it while walking those two great streets of glory that have formed, at one level, arms and letters. I do not say this to boast of parity, but rather to defend absolute aptitude, leaving us with no difference, as if on a level plain of honor in both worlds.

Inca Garcilaso, in the preface to his *Comentarios reales de los Incas,* shared his framework for bridging the Old World and the New and emphasized the unique position that Peru occupied as a cultured empire and nation: "Cuzco, que fue otra Roma en aquel Imperio" [Cuzco, which was another Rome in that empire]. In the same fashion that Spain had once enriched Rome's coffers, now too did America enrich Spain's, providing human and material riches. As Raquel Chang-Rodríguez explains above, the Inca Garcilaso hereby "inverts the proposition: rich lands will . . . produce intelligent offspring, and their wealth will have a positive impact on all born and raised there." Similarly, we can say that Peralta disputes the negative arguments about climate and geographical influences on creole aptitude.[17]

Peralta summarizes that, in the same manner that Rome imposed its language on the Iberian Peninsula and other colonies, and Spain its language on the Americas, so too did the Incas, as conquerors, on the peoples they subjugated:

17. Garcilaso de la Vega, el Inca, *Comentarios reales,* ed. Mercedes Serna (Madrid, 2000), preface.

Política fue de los romanos (como lo es de todos los conquistadores) hacer del propio idioma una más noble cadena de los sujuzgados. . . . Hácese olvido de la libertad el de la lengua y compañía del vasallaje la del uso en la nueva. Los babilonios lo consiguieron brevemente en los hebreos y aun los incas en los peruanos. Costosa pero agradable cultura fue la del lenguaje de aquellos dominantes a los españoles, cuya nación entre todas las demás sujetas tuvo la prerrogativa de unirse después a la romana, de suerte que casi llegó a ser igual de valerosa. (Book 1, cols. 137–138)

It was the practice of the Romans (like all powerful conquerors) to use their language as one more noble chain for the conquered. . . . As one forgets the language, one forgets freedom; and as one accepts a new language, one accepts a new servitude. Babylonians achieved this briefly against the Hebrews, and even the Incas against the Peruvians. The adoption of the language of those conquerors was costly but culturally agreeable to Spaniards, whose nation—among all other subjugated nations—had the prerogative to be combined with the Roman language to the extent that it became almost equally brave.

The Incas had not only learned and dominated the Spanish language, appropriating it to their benefit as the Spaniards had adapted Latin, but also had managed to preserve the speaking and teaching of Quechua: "Estilo que también se experimenta en la América, principalmente en el Perú donde, aunque hay diversos dialectos o lenguas particulares en algunas partes, se conserva en los orígenes de las dicciones la general del Cuzco, y ésta se habla también y en ella enseña, y se predica el Evangelio" (book 1, cols. 126–127). [This is a situation experienced also in America, mainly in Peru where, although there are different dialects and particular languages, the general language of Cuzco is maintained in the origins of words, and this is also the spoken language and the one used in teaching and in preaching the gospel.] Yet the loss of the Inca language follows the same natural order and pattern that characterize the lost languages of ancient civilizations.

¿Qué se hicieron en Babilonia el caldeo, en Egipto el cóptico, el hebreo en Palestina, y otros muchos? ¿En cuántas se ha extinguido no sólo la lengua sino la nación, como . . . se ve en las islas primeras de la América, cuales son la Española y la de Cuba, donde no se halla huella alguna de sus originarios moradores? ¿Quién duda que pudo suceder en España lo que se experimenta en grande parte de los valles del Perú en que por la entrada y dominación de la nación española han perdido los primitivos habitadores su propio idioma y sólo saben el castellano con la misma destreza que los dueños? Esto se ha visto en la misma Cantabria, [donde] hoy no se habla en estas partes el vascuense, que se perdió del todo en ellas. (Book 1, cols. 123–125)

What happened to the Chaldean language in Babylonia, to Coptic in Egypt, to Hebrew in Palestine, and many others? In how many regions have been extinguished not only the language but also the nation . . . as it happened in the first American islands, like Cuba and Hispaniola, where no trace can be found of the original inhabitants? Who doubts that in Spain could have happened what we experience to a large extent in the valleys of Peru, where, after the Spanish arrival and conquest, the native population has lost its language and knows only Castilian, with the same skill as their masters? We have seen this even in Cantabria, where in those areas today they do not speak Basque, which has been totally lost.[18]

There are limited yet pointed references to the hardships both ancient Spain and eighteenth-century Peru endured as colonies, in particular the comparison between the legendary drought that occurred during the reign of Habidis, successor to King Gargoris, and the 1719–1722 drought Peralta had witnessed during the viceregency of Santo Bono: "¿No hemos visto en nuestros [campos] la total infecundidad de los peruanos valles, con tan activo fuego y telón tan tenaz que, habiendo durado cerca de cuarenta años, hubiera hecho poco menos que despobladas sus regiones, si en Chile no hubiera hallado su granero?" (book 1, cols. 219–220). [Have we not seen in our own fields the total infertility of the Peruvian valleys, what with so much fire and persistent smoky haze that, having lasted forty years, it would have made its regions virtually uninhabited were it not for the grain found in Chile?] The conquered Incas owed their decline, not to excessive use of alcohol and confiscation of land, nor to the existence of the *mita* (system of forced Indian labor), but rather to the simple fact of political domination. Last, Peralta expresses that, as idolaters, the Incas raised temples to Pachacamac in the very spirit in which the ancients raised idols to their creator, and the Romans to Hercules. Given that Peralta has been faulted for showing little interest in the Incas, his pronouncements on Inca

18. Peralta theorizes that, as part of God's punishing humankind for its pride, each family or tribe received its own language and that Tubal introduced the Basque language, which betrayed no trace of Phonecian, Carthaginian, or Roman influences (*Historia,* book 1, col. 467).

language and culture paint the canvas of Peru, as a nación, that differs little from Spain in spirit and history.[19]

The Vindication of Creole Identity

Concolorcorvo (Alonso Carrió de la Vandera) in *El Lazarillo de ciegos caminantes* [Guide for Blind Rovers] (1773) portrayed Peralta as a conflicted colonial subject who idled away his time pursuing a defense of the monarchy and analyzing European events with passion at a time when his own under-developed native land was struggling to free itself from the yoke of colonialism. That valid criticism notwithstanding, Peralta was quick to recognize that his status as a creole was responsible for his being denied access to a wider scien-tific and literary audience. To that end he interjected into selected works remarks to the effect that his creole identity enjoined him from achieving greater glory and that, had he been a Spaniard, he would have risen to the heights of his Peninsular counterpart, the commentator Benito Jerónimo Fei-joo, and other European contemporaries. The claim of prejudice against Peralta as a creole appears in the front matter to *Historia*, in the approval letter written by Tomás de Torrejón:

Si floreciera en la Europa, donde son tan fáciles las prensas, las tuviera en continuo afán, con mucha gloria de la nación española y provecho del orbe literario. . . . Mas ésta es una desgracia que . . . sigue a los ingenios peruanos, cortándoles las alas para que, encarcelados en su nido, no puedan prender a otra región el vuelo. . . . Si se ignorase la patria del doctor don Pedro, pudieran disputar esta gloria todas las ciudades de España, como contendieron por Homero las siete más célebres de Grecia. Pero sabiéndose que nació en Lima, debe esta noble y tres veces coronada ciudad rendirle a Dios las gracias de que no hubiese nacido en otra.

If he were to flourish in Europe, where the press is so easily accessible, he would keep it always busy, providing immense glory to Spain and benefit to the literary world. . . . But this is a misfortune that follows Peruvian geniuses, clipping their wings so that, imprisoned in their nest, they cannot fly to another region. . . . If we did not know the birthplace of Dr. Don Pedro, all the cities of Spain could claim this glory, much like the

19. Pedro de Peralta Barnuevo, *Lima triunfante, glorias de la América* . . . (1708) and *Júbilos de Lima y fiestas reales* (1723) (also known by the title *Descripción de las fiestas reales*) contain a history of the origin and natural order of the Incas.

seven most famous cities of Greece for Homer's. However, we know that he was born in Lima, and therefore this noble and thrice-crowned city must thank God that he was not born somewhere else.

Cultural and political considerations take center stage in *Historia* and frame Peralta's response to his colonial situation.[20]

There is merit to probing the representation of creole identity in a work that was to be a corrective and current history of Spain, composed in the spirit of— and obeying the historiographic mission of—early chroniclers and historians of the New World. *Historia* was to fulfill a dual purpose: (1) to establish truth by correcting the "grave errors" of (Peninsular) historians and, (2) to be of service to the nación and to the political sphere. Peralta asserts that he is the best historian to write of Spain's greatness because he has less to gain as a New World subject.

> Y así, de la manera que un grande orador dijo de sí, que ninguno era más
> conveniente que alabase a príncipe que el que era menos necesario,
> puedo decir que ninguno es más propio para escribir de una nación que
> el que es menos preciso, como para la nuestra lo soy yo sin que esta
> libertad diminuya el mérito del amor, ni éste haya embarazado el deseo
> de la exactitud. . . . Su legítima gloria consiste en la pureza de ésta y que
> no vive tan escasa de fama su grandeza que necesite de pedirla prestada al
> afecto de los propios, ni tema que se la gaste el odio de los extraños.
> (Prologue)

> And, therefore, like a great orator once said about himself—that is, no
> one is more suitable to praise a prince than the one who is least needed—
> I can say that no one is more appropriate to write about a nation than the
> one who is least needed, as is the case with me and our country [both
> Spain and Peru], without this liberty's diminishing love's reward and
> without this love's impeding the desire for accuracy. . . . Its legitimate
> glory lies in the latter's purity, and its greatness does not have so little
> fame as to need to borrow fame from the affection of its own [citizens],
> nor as to fear it to be consumed by the hatred of foreigners.

---

20. Alonso Carrió de la Vandera, *El Lazarillo de ciegos caminantes* (1773) (Buenos Aires, 1942), 20; Tomás de Torrejón, in "Approval" letter, unnumbered folio in Peralta, *Lima fundada*. For an appraisal of the discourse on the "natural deficiency" of creoles, see Jerry M. Williams, "Academic and Literary Culture in Eighteenth-Century Peru," *Colonial Latin American Review*, IV (1995), 129–152; Eva M. Kahiluoto Rudat, "The Spirit of Intellectual Independence in the Writings of Enlightened Creoles," *Dieciocho*, XIV (1991), 80–91.

The reward for loving one's country is not the main motivation for accuracy. Peralta strives for impartiality based on self-declared insignificance, disenfranchisement, and self-effacement and seeks to make his own integrity. Born in a distant land and an extended native of Spain's provinces, he considers himself to be less passionate and less compelled than Peninsular historians to defend and engage Spain's history in an objective manner. In order to make history come alive for readers by having them recognize the historical ties that all Peruvians share with Spain, Peralta positions himself as did Peninsular historians who wrote passionately—but with degrees of inaccuracy—about the New World, often without visiting it; instead, those historians viewed the new continent more through their soul than with their eyes. Peralta owns that he writes about a country he has never visited except in his imagination (for despite achieving international recognition, he never left his native Peru).

> Si para escribir las historias de los reinos fuese siempre inviolable requisito el verlos, negaríamos la fe a Tito Livio en lo que habla de España y de Grecia, a Tácito en lo que habla de Alemania y Asia y, sin entendernos a otros tan antiguos, a Herrera y a Solís en lo que refieren del América. Debiendo decirse lo mismo de las descripciones porque ninguno de los que las reducen a la línea en cartas, ni a la pluma en libros, han necesitado ver todas las regiones que han copiado, pues a ninguno ha dado el sol su carro para andarlo todo. (Prologue)

> If to write the history of the kingdoms it should be absolutely essential to see them, then we should deny credibility to Titus Livy for what he says about Spain and Greece, to Tacitus for what he says about Germany and Asia, and also, without referring to others so ancient, to Herrera and Solís for what they tell about America. The same can be said about their descriptions, because not one among those who gives his account in letters or books has had the need to see all the regions that he copied, for to none of them has the sun given its cart to travel all over [the world].

Peralta's view was that the public and scholars should accept on faith his historical method and approach, in much the way that they came to embrace the accounts of Livy and Tacitus. In the end, Peralta's history of conquest was to exceed the feats of modern historians (Saavedra, Ocampo, Morales, Núñez de Castro) and be more suitable for readers than was the labyrinthine and inaccessible history of Spain that Pellicer had produced. It is ironic and yet a fitting tribute to New World prowess that an enlightened creole and subaltern should attempt to write the definitive history of the Spanish Empire.[21]

Peralta addresses the then-popular pseudoscientific theories espoused by Europeans about climatic determinism, which promoted creoles to be victims of a form of capitis diminutio, or loss of legal personality, and where laws of humoral pathology and detrimental effects of geography were forces that impinged negatively on the rational faculties of creoles. Peralta embeds between the lines of *Historia*—and oftentimes presents as digressions or asides—his rejection of such theses and bristles at the errant science behind them: "Siempre ha sido el primer honor de los mortales la nobleza del primitivo suelo donde nacen, la cual, como si el temperamento del clima fuese influencia de la virtud y las propriedades del terreno fuesen privilegios de la sangre, les sirve como de una alcuña universal de la nación en que tiene por estirpe común la patria" (book 1, cols. 1–2). [The nobility of the original native land has always been the first [badge of] honor of mankind, and that nobility—as if the temperament of climate were an influence on virtue and the earthly properties blood privileges—represents to them the universal lineage of the nation whose common ancestry is the homeland.] This and similar remarks point to a geographical determinism that is expressed in advance of Buffon's and Montesquieu's systematically formulated ideas about the influence of climate and geography on human psychology and intellectual capacity.

In the Prologue to *Historia* Peralta shoots his first volley at the crown when he reasons that the American colonies and their peoples enjoy the same relationship with Spain as did Spain with Rome when the former was a colony of the Roman Empire: "Es innegable que aquella proporción que antiguamente tuvo con Roma España cuando fue la provincia más noble de su imperio es la misma que hoy tiene con España el América" (Prologue). [Undoubtedly, the relationship Rome had with Spain during antiquity, when Spain was the empire's noblest province, is the same relationship Spain has with America today.] This locus classicus echoes the tone that Peralta uses to elucidate the question of race and class in America: that in the hegemonic battle Spain is the loser, that it does itself a disservice in promoting and maintaining class and race distinctions, and that Spain too suffers when creoles are divested of rights and opportunities for growth. He uses the case of Seneca to illustrate this point: "Era Séneca extranjero y de provincia conquistada. Vergüenza es de aquellas cortes en que no se premian aun los mismos propios por distantes" (book 4, col. 948).

---

21. Peralta's lack of travel beyond Peru is the subject of Estuardo Núñez, "El no viajar de Peralta," in Núñez, *La imagen del mundo en la literatura peruana* (Mexico City, 1971), 38–39.

[Seneca was a foreigner and from a conquered province. It is a point of shame of those courts, in which even their own people are not rewarded, because they are far off.]

That initial volley is continued by yet another, in book 1, where Peralta subverts the notion of "natural deficiency" by refuting the claim that the American climate is responsible for influencing the virtue of its subjects. To the contrary, American soil nurtures their roots and spirit, producing enriched talents. America and Peru are home to "unas regiones ennoblecidas de más rica materia, de fecundidad más singular" (book 1, cols. 2–3) [ennobled regions of richer substance, of most singular abundance]. In essence, from American ground is mined the rich creole ingenuity that contributes to Spain's economic and spiritual fortune. Within Jorge Cañizares-Esguerra's notion of how epistemologies and identities in the eighteenth-century influenced the writing of history, Peralta's patriotic epistemology and defense of creole aptitude contributed to having "exposed the shortcomings and limitations of Europeans who sought to write natural histories of the New World" and "reflected the longings of the Creole upper classes in Spanish America to have 'kingdoms' of their own."[22]

The question arises whether Peralta could have used his talents more productively to denounce the colonial situation of creoles. There is little evidence to suggest that Peralta rejected or was confused about his creole identity. Though it can be reasonably argued that, as a colonized subject, Peralta perpetuates language "through scholarly pursuits into the splendors of the past," one can find in many of his books positive assertions about his life as a *criollo* (creole), *español-americano* (Spanish American), and *americano* (American). His colonial bilingualism and the ability to distinguish between his adopted cultural language and his native creole language, particularly in popular expressive idioms, are an important characteristic of his discursive project of self-affirmation. Peralta rescues himself through language from otherwise becoming an invisible presence within Hispanic letters. His writings contain astute observations about contemporary issues that affected his career, and he marketed himself as the only creole among fellow academicians who was capable of forming a serious concept about the most arduous political problems. His aim is to be accepted by the mainstream and preserve his integrity: "Así de la una

22. Jorge Cañizares-Esguerra, *How to Write the History of the New World: Histories, Epistemologies, and Identities in the Eighteenth-Century Atlantic World* (Stanford, Calif., 2001), 4. Here I find engaging this essay's dialogue with Mazzotti's cogent interpretation (above) of creole moral superiority that Juan Meléndez espoused in *Tesoros Verdaderos de las Yndias,* and Yolanda Martínez–San Miguel's assertion (above), that the discursive and political struggle of creoles for legitimation was "to prove their rational and physical equality."

manera, habré hecho dos sacrificios, el de mi trabajo, y mi opinión; y de la otra, lograré dos glorias, la de mi celo, y de mi aceptación." [Just as in one way, I shall have made two sacrifices, that of my work and my opinion; in another way, I will achieve two glories, that of my zeal and my acceptance.] As Albert Memmi aptly points out: "The role of a colonized writer is too difficult to sustain. He incarnates a magnified vision of all the ambiguities of the colonized." In the same fashion that Rome prospered from Spain as a colony, and Spain from Peru, so too does Peralta—as a loyal patriot and defender of monarchical sovereignty and the viceroyalty—benefit from his relationship with the court.[23]

In "Relación del estado de los reinos del Perú," which Peralta ghostwrote for the viceroy the marquis de Castelfuerte, he proposes that creoles should constitute the spiritual and material support of the crown and be granted political authority and economic power. Cognizant of how the daily drama of colonialism played itself out in the streets of Lima as well as in literary salons and in government, Peralta reasons that Spain has failed to learn its lesson from the time when it once represented for Rome what America did for the monarchy; both were drained of human and material wealth. Peralta understood that the political and material misfortunes of Spain had contributed to its moral and religious bankruptcy, hence, his attempt to redeem or vindicate Spain through its illustrative history. By vindicating Spain of the imputation of decline and enshrining her cultures and civilizations, Peralta ensured his place in the history of both Spain and Peru and vindicated his aptitude as a creole.[24]

Toward the end of his life, Peralta was conscious of carving for himself a niche in the annals of history. In *Historia,* when he extols renowned historians and chroniclers of Europe and America, whose historical models influenced the composition of *Historia,* he places his own name alongside the names of Pigafetta, Riccioli, Botero, Laet, Cieza de León, the Inca Garcilaso, López de Gómara, Zárate; fathers Acosta, Clancha, Salinas, and Suárez de Figueroa; and Bishop Fernández de Piedrahita. He boasts that the mathematician and botanist Louis Feuillée (1660–1732) had quoted him in "Historical Atlas," in the *Journal des observations physiques, mathématiques, et botaniques* (1714), as had Frézier in *Relation du voyage á la Mer du Sud* (1716). It is Peralta's conviction

23. Peralta, *Lima fundada,* Prologue; Albert Memmi, *The Colonizer and the Colonized,* trans. Howard Greenfield (New York, 1965), 108.

24. [Pedro de Peralta Barnuevo], "Relación del estado de los reinos del Perú que hace el excmo: señor don José Armendaris, marqués de Castel-Fuerte, a su sucesor el marqués de Villagarcía, en el año de 1736," in M. A. Fuentes, ed., *Memorias de los vireyes que han gobernado el Perú, durante el tiempo del coloniaje español* (Lima, 1859), III, 1–369.

that only the ocean and geography separate his acumen from European literary and scientific currents; geographical distance affects his credibility as author and influences how he negotiates his claim to knowledge. From a preenlightened perspective and within the confines of an evolving academic and political world in which ideological aggression is a mainstay, Peralta beholds his acceptance by European thinkers as a confirmation of *nuestra América* (our America) and *nuestra criolla nación* (our creole nation). With this confirmation he confronts his invention by Europe, seeks to reverse disparaging opinions about creoles, and reinvents himself, defending both his identity and native land.[25]

The Legacy of the *Historia*

Peralta embodies the synthesis of the creole writer in transition between Scholasticism and the Enlightenment. *Historia* contests the image of Peralta as a detached, Europeanized intellectual whose writings constitute only a guide to the scholarly pursuits and philosophy of his era. The latter point is important in arriving at an overview of Peralta's pronouncements on creole identity, particularly when we remember that *Historia* was to be not only Peralta's gift to Felipe V and the Spanish Empire but also a thinly veiled challenge to monarchical practices.

The historical-literary vindication of Spain is more than a defense of Spain's glories and excellent qualities. At the core of Peralta's thesis, framed by Spain's architecture of conquest, is the vindication of Peru as a nación, or patria. According to Eva M. Kahiluoto Rudat, "A clear concept of patria and of nation consisting of people with a common origin, born on the same soil" appears in *Historia*. This strong sentiment of American regionalism is expressed in the Prologue, where Peru, compared to Rome's colonies, is painted as the target of twofold victimization:

Era el gobierno de los pretores otra guerra de paz que se hacía a los
sujetos con que el robo civil no era menos valiente que el saco militar, y
la codicia sucedía a la ambición. Era entonces la España la América de
los romanos: semejante en las riquezas y en la extracción de las riquezas.
Desdichada provincia donde dos veces se sacaba la sangre de sus

25. In *Lima fundada*, unlike *Historia*, Peralta cites many of his publications, such as *Historia de España vindicada*, *Imagen política*, *Desvíos de la naturaleza o tratado de el origen de los monstros* (1695), *Júpiter olímpico* (1716), *Templo de la fama vindicado* (1720), *Teatro heroico* (1720), *Fúnebre pompa* (1728), and *Galería de la omnipotencia* (1729).

habitadores a cuyos males sólo les servía la muerte que tomaban de
remedio. (Book 2, cols. 411–412)

The praetorian government was another peaceful war waged against
the subjects, in which civilian robbery was not less brave than military
plunder and in which greed replaced ambition. At that time Spain
became the America of the Romans: alike in wealth and in the pillaging of
wealth. Unfortunate province whose blood was sucked out twice from its
people, whose evils were only cured by the death they chose as a remedy!

From a moralizing perspective, Spain and Peru are the subjects of conquest
because they allow their prosperity and riches to lull them into a sense of
ambition, false security, and tranquility.

Error es de torpe ocio o de necio descuido tener en las riquezas el
incentivo que provoca la invasión sin la defensa que asegura la
quietud. . . . Los españoles, que tenían como presente de la naturaleza
dentro de su casa las riquezas, ni las estimaban como solicitadas ni las
buscaban fuera; y las que pudieran servirles para adquirir extranjeros
dominios, les servían para perder los propios, siendo señuelo de la
ambición ajena lo que pudiera ser instrumento de la propia gloria.
Causa porque ha sido carácter de la España estar expuesta siempre a
la dominación de otras naciones, no por defecto de un valor que ha
mostrado aun a favor de sus conquistadores sino por exceso del ocio o
del contento que induce la abundancia. (Book 1, cols. 227–229)

It is an error of sluggishness or dim carelessness to possess wealth that
provokes an invasion but does not provide a defense to maintain it
secure. . . . The Spanish, who had in their homes all this wealth as a gift
from nature, neither did they value it because it was courted, nor did they
seek it outside; and the wealth that they could have used to acquire
foreign dominions helped them instead to lose their own, and so what
could have been an instrument of their own glory became a magnet for
others' ambition. This is the reason why Spain has been exposed to
domination by other nations, not because of lack of valor—which actually
it has shown even in its conquistadors—but because of excess of leisure
and contentment brought about by abundance.

This critique seemed to foreshadow Spain's impending transatlantic losses.
Divine Providence, according to Peralta, is capable of determining human

affairs, altering governments and laws, favoring chosen rulers in battle, and providing a framework for Peruvian nationhood.[26]

The temporal concept of nation, which paves the way for Spain's providential rise, also distinguishes Peru and other historic and cultural entities with deep roots, namely Celts, Greeks, Carthaginians, Romans, Goths, and Muslim Arabs. Within Peralta's discourse, the articulation of *nuestra España, nuestra criolla nación, nuestra Lima, nuestro suelo, patrio suelo,* and *nuestra lengua* (our Spain, our creole nation, our Lima, our soil, our homeland, our language) are far from contradictory terms: they are affirmative declarations of the continuous political and religious history that frames his New World identity. The importance of Peralta's thesis about conquest and the nación is that, like other Spanish Americans, he contributes to "an intellectual tradition that, by reason of its engagements with the historical experience and contemporary reality of America, was original, idiosyncratic, complex, and quite distinct from any European model."[27]

From 1714 to 1730 we follow a linear trajectory between *Imagen política* and *Historia* (and later *Lima fundada*), where the notion of conquest and heroism is both defined and reinforced by the theory and practice of the pen as a weapon. The line of thought is coherent in following the transition from the employment of arms to shape conquest in the Old and New Worlds to the use of letters to articulate a changing transatlantic political and sociocultural order that fashions the nación. Peralta's ethic of conquest and his promotion of Peru as a nación foreshadow the independence movements and calls for nationhood that occur almost one hundred years later in his native land. The historiographic advances of the past centuries have resulted in a fuller appreciation of colonial Latin American letters, and *Historia* ranks among the most successful histories published in any of the New World colonies—a fact that invites students and scholars alike to reappraise Peralta's locus within the canon of Latin American studies.

26. Eva M. Kahiluoto Rudat, "Lo clásico y lo barroco en la obra literaria de Peralta Barnuevo," *Dieciocho,* VIII (1985), 31–62, 85.

27. D. A. Brading, in *The First America: The Spanish Monarchy, Creole Patriots, and the Liberal State, 1492–1867* (Cambridge, 1991), holds that, despite the cultural ties between Spain and America, the writings of Spanish-American patriots created an intellectual climate that resulted in their distinct American identity (5).

RALPH BAUER

The "Rebellious Muse": Time, Space, and Race in the Revolutionary Epic

In 1825, the Ecuadorian poet José Joaquín Olmedo (1780–1847) published an ode commemorating Simón Bolívar's and Mariscal Antonio José de Sucre's recent military victories over the Spanish and loyalist armies at Junín and Ayacucho, respectively. One of the earliest poems of Spanish-American independence, *La Victoria de Junín* begins on a note of uncertainty.

Trémula, incierta,
torpe la mano va sobre la lira
dando discorde son. . . .

. . . .

Siento unas veces la rebelde Musa,
cual bacante en furor, vagar incierta
por medio de las plazas bulliciosas,
o sola por las selvas silenciosas,
o las risueñas playas
que manso lame el caudaloso Guayas.

Tremulous, uncertain and heavy, my hand runs over the lyre giving a discordant sound. . . . Sometimes I hear the rebellious Muse wandering uncertainly, like a bacchante in a frenzy, through the noisy squares, or alone through the silent forests or the charming shores lapped gently by the mighty Guayas [River].

Indeed, the reader may wonder about this "rebellious Muse" here invoked for inspiration but nowhere to be found in the classical pantheon populating Mount Helicon. While the revolutionary poet could draw on a long tradition of epic poetry that had flourished in Spanish America during colonial times, these poems had celebrated the European conquerors of the Americas, not American liberators from European imperial domination. They were profoundly informed by the notion of *translatio,* or transfer, of a Christian imperium, by the idea that all civilization and religion originated in the East and providentially migrates to the West in the course of a perpetually violent conquest of a (Christian) Aeneas vanquishing a savage (infidel) Turnus. It was this epic story of the conquest that had mythically plotted the neofeudal ideology of the "heroic knight" underlying a distinctly creole identity in colonial Spanish America for at least two hundred years.[1]

In *La Victoria de Junín,* by contrast, the epic account of the battle action is crowned, not by the miraculous appearance of an equestrian Santiago, manifesting God's providence by wreaking havoc among the infidel, but rather by an enormous apparition in the sky that identifies itself as Huayna Cápac (1493–1526?), the eleventh and penultimate Inca ruler before the arrival of the Spanish invaders under Pizarro and Almagro in Peru in 1532. As though a patron saint of Spanish-American independence, Huayna Cápac prophesies a bright future of the American republics.

Miró a Junín, y plácida sonrisa
vagó sobre su faz. "Hijos—decía—
generación del sol afortunada,
que con placer yo puedo llamar mía,
yo soy Huayna-Capac, soy el postrero
del vástago sagrado;
dichoso rey, mas padre desgraciado.
De esta mansión de paz y luz he visto
correr las tres centurias
de maldición, de sangre y servidumbre
y el imperio regido por las Furias." (134)

He looked down at the battle site of Junín, and a calm smile spread over his face. "Children," he spoke, "fortunate descendants of the Sun that with delight I can call my own, I am Huayna-Capac; I am the last sacred offspring, blessed king, but wretched father. From this sanctuary of peace

1. José Joaquín de Olmedo, *Poesías completas de José Joaquín de Olmedo,* ed. Aurelio Espinosa Pólit (Mexico City, 1947), 123–124; E. Caracciolo-Trejo, ed., *The Penguin Book of Latin American Verse* (Baltimore, 1971), 227. In this essay, I am citing Caraciollo-Trejo's (abridged) translation whenever possible. Otherwise I have translated from Espinoza Pólit's edition. Further references to these editions will appear in the text. For a good discussion of the tradition in colonial Latin America, see Margarita Peña, "Epic Poetry," in Roberto González Echevarría and Enrique Pupo-Walker, eds., *The Cambridge History of Latin American Literature* (Cambridge, 1996), I, 231–259, esp. 231.

and light I have watched three centuries pass by—centuries of damnation, of bloodshed and slavery, and of the empire ruled by the furies."

The Inca's miraculous appearance has been the subject of much criticism since almost immediately after the publication of the poem. Even Simón Bolívar, the *libertador* himself, to whom the poem was dedicated, saw in the plan of the poem a "capital defect in its design." In a letter to Olmedo, he questioned the verisimilitude not only of the epic machinery of the apparition—which must have been "lighter than air since he comes from Heaven"—but the historical plausibility that the ancestral Inca would have championed the cause of an independent national creole state. "It hardly seems proper for him to praise indirectly the religion that destroyed him," he wrote, "and it appears even less proper that he does not desire the reëstablishment of his throne, but, instead, give preference to foreign intruders who . . . [are] the descendants of the destroyers of his empire." Yet, subsequent critics of Olmedo's poem have agreed with Bolívar's sense that the Inca Huayna Cápac is "its hero," noting the centrality of this figure in Olmedo's poetic enterprise.[2]

The problem of verisimilitude noted by Bolívar and many later critics since then highlights a set of ideological ambiguities and contradictions in the post-

2. Simón Bolívar, *Selected Writings of Bolivar,* comp. Vicente Lecuna, ed. Harold A. Bierck, trans. Lewis Bertrand (New York, 1951), II, 520–521. Perhaps the most famous later critic of Olmedo's invocation of the Inca apparition has been the eminent literary historian and critic Marcelino Menéndez y Pelayo, who repeats Bolívar's earlier charge of historical distortion; see Marcelino Menéndez Pelayo, *Historia de la poesía hispano-americana* (1893–1895) (Madrid, 1947), I, 376, II, 30–35. For a review of these critiques, see Luis Monguió, "Las tres primeras reseñas de londinenses de 1826 de *La Victoria de Junín*," *Revista iberoamericana*, XXX (1964), 225–237. For later assessments, see Stephen Hart, "Signs of the Subaltern: Notes on Nineteenth-Century Spanish American Literature," *Tesserae: Journal of Iberian and Latin American Studies*, V (1999), 27–35, esp. 31; Inke Gunia and Klaus Meyer-Minneman, "José Joaquín de Olmedo: 'La victoria de Junin: Canto a Bolívar' (1925): legitimación política y legitimidad poética," in Dieter Janik, ed., *La literatura en la formación de los estados hispanoamericanos (1800–1860)* (Frankfurt, 1998), 219–235, esp. 221; Regina Harrison, *Entre el tronar épico y el llanto elegíaco: simbología indígena en la poesía ecuatoriana siglos XIX y XX* (Quito, 1996), esp. 56; Alberto Andino, "Bolívar, Olmedo, y el 'Canto de Junín,'" *Cuadernos hispanoamericanos*, no. 279 (1973), 611–620; Antonio Cornejo Polar, *Sobre literatura y crítica latinoamericanas* (Caracas, 1982), esp. 67–85. As Carolyn F. Smith writes, this epic device in Olmedo's poem is intended to "establish a link between the past and the future" in the Spanish-American historical imagination and signals, as Christopher Conway notes, a "break with colonial discourse" by aiming to "legitimate a concept of autochthonous American culture." The continent's Indians, whether Inca or Aztec, thus become a new pantheon of gods and heroes not unlike that of the classical world. See Smith, "The Sacred-Historical Role of the Inca of Olmedo's 'Canto a Bolívar,'" *Hispania*, LVI (1973), 212–216, esp. 214, 215; Christopher Conway, "Gender, Empire, and Revolution in *La Victoria de Junín*," *Hispanic Review*, LIX (2001), 299–317, esp. 315. On later examples of creole appropriations of native Americans for symbols of national identity in Brazil, see Doris Sommer, *Foundational Fictions: The National Romances of Latin America* (Berkeley, Calif., 1991), 138–171.

colonial rewriting of history by the revolutionary creole offspring attempting to assert their cultural independence from the old centers of European imperial power not only in Spanish America but in former European settler colonies more generally. Throughout the Americas revolutionary poets descended from the former colonial creole elite—such as Olmedo as well as Andrés Bello (1781–1865) or José María Heredia (1803–1839) in Spanish America and the Connecticut Wits Joel Barlow (1754–1812), David Humphreys (1752–1818), John Trumbull (1750–1831), and Lemuel Hopkins (1750–1801) as well as Philip Freneau (1752–1832) in British America—sought to articulate, as Andrew Bush notes with regard to Latin American poets, a "historical theme of emphatically American character" by clinging to the languages and literary forms inherited from Europe, frequently producing poems that have been described as Romantic in content but neoclassical in form. Thus, the Venezuelan poet living in England Andrés Bello explored, in the neoclassical verses of his *Silvas americanas* (1827), the poetic potential of tropical indigenous American plants, such as the pineapple or cocoa, in articulating a distinctly American national identity, while in British America the Connecticut poet Timothy Dwight, in his georgic epic *Greenfield Hill* (1794), appealed to Connecticut's "lightsome vales" as a source of the special virtue of its "generous sons." In their search of models for an autochtonous American cultural identity rooted in the sublime grandeur of the American landscape, postcolonial American creoles began for the first time to look beyond the old imperial boundaries and to develop a hemispheric understanding of New World history and the destiny of the newly created American nation-states. Thus, the Cuban José María Heredia, in such poems as "Niágara" (1824, translated into English by William Cullen Bryant in 1827) became one of the first Spanish-American poets to explore the poetic potential of the continent's natural wonders in neoclassical verse.[3]

3. For a discussion of the distinction between so-called settler and invaded colonies, see Bill Ashcroft, Gareth Griffiths, and Helen Tiffin, eds., *The Empire Writes Back: Theory and Practice in Post-Colonial Literatures* (London, 1989). On Bello and Heredia, see Andrew Bush, "Lyric Poetry of the Eighteenth and Nineteenth Centuries," in González Echevarría and Pupo-Walker, eds., *The Cambridge History of Latin American Literature*, I, 387. On British America, see Leon Howard, "The Late Eighteenth Century: An Age of Contradictions," in Harry Hayden Clark, ed., *Transitions in American Literary History* (New York, 1967), 51–89; Andrés Bello, "Silva, a la Agricultura de la Zona Tórrida," in Elijah Clarence Hills, ed., *The Odes of Bello, Olmedo, and Heredia* (New York, 1920); Timothy Dwight, *Greenfield Hill* (1794) (New York, 1970), 13. For a more comprehensive discussion of the ideological role that the representation of the American landscape played in the letters of the North American Revolution, see Robert Lawson-Peebles, *Landscape and Written Expression in Revolutionary America: The World Turned Upside Down* (Cambridge, 1988); also Myra Jehlen, *American Incarnation: The Individual, the Nation, and the Continent* (Cambridge, Mass., 1986). For a more comprehensive discussion of Heredia's role in the literary

Moreover, revolutionary creoles began to turn to the symbols of America's pre-Columbian past for lending cultural legitimacy to the newly formed independent creole nation-states. Thus, in the 1820s, Bolívar had the ancient Inca temple of Pachacamac reconstructed (which had lain in ruins since the European conquest) while San Martín, a mestizo revolutionary addressing the Araucanians of Argentinia in 1816, proclaimed, "I am an Indian too," in order to mobilize the Indian sectors for his campaign for independence. Similarly, in British America, at the Boston Tea Party, creole revolutionaries dressed up as native American warriors in order to protest imperial mercantilist policies. However, throughout the hemisphere, American creoles could identify with the American landscape and indigenousness only ambivalently, their appropriations of a precolonial American past remaining, for the most part, mythic and elusive.[4]

This essay investigates some of these interrelated ambiguities of a postcolonial creole rewriting of history in Olmedo's poetry in comparison with that of the Anglo-American revolutionary poet Joel Barlow. In their appropriations of a native American past in order to lend their newly created creole nation-states a history apart from that of the European mother country, both revolutionary epics engage with Enlightenment theories about the newness of America and with the problematic legitimacy of the creole nation-states' claim to an indigenous past in light of a continuing native American presence (and, implicitly, claim to that past). Both epics thereby reconceptualize the history of the New World from the spatial expansion of Europe to a progressive temporal plot of historical supersessions in the New World, albeit based on a Eurocentric model, and uphold race as the most important paradigm underlying historical evolution. The poetic license of the epic afforded the revolutionary poet an apt generic vehicle both for the critical engagement with European scientific historiography about the New World and for a remythification of American history from the point of view of the creole nation-state.

The Creole Politics of Indian Carnival

Joel Barlow (1754–1812) had grown up as the son of a fairly well-to-do New England farmer. In the mid-1770s, he matriculated at Yale, but his college career was interrupted by the Revolutionary war, during which he served as

---

history of the nineteenth-century Americas, see Kirsten Silva Gruesz, *Ambassadors of Culture: The Transamerican Origins of Latino Writing* (Princeton, N.J., 2002); Anna Brickhouse, *Transamerican Literary Relations and the Nineteenth-Century Public Sphere* (Cambridge, 2004).

4. The quote from San Martín is from Pedro Henríquez-Ureña, *Literary Currents in Hispanic America* (Cambridge, Mass., 1946), 104.

chaplain in the patriot army. In 1781, he married and settled in Hartford as a lawyer and editor. In 1787, he published *The Vision of Columbus* and was sent to Europe on behalf of the Scioto Associates, a group of businessmen dealing in real estate. In Paris he lived through the events of the French Revolution and for several years divided his time between France and England, writing political pamphlets and books, making a fortune through commerce and speculation, and becoming minister to Algiers in 1796. While in Europe, he continued to write poetry, including his most popular poem, *The Hasty Pudding*. He returned to the United States in 1805, began revising his earlier epic poem, *The Vision of Columbus*, and two years later published it under the new title of *The Columbiad* (1807).

Like *The Hasty Pudding*, *The Vision of Columbus* and *The Columbiad* celebrate things natively American. But, unlike *The Hasty Pudding*, which describes, in four hundred lines of mock-heroic couplets, the making of the famous New England dish, Barlow's historical poems turn to America's indigenous past, drawing widely from the Spanish chronicles of the discovery and conquest and being particularly inspired by Alonso Ercilla y Zúñiga's *La Araucana* and the Inca Garcilaso de la Vega's *Comentarios reales*. The poem, dedicated to Louis XVI in its first edition of 1787 (a dedication that he discreetly dropped in subsequent editions published after the French Revolution) opens with a destitute Columbus despairing in his cell, where he was imprisoned by an ungrateful Ferdinand after Isabella's death, when a seer, or Angel, appears to him and takes him onto the Mount of Vision, from where the continent of America comes into view, and the entire history of the New World leading up to the American Revolution appears before Columbus in form of a prophecy, or "vision."[5]

José Joaquín de Olmedo was born a first-generation creole, on March 19, 1780, to Miguel Agustín de Olmedo, an immigrant from the vicinity of Málaga in Andalucía, and Ana Francisca Maruri y Slavarría, the daughter of a prominent creole family in Guayaquil. José Joaquín's father had held a prominent position in viceregal Peru, serving in various civic functions such as president of the local cabildo, corregidor, judge, and mayor. At age nine, José Joaquín, like many of his contemporaries from the Peruvian creole elite, attended a college run by Dominican monks, the Colegio de San Fernando in Quito, and later the Colegio de San Carlos in Lima. He received a law degree at age twenty-five and began teaching civil law at the Colegio de San Carlos before becoming a

5. For a discussion of the influences of Ercilla and Garcilaso on Joel Barlow, see Ralph Bauer, "Colonial Discourse and Early American Literary History: Ercilla, the Inca Garcilaso, and Joel Barlow's Conception of a New World Epic," *Early American Literature*, XXX (1995), 203–232.

professor at the University of San Marcos. Before the revolution, he served as secretary of the Cortes, or legislature, in Cádiz and, upon his return to Lima in 1817, married Doña Rosa de Icaza. When, in 1820, a group of patriots of Guayaquil, emboldened by Bolívar's victory at Boyacá the year before, approached Olmedo with plans to take part in the general insurrection that was spreading throughout the southern continent, Olmedo supported their cause, became president of the provisional revolutionary government, participated in the constitutional congress of Peru, and, in 1824, accepted Bolívar's commission for the writing of an epic poem commemorating the recent military victories.[6]

The product, *La Victoria de Junín,* manifests the influences not only of the classical epic tradition, such as of Virgil's *Aeneid,* and of the Spanish Renaissance tradition, such as Ercilla's *La Araucana,* but also of the French and British neoclassical tradition. Olmedo was an admirer of "Alejandro Pope," for example, having translated the first epistle of Pope's *Essay on Man.* But he was particularly interested in native American cultures throughout the hemisphere, reading travel accounts such as the barón de Lahontan's *New Voyages to North-America* (1703) and Jonathan Carver's *Travels through the Interior Parts of North-America in the Years 1766, 1767, and 1768* (1778). His proto-Romantic interest in native American cultures of the hemisphere was already manifest in a poem entitled "Canción Indiana," which celebrated the "valor marcial y el amor a la patria . . . de aquellos amables hijos de la naturaleza" [martial valor and patriotic love . . . of those amiable sons of nature].[7]

The appropriation of the symbols of native American culture as a platform for creole resistance to imperial authority has a long history in the colonial Americas, dating back, in Spanish America, to the first-generation creoles' outrage over the New Laws in the 1540s, which revoked their grants of an *encomienda* (a royal grant of Indian tribute and labor) in perpetuity. Thus, one night in the late 1560s in Mexico City, two prominent creoles, the brothers Gil and Alonso González de Avila, dressed up as Indian chieftains and led a proces-

6. On Olmedo's family, see Luis Noboa Icaza, *Estudios sobre Olmedo* (Guayaquil, 1973), 77–86; on his biography more generally, see Francisco Vascones, *Olmedo y sus obras: estudios histórico-critico* (Guayaquil, 1920), 1–78; Darío Guevara, *Olmedo: actor y cantor de la grán epopeya libertadora de América* (Quito, 1958).

7. On the influence of the *Aeneid* on *Victoria de Junín,* see Bush, "Lyric Poetry," in González Echevarría and Pupo-Walker, eds., *The Cambridge History of Latin American Literature,* I, 386–387. For a discussion of the influence of French and Anglo-American texts on Olmedo's "Canción Indiana," see Luis Monguió, "Sobre la Canción Indiana, de Olmedo," in Andrew Debicki, Enrique Pupo-Walker, and Sturgis Leavitt, eds., *Estudios de literatura hispanoamericana en honor a José J. Arrom* (Chapel Hill, N.C., 1974), 71–86. The quote from Olmedo's "Canción Indiana" can be found in *Poesías completas,* 158.

sion of whites disguised as Indian warriors to the house of Martín Cortés, presenting the conqueror's son with a crown of flowers. The entire spectacle was a reenactment of the surrender of the city to Martín's father and a protest against the crown's policy of stripping the creole descendants of what they considered as their natural right of inheritance.[8]

In British America, such carnivalesque charades would have been difficult to imagine during colonial times—the occasional assertion, such as Virginian Robert Beverley's, "I am an *Indian*," notwithstanding. Not until the late eighteenth century, when the real Indian as a dominant cultural presence had all but disappeared from the eastern seaboard, did creole revolutionaries turn to the native American warrior as a symbol of American resistance to British imperial policy. But in colonial Spanish America at large, too, New Spain's cult surrounding the symbols of Aztec culture, such as that of Quetzalcoatl, might have been the exception rather than the rule. Generally, creoles during colonial times found little romantic in native American culture. As Jerry M. Williams shows above, this was particularly true of Peru, where creoles were more likely to look toward Europe in emulation of its social customs, habits, and dress than to an indigenous tradition. In viceregal Peru, the real Indian was too persistent and dangerous a challenge to creole and Spanish hegemony to be regarded with romantic nostalgia. The frequent creole rebellions against the imperial reforms of the Bourbons had failed to expand into a full-blown revolution mainly because of the terrifying specter of Indian uprisings that had haunted colonial creole society since the sixteenth century. Indeed, Peru would experience numerous devastating Indian rebellions under the leadership of self-styled heirs of the ancient Inca dynasts, such as Juan Santos Atahualpa and José Gabriel Condorcanqui Tupac Amaru II, who would have expelled from Peru not only the Peninsular Spanish imperialists but also (and especially) the hated criollo settlers, had the insurgents not been subdued in an extremely bloody and long-lasting war by a coalition of *chapetón* (Peninsular) and creole forces.[9]

8. See Anthony Pagden, "Identity Formation in Spanish America," in Nicholas Canny and Pagden, eds., *Colonial Identity in the Atlantic World, 1500–1800* (Princeton, N.J., 1987), 51–94, esp. 54–55.

9. Robert Beverley, *The History and Present State of Viriginia*, ed. Louis B. Wright (Chapel Hill, N.C., 1947), 9. For a discussion of this rediscovery of the Indian as a postcolonial phenomenon of creole national identity, see Ashcroft, Griffiths, and Tiffin, eds., *The Empire Writes Back*, 143. On the creole appropriation of Quetzalcoatl, see Jacques Lafaye, *Quetzalcóatl and Guadalupe: The Formation of Mexican National Consciousness*, trans. Benjamin Keen (Chicago, 1987). For a good modern account of Juan Santos Atahualpa's rebellion, see Hanne Veber, "Asháninka Messianism: The Production of a 'Black Hole' in Western Amazonian Ethnography," *Current Anthropology*, XLIV (2003), 183–211; on Andean resistance more generally, see Kenneth Andrien, *Andean*

Similarly, the British-American colonies had experienced serious Indian uprisings such as that led by Pontiac, who had mobilized an alliance against the European settlers that included tribes from Lake Superior to the Gulf of Mexico. Not coincidentally did native nations frequently side with the British in the Revolutionary war, for, as native leaders were aware, their interests were guarded better under an imperial than a national order, even though, as Gordon Sayre has argued, the "Indian chief" would later come to function as a "tragic hero" in creole national mythologies throughout the Americas. When, in Spanish America, the creole rebellions led to independence for the various nations between 1808 and 1824, it was only after Spain had itself been invaded by Napoleon. The struggle was carried on mainly by the creole elites who had cobbled together an uneasy alliance with the various subaltern sectors of the colonial societies (mainly mestizos). "None of these men had faith in democratic ideals," writes Arturo Torres-Ríoseco. "They wished to save the colonies of Ferdinand VII, then a prisoner of Napoleon, and to preserve the oligarchical form of government. The great 'liberators'—Bolívar, Belgrano, San Martín, and the others—believed that a liberal monarchy or a perpetual presidency would serve best as a check upon the anarchical tendencies of the masses." "It was only much later that Spanish-American leaders came to prefer the republican form of government."[10]

From this point of view, the American revolutionary wars that brought about the separation from the old European imperial systems present themselves, as Jorge Klor de Alva reminds us, not so much as decolonizing efforts (akin to the struggles for decolonization in twentieth-century Africa and Southeast Asia), but rather as civil wars between different interest groups of Englishmen or Spaniards mostly over economic and political issues—not over cultural ones. For this reason, Lester Langley has characterized only the Haitian revolution as a "revolution from below." By contrast, the Latin American independence movements, he argues, were a "revolution denied," while the Anglo-American rebellion against imperial patrimony was, for the most part, a "revolution from above." Revolutionary British Americans, who "lacked a pervasive sense of class consciousness," refused and therefore failed to deal with issues of social disparity in wealth, Langley continues.

Worlds: Indigenous History, Culture, and Consciousness under Spanish Rule, 1532–1825 (Albuquerque, N.Mex., 2001), 193–232; D. A. Brading, The First America: The Spanish Monarchy, Creole Patriots, and the Liberal State, 1492–1867 (Cambridge, 1991), 306.

10. Gordon M. Sayre, The Indian Chief as Tragic Hero: Native Resistance and the Literatures of America, from Moctezuma to Tecumseh (Chapel Hill, N.C., 2005); Arturo Torres-Ríoseco, The Epic of Latin American Literature (New York, 1942), 44.

Statistically, the United States remained a society of disparities in wealth. Income and wealth were as inequitably distributed in the United States in 1800 as in British America in 1776—this despite the confiscation of loyalist estates, the elimination of primogeniture and entail, and the opening up of the West to settlement.[11]

Moreover, in the United States the Revolution and the postwar definition of the worth of labor left slavery intact as an economic foundation at the same time as it prompted Anglo-Americans to "perceive [slavery] as anomalous or to find more scientific means to justify its retention in a republican society." Despite the abolition of slavery in all the newly independent nations of Spanish America, where Bourbon reform policies, such as the sale of "certificates of whiteness" to mestizos, had previously "blurred social distinctions based on race, instinctively fearful Creoles clung to racial categories to justify their social positions" at a time when traditional descriptions of social status "no longer served to guarantee one's place in the social order." In fact, the racially and socially volatile situation in Spanish America, Langley suggests, might have been one of the principal reasons why the creole elites remained loyal to the imperial crown even after the thirteen British colonies in North America had succeeded in securing their independence.[12]

Thus, if postcolonial criticism often describes European colonialism in the Americas as a variety of "settler colonialism" in reference to creole identities in the early Americas (vis-à-vis the so-called invaded colonies of nineteenth-century European imperialism in Africa and Asia), it must be remembered that, from the point of view of social history, this category is itself a fiction that threatens to perpetuate a colonialist ideology. Clearly, as the historian Francis Jennings would remind us, all "settler" colonies were built on "invaded" territory still claimed by surviving indigenous peoples. From this point of view, the nativism practiced by (post)colonial creoles must be seen not only in the geopolitical light of (post)colonial resistance to imperial authority and assertions of cultural autonomy but also, as critics such as Benita Parry and Kwame Anthony Appiah have argued, in a more local context of (white) creole social

11. Jorge Klor de Alva, "The Postcolonization of the (Latin) American Experience: A Reconsideration of 'Colonialism,' 'Postcolonialism,' and 'Mestizaje,'" in Gyan Prakash, ed., *After Colonialism: Imperial Histories and Postcolonial Displacement* (Princeton, N.J., 1995), 241–278, esp. 250; Lester D. Langley, *The Americas in the Age of Revolution, 1750–1850* (New Haven, Conn., 1996), 62–64.

12. Langley, *The Americas*, 57, 157, 165, 167. On the role that ethnic conflict played in the "breakdown of the Spanish American Empire," see also Jorge I. Domínguez, *Insurrection or Loyalty: The Breakdown of the Spanish American Empire* (Cambridge, Mass., 1980), 28–45.

politics aiming to maintain the elite status they were able to attain in the context of the colonial order.[13]

The Politics of the New World Landscape

Olmedo's *Victoria de Junín* is the most famous poem within an entire corpus of Bolivarian epic poetry that emerged in the context of the Spanish-American revolutions. This literature sought to legitimize Bolívar's political authority, which had frequently been challenged by other local leaders of the creole rebellions. While ostensibly telling the story of the *liberador's* military feats, the most important cultural work these poems performed lay in the cultural and political rationalization of the new order, particularly in their attempt to relocate the origins of Great Colombia (1819–1830), not in the Spanish Empire, but rather in the pre-Columbian past. The history of the Spanish Empire would thus appear merely as a period of interregnum, a histori-cal parenthesis separating an essentially continuous indigenous American his-tory. However, these poems, while otherwise steeped in neoclassical poetics, did not conceive of this continuity of American history in terms of a "recorso" (or reversion) as was the case in the historical imagination of eighteenth-century classical republicanism. Written as they were in the cultural context of the postcolonial Americas, where the European-descended creoles were only one among various social groups who might lay claim to an indigenous past, they conceptualized this continuity in terms of a progressive and prophetic fulfill-ment of an ancient native history that culminates in the creoles' rebellions.[14]

Implicit (and often explicit) in the revolutionary epic's claim for a native origin and teleology of a national history was an active engagement with Enlightenment natural philosophy, especially the theory of the "newness" of the New World, propounded by such prominent European figures as Voltaire, Montesquieu, Buffon, the abbe Raynal, Cornelius de Pauw (eighteenth-century Dutch scholar), and William Robertson, who had held the American environ-ment and climate as inferior to the Old World's, thus explaining the alleged inferiority of the New World's animals and even man, whether indigenous or transplanted. Though critical of the sixteenth-century Spanish Renaissance

13. See Kwame Anthony Appiah, "Out of Africa: Topologies of Nativism," *Yale Journal of Criticism*, II, no. 1 (Fall 1988), 153–178; Benita Parry, "Problems in Current Theories of Colonial Discourse," *Oxford Literary Review*, IX (1987), 27–58.

14. On the corpus of Bolivarian epic poetry, see Antonio Cussen, *Bello and Bolívar: Poetry and Politics in the Spanish American Revolution* (Cambridge, 1992); Conway, "Gender," *Hispanic Review*, LXIX (2000), 299–317.

chronicles of the conquest, Enlightenment philosophy of history had inherited their imperialist teleology insofar as it told the history of the New World as that of translatio imperii, an expansion of European civilization into a New World essentially conceived as a vacant wilderness, devoid of a legitimate culture and history. Karlheinz Stierle has described this early modern ideological formation in terms of an "axis" that shifted in orientation in the Renaissance: "One might say that the dominance of the axis of vertical translation is basic to the medieval conception. . . . The transition from a medieval to a postmedieval model of culture can be understood as a shift from vertical to horizontal dominance." While eighteenth-century natural philosophy secularized the providentialist telos of imperial history, it left its basic spatiohistorical matrix intact, as the cultures of the New World were seen as being at a stage of some former period of European cultural evolution in a telos regarded as universal.[15]

Thus, in 1724 Joseph François Lafitau, in his *Moeurs des sauvages amériquains comparées aux moeurs des premiers temps,* compared the eighteenth-century Huron with the ancient European Spartan, while, in 1800, Joseph-Marie, baron de Gerando declared:

> The philosophical traveller, sailing to the ends of the earth, is in fact, travelling in time. He is exploring the past; every step he takes is the passage of an age. Those unknown islands that he reaches are for him the cradle of human society.

"Progress" happened in Europe, according to this narrative, but nowhere else. Still in the nineteenth century, which increasingly privileged time over space in its historical epistemology, G. W. F. Hegel, the father of modern progressivist theories of history, treated the Americas as an exception to his theory of historical dialectics. In *The Philosophy of History,* Hegel, who had conceived of the idea of a progressive historical development in his contemplation of the meanings of the French Revolution, dismissed the Americas as outside the spirit of history, the recent revolutions in the Americas notwithstanding:

> Of America and its grade of civilization, especially in Mexico and Peru, we have information, but it imports nothing more than that this culture

---

15. Karlheinz Stierle, "Translatio Studii and Renaissance: From Vertical to Horizontal Translation," in Sanford Budick and Wolfgang Iser, eds., *The Translatability of Cultures: Figurations of the Space Between* (Stanford, Calif., 1996), 56. On Renaissance historiography, see also Walter D. Mignolo, *The Darker Side of the Renaissance: Literacy, Territoriality, and Colonization* (Ann Arbor, Mich., 1995), particularly 125–218. On Enlightenment historiography, see Jorge Cañizares-Esguerra, *How to Write the History of the New World: Histories, Epistemologies, and Identities in the Eighteenth-Century Atlantic World* (Stanford, Calif., 2001).

was an entirely national one, which must expire as soon as Spirit approached it. America has always shown itself physically and psychically powerless, and still shows itself so. . . .

. . . And what takes place in America, is but an emanation from Europe.[16]

From an epistemological perspective outside Europe, therefore, liberal Hegelian (and later Marxist and Habermasian) historical dialectics, in their universalizing narratives of the unfolding of a rational system of world history modeled on the experience of Europe, have been subject to intense critique by Latin American philosophers of history, such as the Argentine Enrique Dussel, who argued that the European subject constituted itself by "eclipsing" its (Latin) American other. From the point of view of the (post)colonial periphery such progressivist theories present themselves, as Robert Young has noted, as "simply a negative form of the history of European imperialism." As to why historical development had been suspended in America, scientific explanations were readily at hand. Already during the Renaissance, the natural law theorist Jean Bodin had claimed a connection between the natural environment and the development of human culture. In the eighteenth century, Montesquieu had added the thesis that the American climates and soils made people in general lazy, servile, and degenerate. Also, in 1749, Buffon had published his influential *Histoire naturelle,* in which he had claimed that the American environment specifically was averse to the development of human civilization. Other influential natural historians such as de Pauw, Peter Kalm, and the abbé Raynal were soon to follow. Working within this European rhetorical tradition about the negative influences of America's size, climate, and environment upon the development of culture, Robertson, who had never been to America, arrived in his historical masterpiece at the conclusions that Americans were "destined to remain uncivilized" and that whatever civilization was transplanted to the American soil would inevitably regress and degenerate into barbarity. His discussion of native American culture would serve as a case in point. After his *History* had been first published, one of Robertson's readers, the Jesuit Juan Nuix in his Italian exile, ironically remarked that the "wretched Americans"

16. Joseph-Marie Dégerando [de Gérando], *The Observation of Savage Peoples,* trans. F. C. T. Moore (Berkeley, Calif., 1969), 63; Georg W. F. Hegel, *The Philosophy of History* (1827), trans. J. Sibree (Buffalo, N.Y., 1991), 81–82. For a more extensive critique of this ideology underlying the formation of modern anthropology, see Johannes Fabian, *Time and the Other: How Anthropology Makes Its Object* (New York, 1983).

could be thankful to their Spanish conquerors that they had not "viewed you as Robertson and other philosophers did."[17]

Not surprisingly, pronouncements such as Roberton's had created an outrage also among British- and Spanish-American creoles, such as Thomas Jefferson, who denounced Raynal and Buffon in his *Notes on the Present State of Virginia*, and the Mexican historian Javier Clavigero, who wrote his *Historia antigua de México* in order to "detect some of the many misrepresentations which occur in the history" of Robertson, "which we might swell into large volumes." For creole patriots in Anglo- and Spanish America alike, Robertson's historical discourse about America was anathema in their attempt to write a usable precolonial past.[18]

The creoles' epic celebrations of the New World landscape must be seen as a polemical and political response to this debate about the interrelations between nature and culture in the Americas. Thus, Olmedo finds the origins of American military "victory" and political love of liberty already inherent in the "sublime" qualities of the American landscape, especially the Andes:

Mas los sublimes montes, cuya frente
a la región etérea se levanta,
que ven las tempestades a su planta
brillar, rugir, romperse, disiparse,
los Andes, las enormes, estupendas
moles sentadas sobre bases de oro,
la tierra con su peso equilibrando,
jamás se moverán. Ellos, burlando
de ajena envidia y del protervo tiempo
la furia y el poder, serán eternos
de libertad y de victoria heraldos. (123)

---

17. Enrique Dussel, *The Invention of the Americas: Eclipse of "the Other" and the Myth of Modernity*, trans. Michael D. Barber (New York, 1995); Robert Young, *White Mythologies: Writing History and the West* (London, 1990), 2; John Bodin, *Method for the Easy Comprehension of History*, trans. Beatrice Reynolds (New York, 1945), 269–291. For a discussion of Buffon and the eighteenth-century debate, see Antonello Gerbi, *The Dispute of the New World: The History of a Polemic, 1750–1900*, trans. Jeremy Moyle (Pittsburgh, 1973), 3–34; Lawson-Peebles, *Landscape*, 29–43; William Robertson, *The History of the Discovery and Settlement of America* (New York, 1829), 123, 128; Juan Nuix, *Reflexiones imparciales sobre la humanidad de los Españoles en las Indias contra las pretendidos filósofos y políticos . . .* (Madrid, 1782), 303.

18. Thomas Jefferson, *Notes on the State of Virginia*, ed. William Peden (Chapel Hill, N.C., 1954), 64–65; Francesco Saverio Clavigero, *The History of Mexico* (1780) (New York, 1979), I, xxvii. For a comprehensive discussion of this dispute, see Gerbi, *The Dispute*.

The sublime mountains, however, their faces raised in the ethereal regions, watching the storms flare up, roar, shatter, and vanish at their feet, the huge and marvellous blocks on foundations of gold that balance the earth with their weight, the Andes will never move. Scorning the fury and the strength of foreign envy and peevish time, they will be the eternal heralds of freedom and victory. (226)

The Incas—like the modern Ecuadorians later—developed a superior culture because they were under the invigorating influence and protection of the Andes. In his environmental argument, Olmedo is followed by many other Spanish-American revolutionary poets, who also appealed to the American landscape as an origin for their love of liberty.[19]

As in Olmedo's *Victoria de Junín,* in Barlow's *Vision of Columbus* the American republic also incarnates the virtues already inherent in the natural landscape. However, the historical "dispute" over the nature of the New World also provides the subtext for the dialogues between Columbus and the "Seraph." Thus, Columbus asks with regard to the American man:

> Tell then, my Seer, from what dire sons of earth
> The brutal people drew their ancient birth?
> Whether in realms, the western heavens that close,
> A tribe distinct from other nations rose,
> Born to subjection; when, in happier time,
> A nobler race should hail their fruitful clime.
>
> . . . .
>
> Why various powers of soul and tints of face
> In different climes diversify the race? (52)

While Barlow, in this passage (like Olmedo in his poem), accepts the ideological premise of the determinant influences of the environment on human civilization, he goes on to invert its negative conclusions. Europeans transplanted to America become, in his narrative, not weaker, smaller, and less civilized (as European natural historians had argued) but, rather, stronger, bigger, and more virtuous. As evidence, Barlow observes that Europeans transplanted to America have a "ruddier hue" than those remaining in Europe (55). Both Olmedo and Barlow thus engage in a polemical rewriting of the natural, moral, and political value of American nature vis-à-vis Enlightenment historiography about the New World by accepting its basic premise about the connections between the

19. See Cussen, *Bello and Bolívar,* 74.

natural environment and the development of human culture, albeit by inverting its spatial determinations. The natural environment of the New World makes its creatures, cultures, and political institutions, not weaker and degenerate—but more vigorous and virtuous.[20]

The New World Histories of Olmedo and Barlow

The creoles' acceptance of the basic premise of environmentalist determinism in Enlightenment natural and philosophical history about the New World on the one hand, and the lingering presence of apparently savage peoples in the New World on the other, increasingly forced a logic onto the creole defenders of American nature that emphasized racial essentialism as an explanatory paradigm for why some inhabitants of the New World (such as the European-descended creoles) progressed in culture and civilization while others (such as Africans or native Americans) did not. Thomas Jefferson, for example, aimed to refute the arguments of Buffon that the influence of the natural environment in the Americas had resulted in a "degeneration" of transplanted species by pointing out that Euro-America had already produced a Franklin and a Washington. The achievements of Africans transplanted to the New World, by contrast, such as the poetry of Phillis Wheatley or the letters of Ignatius Sancho, were destined to be "below the dignity of criticism." If Africans transplanted to the New World are inferior, Jefferson suggests, it is not because of the degenerative influences of the American environment but because the African slaves already brought their inferiority along with them from Africa—an argument that contemporaneous Afro-British writers such as Olaudah Equiano refuted.[21]

Thus, if, as Dana D. Nelson has shown, the colonialist representation of race played an important role in the construction of early American national identities, the emergence of the distinct discourses of race and culture in these

20. Joel Barlow, *The Vision of Columbus: A Poem in Nine Books*, 1st ed. (Hartford, Conn., 1787), facs. rpt. in *The Works of Joel Barlow* (Gainesville, Fla., 1970), II; pagination in text follows the 1787 edition. This argument about the natural environment is, as Robert Lawson-Peebles has pointed out, a common (however fateful) rhetorical strategy in American Revolutionary writing (see *Landscape*, 44–57). In his discussions of Crèvecoeur, Freneau, Brackenridge, and Lewis and Clark's journal, Lawson-Peebles shows how these North American creole writers often failed to accommodate the American landscape in their Revolutionary quest for cultural independence by recoiling into European concepts about America. Similarly, Myra Jehlen has illustrated the more or less successful attempts by Jefferson and the Argentinean writer Domingo Faustino Sarmiento to escape the patriarchy of the European literary traditions in their representations of the American landscape (see Jehlen, *American Incarnation*).

21. Jefferson, *Notes on the State of Virginia*, ed. Peden, 267; Olaudah Equiano, *The Interesting Narrative and Other Writings*, ed. Vincent Carretta (New York, 1995), 45.

colonial creole texts must be seen in the larger imperial context of a trans-atlantic debate rationalizing difference in natural history since the sixteenth century. The proto-anthropological discourse of race and culture, in other words, was a (post)colonial rhetorical substitution for a discourse of nature that had underwritten the European settler empires in the New World but that was irreconcilable with creole nationalism and the new structures of imperialism emerging during the nineteenth century. In this regard, the racism of (post)colonial writers such as Jefferson is intimately linked to their defensive creole patriotism, bearing testimony to what Edmund S. Morgan has called an American "paradox" in which the liberal ideology of "equality" among whites came to be founded as the counterpart of an ideology of black racial inferiority and on the material base of black slavery.[22]

In Spanish America, which, for the most part, lacked a liberal tradition and had instead a long patrimonialist tradition of hierarchical inclusivism, the boundaries constructed by ideologies of race were somewhat more permeable than in British America. Nevertheless, the ideological investment in racial boundaries underlying creole patriotism is manifest (though distinctive) also there. In this context, Olmedo's choice in *Victoria de Junín* of Huayna Capac as the mythic founding father of Spanish-American national independence, rather than, say, the first Inca Manco, is significant. Huayna Capac, the last undisputed ruler, had broken with the Inca tradition of marrying exclusively full sisters. Upon his death (due probably to a European disease), the struggle for power between his two eldest surviving sons, Huascar and Atahualpa, half brothers from different mothers, threw the Inca state into the civil war in which the Spanish conquerors found it. Huayna Capac had therefore become something of a pariah for sixteenth-century native or mestizo historians, such as the Inca Garcilaso de la Vega, who had interpreted the subsequent Spanish conquest as God's punishment for Huayna's adulteration of the Incas' royal blood.[23]

22. Dana D. Nelson, *The Word in Black and White: Reading "Race" in American Literature, 1638–1867* (New York, 1992). For a discussion of this in the Anglo-American context, see Edmund S. Morgan, *American Slavery, American Freedom: The Ordeal of Colonial Virginia* (New York, 1975). For the Spanish-American context, see Jorge Cañizares Esguerra, "New World, New Stars: Patriotic Astrology and the Invention of Indian and Creole Bodies in Colonial Spanish America, 1600–1650," *American Historical Review,* CIV (1999), 33–68.

23. It should be noted here that the identity and status of Atahualpa's mother is controversial. The chronicler Pedro Sarmiento de Gamboa claims that Atahualpa was a "bastard." So does Titu Cusi Yupapnqui, who dictated his account of the history of the conquest in 1570, on account of the non-Inca status of his mother. The sixteenth-century chronicler Juan de Betanzos, by contrast, claims that Atahualpa's mother was from Cusco and from a royal *panaca* (descent group). However, neither Titu Cusi nor Betanzos can be assumed to be disinterested here. Titu Cusi attempted to bolster the claim of his father, Manco Inca, to the royal crown. Betanzos, on the

By contrast, Huayna Capac becomes, in Olmedo's revolutionary epic, the father of creole America who had set into motion the teleology of events culminating, not in the return of a native elite, but rather in the ascendancy of the creole avengers of a culture tragically destroyed forever by Spain. Thus, Huayna Capa addresses Bolívar: "Hijo y Amigo y Vengador del Inca! ¡Oh pueblos, que formáis un pueblo solo / y una familia, y todos sois mis hijos!" (136). [Son and friend and avenger of the Inca! Oh, you nations who constitute a single nation and one family, and you are all my sons!] The Inca empire destroyed, the creole avenger becomes the legitimate heir of Huayna Capac: "Tuya es la tierra y la victoria es tuya" (151). [Yours is the land and the victory.] Thus, the American Revolution represents, in Olmedo's poem, the return of the land to its rightful owners—the creole "children" of the (dead) Inca ruler—after it had been usurped by the European conquerors. This creole version of New World history entails the appropriation of a mythic native American past and an erasure of a native present, its plot being underwritten by its progressivist teleology. It is a totalizing plot that absorbs not only local Peruvian history but all parts of the Pan-American hemisphere that had recently become independent from European imperial powers. The history of the Aztecs, whose conquest had preceded that of the Incas, is a case in point. Thus Huayna Capac exclaims: "¡Oh dolor!, ni el solo, ni el primero: / que mis caros hermanos / el gran Guatimozín y Motezuma / conmigo el caso acerbo lamentaron" (135). [O pain, but I was not the only one nor first one, my dear brothers; the great Guatimozin and Motezuma lamented with me the bitter event [of the Conquest].] Even the sixteenth-century archenemy to creole interest in Spanish America—the Indians' *defensor* Bartolomé de las Casas—is now mobilized in Olmedo's historical synthesis for the cause of the creole insurgency—as "el martir del amor americano, / de paz, de caridad apóstol santo" (136) [the martyr of American love, of peace, of apostolic and holy charity].[24]

As in Olmedo's *Victoria de Junín,* Joel Barlow's *Vision of Columbus* projects a similarly totalizing progressivist teleology of history upon the New World designed to rationalize the creole Revolution. And, also like Olmedo, Barlow hereby develops this historical theory in a refutation of Enlightenment histo-

---

other hand, was married to Doña Angelina Yupanqui, Atahualpa's sister, and most likely got most of his information from Atahualpa's descent group. What seems clear enough is that Atahualpa's legitimacy was not recognized by the nobility of Cusco, who favored his half brother Huascar; for a discussion of this, see Ralph M. Bauer, introduction, in Titu Cusi Yupanqui, *An Inca Account of the Conquest of Peru,* ed. and trans. Bauer (Boulder, Colo., 2005).

24. Of course, the real Las Casas had, during the colonial period in the sixteenth century, been much more closely allied with Spanish metropolitan rather than creole interests; see Lewis Hanke, *The Spanish Struggle for Justice in the Conquest of America* (1949; Philadelphia, 1965).

rians such as Robertson: Why, Columbus asks the Seraph, have the Americans —"These tribes [which] have stray'd beneath the fruitful zone / Their souls unpolished and their name unknown"—not produced any great civilizations like the Western world—where "Since that unletter'd, distant tract of time / What arts have shone! / what empires found their place!"? (57–58). As an answer, the Seraph shows Columbus the great civilizations of America: the Aztec and Inca empires. In order to disprove the argument that the present native American inhabitants of the New World have degenerated from the cultural development of these ancient civilizations, Barlow argues that the present native Americans were not the descendants of the Incas and Aztecs at all but rather derive from a savage Asian stock that has not evolved but remained in its unchanging state of barbarity. The founders of the great ancient American civilizations, the Aztecs and the Incas, by contrast, had sprung, not from Asian, but rather from European origins:

> When first thy roving race, the Power reply'd
> Learn'd by the stars the devious sail to guide,
> From stormy Hellespont explored the way,
>
> . . . .
>
> Driven from those rocky straits, a hapless train
> Roll'd on the waves that sweep the western main. (55–56)

For "Europeans" (such as Aztec, Inca, and creole patriots) living in the extremities of the American environment, culture and institutions have the greatest potential to flourish. The "Indians" of Asian stock, by contrast, where "Tartar hosts for countless years, have fail'd" (56)—degenerate in the colds of the North American continent. It was these descendants from classical Greek antiquity, he claims, who built the great empires of Mexico and Peru and who are the real ancestors of Revolutionary Americans.[25]

Thus, the creole rebellion becomes the culmination of a progressive historical development in the New World that began with American antiquity. First, the poet gives a description of Mexico, which becomes America's Egypt. Tenochtitlán is built in "Memphian style"; its temples—in "eastern" and "equal pomp"— are "magnificently great"; and Moctezuma (like the Pharaohs) is "robed in state, high on a golden throne, Mid suppliant kings" (58–60). As in Olmedo's poem, in *Vision* the Spanish conquerors after Columbus, such as the "murderous

---

25. For an extensive discussion of the ideology underlying nineteenth-century Anglo-American fascination with the Aztecs and Incas, see Eric Wertheimer, *Imagined Empires: Incas, Aztecs, and the New World of American Literature, 1771–1876* (Cambridge, 1999).

Cortés," become thereby, not the ancestors of their creole descendants, but rather the epitome of a (Peninsular) Spanish cruelty and oppression (62). In Barlow's account of the second period of the American history, the Inca past becomes America's classical antiquity. Barlow's descriptions of the Inca empire abound in allusions to ancient Greece and Rome. The imperial city of Cuzco, for example, is a place where the "arts of peace" flourish (Pax Augusta) and where processions of "white-robed . . . virgins" can be watched (66). Peace, civic and public virtue prevail throughout. Manco Capac's political system (as we learn in Barlow's "Dissertation," written in prose and inserted between books 2 and 3 into the poem) was "at least equal to those of the most celebrated ancient or modern lawgivers" (86–87). Although Manco Capac's government was—like that of Augustus—despotic, it was "beyond all comparison" in his "artfully contrived" pretensions to divine authority, which linked religion and the state for the sake of his benevolent ends as well as for the benefit of his imperial subjects. In this, Barlow claims, Manco Capac equals the "most enlightened periods of antiquity, [when] only a very few of their wisest Philosophers, a Socrates, a [Cicero], or a Confucius, ever formed a just idea on the subject, or described the Deity as a God of purity, justice and benevolence" (89). Manco Capac is the incarnation of republican virtues. Like Cincinnatus, who was not naturally a warrior, he left his fields in order to defend his patria against the barbarous intruders of the tribe of Zamor. He returns to his wife Oella after subduing his enemies by gentle persuasion and promises of extending his benevolent imperial protection to them (70–71). In the "Dissertation," Barlow emphasizes that in the Inca empire the cultivation of the soil was considered a "divine art" (85). He evokes, in short, the pastoral imagery that William Dowling has called "Connecticut Georgic"—projected, however, onto the native American past as an "Inca Georgic." Revolutionary Americans thus become the direct descendants of the Incas. The British, by contrast, are linked to the barbarous tribe of Zamor, which has invaded the Inca empire and takes Sinchi Roca, Manco Capac's son, captive. The barbarous tribe (like wild "tygers") are about to offer Rocha to their "Gods of gore" in an outrageous blood sacrifice, when Manco Capac appears and engages in an epic battle with Zamor: "The strife is fierce, your fanes and fields the prize, / The warrior conquers or the infant dies" (116). The benevolent Manco Capac, who "knows to conquer, but . . . loves to spare" (124) rescues his son, who in turn, fathers twelve subsequent generations of benevolent government and American civic values.[26]

Analogously, the British—"another Wolfe" (172)—during the Revolutionary

---

26. William C. Dowling, *Poetry and Ideology in Revolutionary Connecticut* (Athens, Ga., 1990), 114.

war take America captive, thereby linking the mythic Rocha to America: "And, with increasing vollies, give the fight / . . . smear'd with clouds of dust, and bath'd in gore / . . . / Your children butcher'd and your villas burn'd" (166–167, 171). But then a new Manco, the heroic Wadsworth, comes to rescue and engages in the epic battle with the British foe: "Reverse the fate, avenge the insulted sky; / Move to the strife, we conquer or we die" (171).

Manco Capac has a prophetic vision of how "future empires from his labours rise" (69). When Tenochtitlán falls, Columbus laments ever discovering America for the Europeans; however, he is consoled by the Seraph that "future years thy rising fame extend," and future "fires of nations" will follow Mexico in America (61). In turn, Pizarro is the reincarnation of Cortés ("Another Cortez" [65]). Equally, when the empire of the "arts of Peace" in Peru is destroyed, the Seraph evokes the prospect of another empire to follow (73). Thus, by linking the Mexican and Peruvian past with the republican present, Barlow creates an American genealogy of republican values.

The New World Bard as Epic Hero

In their epic engagements with a long European tradition of deprecating representations of the New World as weak and degenerate, both poets celebrate their own roles as the cultural liberators. The cultural equivalent of the military defenders of American independence, Olmedo fashions himself, as Darío Guevara has pointed out, as the "cantor de la gran epopeya del Nuevo Mundo" [the singer of the great epic of the New World], who not only chronicles history but, with his pen, participates in and shapes the historical process. Olmedo had therefore written, in a letter to Bolívar, while at work on his poem: "Y es que si me llega el momento de la inspiración y puedo llenar el magnífico y atrevido plan que he concebido, los dos, los dos hemos de estar en la inmortalidad." [If inspiration comes to me and I can fulfill the magnificent and daring plan I have conceived, the two of us will be immortal together.][27]

Barlow's Vision of Columbus, like Olmedo's Victoria, also celebrates the New World poet as cultural warrior. And Barlow perceives his role in writing his historical poem about the American Revolution as similar to Olmedo's. After the battles are fought and won, and experience contradicts a whole historiographic tradition that claimed, with Robertson, that degenerate "Americans have never succeeded in defense of their liberty rights," it is the eyewitness-poet's task to rewrite history from his own, more advanced perspective:

27. Guevara, Olmedo, 10, and quoting Olmedo, 253.

And lo, descending from the seats of art,
The growing throngs for active scenes depart;
In various garbs they thread the welcome land,
Swords at their side or sceptres in their hand,
With healing powers bid dire diseases cease. (204)

Barlow's idea of poetry reflects thus the idea of government in the heroic Inca emperor in the second book of *Vision,* who grounded his authority for his benevolent government by creating the illusion of being the child of the sun. This illusion created by the heroic emperor Manco Capac (the "Guardian" of America) prefigures the rhetorical illusion of the *Vision* created by the Seraph and the poet Barlow himself. The rhetorical counterillusion is, like sun worship, the benign means to the "mighty plan design'd, / To bless the nations and reform mankind" (166).[28]

The Seraph-poet's rediscovery of America is thus more precisely a creole reinvention of America. The poet and recreator of history becomes in Barlow what Cynthia Jordan has called the "new patriarchy" of the learned authority figure of the Republic. In singing about the moderate and benevolent despotism of Manco, which "encouraged the advancement of knowledge, without being endangered by success" (86), Barlow sings about himself as he is trying to renegotiate the progresses and dangers that the Revolutionary zeal brought with them by creating a new, more perfect historical illusion. Thus, each Barlow and Olmedo fashions himself as the revolutionary New World man of letters who leads to cultural independence in analogy to the heroic generals whose military genius led to political independence.[29]

BOTH REVOLUTIONARY epic poets thus attempt to construct an indigenous postcolonial American history rooted in the symbols of the New World landscape and in a mythic native American past; both creole poets similarly engage with Enlightenment historiography about the New World and substitute a discourse of nature for a protoanthropological discourse of race and culture rationalizing colonial difference; and both fashion themselves thereby as literary heroes inspired by their "rebellious Muse," bringing cultural independence analogous to the military hero's bringing political independence. The difference between Olmedo and Barlow, of course, is that, whereas the latter wrote in a historical context in which the real native American and African had, for the

28. Robertson, *History,* 347.

29. Cynthia Jordan, "Old Worlds in New Circumstances: Language and Leadership in Post-Revolutionary America," *American Quarterly,* XL (1988), 491–523, esp. 506.

time being, been excluded from the new nation-state, the former wrote in a context in which the creole nation builders had to reckon with the Indian and African-descended populations and therefore fostered the expectation that independence from Spain would also bring about their freedom. Not coincidentally, throughout independent Spanish America slavery was abolished, and the United States would be absent from the Pan-American Congress that met in Panama in 1826 in order to establish a hemispheric order of free American nation-states—mainly because of the powerful interests of the southern slave states. Thus, like many other Spanish-American Revolutionaries, Olmedo actively lobbied for the rights of (living) Indians, when, for instance, speaking out against the *mita* (tribute labor) before the Cortes of Cádiz. Unlike their Protestant contemporaries in the northern part of the hemisphere, the Spanish-American states did not in principle exclude philosophically (or exterminate physically) the subaltern social sectors upon whose labor and land modernity was being built in the increasingly globalized networks of exchange. Faced with a relative lack in social and racial cohesion that had characterized the societies of Europe and the neo-European outposts of British America, elite Spanish American creoles could not agree to all be equal, for they had failed to disqualify their nonequals as men.[30]

30. On Olmedo's advocacy for the Indians and denouncement of the *mita* before the courts of Cádiz, see Guevara, *Olmedo*, 121–130.

SANDRA M. GUSTAFSON

Natty in the 1820s: Creole Subjects and Democratic Aesthetics in the Early Leatherstocking Tales

Transamerican Cooper

Summing up the impact of James Fenimore Cooper's literary career for an audience of mourners in 1852, William Cullen Bryant eulogized his longtime friend as the author of works whose global reach even a contemporary writer might envy:

> Here we lament the ornament of our country, there they mourn the death of him who delighted the human race. Even now, while I speak, the pulse of grief which is passing through the nations has haply just reached some remote neighbourhood; the news of his death has been brought to some dwelling on the slopes of the Andes, or amidst the snowy wastes of the North, and the dark-eyed damsel of Chile, or the fair-haired maid of Norway, is sad to think that he whose stories of heroism and true love have so often kept her for hours from her pillow, lives no more.

In the distinction that he draws between mourning Cooper "here" and mourning him "there," Bryant propounds a relationship between Cooper the nationalist icon and Cooper the international literary celebrity. As Bryant's remarks suggest, Cooper's works were among the first major cultural exports of the United States, both in Europe and in Latin America, where Cooper became what Kirsten Silva Gruesz has called an "ambassador of culture." Gruesz analyzes the mutually constitutive nature of the national and the transnational literary publics in the nineteenth century in a way that illuminates the relationship between Bryant's "here" and "there," observing that major nineteenth-century writers "appear within the transnational sphere . . . as ambassadorial icons of national cultures." Identifying Cooper as a central instance of the phenomenon of cultural ambassadorship, Gruesz rightly notes the potent "nationalistic desires" that shape international literary reputations in this era while also observing the volatility of national and cosmopolitan literary identities, particularly in postcolonial settings such as those of the Americas. Cooper is a particularly complex instance of this volatility.[1]

From the almost mythic beginning of his literary career, which famously began when he claimed that he could write a better book than an English novelist and met his wife's ensuing challenge by producing *Precaution* (1821), Cooper was deeply committed to the creation of a postcolonial culture in the United States. He rapidly became an icon of American literary nationalism, representing distinctively American figures and historical events in his fiction and, in his nonfiction, articulating a vigorous defense of American institutions in the face of European criticism. Yet Cooper's cultural and political nationalisms were far from simple. His adaptation of British literary models, notably Scott and Shakespeare, is well known. Cooper's reliance on these precursors is best understood in the context of his continuing meditations on patrimony, property, and political life as they shape a society's literature. What did the United States inherit from the British Empire, politically and culturally, and how was that heritage transformed after Independence? What other sorts of paternal relations were available to the new nation? Attempting to answer these questions, Cooper populated his novels with patriarchs of varying nationalities and moral constitutions. In his political writings as well, Cooper manifested a complex and shifting blend of nationalism and dissent born of cosmopolitan experience. A lengthy sojourn in Europe in the 1830s fueled a comparative political and sociological strain in his thought that found much to celebrate in American experience but also much to criticize. His running feud with the media in his homeland over his role as a public figure, which culminated in a successful lawsuit for slander, best reveals his considerable ambivalence about his role as a national icon and ambassador of culture.

Cooper's complicated role as voice for and critic of the United States, positioned between the national and the cosmopolitan, has been well analyzed by an earlier generation of scholars who focused on Cooper's transatlantic experiences. Much modern criticism, however, has tended to present Cooper as the nationalist ideologue of Jacksonian America's most pernicious projects: racial purism and Indian Removal. Such readings rely almost exclusively on *The Last*

---

1. William Cullen Bryant, "The Life, Character, and Genius of James Fenimore Cooper," in *Memorial of James Fenimore Cooper* (New York, 1852), 39–74 (quoted passage, 72–73); Kirsten Silva Gruesz, *Ambassadors of Culture: The Transamerican Origins of Latino Writing* (Princeton, N.J., 2002), 15.

of the Mohicans. When Cooper's criticisms of the United States are addressed, they tend to be cast as evidence of his antidemocratic sensibilities rather than as proof of Cooper's belief in the importance of dissent. In light of modern transatlantic conflicts, it would seem that Cooper's effort to shape a nationalism that takes cosmopolitan exchange seriously has much to teach us.[2]

One arena where the image of Cooper the racial purist and mythographer of the nation has been critically examined is in studies of his hemispheric impact. In her influential *Foundational Fictions,* Doris Sommer describes the enormous popularity of Cooper's fiction in newly independent Spanish-American nations. When Bryant told of the occupants of Andean dwellings and dark-eyed Chilean maidens reading Cooper's works and mourning his death, it seems he was scarcely exaggerating. According to Sommer, Cooper's immense popularity in Latin America was the result of a hunger in these postcolonial societies for models of founding romances that could be adapted to legitimate their own newly national regimes. Sommer's approach to Cooper as a transamerican author portrays him as both a cultural ambassador and a strong literary father to be challenged and revised, Harold Bloom fashion, by his Spanish-American literary offspring. Sommer usefully highlights "Cooper's possibly ambivalent position between classical, clearly defined, signs and romantic evolutionism," an ambivalence that manifests itself in the attractiveness with which he invests Cora in *Mohicans.* According to Sommer, that elusive quality in Cooper's racial thought was eliminated in the Argentine writer Domingo Sarmiento's reading of Cooper in *Facundo* (1845), where Sarmiento produces an unambiguously racist taxonomy of progressive continental domination. In another work Deborah J. Rosenthal reads Cooper the way that Sommer says Sarmiento does, pointing to a contrast between Cooper's monoracial vision of a postcolonial order as depicted in *Last of the Mohicans* and the celebrations of *mestizaje* (or racial mixture) that can be found in the works of a number of Cooper's Spanish-American followers (other than Sarmiento). While the treatment of Cooper as progenitor usefully highlights how Spanish-American writers who came after him variously adapted and responded to his literary models, the

2. Much modern scholarship has examined *The Last of the Mohicans,* a novel that, when read apart from the other works in the series, readily lends itself to incorporation in the Vanishing Indian mythos. Of special importance is Richard Slotkin's influential introduction to the Penguin edition of *Last of the Mohicans* (New York, 1986). In *Regeneration through Violence: The Mythology of the American Frontier, 1600–1860* (Middletown, Conn., 1973), Slotkin offers a truncated reading of *The Prairie* that identifies some of the features of the novel that interest me but calls them the "bare suggestion of a conclusion" (495–496), emphasizing Cooper's return to the series in the 1840s. What I wish to stress here is the importance of viewing the two parts of the Leatherstocking series in their different historical and biographical moments.

approach has the disadvantage of reproducing the cultural hegemony of the United States in the hemisphere while also focusing too narrowly on a single Cooper text and thereby reducing the potential meanings of his fictions.[3]

In this essay I treat Cooper, not as a literary father, but as a contemporary of a group of Spanish Americans writing in the 1820s who expressed the political and cultural difference of the postcolonial Americas through references to indigenous traditions and the indigenous past. Like Cooper, these writers embraced and appropriated aspects of native life and history to define their emerging national identities. In one notable Spanish-American example, José Joaquín de Olmedo's epic poem *La Victoria de Junín: canto a Bolívar* (1825), Olmedo seeks cultural and political legitimacy for a newly independent Peru by depicting the spirit of Inca Huayna Capac as he proclaims Bolívar to be his political descendant and the creole Peruvians as the heirs of the Inca empire—a lineage that Bolívar pointedly rejected in a letter to his friend. Olmedo's controversial strategy in the poem was made possible by a brutal history: creole authorities had wiped out the Inca elite after the rebellion of Tupac Amaru II in the early 1780s, leaving the indigenous population without leadership and the Inca past subject to appropriation. The situation in the United States was somewhat different, though no less brutal, as creole settlers and the United States government faced continued indigenous resistance movements led by such men as Tecumseh and Black Hawk in wars that posed a real challenge to the country's imperial expansion, even as Indian Removal became a reality. Writers in the United States did in some cases stage Olmedo-style appropriations of an indigenous heritage. During the 1820s and 1830s, in the thick of debates over Indian Removal, Tecumseh and native leaders were celebrated as tragic heroes, most notably in a vogue for Indian tragic drama that began in earnest with John Augustus Stone's *Metamora; or, The Last of the Wampanoags* (1829) and lasted through the 1830s. Alternatively, writers turned to a far distant, epic native past associated with the newly imagined Mound Builder culture. In "The Prairies" (1834), perhaps the closest analogue to the Olmedo poem, Cooper's Hispanophile friend Bryant sought a parallel in the lost Mound Builder society to the robust indigenous imperial heritages to be found in Aztec and Inca so-

---

3. Doris Sommer, *Foundational Fictions: The National Romances of Latin America* (Berkeley, Calif., 1991), chap. 2 (quote, 68); and Debra J. Rosenthal, "Race Mixture and the Representation of Indians in the U.S. and the Andes: *Cumandá, Aves sin nido, The Last of the Mohicans*, and *Ramona*," in Monika Kaup and Debra J. Rosenthal, eds., *Mixing Race, Mixing Culture: Inter-American Literary Dialogues* (Austin, Tex., 2002), chap. 7. An anonymous reviewer of this essay takes issue with Sommer's reading of Sarmiento, finding that he mirrors Cooper's ambivalence when he praises the gaucho's oneness with the pampa even as he anticipates the gaucho's demise.

cieties. This advanced Mound Builder society was expunged, Bryant claims in a striking parallel to the Book of Mormon, by "red" barbarians who had themselves conveniently vanished westward, leaving the fertile land empty and almost panting for its new, white possessors, who would recreate the greatness of the American past.[4]

Cooper never imagines so direct an appropriation of a native inheritance for creole citizens of the United States. While he consistently describes the displacement of native communities by creoles as inevitable, often in strongly fatalistic terms, he nevertheless portrays the cultural dynamics of creole-native relations in a much richer and more varied way than Bryant (whose Indians are either dead or missing) or Olmedo (whose Inca is a ghost). Particularly in *The Prairie* (1827), the third Leatherstocking Tale which ends in Natty Bumppo's death, thereby bringing to a close the cluster of novels that he wrote in the 1820s, Cooper portrays a surprising array of relationships between creoles and native Americans. While Bryant's prairies are temporarily vacant, land that is not virgin but rather a still attractive and fertile widow eagerly awaiting a new (white) spouse, Cooper's prairies are broad swaths of topography that only appear to be empty land. In scene after scene of *The Prairie,* what appears to be uninhabited space is revealed to contain multitudes—rival groups of Sioux and Pawnee hunters, the traveling caravan led by patriarch Ishmael Bush seeking "the Eldorado of the West," vast herds of buffalo, groups of federal soldiers, and of course the aging Natty Bumppo, who first appears in a golden haze of natural apotheosis that anticipates his end. The seven years between Cooper's and Bryant's ideologically charged depictions of the heartland cannot explain their radically different portraits of a contested terrain.[5]

One of the main differences between these writers, I would suggest, is their different relationships to Latin America. As a youth, Cooper was drawn to the revolutionary aspirations of Francisco de Miranda, but in the 1820s Spanish-American indigenism and republicanism provided a comparatively distant horizon for him. He did not share the Hispanophile enthusiasms of literary friends and rivals such as Bryant and Irving and Longfellow, preferring to focus on Europe rather than the Southern Hemisphere. Apart from *The Prairie's* Hispanic-American characters, among Cooper's thirty-six novels with their

4. Ralph Bauer discusses Olmedo's poem in his essay in this volume. Gruesz discusses Bryant's "The Prairies" in *Ambassadors,* 48–56. Anthony Pagden treats the figure of the Indian in Spanish-American political thought in *Spanish Imperialism and the Political Imagination: Studies in European and Spanish-American Social and Political Theory, 1513–1830* (New Haven, Conn., 1990).

5. James Fenimore Cooper. *The Leatherstocking Tales* (New York, 1985), I, 889. All further references to this edition will appear parenthetically in the text.

various historical and geographic settings, only two have even loosely defined Spanish-American settings or themes: *Mercedes of Castile; or, The Voyage to Cathay* (1840), which portrays Columbus's voyage to the West Indies; and *Jack Tier; or, The Florida Reef* (1846), which is set in the Florida Keys during the Mexican War. In the early 1820s, perhaps influenced by the promulgation of the Monroe Doctrine in 1823, Cooper advocated knowledge of Spanish as an essential component of education in the United States, believing in the importance of future commercial ties between North and South America. This ambition to bind the hemispheres linguistically met with only limited success even in Cooper's own family; the Coopers did better at mastering French during their long residence in France. Moreover, though his budding friendship with Bryant might have raised his awareness of Latin America in the 1820s, I have found nothing to suggest that he read the literature of the new southern republics. The influence of Spanish-American republicanism and indigenism on Cooper's fiction of the 1820s, then, was diffuse and indirect, but nevertheless important for understanding the full context of Cooper's literary and social thought. Cooper engages in what was at the time a hemispheric intellectual project of uncovering native precedents for national civic life, and the differences with his Spanish-American peers reveal an unfamiliar side of Cooper.[6]

The Cooper that emerges from this juxtaposition is one who does not so readily anticipate the eradication of native peoples as some critics claim but rather, as Sommer notes, reveals substantial ambivalence about the racial and gender taxonomies that his works nevertheless at times reinforce. Perhaps most significantly, Cooper does not turn to vanished indigenous empires to validate civic life in the United States. Rather, he examines contemporary native political life for analogies to the emerging democracy of his own day. Cooper's interest in indigenous forms of government clearly marks *The Last of the Mohicans,* notably in his portraits of the demagogue Magua and the dynamics of debate among the Hurons and the Delawares. But his sympathetic portrayal of native civic life emerges most fully, and is most directly linked to creole practices of civic leadership, in *The Prairie.* This least-read of the Leatherstocking Tales is also the one most openly engaged with the conduct of politics. In *The Prairie* Cooper manifests a complex engagement with native American political practices, finding in them some models (both positive and negative) for demo-

6. Wayne Franklin notes Cooper's early attraction to Miranda's insurgency in *James Fenimore Cooper: The Early Years* (New Haven, Conn., 2007), 68. Robert E. Spiller, *Fenimore Cooper: Critic of His Times* (New York, 1931), 82; Stanley T. Williams notes Cooper's "indifference" to Latin America, apart from his sense of emerging commercial ties, in *The Spanish Background of American Literature* (New Haven, Conn., 1955), I, 223, 390.

cratic republican governance. This novel also depicts the incorporation of an ethnically alien population into the United States. In an instance of what Sommer has called "national romance," Cooper portrays a marriage between Captain Duncan Uncas Middleton (a descendant of the Anglo-American founding couple in *Last of the Mohicans*, Duncan Middleton and Alice Heyward, who also bears the name of Natty's dead Indian "son") and Inez (the daughter of the creole patriarch Don Augustin de Certavallos, a newly Americanized citizen in the recently annexed territory of Louisiana). Significantly, then, Cooper's fullest depiction of native Americans as republicans takes place in the novel where he depicts the integration of Spanish Americans into the society of the United States. Noting that "time was necessary to blend the numerous and affluent colonists of the lower province with their new compatriots" (888), Cooper portrays a cautious mixing of creole societies—one that is almost disrupted first when Inez is kidnapped on her wedding night by the slave-stealing Bush family and again when she becomes the object of desire for two Indian chiefs. Ultimately, though, Middleton and Inez successfully consummate their union, and Don Augustin's wealth and social influence propel Middleton to the highest levels of American politics. The political and familial are still further intertwined as Cooper constitutes a mixed family for Natty when he adopts the Pawnee chief Hard-Heart, who in turn offers a model of heroic civic leadership to future representatives Middleton and Paul Hover. Situated in a transamerican discourse of political and cultural origins, this reading of *The Prairie* offers a more complex, less starkly racist and nationalist Cooper that provides a valuable point of comparison to Spanish-American creole indigenism.

Becoming Creole Subjects in the Age of Democratic Revolution

In its portraits of heroic Indian leadership and its creole inheritors, *The Prairie* registers the impact of Cooper's first encounter with Europe. Begun in the Unites States but largely completed in France, the novel manifests at the level of plot and characterization the profound and somewhat defensive response of an American author confronted with the anti-Americanism that was common in elite European society at this time. *Notions of the Americans,* Cooper's challenge to and tonic for that anti-Americanism, appeared the year following *The Prairie,* and the letters that he wrote as he was finishing the novel are filled with the kinds of resentments that fueled the composition of his subsequent work. Already in his novel we see Cooper reimagining his presentation of American life in response to European critics. Among the most important of these revisions are his depictions of indigenous societies, of native and creole political life, and of the relationships between natives and creoles. These transformations are best read as reflections of Cooper's hopefulness about American democracy, crystallized by his optimism about Andrew Jackson's leadership and a nationalist impulse that emerged strongly in the face of European condescension. In *The Prairie* Cooper's heroic Indians symbolize the value and legitimacy of New World civic forms, offering a corrective to Old World structures of power.

The changes in emphasis across Cooper's Leatherstocking novels reveal the variety of ways that the indigenous inhabitants of the Americas contributed to creole self-imaginings. From the early years of European colonization, creole subjects in the Americas formed themselves and were formed *as creoles* through acts of conscious triangulation with indigenous American and European identities. Measuring the unstable distance between the New World and the Old, creole authors positioned themselves as the tip of the transatlantic triangle, closer to or farther from their two points of reference—and often above them in a moral or social sense. Transcending indigenous and European realities, creoles imagined themselves mounting beyond those worlds both spatially and temporally as they moved along the high road to modernity. Creole authors expressed this view of their societies with unusual urgency and directness during the Age of Revolution, from the beginning of the American Revolution in 1776 until Símon Bolívar's death in 1830. Transforming imperial subjects into republican citizens, revolutionaries north and south rejected Old World structures of authority and identity in favor of republican forms drawn from ancient Greek and Roman models while imbuing these classical antecedents with the indigenous difference that marked off the modern world of the Americas from premodern Europe.

Throughout the Americas the Indian represented an authenticity, a proximity to nature and to a primal social order that in Europe had been buried beneath the cultural, social, and political debris of many centuries. In British North America the republican Indian became an important figure in the 1740s when the rise of classical republican thought sparked a vogue in Indian eloquence that Benjamin Franklin's published version of the 1744 Lancaster Treaty helped to fuel, and it accumulated cultural significance in the 1770s and 1780s, when Thomas Jefferson celebrated native oratory and mythologized the eloquent Logan. During the war anti-British cartoons portrayed the North American colonies as an Indian woman, and Revolutionaries dressed as Indians engaged in acts of resistance in Boston and beyond. Celebration of the republican Indian was somewhat subdued in the United States in the 1780s, as the native "savage" was tied to the supposedly anarchic lower orders in the conflict-filled years leading up to the Federal Constitutional Convention. Interest in the republican Indian never completely disappeared, however, and it reawakened with special vigor in the 1820s when the status and rights of Indians were hotly contested issues. A flurry of novels, autobiographies, speeches, and plays during this decade examined the historical experience of native Americans and the contemporary relevance of Indian life for republican creoles. A similar phenomenon arose in Latin America in the 1820s, where *Incaísmo* became an important intellectual and literary movement in the new Andean republics. Works in the Incaísmo vein typically passed over the actual history of indigenous and creole relations to portray the creoles themselves as equal victims of imperial Spain with the Incas and as inheritors destined to reclaim and fulfill the Inca empire's glories.[7]

The parallel interest in tracing an indigenous heritage for creole nationalism in the Andean republics and the United States during the 1820s developed in competing directions that reflect the different indigenous histories and histories of colonization of the two regions. Bolívar viewed the descendants of the indigenous Andeans as peasants unfit for self-governance. Moreover, he shared to some extent Anglo-American views of Spanish rule, which he characterized as preeminent in "ferocity, ambition, vindictiveness, and greed." Bolívar dismissed the possibility of popular government in Latin America: "As long as our countrymen do not acquire the abilities and political virtues that distinguish our brothers of the north, wholly popular systems, far from working to our advantage, will, I greatly fear, bring about our downfall." He envisioned a

7. See my discussion of the republican Indian and the "savage" speaker in *Eloquence Is Power: Oratory and Performance in Early America* (Chapel Hill, N.C., 2000), 116–117, 138–139, 204–205. Philip J. Deloria describes the Revolutionary and early republican uses of Indian costume in *Playing Indian* (New Haven, Conn., 1998), chaps. 1, 2. The most important literary works from the 1820s that take the North American Indian as their subject include an epic poem, James Wallis Eastburn and Robert Sands's *Yamoyden, A Tale of the Wars of King Philip: In Six Cantos* (1820); autobiographies including *A Narrative of the Life of Mrs. Mary Jemison,* edited by James Everett Seaver (1824), and the two published versions of William Apess's life story; novels such as the first three Leatherstocking Tales of James Fenimore Cooper (*The Pioneers* [1823], *The Last of the Mohicans* [1826], and *The Prairie* [1827]), Lydia Maria Child's *Hobomok* (1824), and Catharine Maria Sedgwick's *Hope Leslie* (1827); and a substantial number of Indian plays, notably John Augustus Stone's *Metamora; or, The Last of the Wampanoags* (1829). Susan Scheckel treats the importance of Indian issues in politics and culture during the 1820s in *The Insistence of the Indian: Race and Nationalism in Nineteenth-Century American Culture* (Princeton, N.J., 1998), chap. 1. For an example of Incaismo in revolutionary Latin America, see José Joaquín de Olmedo, *La Victoria de Junín: canto a Bolívar* (Quito, n.d.). Don Marcelino Menéndez y Pelayo discusses Olmedo's poem in *Historia de la poesía hispano-americana* (Madrid, 1911), 148–149. Antonio Cornejo Polar discusses "el *incaismo*" in *La formación de la tradición literaria en el Perú* (Lima, 1989), 31–35.

strongly centralized, partly hereditary republican government modeled on the Roman Republic to provide elite leadership and strong moral discipline to the lower orders. Yet, despite his distrust of the plebs, in at least one way Bolívar proved committed to a form of equality unknown in the north. In 1816, influenced by his experiences in Haiti, Bolívar proclaimed the abolition of slavery, an act that he repeatedly described as both morally and politically essential to the founding of stable republics.[8]

In the United States a powerful movement toward universal white manhood suffrage transformed the political landscape and made the country into the first popular democracy since ancient Athens. The transformation from an elite republic to a democratic republic inclusive of all white men occurred under the watchful gaze of Europeans, who scrutinized the nation for the social and cultural effects of democracy. Spanish Americans, too, looked to the United States, viewing it variously as a role model or a cautionary example for their emerging republics. After the promulgation of the Monroe Doctrine in 1823 the southern republics saw the country as a potential ally and an imperial threat. Many Americans, in turn, viewed the European and Spanish-American states as competing social and political orders. European monarchies and empires were often seen to present an obstacle to republican progress, particularly when republican revolutionary movements such as the one in Greece met with hostility and repression from threatened monarchs. Spanish-American revolutionary thought offered a complex response and challenge to the American model, one that was more hierarchical but less racial. Some influential American political leaders feared that the Spanish-American republics undermined the institution of slavery in the United States and worried that abolition in the Southern Hemisphere called into question the legitimacy of the white republic of the north.

This international climate of intense political creativity and instability helped focus American attention on the fate of the continent's indigenous peoples. From the Republic's earliest years, concern about world opinion had influenced the government's Indian policy. European travelers' accounts typically incorporated justly caustic observations on the fate of American Indians. Strident American nationalists who championed the nation's history of political progressivism invited bitter and often sarcastic European responses about brutalized natives. In this general climate, three factors contributed most importantly to

8. Both quotations are from Simón Bolívar's most famous early political statement, the "Jamaica Letter" of 1815, in Vicente Lecuna, comp., Harold A. Bierck, Jr., ed., Lewis Bertrand, trans., *Selected Writings of Bolívar*, 2d ed. (New York, 1951), I, 115.

the peculiar shape of the Indian vogue in the United States during the 1820s: the rise of Andrew Jackson to political prominence, and his pursuit of Indian Removal as national policy; the emergence of the country as a political democracy; and the rise of independence movements in Latin America and Greece.[9]

Andrew Jackson's public reputation embodies the paradoxes of the phenomenon that Richard Slotkin has called "regeneration through violence." Jackson's contemporaries described him as a "natural man" whose cultural proximity to the native allowed him to absorb and redeploy Indian traits and abilities in order to destroy actual Indians. In a particularly clear instance of the triangulation that produces creole identity, Jackson earned the fame that fueled his political career both for his defeat of the British at New Orleans in 1815 and for his Indian fighting during that same decade. The defeat of both British and native opponents reenacted the major oppositions of the American Revolution, when most tribes sided with the British and when the Indian threat exacerbated patriot anxieties. The contrast with the independence movement in the Andes, where native resistance had been wiped out forty years earlier, is instructive. Elected president in 1828, Jackson proceeded to implement his Indian Removal policy despite the adverse ruling of the Supreme Court, construing creole entitlement to North American lands as a natural law that superseded human law in order to force eastern native inhabitants west across the Mississippi River.[10]

The paradox of Jacksonian creolism deepens when we pursue the second factor contributing to the Indian vogue: the rapid spread of the suffrage to unpropertied white men and the rise of popular political activism. In the 1820s and 1830s the frontiersman became a synechdochical figure for the common man, the white man of little or no property who in many instances had been excluded from full citizenship rights by the states after the Revolution. Americans in the 1820s saw a connection between democratization and the frontier akin to the one that Frederick Jackson Turner later made explicit in *The Frontier*

9. As president, George Washington feared that America would be classed with Spain in the international court of public opinion unless the nation established a more benign relationship with the continent's native peoples. See my discussion in *Eloquence Is Power*, 261.

10. John William Ward discusses the portrayal of Jackson as "nature's nobleman" in *Andrew Jackson: Symbol for an Age* (New York, 1955), chap. 3. Michael Paul Rogin analyzes Jackson's ambivalent identification with and efforts to distance himself from Indian savagery in *Fathers and Children: Andrew Jackson and the Subjugation of the American Indian* (New York, 1975). Rogin writes: "Jackson began on the frontier. . . . He returned to nature in Indian war. A deadly combat of brothers secured Jackson's birthright, and prepared him to claim national authority" (113). For an elaboration of "regeneration through violence," see Slotkin's influential analysis of early American culture in *Regeneration through Violence,* notably in chap. 13 on Cooper's Leatherstocking cycle.

in American History (1920). In his first, most famous statement of his frontier thesis in "The Significance of the Frontier in American History" (first presented 1893), Turner wrote of the process of creolization as the Indianization of the European:

> The wilderness masters the colonist. It finds him a European in dress, industries, tools, modes of travel, and thought. It takes him from the railroad car and puts him in the birch canoe. It strips off the garments of civilization and arrays him in the hunting shirt and the moccasin. It puts him in the log cabin of the Cherokee and the Iroquois and runs an Indian palisade around him. Before long he has gone to planting Indian corn and plowing with a sharp stick; he shouts the war cry and takes the scalp in orthodox Indian fashion.

The frontier and its main product, the Indianized, egalitarian, and individualistic white man, has been the agent of promoting "democracy here and in Europe," Turner continues. Writing in the "Contributions of the West to American Democracy," Turner described Jackson as the "very personification" of frontier democracy. Turner quoted Albert Gallatin's description of Jackson when he first entered Congress in the 1790s: "A tall, lank, uncouth-looking personage, with long locks of hair hanging over his face and a cue down his back tied in an eel-skin; his dress singular; his manners those of a rough backwoodsman." And he quoted Jefferson on Jackson's inability to speak in the Senate "on account of the rashness of his feelings": "I have seen him attempt it repeatedly and as often choke with rage." Turner's portrait of Jackson pits the rough force of a white male democracy formed on the frontier against the older generation of republicans formed in contact with Europe. Gallatin and Jefferson are the voice of the past, Jackson's the not yet fully articulate voice of the future.[11]

Though Turner's thesis has been challenged and at least partly discredited as an explanation for the spread of the suffrage, with contemporary scholars placing more importance on urban settings than on the frontier, he was right to recognize the important connection between the Indianized frontiersman and the rise of democracy in the minds of Jackson's contemporaries. The frontier loomed large as a laboratory for democracy in the 1820s. *The Prairie*'s Paul Hover starts life as a lowly bee hunter and ends up a state legislator with a knack for humorous speeches and pragmatic wisdom. Early in the novel Paul refers to the immensely popular song "The Hunters of Kentucky," written to celebrate

---

11. Frederick Jackson Turner, *The Frontier in American History* (1920) (New York, 1996), 4, 30, 252–253.

Jackson's victory in New Orleans, a defining act of creole violence that pitted him against both the indigenous inhabitants of the continent and the representatives of the Old World. The song celebrated Kentucky fighters who were "half a horse, / And half an alligator," popularizing a colorful colloquial phrase that would later become associated with David Crockett. In the early 1820s Crockett was a Tennessee state legislator with a growing national reputation, and later in the decade he gained fame as a representative to the federal Congress. There he became an even more radical exponent of democracy than Jackson, defending the rights of squatters and other landless folks in western Tennessee against the eastern Tennessee planters, including Jackson himself. In a move that had been anticipated by the Shaysites and the Whiskey Rebels, Crockett identified the western borderlands with egalitarianism, resisting incursions from the elite-dominated eastern part of the state. Where the earlier instances of border resistance failed, however, Crockett succeeded at the cultural level (though he, too, failed at his political goals of defending squatters' rights). Like Cooper's Hover, Crockett emerged as a tall-talking, good-natured frontier politician with the people's interests at heart, who used his wits, his sense of humor, and his natural verbal skill to triumph over better-educated opponents. It was an image with tremendous appeal and widespread influence in the antebellum period.[12]

The third factor influencing the rise of interest in indigenous peoples during the 1820s was the spread of republican revolution to the southern part of the hemisphere, and to Europe, where the revolutionary resistance in Greece challenged Ottoman control. Patterned after the American Revolution, solicitous of United States support, and yet perceived by some Americans as a threat rather than as a fulfillment of their own example, the Spanish-American independence movements led by Simón Bolívar and José de San Martín involved a dramatically different indigenous population. Where in the United States the native population existed primarily on the nation's borders during the Revolution and was pressed west with increasing urgency and violence in subsequent years, the indigenous Andean peoples were more integrated with the descendants of the Spanish—an integration facilitated, if not indeed enforced, by the extermination of the Inca elite. The most important difference between the northern and southern revolutionary movements in the eyes of many Americans, however, was the clear antislavery position taken by Bolívar after 1815, when he won military assistance from the Haitian government by pledging his commitment

12. First performed in 1822, "The Hunters of Kentucky" remained immensely popular throughout the decades and was used as a campaign song in the 1828 presidential election. John William Ward discusses the song in chap. 2 of *Andrew Jackson* and reproduces a broadside of the song in plate 8.

to liberate slaves. When in the mid-1820s Bolívar proposed a hemispheric congress to be held in Panama that would bring together representatives of the United States with those of the new Spanish-American republics, the proposal sparked three months of intense debates in the United States Congress. Proponents, including Daniel Webster, called on their government to recognize and support its sister republics, and opponents, many from southern states, objected to an alliance with abolitionist governments and feared a threat to the existence of slavery in the United States.

Also in the 1820s, the revolution in Greece against Ottoman control heightened tensions between American supporters of the Greeks and European monarchies fearful for their sovereignty. An international philhellenic movement to support the Greek revolutionaries arose, supported most famously by Lord Byron as well as by the prominent American doctor Samuel Gridley Howe. The revolution also helped to promote transatlantic interest in ancient Greece as a model of democratic political life. The significance of this unprecedented interest in Greek democracy should not be underestimated. For centuries the Athenian experiment had been considered the nadir of civilized political life. Indeed, political philosophy was born and developed for two millennia in an important sense as an effort to present alternatives to the failed Athenian experience. Only in the nineteenth century did democracy undergo a rehabilitation. Studying ancient Athens for the possibilities it revealed about democracy, beginning in the 1820s John Stuart Mill and his circle in England and Edward Everett and George Bancroft in the United States participated in a thoroughgoing reconsideration of the potential for a democratic polity. In 1821 the Harvard Corporation began its display of the popular *Panorama of Athens,* a depiction of ancient Athens whose purchase Everett had championed. Everett also played a role in Daniel Webster's famous 1824 speech to the Senate, in which Webster argued that as the world's leading republic the United States had a duty to defend Greek independence. In this speech Webster also attacked European monarchs opposing the resistance movement, celebrated ancient Greek political life, and highlighted the "white slavery" of Greeks to the Ottoman Turks.[13]

13. Noting that "throughout most of Western history, Athenian democracy per se has been in bad odor," Jennifer Tolbert Roberts observes that "the anti-Athenian tradition has become a crucial building block of Western political thought." See her *Athens on Trial: The Antidemocratic Tradition in Western Thought* (Princeton, N.J., 1994), xi–xii. Thomas Gustafson traces one important element of anti-Athenianism in his discussion of the "Thucydidean moment" when "political and linguistic disorders . . . become one and the same" (*Representative Words: Politics, Literature, and the American Language, 1776–1865* [Cambridge, 1992], 13). The transatlantic interest in Greek democracy is discussed in Nadia Urbinati, *Mill on Democracy: From the Athenian Polis to Representative Government* (Chicago, 2002), 33. George Bancroft, the future Democrat and democratic

During the 1820s, then, political forces both within and without the United States pushed American intellectuals to rethink their republican experiment and to define the meaning of their emerging democracy in relation to other political orders, both past and present. Few writers engaged in this project with the intensity and earnestness of James Fenimore Cooper. He did so in two ways: by writing a mock travel narrative (*Notions of the Americans* [1828]) that purported to view the United States through the eyes of a European bachelor, offering a largely celebratory portrait of American democracy; and by writing the first three Leatherstocking Tales, where by the end of *The Prairie* native American communities emerge as the clearest examples of democratic societies governed by influence and persuasion rather than by law or hierarchy. In these works of the 1820s, Cooper projected newly democratized creole subjects, using the triangulating strategies of creolism that he shared with his Spanish-American peers to define American democrats in relation to Europeans and indigenous Americans.

Creole Indianization and Cooper's Aesthetics of Democracy

Cooper had a complex but, for most of his life, largely positive relationship with the emerging representative democracy that distinguished the United States in the eyes of the world in his day. The son of a self-made man who was both a product of the democratizing forces unleashed by the Revolution and their victim, Cooper was a longtime supporter of Andrew Jackson, defending the most radical positions of Jackson's Democratic Party; a contributor, along with Nathaniel Hawthorne, Walt Whitman, and George Bancroft, to John O'Sullivan's influential Democratic Party organ, the *United States Magazine, and Democratic Review;* and a champion of a version of American democracy that combined a liberal commitment to individual rights with a class-oriented analysis of the distribution of power.[14]

---

historian, studied Greek history in a German university and translated a German history of Greece in 1823. Also during the 1820s, Edward Everett published important essays on ancient and modern Greece in the *North American Review,* including the one that Daniel Webster drew on for his Senate speech in favor of Greek independence. Webster's motion to send a commissioner to Greece ultimately failed. On this speech, see Irving H. Bartlett, *Daniel Webster* (New York, 1978), 101–103. Caroline Winterer traces the shift from a predominantly Roman identification to a Greek-oriented democratic republicanism during the antebellum period, noting the Harvard Corporation's display of the *Panorama of Athens* from 1821, in *The Culture of Classicism: Ancient Greece and Rome in American Intellectual Life, 1780–1910* (Baltimore, 2002), 66–67.

14. Alan Taylor describes the Cooper family's experience with democratic forces on the New York frontier in *William Cooper's Town: Power and Persuasion on the Frontier of the Early American*

Particularly in his writings of the 1820s, Cooper optimistically examined the prospects of the democracy that was unfolding around him. *Notions of the Americans* openly celebrates the egalitarianism and political system of the United States. Writing shortly after his removal to Europe in 1826 at the behest of the American Revolutionary hero General Lafayette, who had become his close friend and who remained a strong proponent of the United States, Cooper offered in *Notions* a defense against the trickle (soon to become a flood) of criticism to be found in European travelers' accounts of the United States. Cooper wrote to an American friend that he found "so much ignorance here concerning America, so much insolence in their manner of thinking of us" that he felt compelled to respond. Originally proposed by Lafayette as an account of his triumphal American tour (1824–1825) that would also correct European misconceptions and "do credit to the country," the book emerged as a celebration of American manners, customs, and institutions in response to European condescension.[15]

The factor that gave such point to the continuing exchange between American and European writers during the second third of the nineteenth century was the linkage that was routinely made in these transatlantic debates between social leveling and political transformation in the United States. From the 1820s through the 1850s, a flood of works—including those by British writers Frances

---

Republic (New York, 1995). An earlier generation of scholars focused on the nature of Cooper's engagement with democracy rather than on his nationalism. In *The Whig Myth of James Fenimore Cooper* (New Haven, Conn., 1938), Dorothy Waples argues that Cooper was a committed Democrat whose democratic principles stemmed from his opposition to the Anglophile mercantile classes that emerged as the strongest wing of the Whig Party (5, 17–19). Arthur M. Schlesinger, Jr., makes a similar argument in *The Age of Jackson* (Boston, 1953), 375–380. In *Political Justice in a Republic: James Fenimore Cooper's America* (Berkeley, Calif., 1972), John P. McWilliams, Jr., offers the best summary perspective on Cooper's politics, noting that Cooper "referred to America as a republic or as a confederated, representative democracy." "For Cooper, the word 'democrat' described no more than a man who believes in republican principle" (28–29). "Cooper insisted that a republican polity must maintain full equality of political rights without depriving society and government of those citizens, superior in merit, principle, and influence, who were necessary to sustain disinterested republican justice" (402)—in other words, Cooper embraced what we have come to call liberal democracy.

15. This defensiveness about America, which he shared with Lafayette, substantially overcame his early intention to distance himself from the work of another Lafayette intimate, Frances Wright, whose *Views of Society and Manners in America* (1821) Cooper decried in 1828 as "nauseous flattery." The works share incidents and tone as well as a vision of the United States as the embodiment and progenitor of a modernity characterized by egalitarian manners and republican government. See Gary Williams, "Historical Introduction," in James Fenimore Cooper, *Notions of the Americans: Picked up by a Travelling Bachelor*, ed. Williams (Albany, N.Y., 1991), xv–xxvii; Wayne Franklin, *The New World of James Fenimore Cooper* (Chicago, 1982), chap. 2 (quotations, 47, 49).

Trollope, Harriet Martineau, and Charles Dickens and those by French writers Alexis de Tocqueville and Michel Chevalier—examined the confluence of what Chevalier's translator referred to in the title as *Society, Manners, and Politics in the United States*. Entering the fray at a relatively early moment, Cooper chose to mimic the travel genre of his European precursors and to narrate the book in the persona of a bachelor European nobleman. The Count travels through the United States in the company of an American named Cadwallader, who is generally a reticent companion (a national tendency, the Count suggests) but who dispenses firsthand knowledge of the country that the Count otherwise lacks and, when provoked, emerges an eloquent defender of his homeland. Thus Cooper enacts through the structure of his narrative what he hoped the work would in fact achieve: his European aristocrat is guided by a knowledge-able American who can set the Count straight about the nation that he pro-poses to evaluate. Unsurprisingly, the resulting account of the United States is largely laudatory.[16]

The evolution of the Count's attitudes toward American society reflects a gradual deepening of knowledge of the forces shaping that society and a grow-ing awareness of the underlying causes of its predominant features. The Count observes in an early letter that already during his stay he has "met with many individuals of manners and characters so very equivocal" that he has had difficulty placing them in a "conventional order." He notes the "singular . . . compound of intelligence, kindness, natural politeness, coarseness and even vulgarity" of many Americans and observes, "One is ashamed to admit that men who at every instant are asserting their superiority in intellect and infor-mation can belong to an inferior condition, and yet one is equally reluctant to allow a claim to perfect equality, on the part of those who are constantly violating the rules of conventional courtesy." The tension between knowledge and ability on the one hand and "conventional courtesy" on the other forms the core of Cooper's explanation for the misunderstandings between Americans and Europeans. Already here the Count reveals his emerging awareness of the alignment of truth with nature, morality, simplicity, and egalitarianism that, as the narrative progresses, Cooper uncovers as the sources of American superi-ority. By letter 10, the Count offers more general comments on "the true State of ordinary American Society," noting nevertheless the difficulty of drawing any reliable conclusions where social distinctions are so blurry and "no acknowl-

---

16. Cooper incorporates Cadwallader's briefer speeches into the text of the Count's letters. His lengthiest, most nationalistic statement appears in Note A (541–564), where among other things Cadwallader explains why the Count should not trust English books on the United States as factual sources.

edged distinctions prevail." Still, he is willing to draw some pointed conclusions in favor of the United States. Americans, he announces, are

> under far fewer artificial forms, than are to be found in almost any other Country. . . . Direct in their thoughts, above the necessity of any systematic counterfeiting, and in almost every instance secure of the ordinary means of existence, it is quite in nature that the American in his daily communications should consult the truth more and conventional deception less, than those who are fettered and restrained by the thousand pressures of a highly artificial state of being.

This tendency to the natural, the truthful, the moral, the simple, the inartificial reflects the most compelling democratic qualities of the nation. "In short," the Count concludes a few pages later, "the whole Country not only in its Government but in all its habits, is daily getting to be more purely democratic." The federal system of government, the Count states further in letter 26 in the midst of a lengthy description of the political scene in Washington, D.C., "is the most Natural Government known," because "it is a superstructure regularly reared on a solid foundation." This, then, is the American democracy that Cooper painted in the 1820s: built on natural principles, liberated from European social and political artifices, emerging as an orderly, intelligent, well-regulated society in which the talented rise to roles of leadership and the masses are wise enough to follow.[17]

In the two Leatherstocking novels that Cooper wrote before leaving for Europe and in *The Prairie,* which he carried with him and finished there in 1827, Cooper already manifested the interest in comparative social analysis that in *Notions* he directs toward the transatlantic divide between the Old World and the New. In these early Leatherstocking Tales Cooper trained his gaze, not on the ocean frontier, but rather on the inland frontier. There he found sites of social and political experimentation where alternative forms of law, patriarchy, and political structure exist in direct competition with one another and can be evaluated for their justness, defined (as in his analysis of Europe and the United States) by their proximity to nature. Four narrative elements reveal Cooper's concern with the meaning and implications of Jacksonian democracy most clearly: his changing depiction of Natty Bumppo; his use of a symbolic to-

---

17. Cooper, *Notions of the Americans,* 77–79, 136, 137, 143, 383. Marvin Meyers contrasts Cooper's optimistic view of American democracy in the 1820s as revealed in *Notions* with his Arnoldian despair over the debasing effects that the masses have on the American middle classes in his novels of the 1830s and 1840s. See *The Jacksonian Persuasion: Politics and Belief* (Stanford, Calif., 1957), chap. 4.

pography; his thematic examination of different forms of patriarchy, most of them failures; and his representation of native American governmental traditions. Tracking these four elements through the early Leatherstocking Tales, we find an emerging skepticism about the modes of hierarchy and dominance that Cooper soon came to criticize in *Notions* as debased, artificial European forms—cultural components of an "*Old* World" that Natty redefines as "a *worn out*, and an *abused*, and a *sacrilegious* world" (1147). In parallel with this overt skepticism about European preeminence, we also see a growing sympathy with the means and goals of a democratic native American civic life. *The Prairie* offers the culminating expression of Cooper's early interrogation of forms of governance in his depictions of Indian leaders and their influence on white creoles.[18]

Critics of *The Prairie*, past and present, attacked Cooper for reprising characters and scenes from the previous two Leatherstocking Tales, and they were right to notice the parallels and repetitions, which are substantial. The point, I take it, is not that Cooper lacked imagination as some suggest, but rather that he was deliberately revising the earlier tales. Some of this recapitulation is filtered through Natty, who rehashes his past and philosophizes on its meaning. The repetition of themes, characters, and scenes is far too pervasive and structural to be accounted for by the fact of having an elderly man preoccupied with the past as a central character, however. Cooper shares his hero's absorption in the narrative past, through plot, setting, and character, which provide his own indirect authorial meditations on the meaning of his previous novels and thereby stage both continuities and disruptions.

The symbolic topography of *The Prairie* registers one striking and thematically salient difference from its predecessors. Setting this novel on the western prairies at a moment of national expansion, Cooper moved from the dramatic Adirondack scenery of his first two Leatherstocking Tales to the rolling plains of the Midwest. As the highest mountain range in the United States at the time, and one that had proved a barrier to westward migration for centuries, the Adirondacks signify natural and social barriers to democracy. It is from the peak of Mount Vision that Judge Temple has his Moses-like vision of the future settlement that he goes on to found there, its name (Templeton) identifying him as its patriarchal founder. The heights of Mount Vision provide the setting for other major events in the novel. The reader witnesses there the opening confrontation over property and propriety between Temple, Natty, and the

18. On the frontier as a "neutral ground" for testing social arrangements, see McWilliams, *Political Justice*, 12.

youth who is eventually revealed to be Oliver Effingham, whose elderly grandfather represents an alternative, and possibly more authentic, patriarchal title to the land that Temple claims as his own, one predicated on his youthful adoption by Chingachgook. The conflagration that kills Chingachgook and provides the occasion for Oliver and Elizabeth to reveal their love for each other likewise takes place on the mountain. The mountain heights clarify perception; sight from there can be visionary (seeing into the future) and revelatory (seeing beyond surfaces to deeper truths). Natty evokes both forms of vision when he contrasts the fire on Mount Vision to the prairie fire in the later novel: "Do you call this a fire! If you had seen what I have witnessed in the Eastern hills, when mighty mountains were like the furnace of a smith, you would have known what it was to fear the flames and to be thankful that you were spared" (1159). Where the steep slopes of the mountains intensify the danger from a fire, the flatness of the prairie allows Natty and his companions to divert the fire that threatens them, to literally fight fire with fire.

In *Mohicans,* rather than being sites of vision and intensified dangers, the great mountain heights are scenes of mortal exposure and precipitous silent death. The most famous fall from a mountain peak in this novel is Magua's headlong pitch into the abyss at the end, a culminating allusion to Milton's Satan, to whom Magua is compared throughout the novel. But this fall is anticipated by falls of several Indians early in the novel, during the fight scene at Glenn's Falls. It is this opening battle that Natty recalls to Duncan Middleton when they first meet in *The Prairie,* asking Middleton whether his grandfather told the young man of "the imp behind the log—and of the miserable devil who went over the fall—or of the wretch in the tree?" It is this last incident that most anticipates Magua's fate and is most lavishly described in *Mohicans;* likewise, Natty dwells on this episode here, noting: "I have been a dweller in forests, and in the wilderness for threescore and ten years, and if any man can pretend to know the world or to have seen scary sights, it is myself! But never before nor since have I seen human man in such a state of mortal despair as that very savage, and yet he scorned to speak or to cry out, or to own his forlorn condition" (1142). Magua, too, is silent as he falls (864).[19]

19. Lora Romero similarly notes that "the fall of dark persons from on high is a virtual theme in *The Last of the Mohicans.*" In a subtle reading, she identifies this figural pattern with a pedagogical discourse of precocity and links Uncas's precocity and death to the Vanishing Indian motif in an effort to tie "momism" to empire and genocide. While Romero's general point is a valuable one, her reading of Cooper manifests the dangers of generalizing from a single Leatherstocking Tale. See "Vanishing Americans: James Fenimore Cooper," in Romero, *Home Fronts: Domesticity and Its Critics in the Antebellum United States* (Durham, N.C., 1997), esp. 36, 48.

The landscape of *The Prairie* differs markedly from the eastern landscapes of the earlier novels, and the changes register the altered social vision that the novel explores. In his introduction Cooper notes that the region is a vast plain, that "there is scarcely an elevation worthy to be called a mountain" and that "even hills are not common" (883). The pervasive metaphor for the prairie landscape, one that was important to Sarmiento in *Facundo* and became ubiquitous in later fiction (notably *Moby-Dick*), is the seascape: "From the summits of the swells, the eye became fatigued with the sameness and chilling dreariness of the landscape. The earth was not unlike the ocean. . . . There was the same waving and regular surface, the same absence of foreign objects, and the same boundless extent to the view" (892). The uniform rolling landscape produces illusions and distortions—we are told, for example, that "the sameness of the surface, and the low stands of the spectators exaggerated the distances" (892)—and these perceptual anomalies are magnified by atmospheric phenomena such as the mists and fogs, or the "flood of fiery light" that surrounds Natty when he first appears, making him appear "colossal" and rendering it "impossible to distinguish its just proportions or true character" (893). The perceptual difficulties here bear a certain kinship with the problems that the Count has in *Notions*, where the democratic "landscape" of society makes it difficult for him to discern social distinctions. A similar figural pattern in which a flat landscape reflects the democratic social order characterizes the opening of Frances Trollope's *Domestic Manners of the Americans* (1832). Trollope, of course, was not a fan of American democracy and the social egalitarianism that seemed especially to mark American culture for European visitors in the antebellum period. Cooper's ambivalence here is palpable. The delusions of the democratic prairie produce the vicious squatter patriarch Ishmael Bush; they also produce the glorified and apotheosized Natty Bumppo, Cooper's great democratic hero and adoptive patriarch.[20]

Patriarchy, with its connections to property rights, is a troubled and troubling institution for Cooper. The patriarchal order identified with Judge Temple in *The Pioneers* is shown to contain property-related injustices that can be reconciled only through marriage of Elizabeth Temple and Oliver Effingham;

---

20. Describing her arrival at the mouth of the Mississippi, Trollope writes: "The shores of this river are so utterly flat, that no object upon them is perceptible at sea. . . . I never beheld a scene so utterly desolate at this entrance of the river. Had Dante seen it, he might have drawn images of another Bolgia from its horrors. One only object rears itself above the eddying waters; this is the mast of a vessel long since wrecked in attempting to cross the bar, and it still stands, a dismal witness of the destruction that has been, and a boding prophet of that which is to come." *Domestic Manners of the Americans* (Harmondsworth, 1997), 9.

the patriarchal order of *Mohicans* is undermined both by the loss of children (Uncas, Cora) and by the deterioration of Munro, but it is refounded for the white characters through the union of Alice Munro and Duncan Heyward. Patriarchy in *The Prairie* is an altogether more complicated phenomenon. Both native and white societies manifest debased forms of patriarchy. Mahtoree is shown to be an unworthy patriarch when he offers to abandon his wife and their infant son in order to marry Inez. Inez's father and the Catholic priest who is her spiritual father are deluded into believing that Inez has experienced something analogous to the assumption and so do not pursue her kidnappers. And then there is Ishmael Bush, who seems to draw his sense of entitlement to the land from his reproductive proficiency: producing more and more children, he feels himself entitled by natural law to the land to support them and is willing to assail anyone who challenges that right.

The unmarried, childless Natty represents the novel's patriarchal ideal. Regularly referred to as "Father" by both white and red characters, he is explicitly in search of an heir to replace his lost "son" Uncas, and he finds one in the idealized Hard-Heart. The most emotionally powerful and ethically justifiable patriarchal bonds in this novel are bonds of choice between a white father and his red adoptive sons. This is a verbal bond: Natty confesses to Hard Heart: "I never was a father, but well do I know what is the love of one. . . . My heart yearns to you, boy, and gladly would I do you good." And Hard Heart replies: "I have heard your words. They have gone in at my ears, and are now within me" (1194–1195). As a verbal bond, patriarchy is restricted to deeds of mutual affection and respectful memory uncomplicated by inheritance and authority.[21]

The thematic movement from hierarchy to democracy across the three novels may be most visible in the changing depictions of native forms of civic life. Central to this transformation is the premise that authority is earned rather than inherited in native communities. But such antipatriarchal forms of government do not guarantee good leadership, as the character of Mahotree reveals. Perhaps the clearest parallels in the early Leatherstocking novels are between the Indian leaders in *Mohicans* and *The Prairie*, the bad Indian demagogues

21. The transition to more democratic forms of patriarchal authority were being negotiated more broadly in American society during these years, notably in relation to the Revolutionary founders. John Adams and Thomas Jefferson had died in a spectacular coincidence on July 4, 1826. Jay Fliegelman traces the emergence of antipatriarchal forms of patriarchy in the eighteenth century in *Prodigals and Pilgrims: The American Revolution against Patriarchal Authority, 1750–1800* (Cambridge, 1982). George B. Forgie discusses the psychological dynamics of patriarchy and inheritance in the "post-heroic" antebellum period in *Patricide in the House Divided: A Psychological Interpretation of Lincoln and His Age* (New York, 1979).

(Magua and Mahtoree) and good Indian sons (Uncas and Hard-Heart). While both Magua and Mahtoree are clearly meant to reveal the dangers of persuasive speech in a government based on popular consent, the political references that accumulate around Mahtoree are much denser than those characterizing Magua. The complicated nature of political consent emerges when Cooper likens Mahtoree to a feudal lord, "some Chevalier of a more civilized race" who speaks "in the haughty tones of absolute power" (1136). Mahtoree is a Napoleonic figure capable of uniting "the powers of reason and force" who in another "state of society" would have been "both a conqueror and a despot" (1189). He impersonates a republican by living simply, yet his republicanism is revealed as false and, like the republicanism in revolutionary France, atheistic (1203). Cooper implies that, like Magua, Mahtoree has been corrupted by contact with whites.

Both Mahtoree and Hard-Heart are described as the "Partizans" of their tribes, a term that unites military might with political leadership while also capturing something of the emerging Jacksonian party system. If Mahtoree is the Napoleon figure, Hard-Heart is an idealized type of Jackson: vigorous in defense of his people, leading through skill rather than inherited authority or wealth. In contrast to the silently heroic and ultimately dead Uncas, Hard-Heart emerges as an exemplary republican leader, who earns his status by heroism and strong leadership—and he survives, first to be adopted by Natty in a newly constructed transracial patriarchal lineage of natural men and democrats (replacing Chingachgook and Uncas), and in the end to tend Natty's prairie grave in a testimony to the lasting civic power of memory. At the end of The Prairie, Natty is apotheosized before an audience of Indians led by Hard-Heart and whites led by Middleton, a dying patriarch supported by his adopted heirs, one white and one red. Middleton buys Natty's tombstone, set up on the prairie to mark the "spot where a just white-man sleeps," and Hard-Heart's Pawnees tend the grave "to the present hour" (1317). In this novel, then, Cooper's representation of native societies offers a celebration of heroic leadership, dignity, and persistence that goes well beyond anything in the previous two tales, which respectively portray the death of Chingachgook and the death of Uncas and collectively represent the passing of the noblest Indians.

The development of Cooper's perspective across the three novels is often registered through changes in Natty's perspective. In Mohicans Natty insists that the almost extinct Delawares were the only truly noble savages, a claim that he reiterates early in The Prairie. Yet in the latter novel Natty changes his mind after meeting Hard-Heart. Rather than dying out forever in the New York wilderness, the Noble Savage lives on in the American prairie.[22] Moreover, Natty's role in *Mohicans* as the policer of racial boundaries in the afterlife, his silent skepticism about the ghostly union of Uncas and Cora that disrupts the hopeful visions of the indigenous and Christian ceremonies, is supplanted in *The Prairie* by a newly accepting view of spiritual union. Considering his own fate in the afterlife, Natty expresses the hope that "the same meaning is hid under different words" and that he and Hard-Heart will one day "stand together . . . before the face of your Wahcondah who will then be no other than my God" (1313).

Indeed, the novel as a whole is framed as a tale of reconciliation. Cooper sets the story at a moment when the debates over the Louisiana Purchase began to fade and "party considerations gave place to more liberal views" (887), and he anticipates the time when the "numerous and affluent colonists of the lower province" would "blend" with "their new compatriots" (888).[23] In what is perhaps the most ideologically vexed moment of the novel for a reader today, Hard-Heart refuses Mahtoree's plea to join forces against the whites and protect native lands. Cooper defends this refusal, despite the fact that he repeatedly raises the issue of native entitlement to their lands, indicating that by rejecting Mahtoree's plan Hard-Heart remains committed to native values of generosity to strangers, thereby casting the proposed pan-Indian alliance (reminiscent of Tecumseh's resistance movement in the previous decade) in an unnatural light. The tending of a just white man's grave is the best substitute that Cooper can provide for clear native title to their homelands.

Such property issues are unresolved and indeed seem unresolvable in Cooper's world. If the only thing that Hard-Heart inherits from his white father is

22. Cooper's 1832 introduction to *The Prairie* significantly reframes the prairies once again, describing them as "the final gathering place of the red men" and noting that in 1804 when the novel is set these remnant nations "dwelt in open hostility" but since that time "the power of the republic has done much to restore peace to these wild scenes" (884–885). Cooper's views on race and indigenous Americans are so difficult to articulate both because he shifts his emphases from one work to the next, and sometimes even in the same work, and also because he reorients a single work with prefatory material composed for later editions. A deeply responsive and context-oriented writer as well as a prolific one, Cooper cannot be pinned down to a single message. My purpose here is to focus on the early Cooper, writing in the first bloom of Jacksonian democracy, not the later disillusioned Cooper.

23. In the quoted passages Cooper emphasizes the way that the "more humble" inhabitants of the region were "swallowed in the vortex which attended the tide of instant emigration" by "a race long trained in adventure and nurtured in difficulties" (that is, white Americans) (888) far more than in blending. The novel as a whole, however, portrays both aspects of this process and, if anything, emphasizes the blending of Anglos and Hispanic Americans in the marriage of Middleton and Inez, a union that helps win Middleton a role in national governance.

the responsibility of tending a grave, the white characters learn something about civic life from their contacts with Hard-Heart. One thing they learn is that political authority that is not founded on property will not perdure: Middleton achieves prominence, not through his military exploits, but through his affiliation with the wealthy Don Augustin; similarly, Paul's political successes follow after he has become "a prosperous cultivator of the soil" (1306). As well, they learn to create social bonds out of language and emotion. Paul becomes a state legislator "notorious for making speeches, that have a tendency to put that deliberative body in good humor" (1306). Middleton's rhetorical style is never portrayed, but Cooper identifies him as "the source from which we have derived most of the intelligence necessary to compose our legend" (1306). Since Middleton has just been described as a member of a "far higher branch of Legislative Authority" than Paul, Cooper would seem to be implying that his novel, based as it allegedly is on Middleton's words, can serve a similar national function to that of Paul's deliberative oratory: binding people in good humor to engage in political action based "on great practical knowledge suited to the condition of the country" and not on "subtle and fine spun theories" (1306). Offering a rebuttal to the European theorists who insisted on the inadequacies of democracy, *The Prairie* provides an account of democracy as a kind of adopted indigenous son for creoles negotiating a transition to a political order based on affect and words rather than hierarchy, power, and force.

Indigenous Identities, Now and Then

In 1990 the new Museo de la Nación opened in a former military government building in Lima, Peru. Remarkably, the museum is entirely devoted to native history, pre-Inca and Inca. Many of the most important artifacts were moved from the previous national history museum, the Museo Nacional de Historia, which remains open and has its own still impressive collection of Inca objects. The national history museum, however, positions those Inca artifacts at the beginning of a historical narrative that extends through the Spanish conquest, the Tupac Amaru II rebellion, and the war for independence. The Museo de la Nación instead identifies indigenous history as national history, a strategy of identification that seemed more plausible during the regime of Alejandro Toledo, the first Peruvian president from an indigenous background. The museum is perhaps best seen as an effect of the intellectual and literary movement of Incaísmo, which originated in the revolutionary 1820s, and which has also importantly influenced the nearly sixty-year-old celebration of Inti Raymi, the reinvented tradition of the Inca festival of the sun held every June in Cuzco.

In contrast to the emphasis on Inca history in Peruvian national self-constructions, the Smithsonian Museum in the United States has become a lightning rod for conflicts about the native past and its role in American national memory. A major repository of Indian bones and artifacts accumulated under ethically dubious if not outright illegal circumstances, the Smithsonian has been involved in an extensive repatriation project. At the same time it has, at last, built a National Museum of the American Indian on the Mall, which opened on September 1, 2004. The museum is constructed of rich golden limestone from Minnesota, a notable contrast with the white marble facades of most of its neighboring buildings. Its opening followed by more than a decade the opening of the nearby United States Holocaust Memorial Museum. Though not directly on the mall and not part of the Smithsonian complex, the Holocaust Museum stirred up a sometimes heated discussion about national identifications when it opened in 1993. Is the Judeo-Christian tradition the true source of United States national meaning, as one representative of the museum argued? The concluding scene of Steven Spielberg's *Raiders of the Lost Ark* (1981), where the ark disappears into the vast Smithsonian vault, implies as much. Why, the museum's critics asked, should a European genocide have precedence in the national memory over United States creole crimes against native Americans and enslaved Africans? But then, again, is the best form for the National Museum of the American Indian one that catalogs genocide and territorial theft, or one that celebrates and perhaps, as in Peru, helps recreate enduring vital traditions? The answer, surely, is both, and this is a balance that the museum attempts to strike.

The complex dynamics of creole national identifications that I want to highlight here cannot be easily captured in a single text, such as *The Last of the Mohicans*. What a reading of *The Prairie* in its specific historical moment and in relation to the first two Leatherstocking Tales helps to foreground about such identifications as they continue to play out in debates over the museums on the National Mall is the subtlety and variety of creole responses to indigenous cultures. Good creole that he was, Cooper defined himself as an American in relation to both indigenous and European traditions. His initial arrival in Europe sparked a nationalist impulse that propelled him away from European traditions and toward a native American heritage that he identified with democracy. While this was not his final resting point, it was an important stop on his intellectual journey as a creole, an ambivalent democrat, and a national icon.

NOTES ON CONTRIBUTORS

Ralph Bauer is an associate professor in the Department of English and Comparative Literature at the University of Maryland, College Park. He is the author of *The Cultural Geography of Colonial American Literatures: Empire, Travel, Modernity* (Cambridge, 2003). He is the editor and translator of Titu Cusi Yupanqui, *An Inca Account of Conquest of Peru* (Boulder, Colo., 2005); he is a coeditor of *The Wadsworth Anthology of American Literature.*

Raquel Chang-Rodríguez is Distinguished Professor of Hispanic Literature at the Graduate Center and the City College of the City University of New York (CUNY). Her publications include *"Aquí, ninfas del sur, venid ligeras": voces poéticas virreinales* (Frankfurt, 2008); *La palabra y la pluma en "Primer nueva corónica y buen gobierno"* (Lima, 2005); and an essay collection in both Spanish and English, *Beyond Books and Borders: Garcilaso de la Vega and "La Florida del Inca"* (Lewisburg, Pa., 2006), *Franqueando fronteras: Garcilaso de la Vega y "La Florida del Inca"* (Lima, 2006). She is the founding editor of *Colonial Latin American Review* and Profesora Honoraria of the Universidad Nacional Mayor de San Marcos.

Lúcia Helena Costigan is associate professor of Luso-Brazilian and Latin American literatures and cultures at the Ohio State University. She has been the recipient of major National Endowment for the Humanities grants. Her publications include *A sátira e o intellectual criolla na colônia: Gregório de Matos e Juan del Valle y Caviedes* (1991) and several edited volumes, such as *Diálogos da conversão: Missionários, indios, negros e judeus no contexto ibero-americano do período barroco* (2005), *From "Excessive Friendships" to Cannibalism Revisited: Brazilian and Spanish Literary and Cultural Encounters* (2005), and is the coeditor of *Research in African Literatures,* XXXVIII, no.1 (Spring 2007), *Lusophone African and Afro-Brzilian Literatures.* Her book *In the Shadow of the Inquisition: The Discourse of New World Letrados of Jewish Heritage* is forthcoming.

Jim Egan teaches in the English Department at Brown University. He is the author of *Authorizing Experience: Refigurations of the Body Politic in Seventeenth-Century New England Writing* (Princeton, N.J., 1999). His current project is a book on Eastern influences on early American literature.

Sandra M. Gustafson is Associate Professor of English at the University of Notre Dame. She is the author of *Eloquence Is Power: Oratory and Performance in Early America* (Chapel Hill, N.C., 2000); the coeditor (with Caroline F. Sloat) of *Cultural Narratives: Textuality and Performance in the United States before 1900* (South Bend, Ind., 2009); and the editor of *Early American Literature.* Her current project is "The Deliberative Imagination in the Early American Republic."

Carlos A. Jáuregui is Associate Professor of Latin American Literature and Anthropology at Vanderbilt University. He is the author of *Canibalia* (winner of the Premio Casa de las Americas, 2005). He has edited *Querella de los indios en las Cortes de la Muerte (1557) de Michael de Carvajal.* He has coedited (with J. Pablo Dabove) *Heterotropias: narrativas de identidad y alteridad latinoamericana;* (with Mabel Moraña) *Colonialidad y crítica en América Latina;* (with Enrique Dussel and Mabel Moraña) *Coloniality at Large: Latin America and the Postcolonial Debate;* (with Joseph S. Mella and Edward F. Fischer) *Of Rage and Redemption: The Art of Oswaldo Guayasamín.*

Yolanda Martínez–San Miguel is Professor of Romance Languages at the University of Pennsylvania. She is the author of *Saberes americanos: subalternidad y epistemología en los escritos de Sor Juana* (Pittsburgh, 1999); *Caribe Two Ways: cultura de la migración en el Caribe insular hispánico* (Ediciones Callejón, 2003); and *From Lack to Excess: Minor Readings of Latin American Colonial Discourse* (Lewisburg, Pa., 2008). She has also edited, with Mabel Moraña, the compilation of essays *Nictimene sacrílega: homenaje a Georgina Sabat de Rivers* (Mexico City, 2003). She has published articles in *Revista de Crítica Literaria Latinoamericana, Revista Iberoamericana, Posdata, Nómada, Revista de Ciencias Sociales, Journal of Caribbean Literatures, Centro Journal, Colonial Latin American Review,* and *Debate Feminista.* Research and teaching areas include colonial Latin American discourses and contemporary Caribbean and Latino narratives; colonial and postcolonial theory; migration and cultural studies.

José Antonio Mazzotti is Professor of Latin American Literature and Chair of the Department of Romance Languages at Tufts University. He has also been President of the International Association of Peruvianists since 1996. He has published *Coros mestizos del Inca Garcilaso: resonancias andinas* (Lima, 1996), *Poéticas del flujo: migración y violencia verbales en el Perú de los 80* (Lima, 2002), *Incan Insights: El Inca Garcilaso's Hints to Andean Readers* (Frankfurt and Madrid, 2008), seven volumes of poetry, and more than fifty articles on Latin American colonial literature and contemporary poetry. He has also edited *Agencias criollas: la ambigüedad "colonial" en las letras hispanoamericanas* (Pittsburgh, 2000), *"Discurso en Loor de la Poesía": Estudio y edición,* by Antonio Cornejo Polar (Berkeley, Calif., 2000), and coedited

The Other Latinos: Central and South Americans in the United States (Cambridge, Mass., 2007), *Edición e interpretación de textos andinos* (Frankfurt and Madrid, 2000), and *Asedios a la heterogeneidad cultural: libro de homenaje a Antonio Cornejo Polar* (Philadelphia, 1996).

Stephanie Merrim is Royce Professor of Comparative Literature and Hispanic Studies at Brown University. Her major publications include *Early Modern Women's Writings and Sor Juana Inés de la Cruz* (1999); "Spectacular Cityscapes of Baroque Spanish America," in Mario J. Valdés and Djelal Kadir, eds., *Literary Cultures of Latin America*, III, *Latin American Literary Culture* (2004); "The First Fifty Years of Hispanic New World Historiography: The Caribbean, Mexico, and Central America," in Roberto González Echevarria and Enrique Pupo-Walker, eds., *The Cambridge History of Latin America*, I, *Discovery to Modernism* (1996); "Sor Juana Inés de la Cruz," in *Encyclopaedia Britannica*.

Susan Scott Parrish is Associate Professor in the Department of English Language and Literature at the University of Michigan. Her book *American Curiosity: Cultures of Natural History in the Colonial British Atlantic World* (Chapel Hill, N.C., 2006) received the Jamestown Prize from the Jamestown-Yorktown Foundation and the Ralph Waldo Emerson Prize from Phi Beta Kappa.

Luis Fernando Restrepo is Professor of Latin American Studies and Comparative Literature and Cultural Studies at the University of Arkansas, Fayetteville. His publications include *Antologia critica de Juan de Castellanos* (Bogota, 2004), *Un nuevo reino imaginanado* (Bogota, 1999), and articles in *Revista iberoamericana, Modern Language Notes, Cuadernos de literatura, Estudios de literatura colombiana* as well as other journals and editions. He has been a Fulbright visiting scholar in Colombia and visiting professor at the Universidad de Antioquia; he was a co-founder of the Colonial Americas Studies Organization (CASO).

Jeffrey H. Richards is professor of English at Old Dominion University. He is the author of *Drama, Theatre, and Identity in the American New Republic* (Cambridge, 2005), and editor (with Sharon M. Harris) of *Mercy Otis Warren: Selected Letters* (Athens, Ga., 2009).

Kathleen Ross is Professor of Spanish at New York University. She is the author of *The Baroque Narrative of Carlos de Sigüenza y Góngora* (Cambridge, 1994) and the translator of Spanish-American poetry, essays, and fiction, including Domingo F. Sarmiento's *Facundo* (Berkeley, Calif., 2003).

David S. Shields is the Euphemia McClintock Professor of Southern Letters in the Departments of English and History at the University of South Carolina. He is editor of *Early American Literature*, author of *Oracles of Empire: Poetry, Politics, and*

Commerce in British America, 1690–1750 (1990) and *Civil Tongues and Polite Letters in British America* (1997), and compiler of the Library of America's *American Poetry: The Seventeenth and Eighteenth Centuries*. He contributed to volumes I and II of *A Hisstory of the Book in America* and to volume I of *The Cambridge History of American Literature*. He has also published scholarship in the history of American performing arts, photography, and regional foodways.

Teresa A. Toulouse is Professor of English at the University of Colorado at Boulder. She is the author of *The Art of Prophesying: New England Sermons and the Shaping of Belief* (Athens, Ga., 1987) and *The Captive's Position: Female Narrative, Male Identity, and Royal Authority in Colonial New England* (Philadelphia, 2007). She is editor, with Andrew Delbanco, of vol. II of *The Complete Sermons of Ralph Waldo Emerson* (Columbia, Mo., 1990).

Lisa Voigt is Associate Professor of Spanish in the Department of Romance Languages and Literatures at the University of Chicago and Visiting Associate Professor in the Department of Spanish and Portuguese at the Ohio State University. She has held a National Endowment for the Humanities fellowship at the Newberry Library and a Mellon fellowship at the Omohundro Institute of Early American History and Culture. She is the author of *Writing Captivity in the Early Modern Atlantic: Circulations of Knowledge and Authority in the Iberian and English Imperial Worlds* (Chapel Hill, N.C., 2009).

Jerry M. Williams is Professor of Spanish and Latin American Studies and Chairperson of the Department of Foreign Languages at West Chester University of Pennsylvania. He is the author of *El Teatro del México colonial: época misionera* (New York, 1992) and *Censorship and Art in Pre-Enlightenment Lima* (Potomac, Md., 1994); editor of *Peralta Barnuevo and the Art of Propaganda: Poltics, Poetry, and Religion in Eighteenth-Century Lima* (Tempe, Ariz., 2001) and of *Peru's Inquisition on Trial: The Vindication of Ana de Castro* (Potomac, Md., 2008); coeditor (with Robert E. Lewis) of *Early Images of the Americas: Transfer and Invention* (Tucson, Ariz., 1993) and (with David F. Slade) of *The Devout World of Peralta Barnuevo: La Galeria de la Omnipotencia and Pasión y Trifuno de Cristo* (Chapel Hill, N.C., 2008). He has published articles on colonial Brazil, religious iconography, and sixteenth-century Latin America. He has received grants from the National Endowment for the Humanities, the United States Department of Education, the Ministry of Culture of Spain, and numerous research fellowships.

Index

Incaísmo, 473, 489

Incas: as colonial power, 21, 382–383, 430–431; preconquest history of, 118, 429, 489; as symbol for creole identity, 282, 444, 446, 458–459, 461, 468; and El Dorado, 380, 382, 388, 393–394, 397; after conquest, 408, 432; and environmental determinism, 456. See also Incaísmo; Indians; Mita; Peru

Indentured servitude, 29, 41–42, 136–140, 142, 150–151. See also Slaves and slavery

Indian criollos: defined, 123, 129–130; in colonial Peru, 130–133

Indian Removal, 367, 466, 468, 475

Indians: and creole identity, 4, 26, 238–239, 306, 364–365, 367, 472–473, 475, 486–489; and religion, 14, 61–100, 209, 270, 273, 284, 300; and colonization, 14–17, 19–24; and languages, 28, 146–147, 358; and resistance, 31, 141, 158–160; and race, 34–35, 466; and minority discourse, 176; and theories of origins, 203; and creole appropriation of symbols and native identities, 211, 213, 258–259, 444–452, 459–460, 468–470

Indio: defined, 335n

Indio ladino: defined, 118

Inquisition, 75, 195, 304–305, 311; and Brazil, 245, 249–251, 253, 259n

Inti Raymi, 490

Ireland: colonial experience of, 16–17

Jackson, Andrew, 472, 475, 479

Jamaica, 106, 110, 112–115, 185

Jefferson, Thomas, 472, 476, 486n; on creole character, 38; on race and slavery, 38–39, 457; on New World climate, 455, 457

Jerez, Francisco de, 382

Jesuits: and Indians, 15, 64, 72, 74, 76, 85, 87, 93, 211, 262; and creoles, 26, 194, 337; and Sor Juana, 193–218; in Mexico City, 193–194, 202–205; and Jews, 243–244; in Brazil, 262; in New Granada, 337, 348–352

Jews (cristãos novos; New Christians): in Brazil, 241–264

João VI (of Portugal), 28

Johnson, Samuel, 113

José de Sucre, Mariscal Antonio, 442

Juan, Jorge, 34, 36–38

Juana Inés de la Cruz, Sor, 82, 168, 179, 189, 304; appropriation of indigenous symbols

by, 84–100; on Eucharist and Aztec sacrifice, 85–90, 209, 212; and the Mexican Archive, 193–218; and Spanish audiences, 205–218

King, William, 359

King Philip's War, 31, 314, 318–319

Kircher, Athanasius, 203, 211–212

La Condamine, Charles de, 34

Lafitau, Joseph François, 453

Language: and interpretation of the New World, 355–372; and Indians, 358; and satire and aesthetic play, 360; and William Byrd II, 366–367; and science and nature, 366–367; and conquest, 430–431

Las Casas, Bartolomé de: and Indians (Aztecs), 22, 72, 76–82, 85, 93, 176, 459; and Oliver Cromwell, 107; rhetorical devices of, 180, 182, 184–187; and critique of colonialism, 342, 344

León Pinelo, Antonio de, 396–398

Lettered city, 26, 83–84, 95–96, 99–100, 201, 403

Levante do Maranhão, 244, 259–263

Lima: creole culture in, 26, 50, 242, 244, 265, 376–379, 386–390, 399, 401–404, 411, 413, 428–429, 438, 441, 447–448, 489

Llano Zapata, José Eusebio de, 428

Loa: defined, 63n, 205. See also Juana Inés de la Cruz, Sor

López de Caravantes, Francisco, 377

López de Gómara, Francisco, 20, 64n

López de Velasco, Juan, 4, 409–410

Louisiana Purchase, 488

Machado, Simão Ferreira, 268, 276–280, 287–288

Manco Capac (11th c.), 461–463

Manco Inca (Manco Capac, 1500–1544), 393–394

Manoa (legendary city), 381

Manoel da Cruz, 286

Manrique de Zúñiga, Alvaro, 204

Mansfield, Edward, 106

Manuel I (of Portugal), 16

Maranhão, 286–287; revolt in, 244, 259–263

Mariana. See Brazil; Minas Gerais

Marriage, 29, 142, 151, 155, 245, 346, 471, 485

Maryland: and Ebenezer Cooke, 39, 145–154; and religion, 40; and race, 139, 153–156; and tobacco, 143; and Thomas Cradock, 153–161

Masías, Juan, 402

Massachusetts, 31. *See also* Boston Tea Party; Bradstreet, Anne; Mather, Cotton; New England; Rowlandson, Mary; Swarton, Hannah

Mather, Cotton: and creole identity, 5, 31, 361; and Hannah Swarton, 313–316, 327–333

Mather, Increase, 238; and Mary Rowlandson, 313–333

Mazombos: defined, 242n

Meléndez, Juan, 32–33, 398–403

Mendieta, Gerónimo de, 76, 213

Mendoza, Antonio de, 302

Mendoza, Pedro de, 383

Menores: defined, 14

Mestizaje: defined, 34, 177, 197, 467

Mestizos and mestizas: defined, 34–35, 180n, 335n; in colonial Peru, 121–123, 126; in Brazil, 242–243; in New Granada, 334–354; and revolutionary creoles, 450–451

Meta (legendary country), 379

Mexía de Fernangil, Diego, 268–275, 280, 289–290

Mexica. *See* Aztecs

Mexico: and Spain, 14; creole consciousness in, 26, 199–205, 293–312; and religion, 61–100; and British hopes for expansion, 104; Jesuits in, 193–194, 202–205; literature of, 193–218; Franciscans in, 194, 215; and Egypt, 203, 211–212, 460; Indians in, 294, 300–301, 306

Middle Ages, 64, 67–68, 74n

Minas Gerais, 265–268, 276–280, 286–290

Mining: and Spanish exploitation of New World, 19, 200; and wealth of Peru, 112, 377, 383; and boomtowns and creole identity, 265–290; in New Granada, 336, 343

Minority discourse, 44–45; colonial writings as, 162–190; and colonialism, 171–180; defined, 173; and colonial rhetoric, 187–190

Miranda, Francisco de, 469

Mita (*mit'a*): defined, 343, 432, 464; in Peru, 377n

Modyford, Thomas, 110–111

Mogrovejo, Toribio de, 386–387, 403–404

Monroe Doctrine, 470, 474

Montalvo, Francisco Antonio de, 399, 403–406

Montesinos, Antón de, 22

Morales, Ambrosio de, 425, 427

Morcillo Rubio de Auñón, Diego, 281, 284, 286, 290

Moret, Jean, 427

Morgan, Henry, 106, 110–112

Motolinía, Toribio de Benavente, 65, 70–71

Mound Builder society, 468–469

Mountain of Silver, 382–383. *See also* El Dorado; El Paititi

Muiscas, 337–344; origins of, 338–339; and religion, 338–339, 352; in New Granada, 339–344, 351–352, 354; wealth, knowledge, and labor of, 343–344, 350–353

Muñoz de Collantes, Diego, 352

Muñoz de Collantes, Juan, 345

Nation (*nación*): defined, 27n, 415; early modern understanding of, 280n; as ethnic group, 376, 378; in Peru, 377–378, 407–408, 414, 439–441

Nationalism: in New World, 2, 100, 407–408, 458, 466–467, 473; and Spain, 12; and minority discourse, 162–163, 169. *See also* Nation

Nativism, 253, 451. *See also* Fernández de Piedrahita, Lucas

Navarra y Rocafull, Melchor de, 403

Nebrija, Antonio, 344, 416

Netherlands, the, 27, 57, 110, 151, 167, 230, 251–254, 386

New England: and Indians, 19–20, 31; creole identity in, 31, 219–240, 313–333; and Anne Bradstreet, 219–220, 235–239

New English, 16–17

New Granada, 334–354

New Laws, 24, 176, 343, 448

New World: early modern perceptions of, 2, 5–6, 17, 55, 121–122; as empty, 17, 453, 469; Spanish debate over conquest of, 20–26, 80–82; and race, 33, 36–37; and nature, 368–371; as a paradise, 375, 396–398, 404; saints of, 386–387. *See also* Creolization; Environmental determinism

Nichols, Philip, 105

North Carolina, 356, 362–364, 366

Religion (*cont.*)
and creole syncretism in Mexico, 210–211;
and New World saints, 386–387; and race,
401–402. *See also* Franciscans; Jesuits;
Jews; Puritans

Repartimiento: defined, 24

Repartos: defined, 23

Restoration (of Stuart monarchy), 31, 101, 109,
144, 326

Revel, James, 136–142, 144–146, 148–150,
160–161

Revolutionary: defined, 179n

Revolutionary creoles: and Indian symbols
and images, 444–452, 460; and rewriting
history, 452–457, 460; and America,
463–464

Robertson, William, 6, 452, 454–455, 460,
462

Rome, colonies of, 12–13, 17, 430, 436,
438–439

Rosas de Oquendo, Mateo, 201

Rose of Lima (Rosa de Santa Maria), 386–
387, 401

Rowlandson, Joseph, 313, 320n, 321

Rowlandson, Mary: and tobacco, 143; captivity narrative of, 238, 313–333

Rueda, Lope de, 382

Rústicos: defined, 14

Sá e Menezes, Francisco de, 260n, 262

Safios: defined, 32, 399

Sahagún, Bernardino de, 5n, 64, 70–71, 213

Salazar y Alarcón, Eugenio de, 203–204, 215

Salinas, Buenaventura de, 387–391, 395, 403

Saltonstall, Nathaniel, 322

Sambenito: defined, 245

Sánchez, Miguel, 199, 215, 218

San Martín, José de, 446–447, 477

San Martín, Juan de, 344

Satire, 359–362; and creole identity, 358–359;
and William Byrd II, 361–362

Science: language of, 358–359; and William
Byrd II, 361–362, 365; and New World, 371

Sebastião (of Portugal), 16, 245–246, 248,
250–251

Sepúlveda, Juan Ginés de, 79

Sertão: defined, 266

Sesmerias: defined, 15

Sex: and women, 130–133; and race, 155, 157–
158; and creole stereotypes, 172; and Indians, 346–347, 364–365

Sidney, Philip, 219, 222–223, 227, 230–239

Sigüenza y Góngora, Carlos de, 27, 82–84,
189, 201–204, 211–215, 262–264, 295, 304,
306–312, 378

Simón, Pedro, 341

Slaves and slavery: and etymology of creole, 3,
6, 376; in Brazil, 15–16, 242–243; in British
America, 20, 29–30, 41–42, 107, 139–140,
150, 153–159, 451, 490; and Indians, 22, 108;
and race, 38, 42, 120, 457–458; Simón
Bolívar on, 464, 474, 477–478. *See also* Africans; *Encomienda* and *ecomenderos;* Indentured servitude

Sloane, Hans, 359

Smithsonian Institution, 490

Solano, Francisco, 386–387, 403–404

Souza, Tomé de, 15

Space and spatial concepts: in theory, 166–
168; and Englishness and creolism, 223–
226, 233, 236, 239; and Puritans, 317; and
gender, 320–321

Spain: and creolization, 3–4; and colonialism,
13–16; and Portugal, 15, 248, 259; and Great
Britain, 19, 101–117; and debate about New
World Conquest, 21–24, 402, 414; and religion, 40, 294; and New World wealth, 109,
377, 392–393, 397; and Sor Juana, 195, 205–
218; and Jews, 241, 246–248; and the
Netherlands, 253; as *patria,* 304; and Peru,
388, 414, 440; and Pedro Peralta Barnuevo,
416–419, 425, 429, 438

Spanish Americas: compared to British and
Portuguese American colonies, 2–3; and
definition of colonialism, 12–13; and religion, 14, 40, 61–100; and debate about
New World conquest, 20–26, 80–82; and
Indians, 23–24, 347n; and British Americas,
31–32, 106–117; and race, 34–38; and independence, 442–446; and creole resistance,
448–449

Spenser, Edmund, 16

Spotswood, Alexander, 361

Stone, John Augustus, 468

Suárez de Avila, Juan, 295, 301

Suárez de Peralta, Juan, 200, 294–306, 310–311